An Introduction to Juvenile Justice

An Introduction to
Juvenile
Justice

Dr. Frank Merenda

Marist College

New York   Oxford

OXFORD UNIVERSITY PRESS

Oxford University Press is a department of the University of Oxford.
It furthers the University's objective of excellence in research, scholarship,
and education by publishing worldwide. Oxford is a registered trade mark of
Oxford University Press in the UK and certain other countries.

Published in the United States of America by Oxford University Press
198 Madison Avenue, New York, NY 10016, United States of America.

© 2022 by Oxford University Press

Library of Congress Control Number: 2021947674

ISBN: 978-0-190-85283-2

For titles covered by Section 112 of the US Higher Education
Opportunity Act, please visit www.oup.com/us/he for the latest
information about pricing and alternate formats.

Printing number: 9 8 7 6 5 4 3 2 1
Printed by Sheridan Litho Offset
United States of America

Dedication

To my wife, Lisa, for her unbroken understanding and endearments.

To my children, Frank, Marc, and Kayla, for their patience and love.

To the rest of my family and friends for their kindness and support.

Brief Contents

Contents

3 Theories of Delinquency 45

SECTION 2 ▬▬▬▬▬▬▬▬▬▬▬▬▬▬▬▬▬▬▬▬▬▬▬▬▬

 ### The Juvenile Offender: A Small Adult?   71

 ### Gangs and Juveniles   93

6 Juvenile Victims 117

SECTION 3

 The Police and Juveniles   159

 Juvenile Courts   185

Juvenile Corrections   209

10 Interventions and Diversion 251

SECTION 4

13 Juvenile Justice: Trends and Reforms   333

Preface

The aim of this work was to create a highly accessible, student-friendly introductory text for college undergraduates. The text begins by framing the juvenile justice system's historical context and then takes students on a journey through the system's development, its practical and theoretical approaches, and the effects of the system on those within it and on society at large. Throughout the text, the author has provided multiple perspectives, including a worldview comparison at the end of each chapter, practical applications, victim impact, disparities within the system, and its changing role. A variety of online resources to accommodate a multitude of learning styles have also been provided to ensure students' success. The final chapters discuss contemporary issues that are being faced in the early 21st century; for example, a larger chapter discusses the historical and contemporary media impact on juveniles, cybercrimes, and juvenile justice trends and reforms.

The Approach of This Text

On any given day, the United States incarcerates over 40,000 juveniles, many of whom end up in formal detention centers. Although this number is lower than in previous years, the United States, as compared to any other developed country, remains at the top of the list for youth confinement. The theme of this text is to not only provide students with what they need to know regarding the essentials of the juvenile justice system, but also provide a variety of perspectives, including worldviews, theories, and practical applications. The intention of this text is to provide students with a well-rounded and impartial representation of the topics covered in each chapter in order to promote independent critical thinking.

Features and Benefits

- A student-friendly, comprehensive overview of the juvenile justice system, ranging from how and why it was formed to what it has become and its current challenges
- Contemporary laws and public opinions concerning solitary confinement, life in prison, formal detention, and disparities across age, race, gender, and socioeconomic status
- An entire chapter covers digital age issues facing youth in the early 21st century, including social media, cyberharassment, cyberbullying, sexting, child pornography, and abduction. This chapter also covers the interchangeable role of the offender and the victim.
- A worldview section is also included at the end of each chapter, which allows students to have a broader perspective of the concepts presented and compare and contrast a variety of factors within and outside the system.
- An individual and larger chapter examines the effects of media violence and present-day virtual reality video games. The chapter addresses increased media violence and realism as well as increased accessibility by juveniles as compared to years ago, when many of the studies were conducted.

- An in-depth look at juvenile victims, with additional text specifically describing how they are treated by the system, the outreach that is done, their satisfaction, and their role within the many stages of the justice process
- A broader scope of juvenile corrections, including a detailed look at its evolution to community-based treatment and additional sections on solitary confinement, life sentences, victimization and bias, and aftercare
- A variety of textbook resources, discussion questions, and online resources are included to accommodate the varied learning styles of all students to ensure the success of the learner.

Organization of the Text

Section 1 encompasses how the juvenile justice system was formed and how delinquency is measured. We also look at juvenile crime trends, violent crimes by juveniles, and their resulting prosecution as adults. Finally, we explore why juveniles commit crimes. Specifically, we examine both classical and positivist theoretical perspectives from the 1700s and 1800s to modern day.

Section 2 addresses a new class of juvenile delinquents, deemed superpredators. We examine how states classify juveniles in the same way they classify adult offenders and how in some cases punishment is disproportionally applied across this population. We then discuss continued offending by juveniles and their presence in gangs. We further explore current trends and interventions to protect children from joining gangs and to help them get out. Finally, we examine the impact of crime on juvenile victims and how victimization comes in many forms. We discuss how juvenile victims are treated by the justice system, the role they play, and the resources provided to support them and their families.

Section 3 discusses the core bodies that make up the system and interventions that have been put in place to avoid formal processing when possible and society's changing attitudes toward this process. National and world perspectives are addressed. The police are discussed in terms of their varied roles in the system and as primary gatekeepers. The section also examines how the police have participated in preventive measures to combat delinquency. One chapter looks inside the courts at the offender process and its effects on victims and their families. Next, correctional methods and statistical trends are presented with regard to how sanctions are applied across race, age, gender, and socioeconomic status, along with additional sections covering recent legislation affecting solitary confinement, life sentences, and alternative community-based treatment programs and aftercare. Finally, intervention and diversion methods used by the system to handle matters informally, from wilderness programs to foster care and group homes, are discussed.

Section 4 looks at contemporary and growing issues that affect everyone associated with the juvenile justice system, especially our youth. The first chapter in this section addresses the evolution and impact of media violence (television, movies, video games, and online), its accessibility by youth, and its overall impact on aggression and violence. The next chapter examines a wide range of cybercrimes that not only affect our youth but also have turned victims into offenders in the digital age. The text concludes by presenting current trends and reforms of the system as they relate to political, social, and financial interests, both nationally and around the world.

About the Author

Dr. Merenda is an associate professor in the Department of Criminal Justice at Marist College in Poughkeepsie, New York. He received his doctorate from St. John's University and his Master's of Public Administration from Harvard University, where he was awarded the 2012 Harvard University Presidential Fellowship for Public Service.

Dr. Merenda has worked with juveniles in a variety of capacities for over 25 years. Prior to entering academia, Professor Merenda worked for the New York City Police Department, performing various roles. Many of these positions enabled him to interact with or assess policy concerning juveniles. He retired as a police captain after completing 20 years of dedicated service.

Professor Merenda has been teaching criminal justice courses for over a decade, specializing in juvenile justice and delinquency courses. He extends his teaching outside the classroom by being actively involved with the community. He has organized large-scale events to raise awareness for youth homelessness and children impacted by a multitude of adversarial environmental conditions.

Dr. Merenda has published several scholarly works examining intervention and diversionary strategies. He continues to be an advocate for juvenile justice reform and the adoption of community-based programs that aim to better serve today's youth.

He lives with his wife, three children, two dogs and two cats in New York.

Acknowledgments

I am so appreciative of the hard work and dedication of the staff at Oxford University Press, especially executive editor Steve Helba and assistant editor Sonya Venugopal for their guidance and unwavering support throughout the development and production process.

An Introduction to Juvenile Justice

Children of the Industrial Revolution

History of the Juvenile Justice System

CHAPTER OUTLINE

LEARNING OBJECTIVES

At the end of the chapter, students will be able to

Compare the similarities in the punishment of children within the American colonies and the rest of the world during the 17th and 18th centuries;

explain the philosophical difference between the early reformers in the 1800s, who created the Houses of Refuge, compared to the Child Savers, who advocated for a juvenile court;

describe the Progressive Era and the challenges society faced;

describe the purpose of the 1974 Juvenile Justice and Delinquency Prevention Act passed by Congress;

describe the four Ds that have emerged from the juvenile justice system's evolution from the 20th century to the present;

define the term juvenile super predator, where it originated, and the societal changes that occurred; and

compare the evolution of the juvenile justice system in the United States with other systems around the world.

Keywords

Bridewell
Child Savers
Code of Hammurabi
Community-based alternatives
Cottage system
Decriminalization
Deinstitutionalization
Diversion
Due process
England's poor laws

English Common Law
Enslaved
House of refuge
Indentured servants
Net widening
New York Society for the Prevention
  of Pauperism
Parens patriae
Patriarchal system
Placing-out system

Progressive Era
Roman Laws of the 12 Tables
Sight and sound separated
Society for the Reformation of Juvenile
  Delinquents
Status offense
Stubborn Child Law
Superpredator

Introduction

The United States, much like the rest of the world, has a separate system of criminal justice dedicated solely to the handling and processing of juveniles who commit acts that would be considered a crime if they were committed by an adult. This separate structure is known as the juvenile justice system, but it did not always exist. From the 1600s to the 1800s, law enforcement, the courts, and corrections treated adults and children (usually age 7 or older) nearly the same. Society allowed for whipping, torture, and even execution of individuals, including juveniles, who committed even the most minor offenses. How could a civil society behave in such a manner? The unfortunate truth is that there were few options within the criminal justice system when a child committed a crime. During this time, a separate juvenile justice system had not yet been created. Therefore, a child who committed a criminal act could either be let go or disciplined within the system that processed and punished adults. Severe sanctions were delivered in the name of deterrence and punishment, and this occurred all over the globe. As centuries passed, people started to examine how we as a society were treating our youth, and it is through these efforts that our juvenile justice system was created and continues to evolve.

Children as Property and Small Adults

In Massachusetts in 1691, if a child of 16 disobeyed their parents, they could be put to death. Retribution of this kind was under the authority of the **Stubborn Child Law**, inspired by God-fearing Puritans. They believed that only swift and strict punishment would protect communities from God's wrath (Sutton, 1988). Although the punishment in other colonies may not have been as harsh, sanctions would be similar to what were given to adults who committed offensive acts at the time, including whipping, caning, and mutilation. This occurred because children and adults were thought of as being the same, according to the law. Children were considered property with regard to their role in society and at a young age were described as small adults in terms of responsibility for a criminal act. But this type of thinking did not originate in the United States. It had existed elsewhere for more than 4,000 years and was eventually adopted by European countries, England being the most prevalent and influential to the United States (Quigley, 1996).

King of Hammurabi of Babylon

The Code of Hammurabi

The **Code of Hammurabi** was created in the 18th century B.C., more than 4,000 years ago, carved on a 7.5-foot stone pillar. Much like the Stubborn Child Law in Massachusetts, it authorized strict punishment for disobedient children. Specific penalties included cutting off the tongue for deserting one's adoptive home, putting out one's eyes for rejecting one's adoptive mother or father, and chopping off a child's hand for striking one's father (further discussed in chapter 3).

Roman Laws of the 12 Tables

In 450 B.C. Rome, the **Roman Laws of the 12 Tables** gave a child's father the right of life and death over his natural son. These laws applied to children who had reached puberty, age 14 for boys and 12 for girls; younger youth were not considered responsible for their actions. Nonetheless, once a child reached puberty, even death by hanging could be imposed (Bernard & Kurlychek, 2010).

Much like in ancient Rome, the common theme of families, specifically fathers, being responsible for their children's care and permitted to exercise corporal punishment continued into the Middle Ages (the 16th and 17th centuries) in Europe. Europe was undergoing an economic transformation, from peasants who had received land from kings to grow crops for their personal use (feudal system) to lords, creating a trade-oriented system that resulted in more work and imposed increased fees (Epstein, 2009). Families were eventually displaced because they could not afford to live under these new conditions, and they looked for work elsewhere. As impoverished families traveled to urban towns searching for work, they were rejected, as was the case in England through the creation and enforcement of poor laws from the 1500s into the early 1600s.

England's Poor Laws

England's poor laws prevented peasants from entering guilds (worker's unions), which in turn prevented them from getting jobs (Quigley, 1996). Society feared these peasants would work for lower wages and therefore take jobs away from current workers. This widespread lack of work resulted in widespread vagrancy. At the time, families had the dual responsibility to care for dependent children and deliver punishment to control wayward youth. For adults and children alike, other statutes were enacted through poor laws that would punish "intentional" vagrancy by having one's ears burned as punishment for a first offense and death by hanging for a second offense.

Only those who were homeless through no fault of their own, as determined by the government, were given relief through poor laws. Parishes were directed by Parliament to provide essentials through charitable donations. This relief system was enacted in 1597 by Queen Elizabeth the First, and strained families who could no longer control their children had them placed with "better able," wealthier families. However, there

Bridewell Prison, London. Bridewell Prison was the first house of correction in England, established in 1553. Over its 300 years of operation, Bridewell became the basis for future orphanages, workhouses, and prisons. Within just three years of its initiation, similar institutions spread all over Europe. The word "bridewell" became synonymous with "large prison."

were no mandates placed on those new families to teach a trade to the children, and they were allowed to assign boys to work their farm and girls to cook and clean. In other areas in England, formal institutions were erected to house and control wayward youth, the first of which was created in 1555 London, called the **Bridewell**. The institution was named after an ancient holy well (St Bridget's well) next to the facility (formerly a king's castle). Bridewells, also considered houses of correction, spread all over England and accepted all types of children: vagrants, destitute, sick, orphaned, and criminal.

Eventually, institutionalizing youth became the mainstay of societies, and parishes were also stripped of their mission to relieve the poor. New poor laws were enacted in the next century in England that created new institutions, called workhouses. Now, instead of a youth or family receiving aid directly, they had to work in a government facility in exchange for food, shelter, and medicine (Fox, 1970).

Colonial America

Other families sought relief in colonial America in the 1600s. Soon, many Europeans were either volunteering or coerced to settle in colonies. This was accomplished via an agreement that poor children and adults would work as **indentured servants** and eventually win their freedom.

Enslavement

In 1619, for example, the colony of Virginia made an agreement regarding a shipment of poor and orphaned children from England. African adults and children were also brought to the colonies during this time but were **enslaved**; they were not given the opportunity to win their freedom and remained in servitude for the rest of their lives (Ward, 2012). Native American children in the early 1600s were kidnapped, and attempts were made to raise them as Christians and put them to work (Clews, 2009; Taylor & Foner, 2010). Many of these practices continued into the next century.

Tithing Men

In 17th-century colonial America, initially, parents were solely responsible for the morality, education, and punishment of their children. Eventually, the colony appointed tithing men. These disciplinarians assisted government officials, such as town councilmen and constables, with visiting families who did not fulfill their financial contributions and self-discipline (Mason, 1996). However, this system was not successful, and by the 18th century, although parents were still held legally responsible for their children, wayward children were put into apprenticeships. Many destitute children from low-income families were contracted out to other families, much like the European settlers, as indentured servants. As time passed, there were fewer apprenticeships, and more young people were assigned to be part of the labor force. By the early 19th century, children comprised over half the workforce in industries such as cotton mills. As the Industrial Revolution spread throughout America, factories continued to replace farming and other family-based means to survive, and as in Europe, families were weakened and displaced. More juveniles were left homeless to fend for themselves. The increase of impoverished children, urbanization, and immigrant growth in the early 19th century caused a fear of losing social control over society's youth. In an effort to control these youths and prevent them from committing illegal acts, special interest societies began to emerge (Fox, 1970).

Reforms in the 1800s

The United States, much like other countries, still had a **patriarchal system** in the late 18th and early 19th centuries, with the father as the head of the family and responsible for controlling his children and providing for them. However, some people in communities, especially the upper class, felt families alone could no longer control society's underprivileged and potentially delinquent youth and believed that organizations and government needed to step in. Rather than the failed solutions of apprenticeships and indentured servants, communities felt new solutions were necessary. During this time, societies typically had only two choices when dealing with children who committed crimes: either imprison them with adults or ignore the offense and let them go. It is within that environment, and because of societal criticisms, that advocates for change emerged.

In 1817, a group of wealthy Americans who wanted to set up controls for poor individuals who were believed to be desperate and likely to commit crimes formed the **New York Society for the Prevention of Pauperism**. They initially targeted taverns and other places that sold alcohol or in some way contributed to individuals becoming destitute. Their efforts then expanded to include impoverished and vagrant children. An 1818 report written by one of the society's members, John Griscom, detailed, among other things, the links between poor and needy youth and delinquency. Around the same time, further studies of prisons by the society revealed abusive conditions and the ill effects of imprisoning adults and children together. These reports prompted the notion of creating an alternate form of detention for children that would focus on education and work rather than punishment.

The New York House of Refuge, as it was in 1855

In 1824, the society reorganized to become the **Society for the Reformation of Juvenile Delinquents**. They proposed an institution that would relieve impoverished families of the responsibility to care for their desolate or wayward children and at the same time protect children, rather than enslave them. The goal would be to "re-educate and rehabilitate" both children in need of care and those who had committed illegal acts (Juvenile Justice History Center, 2016; Schlossman, 1983). On January 1, 1825, with approval from the New York State Assembly, a much-advocated-for alternative for youth in New York City was created, a safe haven, a **House of Refuge**.

Houses of Refuge

Houses of Refuge were mostly privately run juvenile reformatories that educated and rehabilitated youth through moral, industrial, and general education until they entered adulthood, generally at 21 years of age (Binder et al., 1997). This would be accomplished through praying, attending classes, and working. However, these youth were also punished, similar to individuals who were in prisons, by being put in leg irons and whipped if they were disobedient. One year after the first House of Refuge was created in New York City, the state-run Boston House of Reformation was started, and in 1828, the Philadelphia House of Refuge was formed. Because they were considered preventative institutions, they could admit both children convicted of crimes and destitute children alike (Schlossman, 1983). As years passed, Houses of Refuge became overcrowded. For example, within a decade, New York's House of Refuge went from its original admittance of 6 boys and 3 girls to being responsible for over 1,000 children (New York State Archives, 1989). More states eventually began to take over these institutions in an attempt to regulate them, much like the first state-run reformatory school in Boston in 1826. Still, because of their continued reliance on discipline and overcrowded conditions, they received substantial criticism.

By the middle of the 19th century, more alternatives were emerging. The **cottage system** attempted to do away with one large, heavily populated facility and replace it with smaller buildings (cottages), each holding approximately 40 youth. The goal was to improve outcomes through more individualized rehabilitative care.

The **placing-out system** was another alternative in the mid-1800s. From what were considered urban slum areas, thousands of children and teens were convinced to board trains and travel to other states. They were to be placed on farms with foster families to learn skills and build moral character through work and guidance. Unfortunately, these families provided less skills training and more physical labor, with little moral guidance (Binder et al., 1997).

Separate institutions for females were also being built with a focus on teaching domestic and child-rearing skills, as well as military schools, which were usually reserved for youth coming from upper-class families. Even with an array of institutional and placement options, the grim realities of these detention centers became overwhelmingly apparent. Table 1.1 presents fact and fiction in relation to Houses of Refuge.

Not only did Houses of Refuge receive substantial criticism for their delivery of harsh treatment and poor conditions, but also the legality of removing children from a home and placing them in a reformatory began to be questioned. States justified their actions of taking over as guardians, even when it was at the behest of parents, by asserting that they were acting in the child's best interests.

Parens Patriae

Parens patriae is Latin for "parent of the country" and has its roots in **English Common Law**—societal customs and traditions enforced by judgments of the court. During feudal times, it gave the father-of-his-country role to their kings (Schlossman, 1983, p. 962).

TABLE 1.1 House of Refuge/Reformatory School Fiction and Fact	
FICTION	**FACT**
Institutions were an alternative to adult imprisonment.	Most of the children institutionalized had not committed any crime.
Any child in need of care or who committed an offense would be taken in.	By 1860, over half of the occupants were mostly poor Irish immigrants. African American children were excluded and housed in segregated facilities.
Children received education (taught reading, writing, and arithmetic).	Very few children were actually taught.
Children were permitted to worship according to their individual moral and religious obligations.	Children underwent forced religious conversion to Protestantism.
A variety of inducements to correct behavior were utilized, and unlike the punishment received by adults, the goal was to reeducate and rehabilitate.	Punishments were no different than what adults would receive and included shackles, deprivation of food except bread and water, physical abuse (beatings), and even solitary confinement.
Numerous skills were provided to assist children with reentering and becoming productive members of society.	Often, the sole skill taught was training to work in a factory.
The children were happy.	Children often tried to escape.

In the United States, the parens patriae doctrine "has had its greatest application in the treatment of children, mentally ill persons, and other individuals who are legally incompetent to manage their affairs" ("Parens Patriae," 2008, p. 1). It allows the state to act as the ultimate guardian of all children within its jurisdiction and to intervene to protect the best interests of the child.

In the 1800s, the concept of parens patriae was relied on as justification for states to send a child to a House of Refuge or another type of reformatory, even without the parents' consent. This notion was first challenged in 1838 in Pennsylvania's Supreme Court in *Ex parte (for) Crouse*.

Ex Parte Crouse

In 1838, Mary Ann Crouse was sent to the Pennsylvania House of Refuge after her mother complained to the court that her daughter was unruly and "incorrigible" and should be sent to a House of Refuge. Mary Ann's father later argued that there was no trial and therefore her "imprisonment" was unconstitutional. The court ruled that "the House of Refuge was a reformatory rather than a jail, and Mary Ann's behavior could be reformed as long as she remained there" (*Ex parte Crouse*, 1838). The court decided that the state had the right to intervene on behalf of the child's best interests. This case validated the legal doctrine of parens patriae in the United States.

Reformatories continued to receive criticism, however, and there was growing opposition against institutionalizing youth and finding effective alternatives. In 1841, the poverty-stricken society was riddled with vagrancy, and many individuals were taken into custody for minor offenses, such as being intoxicated in public. John Augustus, a bootmaker by trade, joined the Washington Total Abstinence Society. This society put up bail for men and women arrested for public drunkenness to keep them out of prison and teach them skills to get them back on their feet. Augustus later advocated for children who committed petty crimes and convinced judges to forego sentencing youth to institutions for a fee (bail) and to allow him to teach the children skills and find them jobs. Augustus started with 3 children (2 girls and 1 boy), and over the next 18 years, he prevented over 1,900 juveniles and adults from being sent to reformatories and prisons (Binder et al., 1997). It is believed that he set the course for modern-day probation, and in 1859, Massachusetts passed the first probation statute based on Augustus's work. This created an official probation system that quickly spread to other states. Because of his work and how he inspired this new diversionary system, John Augustus is considered the Father of Probation.

Despite the creation of a formal probation system, many children continued to be removed from families and placed in institutions in the name of rehabilitation. Unfortunately, reformatories such as the Houses of Refuge continued to receive criticism for harsh discipline, a work-filled environment, and other detrimental conditions. It was not until more than 30 years after the Crouse decision that the broad scope of parens patriae, which continued to allow states to institutionalize children, many of whom had not committed crimes, was challenged. State intervention without procedural safeguards was found legal in the

The "Father of Probation" John Augustus

Crouse case. The question is, Was the notion of parens patriae a conduit for rehabilitation or a catalyst for boundless punishment?

O'Connell v. Turner, 1870

In 1870, Daniel O'Connell, age 14, was sent to the Illinois Reform School for the charge of being "destitute of proper parental care thereby wandering about the streets, or causing criminal mischief, or growing up idle" (*O'Connell v. Turner*, 1870). This decision was against the child's parents' wishes, and an appeal was filed based on O'Connell not having committed a crime, yet having his liberty taken away. The Illinois Supreme Court reviewed the case and ordered Robert Turner, the superintendent of the reform school in Illinois where Daniel was sent, to show cause for his detention. After reviewing the facts, the court's opinion was that parents have a right to care for and educate their children, which cannot be prevented by the court without gross negligence. The higher court further ruled that the state imprisoning youth for "moral welfare and the good of society" without committing a crime was unconstitutional. This preeminent ruling weakened the government's unbridled intervention through parens patriae, limiting its application to either situations of total unfitness of parents or criminal offenders.

With declining state control over society's wayward youth, upper-class society once again feared a rise in delinquency and a threat to societal structure. Both children and society needed to be saved.

Child Savers in the Progressive Era (1890–1920)

As industry continued to grow, leaving behind displaced families, attempts were being made by social activists to combat the potential ill effects. This time in history was considered the **Progressive Era**, "a period of widespread social activism and political reform across the United States" (Buenker et al., 1986, p. 3). Houses of Refuge continued to fail at decreasing delinquency and were believed to be incapable of providing for the children residing within them. Additionally, after the O'Connell case limited the government's power, courts were restricted to having jurisdiction only over those juveniles who committed crimes, giving the responsibility of the child back to the family. Although some courts ignored the outcome of the O'Connell case, neglected and impoverished children continued to roam the streets, generally ungoverned. An alternate way to control all youth, whether criminal, wayward, or destitute, was believed necessary. The wealthier class feared that the link between pauperism and delinquency, written about by the Society of Pauperism earlier in the 1800s, was a ticking time bomb, soon to disrupt their societal class.

The Creation of the Juvenile Court

Social activists composed of prominent and wealthy wives and daughters of businessmen and politicians led the push to find a better way to handle all juveniles in the name of social reform. Later in the 19th century, they formed a group that again advocated that it was the state's responsibility to ensure that poor, destitute children were taken care of, not through failed institutional punishment, but through rehabilitation. This group of reformers, composed mostly of women, purported that their purpose was to save children and, as such, named their society **Child Savers**. Some critics argue that their goal was to save society (Platt, 1977).

This new society was involved in social activism, as were previous groups, such as the Society for the Prevention of Juvenile Delinquents. Still, these founders differed from the founders of the House of Refuge in that they did not believe institutionalizing children was necessary or even useful in reforming youth. Not only were reformatories failing, as indicated by rising delinquency and the number of destitute children, but also they became so overcrowded it was feared they could no longer house the growing juvenile population. An alternative way of saving the youth was deemed not only necessary but also an impending priority.

The group believed that staying with families (with government intervention and supervision) was important to a child's rehabilitation and that community and churches should be involved as well. They also regularly distributed food and clothing and provided temporary shelter to vagrant children when necessary.

Child Savers advocated for government intervention and purported that parens patriae should be broadened to include neglected and abandoned children, because it was the state's responsibility to act in the child's best interest. They believed that children should not be held responsible for their crimes because they were developmentally different from adults. The focus should be on the child's individual circumstances or needs, not the details of the crime itself.

Illinois Juvenile Court Act of 1899

Although there were attempts in other states to treat juveniles separately, for example, separate trials in Massachusetts and separation of juveniles in courts and penal institutions in New York, it was ultimately the influence of the Child Savers that prompted the passage of the Illinois Juvenile Court Act of 1899, which authorized the first juvenile court in the United States. The act gave the court broad jurisdiction over neglected, dependent, and delinquent children under the age of 16. Unlike the goal of adult criminal court, which was to punish, the juvenile court's overarching goal was to rehabilitate (Butts, 2002; National Research Council and Institute of Medicine, 2001).

The act also required the separation of incarcerated juveniles from adults and barred any child's detention under age 12. It also provided for informal and nonadversarial court proceedings. The benefits and formation of a juvenile court quickly spread, and by 1925, there was a juvenile court in all but two states, Maine and Wyoming (Schlossman, 1983). By 1945, there were juvenile courts in every state, all with the goal to rehabilitate as opposed to punish.

It is important to note that although the establishment of the juvenile court diverted youth from the punitive nature of a criminal court, it expanded the government's social control over juveniles, termed **net widening**, through court supervision and treatment centers (Bilchik, 1999; National Research Council and Institute of Medicine, 2001). Net widening describes the treatment of youth who are involved with the justice system for minor offenses and social issues, who otherwise might have had the incident handled outside the system or informally. It also describes intrusive sanctions by the court, such as community activities and education requirements, that impose further social control (Cate, 2016). These types of mandates exist because of the informal nature and rehabilitative goal of the juvenile court; however, if violated, they could result in formal detention and a greater number of incarcerated youth.

Juveniles were brought before the court for a variety of reasons, but all were treated with the goal of rehabilitation in mind. Those who had committed an offense were charged not with the crime, but with a delinquent act. As such, the court was civil

TABLE 1.2 Key Provisions of the 1899 Illinois Juvenile Court Act
1. Distinguish between criminal and noncriminal juveniles
2. Informal procedures were developed to handle juvenile cases
3. Children and adults must be separated not only in court proceedings, but also in confinement
4. Established a system of probation to assist the courts

Source: National Research Council and Institute of Medicine (2001).

in nature, and instead of handing down criminal sanctions, "treatment" came in the form of warnings, supervised probation, and training school/reformatory confinement. These treatment types could last until the child was rehabilitated or turned 21 (Butts, 2002). With this expanded authority, courts could also bring before them and provide "treatment" to noncriminal children, who were handled the same way as delinquents, sometimes against the will of their parents.

Commonwealth v. Fisher, 1905

In *Commonwealth v. Fisher*, a juvenile accused of larceny was taken into the custody of the court and sent to a reformatory school for 7 years. The case was appealed to the superior court in Pennsylvania, stating that it was unconstitutional for Fisher to be taken into custody without formal due process and that his right to trial by jury was denied. The superior court made the following decision in 1905 regarding the constitutional rights of juveniles in juvenile court:

> The natural parent needs no process to temporarily deprive his child of its liberty by confining it in his own home, to save it and to shield it from the consequences of persistence in a career of waywardness, nor is the State, when compelled, as Parens Patriae, to take the place of the father for the same purpose, required to adopt any process as a means of placing its hands upon the child to lead it into one of its courts. When the child gets there and the court, with the power to save it, determines on its salvation, and not its punishment, it is immaterial how it got there. (Bernard & Kurlychek, 2010, p.84)

The court went on to explain that since juveniles are not accused of or tried for crimes, but instead taken into custody for delinquent acts, the constitutional rights of due process do not pertain to these "noncriminal cases." This ruling affirmed that the court's role under parens patriae was constitutional and that it could supersede the rights of the child or their parents. Over the next 60 years, the juvenile justice system's constitutionality generally went uncontested, with those cases that did allege unconstitutionality dismissed based on the Fisher ruling.

Criticism ensued of the court's fairness and effectiveness, questioning features such as informal proceedings, discrimination (children from low-income families were generally brought before the court while affluent families remained intact), and lack of due process. The courts' ability to detain and incarcerate children without a formal trial was reminiscent of prior proceedings associated with Houses of Refuge and was now having the same ill effects in the juvenile courts.

Federal Intervention

It was not until 1909 that the federal government began to take part in the juvenile justice system discussion, at the White House Conference on Children and Youth, which debated the institutionalization of dependent and neglected youth. Although many at the conference agreed with the preservation of family, removals to institutions continued. In 1912, the United States Children's Bureau was established. Along with the National Probation Association, it advocated for a standard juvenile court act to address the informality and inconsistency of juvenile courts throughout the states. In 1936, federal funds began to be utilized to care for neglected, abused, and delinquent children. The federal government then passed the first Juvenile Court Act in 1938, which limited sentencing terms for all juveniles to the age of 21 and reiterated the Illinois juvenile court act's key provisions of rehabilitation and treating juveniles separate from adults. Prior to 1938, no federal legislation provided special treatment for children (Bremner & Barnard, 1974).

By the end of the 1960s, the Supreme Court began to intervene by again examining the effects of parens patriae as it applied to juvenile proceedings and its use as a critical component for denying children the constitutional rights that were otherwise guaranteed to adults (see Chapter 8, "Juvenile Courts," for a detailed account of landmark cases that helped restructure the juvenile justice system). The juvenile justice system was evolving into a system with four primary focuses: due process, decriminalization, deinstitutionalization, and diversion.

The D-Word

Sociologist LaMar Empey illustrated four Ds emerging from the developing juvenile justice system (Empey, 1976). Because of the nature of the juvenile justice system, the rights guaranteed to adults in the criminal court system were not always guaranteed to juveniles. The logic was that the juvenile court process was, in fact, not criminal but civil in nature, and children were not criminally punished but instead morally rehabilitated. As such, constitutional guarantees of due process should not apply to them. We have seen this logic challenged in the courts as the system has evolved, because without due process, juveniles were not only denied procedural rights but also, as a result, sanctioned more harshly than adults would have been for the same offenses. Ultimately, it was decided that when sanctions could include loss of liberty, the courts had an obligation to apply due process based on the act, regardless of the age of the offender or the court system. Therefore, our first emerging D, which was part of the juvenile justice system's evolution, is **due process**—procedural rights guaranteed by the Constitution.

The second D has arisen from the system's overall goal to rehabilitate instead of punish. It was believed that these children were affected by external conditions such as poverty (initially, the focus was on biological factors; see Chapter 3) and could therefore be changed. Still, while adults were punished in a criminal court for crimes they committed, minors were processed in a juvenile court for delinquent acts and **status offenses**, acts considered illegal based on one's age, such as truancy and running away, that if committed by an adult would be legal. The criminality of the act and its punishment were not to be the only focus; instead, the delinquent act's causes were to be addressed and attempts to rehabilitate the whole individual should be made. Therefore, our second D is **decriminalization**, a shift from criminalizing acts such as status offenses to focusing on the child and their rehabilitation (decriminalization plays a role and can be applied in all aspects of juvenile justice, as we will see in the following chapters).

As institutions continued to fail at reducing delinquency and providing a rehabilitative environment, the themes of **deinstitutionalization** and **diversion** become another priority into the 1970s, as the federal government continued to pass legislation akin to the new strategy of community-based rehabilitation. As the system developed, there was a shift in focus that emphasized nondetention by providing alternatives to formal placement, such as at-home court supervision, counseling, mediation, and other government services that could keep juveniles out of an institution and at the same time rehabilitate them.

Shifting Focus

Community-Based Alternatives

In 1967, the President's Commission on Law Enforcement spoke out against remanding youth to costly, low-performing institutions and instead advocated for **community-based alternatives**—supervision and services provided outside locked facilities to avoid stigmatizing youth and subjecting them to the poor conditions associated with detention centers. Therefore, in the 1970s, community-based programs, diversion, and deinstitutionalization became the focus of federal policy. Because of this emphasis on rehabilitating juvenile delinquents by means other than institutional care and solidifying these initiatives, on September 7, 1974, Congress passed the Juvenile Justice and Delinquency Prevention Act.

1974 Juvenile Justice and Delinquency Prevention Act

The intent of the Juvenile Justice and Delinquency Prevention Act was to not only set standards and procedural rights for juveniles who came under federal jurisdiction, but also assist states in preventing delinquency and improving the juvenile system as a whole (Office of Juvenile Justice and Delinquency Prevention, 2010). The Office of Juvenile Justice and Delinquency Prevention was created through the act to support these efforts. Emphasis was put on deinstitutionalizing youth through community-based alternatives and keeping children **sight and sound separated** from adults—disallowing all contact with adult offenders when juveniles were housed in the same facility. The practice of keeping juveniles sight and sound separated from adult offenders has spread throughout the juvenile process (police, courts, and corrections), as we will see in the upcoming chapters.

The act allowed for grants to be given to states that adhered to the act's provisions. Although many states did follow specific guidelines, others had different solutions to juvenile crime (Schwartz, 1989). Between 1978 and 1981, nearly half of the other states were passing strict legislation, not only changing the definition of a juvenile delinquent by lowering the age to qualify but also by automatically mandating juveniles to be tried in adult criminal court for particular offenses. This type of legislation, which also set forth mandatory minimum sentencing, resulted in a 50% increase in detention between 1977 and 1985 (National Research Council and Institute of Medicine, 2001).

The Juvenile Justice and Delinquency Prevention Act, which still governs the juvenile justice system, has been reauthorized throughout the years to broaden its scope, including new requirements for states to receive federal funding (see Figure 1.1). It was last reauthorized in 2018 to expand funding for initiatives such as removing criminally adjudicated youth from adult prisons (except under extreme circumstances) and setting forth further accountability. See Chapter 4, "Juvenile Offenders," and Chapter 13, "The Future of Juvenile Justice," for a more in-depth look at recent amendments and future goals of the act.

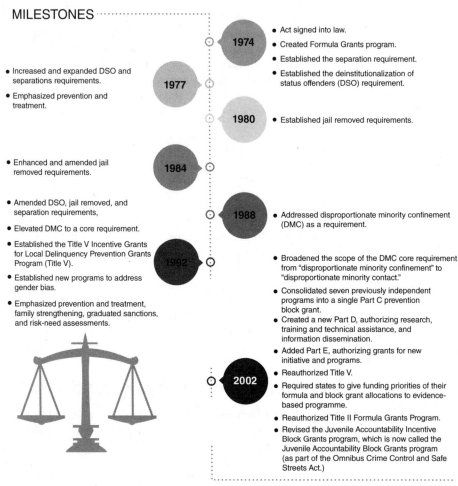

MILESTONES

1974
- Act signed into law.
- Created Formula Grants program.
- Established the separation requirement.
- Established the deinstitutionalization of status offenders (DSO) requirement.

1977
- Increased and expanded DSO and separations requirements.
- Emphasized prevention and treatment.

1980
- Established jail removed requirements.

1984
- Enhanced and amended jail removed requirements.

1988
- Addressed disproportionate minority confinement (DMC) as a requirement.

1992
- Amended DSO, jail removed, and separation requirements,
- Elevated DMC to a core requirement.
- Established the Title V Incentive Grants for Local Delinquency Prevention Grants Program (Title V).
- Established new programs to address gender bias.
- Emphasized prevention and treatment, family strengthening, graduated sanctions, and risk-need assessments.

- Broadened the scope of the DMC core requirement from "disproportionate minority confinement" to "disproportionate minority contact."
- Consolidated seven previously independent programs into a single Part C prevention block grant.
- Created a new Part D, authorizing research, training and technical assistance, and information dissemination.
- Added Part E, authorizing grants for new initiative and programs.

2002
- Reauthorized Title V.
- Required states to give funding priorities of their formula and block grant allocations to evidence-based programme.
- Reauthorized Title II Formula Grants Program.
- Revised the Juvenile Accountability Incentive Block Grants program, which is now called the Juvenile Accountability Block Grants program (as part of the Omnibus Crime Control and Safe Streets Act.)

Figure 1.1 Juvenile Justice and Delinquency Prevention Act

Juvenile Justice and Delinquency Prevention (JJDP) Act: [Pub. L No. 93-415, 42 U.S.C. § 5601 et seq.]

The 1980s and 1990s: The Years of the "Juvenile Superpredator"

During the 1980s and 1990s, despite new government efforts, juvenile crime not only continued to rise but also hit record numbers for a variety of offenses, including violent crimes. Experts in the field not only looked for causes, but also were clear about the need for quick solutions to avoid what was believed to be an imposing epidemic of youth crime. Alleged reasons ranged from economic conditions affecting families to the widespread drug epidemic facing the nation. Academics such as James Fox and James Q. Wilson stressed the impending doom society was about to endure regarding an epic rise in crime. Criminologist and political scientist John Dilulio spoke to then–U.S. president Bill Clinton at a dinner centered on juvenile crime. The conversation spoke to youth's unremorseful violence and the bleak future ahead if immediate and severe action were not taken. Dilulio used the term **superpredator** to describe this class of violent youth who demonstrated no remorse and no empathy.

Society listened, and states began passing more legislation that moved away from emphasizing education and rehabilitation for all children to a more punitive response for juveniles committing violent crimes. The notion that children who commit adult crimes should be prosecuted as adults rang out in courts all over the country, resulting in many transfers and prosecutions of children in adult criminal court. However, violent crime did not continue to grow; instead, beginning in 1994, it began to decline. Most scholars who had warned of this impending rise of superpredators regrettably acknowledged their fallacy because a relatively small number of juveniles were accounting for the majority of juvenile crime. We see this currently with both adults and children, where a small number of individuals are responsible for the majority of crimes (National Research Council, 2013). See Chapter 4, "Juvenile Offenders," for a more in-depth look at juvenile predators and legislation that was created to combat their effects.

The 21st Century

In the 21st century, states have tried to balance their treatment of juveniles, realizing a boilerplate formula based solely on the crime or strictly on the person committing the crime is not the answer. As we will see in the following chapters, however, there is still a reliance on measuring juvenile crime (and theorizing its causes) in terms of treatment of juveniles within the system and the policies that support it.

Worldview

The United Nations

The United Nations declared 1980 "**the year of the child**," holding the sixth U.N. Congress on the prevention of crime. At that time, a paper was presented by Dahn Batchelor, a criminologist, regarding the need for a bill of rights for young offenders. The paper was supported, and drafting of policy began at a conference in Beijing, China, eventually called the United Nations Standard Minimum Rules on the Administration of Juvenile Justice (it is also known as the Beijing Rules, after the location where it was drafted). It mandated separate treatment for children as compared to adults and advocated for two main objectives of any juvenile justice system. One is the promotion of the well-being of the child and the other is fair punitive sanctions based "not only the gravity of the offense but also of personal circumstances" (U.N. General Assembly, 1985, p. 5).

In 1989, the United Nations sought to recognize specific children's rights worldwide in the Convention on the Rights of the Child. The convention was adopted by the U.N. General Assembly and came into effect in 1990. As a result of that convention, a child, defined by the U.N. as anyone under the age of 18, was said to be entitled to 40 specific rights without regard to race, sex, or religion. All of the rights stemmed around acting in the best interest of the child and included such mandates as no child being the subject of torture or other degrading treatment or punishment, respect of the child's lawful rights of privacy, separation from adults, and focus on rehabilitation with imprisonment as a last resort. In the early 21st century, 196 countries have ratified the act, including every member of the U.N. except the United States. The United States has not attempted approval through the Senate because of what some describe as conflicts with the U.S. Constitution and the act's repetitive nature with regard to what the United States has already implemented.

Many counties, like the United States, have undergone changes in their juvenile systems, having passed legislation shifting their goals to focus on rehabilitation. The just treatment of juveniles and alignment to the mandates set by the U.N. and other entities have set standards for how to effectively administer juvenile justice and to whom.[1]

AUSTRALIA

In Australia, a juvenile is defined as a youth age 10 to 17 (the age in Queensland is 10 to 16). This is a more streamlined definition than that of the United States, because the United States has over 51 variations of minimum and maximum ages to define a juvenile delinquent. Australia's juvenile justice system began in 1895, but was riddled with conflicting objectives resulting from a lack of legislation. Australia's juvenile justice system underwent many changes, including its overarching goal, just as the juvenile justice system has in many other countries. Through the implementation of various acts similar to the Juvenile Prevention Act in the United States, such as the Youth Court Act, the Youth Offenders Act, and the Children and Young People Act, a more unified system was created. Australia's current system includes community-based sentencing options, reduced or split sentencing between imprisonment and community supervision, and therapeutic and mediation diversion programs, all with goals of rehabilitation (Australian Bureau of Statistics, 2013; Australian Institute of Health and Welfare, 2013; Blagg, 2009; Richards, 2009).

FRANCE

In France, children can be taken into custody and found criminally responsible at any age. However, France has three distinct approaches to handle juveniles, each with its own method and objective. Children, at any age up to 9, can be found criminally responsible, but the youth can only be provided with assistance from the court regarding protection and education. No criminal penalty or educational sanctions can be applied. From ages 10 to 13, a judge can order educational sanctions, including mandatory civic education and restitution to the victim, all of which will create a criminal record for the child. Violation of any of these sanctions can result in the 10- to 13-year-old being placed in some kind of formal detention. Children from 13 to 16 years old can receive educational sanctions or criminal penalties, but sentences are half those for adults. Finally, children aged 16 to 18 receive the same penalties as an adult would; however, there is discretion to give them a lesser criminal sentence or, if appropriate, educational sanctions.

Until the 1600s, before the passage of this legislation, parents could have their children imprisoned without having to give any reason. It was not until 1945 that France began to formalize some kind of juvenile justice system, where the focus went from imprisonment to education and counseling, but on a case-by-case basis (Dunkel et al., 2010).

INDIA

India housed adults and juveniles in prison together until 1960. The passage of the Children's Act in 1960 mandated their separation. In 1992, India endorsed the U.N. Convention on the Rights of the Child, and through India's Juvenile Justice Care and Protection Act of 2000, further steps have been taken to protect youth within India's juvenile

---

[1]Countries were selected based on available and relevant data.

justice system. This act provides a framework that many consider one of the most advanced in all of Asia (Penal Reform International, 2014). There is no longer a juvenile court, but instead a juvenile board with two entities at work within this structure, the Children's Court and the Welfare Board. Both minors who have committed criminal offenses and those considered vulnerable because of poverty or neglect are addressed through this system.

The Apprentices Act of 1850 was India's first legislation to address children who committed crimes. It set forth a separate definition for a juvenile delinquent based on gender, for boys up to age 15 and girls up to 17. Eventually, through the Juvenile Justice Act of 2000, the age was changed to 17 for both boys and girls, with a minimum age of 7.

The Juvenile Justice Act of 2000 also absolves any minor under the age of 18 from trial through criminal court. If a juvenile is found guilty, unlike in the United States and many other countries that can keep youth in a detention facility up until age 21 or sometimes even older, India's maximum sentence for a child, even for murder, is 3 years in a detention facility (Cavadino & Dignan, 2011). Options of community service and probation are also available. Like France, India has age bands that can receive different punishment or rehabilitation; thus, minors between the ages of 7 and 12 are treated differently than those 13 to 17.

In 2015, a revision to the Juvenile Justice Care and Protection Act extended the 3-year maximum sentence for minors ages 16 and 17 who commit heinous crimes. It allows them to be punished with the same sentencing as adults, excluding life sentences or death (Agarwal & Kumar, 2016; Cavadino & Dignan, 2011).

ITALY

Italy established its first juvenile court in 1934; however, like other countries' systems, initially, the focus was not on rehabilitation, but imprisonment. The 1988 Juvenile Justice Procedural Reform Act reorganized Italy's juvenile justice system with goals of minimizing involvement with the criminal justice system, imprisonment only when no other options are available, and positive embrace of adjudicated youth (Istituto Don Calabria, 2013).

The minimum age of criminal responsibility in Italy is 14, and if imprisoned, a youth can stay in a juvenile detention center until the age of 21 before being transferred to any other form of detention. A 1994 Constitutional Court ruling prohibited life sentences without parole for minors in Italy. The United States prohibits mandated life sentences without parole for juveniles in most cases, but it can be imposed by judges in extreme situations (*Miller v. Alabama* and *Jackson v. Hobbs*, 2012).

However, if a juvenile goes to trial in Italy, the judge only has one option: imprisonment with some leeway to suspend sentencing. There are many options before trial that can be utilized, such as dismissal or pretrial probation, and higher courts have stressed their utilization before the case goes to trial. Typically, only minors found guilty of serious crimes are sent to Italy's formal detention centers (Istituto Don Calabria, 2013).

COLOMBIA

Colombia's juvenile justice system also initially made little distinction between the punishment of children and that of adults. It incarcerated them together, as did many of the other countries you have been reading about. Their system changed through the 1989 Code of Minors and the 1991 Childhood and Adolescence Act, both of which advocated for handling and keeping juveniles separate during adjudication and in detention. Now only juveniles aged 14 to 18 can be held criminally responsible. Since the early 2000s, after prior laws were changed to adhere to the U.N. Convention on the Rights of the Child, only serious criminal offenses by juveniles can result in prosecution. Further, detained juvenile delinquents can remain under the auspices of the juvenile system until age 25 (Zalkind & Simon, 2004).

There is a current political push to have minors over the age of 15 accused of more severe crimes to be charged as adults. Currently, no juvenile in Colombia, regardless of the crime, is processed through adult criminal court. This differs from the United States. For example, in Florida and Pennsylvania, all homicide cases must be filed in adult court regardless of the offender's age.

SOUTH AFRICA

South Africa traditionally had limited diversion options. In 2000, there were 4,158 South African youths under age 18 in youth prisons, the second highest number in custody behind the United States. In 2009, the Child Justice Act provided for more diversionary options, and now there are two options: care centers and prisons. During this time, 20,000 youths were diverted to child and youth centers. The act also limits the placement of juveniles in prison. Those under age 14 cannot serve prison sentences, regardless of the crime committed. For others, imprisonment should be a last resort. The act also encourages family group counseling and victim offender mediation in an effort to target low-risk youth for reduced incarceration and rehabilitation (Gallinetti, 2009).

CHINA

China did not have a juvenile justice system until juvenile crime doubled across the country into the 1980s, just as it was increasing in many other countries worldwide, including the United States. This was generally theorized to be the result of poor economic conditions, drug and family abuse, and weakened family structure (Liu, 2015). China's 1979 "one-child law" (updated to the "two-child law," effective 2016) has also been said to have exacerbated the rise in crime (Edlund et al., 2007). In 1991, China enacted the Law on the Protection of Minors. It held the government, schools, families, and society responsible overall for instilling discipline and culture. Ultimately, it was the parent's duty to punish children who committed crimes before the age of 16, but for more severe crimes, the government could assume responsibility. In 1994, China passed the Law on Prevention of Juvenile Delinquency that established goals of "protecting juveniles in all facets of life." Since the law's passage, a juvenile delinquent with no prior record can have the case dismissed, or the juvenile may be required to apologize or compensate the victim. In Chinese courts, judges are expected to use imprisonment as the last possible punishment and can suspend the sentence if a juvenile is deemed a minimal risk and if there is a responsible family environment. In the United States, the percentage of youth imprisoned after a trial is about 27%, and this figure is even lower in many other European countries. Although China's Prevention of Juvenile Delinquency Act officially calls for imprisonment as a last resort, community-based sanctions are limited in China; therefore, judges incarcerate upward of 60% of their delinquent youth (Snyder & Sickmund, 2014).

Wrap-up

The overarching goal of the juvenile justice system is rehabilitation. However, this was not always the case. We have seen how societies worldwide historically handled their youth and the progression from the days of harsh punishment and lack of distinction between children and adults. The United States adopted many of these systems in the 1600s and 1700s; however, governments and parliaments around the world came to realize a more uniform and institutional method of controlling youth was necessary. In the early 1800s, the U.S. government began interventions, and juvenile reform centers were created, but not without shortcomings and criticism for poor results and abuses within those institutions. The second half of the 19th century brought a progressive era that set the pathway for Child Savers to advocate for the separate treatment of juveniles and nondetention alternatives. These local, child-focused efforts, along with state and federal oversight, have led to our modern-day juvenile justice system. Figure 1.2 shows a juvenile justice history timeline.

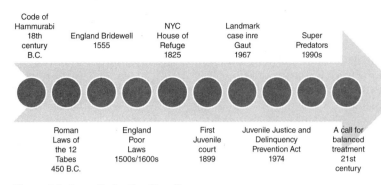

Figure 1.2 Juvenile Justice Timeline

Discussion Questions

1. What did American colonies have in common with the rest of the world during the 17th and 18th centuries?
2. Explain the various philosophies during the 1800s regarding treatment and confinement of juvenile delinquents and juveniles in need.
3. What are the four Ds in the juvenile justice system from the 20th century to the present?
4. Describe the challenges faced during the Progressive Era.
5. List and describe community-based alternatives within the juvenile justice system.
6. What was the purpose of the 1974 Juvenile Justice and Delinquency Prevention Act?
7. Define the term juvenile superpredator and its effects on society at the time.
8. How is the justice system in the United States different from that of other countries around the world?

ONLINE RESOURCES

U.S. Department of Justice, Office of Justice Programs http://www.ojp.gov
Youth.gov http://www.youth.gov
Juvenile Justice Center of Philadelphia http://www.juvenilejustice.org
National Institute of Justice Crime Solutions http://www.crimesolutions.gov
National Criminal Justice Reference Service http://www.ncjrs.gov

Definitions

Bridewell—England's formal institutions to house and control wayward youth, the first of which was in 1555, also considered houses of correction

Child Savers—a group of reformers, composed mostly of women, with the intention to save children, and some argue to save society

Code of Hammurabi—created in the 18th century B.C., it authorized strict punishment for disobedient children

Community-based alternatives—supervision and services provided outside locked facilities

Cottage system—attempted to do away with one large, overcrowded facility and replace it with smaller buildings (cottages), each holding approximately 40 youth

Decriminalization—a shift from a focus on the criminal offense to a focus on the child

Deinstitutionalization—reduction of imprisonment of juveniles

Diversion—diverting juveniles from institutions to a more rehabilitative environment

Due process—procedural rights guaranteed by the Constitution

England's poor laws—prevented peasants from entering guilds (worker's unions), which in turn prevented them from getting jobs. Only those who were homeless through no fault of their own, as determined by the government, were given relief through poor laws.

English Common Law—societal customs and traditions enforced by judgments of the court

Enslaved—individuals that are in servitude for their entire life with no opportunity to gain their freedom

Houses of Refuge—1800s juvenile reformatories that educated and rehabilitated youth through moral, industrial, and general education until the child entered adulthood

Indentured Servant—individuals who would receive their freedom after fulfilling a work contract that typically only provided room and board.

Net widening—expansion of the government's social control over juveniles through intrusive sanctions involving court supervision and conditional release

New York Society for the Prevention of Pauperism—An organization established in 1817 by a group of wealthy Americans who provided assistance to poor individuals and later expanded their efforts to include impoverished and vagrant children.

Parens patriae—Latin for "parent of the country," allows the government to intervene in juvenile matters in the best interest of the child

Patriarchal system—in the early 1800s, the father was head of the family and responsible for controlling his children and providing for them

Placing Out System—An alternative to reformatories in the mid-1800s whereby children and teens were placed on farms with foster families with the intention to learn skills and build moral character through work and guidance.

Progressive Era (1890–1920)—a period of widespread social activism and political reform across the United States

Roman Laws of the 12 Tables—in 450 B.C. Rome, gave a child's father the right of life and death over his natural son

Sight and sound separated—disallowing juveniles any contact with adult offenders when housed in the same facility

Society for the Reformation of Juvenile Delinquents—Formally the New York Society for the Prevention of Pauperism, and in 1824, reorganized to focus more on wayward children and providing them with rehabilitative care.

Status offense—an offense that only applies to minors, whose actions would not be considered unlawful if they were adults

Stubborn Child Law—inspired by God-fearing Puritans who believed only swift and strict punishment would protect communities from God's wrath. Permitted the death of a 16-year-old boy who was incorrigible.

Superpredator—a class of violent youth described as having demonstrated no remorse and no empathy

References

Agarwal, S., & Kumar, N. (2016). Juvenile Justice (Care and Protection of Children) Act 2015: A review. *Space and Culture, India, 3*(3), 5–9.

Australian Bureau of Statistics. (1982–2013). *Prisoners in Australia* (various issues) (ABS Cat. 4517.0). 1982–1993 published by the Australian Institute of Criminology.

Australian Institute of Health and Welfare. (2013). *Youth detention population in Australia 2013* (Juvenile Justice Series 13, Cat. J.U.V. 31).

Bernard, T. J., & Kurlychek, M. C. (2010). *The cycle of juvenile justice* (2nd ed.). Oxford University Press.

Binder, A., Geis, G., & Bruce, D. D., Jr. (1997). *Juvenile delinquency: Historical, cultural, and legal perspectives* (2nd ed.). Anderson.

Blagg, H. (2009). *Youth justice in Western Australia*. Commissioner for Children and Young People.

Bremner, R. H., & Barnard, J. (1974). *Children and youth in America: A documentary history.* Harvard University Press.

Buenker, J. D., Burnham, J. C., & Crunden, R. M. (1986). *Progressivism*. Schenkman.

Butts, J. A. (2002). Juvenile justice: Juvenile court. In J. Dressler (Ed.), *Encyclopedia of crime and justice* (2nd ed., Vol. 3, pp. 937–947). Macmillan Reference USA. http://link.galegroup.com/apps/doc/CX3403000164/UHIC?u=gray02935 &xid=79ec3894

Cate, S. (2016). Devolution, not decarceration: The limits of juvenile justice reform in Texas. *Punishment & Society, 18*(5), 578–609.

Cavadino, M., & Dignan, J. (2011). Penal systems: A comparative approach. SAGE.

Clews, E. W. (2009). *Educational legislation and administration of the colonial governments.* Biblio Bazaar.

Commonwealth v. Fisher, 213 Pa. 48, 62A 198, 199, 200 (1905).

Convention on the Rights of the Child. (1989). *Human rights.* https://treaties.un.org/Pages/ViewDetails.aspx?src=TREATY&mtdsg_no=IV-11&chapter=4&lang=en

Dunkel, F., Gensing, A., Burman, M., & O'Mahony, D. (2010). *Juvenile justice systems in Europe: Current situation and reform developments.* Forum Verlag Godesberg.

Edlund, L., Li, H., Yi, J., & Zhang, J. (2007). *Sex ratios and crime: Evidence from China's one-child policy* (Contract 3214). Institute for the Study of Labor.

Empey, L. (1976). Childhood, delinquency, and social reform. In M. Klein (Ed.), *The juvenile justice system* (pp. 27–28). Sage.

Epstein, S. (2009). *An economic and social history of later medieval Europe, 1000–1500.* Cambridge University Press.

Ex parte Crouse, 4 Whart. 9 (Pa. 1838).

Fox, S. J. (1970, June). Juvenile justice reform: A historical perspective. *Stanford Law Review, 22,* 1187–1239.

Gallinetti, J. (2009). *Getting to know the Child Justice Act.* Child Justice Alliance,

Istituto Don Calabria. (2013). *Italy National Report—J.O.D.A.—Juvenile offenders detention alternative in Europe.* International Juvenile Justice Observatory.

Jackson v. Hobbs, 132 S. Ct. 2455 (2012)

Krisberg, B. (1996). *The historical legacy of juvenile corrections, correctional trends, juvenile justice programs, and trends.* American Correctional Association.

Liu, J. (2015). *China's juvenile justice: A system in transition. National statistics of China 2012.* https://www.researchgate.net/publication/281612947_China's_Juvenile_Justice_A_System_in_Transition

Lopez, D. E. (n.d.) *Strengthening rehabilitation and reintegration of youth offenders.* United Nations International Children's Emergency Fund.

Manfredi, C. P. (1998). *The Supreme Court and juvenile justice.* University Press of Kansas.

Mason, M. A. (1996). *From father's property to children's rights: The history of child custody in the United States.* Columbia University Press.

Miller v. Alabama, 567 U.S. 460 (2012)

Munyo, I. (2013, November). *Youth crime in Latin America.* Brookings Global.

National Research Council. (2013). *Reforming juvenile justice: A developmental approach.* National Academies Press.

Office of Juvenile Justice and Delinquency Prevention. (2010). *Guidance manual for monitoring facilities under the Juvenile Justice and Delinquency Prevention Act of 1974, amended* (3rd ed.). U.S. Department of Justice.

National Research Council and Institute of Medicine. (2001) *Juvenile crime, juvenile justice.* National Academies Press.

New York State Archives and Records Administration, Golding, E. A., & Roe, K. (1950–1989). *The greatest reform school in the world: A guide to the records of the New York House of Refuge.* University of the State of New York.

O'Connell v. Turner 55 Ill. 280; 1870 Ill. LEXIS 355 (1870).

Parens patriae. (2008). *West's Encyclopedia of American Law* (2nd ed.). Thomson/Gale.

Penal Reform International. (2014). *When the crime overshadows the child: International standards and national practice in reconciling serious crime and childhood.*

Platt, A. M. (1977). *The child savers—The invention of delinquency* (2nd ed.). University of Chicago Press.

Quigley, W. P. (1996). Five hundred years of English poor laws, 1349–1834: Regulating the working and nonworking poor. *Akron Law Review, 30*(1), 73–128.

Rausch, S. (1983). Court processing versus diversion of status offenders: A test of deterrence and labeling theories. *Journal of Research in Crime and Delinquency, 20,* 39–54.

Richards, K. (2009). *Juveniles' contact with the criminal justice system in Australia.* Australian Institute of Criminology.

Rollings, K. (2008). *Counting the costs of crime in Australia: A 2005 update* (Research and Public Policy Series 91). Australian Institute of Criminology.

Rosenheim, M. K. (1983). Juvenile justice: Organization and process. In S. Kadish (Ed.), *Encyclopedia of crime and justice* (Vol. 3, pp. 969–977). Free Press.

Schlossman, S. (1977). *Love and the American delinquent: The theory and practice of progressive juvenile justice, 1825–1920.* University of Chicago Press.

Schlossman, S. (1983). Juvenile justice: History and philosophy. In S. H. Kadish (Ed.), *Encyclopedia of crime and justice* (Vol. 3, pp. 961–969). Free Press.

Schwartz, I. M. (1989). *Justice for juveniles: Rethinking the best interests of the child.* Lexington Books.

Snyder, H. N., & Sickmund, M. (2014). *Juvenile offenders and victims: A national report* (NCJ Publication 153569). U.S. Department of Justice.

Sutton, J. R. (1988). *Stubborn children: Controlling delinquency in the United States, 1640–1981.* University of California Press.

Taylor, A., & Foner, E. (2010). *American colonies: [The settling of North America].* Penguin Books.

U.N. General Assembly. (1985, November 29). *United Nations standard minimum rules for the administration of juvenile justice ("The Beijing Rules"): Resolution/adopted by the General Assembly* (A/RES/40/33). https://www.ohchr.org/documents/professionalinterest/beijingrules.pdf

Ward, G. (2012). *The Black Child-Savers: Racial democracy and juvenile justice.* University of Chicago Press.

Zalkind, P., & Simon, R. J. (2004). *Global perspectives on social issues: Juvenile justice systems.* Lexington Books.

2

Juvenile Delinquency: Definitions, Scope, and Crime Measures

CHAPTER OUTLINE

LEARNING OBJECTIVES

At the end of the chapter,
students will be able to

define juvenile delinquency,

compare and contrast local and
federal laws regarding juveniles,

analyze and describe various
crime reporting tools,

explain self-reports,

describe additional sources that
measure the treatment of juveniles, and

compare and contrast crime
measuring tools around the
world.

Keywords

Dark figure of crime
Developmental Victimization Survey
Easy Access to Juvenile Court Statistics
Easy Access to UCR FBI Arrest Statistics
Felony
Hierarchy rule
International Self-Report Delinquency
   Study
Juvenile delinquency
Longitudinal study
Misdemeanor

National Center for Juvenile Justice
National Council of Juvenile and Family
   Court Judges
National Crime Statistics Exchange
National Crime Victimization Survey
National Incident-Based Reporting
   System
National Youth Survey–Family Study
Office of Juvenile Justice and
   Delinquency Prevention
Part I index crimes

Part II index crimes
Reliability
Self-reports
Statistical Briefing Book
Summary Reporting System
Uniform Crime Report
Validity
Victimization surveys
Youth Risk Behavior Surveillance System

Introduction

As we saw in Chapter 1, the general public has always paid close attention to its youth and controlling their actions within society. Chapter 1 detailed incarceration strategies that began in the 1800s to suppress juvenile delinquency based on the notion that there was a strong link between destitute youth and crime. In the 21st century, society turned to creating policies that relied on crime measuring tools as a strategy to reduce juvenile delinquency. Various forms of measuring crime were developed to interpret trends, victimization, juvenile delinquency, and crime overall. As we will see, there are numerous measuring tools not only across the United States, but also around the world, and the pros and cons of each tool are just as numerous.[1]

Juvenile Delinquency

The Department of Justice defines **juvenile delinquency** as "the violation of the law of the United States committed by a person prior to his eighteenth birthday, which would have been a crime if committed by an adult" ("Easy Access to Juvenile Court Statistics," 2017, p. 1). The federal government provided a general definition, but individual states not only interpret the act of delinquency differently but also independently decide which offenders it applies to (U.S. Attorney's Manual, 1997).

Not All States Laws Are Created Equally

Although the federal government has set guidelines for how to define and assess juvenile delinquency, each state has the ability to create its own definition of what a juvenile

---

[1]Later chapters will address the issues these crime measuring tools reveal, such as disproportionate arrest data, theoretical causes for these offenses, and efforts to support juveniles and promote change.

delinquent is. Generally, a juvenile delinquent is any minor (as defined by the given state) who commits an act that would be considered a crime if committed by an adult.

As of the latest statistics published in 2017, 42 states allow the juvenile court to have jurisdiction for a child considered a juvenile delinquent up to age 17, 6 set jurisdiction up until 16, and 2 states, New York and North Carolina, only protect a child within the juvenile court up until age 15 (Office for Juvenile Justice and Delinquency Prevention [OJJDP], 2017a).[2] Falling under the auspices of the juvenile court puts the focus on rehabilitation as opposed to punishment, as seen in criminal court.

As an example of just how much of a difference state statutes make, if a 17-year-old in California is arrested for vandalism, a misdemeanor, they would be considered a juvenile delinquent under the jurisdiction of California's juvenile justice system. They would be afforded certain protections in terms of sentencing and treatment, with an overall goal of rehabilitation. However, if that same juvenile commits the same crime in Texas, they would be prosecuted in adult criminal court because no one age 17 or older in Texas can qualify for juvenile court. They would not fall under the juvenile justice system's jurisdiction or be afforded any of its protections, and the overarching goal would be to punish, reflective of the adult sentencing they would receive. Differences in state laws not only make it difficult to assess court jurisdiction for how the juvenile is processed, but also make it challenging to measure juvenile crime and create appropriate policies.

When we look at crime measuring tools and the resulting data used to measure juvenile crime, because there are differences in who an individual state considers a juvenile, most juvenile crime data and resulting comparisons for trends generally include individuals under the age of 18.

Collecting accurate crime data is essential to create policies and initiatives appropriately and effectively. As we are about to see, there are no perfect crime measuring methods, although many reveal patterns, trends, and an overall outlook of crime.

Measuring Crime in the United States

The United States has two main ways of collecting crime data: through law enforcement agencies and through **self-reports** via **victimization surveys**, surveys that solicit self-reporting data from crime victims and those affected by crime.

Uniform Crime Reporting Program

In the 1920s, the International Association of Chiefs of Police, a nonprofit organization of police chiefs that still exists in the early 21st century, and the Social Science Research Council worked to create a uniform, national set of crime statistics that could be analyzed and relied on for crime reduction and other initiatives. They formed a committee and determined seven offenses for crime rate comparisons. These crimes were all **felonies** (crimes punishable with more than 1 year in jail) and were tagged **Part I index crimes**. They initially included murder and nonnegligent manslaughter (willful killing of a human being), forcible rape,[3] burglary, aggravated assault, larceny, and motor vehicle

---

[2]In 2016, legislation was passed to raise the age for juvenile court jurisdiction in both New York and North Carolina to 17 in 2018 and to 18 in 2019.

[3]In 2013, the FBI expanded their rape definition to include any penetration by force or unlawful statutory actions, including **statutory rape**, in which the victim is not of a mental state to consent, including being under the age of consent.

theft (an eighth crime, arson, was added under a congressional directive in 1979). U.S. police departments began voluntarily providing monthly data. In January 1930, the first report was published by the International Association of Chiefs of Police after receiving crime data from 430 municipalities across 43 states. Later, in June 1930, legislation was passed to allow the FBI to assume responsibility for collecting, preserving, and publishing these crime data, as they still do today under the auspices of the Justice Department. In 2017, over 18,000 police entities voluntarily provided crime data for the **Uniform Crime Report** (UCR) program (Department of Justice [DOJ], 2017a).The current UCR program consists of four types of data collection by police agencies, the Law Enforcement Officers Killed and Assaulted program, the Hate Crime Statistics program, the **Summary Reporting System** (SRS), and the **National Incident-Based Reporting System** (NIBRS). The UCR program publishes annual and preliminary semiannual reports for all of the data collected (National Academies of Sciences, Engineering, and Medicine, 2016).

Summary Reporting System

The SRS of the UCR program is the standard and most widely cited method of measuring crime in the United States (James, 2008; National Academies of Sciences, Engineering, and Medicine, 2016).

The SRS data include a breakdown of complaints by victims and offenders' arrests disaggregated by location, gender, race, ethnicity, and age. This type of data collection can provide some insights into the propensity and type of crime by many groups, including juveniles. The SRS has both strengths and limitations (DOJ, 2017a). It is based on complaint reports to the police, and although communities can be encouraged to report crimes, not all crime is reported. The **dark figure of crime** comprises the offenses that go unreported to the police for a variety of reasons, such as embarrassment, fear of repercussions, or a belief that nothing will be done (Bureau of Justice Statistics [BJS], 2017). There have also been issues of proper discretion by police departments regarding the interpretation of reported offenses and determining what crime classification would be most appropriate.

Although the SRS also includes **Part II index crimes**, including **misdemeanors** (punishable by less than a year in jail), when crime is reported as being either up or down, this usually refers only to the eight felony Part I index crimes. This can lead to a misconception by the public of what type of crime is down and what is up. For example, whereas felony assault is a Part I index crime, all other misdemeanor assaults, such as ones that may be occurring in and around schools, are not included in this category. Solely relying on reports of Part I crimes being down can be misleading in terms of crime trends occurring among youth, among whom the majority of arrests are for nonfelony offenses (OJJDP, 2020).

The SRS additionally follows a **hierarchy rule**, meaning that only the most serious crime within a given incident is reported. For example, if a robbery occurred and the victim was murdered, only the murder statistic would be reported in the SRS, not the robbery. Further, as the description indicates, the system is summary based and thus reports the total number of crimes a population has experienced as opposed to providing more specific details regarding any given incident. A summary-based system makes it simpler for law enforcement to report regularly. Still, it excludes data that could be essential for analyzing particular issues a given community could be experiencing and implementing strategies that would be most effective. Practitioners in the field, researchers, and policy makers recognized that an additional crime measuring tool was needed.

Juvenile Data Collection

The UCR program considers a juvenile an individual under 18 years of age, regardless of state definition. The program does not collect data regarding police contact with a minor who has not committed an offense, nor does it collect data on situations in which police take a juvenile into custody for their protection, such as in neglect cases.

- Arrests of juveniles for all offenses decreased 8.4% in 2015 when compared with 2014; arrests of adults decreased 3.0% (see Table 2.1 for an example of how this is reported).

National Incident-Based Reporting System

In 1989, the FBI and the BJS began to implement the NIBRS as an alternate reporting system. As indicated by its name, this system provides more incident data, such as additional details about each specific crime incident, as opposed to just summary data reported by the SRS. The NIBRS collects information about victims, offenders, property, and arrests, but differs from the SRS in that it provides 57 offense classifications, with up to 10 offenses per incident (remember that because of the SRS's hierarchy rule, only the most serious crime is reported per incident). Regarding juveniles, the NIBRS provides data on not only the age of the offender, but also the age of the victim (DOJ, 2017a).

The NIBRS also collects data on homicide and assault offenses at schools and colleges, gang violence, firearm data, and reports on age groups most affected by various crime incidents. It expands data collection to include offense definitions and can provide information on correlations between offenses, property, victims, offenders, and arrestees. It has also expanded data to include victim-to-offender relationships and provides additional crime details such as weapon information for all violent offenses, drug- and computer-based crimes, type of injury per victim, incident location, date, and time. Table 2.2 illustrates some of the data that NIBRS collects.

Unfortunately, because participation is voluntary and because this type of extensive data collection and reporting is much more time-consuming than SRS data collection, it has not been adopted by all of the agencies that provide information for the SRS. Therefore, the FBI has maintained both the SRS and the NIBRS (see Table 2.3). In 2016, only about a third of all reporting police entities had adopted this crime measuring tool, and the rest continued to report through the SRS's standards and guidelines. Mandates have been put in place to completely replace the summary system with the NIBRS in 2021. Prior to this, an alternate means to be able to report on more in-depth incident data, representative of the U.S. population, was implemented (DOJ, 2017a).

National Crime Statistics Exchange

In 2012, in a joint effort, the FBI and the BJS established an interim and transitional tool to provide more specific national crime data to the public and assist all law enforcement agencies in using the NIBRS to report their offense data. The **National Crime Statistics Exchange** consists of 400 strategically identified agencies that were already reporting through the NIBRS. The data from these strategically placed agencies could be representative of crime nationally. These efforts are currently underway (BJS, 2017, 2020).

TABLE 2.1 Arrest Trends, 2014–2015

	NUMBER OF PERSONS ARRESTED														
	TOTAL ALL AGES			**UNDER 15 YEARS OF AGE**			**UNDER 18 YEARS OF AGE**			**18 YEARS OF AGE AND OVER**		
OFFENSE CHARGED	**2014**	**2015**	**PERCENT CHANGE**	**2014**	**2015**	**PERCENT CHANGE**	**2014**	**2015**	**PERCENT CHANGE**	**2014**	**2015**	**PERCENT CHANGE**
TOTAL[1]	**7,967,934**	**7,689,755**	**−3.5**	**197,475**	**180,987**	**−8.3**	**709,317**	**649,970**	**−8.4**	**7,258,617**	**7,039,785**	**−3.0**
Murder and nonnegligent manslaughter	7,044	7,519	+6.7	41	47	+14.6	488	521	+6.8	6,556	6,998	+6.7
Rape[2]	14,991	15,934	+6.3	939	991	+5.5	2,356	2,515	+6.7	12,635	13,419	+6.2
Robbery	64,612	66,138	+2.4	2,533	2,348	−7.3	12,597	12,347	−2.0	52,015	53,791	+3.4
Aggravated assault	269,114	271,650	+0.9	7,033	6,667	−5.2	21,579	20,503	−5.0	247,535	251,147	+1.5
Burglary	171,437	156,419	−8.8	8,052	7,543	−6.3	28,386	25,527	−10.1	143,051	130,892	−8.5
Larceny-theft	891,541	838,874	−5.9	35,758	31,006	−13.3	126,889	113,114	−10.9	764,652	725,760	−5.1
Motor vehicle theft	47,027	53,315	+13.4	1,917	2,055	+7.2	8,182	9,236	+12.9	38,845	44,079	+13.5

Source: Department of Justice (2017b).

TABLE 2.2 Offenders' Age Category by Offense, 2017

OFFENSE CATEGORY	TOTAL OFFENDERS[1]	AGE CATEGORY		
		ADULT	**JUVENILE[2]**	**UNKNOWN**
Total	5,266,175	3,901,203	501,503	863,469
Crimes against persons	1,382,797	1,138,370	163,516	80,911
Assault offenses	1,262,885	1,050,827	142,128	69,930
Homicide offenses	6,561	5,339	419	803
Human trafficking offenses	462	402	21	39
Kidnapping/abduction	20,475	18,012	874	1,589
Sex offenses	86,970	59,803	18,806	8,361
Sex offenses, nonforcible	5,444	3,987	1,268	189
Crimes against property	2,600,568	1,605,848	232,738	761,982
Arson	10,236	5,360	2,404	2,472
Bribery	446	404	23	19
Burglary/breaking & entering	279,790	149,043	24,012	106,735
Counterfeiting/forgery	81,880	63,896	1,811	16,173
Destruction/damage/vandalism	456,273	261,855	59,875	134,543
Embezzlement	21,657	19,898	725	1,034
Extortion/blackmail	2,697	1,478	232	987
Fraud offenses	237,564	157,452	6,528	73,584
Larceny/theft offenses	1,197,252	749,912	103,159	344,181
Motor vehicle theft	147,882	79,942	14,063	53,877
Robbery	101,021	62,555	12,921	25,545
Stolen property offenses	63,870	54,053	6,985	2,832
Crimes against society	1,282,810	1,156,985	105,249	20,576
Animal cruelty	3,115	2,620	116	379
Drug/narcotic offenses	1,122,416	1,027,739	85,353	9,324
Gambling offenses	1,237	1,128	38	71
Pornography/obscene material	13,399	6,250	6,026	1,123
Prostitution offenses	12,515	12,153	138	224
Weapon law violations	130,128	107,095	13,578	9,455

[1] Offenders are counted once for each offense type to which they are connected. Neither the offender data nor the offense data for the 1,665,707 incidents reported with unknown offenders were used in constructing this table.
[2] For this table, a juvenile is an offender under the age of 18.
Source: Department of Justice (2017b).

TABLE 2.3 Comparison of the Summary Reporting System and the National Incident-Based Reporting System

SUMMARY REPORTING SYSTEM	NATIONAL INCIDENT-BASED REPORTING SYSTEM/ NATIONAL CRIME STATISTICS EXCHANGE
Total number of crimes	Specific victim, offender, property, and arrest details
Hierarchy rule	Up to 10 offenses per incident
Limited information on victims, including juveniles	More information on all victims, including juveniles
Limits range of Part I offense categories (combines many attempted and completed crimes)	Broader range of offense categories (separates attempted and completed crimes)

Source: Department of Justice (2017a).

What If Victims Are Hesitant to Report a Crime to the Police?

Self-Reports: Victimization Surveys

Surveys are one way to solicit data regarding a particular subject. With regard to crime, they enable individuals who do not want to report an incident to the police for a variety of reasons (distrust, belief that it will not help) and can be used to combat the dark figure of crime. When analyzing survey results, it is important to look at a variety of factors to ensure that every effort was made to achieve impartial results that have good **validity** (the extent that the questions measure what they are intended to measure) and **reliability** (consistency of a measure). When evaluating statistical surveys and their results, experts agree it is important to keep the following in mind:

1. Who is sponsoring the survey?
2. Who is conducting the survey?
3. Where is the sample of the population coming from?
4. Does the sample represent the rest of the population?
5. What environment were the questions asked in?
6. Who asked them?
7. How were they asked (personally, paper, computer)?
8. What were the specific questions, and how were they phrased?
9. Were the people being tested paid? (Dillman et al., 2014)

Many crime surveys have been geared toward the criminalization of youth throughout the years, both as the offender and as the victim.

The National Youth Survey–Family Study

The **National Youth Survey–Family Study** began in 1976 and was initially called the National Youth Survey. At that time, 1,725 adolescents between the ages of 11 and 17, as well as a parent/guardian, were interviewed. In 2000, "Family Study" was added to the name because the participants were no longer youths. For over 30 years, this **longitudinal study** (a research design that entails repeated observations over a long period of time, usually many years) examined changing attitudes and behaviors regarding career goals, community and family involvement, and attitudes about violence, drugs, values, and victimization. Additional questions covered family relationships, education, and employment. In 2002, researchers began collecting DNA from the respondents to study relationships between specific genes and measured behaviors (National Youth Survey, 2015).

Information from these studies has been used to create initiatives and policy recommendations regarding youth in America. In 1993, researchers began interviewing the partners and children of the original respondents, and by 2011 those original respondents were aged 46 through 55.

The Youth Risk Behavior Surveillance System

The **Youth Risk Behavior Surveillance System** (YRBSS) was developed in 1990 to monitor "priority health risk behaviors that contribute markedly to the leading causes of death, disability, and social problems among youth and adults in the United States" (Centers for Disease Control and Prevention, 2019, p. 2). The YRBSS includes "national, state, territorial, tribal government, and local school-based surveys of representative samples of 9th through 12th-grade students" (Centers for Disease Control and Prevention, 2019, p. 2). These surveys are conducted every 2 years, usually during the spring semester. They collect information on behaviors that can present during childhood and early adolescence and include

- behaviors that contribute to unintentional injuries and violence,
- sexual behaviors related to unintended pregnancy and sexually transmitted diseases,
- alcohol and other drug use,
- tobacco use,
- unhealthy dietary behaviors, and
- inadequate physical activity.

In addition, according to the 2019 National YRBS Data Users Guide, "the YRBSS monitors obesity and asthma and other priority health-related behaviors plus sexual identity and sex of sexual contacts. From 1991 through 2015, the YRBSS has collected data from more than 3.8 million high school students in more than 1,700 separate surveys" (Centers for Disease Control and Prevention, 2019, p. 1).

Based on survey results, the YRBSS can

- determine health behaviors and assess changes,
- examine the co-occurrence of health behaviors,
- provide comparable data including among subpopulations of youth, and
- monitor progress toward healthy well-being objectives.

Developmental Victimization Survey

The **Developmental Victimization Survey** was created in 2002. Its purpose is to reveal victimizations that can be broken down by gender, race, and developmental stage. The questionnaire was developed by the Crimes Against Children Research Center. Telephone interviews of a nationally representative sample of 2,030 children ages 2 to 17 years are conducted annually. Individuals age 10 and older speak with an interviewer themselves, and primary caregivers (usually a parent) speak on behalf of children under 10. The survey measures 34 forms of victimization that occurred in the prior year, grouped into five areas.

> *Standard crimes* include robbery, personal theft, vandalism, assault with a weapon, assault without a weapon, attempted assault, kidnapping, and bias attack. *Child maltreatment* includes physical abuse of caregivers, emotional abuse, neglect, custodial interference, or family abduction. *Peer and sibling victimization* include gang or group assault, peer or sibling assault, nonsexual genital assault, bullying, emotional bullying, and dating violence. *Sexual victimization* includes sexual assault by a known adult. *Indirect victimization, including witnessing criminality.* (Crimes Against Children Research Center, n.d., p. 1)

Analyses of these data are ongoing.

The largest survey still utilized in the early 21st century is the **National Crime Victimization Survey** (NCVS), run by the BJS. The NCVS is an essential tool for quantifying the delinquency and violence problem in the United States. Although we have read about other types of surveys, the NCVS continues to be the primary victimization measure of crime in the United States (BJS, 2016).

National Crime Victimization Survey

The NCVS began in 1973 under the auspices of the BJS. This survey provides self-reported details of crime incidents, victims, and trends. The BJS redesigned the survey in 1993. Questions were updated to better solicit crime data from victims, survey methods were updated, and the extent of crimes measured was broadened. The NCVS gathers detailed information regarding the frequency and nature of rape and other sexual assaults, personal robbery, aggravated and simple assault, household burglary, theft, and motor vehicle theft. It does not measure homicide or commercial crimes (e.g., burglaries of stores). The NCVS is a national survey and cannot break down data by state or locality (Donziger, 1996).

Telephone interviews with approximately 43,000 households twice a year, resulting in a sample of 150,000 individuals, are conducted annually by the U.S. Census Bureau on behalf of the BJS. Persons age 12 or older can be interviewed, and households stay in the sample for 3 years. New households rotate into the sample on an ongoing basis (BJS, 2016).

The NCVS collects information on crimes suffered by individuals and households, including those not reported to the police, in order to include the usually unaccounted-for dark figure of crime. It also provides reasons victims give for reporting or not reporting crimes.

The survey provides information about victims (age, sex, race, ethnicity, marital status, income, and educational level), offenders (sex, race, approximate age, and victim-to-offender relationship), and crimes (time and place of occurrence, use of weapons, nature of the injury, and economic consequences). Questions also cover experiences victims had with the criminal justice system, protective measures used by victims, and any substance abuse by offenders. Supplements are intermittently added to the survey to obtain specific information on topics like crime in school (BJS, 2016).

Issues with self-reports include the following:

- Not everyone will admit to illegal acts.
- Participants may forget or exaggerate crimes.

- Participants may be confused about what they are being asked for.
- The data collected are from a sample, not the entire population.

Comparing the Big Three: SRS, NIBRS, and NCVS

The SRS, NIBRS, and NCVS define serious crimes similarly and report on crimes such as rape, robbery, aggravated assault, burglary, theft, and motor vehicle theft. The NCVS includes crimes reported to police, like the SRS and NIBRS, but also crimes that were not reported to law enforcement. The NCVS excludes but the SRS and NIBRS include homicide, arson, commercial crimes, and crimes against children under age 12. While both the SRS and the NIBRS collect data on offenses reported to law enforcement, only arrest data for simple assaults and sexual assault other than rape are included in the SRS. The NIBRS collects arrest data on nearly 60 offenses.

There are also some differences in the definitions of less violent crimes. For example, the SRS and NIBRS define burglary as the unlawful entry or attempted entry of a structure to commit a felony or theft within. The NCVS, anticipating that victims would not know the offender's intentions, defines burglary as the unlawful entry or attempted entry of a residence by an individual.

The SRS and NIBRS rates for these crimes are reported per capita (number of crimes per 100,000 persons), whereas the NCVS rates are reported per household (number of crimes per 1,000 households). Because the number of households may not grow at the same rate as the total population each year, trend data may not be comparable between the systems. As mentioned previously, the SRS and NIBRS's data represent the population, whereas the NCVS provides sampling data, which would be subject to a margin of error (DOJ, 2017a; U.S. Attorney's Manual, 1997).

Finally, strengths of the SRS and the NIBRS include capturing crimes reported to police all over the country, and the UCR program provides an additional homicide report that gives the number and nature of homicides across the nation. The NCVS excels by providing not only information on the quantity and types of crimes committed by offenders that go unreported, but also detailed victimization information, including information for juveniles.

Access to Data Measuring Tools

Office of Juvenile Justice and Delinquency Prevention

The **Office of Juvenile Justice and Delinquency Prevention** (OJJDP) is part of the Office of Justice Programs in the U.S. DOJ. It supports cities, towns, states, and tribal territories in developing juvenile justice programs.

Statistical Briefing Book

The OJJDP **Statistical Briefing Book** was developed by the National Center for Juvenile Justice and allows anyone to access juvenile crime, youth involved in the system, and victimization data from a variety of sources, including the UCR program via the OJJDP's website. In addition, it provides detailed statistics on a variety of juvenile justice topics ("Easy Access," 2017).

Easy Access to Juvenile Court Statistics

Easy Access to Juvenile Court Statistics was created to assist in analyzing national estimations of juvenile court cases throughout the country. This analysis can provide users with information on the age, sex, and race of juveniles involved in these cases. It can also provide information on referral, detention, adjudication, and case disposition. Demographic characteristics of justice involving youth and how juvenile courts process these cases are also available ("Easy Access," 2017). Chapter 8 will explore the juvenile court process and treatment of juveniles from various demographics in greater depth.

Easy Access to UCR FBI Arrest Statistics

Easy Access to UCR FBI Arrest Statistics was developed to "provide access to juvenile arrest statistics at the national, state, and county levels" (OJJDP, 2017b, p. 1). Arrest statistics are presented for 29 detailed offense categories. Displays can be selected based on counts or rates for juveniles, adults, or all ages combined.

National Center for Juvenile Justice

The **National Center for Juvenile Justice** is the research division of the **National Council of Juvenile and Family Court Judges**. It is the oldest juvenile justice research group in the United States. It has provided open access to crime and delinquency data from national and international studies since 1973 ("Easy Access," 2017).

As we can see, there are many resources for collecting and assessing data points for juvenile delinquency and crime. These tools enable stakeholders to not only be aware of the current state of crime, but also develop strategies to appropriately and effectively address it. This is vital not only to the United States, but also to countries around the world.

Worldview

Measuring Delinquency and Crime Around the World

Much like the United States, countries across the globe track their juvenile crime in various ways, relying on data from both law enforcement and victimization surveys.[4] According to the World Health Organization (2020), an average of 200,000 homicides occur each year among youth. Globally, 84% of youth homicide victims are males, and in every country, males also make up the majority of offenders. Crime measuring tools are therefore relied on for policy decisions on an international level. In the years 2000–2016, rates of youth homicide decreased in most countries, with greater decreases occurring in high-income countries. Strategies that include analyzing crime data remain the primary source for keeping those crime rates down (World Health Organization, 2020).

---

[4]The countries discussed in this section were selected based on available and current data relevant to the chapter.

AUSTRALIA

Australia collects national crime statistics in two ways: *administrative data*, or data taken from state and territory police forces, courts, hospitals, and community services, and *crime victimization surveys*, or self-reporting.

Since 1993, state and territory police forces have provided crime data to Australia's Bureau of Statistics (ABS). Data are then compiled and published. Each state or territory in Australia also publishes its own crime statistics through administrative data and surveys. Similar to the United States and other countries that also rely on police data to measure crime, Australia faces limitations, such as only having data on offenses reported to police. Other issues include indigenous communities handling criminality internally, particular groups such as women and children having low reporting issues, and the police discretion to record crime only if they feel it is warranted, even if a crime was committed (ABS, 2014). Other difficulties include differences in states' and territories' legislation and differences in administrative and recording practices. One recommendation to alleviate some of the differences between states and territories was to have the Australian Federal Police, as a national body, serve in a leadership role to establish a consistent national police data collection method (ABS, 2014). Crimes included in the administrative data include

- homicide and related offenses (including murder, attempted murder, and manslaughter, but excluding driving causing death and conspiracy to murder);
- assault;
- sexual assault;
- kidnapping/abduction;
- robbery;
- blackmail/extortion;
- unlawful entry with intent;
- motor vehicle theft; and
- other theft. (ABS, 2014)

Unlike the U.S. SRS, however, there is no hierarchy rule, meaning that lesser offenses in one incident are also recorded, rather than just the offense determined to be the most serious. The recording of only the highest crime in an incident has received criticism in terms of misrepresenting the total number of crimes (Donziger, 1996; Mosher et al., 2010).

The ABS also conducts a national crime victimization survey. However, the survey is not published every year, creating gaps of up to 4 years. This type of sporadic publishing and resulting lack of annual statistics prevents establishing timely trends and comparisons. Local communities and organizations collect other smaller, more specific crime data. The Australian Crime Commission produces the Australian Illicit Drug Data Report, and the Australian Institute of Criminology facilitates programs monitoring violence within families.

As we have discussed, one of the issues with relying on police data is the dark figure of crime. To address this lack of reporting, Australian crime victimization surveys attempt to solicit unreported crime through interviews within the community. However, these surveys are based on a sample of the population and are subject to sampling errors (Australian Institute of Health and Welfare, 2013).

CANADA

Statistics Canada has used four versions of crime measuring tools, created in 1962, 1988, 1998, and 2004, all equivalent to the U.S. SRS and NIBRS. They currently use their original crime measuring tool, UCR1.0, which is summary based like the U.S. SRS, as well as the UCR2.0, created in 2004, which collects incident data like the U.S. NIBRS. The survey is currently administered as part of the National Justice Statistics Initiative (*Statistics by Subject*, 2018).

The UCR, also known as UCR1, was created in 1962 and collects summary data for approximately 100 criminal offenses. All 1,000 police entities provide statistical data, so the program is not voluntary like the U.S. UCR. Data for the incident-based UCR2 are collected from police records management systems and are submitted on a monthly basis.

Canada has a hierarchy rule, like the U.S. SRS reporting process. However, the incident-based UCR2 version allows up to four violations per incident. All areas in Canada are surveyed under the UCR2 program. In 2016, 159 police services provided data for the UCR2 survey, representing 99% of Canada's population (*Statistics by Subject*, 2018). Both the UCR1 and the UCR2 provide offense and arrest data for youth and adults, along with other data points.

Statistics Canada also developed a victimization survey called the General Social Survey. Data from this survey include victimization experiences of individuals age 15 and older. Like the victimization survey in Australia, Canada conducts this survey sporadically, every 5 years. Canada also mandates its citizens to respond to certain surveys, such as surveys soliciting labor, socioeconomic, and agriculture information.

In 2009, a new crime tool was introduced called the Crime Severity Index. The Police Information and Statistics Committee of the Canadian Association of Chiefs of Police asked Statistics Canada to create a new crime measuring tool that would address traditional crime rate reporting limitations. This new tool tracks crime data back to 1998 and, unlike the UCR, weighs various crimes differently. It not only provides the total number of crimes that are up or down but also can provide details on the severity of a crime. For example, in the United States, the total number of Part I index crimes is added and compared to the previous year to indicate if crime is up or down, regardless of whether the majority of those crimes are considered more or less serious. The Crime Severity Index in Canada additionally evaluates each category of crime and assigns a severity rating. For example, if instances of murder are down and instances of car theft are up, causing the overall crime rate to be up, the overall severity rating may still be reported as down.

The Crime Severity Index helps answer such questions as, Is the crime now coming to the attention of police more or less serious than it was prior? and Is police-reported crime in a given city or province more or less serious than in Canada overall? (*Statistics by Subject*, 2018). The new index is meant to coexist with the other crime measuring tools to provide a variety of useful data.

ITALY

Italy's equivalent to the traditional U.S. SRS program is the Statistics of Offenses, which began in 1955. The Ministry of Interior collects and publishes data. Statistics are calculated based on recorded crimes, victims, and suspects. Police statistics are based on approximately 30 crimes. Data are collected by police at the local level and provided monthly to the Italian National Institute of Statistics (Italian National Institute of Statistics, n.d.).

The Italian National Institute of Statistics also administers a general victimization survey and other specialized surveys, such as the Violence Against Women and Family Survey. The first victimization survey was carried out in 1997/1998 and is updated every 5 to 6 years. Data are collected over the phone by only female interviewers. Interviewers are personally recruited and trained for 5 days (3 days of theoretical and 2 days of technical training). They are monitored daily and evaluated. The survey has a sample of 60,000 households, wherein only one person aged 14 and over is interviewed (remember that the U.S. NCVS interviews those age 12 and over). The survey collects data on predatory crimes, such as child molestation, and certain types of crimes against the person, such as robbery and assault.

The Italian victimization survey shares the common objective of uncovering the dark figure of crime. Italy estimates that their unreported crime is approximately 70% for crimes such as robbery, burglary, bag snatching, assaults, and other violent crimes. It is estimated that only 7% of rapes are reported (Italian National Institute of Statistics, n.d.; Muratore & Sabbadini, 2008). Their hope is that victimization surveys will continue to uncover these unreported crimes and help differentiate between perception and reality with regard to the crime rate. In Chapter 4, we will see how perception can be misguided and result in haphazardly created policies that can do more harm than good.

Before the 1990s, administrative statistics were the only source of data in Italy. However, the dual method of collecting crime data that has become common in the United States is also becoming more popular all over the world.

FRANCE

The National Observatory of Delinquency and Criminal Responses in France is a department of the National Institute of Higher Studies of Security and Justice. Its primary purpose is to provide statistics on crime and delinquency and its mission is to collect statistical data from all government departments and any public or private bodies in France with related information. These data are analyzed and published monthly.

In 2005/2006, France began publishing its own national victimization survey, Living and Security Environment, through the Institute of Statistics and Economic Studies (2016). This is the first survey to measure, among other criminal activity, trends in delinquency beyond what has been reported to the police. The objective of this survey is to collect self-reported crime data as well as information from victims and nonvictims regarding living environment and safety. The survey was initially conducted annually through phone interviews with individuals age 14 or older. In 2009, the eligible interviewing age was lowered to 10. Participants can also fill out confidential questionnaires, but this option is only for individuals between the ages of 18 and 75. In 2007, the annual victimization survey became a stand-alone survey devoted to trends in delinquency, awareness, and other victims of violence. In 2016, data from approximately 15,000 households and almost 23,000 individuals were collected (Institute of Statistics and Economic Studies, 2016).

ENGLAND AND WALES

England and Wales have multiple ways of measuring crime data for adults and children. Crime data reported to the police are published yearly and are based on crime statistics reported by the police. Police-recorded crime statistics are based on data from all 44 police entities in England and Wales. They also administer the Crime Survey for England and Wales (previously called the British Crime Survey). The survey is administered to 35,000 households through the Office of National Statistics. Previous results of this study have indicated that only 4 in 10 crimes are reported to the police. The Crime Survey also covers new and emerging crimes, such as fraud and online crime.

The survey provides information about the nature of offenses, such as the location and timing of crimes, offenders' characteristics, and the relationship between victims and offenders.

TABLE 2.4 Two Forms of Measuring Crime in England and Wales

CRIME SURVEY	POLICE-RECORDED CRIME STATISTICS
STRENGTHS	
Large, nationally representative sample survey providing a good measure of long-term crime trends for the offenses and the population it covers (that is, those residents in households)	Broader offense coverage and population coverage than the Crime Survey for England and Wales
Consistent methodology over time	Good measure of offenses that are reported to the police
Covers crimes not reported to the police and is not affected by changes in police recording practices; therefore, it is a reliable measure of long-term trends	Primary source of local crime statistics and for lower volume crimes (for example, homicide)
Coverage of survey extended in 2009 to include children aged 10	Provides whole counts (rather than estimates that are subject to sampling variation)
Independent collection of crime figures	Time lag between occurrence of crime and reporting results tends to be short, indicating emerging trends
LIMITATIONS	
Survey is subject to error associated with sampling and respondents recalling past events	Excludes offenses that are not reported to or not recorded by the police and does not include less serious crimes
Excludes crimes against businesses and those not resident in households (for example, residents of institutions or visitors)	Trends can be influenced by changes in recording practices or police activity
Previously excluded fraud and cybercrime	Concerns exist about the quality of recording—crimes may not be recorded consistently across police forces, so the actual level of recorded crime may be understated

Source: Office for National Statistics (2015).

Since 2009, the survey has included a separate questionnaire to solicit victimization experiences of young people aged 10–15. Young people are selected to participate in this dedicated youth section from the same households selected for the adult survey. Interviews are conducted with the permission of a parent or guardian (Office for National Statistics, 2015).

WORLDWIDE VICTIMIZATION SURVEY
The **International Self-Report Delinquency Study (ISRD)** is a worldwide victimization survey created by the Dutch Research and Documentation Center. It has undergone three stages with the assistance of researchers all over the globe. It collects international data on juvenile delinquency and victimization by observing and comparing differences, similarities, and trends in juvenile offending and victimization between countries. The primary focus is Europe, but the sample also includes a number of non-European countries. The three core objectives of the ISRD are "(1) to measure the prevalence and incidence of offending and

victimization; (2) to test theories about correlates of offending and victimization; and (3) to develop policy-relevant recommendations" (Enzmann et al., 2015, p. 3).

The ISRD uses a standardized self-report survey conducted in school settings among students in Grades 7, 8, and 9 (or equivalent grades for children aged 12–15), randomly selected from schools in a minimum of two cities per country. Each country has a goal of 1,800 participants.

ISRD1: 12 countries participated (1992–1993)

ISRD2: 32 countries participated (2005–2007)

ISRD3: 39 countries participated (2012–2019)

The ISRD2 study was conducted in 32 countries. Sampling was conducted in school classes with a goal of 2,100 youths per participating country. The survey was distributed to children between the seventh and ninth grades. Students filled out the questionnaires under the supervision of the researchers or teachers.

The third stage of the ISRD, the ISRD3, an international collaborative study of delinquency among seventh, eighth, and ninth graders, is currently underway (Enzmann et al., 2015). First results from the ISRD3 were published in 2017 and address theories such as social bonding and the implications of youth exhibiting a reluctance to self-report victimization and criminality around the world (Neissl, 2017).

Wrap-up

As we have seen, measuring crime in a variety of modalities is essential for accurately establishing trends and victimization to then create effective initiatives and appropriate policies. Most countries have a system that both gleans crime data reported to the police and provides opportunities for victims to self-report. This is done to reveal victim/offender information and the dark figure of crime. As we will see in future chapters, society can be influenced by a variety of factors in addition to crime data when determining how to understand, address, and assist the juvenile population.

Discussion Questions

1. Should states be able to define what a juvenile delinquent is, or should a single definition be adopted?

2. What are the benefits and shortcomings of crime measuring tools that rely on data reported to the police?

3. Compare and contrast the UCR's SRS and the NIBRS.

4. What are the benefits and shortcomings of crime measuring tools that rely on self-reports?

5. What is the purpose of the OJJDP?

6. List and describe additional surveys that have been created to solicit other information about the treatment of juveniles within the system.

7. How are the measuring tools in the United States different/similar to those used in other countries around the world?

ONLINE RESOURCES

National Academies Press http://www.nap.edu
Office of Justice Programs http://www.ojp.gov
Youth.Gov http://www.youth.gov
Juvenile Justice Center of Philadelphia http://www.juvenilejustice.org
National Institute of Justice: Crime Solutions http://www.crimesolutions.gov
U.S. Department of Justice: Office of Justice Programs http://www.ncjrs.gov

Definitions

Dark figure of crime—crimes that go unreported to police

Developmental Victimization Survey—a study designed to assess a comprehensive range of childhood victimizations across gender, race, and developmental stage

Easy Access to Juvenile Court Statistics—developed to "facilitate independent analysis of national estimates of delinquency cases processed by the nation's juvenile courts" ("Easy Access," 2017, p. 2)

Easy Access to UCR FBI Arrest Statistics—provides access to juvenile arrest statistics at the national, state, and county levels

Felonies—crimes punishable by more than 1 year in jail

Hierarchy rule—states that only the highest crime within a given incident is reported on the Uniform Crime Report's Summary Reporting System

International Self-Report Delinquency Study—a worldwide victimization survey created by the Dutch Research and Documentation Center that has undergone three stages with the assistance of researchers all over the globe

Juvenile delinquency (federal definition)—"the violation of the law of the United States committed by a person prior to his eighteenth birthday, which would have been a crime if committed by an adult" ("Easy Access," 2017, p. 1)

Longitudinal study—a research design that entails repeated observations over a long period of time, usually many years

Misdemeanors—crimes punishable by less than a year in jail

National Center for Juvenile Justice—the research division of the National Council of Juvenile and Family Court Judges providing open access to the public to national and international studies on crime and delinquency

National Crime Statistics Exchange—400 strategically identified agencies that are being used to create a nationally representative system and assist with transitioning law enforcement agencies to report crime through the National Incident-Based Reporting System

National Crime Victimization Survey—a survey that provides self-reported details of crime incidents, victims, and trends

National Incident-Based Reporting System—method of collecting and reporting detailed incident crime data in the United States

National Youth Survey–Family Study—a longitudinal juvenile study looking at changing attitudes, beliefs, and behaviors

Office of Juvenile Justice and Delinquency Prevention—part of the Office of Justice Programs, U.S. Department of Justice, it supports cities, towns, states, and tribal territories in developing juvenile justice programs

Part I index crimes—murder and nonnegligent manslaughter; forcible rape, and after 2013, nonforcible rape; burglary; aggravated assault; larceny; motor vehicle theft; and arson, listed on the Uniform Crime Report

Part II index crimes—other crimes listed on the Uniform Crime Report

Reliability—consistency of a measure

Self-reports—reporting criminality or victimization through surveys and questionnaires

Statistical Briefing Book—developed by the National Center for Juvenile Justice; allows anyone to access juvenile crime, youth involved in the system, and victimization data from a variety of sources

Summary Reporting System—method of collecting summary-based crime data in the United States

Uniform Crime Reporting—consists of data collection tools used by law enforcement to report crime data in the United States

Validity—the extent to which the questions measure what they are intended to measure

Victimization surveys—surveys that solicit crime and victimization data through self-reporting

Youth Risk Behavior Surveillance System—monitors risky behavior that contributes to the leading causes of death, disability, and social problems among youth and adults in the United States

References

Australian Bureau of Statistics. (2014). *Measuring crime.* Parliament of Australia. https://www.aph.gov.au/Parliamentary_Business/Committees/House_of_Representatives_Committees?url=laca%2Fcrimeinthecommunity%2Freport%2Fchapter4.pdf

Australian Institute of Health and Welfare. (2013). *Youth detention population in Australia 2013* (Juvenile Justice Series 13, Cat. JUV 31).

Bureau of Justice Statistics. (2017). *National Crime Statistics Exchange (NCS-X).* https://www.bjs.gov/content/ncsx.cfm

Bureau of Justice Statistics. (2020). *National Crime Statistics Exchange (NCS-X).* https://nibrs.search.org/nibrs-admin/

Centers for Disease Control and Prevention. (2019). *2019 National YRBS Data Users Guide.* https://www.cdc.gov/healthyyouth/data/yrbs/pdf/2019/2019_National_YRBS_Data_Users_Guide.pdf

Crimes Against Children Research Center. (2019, July 2). *Developmental Victimization Survey.* http://www.unh.edu/ccrc/developmental_victimization_survey.html

Department of Justice. (2017a). *The nation's two crime measuring tools.* https://ucr.fbi.gov/crime-in-the-u.s/2017/crime-in-the-u.s.-2017/topic-pages/nations-two-crime-measures#:~:text=The%20U.S.%20Department%20of%20Justice,Crime%20Victimization%20Survey%20(NCVS)

Department of Justice. (2017b). *National Incident Based Reporting System.* https://ucr.fbi.gov/nibrs/2017/tables/data-tables

Dillman, D. A., Smyth, J. D., & Christian, L. M. (2014). *Internet, phone, mail, and mixed-mode surveys: The tailored design method.* John Wiley & Sons.

Donziger, S. R. (1996). *The real war on crime: The report of the National Criminal Justice Commission.* HarperPerennial.

Easy Access to Juvenile Court Statistics. (2017). National Center for Juvenile Justice. https://www.ojjdp.gov/ojstatbb/ezajcs/

Enzmann, D., Marshall, I. H., Killias, M., Junger-Tas, J., Steketee, M., & Gruszczynska, B. (2015). *Second International Self-Reported Delinquency Study, 2005–2007* (ICPSR34658-v2). Inter-university Consortium for Political and Social Research [distributor]. https://doi.org/10.3886/ICPSR34658.v2

Institute of Statistics and Economic Studies. (2016). *Victimization survey—Living environment and security/CVS.* https://www.insee.fr/en/metadonnees/source/s1115

Italian National Institute of Statistics. (2019, May 17). *Justice.* https://www4.istat.it/en/about-istat

James, N. (2008). *How crime in the United States is measured.* Congressional Research Service.

Mosher, C. J., Miethe, T. D., & Hart, T. C. (2010). *The mismeasure of crime.* Sage.

Muratore, M. G., & Sabbadini, L. L. (2008). *New developments on crime statistics concerning population survey in Italy.* National Institute of Statistics.

National Academies of Sciences, Engineering, and Medicine. (2016). *Modernizing crime statistics: Report 1: Defining and classifying crime.* National Academies Press.

National Youth Survey. (2015, April 20). Criminal Justice. http://criminal-justice.iresearchnet.com/crime/school-violence/national-youth-survey/

Neissl, K. (2017). *First results for ISRD3.* Northeastern University.

Office for Juvenile Justice and Delinquency Prevention. (2017a). *Statistical briefing book.* U.S. Department of Justice. http://www.ojjdp.gov/ojstatbb/structure_process/qa04102.asp?qaDate=2016

Office of Juvenile Justice and Delinquency Prevention. (2017b). *Easy access to FBI arrest statistics.* U.S. Department of Justice. https://www.ojjdp.gov/ojstatbb/ezaucr/

Office for Juvenile Justice and Delinquency Prevention. (2020) *Statistical briefing book.* U.S. Department of Justice. https://www.ojjdp.gov/ojstatbb/crime/qa05101.asp?qaDate=2019

Office for National Statistics. (2015). *Crime Survey for England and Wales.* https://www.crimesurvey.co.uk/en/AboutTheSurvey.html

Statistics by subject—Crime and justice. (2018, January 13). Statistics Canada. Retrieved January 14, 2018, from https://www.statcan.gc.ca/eng/subjects/crime_and_justice

U.S. Attorney's Manual. (1997). *Constitutional protections afforded to juveniles.* https://www.justice.gov/usam/criminal-resource-manual-38-juvenile-defined

World Health Organization. (2020). *Youth violence.* http://www.who.int/mediacentre/factsheets/fs356/en/

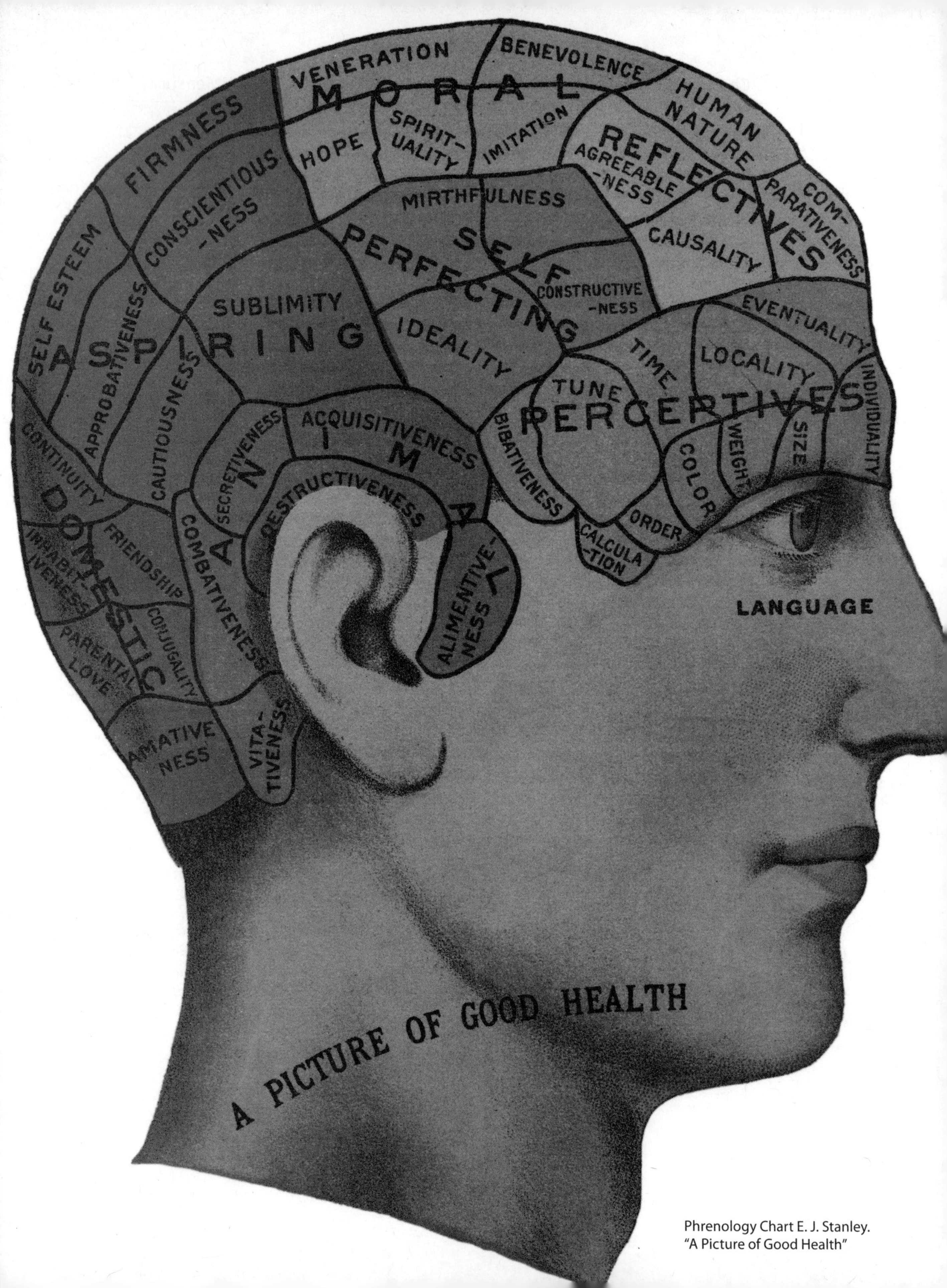

Phrenology Chart E. J. Stanley.
"A Picture of Good Health"

Theories of Delinquency

LEARNING OBJECTIVES

At the end of the chapter, students will be able to

describe the historical development of the theoretical causes of delinquency and crime;

describe the two major philosophical schools of thought and their application to the past and present handling of juvenile delinquents;

describe the key differences in biological, psychological, and sociological theories;

evaluate what role the Enlightenment played in advancing criminological theory;

discuss how positivism influenced our current juvenile justice system;

explain the pros and cons of two theories from each philosophical school of thought; and

compare and contrast theoretical philosophies of the United States and around the world.

Keywords

Classical criminology
Consequentialism
Criminal atavism
Criminological theory
Demonological theory
Deterrence theory
Differential association
Doli incapax
Ego

Enlightenment period
Eye for an eye
General deterrence
Hammurabi's Code
Hedonistic calculus
Id
Phrenology
Positivist school of thought
Prosocial bonds

Psychopathology
Puritans
Situational crime prevention
Social disorganization theory
Social ecology
Specific deterrence
Superego
Theory
Utilitarianism

Introduction

Throughout history, even before creating our justice system, society has attempted to figure out why individuals commit crimes. As we read in Chapter 1, early in the 1600s, juveniles and adults were generally treated the same in terms of the harsh punishments that were carried out. The belief was that only severe punishment could curtail offending and appease supernatural beliefs, even for the most minimal of crimes. Our youth, who were considered "small adults," were no exception. As societies around the world progressed into the 18th and 19th centuries, a new school of thought emerged for explaining criminality, called classical criminology. This new philosophy revolved around the notion that everyone, including juveniles, possessed free will and rational choice.

What is a Theory?

Juvenile minds were thought to be the same as adult minds in terms of development and rational motives for delinquency; criminality was believed to stem from making rational choices. As years passed, as a result of the limited explanations that classical criminology could offer as to why individuals made those choices, another school of thought, referred to as positivism, was developed. Positivist theorists sought to consider other causes for crimes beyond rational choice, ranging from physical and biological to psychological, environmental, and sociological factors. In this chapter, we will take an introductory look at classical, positivist, and modern theories of crime and delinquency.

What Is a Theory?

A **theory** can simply be defined as trying to explain something, and as such, **criminological theory** attempts to explain criminal and delinquent behavior (Byrne & Hummer, 2016). Criminological theories are based on various underlying causes, such as rational choice and biological and psychological factors, as well as external causes, such as environmental and social learning, (as shown in Table 3.1, later in the chapter).

Before Taking an Eye for an Eye

Throughout Europe and colonial America during the 17th and 18th centuries, individuals committing crimes were often looked on as deviant and as being influenced by supernatural and evil spirits, sometimes referred to as **demonological theory**. It was therefore believed that to curtail crimes and appease God(s), punishments had to be very harsh and often outweighed the criminal act itself. It was not uncommon at this time to fight in a battle to the death to prove one's innocence through victory or to have a hand cut off for stealing a loaf of bread, be branded a thief for stealing cattle, be whipped for not attending church, or, because children were no exception, have your tongue cut out for talking back to your parents (Cox, 2003).

Specifically, in colonial America, this type of justice was supported by **Puritans**, a religious group that was part of a movement that was separating from the Catholic Church. Puritans had populated other parts of the world, but migrated to parts of colonial America in the 1600s, initially occupying Massachusetts Bay before spreading to other parts of New England. Eventually, they spread across all colonial America. Puritans believed in a strict moral code to keep people in line, including attending church regularly, remaining faithful to your spouse, and being intolerant of even the most minor crimes and deviance. They feared that violating this moral code without harsh repercussions would be met with God's wrath and invite the devil's influence on every member of the community. Therefore, all members, including the children, were punished severely and by all accounts disproportionally for the offense to appease God and deny evil (U.S. History, 2021). It was also during this time that perceived "supernatural" occurrences, including weather changes and "witchcraft," existed and influenced behavior. Evil spirits were believed to be as real as God and were thought to prey on society's most vulnerable and weak, thought to be women and children.

Toward the end of the colonial period, supernatural reasons for crime and deviance gave way to a new school of thought termed rationalism. This shifted the focus from appeasing God to avoid his wrath to the belief that God had given individuals the ability to reason right from wrong and freely choose whether to commit crimes (Blanshard, 2016).In the early 21st century, society acknowledges that a child's brain is still developing until they reach the age of 24 and that youth are impulsive, not rational (Steinberg, 2017); applying the notion of rationalism to youth would cause youth to be held more culpable for their actions.

The Enlightenment Period

The **Enlightenment period**, also known as the age of reason, occurred between 1685 and 1815. It was during the Enlightenment that societies moved away from theorizing that people committed crimes because of supernatural causes and religious factors, such as influence from the devil. It challenged society's thinking in Britain, France, Europe, and America regarding authority and their way of thinking. During this time, contributions such as books, essays, inventions, scientific discoveries, and conceptualizing laws and punishment flourished, all with the goal of improving humanity through rational change ("Enlightenment," 2019). There was a growing belief that reason and knowledge could benefit humankind by providing and dispelling explanations for events such as lightning as a natural occurrence instead of God's wrath for misbehavior.

Growing acceptance that individuals commit crimes because of their own free will and not because of external supernatural forces also brought with it the idea that to curtail delinquency and criminality, the punishment need only be proportionate to the offense. Fair and just penalties serving to dissuade an individual's rational choice to commit a crime have also been called an **eye for an eye**. The expression eye for an eye originated from the ancient Mesopotamian Empire in the 18th century B.C.

Hammurabi's Code

This expression was part of **Hammurabi's Code**, a code of laws enacted by the Babylonian king of Mesopotamia, Hammurabi, that read, "If a man has destroyed the eye of a man of the gentleman class, they shall destroy his eye." It can also be found in the Christian Bible in Deuteronomy 19:21, "Life shall go for life, eye for an eye, tooth for a tooth." This saying puts forward the notion that the punishment should fit the crime. Although sometimes misinterpreted, it incorporates the idea that it is unnecessary to impose severe repercussions because individuals rationalize their actions. The belief that fair and proportionate punishment would be enough to quell rational choices for misbehavior became the foundation for classical criminology.

Classical Criminology

With its emphasis on rationality and reason, the Enlightenment spawned influential scientists, researchers, philosophers, and other persuasive minds at the time. One such influential figure was Cesare Beccaria, who eventually would be called the Father of Classical Criminology. Beccaria was an economist and criminologist. He believed that the government and its justice system were inefficient and its harsh punishments were misguided and ineffective. In 1764, he wrote "Crimes and Punishments," in which he advocated for immediate but fair sentences and condemned capital punishment and any forms of torture, practices he felt were neither humane nor effective deterrents for crime. He believed that punishment did not need to be excessive to prevent offending. Beccaria's belief that adults and children made rational choices and weighed the benefits and consequences of their actions when deciding to commit crimes and delinquency helped to form the core of classical criminology. **Classical criminology** asserts that all criminal behavior is a product of rational choice and free will, and to deter it, punishment should be swift and fit the crime.

We can think of classical criminology as a philosophical school of thought, an umbrella that covers several associated theories that rely on the principles of free will and rational choice as being the reasons why one decides to commit a crime and hypothesizes how to deter it.

Deterrence Theory

According to Beccaria and **deterrence theory**, crime and delinquency can be deterred by both general and specific efforts. **General deterrence** can occur when punishment is applied to an individual and the general population is dissuaded from committing crime. For example, if a juvenile receives a sentence of 6 months in a detention facility, according to Beccaria, it will deter other juveniles who might be weighing the benefits and consequences of committing their own offense. **Specific deterrence** occurs when the penalty is applied to an individual to deter that specific individual from reoffending. It should be noted that these forms of deterrence are not mutually exclusive, because applying an appropriate punishment can deter both the specific individual and the general public from offending in the future. Deterring crime in this manner reformed thinking at the time and provided answers to not only how adults and children decide to commit crimes, but also how to control that behavior. Beccaria's work inspired many other philosophers and theorists, including Jeremy Bentham.

Utilitarianism

Jeremy Bentham was an English philosopher who furthered Beccaria's work, focusing on the philosophy that the potential consequences of an act determine behavior. His moral philosophy, **utilitarianism**, argued that it is the overall benefit (amount of utility) from an action that is most important. He, too, believed that people were rational and theorized that the choices people make were guided by maximizing benefits (pleasure) and minimizing negative consequences (pain). He used the term **hedonistic calculus** to describe this phenomenon, hedonistic meaning pleasure-seeking and calculus meaning the conscious or subconscious method of attaining it. Bentham believed that people's criminal behavior could be controlled by having proportionate consequences for one's actions, also known as **consequentialism**. For example, if a teenager chose to commit armed robbery, the government would not need to brand them with a hot iron or cut off their hands to punish them and prevent reoffending. The consequences of one's chosen actions would only need to outweigh the benefits of the crime to prevent it and avoid recidivism.

Both Bentham and Beccaria would be known as utilitarian philosophers, and their philosophy of rational choice has spawned other related theories.

DEEPER DIVE

Jeremy Bentham, 1748–1832

Upon his death, Jeremy Bentham allowed his body to be "dissected," which was illegal and uncommon at the time, for the greater good of medical science. This was in adherence to his moral philosophy of utilitarianism, focusing on the overall good of society. He also asked for his body to be preserved, and in 1850, it was donated to University College London, where it rests today.

Bentham's head was not preserved well and was replaced with a replica. For many years, Bentham's actual head with glass eyes sat below the wax head, as shown in the photo.

For more information, visit UCL Jeremy Bentham https://blogs.ucl.ac.uk/transcribe-bentham/jeremy-bentham/

Jeremy Bentham, 1748–1832

Rational Choice Theory

A more contemporary theory, akin to the notion that individuals are rational decision-makers and often weigh the benefits and consequences of an act before making a choice, was termed rational choice theory. Rational choice theory, proposed by researchers Derek Cornish and Ronald Clarke in 1986, was not only applied to delinquency and crime but also to economics, whereby people conduct a cost and benefit analysis. If the benefits outweigh the costs, this theory, founded in utilitarianism, suggests that crime will occur (Gul, 2009). Expanding on Beccaria's mantra that individuals weigh the benefits and consequences of crime, rational choice theory also considers that other factors may contribute to making that choice, such as personal traits, social conditions, and attitudes toward crime in general. Some rational choice theorists also acknowledge that some crimes may be more spontaneous and based on opportunity (Pratt, 2008).

Routine Activities Theory

Routine activities theory, developed by Lawrence Cohen and Marcus Felson in 1979, initially tried to explain the rise in crime after World War II. They hypothesized that it was a change in one's routine that presented more opportunities for crime to occur. According to Marcus and Felson, as the result of an increase of women in the workforce, more opportunity for criminals was created (Miro, 2014). Accordingly, they believed that for a crime to occur, there needed to be three elements: a motivated offender, a victim, and an opportunity, also referred to as a lack of guardianship. Guardians can be in the form of the police, being in the company of others, or even a home security system. For example, if there is a motivated offender and an available victim, but there are also police patrolling in the area, there would be no opportunity, and therefore crime would not occur. This theory can also be applied to methods of protecting potential child victims, whereby children can stay in groups, travel with friends, and avoid high-crime areas.

Situational Crime Prevention

Finally, the premise of rationality and opportunity as the catalyst for crime helped shape the perspective of **situational crime prevention** developed by criminologist Ronald Clarke. Situational crime prevention is a strategy that combines the theoretical principles of rational choice, routine activities, and elements necessary for a crime to explain and potentially prevent illicit behavior. Based on this philosophy, to avoid the occurrence of criminality, there needs to be a reduction of opportunity while decreasing its benefits and increasing negative consequences. This perspective also provides "opportunity-reducing" techniques, such as methods for strengthening security, which has been adopted by many law enforcement agencies as part of their crime control strategies (Clarke, 1995; Fennelly & Perry, 2018).

As discussed, theorists continued to consider other factors beyond solely weighing benefits and consequences in choosing to commit crimes. These additional considerations include biological and psychological influences, social experiences, and other types of environmental factors. This set the stage for a new school of thought called positivism and applications of more contemporary theories explaining delinquency (Pratt, 2008).

Positivism—The Second Umbrella

The **positivist school of thought** began in the mid-1800s, and unlike classical criminology, it looked to factors beyond rational choice to explain delinquency and criminology. Positivist thought would eventually take the position that youth differed from adults in terms of their premature biological makeup, susceptibility to external influencers, and overall development. This mindset also influenced reformers to advocate for the creation of the juvenile justice system, with its goal of rehabilitation as opposed to the historical punitive measures that did not consider these distinguishing factors.

Positivism has continued to grow, first considering both physical and biological theories and then exploring psychological, environmental, and sociological reasons to explain crime and delinquency.

Biological/Physical Theories of Crime

One of its first positivist theorists, also called the Father of Positivism and Criminology (Lindesmith & Levin, 1937), was Cesare Lombroso. In his manuscript *The Criminal Man*, in 1876, the causation of crime was refocused on biological and physical factors contributing to a large portion of criminality. Lombroso advocated for the notion that some criminals were born bad and that certain physical attributes/anomalies could be strong indicators for juvenile delinquency and adult criminality. Expanding on the philosophy of Charles Darwin, a biologist known for his theory of natural selection, Lombroso also believed that a focus on evolution should be applied to the development of individuals. As a result, Lombroso put forward the idea of **criminal atavism**, meaning that the possession of unique physical features (anomalies) reminiscent of primitive man is a potential cause for criminality. He described a person who has not physically developed, an evolutionary throwback to more primitive times, as having a strong potential for delinquent behavior and eventually becoming a criminal. Criminals were not as biologically evolved compared to noncriminals.

Lombroso also believed that there were biological traits that were inherited and could also be predictors of criminality. Enrico Ferri, a protégé of Lombroso, coined the phrase akin to this philosophy, that some people are just "born bad."

Lombroso was famous for examining the dead bodies of criminals and, as such, looked for what he considered primitive commonalities among them. In the early 1870s, he studied the corpse of Giuseppe Villella, a former prisoner. He discovered an indentation in Villella's skull that was commonly found on apes' skulls, reinforcing the idea of criminal atavism and prompting Lombroso's writings. Franz Galli first proposed this type of examination to link the skull's bumps, flatness, and indentations to personality traits stemming from the brain in the early 19th century. It was known as **phrenology**, literally translated from Greek as mind knowledge (Jones et al., 2018). The 27 locations (indicators) were mapped out on the skull (as shown in the diagram that opens this chapter) and were believed to reveal certain personality traits, including being prone to criminality or deviance.

Lombroso continued his examinations of anomalies similar to primitive man and apes, whose aggressive and violent behavior he believed could be adopted by anyone who shared those physical features (Little, 2019). Lombroso continued to examine the dead bodies of criminals and record the commonalities between them to create a sort of typology for individuals he believed were more prone to criminality. He identified such primitive characteristics of children and adults alike as possessing big teeth, longs arms, excessive hair, premature wrinkles, a large head, and protruding ears. Although Lombroso believed that these traits were inherited and provided explanations for crimes being committed, he believed they only accounted for approximately a third of all criminals. He accepted that the remainder of criminality was caused by other factors associated with one's environment, such as addictions, lack of education, and even climate, some of which are considered causes for delinquency in the early 21st century. Critics of Lombroso argue that when evidence of criminality from his collection of dead bodies

DEEPER DIVE

Skull Display at the Cesare Lombroso Museum

Visitors are met by Lombroso's actual full skeleton (as Lombroso requested) as they enter through the museum's doors.

For more information about this museum, you can visit Cesare Lombroso's Museum of Criminal Anthropology https://www.atlasobscura.com/places/cesare-lombrosos-museum-of-criminal-anthropology

Cesare Lombroso Museum. The Cesare Lombroso Museum, located in Turin, Italy, is open to the public and displays the many skulls that Cesare examined to identify commonalities among known criminals.

was statistically compared to the general public's crime potential, there were no significant differences. In other words, any random pool of individuals with or without his described primitive traits had the same likelihood of criminality.

As we have mentioned, the crime rate increased after World War II, and while classical methods to control crime by changing routines persisted, so did the notion of biological/physical causes for crime. During the 1940s, William H. Sheldon followed Cesare Lombroso's path by developing constitutional psychological theory, a classification system that correlated personality traits to one's body makeup. Described as a somatotype, classifications included ectomorphs for slim bodies, endomorphs for those who were heavy-set, and mesomorphs for those who were muscular. Sheldon focused on juveniles with regard to characterizing those who were mesomorphic (muscular) as more likely to engage in delinquency. Other researchers, such as Eleanor and Sheldon Glueck during the 1950s, supported William Sheldon's theory, finding support for a mesomorphic link to delinquency. As advances continued in the social and behavioral sciences, other biological causes of crime, such as biochemical makeup and brain function, were explored and eventually led to a conglomerate of psychological theories to further explain delinquency and crime.

Psychological Theories

As time progressed, less attention was given to physical qualities as indicators of crime and more attention was directed to psychological causes. Some viewpoints revolved around the notion that individuals, specifically juveniles, commit crimes because of early childhood experiences and subconscious processes within psychodynamic theory. Other explanations focused on an individual's perception of the world around them, known as cognitive theory.

Psychodynamic Theory—Id, Ego, Super Ego, Oh No

Psychodynamic theory, also known as the psychoanalytical perspective, gained momentum in the mid-19th century and was supported by Sigmund Freud to explain criminal behavior. Freud focused on early childhood and psychological development as causes for children to be more or less prone to delinquency and criminal behavior into adulthood. He believed subconscious processes could affect one's personality (Freud, 1933).

According to Freud and his psychoanalytical perspective, personality, including a criminal personality, comprises a variation of three distinct facets of the subconscious, namely, the id, the ego, and the superego. The **id** is most representative of a child's personality, one that is impulsive and of a primitive drive without considering the consequences of one's actions. Freud believed that an individual driven by their id who desires something would do whatever it takes to fulfill that need in order to experience instant gratification, regardless of the repercussions. Known as the pleasure principle, this process begins at birth with unconscious drives toward food and other necessities. This can continue throughout one's life as an impulsive drive for other desires. While Freud believed that the id could serve as a survival mechanism for infants, he also believed that it can be destructive as one gets older and may lead to delinquency. In contrast, the ego is believed to balance the need for fulfillment by instilling the reality that either instant gratification most often is not plausible or the consequences of one's impulsive actions need to be considered to function appropriately in society. The **ego** can be regarded as a component of one's decision-making. The third subconscious element that drive's one's personality, according to Freud, is the **superego**, also known as one's conscience. The superego adheres to the norms of society and strict morality.

It is important to note that these elements do not function independent of each other and can exist at different levels of consciousness. According to Freud, in a healthy, developed individual, the ego serves as a mediating force between the id's need for instant gratification and the superego's striving for high morality. For those prone to criminality, according to a psychodynamic perspective, the ego and superego did not develop and do not function properly. This could be a result of negative factors occurring during childhood, such as neglect or inadequate nurturing, causing the id to have a stronger influence. This could lead to what Freud referred to as low mental functioning. There are also mental conditions that fall within the psychodynamic theory that can cause aggressive and deviant behavior; these include oppositional defiant, schizophrenia, and bipolar disorders. For more information regarding these disorders, visit http://www.aacap.org/.

Cognitive Theory

Cognitive theory focuses on the way individuals perceive the world around them as a potential cause for criminality. In the 19th century, Jean Piaget, a psychologist who focused on child development, applied moral and intellectual development to how events are perceived and how this continues to develop through one's lifetime. Lawrence Kohlberg, a psychologist who focused on stages of moral development, extended this notion by describing developmental levels that are necessary for healthy growth. According to Kohlberg, the first level should occur in the primary grades and center around compliance and adherence to social norms because of fear of punishment. At this level, children should exhibit behavior independent of others and in the fulfillment of one's interests.

As one becomes a young adult, they should enter the second level, whereby moral reasoning is incorporated in their judgments of others and genuine concern for how others, namely, society as a whole, think of and judge them. They recognize society's rules and laws as right and wrong and reject criminality because of its unacceptance and conceived punishments. The final level involves a social contract and a desire for laws to be grounded in social justice. According to Kohlberg, criminality stems from a lack of development in moral judgments and perspectives through these levels.

In addition to internal childhood processes, perceptions of the world, and moral development affecting one's behavior, theories focusing on external social experiences and learned behavior were considered in explaining one's conduct.

Behavioral/Sociological Theories

Behavioral theorists attempt to explain one's behavior, including maladaptive behavior, as a result of life experiences. Specifically, they focus on one's interaction with their environment, either being encouraged through reward or dissuaded via punishment. Unlike utilitarianism, however, they consider an ongoing process of conditioning rather than just the utility of isolated events. According to behaviorists, delinquent or criminal behavior that has been experienced and has not been discouraged will continue throughout adolescence and adulthood.

Differential Association Theory

In 1939 and with revisions in 1947, Donald Sutherland put forward the notion that behavior is learned and is prevalent across all classes (Wood & Alleyne, 2010). This learning can occur within one's family and other contexts where one's time is spent, such as within social institutions and peer groups. Adopting behavior by observing it can be positive for a child when it comes to learning how to get dressed or tie their shoes, but other actions, such as deviance, can also manifest in the observer's behavior. According to Sutherland, when children find themselves interacting with individuals who support and exhibit deviance, they, in turn, will engage in similar behavior, a phenomenon he termed **differential association** (Matsueda, 2010; Vinney, 2019). In a sense, these children will change any disparity in their own behavior in order to assimilate to what they observe, even if it is delinquency. Sutherland later borrowed from classical utilitarian thought and added differential reinforcement to explain that learned delinquent behavior can be interrupted by proper punishment or reinforced by it being permitted. Sociologist Ronald Akers further developed this theory by asserting that multiple behaviors can be adopted if they occur frequently enough by people around an individual and that, if reinforced, they can change an individual's conventional values, justification, and attitudes (Akers, 1973).

Learning has also been theorized to occur through modeling behavior. Albert Bandura, a prominent psychologist in the 20th century, extends behavioral theory by rejecting that people have innate tendencies toward crime. Instead, he asserts that behavior is learned not only through punishment and rewards (conditioning) but also through modeling observed behavior, known as **social learning theory** (Bandura, 1978).

In his famous Bobo doll experiment, Bandura had one group of young children view adults acting violently toward a life-size doll. Children were then left alone in the room

DEEPER DIVE

Bobo Doll Experiment

In 1961 at Stanford University, Albert Bandura tested his theory that behavior is learned through social learning and imitation as opposed to having biological and genetic causes. He found that children who observed aggressive behavior were more likely to act in the same manner than children who did not observe such behavior, in this case toward a "Bobo doll."

Bandura concluded that a child's behavior is not only learned through punishment and rewards, but also based on what they observe and, in turn, model.

For more information, you can visit Very Well Mind https://www.verywellmind.com/bobo-doll-experiment-2794993

Top: adult models violent behavior toward the "Bobo doll." Middle and bottom rows: children left alone with the doll behaved in the same manner.

with the doll, and without any provocation, they began to also act violently toward it, seemingly modeling the behavior observed previously. In the context of families, behaviorists may apply this modeling to children being exposed to violence by family members, for example, as being more likely to act violently during their own lives. This theory has also been applied to adversarial and crime-ridden environments outside the family, as well as exposure to violence being portrayed in the media including movies, television, and video games, potentially causing criminal behavior (see Chapter 11, "Media Evolution and Its Effects on Juveniles").

Social disorganization theory, developed by researchers Clifford Shaw and Henry McKay in the 1940s and still studied in the early 21st century, moves away from individual characteristics causing delinquency and crime and refocuses on environmental conditions. It relates behavior to **social ecology**, described as interactions between communities and resources influencing illicit behavior. The notion of individuals being affected by environmental conditions was developed further by other researchers, including Robert Sampson, in the 1990s. Sampson describes neighborhood influences such as poverty, instability, and segregation of race and ethnicity affecting delinquency to explain why illegal activity forms in clusters within cities instead of being evenly distributed. In essence, social disorganization in communities in terms of not sharing common interests and norms and lack of cohesiveness to address problematic issues could lead to increased criminality in those places (Wickes & Sydes, 2017).

Social Control Theory

In the 1960s, sociologist Travis Hirschi built on a growing consensus that attributed behavior to one's social environment in terms of expectations and the constraints it puts on the individual, known as social control theory. Hirschi stressed that ties to various aspects of society could control maladaptive behavior (McMurtry & Curling,

2008). He theorized about the importance of **prosocial bonds**—positive relationships with institutions and communities. These bonds result in an attachment to these institutions, sharing in their values and beliefs, and commitment to positive and productive activities. According to Hirschi, weak social bonds can lead to delinquency, where a juvenile who does not feel like they belong to any group, institution, or society may believe they do not have to abide by its rules. In a sense, social bonding extends social control theory by broadening it to stress the importance of ties to multiple facets of society. A child can either feel a part of/controlled by any institution and be committed to following its rules and laws or isolate themselves, resulting in weak obligatory social ties, leading to delinquency.

Self-Control Theory: "General Theory of Crime"

Created by criminologist Michael Gottfredson and sociologist Travis Hirschi in 1990, self-control theory, also described as the general theory of crime, attempts to combine the classical school's reasons for crime such as rational choice and weigh its benefits with a positivist view to explain what those choices are based on.

Self-control theory argues that low self-control causes an individual to seek gratification based only on self-interest. Unlike social control theory, self-control theory focuses on the individual and their own ability to control their behavior and moves away from focusing on the influences of bonds with society. It considers factors that affect poor choices such as being impulsive, short-sighted, and self-centered, all of which can not only cause participation in risky, nondeviant behavior but also lead to deviance and adult criminality (Siegel & McCormick, 2006). According to Gottfredson and Hirschi, low self-control can occur during childhood as a result of a lack of supervision, affection, nurturing, and discipline and is consistent with delinquency (Gottfredson & Hirschi, 1990, 1993).

Although proposed as a general theory of crime, other socialization theories have suggested additional causes of illicit behavior and have linked these concepts to more modern views.

Strain, Anomie, and General Strain Theory

Strain theory focuses on the inability to obtain what society considers necessary and essential achievements in life, such as advanced education, gainful employment, wealth, and power. When youth, for example, especially those facing numerous obstacles, fall short of achieving such status, it creates strain (stress/pressure). According to strain theory, this can lead to illicit behavior to obtain those things that are believed by some to be otherwise unattainable. Strain theory is based on anomie theory, created by Emile Durkheim and developed in 1938 by Robert Merton, which focused on circumstances where society has set predefined goals, but based on societal conditions, there are no clear (normative) ways to achieve those goals, creating a state of anomie—normlessness and hopelessness. This creates differing views (including criminality) of how to obtain those goals and sometimes deviant or rebellious behavior rejecting them (Baumer, 2016). General strain theory, developed by Robert Agnew, is based on anomie and strain theory, but instead of focusing on indistinct methods and lack of resources discouraging and preventing the achievement of goals, it extends strain theory by looking at other factors that can cause anxiety and wrongdoing. This includes factors such as criminal environments and lack of coping skills that can lead to negative emotions and depressive or violent behavior (Agnew, 1992; Wickert, 2019). Strain can also cause juveniles to identify and embrace their adverse conditions within smaller offshoot groups of society, known as subculture theory.

Subculture Theory and Cultural Transmissions

Subculture theory, developed by theorist Albert Cohen in 1955, addresses those individuals and their associated deviance, which, although it is rejected within the broader culture, has been accepted within smaller groups whereby distorted values and customs are shared. Cohen applied strain theory principles, asserting that like-minded individuals who feel they cannot achieve the benchmarks society has set for them and in turn have engaged in delinquent behavior will sometimes form their own juvenile groups. These "subgroups" will often have altered conventional standards. This can include delinquent acts, dropping out of school, participating in illicit means to obtain money and status, and other forms of violent behavior. These forms of conduct are not only accepted by the group but also often encouraged, such as seen in gang culture (Barton, 2006; Bernard, 2019; see Chapter 5, "Gangs and Juveniles," for more information on gang culture). The acceptance of these beliefs can be passed down from generation to generation, known as cultural transmissions. Although these cultural transmissions can be norms and values of a particular area or group, such as family dynamics and noncriminal activities and beliefs, other norms can revolve around deviance and criminality. However, it is believed that cultural norms may not automatically determine one's behavior. Behavior can also depend on how a person's culture is interpreted based on individual perspectives that consider other facets of one's life, such as other cultures, external groups affiliations, and environments the individual may be exposed to, socialize within, and potentially adopt (Barnett & Casper, 2001). Adopting less popular values and customs has also resulted in society labeling individuals, including juveniles. This occurs especially if their actions lead to maladaptive conduct or trends in criminal behavior (see Superpredators in Chapter 4) and can be seen as a modern-day form of branding (Greer & Reiner, 2014).

Labeling Theory

Using labeling theory, initially developed by sociologist Howard Becker in 1963, attaching a negative stigma to a child by society has been argued to produce adverse effects and cause further delinquency (Shulman, 2005; Skaggs, 2016). In 1967, sociologist Edwin Lemert described this negative perception by the child as being twofold. First, when a youth becomes involved with the juvenile justice system through some form of delinquency or illicit behavior, termed **primary deviance**, they are given the label juvenile delinquent/offender. According to Lemert, if a juvenile believes that society has determined they are a criminal, they will begin to internalize and self-identify with that label and continue to live up to that stigma, what Lemert terms **secondary deviance** (Rosenberg, 2010). Stanley Cohen, a sociologist, advanced labeling theory by suggesting that other sources of information, such as the media, contributed to society's perceptions of the offender and the offender's negative responses to those assessments. Labeling theory continued to evolve into the 20th century and began to consider informal but negative labels given within families and stereotypes by communities within society (Liu, 2000). Although this theory does not address why delinquency occurred in the first place and critics believe more evidence is needed to understand the effects of labeling, there is ongoing support and acknowledgment of the detrimental effects of labeling youth (Bernburg, 2019; Restivo & Lanier, 2015).

Biosocial Theory

Theories do not necessarily have to be isolated from each other. Various aspects can be combined, as we see in biosocial theory, influenced in the 1970s by biologist Edward Osborne Wilson. He illustrated how, although biological causes for delinquency may exist, they do not function independently and can be intertwined and evolve with social conditions considering both nature and nurture factors (McMurtry & Curling, 2008). Modern biosocial theory examines how sociological factors such as environment and social learning intertwine with biological development. According to this theory, genetic predispositions may cause individuals to be more prone (predisposed) to engage in delinquency and criminality in specific social settings. For example, suppose a child has a biological learning disability. In that case, the learning disability can negatively interact with a stressful, nonaccommodating learning environment and cause frustration, which may lead to antisocial and aggressive delinquent behavior. Additionally, recognized disorders such as attention-deficit/hyperactivity disorder and conduct disorder may be exasperated under certain social/environmental conditions, leading to maladaptive behavior (Schilling et al., 2011). Although biosocial theory has been criticized for not explaining varied reactions when there are similar biological and social conditions, the combinations of nature and nurture causes of delinquency continue to be explored (Wells & Walsh, 2019).

Life Course Theory

The integration of theoretical explanations for crime is additionally discussed within life course theory, also known as developmental theory. This theory asserts that a culmination of social, economic, environmental, and other factors throughout one's life can cause variation in delinquency and criminality (Fox & Farrington, 2016). Many theorists have considered factors throughout one's life that affect behavior. In 1993, Terrie Moffitt, a psychologist, described a developmental life course theory that focuses on two groups of offenders based on the onset of criminality. One group she calls adolescence-limited offenders, whose criminality begins in the teenage years but will cease (age out) as they become young adults. The other group is called life course–persistent offenders, who display delinquent behavior in childhood that persists and may even worsen throughout their lives. According to Moffitt, these two types of offending depend on risk and environmental factors the child is exposed to early in life, such as broken homes, poverty, and other adverse environmental conditions (Moffitt, 2003). Researchers John Laub and Robert Sampson conducted a longitudinal study of delinquent boys until they reached age 70 to further investigate life course theory. They found that whether or not criminality begins at a young age, it is not predictive or consistent throughout one's life, but instead fluctuates based on a variety of environmental and social factors reflective of disrupted, weakened, or removed social bonds and informal social controls. These can include interpersonal ties with family, school, and work (Sampson & Laub, 2003; Sweeten, 2010). Criminologist David Farrington also theorized about external environmental factors contributing to chronic offending for juveniles throughout their lifetime. More recently, he focused on protective factors. One of them is self-control, which can help juveniles at risk for delinquency to become resilient, a concept that has been focused on within resiliency theory (Carlsson & Sarnecki, 2015; Farrington et al., 2016; Reid, 2019).

TABLE 3.1 Summary of Theories

SCHOOL OF THOUGHT	THEORY	PHILOSOPHY	DEVELOPED BY
CLASSICAL CRIMINOLOGY			
	Deterrence theory	Utilitarianism/consequentialism	Cesare Beccaria and Jeremy Bentham
	Rational choice	Utilitarianism/consequentialism	Derek Cornish and Ronald Clarke
	Routine activities	Opportunity/elements of a crime	Lawrence Cohen and Marcus Felson
POSITIVIST			
Biological/ physical	Phrenology	The physical shape of the skull	Franz Galli
	Criminal atavism	Primitive physical features	Cesare Lombroso
	Constitutional theory	Body types (ectomorphs, endomorphs, and mesomorphs)	William Sheldon
Psychological	Psychodynamic	Subconscious—id, ego, superego	Sigmund Freud
	Cognitive theory	Perceptions and maturity	Jean Piaget and Lawrence Kohlberg
Behavioral/ sociological	Differential association	Adopting behavior	Donald Sutherland
	Social learning theory	Learning and modeling	Albert Bandura
	Social disorganization	Environmental conditions and social ecology	Clifford Shaw, Henry McKay, and Robert Sampson
	Social control theory	Social bonds	Travis Hirschi
	Self-control theory: "general theory of crime"	Individual constraints	Travis Hirschi and Michael Gottfredson
	Strain, anomie, and general strain theory	Stress and pressure by society, lack of resources, guidance, and other environmental conditions	Emile Durkheim, Robert Merton, and Robert Agnew
	Subculture	Acceptance by smaller sects (subgroups) of society, cultural	Albert Cohen
	Cultural transmissions	Norms and values passed down or exposed to	Albert Cohen
	Labeling theory	Internalizing stigmas, primary and secondary deviance, and stereotypes	Howard Becker, Edwin Lemert, and Stanley Cohen
	Biosocial theory	Combining developmental and environmental influences and predispositions	Edward Wilson
Life course	Developmental theory	Combining developmental and environmental influences and fluctuations over the course of one's life	Terrie Moffitt, John Laub and Robert Sampson, David Farrington
Resilience	Resiliency theory and challenge model	Building coping skills and positive perspectives and perceiving adversity as a challenge for healthy development	Michael Rutter and James Neill

Resilience Theory

Resilience is the ability to cope with and recover from an adversarial event or obstacle and can be perceived as a challenge one can overcome by focusing on their strengths versus weaknesses, also known as the challenge model of resiliency theory (Merenda et al., 2020). Theorized by Michael Rutter in 1987 and developed further by James Neill, resilience should be viewed as a process. This process utilizes coping skills for children, for example, to positively deal with life stressors that may otherwise be handled poorly and potentially lead to juvenile delinquency and criminality (Booth & Neill, 2017). According to Neill, the development of protective factors such as maturity, socialization, and conflict resolution skills can be drawn on when faced with adversarial events. Juveniles who have developed these skills, who may otherwise be at risk for delinquency because of a culmination of risk factors inherent to adverse environmental conditions, may be able to respond positively by viewing these conditions as challenges as opposed to adversities.

The concept of resilience has also been implemented in rehabilitation and diversion programs offered to youth as a method to avoid reoffending and even prevent offending in the first place (Booth & Neill, 2017; Merenda, 2020; Zimmerman, 2013). Also, see Chapter 10, "Interventions and Diversions."

Worldview

Theoretical Causes of Delinquency Around the World

UNITED NATIONS: GUIDELINES FOR THE PREVENTION OF JUVENILE DELINQUENCY

A variety of theoretical concepts to explain delinquency and crime exist not only in the United States, but also around the world. The United Nations Guidelines for the Prevention of Juvenile Delinquency explain juvenile delinquency as the result of immaturity and part of the life course, with most juveniles aging out during adolescence. The U.N. has also spoken about subculture theory or, as stated in the guidelines, lifestyle systems created by families, neighborhoods, and media that establish norms, which can include deviance and violence. Additionally, the U.N. has acknowledged environmental factors such as economics, socialization, and peer pressure as possible causes of delinquency and criminality alike. As such, in 1990, the U.N. Guidelines for the Prevention of Juvenile Delinquency were amended and the notion was put forward that juvenile justice systems around the world should utilize a multitude of resources, such as social services and rehabilitative programs, that should focus on the variety of causes of delinquency. Punishment should be used as a last resort. Many countries have adopted this philosophy and have designed their juvenile justice systems accordingly. In contrast, others have instituted their theoretical perspectives of what factors manifest delinquency and have developed their own ways of controlling it.[1]

---

[1]The following countries were selected based on the extent of associated content available.

AFRICA

According to the U.N. Department of Economic and Social Affairs (2019), the juvenile population in Africa has been rising steadily, and children are expected to make up two thirds of the population by 2050. Unfortunately, Africa's juvenile crime and delinquency are also increasing in many areas (Cheteni et al., 2018). Researchers have theorized that environmental factors such as a poor economy, unemployment, overcrowded living conditions, lack of essential services, and child abandonment cause the majority of delinquency among their youth. Social disorganization theory addresses detrimental environmental conditions as a catalyst for delinquency. In 2008, the Child Justice Act was established to create a separate system for juveniles similar to that in the United States in terms of treating juveniles differently by addressing these causes and acting in the best interests of the child (Terblanche, 2012).

ASIA

Much of the crime occurring in Asia has been attributed to its juvenile population. This is across both genders, with female delinquency rising. Particularly, young people in countries in Asia located near the "Golden Crescent" or "Golden Triangle," areas known for major narcotic sales, are becoming addicted to drugs as a result of these environmental factors. This has created a subculture of dependency and human trafficking that is being dealt with in various ways, including imposing adult punishments (Semise et al., 2015). For example, according to the National Crime Records Bureau (2015), juvenile crimes increased 47%, from 22,740 cases in 2010 to 33,526 cases in 2014. In 2015, their Juvenile Justice Care and Protection of Children Act was amended to permit children ages 16–18 to be tried as adults for "heinous" crimes (Durham, 2015; Institute for Policy Research, 2015). One of the reasons for the amendment was the lenient prosecution of a rape incident of a teenage girl by teenage boys in 2015, which the boys posted on social media. India's government found that half of all juvenile crimes were committed by teenagers and determined that the cause for their behavior was that they rationalized they could get away with it. The minister of women and child development believed imposing harsher consequences through this amendment would deter other teens from committing similar acts (general deterrence) by showing them that they would be tried as adults and face comparable penalties (Arikatti, 2015; Durham, 2015). As discussed earlier in this chapter, deterrence theory falls under classical criminology, the belief that crimes are committed based on rational choice and can be deterred by having the consequences outweigh the benefits. This is similar in the United States and other countries around the world, whose youth would otherwise fall under the juvenile justice system's jurisdiction if not for the type of violent crime committed, causing them to be prosecuted under the adult criminal justice system and face harsher sentences.

Juveniles under age 16 in India still fall under the jurisdiction of their juvenile system. A system with the goal of rehabilitation and the belief that those youth were influenced by various external environmental factors and family conditions necessitates more rehabilitation and fewer punitive consequences (Agarwal & Kumar, 2016; Kumar, 2017).

LATIN AMERICA

Much like the United States, Latin America relied on a positivist school of thought to explain crime. Initially, however, many Latin American countries such as Argentina, Mexico, Brazil, and Chile turned to the ideas of Cesare Lombroso's biological and physical causes of crime, which they referred to as anthropology theory in the 1800s (Olmo, 1999). During this time, criminologists relied on physical characteristics and then inferior personality traits to identify individuals who were prone to criminality. In the early 1900s, Argentina, through the efforts of Dr. Jose Ingenieros, a forensic doctor, rejected Lombroso's biological focus and turned to psychological influences for criminal behavior, what he termed **psychopathology**—the study of abnormal psychological functioning. These types of theoretical explanations of crime, however, seemed to be polarized from their justice system, which remained focused on punitive repercussions for offenses (Olmo, 1999). It was not until the 21st century that a shift in juvenile proceedings occurred, taking into account other causes for delinquency and needed rehabilitation.

Latin American countries are also plagued with vast variations in homicide rates and other violent crimes, creating weakened communities and institutions (Vilalta et al., 2016). Honduras and El Salvador reflect the highest occurrences and Chile and Uruguay the lowest. The variation in criminality and juvenile delinquency has been explained by applying sociological theory, specifically attributing it to a lack of social controls and poor social bonds (Rivera, 2016). While these causes are recognized, there exists a very punitive-oriented justice system resulting in mass incarceration and allegations of deteriorating conditions and human right violations in many Latin American countries (Blaustein, 2016; Rivera, 2016).

CANADA

In 1908, the Juvenile Delinquents Act was passed in recognition that juveniles needed a justice system separate from adults that could treat what were believed to be causes of delinquency, such as immaturity, inadequate schooling, socioeconomic factors, and other detrimental environmental conditions. The intervention focused on a child's development and was believed to be the best solution (Department of Justice Canada, 2004; Tanner, 2001).

Crime increased in Canada in the 1960s, and much like when juvenile crime rose in the United States in the latter part of the 20th century, a new "get tough on crime" mantra swept across the country. In Canada, the Juvenile Delinquents Act was being called too lenient and ineffective by many. Although some individuals fought for its continuance, this debate led to the creation of the Young Offenders Act in 1981 (also see Chapter 4, "Juvenile Offenders"). Although it required that adults and juveniles be kept separate from each other, this act advocated for holding juveniles more accountable for their actions (Bala, 2015; Bala & Anand, 2004, 2012). This led to high incarceration rates in Canada's jurisdictions to deter delinquency and criminality, based on the belief that juveniles were rational and should be held responsible for their acts.

The Young Offenders Act has been amended several times and was renamed the Youth Criminal Justice Act in 2003. The act has been amended to appease both punitive and rehabilitation philosophies. It advocates for youth being held responsible for criminal acts through punitive consequences, specifically for violent and repeat offenders. It also recognizes that a juvenile's immaturity and other external factors can lead to delinquency, necessitating a more rehabilitative response (Bala, 2015; Department of Justice, 2015). As a result, Canada implements a variety of theories and approaches regarding the contributing factors and methods to address juvenile delinquency (Bala, 2015).

AUSTRALIA

The notion of life course theory and cognitive brain development based on one's growth, maturity, and aging out of crime has been incorporated into Australian legislation in terms of managing their youth. It also was the basis of formulating their legal doctrine of **doli incapax**, meaning the child is incapable of criminal intent (Fitz-Gibbon & O'Brien, 2019;

Ian Freckelton, 2017). This perspective has become the default in their justice system when handling youth cases. The court presumes that a child under age 14 is not criminally responsible for their actions because of a lack of development and cognitive ability. The prosecution must refute this to go to trial and convict the youth of a crime. The notion of doli incapax aligns with the U.N.'s guidelines from their Convention on the Rights of the Child, which advocates for children to be viewed separately from adults in terms of their development and, as such, treated differently by the courts (Australian Institute of Health and Welfare, 2019; Richards, 2011). However, Australia can also instill punitive measures for children as young as 10 years old if deemed necessary by the prosecutor and accepted by its courts. This has led to a national debate around changing the federal law to raise the age of criminal responsibility so that no potential for criminal prosecution would exist (Fitz-Gibbon & O'Brien, 2019).

GERMANY

In 1953, after the world war, many German families and their children were displaced, and laws were changed to allow juveniles up to 21 to be protected by the juvenile justice system. Their philosophy, which continues in the early 21st century, was based on the need to rehabilitate youth who were believed to be delinquent as a result of environmental factors such as poverty and lack of intellectual development, instead of criminalizing and punishing their behavior. As with many European countries, the notion of psychosocial and cognitive development connections to children and young adults' impulsive nature has been widely accepted and reflected in their justice systems (Pruin & Dünkel, 2015).

In Germany, the focus is on building cognitive and social skills and developing self-control to increase empathy, moral reasoning, and problem-solving skills. Germany currently has one of the lowest juvenile incarceration and recidivism rates in the world (Matthews et al., 2018; Robinson & Kurlychek, 2019; Schiraldi, 2018). For more information, see https://www.vera.org/publications/sentencing-and-prison-practices-in-germany.

Wrap-up

Since the notion of supernatural causes for illicit and maladaptive behavior was dispelled in the 1600s, there have been two main schools of thought regarding the causes of delinquency and crime for both children and adults. First, classical criminology suggested that adults and children alike commit crimes based on rational choice. According to utilitarianism, rational choice is based on weighing the benefits and consequences of an act. To deter crime, punishments need only be harsh enough to outweigh its benefits. Second, positivism considers many other potential causes of crime beyond rationality, such as biological, physical, psychological, environmental, and sociological reasons.

Initially, positivism focused on inherent traits and physical anomalies as explanations for crime and then focused on psychological causes, including the subconscious mind. However, other questions remained unanswered regarding the effects of environmental conditions, developmental experiences, and interactions with society, especially among our youth. This led researchers to explore sociological influences of crime and changes that may occur during one's life course, including self-control, maturity, development of protective skills, and perspectives of the world around them. Theories continue to be developed to establish the causes of delinquency, not only to better provide rehabilitation for justice-involved youth but also to potentially prevent them from entering the juvenile justice system in the first place.

Discussion Questions

1. Explain how classical criminology played a role in how children were treated and punished by society in the 18th and early 19th centuries.
2. Discuss how positivism has guided our current juvenile justice system.
3. Which theory best describes the environmental risks youth face and methods to overcome those risks?
4. What role did the Enlightenment period play in criminological theory?
5. Choose two theories from both classical criminology and positivism and discuss their pros and cons.
6. Evaluate theoretical similarities and differences between the United States and other countries around the world.

ONLINE RESOURCES

Office of Juvenile Justice and Delinquency Program http://www.ojjdp.gov
Office of Justice Programs http://www.ojp.gov
National Partnership for Juvenile Services http://www.npjs.org
Youth.gov http://www.youth.gov
Juvenile Justice Information Exchange http://www.jjie.org
The United States Department of Justice http://www.justice.gov
Coalition for Juvenile Justice http://www.juvjustice.org
Justice Center; the Council of State Governments http://www.csgjusticecenter.org
American Academy of Child & Adolescent Psychiatry http://www.aacap.org/
Vera Institute of Justice https://www.vera.org
Cesare Lombroso's Museum of Criminal Anthropology https://www.atlasobscura.com/places/cesare-lombrosos-museum-of-criminal-anthropology
Very Well Mind: Bobo Doll Experiment https://www.verywellmind.com/bobo-doll-experiment-2794993

Definitions

Classical criminology—asserts that all criminal behavior is a product of rational choice and free will

Consequentialism—criminal behavior could be controlled by having proportionate consequences for one's actions

Criminal atavism—the possession of unique physical features (anomalies) reminiscent of primitive man as a potential indication for criminality

Criminological theory—attempts to explain criminal and delinquent behavior through a variety of underlying causes

Demonological theory—individuals committing crimes were often looked at as deviants and as being influenced by supernatural and evil spirits

Deterrence theory—crime can be deterred by both general and specific efforts

Differential association—interacting with individuals who exhibit deviance and support the same, and, in turn, engage in similar behavior

Doli incapax—incapable of criminal intent

Ego—balances the need for gratification and the consequences of one's impulsive actions

Enlightenment period—also known as the age of reason, reflected a move away from theorizing that people commit crimes as a result of supernatural causes and religious factors toward a growing belief that reason and knowledge could benefit mankind

An eye for an eye—fair and just penalties serving to dissuade an individual's rational choice to commit a crime

General deterrence—occurs when punishment is applied to an individual and the general population is dissuaded from committing crime

Hammurabi's Code—a code of laws enacted by the Babylonian king of Mesopotamia, Hammurabi

Hedonistic calculus—hedonistic, meaning pleasure-seeking, and calculus, meaning the conscious or subconscious method of attaining it

Id—subconscious impulsive and primitive drive that does not consider the consequences of one's actions

Phrenology—linking the bumps, flatness, and indentations on one's skull to criminal personality traits

Positivist school of thought—considers factors beyond rational choice, such as biological, psychological, environmental, and social factors, to explain delinquency and criminology

Primary Deviance—when a youth becomes involved with the juvenile justice system through some form of delinquency or illicit behavior

Prosocial bonds—positive relationships with institutions and communities

Psychopathology—the study of abnormal psychological functioning

Puritans—a religious group that was part of a movement separating from the Catholic Church

Secondary Deviance—delinquency or illicit behavior as a result of a juvenile believing that society has labeled them as a criminal and behaving in that manner.

Situational crime prevention—a perspective that combines the theoretical principles of rational choice, routine activities, and elements of a crime to explain and ultimately avoid illicit behavior

Social disorganization—focuses on environmental conditions and lack of community cohesiveness leading to crime

Social ecology—described as interactions between communities and resources influencing illicit behavior

Specific deterrence—occurs when the punishment is applied to an individual to deter that particular individual from reoffending

Superego—also known as one's conscience; the superego adheres to the norms of society and strict morality

Social Learning Theory—asserts behavior is learned through modeling observed behavior.

Theory—an attempt to explain something

Utilitarianism—argues that it is the overall benefit (amount of utility) from an action that is most important and that people seek to maximize pleasure and minimize pain

References

AgarwalS., & Kumar, N. (2016). Juvenile Justice (Care and Protection of Children) Act 2015: A review. *Space and Culture, India, 3*(3), 5–9. https://doi.org/10.20896/saci.v3i3.165

Agnew, R. (1992). Foundation for a general strain theory of crime and delinquency. *Criminology, 30*(1), 47–88.

Akers, R. L. (1973). *Deviant behavior: A social learning approach.* Wadsworth.

Arikatti, C. (2015). Juvenile Justice Act, 2015: A major backward step in juvenile justice. *Legal Service India.* http://www.legalserviceindia.com/legal/article-1074-juvenile-justice-act-2015-a-major-backward-step-in-juvenile-justice-system.html

Australian Institute of Health and Welfare. (2019). *Youth justice in Australia 2017–18* (Cat. JUV 129).

Bala, N. (2015). Changing professional culture and reducing use of courts and custody for youth: The Youth Criminal Justice Act and Bill C-10. *Saskatchewan Law Review, 78,* 127–180.

Bala, N., & Anand, S. (2004). The first months under the Youth Criminal Justice Act: A survey and analysis of case law. *Canadian Journal of Criminology and Criminal Justice, 46*(i), 251–271.

Bala, N., & Anand, S. (2012). *Youth criminal justice law* (3rd ed.). Irwin Law.

Bandura, A. (1978). Social learning theory of aggression. *Journal of Communication, 28*(3), 12–29.

Barnett, E., & Casper, M. (2001). A definition of "social environment." *American Journal of Public Health, 91*(3), 465.

Barton, S. W. (2006). General strain, street youth, and crime: A test of Agnew's revised theory. *Criminology, 42*(4), 457–484.

Baumer, E. P. (2016). Anomie. In *Oxford Bibliographies in Sociology.* https://doi.org/10.1093/obo/9780195396607-0006

Becker, H. S. (1963). *Outsiders: Studies in the sociology of deviance.* Free Press.

Bernard, T. J. (2019). Albert Bandura. In *Encyclopedia Britannica.* https://www.britannica.com/biography/Albert-Cohen-American-criminologist

Bernburg J. G. (2019). Labeling theory. In M. Krohn, N. Hendrix, G. Penly Hall, & A. Lizotte (Eds.), *Handbook on crime and deviance.* Handbooks of Sociology and Social Research. Springer.

Blanshard, B. (2016). Rationalism. In *Encyclopedia Britannica.* https://www.britannica.com/topic/rationalism

Blaustein, J. (2016). Exporting criminological innovation abroad: Discursive representation, "evidence-based crime prevention" and the post-neoliberal development agenda in Latin America. *Theoretical Criminology, 20*(2), 165–184. https://doi.org/10.1177/1362480615604892

Booth, J. W., & Neill, J. T. (2017). Coping strategies and the development of psychological resilience. *Journal of Outdoor and Environmental Education, 20*(1), 47–54.

Byrne, J., & Hummer, D. (2016). An examination of the impact of criminological theory on community corrections practice. *Federal Probation, 80*(3), 15–25.

Carlsson, C., & Sarnecki, J. (2015). *An introduction to life-course criminology.* Sage.

Cheteni, P., Mah, G., & Yohane, Y. K (2018). Drug-related crime and poverty in South Africa. *Cogent Economics & Finance, 6*(1), 1534528.

Clarke, R. V. (1995). Situational crime prevention. *Crime and Justice, 19*, 91–150.

Cox, J. (2003). Bilboes, brands, and branks: Colonial crimes and punishments. *Colonial Williamsburg Journal.* https://research.colonialwilliamsburg.org/Foundation/Journal/spring03/branks.cfm

Department of Justice. (2015). Criminal Offences. https://www.justice.gc.ca/eng/cj-jp/victims-victimes/court-tribunaux/offences-infractions.html

Department of Justice Canada. (2004). *The evolution of juvenile justice in Canada* https://publications.gc.ca/collections/Collection/J2-248-2004E.pdf

Durham, M. G. (2015). Scene of the crime: News discourse of rape in India and the geopolitics of sexual assault. *Feminist Media Studies, 15*(2), 175–191. https://doi.org/10.1080/14680777.2014.930061

Enlightenment. (2019). *History.* https://www.history.com/topics/British-history/enlightenment

Farrington, D. P., Ttofi, M. M., & Piquero, A. R. (2016). Risk, promotive, and protective factors in youth offending: Results from the Cambridge study in delinquent development. *Journal of Criminal Justice, 45*, 63–70. https://doi.org/10.1016/j.jcrimjus.2016.02.014

Fennelly, L. J., & Perry, M. A. (2018). *Situational crime prevention theory and CPTED.* CRC Press.

Fitz-Gibbon, K., & O'Brien, W. (2019). A Child's Capacity to Commit Crime: Examining the Operation of Doli Incapax in Victoria (Australia). *International Journal for Crime, Justice and Social Democracy, 8*(1), 18–33. https://doi.org/10.5204/ijcjsd.v8i1.1047

Fox, B. H., & Farrington, D. P. (2016). Is the development of offenders related to crime scene behaviors for burglary? Including situational influences in developmental and life-course theories of crime. *International Journal of Offender Therapy and Comparative Criminology, 60*(16), 1897–1927. https://doi.org/10.1177/0306624X15621982

Freud, S. (1933). New Introductory Lectures on Psycho-Analysis. In J. Strachey et al. (Trans.), The Standard Edition of the Complete Psychological Works of Sigmund Freud, Volume XXII. London: Hogarth Press.

Gottfredson, M. R., & Hirschi, T. (1990). *A general theory of crime.* Stanford University Press.

Gottfredson, M. R, & Hirschi, T. (1993). A control theory interpretation of psychological research on aggression. In R. B. Felson & J. T. Tedeschi (Eds.), *Aggression and violence: Social interactionist perspectives* (pp. 47–68). American Psychological Association. https://doi.org/10.1037/10123-002

Greer, C., & Reiner, R. (2014). Labelling, deviance, and media. In G. Bruinsma & G. Weisburd (Eds.), *Encyclopedia of criminology and criminal justice* (pp. 2814–2823). Springer. https://doi.org/10.1007/978-1-4614-5690-2_181

Gul, S. (2009). An evaluation of the rational choice theory in criminology. *Girne American University Journal of Social and Applied Science, 4*(8), 36–44.

Ian Freckelton, Q. C. (2017). Children's responsibility for criminal conduct: The principle of doli incapax under contemporary Australian law. *Psychiatry, Psychology and Law, 24*(6), 793–801. https://doi.org/10.1080/13218719.2017.1379892

Institute for Policy Research. (2015). PRS legislative research: Juvenile Justice (Care and Protection of Children) Bill, 2014. http://www.prsindia.org/uploads/media/Juvenile%20Justice/Legislative %20Brief%20Juvenile%20Justice%20Bill.pdf

Jones, P., Alfaro-Almago, F., & Jbabdi, S. (2018). An empirical, 21st-century evaluation of phrenology. *Cortex, 106*(3), 26–35.

Kumar, C. (2017, December 17). What drives crime by juveniles in India. *Times of India.* https://timesofindia.indiatimes.com/india/what-drives-crime-by-juveniles-in-india/articleshow/62236088.cms

Little, B. (2019, August 8). *What Type of Criminal Are You? 19th-Century Doctors Claimed to Know by Your Face.* HISTORY. https://www.history.com/news/born-criminal-theory-criminology

Liu, X. (2000). The conditional effect of peer groups on the relationship between parental labeling and youth delinquency. *Sociological Perspectives, 43*(3), 499–514.

Lindesmith, A., & Levin, Y. (1937). The Lombrosian Myth in Criminology. *American Journal of Sociology, 42*, 653–671.

Matsueda, R. L. (2010). Sutherland, Edwin H.: Differential association theory and differential social organization. In F. T. Cullen & P. Wilcox (Eds.), *Encyclopedia of criminological theory* (pp. 899–907). Sage.

Matthews, S., Schiraldi, V., & Chester, L. (2018). Youth justice in Europe: Experience of Germany, the Netherlands, and Croatia in providing developmentally appropriate responses to emerging adults in the criminal justice system. *Justice Evaluation Journal, 1*(1), 59–81. https://doi.org/10.1080/24751979.2018.1478443

McMurtry, R., & Curling, A. (2008). Review of the roots of youth violence. Ontario Ministry of Children, Community and Social Services. http://www.children.gov.on.ca/htdocs/English/professionals/oyap/roots/index.aspx

Merenda, F. (2020). Adventure-based programming with at-risk youth: Impact upon self-confidence and school attachment. *Child & Youth Services*. https://doi.org/10.1080/014935X.2020.1829465

Merenda, F., Ostrowski, S., & Merenda, F., II. (2020). Building blocks of resilience: Applications for justice-involved youth. *Journal of Applied Juvenile Justice Services*, 112–130.

Miró, F. (2014). Routine activity theory. *The encyclopedia of theoretical criminology*, 1–7. https://doi.org/10.1002/9781118517390.wbetc198

Moffitt, T. E. (1993). "Life-course-persistent" and "adolescence-limited" antisocial behaviour: A developmental taxonomy. *Psychological Review, 100*(4), 674–701.

Moffitt, T. E (2003). Life-course persistent and adolescence-limited antisocial behavior. *Causes of conduct disorder and juvenile delinquency*, 49–75.

National Crime Records Bureau. (2015). *Crime in India*. Government of India. https://ncrb.gov.in/en/crime-india-year-2015

Olmo, R. D. (1999). The development of criminology in Latin America. *Social Justice, 26*(2), 19–45.

Pratt, T. C. (2008). Rational choice theory, crime control policy, and criminological relevance. *Criminology and Public Policy, 7*(1), 43–52.

Pruin, I., & Dünkel, F. (2015). *Better in Europe? European responses to young adult offending*. Universitat Greifswäld. https://www.t2a.org.uk/wp-content/uploads/2016/02/T2A_Better-in-Europe.pdf

Reid, D. (2019) *Resilience theory: What research articles in psychology teach us*. Positive Psychology. https://positivepsychology.com/resilience-theory/

Restivo, E., & Lanier, M. M. (2015). Measuring the contextual effects and mitigating factors of labeling theory. *Justice Quarterly, 32*(1), 116–141. https://doi.org/10.1080/07418825.2012.756115

Richards, K. (2011). What makes juvenile offenders different from adult offenders? *Trends & Issues in Crime and Criminal Justice*, 409. https://aic.gov.au/publications/tandi/tandi409

Rivera, M. (2016). The sources of social violence in Latin America: An empirical analysis of homicide rates, 1980–2010. *Journal of Peace Research, 53*(1), 84–99.

Robinson, K., & Kurlychek, M. (2019). Differences in justice, differences in outcomes: A DID approach to studying outcomes in juvenile and adult court processing. *Justice Evaluation Journal, 2*(1), 35–49. https://doi.org/10.1080/24751979.2019.1585927

Rosenberg, M. J. (2010). Lemert, Edwin M.: Primary and secondary deviance. Sage. https://dx.doi.org/10.4135/9781412959193.n151

Sampson, R. J., & Laub, J. H. (2003). Life-course disasters? Trajectories of crime among delinquent boys followed to age 70. *Criminology, 41*(3), 555–592.

Schilling, C. M., Walsh, A., & Yun, I. (2011). ADHD and criminality: A primer on the genetic, neurobiological, evolutionary, and treatment literature for criminologists. *Journal of Criminal Justice, 39*(1), 3–11.

Schiraldi, V. (2018). *In Germany, it's hard to find a young adult in prison*. The Crime Report. https://thecrimereport.org/2018/04/10/in-germany-its-hard-to-find-a-young-adult-in-prison/

Semise, K. E., Radzilani-Makatu, M., & Nkoana, S. E. (2015). Identification of causes of criminal behaviour among youth of Muledane Village, Vhembe District municipality. *Journal of Social Sciences, 44*(1), 46–52. https://doi.org/10.1080/09718923.2015.11893458

Shulman, D. (2005). Labeling theory. In G. Ritzer (Ed.), *Encyclopedia of social theory* (Vol. 1, pp. 427–428). SAGE. https://doi.org/10.4135/9781412952552.n161

Siegel, L. J., & McCormick, C. (2006). *Criminology in Canada: Theories, patterns, and typologies* (3rd ed). Thompson.

Skaggs, S. L. (2016). Labeling theory. In *Encyclopedia Britannica*. https://www.britannica.com/topic/labeling-theory

Steinberg, L. (2017). Adolescent brain science and juvenile justice policymaking. *Psychology, Public Policy, and Law, 23*(4), 410–420.

Sweeten, G. (2010). Sampson, Robert J., and John H. Laub: Age-Graded Theory of Informal Social Control. *F. Cullen & P. Wilcox, Encyclopedia of Criminological Theory. Thousand Oaks, CA: Sage.*

Tanner, J. (2001). *Teenage troubles: Youth and deviance in Canada*. Oxford University Press.

Terblanche, S. S. (2012). The Child Justice Act: A detailed consideration of Section 68 as a point of departure with respect to the sentencing of young offenders. *PER: Potchefstroomse Elektroniese Regsblad, 15*(5), 435–475. http://www.scielo.org.za/scielo.php?script=sci_arttext&pid=S1727-37812012000500014&lng=en&tlng=en

United Nations, Department of Economic and Social Affairs, Population Division. (2019). *World population prospects 2019: Highlights* (ST/ESA/SER.A/423). https://population.un.org/wpp/Publications/Files/WPP2019_Highlights.pdf

U.S. History (2021). *Puritan life*. ushistory.org. https://www.ushistory.org/us/3d.asp.

Vilalta, C. J., Castillo, J. G., & Torres, J. A. (2016). *Violent crimes in Latin American cities*. Inter-American Development Bank. https://publications.iadb.org/publications/english/document/Violent-Crime-in-Latin-American-Cities.pdf

Vinney, C. (2019). *Sutherland's differential association theory explained*. ThoughtCo. https://www.thoughtco.com/differential-association-theory-4689191

Wells, J., & Walsh, A. (2019). Biosocial theories in criminology. In *Oxford research encyclopedia of criminology*.

Retrieved December 28, 2019, from https://oxfordre.com/criminology/view/10.1093/acrefore/9780190264079.001.0001/acrefore-9780190264079-e-245

Wickes, R., & Sydes, M. (2017). Social disorganization theory. In *Oxford bibliographies in sociology.* https://doi.org/10.1093/obo/9780199756384-0192

Wickert, C. (2019). *General strain theory.* SozTheo. https://soztheo.de/theories-of-crime/anomie-strain-theories/general-strain-theory-agnew/?lang=en

Wood, J., & Alleyne, E. (2010). Street gang theory and research: Where are we now and where do we go from here? *Aggression and Violent Behavior, 15*(2), 100–111. https://doi.org/10.1016/j.avb.2009.08.005

Zimmerman, M. A (2013). Resiliency theory: a strengths-based approach to research and practice for adolescent health. *Health education & behavior: the official publication of the Society for Public Health Education, 40*(4), 381–383. https://doi.org/10.1177/1090198113493782

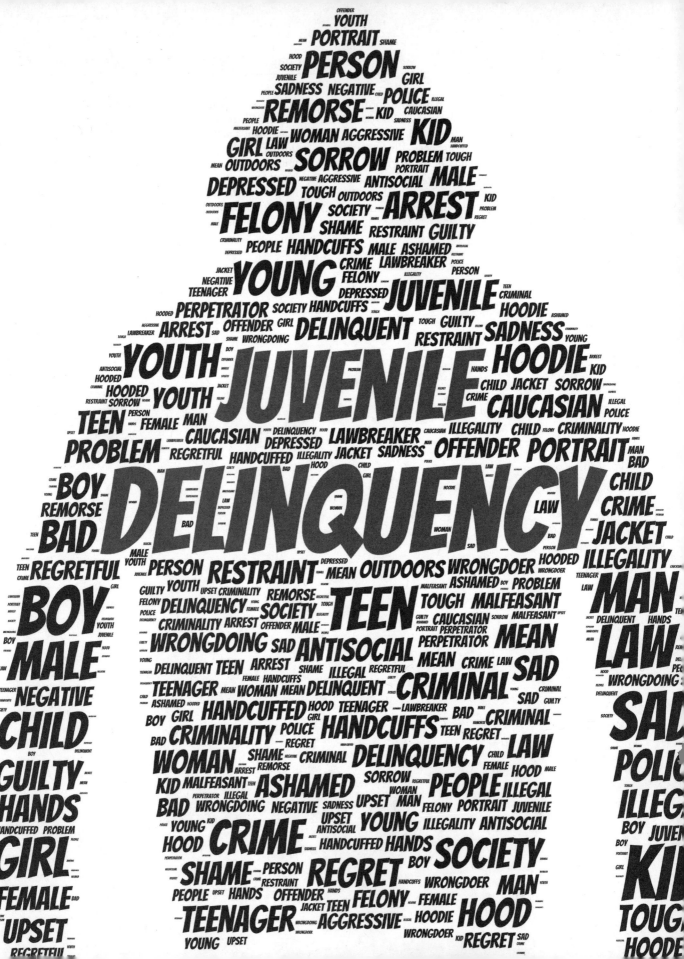

The Juvenile Offender: A Small Adult?

LEARNING OBJECTIVES

At the end of the chapter, students will be able to

compare and contrast a juvenile delinquent and a juvenile offender,

explain local and federal laws regarding juveniles,

define the superpredator and its evolution of reality versus myth,

analyze the cycle of juvenile justice, and

compare and contrast the reaction of countries around the world to juvenile crime.

The chapter opening image is a stereotypical depiction of how some stakeholders in society perceived juvenile offenders in the mid-80s into the early 1990s; focus was on the crime rather than the child and the causes behind their illicit and maladaptive behavior.

Keywords

Anti–Gang and Youth Violence Act
Council on Youth Violence
Cycle of juvenile justice
Demography studies
Juvenile Crime Control Act

Juvenile delinquents
Juvenile Justice and Delinquency
 Prevention Act
Juvenile offender
Juvenile Offender Act of 1978

National Youth Violence Prevention
 Resource Center
Superpredators
Violent Crime Control and Law
 Enforcement Act of 1994

Introduction

As we have seen in Chapters 1 and 2, predicting who will commit crimes and where they will be carried out can keep societies safe. Chapter 1 described society's monitoring of poverty and destitute children as a way to predict crime. Chapter 2 forecasted offending through crime tools such as the Uniform Crime Reporting Program and various victimization surveys and Chapter 3 looked at theoretical causes. In Chapter 4, we will learn how society has perceived juvenile crime and adjusted policies accordingly to keep the crime rate down. As we will see, perception does not always accurately forecast the future.

The juvenile Offender: A Modern-Day Small Adult?

Before the Progressive Era and the creation of institutions such as the juvenile justice system in 1899, children at a certain age and adults were treated similarly. Although age was sometimes a consideration in terms of culpability and sanctions, societies dating back to 400 B.C. did not always consider a child's ongoing development when deciding on "appropriate" sentences, as we do in the early 21st century. Children were often considered small adults in early American history and, in turn, were treated as such. In contemporary times, society generally views juveniles not as small adults, but as a group that should be treated differently with a focus on rehabilitation because of their still-developing minds and their social and environmental influences (Booth & Neill, 2017; Merenda et al., 2020; Office of Juvenile Justice and Delinquency Prevention [OJJDP], 2019a,b; Van Breda, 2018). This group of children are considered **juvenile delinquents**, defined as any minor (as defined by the given state) who commits an act that would be considered a crime if committed by an adult. Juvenile delinquents are processed under the jurisdiction of the juvenile justice system with a goal of rehabilitation as opposed to punishment. However, there is a special category given to those juveniles who, although their age fits within the state definition of a juvenile delinquent, will be prosecuted as adults in adult criminal court and subjected to adult sanctions because of the type of crime they commit. Many believe this legislative shift in how society treats this category of juveniles was spawned from a single incident in New York City.

On March 19, 1978, Willie Bosket, a 15-year-old, shot three individuals in three separate armed robberies, killing two of them on a New York City subway. As a result of his crime spree, and in keeping with the juvenile justice system's goal, he was sentenced to only 5 years in a juvenile detention center. An adult would have received 25 years to life in a maximum secured prison at the time. There was public outcry that New York State's Division for Youth did not punish Bosket appropriately for his heinous crimes. In June of the same year, Governor Hugh Carey, who was up for reelection, responded by initiating and signing into law (in the course of 2 weeks) the **Juvenile Offender Act of 1978**. This law was also known as the Willie Bosket Law. Many acknowledged that this new legislation emerged out of frustration and fear emanating from this single case. At the time, Peter Edelman, director of the Division of Youth, proclaimed this new law would waive "whole categories of kids to adult court law." Youth as young as 13 could now be tried as adults in adult courts with adult sentences. The juvenile offender was born in New York.

Soon after, Florida, Texas, and Illinois adopted similar laws, and a domino effect began to occur as other states passed similar legislation. By 1997, because of this trend and an increase in juvenile crime in the late 1980s and into the 1990s, all 50 states had legislation that allowed youth deemed "juveniles offenders" (or a similar term), sometimes as young as 10 years old, to be tried as adults.

This adult category for juveniles varies from state to state and even federally; they are sometimes referred to as a **juvenile offender** or simply as a juvenile adult transfer. Regardless of the term used, by the late 1990s, juvenile incarceration rates had more than doubled.

Federal Juvenile Delinquency Code

The U.S. Attorney's *Criminal Resource Manual* (U.S. Attorney's Manual, 1997) sets forth guidelines regarding the prosecution and treatment of a juvenile. It defines a juvenile delinquent and the act of juvenile delinquency as follows:

> A "juvenile" is a person who has not attained his eighteenth birthday, or for the purpose of proceedings and disposition under this chapter for an alleged act of juvenile delinquency, a person who has not attained his twenty-first birthday, and "juvenile delinquency" is the violation of a law of the United States committed by a person before his eighteenth birthday which would have been a crime if committed by an adult or a violation by such a person. (U.S. Code Title 18, part IV, Cptr. 403 §5031, definition)

Federally, there is also substantial discretion when it comes to which court the juvenile will be processed in.

> The act imparts considerable prosecutorial discretion as to whether an accused will be tried as an adult even though the criminal conduct charged qualifies as an act of juvenile delinquency. The government may bring a motion to transfer a juvenile defendant to the district court for prosecution as an adult if the juvenile is at least fifteen years of age, and the government alleges that the juvenile committed certain enumerated transferrable offenses (e.g., violent crimes or controlled substance violations). The government may also implement the mandatory transfer of a **juvenile offender** who has previously committed certain crimes. (U.S. Department of Justice, 2015, p. 2)

In addition to providing their own definitions and guidelines to process a juvenile in adult court, individual states have created their own interpretations and juvenile justice system procedures. In fact, every state and the District of Columbia, independent of the federal system, has its own system and governing laws (McCord et al., 2001).

State Laws

All states are still not equal. One of the first actions taken during the juvenile process is determining whether a case should be processed in adult criminal court rather than in juvenile court. All states have their own provisions for trying certain juveniles as adults in criminal court, sometimes referred to as an *adult transfer* to criminal court. For example, as of 2019 in New York, a juvenile delinquent is a child between the ages of 7 and 17 who has committed an offense. Juvenile delinquency cases are heard in the juvenile division of *family court* or *specialized juvenile courts.* However, a youth as young as 13 years old who has committed a serious felony may be tried as an adult in criminal court even though their age qualifies them for juvenile court jurisdiction. If found guilty, the youth is considered a juvenile offender and is subject to more severe penalties than a juvenile delinquent. Although 13 is the minimum age at which New York will prosecute a juvenile as an adult (meaning someone under 13, no matter the offense, would never be tried as an adult), all states have different minimum ages and designated crimes for a child to be prosecuted as an adult. Some states even have no minimum age (see Table 4.1). We will explore the specific ways these transfers take place in Chapter 8, "Juvenile Courts."

The upper age of jurisdiction is the oldest age at which a juvenile court has original authority over an individual for law-violating behavior. New legislation was passed in 2017 for both North Carolina and New York to raise the age to be prosecuted as an adult to 17 and then to 18 by 2019 (see Figure 4.1).

Juvenile Crime Trends

Although states and even the federal government have always been able to try juveniles as adults, it was not until the period between the 1980s and 1990s that jurisdictions were incentivized to create stricter policies, partly as a result of federal funding but mostly because of overwhelming fear.

1980s Into the Early 1990s: Juvenile Crime

> "A Crime Spree and the Worst Is Yet to Come." Dan Rather, CBS News, 1995
> "Teen Crime Bomb Set to Explode." Chelsea Stahl, NBC News, 1995
> "Teen-Age Gangs Are Inflicting Lethal Violence on Small Cities." Erik Eckholm, *New York Times*, 1993
> "A Judge Has Sentenced Two Boys for Killing Another Child Who Refused to Steal Candy for Them." Peter Jennings, ABC, 1996

During the late 1980s, after many prior strides to maintain the goal of the juvenile system, including the creation of the Juvenile Justice and Delinquency Prevention Act and its revisions (discussed later in this chapter), juvenile crime was rising, and society took notice. According to the crime measuring tools described in Chapter 2, by 1994, teenage murder arrests rose over 150%; they had more than doubled over the previous 9 years (Figure 4.2). Although the exact cause(s) were unknown, homicides committed by teens with guns and those related to drugs had also doubled from 1985 to 1994. This led experts to believe the proliferation of available guns and drugs, specifically crack cocaine at the time, coupled with a suffering economy and prevalence of gangs, could all be contributing factors. However, much more attention was given to stopping the violence than to figuring out why it was happening. An overwhelming fear of communities

TABLE 4.1 Statutory Exclusion Provisions Vary Considerably With Respect to Minimum Age and Offense Criteria

STATE	MINIMUM AGE FOR STATUTORY EXCLUSION	STATUTORY EXCLUSION OFFENSE AND MINIMUM AGE CRITERIA							
		ANY CRIMINAL OFFENSE	CERTAIN FELONIES	CAPITAL CRIMES	MURDER	CERTAIN PERSON OFFENSES	CERTAIN PROPERTY OFFENSES	CERTAIN DRUG OFFENSES	CERTAIN WEAPON OFFENSES
Alabama	16		16	16				16	
Alaska	16		16			16	16	16	16
Arizona	15		15		15	15	15		15
California	14				14	14			
Florida	NS		NS		16	NS	16	16	
Georgia	13		13		13	13			
Idaho	14				14	14	14	14	
Illinois	13		15		13	15			15
Indiana	16	NS			16	16			16
Iowa	NS		16					16	16
Louisiana	15				15	15			
Maryland	14			14	16	16			16
Massachusetts	14				14				
Minnesota	16				16				
Mississippi	13		13	13					
Montana	17				17	17	17	17	17
Nevada	NS	16	NS		16	NS			
New Mexico	15				15	15			
New York	13				13	13	14		14
Oklahoma	13		13		13	13			
Oregon	15		15		15	15			
Pennsylvania	NS				NS	NS			
South Carolina	16		16						
South Dakota	16		16						
Utah	16		16		16	16	16		16
Vermont	14		14		14	14	14		
Washington	16				16	16	16		
Wisconsin	10				10	10			

NS = No minimum age statute exists (there is no minimum age to be prosecuted as an adult by law).

Source: Office of Juvenile Justice and Delinquency Prevention (2016).

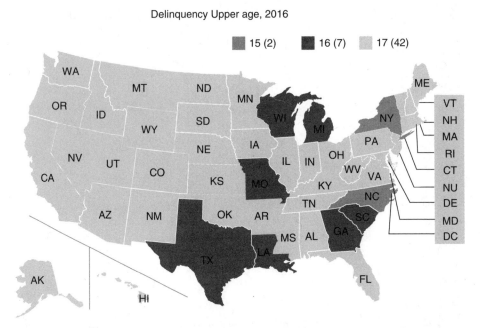

Figure 4.1 **Upper Age of Juvenile Court, Original Jurisdiction Across the United States.**

- The upper age of jurisdiction is the oldest age at which a juvenile court has original jurisdiction over an individual for law violating behavior. An upper age of 15 means that the juvenile court loses jurisdiction over a child when they turn 16; an upper age of 16 means that a juvenile court loses jurisdiction when a child turns 17; and an upper age of 17 means that a juvenile court loses jurisdiction over a child when they turn 18.

- State statutes define which youth are under the original jurisdiction of the juvenile court. These definitions are based primarily on age criteria. In most states, the juvenile court has original jurisdiction over all youth charged with a criminal law violation who were below the age of 18 at the time of the offense, arrest, or referral to court. Some states have higher upper ages of juvenile court jurisdiction in status offense, abuse, neglect, or dependency matters - often through age 20.

- Many states have statutory exceptions to basic age criteria. The exceptions, related to the youth's age, alleged offense, and/or prior court history, place certain youth under the original jurisdiction of the criminal court. This is known as *statutory exclusion*.

- In some states, a combination of the youth's age, offense, and prior record places the youth under the original jurisdiction of both the juvenile and criminal courts. In these situations where the courts have concurrent jurisdiction, the prosecutor is given the authority to decide which court will initially handle the case. This is known as *concurrent jurisdiction, prosecutor discretion*, or *direct filing*.

Source: OJJDP Statistical Briefing Book.

being affected spread from the inner cities to the suburbs, provoked by experts in the field and sensationalized stories of violence (Krisberg et al., 2009).

Among this uprise were especially brutal incidents of youth crime that made headlines all over the country. One such incident that received national attention, including the attention of the president of the United States, was the murder of an 11-year-old boy by other teens in Chicago.

In September 1994, the body of 11-year-old Robert Sandifer was found by an underpass. Sandifer had been killed by a 14-year-old who was accompanied by his 16-year-old brother. The teens told police the killing took place because Sandifer had killed a 14-year-old girl earlier. They all belonged to Chicago's Black Disciples gang. While other gang violence and overall juvenile crime were being discussed, this case was included in a radio address to the nation on September 10, 1994, by then-president Bill Clinton (Clinton, 1994).

All across our country this week, Americans came back from vacation. Our children are back in school, and for many families, this is what they regard as the real new year. As we get back to the business of our lives, it's a good time to stop and think about the work we have ahead of us as a nation.

Unfortunately, that work includes a stark fact about our children. Too many of them are growing up in fear. All too many are growing up without mainstream society's values, without knowing the difference between what's right and wrong, and without believing that it makes a difference whether they do right or wrong.

By now, nearly all of us know the story of Robert Sandifer, known as Yummy to his friends. He was first arrested when he was eight years old. A couple of weeks ago, when he was only 11, he became a suspect in the gang shooting of an innocent girl named Shavon Dean. Several days later, that boy died himself in what Chicago police say was yet another gang-related killing.

The number of gang homicides has nearly tripled since 1980 in Robert and Shavon's hometown. And all across America, too many decent people have felt the anguish of losing a child to the meanness of the streets. At younger and younger ages, boys and girls are turning to gangs and guns.

The growing fear that was building through media reports and by experts in the field now seemed to reach its peak.

A Society Once Again Scared by Its Youth

Reminiscent of what we read in Chapter 1, there has been some debate as to whether the creation of the juvenile court was prompted by a genuine motivation to keep vulnerable children safe, a frightened society secure, or a combination of both. In response to the prevalence of gang-involved crime (discussed further in Chapter 5), a rising crime rate among juveniles (Figure 4.3), and testimony by experts that the worst was yet to come, President Clinton announced, in the same radio address, the creation of what many consider the most influential crime bill in U.S. history.

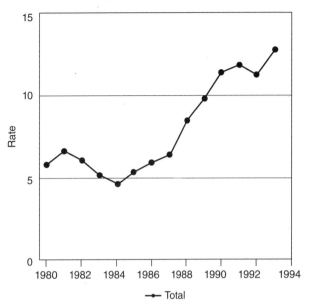

Figure 4.2 Teenage Murder Arrest Rates, 1980–1994

Note: Rates are arrests of persons ages 10-17 per 100,000 persons ages 10-17 in the resident population.

Source: OJJDP Statistical Briefing Book.

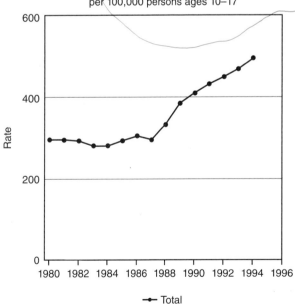

Figure 4.3 Teenage Violent Crime Arrest Rates, 1980–1994

Note: Rates are arrests of persons ages 10-17 per 100,000 persons ages 10-17 in the resident population. The Violent Crime Index includes the offenses of murder and nonnegligent manslaughter, rape, robbery, and aggravated assault.

Source: OJJDP Statistical Briefing Book.

The Violent Crime Control and Law Enforcement Act of 1994: U.S. Department of Justice

"It was the largest crime bill in US history" (Government Tracker, 2004, p. 1), providing for 100,000 new police officers and millions of additional funding for prisons and prevention programs for states willing to pass tougher laws for juveniles. The **Violent Crime and Law Enforcement Act** specifically authorized adult prosecution of children 13 and older who commit certain violent crimes. It also advocated for harsher penalties for the sale or transfer of a firearm to juveniles and possession of certain firearms by minors. It set out to deter children's exploitation by tripling the maximum penalties for using children to distribute drugs and drug sales in or near a protected zone, that is, schools, playgrounds, video arcades, and youth centers. It also created a federal "3 strike rule": mandatory life imprisonment without the possibility of parole for three or more serious violent felonies or drug trafficking convictions. Some aspects of the bill did devote billions of dollars in additional funds to have more police in neighborhoods working with the community and grants for supervised after-school, weekend, and summer programs for youth at risk for delinquency. But because of the prevalent get-tough tactics that this bill included, it received widespread criticism for years to come (Hawkins et al., 2003).

Although these new stricter measures were put in place, many experts believed they were not enough. Scholars and stakeholders spoke of something worse coming, individuals who were going to cause the most violence the country had ever seen. Who were they warning us about? Our nation's children!

The Coming of the Superpredators: "A New Breed of Criminal"

> America is now home to thickening ranks of juvenile "Super Predators"—radically impulsive, brutally remorseless youngsters, including ever more pre-teenage boys who murder, assault, rape, rob, burglarize, deal deadly drugs, join gun-toting gangs and create serious communal disorders —John DiIulio, criminologist (Joyner, 2019, p. 3)

Criminologists John DiIulio and James Fox and other social scientists and notable figures were influential during the 1980s' and 1990s' rise in juvenile crime. Mr. DiIulio even spoke to Congress, helping mold the "get tough" 1994 Crime Bill. However, despite the government's new efforts in 1994, juvenile crime was still perceived as rising (although actual stats revealed something very different; see Figure 4.4). James Fox was quoted in the mid-1990s as saying, "By 2005, we may very well have a blood bath of teenage violence." James Q. Wilson also was critical of the juvenile court process:

> The court was founded on the principle of acting in loco parentis [Latin for in the place of a parent], we need a juvenile court that will be much more heavily funded than the present ones are, that will take very seriously the first signs of repeat offending among juveniles and will be very serious about the penalties they impose. —James Q. Wilson, social scientist (Wilson, 1996)

John DiIulio also warned that the United States would see a rise in the rate of youth violence in the time between the mid-1990s and the mid-2000s. But what were these predictions based on?

John DiIulio looked at **demography studies**—the study of human populations and their size, composition, and distribution—and warned of a bleak and violent future. He predicted future patterns of youth crime based on the fact that teenage homicide rates more than doubled between 1984 and 1994. He estimated that by the year 2000, based on the previous crime trend and demography studies showing that there would be a million more youth aged 14 to 17 by that date, there would be a doubling or tripling of youth violence if no action were taken. DiIulio used the term "**superpredator**" to describe the current and future class of violent youth that, according to him, demonstrated no remorse and no empathy.

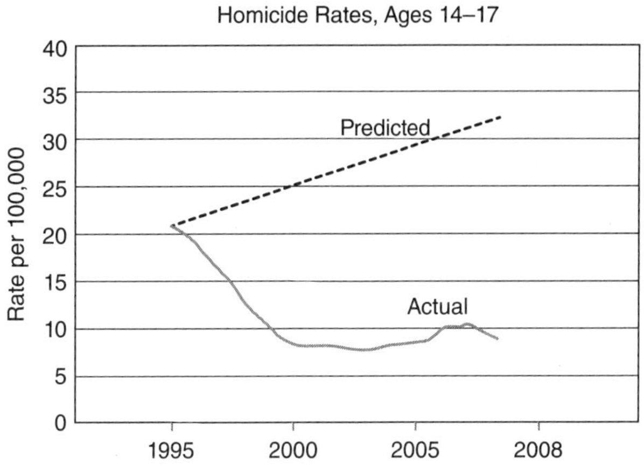

Fear Continues to Grow . . .

We also have to have an organized effort against gangs, just as in a previous generation, we had an organized effort against the mob. We need to take these people on; they are often connected to big drug cartels; they are not just gangs of kids anymore. They are often the kinds of kids who are called super predators. No conscience. No empathy. We can talk about why they ended up that way, but first, we have to bring them to heel. —First Lady Hillary Clinton, 1996

"Wake up! Our youngest career criminals are getting away with the most heinous crimes over and over again, and it's not just gang warfare." —Representative Porter J. Goss of Florida

Figure 4.4 Predicted versus Actual Juvenile Crime Rates, 1995–2008

Source: U.S. Department of Justice, Bureau of Justice Statistics

On January 7, 1997, the **Juvenile Crime Control Act** was introduced to Congress by Representative Bill McCollum of Florida and supported by others in the House of Representatives. This was to be a follow-up to the 1994 Crime Bill with an even greater emphasis on controlling youth crime through punitive measures.

Colleagues in the House supported this bill and vocalized the consequences of not passing more stringent legislation to prosecute juveniles. Gang crime was a major component cited and addressed in the 1994 Crime Bill. Although representatives acknowledged a decrease in juvenile crime, they stressed that juveniles still committed a fifth of all violent crimes committed by individuals under the age 18. The bill specifically would offer $1.5 billion of federal funding to states that would strengthen their juvenile justice systems, including building more prisons, hiring more staff, developing alternative forms of punishment, and establishing drug court programs for youth. However, as a condition of receiving these federal grants, states would have to agree to four stipulations:

- Prosecute all children 15 or older who commit "serious violent crime" as adults.
- Track and increase penalties for repeat offenders.
- Take away confidentiality rights from "juvenile offenders," juveniles being processed as adults, making their criminal records public.
- Allow judges to go after parents or guardians of convicted minors for lack of supervision.

Although President Clinton had previously advocated for tougher sanctions against juveniles in his 1994 Crime Bill, he was publicly criticized for the new bill being more punitive and less rehabilitative, focusing more on enforcement and not on intervention or prevention. The bill was passed by the House on May 8, 1997, but was never passed by the Senate (GovTrack, 2021).

The president supported a separate bill, the **Anti–Gang and Youth Violence Act**, which was introduced, but stalled in the Senate that same year. Nonetheless, although the president advocated for prevention programs and centers for drug abusers, he also warned that the nation "must act now" because of the increasing youth population. He cautioned that the number of children in school exceeds even the baby boom population, echoing the warning of John DiIulio, James Fox, and others of the yet-to-come superpredators. This act, too, ultimately failed in the Senate.

Although Clinton's additional legislation failed, the message of fear seemed to pass and was instilled on the nation. In 1997, 12 states had already met the strict conditions required by the Anti–Gang and Youth Violence Act. Although no further acts passed, within 3 years of the proposal of these acts, nearly all states had adopted additional laws that allowed for more youth to be tried and treated as adults, including removing confidentiality of any criminal records for juvenile offenders. These laws moved away from an emphasis on education and rehabilitation toward a more punitive response for youth who committed violent crimes. The notion that children who commit adult crimes should be prosecuted as adults rang out in courts all over the country, resulting in many transfers and prosecutions of children to adult criminal court.

> The Justice Policy Institute's poll showed Americans overwhelmingly believe youth crime is still on the rise when in fact, it had been falling sharply for four years, an over-reaction by the public and politicians to youth violence."
> —Vincent Schiraldi, director, December 31, 1999

Myth Versus Reality

Although predictions led to panic, fortunately they did not lead to reality. Violent crime among youth did not continue to grow, but instead declined. Murder committed by youth aged 10 to 17 fell almost 70% from 1994 to 2011 (see Figure 4.4) (OJJDP, 2016). Many experts believe that it was not looming sanctions that fostered the continued decline, but instead debate an improving economy, better policing, less availability of guns, and the end of the crack epidemic as potential causes (Blumstein & Wallman, 2006). It was also accepted that a small number of juveniles were responsible for a large number of arrests. We see this with both adults and children, where a small number of individuals are responsible for the majority of crimes (National Research Council, 2013). Many scholars who had cautioned of the rise of the superpredators acknowledged their fallacy when the impending horde society was warned of did not materialize.

We saw that in the 1980s and 1990s, although juvenile crime was declining, perception and fear seemed to drive policy changes. This can create a never-ending cycle of volatile and ineffective policies if legislation is passed based on the perception of crime rather than its reality (Bernard, 1992).

The Cycle of Juvenile Justice

Thomas J. Bernard examined how and why juvenile policies were created over the past 200 years. Based on his research, he discussed the **cycle of juvenile justice**: Society perceives that juvenile crime is at its worse and, as a result, reexamines and continually changes the current policy (see Figure 4.5). If the current legislation is interpreted as harsh, then new, more lenient policies will be implemented. If the current law is interpreted as lenient, then new, harsher policies will be implemented. Bernard and Kurlychek (2010) also discussed a cycle of reforms controlled by stagnant notions that have led to a recycling of old strategies and perspectives rather than creating new ones based on what has been learned. Bernard discussed other causes for this cycle, purporting that no policy can solve youth crime if it arises from social conditions and inequalities as opposed to legitimate needs of the juvenile justice system.

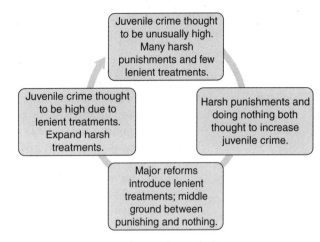

Figure 4.5 The Cycle of Juvenile Justice

Grants and Act Revisions Affecting Juveniles

During the 1980s and 1990s, most states revised their juvenile justice systems to include more punitive measures and more youth being tried as adults. In 1997, Congress created the Juvenile Accountability Block Grant, allowing the attorney general to provide grants to states to strengthen their juvenile justice systems through accountability within their juvenile populations. According to Finklea (2012, p. 2), "Juvenile justice, in general, has thus moved away from emphasizing the rehabilitation of juveniles and toward a greater reliance on sanctioning them for their crimes."

Block Grant Act

The House of Representatives appropriated funding for the **Juvenile Accountability Incentive Block Grants Act** in 1997, and the program began in 1998 (Albert et al., 2000). It provided block grants to state and local governments as financial incentives to increase "accountability" within their juvenile justice systems. Although Congress did not specifically define what was meant by accountability, the guidelines and administrative rules described individual policies that would demonstrate enhancing the offender's responsibility. This included prosecuting juveniles who commit serious violent crimes as adults, expanding sanctions within the juvenile court, holding parents responsible for seeing that their children obey court orders, and making records of those juveniles prosecuted as adults public. Although states only had to consider these revisions in their laws to receive funds, many carried them out. For example, even at its inception, most states began to prosecute serious juvenile offenders as adults (Parent & Barnett, 2003). Throughout the 1990s, 47 states passed laws that modified traditional juvenile court confidentiality agreements, 45 states passed laws making it easier to transfer juveniles into the adult criminal justice system, and most states expanded sentencing options for minors. More punitive measures were incorporated for juvenile justice programs during this time through a series of revisions to the **Juvenile Justice and Delinquency Prevention Act** (JDDPA) that added additional juvenile accountability to federal grant programs (Congressional Research Service, 2015; Finklea, 2012). However, the JJDPA did continue to revise and add to its core components regarding rehabilitation, treating children differently than adults, and unbiased deinstitutionalization.

Juvenile Justice and Delinquency Prevention Act Revisions

The Juvenile Justice and Delinquency Prevention Act of 1974 experienced changes throughout this time in history. As discussed in Chapter 1, it focused on rehabilitating juveniles by means other than institutional care. It also helped states prevent delinquency and improve the juvenile system as a whole (OJJDP, 2010). The JJDPA had three main components: it created entities within the federal government that were dedicated to coordinating and administering national juvenile justice efforts; it established grant programs to assist the states with running their juvenile justice systems, and it put into effect core mandates that states had to adhere to in order to be eligible to receive grant funding. The act allowed grants to be given to states, territories, and the District of Columbia that adhered to the act's main provisions (Act 4, 2007). These provisions, also known as "core protections," are as follows.

DEINSTITUTIONALIZATION OF STATUS OFFENDERS

Youth charged with status offenses and abused and neglected children involved with the courts may not be placed in secure detention or locked confinement. As you read in Chapter 1, a status offense is an offense that only applies to minors whose actions would not be considered unlawful if they were adults. Examples include truancy, running away, curfew violations, and possession or use of alcohol. Juveniles who commit a status offense may not be held for an extended time (more than 24 hours) and cannot be confined in secure adult facilities for any length of time. These protections advocate for children who solely commit status offenses to receive community-based sanctions such as day treatment, counseling, family support, and, in some instances, alternative education. The idea is to move the focus from punishment to finding the root causes of their behavior.

In 1980, the deinstitutionalization of status offenders was amended to include a valid court order exception. This allowed judges who had previously adjudicated a status offense and imposed a court order to not reoffend (including committing another status offense) to put juveniles who violated the order in locked detention.

ADULT JAIL AND LOCK-UP REMOVAL (JAIL REMOVAL)

Juvenile delinquents are not allowed to be detained in adult jails for an extended period of time (over 24 hours). However, this does not apply to those whom the individual state considers juvenile offenders or adult transfers.

"SIGHT AND SOUND" SEPARATION

In those instances when status offenders or juvenile delinquents are temporarily placed in formal detention, "sight and sound" contact with adults is prohibited. Children cannot be confined next to adult cells or share any other space.

DISPROPORTIONATE MINORITY CONTACT

Historically, youth of color have experienced harsher punishments than White youth (Campbell et al., 2018). States are mandated to address disproportionate minority contact by gathering statistics and assessing the causes. Despite efforts, youth of color make up the majority of the youth in the juvenile justice system.

In 1974, the JJDPA only included the first two protections, the deinstitutionalization of status offenders and sight and sound separation. The jail removal provision was added in 1980 in response to findings that showed youth incarcerated in adult facilities had "a high suicide rate, physical, mental, and sexual assault, inadequate care and programming, negative labeling, and exposure to serious offenders and mental patients" (Jenson & Fraser, 2011, p. 76). The disproportionate minority contact requirement was added to the JJDPA in 1992, but stood for disproportionate minority confinement. It was then changed from "disproportionate minority confinement" to "disproportionate minority contact" in 2002. The change to contact occurred as a result of increasing evidence that African American youth had disproportionate contact with the juvenile justice system at almost every point (Piquero, 2008).

According to the Coalition for Juvenile Justice (2009, p. 1), "With youth of color making up one-third of the youth population but two-thirds of youth in contact, this provision requires states to gather information and assess the reason for disproportionate minority contact." Studies still indicate that youth of color receive harsher sentences and are more likely to be incarcerated than White youth for the same offenses (American Bar Association, 2016; OJJDP, 2016). According to Shannon and Hauer (2018, p. 330), "Disproportionate minority contact (DMC) in the US juvenile justice system persists."

COMPLIANCE MONITORING

States are monitored for compliance with the core protections of the JJDPA and receive grant funds based on their compliance level. Full compliance was considered achieved under the following circumstances: States must submit an annual report that provides data on compliance of the first three protections along with a 3-year plan and updates. For a state to indicate compliance with the fourth component, disproportionate minority contact, they must demonstrate progress each year to address and improve efforts to reduce the disproportionate rate of contact with youth of color (Coalition for Juvenile Justice, 2009). The standard does not mandate states to show improvements, but they must make efforts to identify discrepancies through data collection and then make intentional plans to address disparities (National Research Council, 2013). In 2018, the JJDPA was amended to hold states more accountable and each core component was further amended (OJJDP, 2019b; see Chapters 7–9).

Juvenile Justice and Delinquency Prevention Act Timeline

1984   Enhanced and amended jail removal requirements.

1988   Addressed disproportionate minority confinement as a requirement

1992   Amended deinstitutionalization of status offenders, jail removal, and separation requirements

Elevated disproportionate minority confinement to a core requirement

Established the Title V Incentive Grants for Local Delinquency Prevention Grants Program (Title V)

Established new programs to address gender bias

Emphasized prevention and treatment, family strengthening, graduated sanctions, and risk-need assessments

2002   Broadened the scope of the disproportionate minority confinement core requirement to disproportionate minority contact

Consolidated seven previously independent programs into a single Part C prevention block grant

Created a new Part D, authorizing research, training and technical assistance, and information dissemination

Added Part E, authorizing grants for new initiatives and programs

Reauthorized Title V

Required states to give funding priorities of their formula and block grant allocations to evidence-based programs

Reauthorized Title II Formula Grants Program

Revised the Juvenile Accountability Incentive Block Grants program, which is now called the Juvenile Accountability Block Grants program (as part of the Omnibus Crime Control and Safe Streets Act) (OJJDP, 2016, p. 1)

Federal Recommendations for Further Improvements for the JJDPA

Members of Congress and the American Bar Association have advocated not only for the JJDPA's reauthorization, but also for improvements to its major components. These recommendations include the following:

- *End detention or jailing of noncriminal status offenders*: Eliminate the valid court order exception that states have used to detain nondelinquent status offenders. This includes youth who violate curfew or alcohol and tobacco laws, those who are truant, and those who are runaways.
- *Additional provisions*: Promote state efforts to expedite access to qualified counsel and informing youth of their ability to seal or expunge their records.
- *Community-based alternatives to detention*: Improve assessment and treatment for mental health and substance abuse needs, diversion efforts, and greater accountability.
- *Reduce racial and ethnic disparities*: "Youth of color are disproportionately over-represented and subject to more punitive sanctions than similarly-charged/situated white youth at all levels of the juvenile justice system. Legislation should require States and localities to plan and implement data-driven approaches, set measurable goals for disparity reduction, collect data, and publicly report on progress each year." (American Bar Association, 2016, p. 2)

As part of the Consolidated Appropriations Act, 2020 (Public Law 116-93), $320 million has been allocated toward juvenile justice programs, the largest amount in almost a decade (Congressional Research Service, 2020).

Just the Facts: A Return to Statistical Data

In 1999, the White House (under the leadership of then-president Bill Clinton) created the **Council on Youth Violence**. The initial objective was to coordinate federal youth violence prevention activities. In conjunction with the Centers for Disease Control and Prevention and other federal agencies, the council developed the **National Youth**

Violence Prevention Resource Center. Its purpose was to serve as a central database for statistics and additional information on youth violence and youth violence prevention strategies, all accessible by the public. As technology progressed, the center eventually utilized technology by means of a website (www.safeyouth.org), allowing easy access to a variety of information about youth violence, contributing factors, and prevention (Criminal Justice, 2010). In 2007, the center expanded its efforts to encourage and facilitate community youth violence prevention programs between local government and community leaders and provide assistance in creating programs and policies; these efforts continue in the early 21st century.

Worldview

The World Health Organization (2002) reported that juvenile crime on average increased across the globe in many countries in the late 1980s and into the 1990s, much like in the United States, for reasons from low economies to drug prevalence. The 8th United Nations (U.N.) National Congress on the Prevention of Crime and Managing Criminal Justice referred to youth crime as a growing problem worldwide in 1994 (Winterdyk, 2002). In 1995, the U.N. 9th National Congress further concluded that the average age of onset of criminal behavior was falling, and "by the year 2000, more than 50% of the world population will be under the age of 15 . . . [this] highlights the seriousness of the problem of juvenile delinquency and youth crime" (United Nations, 1995, p. 17). Countries around the world experiencing or fearing this rise in crime reacted much like the United States in terms of creating policies that held juveniles more accountable at younger ages and allocated harsher adult sentencing, although there were some exceptions.

Although many European countries and Canada experienced a rise in juvenile crime during the same period as the United States, not all reacted the same as the United States in terms of tougher sanctions and transfers to adult courts.

AUSTRIA
The 1988 Youth Court Law of Austria described juvenile offending as "a normal step in development for which restorative justice, not punishment, is the appropriate response" (Institute of Medicine and National Research Council, 2001, p. 20). Restorative justice can include the victim, the offender, and possibly community stakeholders attempting to resolve the incident informally through accountability and sometimes restitution (Posick, 2019; D. B. Wilson et al., 2017; see Chapters 6 and 13 for more information on this type of community-based treatment).

GERMANY
The rest of Europe also experienced a dramatic rise in juvenile violent crime from the mid-1980s to the early 1990s. In Germany, there were even higher increases in youth violence during this time. In 1984, approximately 300 per 100,000 children ages 14 to 18 were suspected of violent crime; this number increased to 760 per 100,000 by 1995 (Pfeiffer, 1998). In the early 1990s, unemployment was also rampant in Germany, especially after the fall of the Berlin Wall. Many individuals who were previously under communist rule came to western European nations. Unemployment, alcohol use, and unstable and abusive families all were cited as potential contributing factors to this increase in violence (Pfeiffer, 1998). Despite this rise in juvenile

crime, Germany continued to emphasize diversion and educational sanctions, keeping their moderate sentencing practices intact (Dunkel & Heinz, 2017). Other countries reacted much like the United States in the 1980s and 1990s.

ENGLAND AND WALES

Although in the early 1980s England and Wales provided community-based sanctions for young offenders and were moving away from institutional placements, this was reversed in the 1990s because of the sudden rise in juvenile violence. In England in 1986, about 360 of every 100,000 children ages 14 to 16 were arrested for violent crimes. In 1994, that number increased by over 60%. The U.K. Criminal Justice and Public Order Act of 1994 made it easier to place juvenile delinquents under the age of 15 in juvenile correctional facilities and extend the maximum sentences. According to the Institute of Medicine and National Research Council (2001, p. 21), "the UK Crime and Disorder Act of 1998 moved the English juvenile justice system even further toward a punitive, offense-based model."

AUSTRALIA

Reported crime in Australia rose by almost 66% between 1980 and 1990. Violent crime increased sporadically by about the same percentage between 1973 and 1990. The greatest number of arrests for violent crime were for individuals 18 years of age. The peak age for theft and burglary was 15. As we read in Chapter 1, the legal age of criminal responsibility in Australia is 10. Only individuals over 17 are processed as adults. However, if a juvenile is found to have committed a particular act in juvenile court, they could be sent to adult prison. This is done rarely and occurs on a case-by-case basis. But with a decade of growing crime between 1980 and 1990, in 1991, offenders aged 16 were being transferred to adult prison, again a prior rare occurrence. In the early 21st century, Australia has 884 juvenile institutions (Australian Bureau of Statistics, 2014).

ITALY

Between 1986 and 1991, juvenile crime more than doubled compared to the consistent number of juvenile crime cases in the years prior. Drug offenses tripled, crimes by children under 14 rose from 2,500 arrests to almost 10,000, and property crimes committed by children ages 14 to 17 more than doubled between 1986 and 1993. Suggested causes ranged from the proliferation of drugs to minors being used by organized crime. Parents can be held civilly responsible for their child's actions in Italy, and courts generally do not send juveniles to formal detention. Only 1% of their youth end up in jail; however, youth aged 14 to 18 can now be tried as adults (Italy National Report, 2013).

CANADA

Beginning in 1985, juvenile crime continued to rise each year, and in 1991, police-reported juvenile crime reached its highest level in Canada's history (9,126 per 100,000 youth), since it began recording crime in 1962. Some believe the causes were drug use and poor socioeconomic conditions. In contrast, others believe it resulted from an overreliance on incarceration after the creation of the Young Offender Act of 1984. Historically, the age of criminality was 12 years old in Canada, and a juvenile could only be sentenced to a maximum sentence of 3 years regardless of the crime committed. In 1996, the maximum sentence was increased to 10 years with an additional provision that now allowed 16-year-olds to be tried as adults and potentially be sentenced to life in prison.

Since 1991, youth crime has seen steady decreases, with possible causes stemming from an improved economy and increased policing, as were experienced in the United States, to changing values in Canada (Ouimet, 2004; Taylor-Butts & Bressan, 2009). It was also speculated that the creation of the Youth Criminal Juvenile Act that came into effect in 2003, which seemed to have replaced reliance on formally charging youth with warnings and referrals, continued the downward trend of juvenile arrests (Taylor-Butts & Bressan, 2009). In 2012, however, legislation was passed as a provision to the Youth Criminal Juvenile Act that lowered the age to 14 for juveniles to be prosecuted as adults for certain violent crimes (Canada Department of Justice, 2017).

TABLE 4.2 International Comparisons of Juvenile Justice Systems

COUNTRY	MINIMUM AGE OF CRIMINAL RESPONSIBILITY	AGE OF ADULT CRIMINAL RESPONSIBILITY	COURT THAT HANDLES JUVENILES
Australia	10[a]	16–17[b]	Children's courts, which are part of the criminal justice system and deal with juveniles charged with a crime
Austria	14	19	Special sections in local and regional courts; youth courts
Belgium	16–18	18	Special juvenile courts
Denmark	15	18	No juvenile court
England and Wales	10	18	Youth courts
France	13 (unofficial)	18	Children's tribunals; youth courts of assizes
Germany	14	18	Single sitting judge; juvenile court; juvenile chamber
Hungary	14	18	Special sections of regular courts
Italy	14	18	Separate juvenile courts
Japan	14	20	Family courts
The Netherlands	12	18	Special juvenile courts
New Zealand	14; 10 for murder and manslaughter	18	Youth courts
Russia	16; 14 for certain crimes	18	No juvenile court
Sweden	15	18	No juvenile court

Source: From Weitekamp et al. (1999).

INDIA

According to the National Crime Records Bureau, juvenile crime rose 100% to 300% across India between 2005 and 2015. The total number of crime incidents in 2005 was 18,931 and reached 49,400 in 2015.

Juveniles under 18, regardless of their crime, were prosecuted in "youth court," generally with a maximum sentence of 3 years. However, in 2014, because of rising crime and because one assailant from a gang rape, just shy of his 18th birthday, received only a 3-year juvenile sentence, a bill to lower the age to 16 for longer adult sentencing for rape and other crimes was passed in 2015 (Agarwal & Kumar, 2016).

Wrap-up

Despite available crime measuring tools, society seems to have been swayed throughout history to rely more on fear than on facts. Although the 1980s and 1990s saw an increase in crime, predictions that an increase in the juvenile population would result in even higher crime rates never came to fruition. Nonetheless, society continued to change policies and prosecute children as adults. As we have learned, however, just as there are many contributing factors to fluctuating juvenile crime rates, there are as many nonpunitive approaches to effectively address them.

Discussion Questions

1. Should individual states define what a juvenile offender is, or should the country adopt a single definition?
2. How does the cycle of juvenile justice affect contemporary policymaking?
3. What was the purpose of the 1974 Juvenile Justice and Delinquency Prevention Act, and how did it shift its focus in the 1990s?
4. Define the notion of the juvenile superpredator and its effects on society at the time.
5. Explain why or why not juveniles should ever be treated as an adult based on the crime they committed.
6. How did the rest of the world react to increases in juvenile crime?

ONLINE RESOURCES

The National Academies Press http://www.nap.edu
Office of Juvenile Justice and Delinquency Program http://www.ojjdp.org
US Department of Justice http://www.ncjrs.gov

Definitions

Anti–Gang and Youth Violence Act—introduced, but stunted in the Senate; an act that called for stricter prosecution and sentencing for violent youth

Council on Youth Violence—in 1999, the White House created this council to assist with youth violence transparency and prevention strategies

Cycle of juvenile justice—Thomas J. Bernard used this term to describe how society seems always to think that juvenile crime is at its worse and, as a result, will examine the current policy. If the current policy is interpreted as harsh, then new, more lenient policies will be implemented to reduce "crime." If the current policy is interpreted as lenient, then new, harsher policies will be implemented.

Demography studies—the study of human populations and their size, composition, and distribution

Juvenile Crime Control Act—a failed follow-up to the 1994 Crime Bill with more of an emphasis on controlling youth crime through punitive measures

Juvenile delinquent—any minor who commits an act that would be considered a crime if committed by an adult

Juvenile Justice and Delinquency Prevention Act—set policies to keep adults and juveniles separated and provided funding

Juvenile offender—a juvenile who is being prosecuted as an adult for committing specific serious crimes as determined by individual states

Juvenile Offender Act of 1978—set policies to keep adults and juveniles separated and provided funding

National Youth Violence Prevention Resource Center—developed by the Council on Youth Violence, its purpose was to serve as a central database for statistics and other information on youth violence and youth violence prevention strategies, all accessible by the public

Superpredators—a term presented by criminologist John DiIulio to describe youth who he felt were impulsive and remorseless for their violent crimes

Violent Crime Control and Law Enforcement Act of 1994—sponsored by the U.S. Department of Justice, this bill specifically authorized adult prosecution of children age 13 and older who commit certain violent crimes. It also provided for stricter penalties for juvenile offenders and the sale or transfer of a firearm to juveniles and their possession of certain firearms.

References

Act 4 Juvenile Justice Working Group. (2007). *The Juvenile Justice and Delinquency Prevention Act: A fact book.* http://www.campaignforyouthjustice.org/Downloads/Resources/jjdpafactbook.pdf

Albert, R. L., Tuell, J. A., Holloway, C., Martin, S., Matese, M., & Tompkins, E. (2000). *Juvenile Accountability Incentive Block Grants Program: Guidance manual.* Office of Juvenile Justice and Delinquency Programs. https://www.ojp.gov/sites/g/files/xyckuh241/files/archives/documents/jaibg_guidance_manual.pdf

American Bar Association. (2016). Juvenile Justice and Delinquency Prevention Act. https://www.americanbar.org/advocacy/governmental_legislative_work/priorities_policy/criminal_justice_system_improvements/juvenile_justice_delinquency_prevention_act/

Agarwal, S., & Kumar, N. (2016). Juvenile Justice (Care and Protection of Children) Act 2015: A review. *Space and Culture, India, 3*(3). 5–9. https://doi.org/10.20896/saci.v3i3.165

Australian Bureau of Statistics. (1982–2013). *Prisoners in Australia* (various issues) (ABS Cat. 4517.0). 1982–1993 published by Australian Institute of Criminology.

Australian Bureau of Statistics. (2014). *Measuring crime.* https://www.aph.gov.au/Parliamentary_Business/Committees/House_of_Representatives_Committees?url=laca/crimeinthecommunity/report/chapter4.pdf

Bernard, T. J. (1992). *The cycle of juvenile justice.* Oxford University Press.

Bernard, T. J., & Kurlychek, M. C. (2010). *The cycle of juvenile justice* (2nd ed.). Oxford University Press.

Bilchik, S. (1999). *Juvenile justice: A century of change.* 1999 National Report Series, Juvenile Justice Bulletin. https://www.ncjrs.gov/html/ojjdp/9912_2/juv1.html

Binder, A., Geis, G., & Bruce, D. D., Jr. (1997). Juvenile delinquency: Historical, cultural, and legal perspectives (2nd ed.). Anderson.

Blumstein, A., & Wallman, J. (2006). The crime drop and beyond. *Annual Review of Law and Social Science, 2*(1), 125–146.

Booth, J. W., & Neill, J. T. (2017). Coping strategies and the development of psychological resilience. *Journal of Outdoor and Environmental Education, 20*(1), 47–54.

Bremner, R. H., & Barnard, J. (1974). *Children and youth in America: A documentary history.* Harvard University Press.

Buenker, J. D., Burnham, J. C., & Crunden, R. M. (1986). *Progressivism.* Schenkman.

Bureau of Justice Statistics. (2011). *Homicide trends in the United States, 1980–2008.* U.S. Department of Justice. https://www.bjs.gov/content/pub/pdf/htus8008.pdf

Bureau of Justice Statistics. (2016). *Data collection: National Crime Victimization Survey (NCVS).* https://www.bjs.gov/index.cfm?ty=dcdetail&iid=245

Bureau of Justice Statistics. (2017). *National Crime Statistics Exchange.* https://www.bjs.gov/content/ncsx.cfm

Campbell, N. A., Barnes, A. R., Mandalari, A., Onifade, E., Campbell, C. A., Anderson, V. R., … & Davidson, W. S. (2018). Disproportionate minority contact in the juvenile justice system: An investigation of ethnic disparity in program referral at disposition. *Journal of ethnicity in criminal justice, 16*(2), 77-98.

Canada Department of Justice. (2017). *The Youth Criminal Justice Act summary and background*. https://www.justice.gc.ca/eng/cj-jp/yj-jj/tools-outils/back-hist.html

Clinton, W. J. (1994, September 10). *William J. Clinton: The president's radio address—September 10, 1994* [Audio recording]. American Presidency Project. http://www.presidency.ucsb.edu/ws/index.php?pid=49062

Coalition for Juvenile Justice. (2009). *Disproportionate minority contact*. http://www.juvjustice.org/juvenile-justice-and-delinquency-prevention-act/disproportionate-minority-contact

Congressional Research Service. (2015). *Juvenile justice: Legislative history and current legislative issues*. https://www.everycrsreport.com/files/20150714_RL33947_576842b03c2f25c8753b141f57396689e687945b.pdf

Congressional Research Service. (2020). *Juvenile justice funding trends*. https://fas.org/sgp/crs/misc/R44879.pdf

Criminal Justice. (2010). *Crime prevention programs*. http://criminal-justice.iresearchnet.com/system/crime-prevention-programs/

Dunkel, F., & Heinz, W. (2017). Germany. In S. Decker & N. Marteache (Eds.), *International handbook of juvenile justice*. Springer. 305-326.

Finklea, K. (2012). *Juvenile justice: Legislative history and current legislative issues*. Congressional Research Service.

GovTrack. (2021). H.R. 3—105th Congress: Juvenile Crime Control Act of 1997. https://www.govtrack.us/congress/bills/105/hr3

Hawkins, D. F., Myers, S. L., & Stone, R. N. (2003). *Crime control and social justice: The delicate balance*. Greenwood Press.

Institute of Medicine and National Research Council. (2001). *Juvenile crime, juvenile justice*. National Academies Press. https://doi.org/10.17226/9747

Italy National Report. (2013). *JODA—Juvenile offenders detention alternative in Europe*. European Union.

Jenson, J. M., & Fraser, M. W. (2011). *Social policy for children and families: A risk and resilience perspective* (2nd ed.). Sage.

Joyner, R. (2019). Managing a maximum security jail: A new approach. *American Jails, 33*(4), 35.

Krisberg, B., Hartney, C., Wolf, A., & Silva, F. (2009, February). Youth violence myths and realities: A tale of three cities. National Council on Crime and Delinquency. http://nccd-crc.issuelab.org/research/0/program/Reports/filter/date

McCord, J., Widom, C. S., & Crowell, N. A. (2001). *Juvenile crime, juvenile justice*. National Academies Press.

Merenda, F., Ostrowski, S., & Merenda, F., II. (2020). Building blocks of resilience. *Journal of Applied Juvenile Justice Services*, 112–130.

Moral poverty. (1995, December 15). *Chicago Tribune*. http://articles.chicagotribune.com/1995-12-15/news/9512150046_1_crime-talking-bomb/4

National Research Council. (2013). *Reforming juvenile justice: A developmental approach*. National Academies Press.

Office of Juvenile Justice and Delinquency Prevention. (2010). *Guidance manual for monitoring facilities under the Juvenile Justice and Delinquency Prevention Act of 1974, as amended* (3rd ed.). U.S. Department of Justice.

Office of Juvenile Justice and Delinquency Prevention. (2016). *Jurisdictional boundaries*. U.S. Department of Justice. http://www.ojjdp.gov/ojstatbb/structure_process/qa04101.asp?qaDate=2016

Office of Juvenile Justice and Delinquency Prevention. (2019a). *Model programs guide*. U.S. Department of Justice. https://www.ojjdp.gov/MPG/Topic/Details/73

Office of Juvenile Justice and Delinquency Prevention. (2019b). *Juvenile Justice and Delinquency Prevention Act reauthorized*. https://www.ojjdp.gov/enews/19juvjust/190107.html

Ouimet, M. (2004). Explaining the American and Canadian crime drop in the 1990's. *Champ pénal/Penal field, 1*.

Parent, D., & Barnett, L. (2003). *Juvenile Accountability Incentive Block Grant Program: National evaluation*. National Criminal Justice Reference Service.

Pfeiffer, C. (1998). *Trends in juvenile violence in European countries*. U.S. Department of Justice.

Piquero, A. R. (2008). Disproportionate minority contact. *The Future of Children, 18*(2), 59–79.

Posick, C. (2019). Restorative justice. In *The encyclopedia of women and crime*. https://doi.org/10.1002/9781118929803.ewac0437

Shannon, S. K., & Hauer, M. (2018). A life table approach to estimating disproportionate minority contact in the juvenile justice system. *Justice Quarterly, 35*(2), 330-355.

Taylor-Butts, A., & Bressan, A. (2009). Youth crime in Canada, 2006. *Juristat, 28*(3), Article 85-002-X. https://www150.statcan.gc.ca/n1/pub/85-002-x/2008003/article/10566-eng.htm

United Nations (1995), United Nations Ninth United Nations Congress on the Prevention of Crime and the Treatment of Offenders (A/CONF.169/Rev.1). Vienna: UN Crime Prevention and Criminal Justice Branch

U.S. Attorney's Manual. (1997). *Constitutional protections afforded to juveniles*. https://www.justice.gov/archives/jm/criminal-resource-manual-38-juvenile-defined

U.S. Department of Justice. (2015, September). *117. Federal Juvenile Delinquency Code*. https://www.justice.gov/usam/criminal-resource-manual-117-federal-juvenile-delinquency-code

Van Breda, A. D. (2018). A critical review of resilience theory and its relevance for social work. *Social Work, 54*(1), 1–18.

Violent Crime Control and Law Enforcement Act of 1994, H.R. 3355 (103rd) (2004). https://www.govtrack.us/congress/votes/103-1994/h416

Weitekamp, E. G. M., Kerner, H.-J., & Trueg, G. (1999). *International comparison of juvenile justice systems*. Paper prepared for the National Research Council Panel on Juvenile Crime: Prevention, Treatment, and Control. Washington, D.C.

Wilson, D. B., Olaghere, A., & Kimbrell, C. S. (2017). *Effectiveness of restorative justice principles in juvenile justice: A meta-analysis.* U.S. Department of Justice. https://www.ncjrs.gov/pdffiles1/ojjdp/grants/250872.pdf

Wilson, J. Q. (1996, December 10). *What, If Anything, Can the Federal Government Do About Crime?* [Presentation].

University of California at Los Angeles, National Institute of Justice Perspectives on Crime and Justice Series, Washington, DC, United States.

Winterdyk, J. (2002). *Juvenile justice systems: International perspectives.* Canadian Scholars Press.

World Health Organization. (2020). *Youth violence.* https://www.who.int/violence_injury_prevention/violence/world_report/factsheets/en/youthviolence-facts.pdf

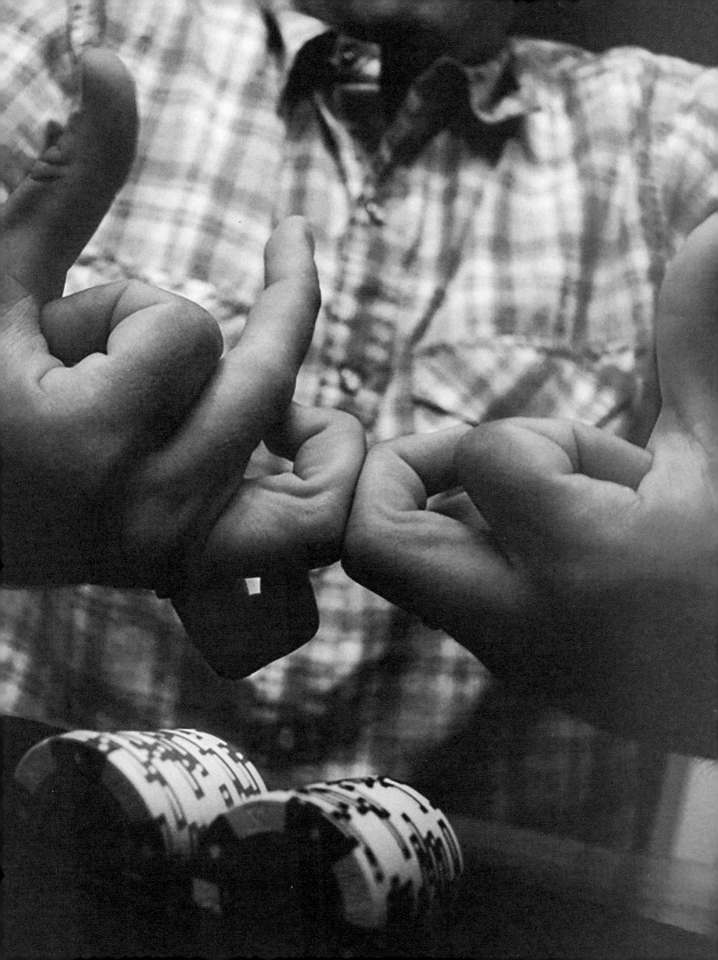

Gangs and Juveniles

CHAPTER OUTLINE

LEARNING OBJECTIVES

At the end of the chapter, students will be able to

describe the historical development of gangs,

describe the major causes of gang development,

describe the key components of gang culture,

evaluate associated theories of why youth join gangs,

discuss the prevalence of gangs and gang activity, and

compare and contrast gang activity and interventions within the United States and around the world.

Keywords

Born in

Cliques

Collective (group) response

Crews/sets

Crowds/clubs

Delinquent subcultures

Differential association

Differential opportunity

Gang

Generational

Jumped in

Larkin

Protective factors

Risk factors

Sexed in

Social control theory

Social disorganization

Social ecology

Strain theory

Street gangs

Transnational gangs

Youth gangs

Introduction

As we read in Chapter 3, "Theories of Delinquency," youth are susceptible to various influences and will even form subgroups within society to feel accepted, cope with stressors, and build self-esteem. Researchers believe that potential gang members, including children, think that becoming part of a gang will fulfill these needs and achieve goals that they think society has set for them. In this chapter, we will examine the history of gangs, how they are defined, and the various types. Specifically, we will examine where and when gangs began, recruitment practices, theoretical perspectives regarding why children join, the prominence of gangs in the United States and around the world, and interventions to not only encourage youth to leave a gang but also prevent them from joining in the first place.

So, What Is a Gang?

The definition of a gang differs from the federal level to the state level, from state to state, and from locality to locality. This is because legislation differs in terms of defining a gang, categorizing the activities of its members, and ultimately the level of punishment given for illicit gang activity.

Federal Definition

The Department of Justice and Homeland Security describes a gang as having a minimum of three members who collectively adopt a group identity through, for example, a common name, color, and hand signs, which they use to create fear or intimidation and engage in criminal or delinquent behavior. They also describe other gang characteristics such as participating in regular meetings, specific rules, providing physical protection, structure, and territorial rights (National Institute of Justice, 2011).

State Definition

State definitions vary but have common themes, as illustrated by legislation in California, where they use the term **street gang** to mean

> any ongoing organization, association, or group of three or more persons, whether formal or informal, having as one of its primary activities the commission of one or more of the criminal acts . . ., having a common name or common identifying sign or symbol, and whose members individually or collectively engage in or have engaged in a pattern of criminal gang activity. (California Street Terrorism Enforcement and Prevention Act, 1988)

Youth Gangs

There is also sometimes a distinction between a gang and a youth gang. **Youth gangs** have been defined by the National Gang Center and the National Institute of Justice as a group of youth or young adults willing to identify as a gang (Office of Juvenile Justice and Delinquency Prevention [OJJDP], 2019). The youth gang has characteristics such as leadership structure, geographic territory, an identifiable gang name and symbols, having regular meetings, and collectively performing crimes or delinquency. Members typically range in age from 12 to 24. It is important to note that although there is a distinct definition associated with youth gangs, minors can be found in almost every gang. Their membership is sometimes even **generational**, participation that occurs from generation to generation (see "Subculture Theory and Cultural Transmissions" in Chapter 3).

It is also important to remember that, although they are in the minority, not all "gangs" engage in criminal behavior, and groups of individuals are not automatically termed a gang, even if they self-identify and have some sort of structure. These other entities have been termed **cliques**, a small group of friends, or **crowds/clubs**, loosely organized groups of teens who share activities and attitudes (Bornstein & Lamb, 2015).

Although there are different definitions of gangs, we do see common federal and state criteria. The basic definition describes a **gang** as a group of three or members with a self-identity and hierarchy who engage in criminal or delinquent behavior (U.S. Department of Justice, 2019).

History of Gangs: Why and How Did They Form?

Not only are there a variety of definitions for a gang, but also there is some debate on when gangs began. Although one of the common characteristics defining a gang is having a structure or hierarchy, a much looser classification existed in 12th-century England, where seemingly unstructured groups of individuals involved in illicit behavior were sometimes referred to as a gang. Because there was no formal gang designation during that time, some historians believe that these types of groups existed and performed crimes even earlier than the 12th century.

17th-Century London

It was not until the early 17th century in London that more structured gangs that met the defining criteria of the 21st century were discovered. These gangs identified themselves with such names as "Hectors," "Bugles," and "Dead Boys," to mention a few. These gangs began distinguishing themselves from each other through colors and establishing rival groups, who seemed to mostly target each other, as is often seen today.

18th- and 19th-Century America

In the United States, gangs emerged in the late 1700s after the American Revolution; however, based on historical accounts, they only engaged in petty crimes (Howell & Moore, 2010; Sante, 1991). After America declared independence in 1776 and through the early 1900s, large waves of immigrant families from all over Europe settled in the United States, particularly in the Northeast and Midwest. Many suffered from poverty and were often discriminated against. Proper housing and social services were strained and resulted in overpopulated and deteriorating living conditions. Gangs formed to overcome these conditions through illicit behavior and sought to protect fellow immigrants who were fearful of being victimized because of their ethnicity and culture.

Initially, as we read in Chapter 1, juveniles were displaced because the American Revolution caused many families to lose their jobs. As a result, juveniles roamed the streets and sometimes formed groups that engaged in petty crimes and fought other youth groups over territory. Large-scale immigration continued, and as overpopulated and vulnerable clusters of communities emerged, so did more ethnic-based and ethnic-mixed gangs.

In the 1800s, Ellis Island in New York City served as a major port of entry for millions of immigrant families, the majority of which were English, Irish, and German. Poverty and overcrowded conditions in the lower east side of the city created an urgent need for housing. Residents of an area known as the Five Points, because of a five-pointed intersection, began abandoning their homes and fleeing the location because a body of water that was used for drinking and growing vegetation became polluted and disease infested after years of contamination from local commercial waste. As a solution, the pond's

---

DEEPER DIVE

Five Points (New York City)

Five Points in the 1800s was an area on the lower east side of New York City that was notorious for violent crime. This resulted in the area having one of the highest homicide rates in the United States at the time. This densely populated and deteriorating area also spawned some of the most notorious and violent gangs.

For more information, visit Five Points NYC https://www.thoughtco.com/five-points-ny-notorious-neighborhood-1774064

Five Points, New York City, 1827

water supply had been filled with dirt, but it began to give off noxious gases because of the buried vegetation and created flooding conditions and weakened foundations of homes as a result of poor engineering. The empty spaces were then subdivided and overrented by landlords to emancipated African Americans from the South and newly arriving immigrants, thereby overpopulating the area. Living conditions continued to deteriorate, with few or no public services such as medical care or proper maintenance of the area's infrastructure. Immigrants occupied this area in high numbers. The lack of resources resulted in the spread of deadly diseases, continued mass unemployment, and the emergence of a variety of gangs that engaged in rampant criminal and violent behavior.

In the late 19th century, five main gangs formed on the East Coast of the United States, with members ranging in age from their early teens to their mid-20s. Such gangs as the Smiths's Vly gang, the Bowery Boys, and the Broadway Boys were predominantly White and Irish, and the Fly Boys and Long Bridge Boys were African American (Howell & Moore, 2010). As time went on, gangs became more structured and more violent, as seen by another group, the Five Points Gang, recognized as one of the most well known and violent gangs during this time. The Five Points gang even recruited the infamous Al Capone from another gang (the James Street gang) to be one of its members. Other gangs, such as the Whyos, not only engaged in violence for their self-gain, but also contracted their services out to nonmembers, including such things as breaking noses and biting off ears for various fees (see Table 5.1).

In the early 1900s, Mexican immigration occurred from El Paso to Los Angeles and was met with controversy and violence. Preexisting gang culture was believed to be spread among youth who called themselves Pachucos. Pachucos became known in America as those who distinguished themselves by their dress, often wearing "zoot suits," and by their alleged association in street gangs. Media outlets described these groups as having large memberships and a street presence that included engaging in delinquency and criminal behavior (Bigalondo, 2017; Navarro, 2019).

In the 1950s and 1960s, new gangs formed with the migration of African Americans from the south and settlement of Latino populations in the western and northern parts of the United States for many of the same reasons facing European immigrants. Mixed ethnic-based gangs began to emerge as well across the United States, including within Hispanic/Latino and Asian populations (Howell & Moore, 2010).

TABLE 5.1	1800s Whyos Gang
CRIMINAL SERVICE	FEE
Punch out	$2
Black eye	$4
Nose and jaw broke	$10
Leg or arm broke (your choice)	$19
Ear chewed off	$15
Stabbing	$25
"The big job" (murder)	$100+

Source: Newton (2008, p. 16).

Man wearing a "zoot suit"

Upsurge in Youth and Gang Violence

After World War II, new ethnic groups migrating to various dissimilar "ethnic predominant neighborhoods" began turf wars, including those between African American, Latino, and European youth gangs. Gangs in Chicago, Los Angeles, and the southern region of the United States were also emerging. These gangs included members who shared similar ethnicities; however, multiethnic gangs were prominent as well. Reasons similar to those in earlier times existed for the emergence of these gangs, such as the disorganization of cities and diverse cultures and ethnic groups populating small, deteriorating spaces (Thrasher, 1927, 2013). Although not all gangs participated in criminal behavior at the time, the majority did, ranging from petty street fights to armed robbery and murder.

As we read in Chapter 2, in the 1980s and into the early 1990s, violent youth crime soared to record highs. The juvenile arrest rate for murder shot up 167% between 1984 and 1993 alone (Butts & Travis, 2002). Many criminologists believe the rise in gangs and drugs was primarily responsible for what many called an epidemic. In response, the federal government imposed the Violent Crime Control and Law Enforcement Act of 1994. This act, also known as the Crime Bill, advocated for stricter legislation through state incentives for more severe punishments for multiple convictions of drug sales and violent crimes. Incentives were also offered to states that implemented anti-gang programs and policy changes for gang members, namely, youth, which would reduce the maximum age to be prosecuted in a juvenile court, thereby allowing more juveniles to be processed as adults and adult sentences to be imposed (U.S. Department of Justice, 1994). Although gang activity has continued into the early 21st century, despite forecasts of a continued upsurge in violent gang activity and violent crime by youth overall, juvenile crime began to plummet in the early 1990s. That trend continues into the 21st century.

Modern-Day Gangs in the United States

Modern-day gangs are still prevalent across the United States and around the globe. Many gangs also serve as anchors for **crews/sets**—subsets of street gangs centered on specific blocks or housing developments that are considered "turf based." They also incorporate the name of the street on which the gang operates into their name, for example, the 196th Street Boyz. Although they usually comprise a small group and lack hierarchy, these crews or sets can be seen in many states carrying out gang activities, spreading their gang identity and embracing gang culture.

CREWS AND SETS

- Subset of street gangs
- "Turf based": centered on specific street blocks or housing developments
- Adopt the street into their name, such as the 225th Street Guyz
- Loosely organized, spreading identity through signs, graffiti, and gang activities
- Gang culture

Gang Culture

Please note that gang culture is constantly changing and evolving.

3 Rs: Reputation, Respect, and Revenge

The 3 Rs of gang culture are what many gangs consider both their personal and their collective creed. All members want a reputation that aligns with their gang values, motives, and actions. This is akin to the respect they expect to receive and will do just about anything to earn and maintain. Showing disrespect by entering another gang's turf, attacking a fellow gang member, or even just being part of a rival gang can spawn violence and even murder (Bjorgo, 2016).

Self-Identity and Communication

Traditionally, members self-identify their gang status through their own language, clothing, signs, colors, graffiti, and expressions. In this way, gangs can recognize not only fellow associates but also rival gang members. Communicating in code through hand signs and graffiti also helps to ensure that only fellow gang members are able to understand them and to keep messages hidden from law enforcement. As we will see later in the chapter, as gang intelligence increased among law enforcement, the level of sophisticated communication between gang members also changed.

Initiations—Getting In

Gang initiations can range from having to murder a rival gang member to showing your loyalty to the gang by taking a police officer's gun. Other initiations include assaulting civilians; being beaten up by potential gang members, called getting "**jumped in**"; and sometimes females having to have sex with several gang members, known as being "**sexed in**." Members can also be "**born in**," meaning their parent(s) or older relative(s) were gang members. For example, initiations to the Latin Kings gang and rival gangs the Crips and MS-13 include being jumped in, being beaten up by present members, and getting sexed in. MS-13 members will beat a potential member for 13 seconds as part of their initiation. The Bloods gang requires new members to slice the face of someone they do not know so severely that it would require 150 stitches, referred to as giving someone a "buck fifty" (Covey, 2015; Descormiers & Corrado, 2016; Hansen & Freitag, 2017). Other gangs engage in other forms of violence for the gang, known as "getting wet" as part of their initiation process.

Gangs communicate in code through hand signs, tattoos, and graffiti.

Getting Out

Getting out of a gang may require money, being almost beaten to death, secretly moving away and hiding, or becoming pregnant; for some gangs, members are never able to leave (Covey, 2015). Many initiatives have taken place to help members, especially youth, get out of a gang, but they have been met with mixed results, including resistance stemming from fear of their gang's punishment, ranging from assaulting or murdering the members and their families.

Gang Trends

According to the latest National Gang Report from the Federal Bureau of Investigation (FBI), threats to law enforcement are an increasing trend. Survey results reveal that although actually carrying out threats has remained the same, a third of law enforcement agencies show increases in the number of threats and their "boldness." Threats utilize various modes of communication, including emails and phone calls to officers' workplaces and even their homes, through social media and even in person (Federal Bureau of Investigation, 2019).

Another trend that has been noted in the FBI report is the corruption of prison staff. Although gang suppression efforts have resulted in gang members' incarceration, many of these individuals still carry out illicit activities both inside and outside prisons. Some prison staff have been bribed to provide favors ranging from assisting in smuggling drugs to giving cell phones to incarcerated members so that they can continue to run things on the street.

Motorcycle gangs have also shown progression in obtaining "white-collar" jobs and businesses. Service industries such as tattoo and repair shops generate cash that can then be funneled to a gang to carry out illicit activities.

Finally, general trends among all gangs can be seen in their efforts to recruit members and gain influence and money. Gangs are increasing their involvement in sex trafficking, prostitution, and connecting with other organized crime entities, including transnational gangs. Members are also infiltrating the military and areas of the criminal justice system by obtaining jobs and volunteering in these agencies. The use of social media and other forms of technology is also increasing to support the efforts to bolster their identity, power, and financial status (Federal Bureau of Investigation, 2019).

Prominent Gangs Across the United States

As mentioned earlier in the chapter, although there are sometimes varying definitions for youth gangs based on specific age groups, among other characteristics, youth can be found in all of the gangs discussed in this section. Some of these gangs were formed by young people and then developed into mixed-age gangs, some of which direct their efforts to recruit more youths.

Asian Boyz

The Asian Boyz gang, also identified as ABZ, began in California in the 1970s and is considered one of the largest Asian gangs in the United States. Initially, they sought to protect immigrants who were threatened by other gang members. The gang has active members of all ages across 14 states in 28 cities and is mostly composed of Cambodian and Vietnamese members. This street gang has an estimated 2,000 members, some of whom have been discovered joining the U.S. military and attempting to traffic drugs. Other gang activities include drug sales and violent crimes, including assaults and homicides (Federal Bureau of Investigation, 2012; U.S. Department of Justice, 2008).

Bloods

Initially established in Los Angeles as the Pirus gang, its original purpose was to protect members from rival Crip gang members. In 1972, this alliance of non-Crip members transformed into what is now known as the Bloods. The Bloods have grown to be a national gang with a membership of approximately 25,000 known members. They are an association of structured and unstructured subsets that have adopted a single gang culture. Large, national-level Bloods gangs include Bounty Hunter Bloods and Crenshaw Mafia Gangsters. Most members are African American males. Bloods gangs are active in 123 cities in 37 states. The primary source of income for Bloods gangs is the distribution of cocaine and marijuana. They are also involved in other criminal activities, including assault, burglary, robbery, and homicide (Bloods, 2017).

Crips

The Crips gang is considered one of the largest gangs in the United States, with an estimated membership of more than 50,000. Most members are African Americans under the age of 25. The gang originated in Los Angeles in 1969 and has since spread to 221 cities in 41 states(U.S. Department 2021). They are also considered one of the most violent gangs, engaging in mass murders and other violent crimes and view Bloods gang members as one of their primary adversaries. Subsets of the Crips include Shotgun Crips and Insane Gangster Crips. (Decker & Curry, 2017; U.S. Department of Justice, 2008, 2021).

Gangster Disciples

The Gangster Disciples gang began in Chicago in the 1960s. Their leader is referred to as the chairman. Members are predominantly African American, and membership ranges between approximately 25,000 and 50,000. Members range in age from preteens to individuals in their 60s and 70s. Initially, the gang was formed in the fight for civil rights and to cope with conditions in impoverished communities. The gang has members in 33 states. Like other gangs, their members take part in drug distribution, money laundering, and murder. However, they also advocate for activism and forming strong families and communities (Drug Enforcement Agency, 2017).

Mara Salvatrucha: MS-13

Mara Salvatrucha (MS-13) originated in Los Angeles, California, in the 1980s and has members in and outside the United States. Initially, the gang focused on protecting fellow Salvadorian immigrants. Mara is a slang word for gang, and Salva is short for Salvador. Other members are from Mexico, Guatemala, and Honduras. The gang has a reputation for extreme violence and using machetes to kill their enemies.

Their nown members span across 46 states, and MS-13 is considered a transnational gang, meaning they also have members in other countries (Federal Bureau of Investigation, 2019). The gang is also known for recruiting at-risk youths from neighborhoods of low socioeconomic status. Membership is estimated between 30,000 and 50,000 worldwide.

Barrio 18 (18th Street)

18th Street gang members mostly occupy Los Angeles, where the gang originated. There are approximately 30,000 to 50,000 active members across 28 states in various sets. The gang leaders refer to themselves as "Palabreros." The majority of members are from Mexico and Central America; no women are allowed in the gang. Since its beginning in the 1960s, the gang has made active recruitment efforts in elementary and middle schools. They are organized by strict laws that are enforced by executing members who disobey them. Their main rival is MS-13, and according to the Justice Department, they are responsible for the high homicide rate in Central America (Seelke, 2016). The gang's revenue comes from a myriad of illicit behaviors, including marijuana, cocaine, fraud, and extortion (Dudley, 2015).

Almighty Latin King Nation

The Almighty Latin King Nation gang (also known as Latin Kings, Almighty Latin King, and Queen Nation) originated in Chicago in the 1960s, and most of its members occupy that area; however, Latin King members can be found across the United States.

DEEPER DIVE

Barrio 18 Gang Rules

- Attend meetings
- Speak the truth
- Respect the "palabreros"
- Be a good example to recent members
- Do not walk around drunk or sleep in the streets
- Respect relatives of the gang members, including their girlfriends
- No crack
- Fight with the enemy, not among themselves
- Do not mention "the letters" (MS-13)
- Do not use a red bandanna or red hat (rival gang colors)
- Search out weapons for the gang
- Take revenge
- Do not leave any members behind
- Do not graffiti in red
- Do not talk about gang business around outsiders
- Members who want to tattoo their faces need to ask permission
- Carry out "a mission" before getting initiated (getting beaten up for 18 seconds by four members while another counts)
- Do not allow women into the gang (since the year 2000)
- No rape
- No snitching

Source: Dudley, 2016: insightcrime.org

They are known for being highly structured, and members have been arrested for engaging in drug distribution as well as many other violent crimes. Although they were initially dominated by Mexican and Puerto Rican members, associates can now be from any nationality. The gang was originally formed to protect against racial prejudice but later began to engage in a wide range of criminal activity both outside and inside the United States and its prison systems. Their active gang members and subsets are located in 158 cities across 34 states, with a total membership between 25,000 and 35,000 (North Carolina Gang Investigators Association, 2015; Richmond & Spence, 2013).

Vice Lord Nation

Originating in the 1950s in Chicago, Vice Lord Nation is considered one of Chicago's oldest and largest gangs. Initially, the gang was formed in a training school by a group of young African American youth as a form of protection and to make money through illicit activities. The gang is still involved in criminal activity such as drug trafficking and violent crimes, including murder. They currently have approximately 30,000 to 35,000 members spanning 74 cities in 28 states, most of whom are African American males (North Carolina Gang Investigators Association, 2015).

Trinitarios

The Trinitarios gang was initially formed in New York in the 1980s but has spread to 10 states across the country and is considered the country's largest Dominican gang. The gang is primarily made up of individuals from the Dominican Republic and was constructed in prisons across New York. Members initially provided protection for Hispanic inmates who were serving time. They are now also considered a street gang, with an approximate membership of 30,000. The gang continues to grow, and members have been found recruiting in high schools for new members. Their rivals include the Bloods and the Latin Kings. The Trinitarios made headlines in 2018 for mistakenly killing a 15-year-old boy, who they thought belonged to a rival gang, with a machete. Other illicit activities include robbery, assault, and drug trafficking (Bharara, 2014; Terrorism Research & Analysis Consortium, 2020).

Although officially many of these gangs originated/were prominent on the East and West Coasts of the United States, subsets and additional gangs existed throughout the United States and continue to do so in the early 21st century.

Prevalence of Gangs: Gang Statistics

Just as juvenile crime declined in the early 1990s, so did gang activity. However, unlike juvenile crime, which continued to decrease, gang activity and membership again began to rise between 2001 and 2005 and have remained relatively constant, with some fluctuations based on population density, location, and other circumstances (National Gang Center, 2019). According to the OJJDP, there are an estimated 30,700 gangs with over 800,000 known members across 3,100 jurisdictions, many of which involved in drug sales, violent crimes, and homicide (OJJDP, 2019).

Gang problems reported by respondents include observed illicit behavior. Replicated from National Gang Center (2019).

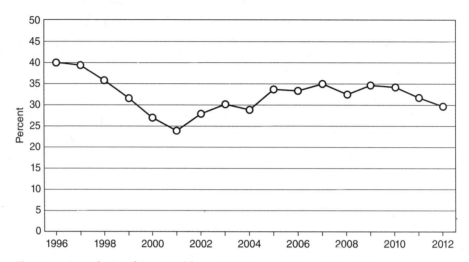

Figure 5.1 Prevalence of Gang Problems in Study Population, 1996–2012

The above statistics are the latest available according to the National Gang Center (2019) Additionally, these numbers are estimated and most likely less than actual figures due to more concealed efforts by contemporary gangs in how they look/self-identify and communicate (see "Gang Intelligence Strategies" later in the chapter).

Source: National Gang Center (2019).

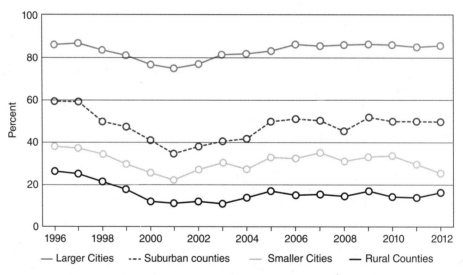

Figure 5.2 Prevalence of Gang Problems by Geographic Area, 1996–2012

Source: National Gang Center (2019).

Gangs in Schools

Gang activity and members' self-identification can be seen across schools in the United States as well. According to the 2018 *Indicators of School Crime and Safety Report* sponsored by the Institute of Education Sciences, gang activity in urban, sub-urban, and rural area schools across the country is down. According to the report, which surveyed students from ages 12 to 18, between 2001 and 2017, gang activity

TABLE 5.1 Number of Gang Related Homicides

	2007		2008		2009		2010		2011		2012		PERCENT CHANGE, PREVIOUS 5-YEAR AVERAGE TO 2012
	N	% TOTAL	N	% TOTAL	N	% TOTAL	N	% TOTAL	N	% TOTAL	N	% TOTAL	
Agencies reporting gang activity	992	—	921	—	1,050	—	1,026	—	928	—	999	—	—
Agencies reporting gang homicide statistics	890	—	768	—	910	—	860	—	739	—	829	—	—
Coverage rate (%)	—	89.7	—	83.4	—	86.7	—	83.8	—	79.6	—	83.0	—
Total gang homicides	1,975	100.0%	1,659	100.0%	2,083	100.0%	2,020	100.0%	1,824	100.0%	2,363	100.0%	23.6
Cities with populations over 100,000	1,215	61.5%	1,022	61.6%	1,123	53.9%	1,272	63.0%	1,242	68.1%	1,587	67.2%	35.1
Suburban counties	477	24.2%	357	21.5%	597	28.7%	439	21.7%	338	18.5%	408	17.3%	–7.6
Cities with populations of 50,000–100,000	215	10.9%	204	12.3%	274	13.2%	209	10.3%	198	10.9%	255	10.8%	15.9
Smaller areas	68	3.4%	76	4.6%	89	4.3%	100	5.0%	46	2.5%	113	4.8%	b

bNot presented because of the small base rate. "Smaller areas" refers to all cities with populations below 50,000 and rural counties combined.
Source: National Gang Center (2019).

dropped from 20% to 9% in education settings (Institute of Education Services, 2018; U.S. Department of Justice, 2019).

Despite this drop within schools, youths continue to join gangs through both recruitment and seeking out membership because of various social and environmental reasons (Ritter et al., 2019).

Why Youths Join Gangs: Theoretical Approaches

In 1927, Frederic Thrasher was one of the first researchers to study various aspects of gangs. His study of 1,313 gangs in Chicago spawned the attention of law enforcement and social and behavioral scientists who wanted to explore the root causes for joining a gang, its effects, and methods of intervention. Thrasher focused on **social disorganization**—weak social controls such as broken homes, inadequate schools, unemployment, and lack of resources within impoverished communities—as a cause for gang membership. Specifically, Thrasher theorized that individuals within these types of environments would seek out subgroups to provide what larger society did not. As you read in Chapter 3, Shaw and McKay further developed this theory by focusing on environmental conditions, specifically **social ecology**, described as interactions between communities and resources influencing illicit behavior. This can occur in economically declining, unstable, and criminal neighborhoods where children who live without adequate resources and who are exposed to adverse elements in society can succumb to these environmentally disorganized and substandard conditions. This may result in adopting and engaging in criminality themselves or seeking out subgroups that they believe can provide for their needs, such as gangs (also review subculture theory and social disorganization theory in Chapter 3).

Also discussed in Chapter 3 and applicable to the motivation to join a gang, Donald Sutherland created the theory of **differential association**. According to Sutherland, individuals of any socioeconomic class can learn to become criminals by associating with other criminals who establish such behavior as acceptable and normal (Vinney, 2019; Wood & Alleyne, 2010). Differential association considers these factors in addition to environmental factors to explain the influence of gangs (Kissner & Pyrooz, 2009). Other researchers also found little evidence of a link solely between low socioeconomic status and gang activity (Wood & Alleyne, 2010). Ronald Akers furthered this theory and its application to join a gang by asserting that frequent associations can also change one's morals, beliefs, and perceptions (Kissner & Pyrooz, 2009).

Albert Cohen, in the 1950s, discussed strain and subculture theory and their implications for gang membership. As you learned in Chapter 3, **strain theory** focuses on the strain society puts on individuals to obtain wealth and power and one's response when few resources are provided to achieve these goals. Cohen examined groups experiencing strain as a result of unequal opportunities and forming subculture in what he termed a **collective (group) response**. Cohen suggested that youth join gangs not only to relieve this strain but also, in a sense, to lash out at those in society whom they believe are responsible for their situation. Cohen wrote *Delinquent Boys* in 1955 in an attempt to explain youth gangs and delinquency. He described **delinquent subcultures** as having an organized set of norms and beliefs accepting of criminality. Delinquency is an accepted pattern for adolescents in these subcultures (Bernard, 2020).

The notion of unequal opportunity, also known as the theory of **differential opportunity**, was developed by Cloward and Ohlin in the 1960s and is sometimes referred to as a general theory of delinquency. In relation to maladaptive behavior and juveniles becoming gang members, it acknowledges the connection between weak social controls and individuals holding society and an unfair distribution of resources responsible for their lack of legitimate opportunities (social disorganization and ecology and strain theory) and that criminal behavior can be learned through association (differential association). However, it adds that individuals may also join gangs to obtain illegitimate opportunities that otherwise would be unavailable to them to gain status in society or within their own subgroup (Cloward & Ohlin, 1960).

As you have read, **social control theory** was developed by Travis Hirschi, whereby bonds with social institutions/entities such as family, school, and work control the behavior of those associated with them. When these social controls do not exist because of weak social bonds, youth will seek out other groups to belong to, and this includes gangs. It has also been recognized that social controls can draw individuals out of gangs, such as members wanting to start a family, get a job, and join the military (Thornberry, 2006).

In the 1980s, some researchers focused on risk and protective factors to explain susceptibility to delinquency and association with gangs (Bishop et al., 2017). **Risk factors** can include personal or environmental factors leading to poor development, including engaging in delinquent and criminal behavior. **Protective factors** are the skills and attitudes juveniles can adopt, which can aid in positive growth and socialization (see Chapter 10, "Interventions and Diversion"). Resiliency theory focusing on risk and protective factors shows that these types of risks can create obstacles and adversarial conditions, but that they can be overcome and coped with.

In the 1990s, gang activity across the United States rose from 17 states reporting occurrences in the 1970s to every state reporting the presence of gangs by the late 1990s. Additionally, the number of cities with gang activity rose from 270 to 2,547 in 1998, an 843% increase (Howell, 2019). In response, the Office of Juvenile Justice and Delinquency Prevention created the National Youth Gang Center to track and research gang activity. It authorized four longitudinal studies to examine potential causes of gang involvement. Various developmental theories were created from this research. Such theories consisted of Rolf Loeber's developmental pathways theory, which focused on disruptive behavior from childhood to adolescence (Loeber et al., 1993), and Thornberry and Krohn's interactional theory, in which behavior results from what is learned from interactions within society, the strength of social bonds over one's life, and the age of deviant onset (Thornberry et al., 2003). Howell and Egley (2005) compiled risk factors for joining gangs in their developmental model of gangs that may exist within families, individuals, schools, peers, and community domains throughout one's life course from preschool to adolescence. As mentioned previously, although the presence of risk factors within these contexts can increase the likelihood of delinquency and even joining a gang, protective factors within these same constructs can also provide coping mechanisms over the course of one's life to resist delinquent groups (Bishop et al., 2017; Gilman et al., 2014; Merenda, 2020).

The study of factors influencing maladaptive behavior and the seeking out of subcultures such as gangs have prompted interventional strategies to address these influences and combat gang membership and associated illicit activities.

Gang Intervention Programs

Gang involvement continues to be a prevalent issue in the United States. In turn, many interventions and suppression programs have been developed.

- In 1993, the Cook County Juvenile Temporary Detention Center in Chicago, Illinois, created the Broader Urban Involvement and Leadership Development (Project BUILD) program for juveniles in detention. It serves as an intervention to avoid recidivism and potential adult offending for justice-involved youth. The program was designed to help these individuals cope with tentative conditions and adversarial events in their communities, including lack of resources and drug and gang activity. The program also provides counseling and work skills training and has proven to be effective in reducing recidivism since its inception (Howell et al., 2017; Lurigio, 2000; National Institute of Justice, 2013).

- Gang Resistance Education and Training is a proactive program designed for all middle school students and was created in 1991 by the Phoenix, Arizona, Police Department. It is delivered through local police departments and focuses on gang prevention. It, too, has had positive results, including reducing potential risk factors for joining gangs, creating negative views of gang life, and promoting positive police relations (Esbensen et al., 2013). Also see Gang Resistance Education and Training (2019).

- The Youth Advocate Program is located in 28 states and the District of Columbia. It aims to both prevent youth from joining gangs and provide support for leaving a gang. The program takes a holistic approach by focusing on the youth and their family, as well as environmental factors that can lead to delinquency and gang involvement. To combat risk factors, program mentors provide services in the youth's school and community. The program's other services include weekly contact, mediation, gang intervention, emergency funds, relocation services, and life skills development. The Youth Advocate Program serves over 20,000 families a year (Youth Advocate Programs, 2020).

- Peer-run intervention programs have also been found to be helpful for youth who may feel more comfortable interacting with others around their age. The Gang Rescue and Support Project (GRASP) is one such program. The free program is run not only by youth but also by juveniles who were prior gang members. It is focused on youth who are considered at risk of joining a gang or who are present members. The program has been around for over half a century and works with not only with the youth participants, but also their families, as well as families of gang victims. The program is involved in providing parent awareness training, job training, and community and school outreach (Gang Rescue and Support Project, 2020).

Additional Efforts

The Office of Juvenile Justice and Delinquency Prevention, in coordination with the National Gang Center, has created a gang model that provides community stakeholders with an overview of gang activity, associate theories, and five proven core strategies to assist with gang prevention. These strategies include mobilizing communities to engage in specific interventions and suppression strategies and overall organizational change (National Gang Center, 2019; OJJDP, 2019). Also see https://www.nationalgangcenter.gov/Comprehensive-Gang-Model/Online-Overview.

There are also programs to suppress existing gang activity carried out by law enforcement across the United States. Operation Cease Fire, now known as Group Violence Intervention, originated in Boston, Massachusetts, but has spread all over the country to such cities as Los Angeles, Cincinnati, and New York City. The program advocated a zero tolerance for gang activity, specifically youth homicide. Gang leaders were invited to sit down with agency representatives from the district attorney's office, probation, and parole to law enforcement. Gang members were told that these agencies can be used as a resource to prevent ongoing violence through cooperation or serve as a consequence akin to a zero-tolerance response for continued criminality. Zero tolerance included maximum sentences without probation, meant to deter further gang activity. There has been a trend of reducing youth homicides across many states in the United States. These reductions have been attributed to various intervention and suppression strategies, including those found within this program (Braga & Weisburd, 2012; Howell, 2019).

Gang Intelligence Strategies

Traditionally, members have used special vocabulary, clothing, signs, colors, graffiti, and names. However, as law enforcement has been able to identify gang members in this manner and gather intelligence, some gang members have tried to be more covert in self-identifying and communicating. They have transitioned from donning traditional colors to wearing ambiguous white T-shirts and have added communication methods such as descriptive postings on social media. According to the FBI's National Gang Report, social media and technology in general, including the use of cellular phones and associated applications, play an "essential role" in gang activity. Such online activities include meetings, recruiting, and illicit activities, including targeting rival gangs. Although technology has allowed gangs to operate more covertly, it has also enabled law enforcement to focus resources on monitoring these online activities (Federal Bureau of Investigation, 2019).

Operation Crew Cut is a suppression program that takes advantage of the use of technology by gangs and crews. It targets social media and monitors postings of past

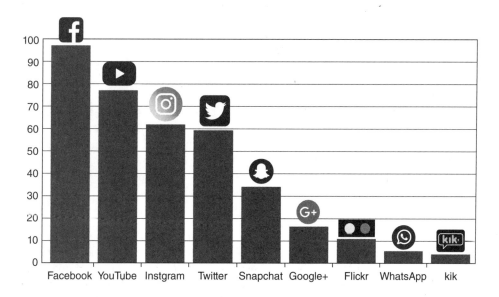

Figure 5.3 Social Media Platforms Most Frequently Reported to be Used by Street Gang Members

Source: National Gang Report 2015.

incidents and future violence, witness intimidation, and recruitment. The program has been cited for a reduction in gang activity and associated crime in such areas as New York City and Chicago. However, criticisms include assertions that this type of public monitoring may violate Fourth Amendment rights and could turn innocent participants into suspects (New York City Bar, 2021).

The National Gang Center has provided additional resources for law enforcement to combat the proliferation of gang activity. Also see https://www.nationalgangcenter.gov/SPT/Program-Matrix for more programs and their measured effectiveness.

Worldview

Gang Prevalence Around the World

LATIN/CENTRAL AMERICA

As we have read in previous chapters, Latin American countries have significant variations in their rates of violence and homicide (Blaustein, 2016; Rivera, 2016). El Salvador, Honduras, and Guatemala collectively make up what is known as the Northern Triangle, an area plagued by the highest homicide rates not only in Latin America but also in all other countries around the world. The Northern Triangle is known for corruption, poverty, and chronic violence, much of which stems from gang activity (Cheatham, 2019). **Transnational gangs**, those whose memberships span across countries, such as MS-13 and M-18, are prominent in this region. Despite efforts by the government to minimize acts of violence, including between MS-13 and M-18 members, violence continues. Although legislation imposing stricter penalties has been directed toward gang members and has resulted in mass incarceration, gangs have been known to run these prisons, and their membership continues to grow (Cheatham, 2019; Olate et al., 2015).

AUSTRALIA

Gangs could be seen in Australia in the 19th century, one of the most prominent being the Rocks Push. They were named after the location where they originated, called the Rocks, located in Sydney, and were considered a "Larkin" gang. **Larkin** is an Australian term for a young person who disregards societal rules and laws. Other Larkin gangs at the time included the Gibb Street Mob, Forty Thieves, the Straw Hat, and Miller's Point Push gang. These youth gangs engaged in theft, assault, and other minor crimes. Other groups emerged in the 20th century, such as the Four Aces, Madonna's Mob, and the 5T gang in Sydney and Melbourne, whose activities included drug distribution and murder (Covey, 2010).

Most recently, Australia has seen an rise in a subculture of motorcycle gangs that have expanded on traditional gang crime, from drug distribution and violence to money laundering and working with other criminal enterprises. This has prompted severe punishments for gang activity indicative in the recent passage of the Police Offences Amendment Bill in 2018, which provides additional tools for law enforcement to investigate and for their justice system to aggressively prosecute gang-related crime (Monterosso, 2018).

CANADA

Canada reports having 434 youth gangs with approximately 7,000 members across their provinces. Canada defines a youth gang as one whose youth members "self-identify as a group and are generally perceived by others as a distinct group engaging in delinquent incidents that produce negative responses from the community and law enforcement agencies"

(Public Safety Canada, 2018a, p. 1). The majority of youth gangs are composed of boys under 18. The Canadian Police Survey on Youth Gangs revealed that gang activity is widespread and, although not as prominent as in the United States, does seem to be a growing problem (Public Safety Canada, 2018a). In 2017, the homicide rate for all of Canada was at its highest in 10 years, and officials contribute this rise to gang-related violence. However, gang-related homicides declined by 5% in 2018, the first decrease since 2014 (Statistics Canada, 2018; Roy & Marcellus, 2019). Programs to combat youth gang proliferation included the Gang Prevention Strategy, which focused on children ages 13 to 25 who were considered at risk for joining a gang. The program sought to teach these youth about the consequences of gang involvement, encourage prosocial bonds with various facets of society, decrease risk factors, and change any positive attitudes about gangs in general. More recently, the Youth Violence Reduction Partnership was developed. The program relies on collaboration between the police, probation, community organizations, and other stakeholders along with families to provide support, supervision, and a path toward education and employment. Currently, six sites across Canada have implemented this strategy. Although evaluations of the program's effectiveness are still being conducted, completed assessments reveal that this kind of support for families is essential for supporting youth (Public Safety Canada, 2018a, 2018b, 2018c, 2018d).

EUROPE

The number of youth gangs in many countries in Europe has increased (Fraser et al., 2018). In the United Kingdom, an increase in youth gangs and associated violence has been a catalyst for new gang policies. Gangs in Europe are a more recent phenomenon, and not much attention was attributed to them until the late 19th and early 20th centuries. Although there is some debate regarding a gang's definition, as in the United States, researchers have defined a youth gang as a street youth group that identifies through their illicit behavior. However, other countries such as Sweden, Italy, and France do not have a strict definition (Fraser et al., 2018; Uberto et al., 2005).

Many countries in Europe have attempted to combat youth gangs through specialized units, intelligence gathering, and communication among agencies. In Spain, a multiagency approach entitled Police Coordination and Intervention Plan Against Organized Violent Juvenile Groups, updated by their state secretary in 2009, is used to combat gang activity and includes increases in monitoring gang activity, training police, and community outreach.

In 2010, France developed strategies to combat criminal gang activity with the goals of preventing criminality, intergang fighting, and trafficking. They implemented a "gang shutdown strategy" to achieve these goals through real-time gang intelligence gathering, partnerships with other government agencies, and community outreach. In 2007, the United Kingdom began a program similar to the U.S. Cease Fire strategy entitled the Tackling Gangs Action Plan. It involves various agencies coordinating efforts to reduce gang violence, the result of which has been mixed in terms of the prevalence of gangs and gang activity (Fraser et al., 2018). Finally, although in Portugal there is no official definition for a youth gang, interventions have been put in place, such as *Programa Escolhas*, which advocates for working with families in areas where youth are considered at higher risk of becoming part of a gang and sends out multidisciplinary teams to address social problems that communities may be facing (Fraser et al., 2018).

AFRICA

Gangs were initially formed for protection in Africa in the 19th and 20th centuries (Bangstad, 2005). In the 1930s, youth gangs, such as the Bo-Tsotsi, participated in the antiapartheid resistance movement in Soweto (Glaser, 2000; Petrus & Kinnes, 2019). In the 1990s, gangs became more organized and exploited communities riddled with unemployment and poverty. Gangs in South Africa have also protected impoverished communities and have provided necessities such as food and supplies. In the Western Cape of Africa, gang violence has increased, accounting for almost 20% of all homicides, totaling 745 murders from 2017 to 2018. These gangs also engage in drug activity and the sale of stolen goods, which have prompted gang wars in this region (Petrus & Kinnes, 2019). Most recently, there have been interagency efforts such as Operation Combat to reduce rising gang violence. These strategies focus on arresting and prosecuting anyone involved, including high-ranking gang members, through the Prevention of Organized Crime Act. Although this operation and its supporting act were intended to reduce organized crime and illicit gang activity, violence in general continues to rise, as does the illegal activity of those incarcerated, who continue to maintain control over gangs within and outside prisons (United Nations Office on Drugs and Crime, 2012).

Wrap-up

The proliferation of gangs in the United States has grown exponentially since the 1800s, and this trend can be found across the globe. Although the definition of different types of gangs varies, including youth gangs and gangs in general, the term usually refers to an organized group engaging in delinquent or criminal behavior. Although they began with petty crimes, gangs have elevated their crimes to assaults and murder, and this type of criminality has spread not only across the United States but also transnationally. Youth join gangs for various reasons, such as strain from society creating the need to form subcultures such as those found in gangs, which offer acceptance and a sense of belonging. Gangs exist on the streets, in prisons, and even in schools, where illicit activity and recruiting can be seen. Private and public institutions have made efforts to combat gangs both by intervention practices and by punitive measures despite gangs' efforts to conceal their activities, and their culture is constantly evolving. Although gang rituals and patterns of violence continue to plague many cities and countries around the world, joint efforts between governments and communities continue to not only disrupt gang activity but also stop it before it begins.

Discussion Questions

1. Explain the historical development of gangs in and outside the United States.
2. What were the causes of gang development in the United States and around the world?
3. Describe how gang culture has changed and the reasons why.
4. Choose and discuss which theories you believe best explain why youth join gangs.
5. Discuss current trends in gang activity and how they help or impede police investigations.
6. Evaluate gang activity and interventions between the United States and other countries around the world.

ONLINE RESOURCES

FBI Vault https://vault.fbi.gov
National Youth Gang Center: U.S. Department of Justice, Office of Juvenile Justice and Delinquency Prevention https://ojjdp.ojp.gov/sites/g/files/xyckuh176/files/pubs/gun_violence/sect08-f.html

National Gang Center PDF https://www.nationalgangcenter.gov/Content/Documents/Gangs-
in-Schools.pdf
National Gang Center https://www.nationalgangcenter.gov
U.S. Department of Justice https://www.ncjrs.gov/gangs/

Definitions

Born in—getting into a gang because one's parent(s) or older relative(s) were gang members

Cliques—a small group of friends

Collective (group) response—groups (e.g., gangs) responding to strain as a result of unequal opportunities

Crews/sets—subsets of street gangs centered on specific blocks or housing developments that are considered "turf based"

Crowds/clubs—loosely organized groups of teens who share activities and attitudes

Delinquent subcultures—having an organized set of norms and beliefs accepting of criminality

Differential association—individuals learn to become criminals by associating with other criminals who establish such behavior as acceptable and normal

Differential opportunity—individuals joining gangs or other like groups to obtain illegitimate opportunities that otherwise would be unavailable to them to gain status in society or within their own subgroup

Gang—a group of three or members with a self-identity and hierarchy who engage in criminal or delinquent behavior

Generational—participation that occurs from generation to generation

Jumped in—being beaten up by potential gang members to join a gang

Larkin—an Australian term for a young person who disregards societal rules and laws

Protective factors—skills and attitudes that juveniles can adopt and that aid in positive development and socialization

Risk factors—personal or environmental factors leading to poor development, including engaging in delinquent and criminal behavior

Sexed in—females having to have sex with several gang members to join a gang

Social control theory—bonds with social institutions/entities such as family, school, and work, which control the behavior of those associated with them

Social disorganization—weak social controls such as broken homes, inadequate schools, and lack of resources within impoverished communities

Social ecology—interactions between communities and resources influencing illicit behavior

Strain theory—focuses on the strain society puts on individuals to obtain wealth and power and one's response when few resources are provided to achieve these goals.

Street gangs—groups that have large memberships, a hierarchy, and a street presence that includes engaging in criminal behavior

Transnational gangs—those whose memberships span across countries

Youth gangs—a group of youth or young adults willing to identify as a gang with characters such as leadership structure, geographic territory, identifiable gang names and symbols, having regular meetings, and collectively performing crimes or delinquency

References

Bangstad, S. (2005). Hydra's heads: PAGAD and responses to the PAGAD phenomenon in a Cape Muslim community. *Journal of Southern African Studies, 31*(1), 187–208. https://rl.talis.com/3/notts/items/06F518C9-8731-2153-8DFA-435D42628BBE.html

Bernard, T. J. (2020, November 21). Albert Cohen. In *Encyclopedia Britannica*. https://www.britannica.com/biography/Albert-Cohen-American-criminologist

Bornstein, M. H., & Lamb, M. E. (2015). Developmental Science: An Advanced Textbook (7th ed.). Psychology Press.

Bharara, P. (2014). *Members of violent Trinitarios gang found guilty in Manhattan Federal Court in connection with racketeering, murder, attempted murder, and narcotics offenses.* Department of Justice. https://www.atf.gov/news/pr/members-violent-trinitarios-gang-found-guilty-manhattan-federal-court-connection

Bigalondo, A. I. (2017). Living/leaving la vida loca: On barrios, Chicano youth and gangs. ODISEA. *Revista de estudios ingleses, 15*, 89–99.

Bishop, A. S., Hill, K. G., Gilman, A. B., Howell, J. C., Catalano, R. F., & Hawkins, J. D. (2017). Developmental pathways of youth gang membership: A structural test of the social development model. *Journal of Crime and Justice, 40*(3), 275–296. https://doi.org/10.1080/0735648X.2017.1329781

Bjorgo, T. (2016). Violent youth gangs. In T. Bjørgo (Ed.), *Preventing crime* (pp. 71–116). Palgrave Macmillan.

Blaustein, J. (2016). Exporting criminological innovation abroad: Discursive representation, 'evidence-based crime prevention' and the post-neoliberal development agenda in Latin America. *Theoretical Criminology, 20*(2), 165–184. https://doi.org/10.1177/1362480615604892

Braga, A. A., & Weisburd, D. L. (2012). The effects of focused deterrence strategies on crime: A systematic review and meta-analysis of the empirical evidence. *Journal of Research in Crime and Delinquency, 49*(3), 323–358.

Butts, J. A., & Travis, J. (2002). *The rise and fall of American youth violence, 1980 to 2000.* Urban Institute: Justice Policy Center.

California Street Terrorism Enforcement and Prevention Act. California Penal Code, §186.22(f) (1988).

Cheatham, A. (2019). *Central America's turbulent Northern Triangle.* Council on Foreign Relations. https://www.cfr.org/backgrounder/central-americas-turbulent-northern-triangle

Cloward, R., & Ohlin, L. (1960). *Delinquency and opportunity: A theory of delinquent gangs.* Free Press.

Cohen, A. K. (1955). *Delinquent boys; The culture of the gang.* Free Press.

Covey, Herbert H. C. (2010). *Street gangs throughout the world.* Springfield, Ill: Charles C. Thomas.

Covey, H. C. (2015). *Crips and Bloods: A guide to an American subculture.* Greenwood.

Decker, S. H., & Curry, G. D. (2017). Crips. In *Encyclopedia Britannica.* https://www.britannica.com/topic/Crips

Descormiers, K., & Corrado, R. R. (2016). *The right to belong: Individual motives and youth gang initiation rites.* Routledge. https://doi.org/10.1080/01639625.2016.1177390

Drug Enforcement Agency. (2017). *Cartels and gangs in Chicago.* https://www.dea.gov/sites/default/files/2018-07/DIR-013-17%20Cartel%20and%20Gangs%20in%20Chicago%20-%20Unclassified.pdf

Dudley, S. (2015). *Barrio 18 in El Salvador: A view from the inside.* Insight Crime. https://www.insightcrime.org/news/analysis/barrio-18-el-salvador-view-from-inside/

Esbensen, F., Osgood, D. W., Peterson, D., Taylor, T. J., & Carson, D. C. (2013). Short and long-term outcome results from a multi-site evaluation of the GREAT program. *Criminology & Public Policy, 12*(3), 375–411.

Federal Bureau of Investigation. (2012). *National gang threat assessment—emerging trends.* National Gang Intelligence Center. https://www.fbi.gov/file-repository/stats-services-publications-2011-national-gang-threat-assessment-2011%20national%20gang%20threat%20assessment%20%20emerging%20trends.pdf/view

Federal Bureau of Investigation. (2019). *National gang report: 2015.* National Gang Intelligence Center. https://www.fbi.gov/file-repository/stats-services-publications-national-gang-report-2015.pdf/view

Fraser, A., Ralphs, R., & Smithson, H. (2018). European youth gang policy in comparative context. *Children & Society, 32*(2), 156–165. https://doi.org/10.1111/chso.12265

Gang Rescue and Support Project. (2020). *Who are we?* Grasp Youth. https://graspyouth.org/

Gang Resistance Education and Training. (2019). GREAT Program. Institute for Intergovernmental Research. https://www.great-online.org/

Gilman, A. B., Hill, K. G., Hawkins, J. D., Howell, J. C., & Kosterman, R. (2014). The Developmental Dynamics of Joining a Gang in Adolescence: Patterns and Predictors of Gang Membership. *Journal of research on adolescence : the official journal of the Society for Research on Adolescence, 24*(2), 204–219. https://doi.org/10.1111/jora.12121

Glaser, C. (2000). *Bo-Tsotsi: The youth gangs of Soweto, 1935–1976.* David Philip.

Hansen, L. L., & Freitag, M. E. (2017). "Come on now, I want to see blood!": Choreographed violence in gang initiation rites. In *Violence and society: Breakthroughs in research and practice* (pp. 805–822). IGI Global.

Howell, J. C. (2019). Youth gangs: Nationwide impacts of research on public policy. *American Journal of Criminal Justice: AJCJ, 44*(4), 628–644. https://doi.org /10.1007/s12103-019-09485-5

Howell, J. C., Braun, M. F., & Bellatty, P. (2017). The practical utility of a life-course gang theory for intervention. *Journal of Crime and Justice, 40*(3), 358–375.

Howell, J. C., & Egley, A., Jr. (2005). Moving risk factors into developmental theories of gang membership. *Youth Violence and Juvenile Justice, 3*(4), 334–354. https://doi.org/10.1177/1541204005278679

Howell, J. C., & Moore, J. P. (2010). History of street gangs in the United States. *National Gang Center Bulletin*, no. 4 (May), 1–24. https://www.nationalgangcenter.gov/content/documents/history-of-street-gangs.pdf

Institute of Education Sciences. (2018). *Indicators of school crime and safety: 2018.* U.S. Department of Education. https://nces.ed.gov/pubs2019/2019047.pdf

Kissner, J., & Pyrooz, D. C. (2009). Self-control, differential association, and gang membership: A theoretical and empirical extension of the literature. *Journal of Criminal Justice, 37*(5), 478-487.

Loeber, R., Wung, P., Keenan, K., Giroux, B., Stouthamer-Loeber, M., Van Kammen, W. B., & Maughan, B. (1993). Developmental pathways in disruptive child behavior. *Development and Psychopathology, 5*(1–2), 103–133.

Lurigio, A. J. (2000). Drug treatment availability and effectiveness: Studies of the general and criminal justice populations. *Criminal Justice and Behavior, 27*(4), 495-528.

Merenda, F. (2020). Adventure-based programming with at-risk youth: Impact upon self-confidence and school attachment. *Child & Youth Services.* https://doi.org/10.1080/0145935X.2020.1829465

Monterosso, S. (2018). From bikers to savvy criminals. Outlaw motorcycle gangs in Australia: Implications for legislators and law enforcement. *Crime, Law, and Social Change, 69*(5), 681–701. https://doi.org/10.1007/s10611-018-9771-1

National Gang Center. (2019). *National Youth Gang Survey analysis.* https://www.nationalgangcenter.gov/Survey-Analysis/Prevalence-of-Gang-Problems#prevalence youthgang

National Institute of Justice. (2011). *What is a gang? Definitions.* https://nij.ojp.gov/topics/articles/what-gang-definitions

National Institute of Justice. (2013). *Program profile: Project BUILD.* https://www.crimesolutions.gov/ProgramDetails.aspx?ID=335

Navarro, J. (2019). Chicano/a gang narratives. In P. Rabinowitz (Ed.), *Oxford research encyclopedia of literature.* Oxford University Press.

North Carolina Gang Investigators Association. (2015). *Gang identifiers.* http://www.ncgangcops.org/gangs.html

Newton, M. (2008). *Gangs and gang crime.* Chelsea House.

New York City Bar. (2021, April 27). *Concerns about the New York City Police Department's Criminal Group Database and associated policing practices.* https://www.nycbar.org/member-and-career-services/committees/reports-listing/reports/detail/nypds-criminal-group-database-and-associated-practices

Office of Juvenile Justice and Delinquency Prevention. (2019). *Gang violence prevention.* https://ojjdp.ojp.gov/programs/gang-violence-prevention

Olate, R., Salas-Wright, C. P., Vaughn, M. G., & Yu, M. (2015). Preventing violence among gang-involved and high-risk youth in El Salvador: The role of school motivation and self-control. *Deviant Behavior, 36*(4), 259–275. https://doi.org/10.1080/01639625.2014.924364

Petrus, T., & Kinnes, I. (2019). New social bandits? A comparative analysis of gangsterism in the Western and Eastern Cape provinces of South Africa. *Criminology & Criminal Justice, 19*(2), 179–196. https://doi.org/10.1177/1748895817750436

Public Safety Canada. (2018). *Youth gangs in Canada: What do we know?* https://www.publicsafety.gc.ca/cnt/rsrcs/pblctns/gngs-cnd/index-en.aspx

Public Safety Canada. (2018b). *Crime prevention inventory.* https://www.publicsafety.gc.ca/cnt/cntrng-crm/crm-prvntn/nvntr/index-en.aspx?s=3

Public Safety Canada. (2018c). *Youth Violence Reduction Partnership (YVRP).* https://www.publicsafety.gc.ca/cnt/cntrng-crm/crm-prvntn/nvntr/dtls-en.aspx?i=10017

Public Safety Canada. (2018d). *Gang prevention strategy.* https://www.publicsafety.gc.ca/cnt/rsrcs/pblctns/gng-prvntn-strtgy/index-en.aspx

Richmond, S. A., & Spence, P. R. (2013). Loitering. In J. I. Ross (Ed.), *Encyclopedia of street crime in America.* SAGE.

Ritter, N. Simon, T. R., & Mahendra, R. R. (2019). *Changing course: Preventing gang membership.* National Institute of Justice. https://nij.ojp.gov/topics/articles/changing-course-preventing-gang-membership#citation—0

Rivera, M. (2016). The sources of social violence in Latin America: An empirical analysis of homicide rates, 1980–2010. *Journal of Peace Research, 53*(1), 84–99. https://doi.org/10.1177/0022343315598823

Roy, J., & Marcellus, S. (2019). *Homicides in Canada, 2018.* Statistics Canada. https://www150.statcan.gc.ca/n1/pub/85-002-x/2019001/article/00016-eng.htm

Sante, L. (1991). *Low life: Lures and snares of Old New York.* Vintage Books.

Seelke, R. (2016). *Gangs in Central America.* Congressional Research Service. https://fas.org/sgp/crs/row/RL34112.pdf

Terrorism Research & Analysis Consortium. (2020). *Los trinitarios.* https://www.trackingterrorism.org/group/trinitario-los-trinitarios

Thornberry, T. P. (2006). Membership in youth gangs and involvement in serious and violent offending. In A. J. Egley, C. L. Maxson, J. Miller, & M. W. Klein (Eds.), *The modern gang reader* (pp. 224–232). Roxbury.

Thornberry, T. P., Krohn, M. D., Lizotte, A. J., Smith, C. A., & Tobin, K. (2003). *Gangs and delinquency from a developmental perspective.* Cambridge University Press.

Thrasher, F. M. (1927). *The gang—a study of 1,313 gangs in Chicago.* University of Chicago Press.

Thrasher, F. M. (2013). *The gang: A study of 1,313 gangs in Chicago.* University of Chicago Press.

United Nations Office on Drugs and Crime (2012). Model Legislative Provisions against Organized Crime. https://www.unodc.org/documents/organized-crime/Publications/Model_Legislative_Provisions_UNTOC_Ebook.pdf

U.S. Department of Justice. (1994). *Violent Crime Control and Law Enforcement Act of 1994.* https://www.ncjrs.gov/txtfiles/billfs.txt

U.S. Department of Justice. (2008). *Attorney general's report to Congress on the growth of violent street gangs in suburban areas.* https://www.justice.gov/archive/ndic/pubs27/27612/appendb.htm

U.S. Department of Justice. (2019). *Gangs.* https://www.ncjrs.gov/gangs/

U.S. Department of Justice (2021). *Criminal Street Gangs.* https://www.justice.gov/criminal-ocgs/gallery/criminal-street-gangs

Uberto, G., Tremblay, R. E., Vitaro, F., & McDuff, P. (2005). Youth gangs, delinquency, and drug use: A test of the selection, facilitation, and enhancement hypotheses. *Journal of Child Psychology and Psychiatry, 46*(11), 1178–1190.

Vinney, C. (2019). *Sutherland's differential association theory explained.* ThoughtCo. https://www.thoughtco.com/differential-association-theory-4689191

Wood, J., & Alleyne, E. (2010). Street gang theory and research: Where are we now and where do we go from here? *Aggression and Violent Behavior, 15*(2), 100–111. https://doi.org/10.1016/j.avb.2009.08.005

Youth Advocate Programs. (2020). *Gang prevention, gang intervention.* https://www.yapinc.org/Portals/0/Docs/Gang%20Prevention-Intervention.pdf

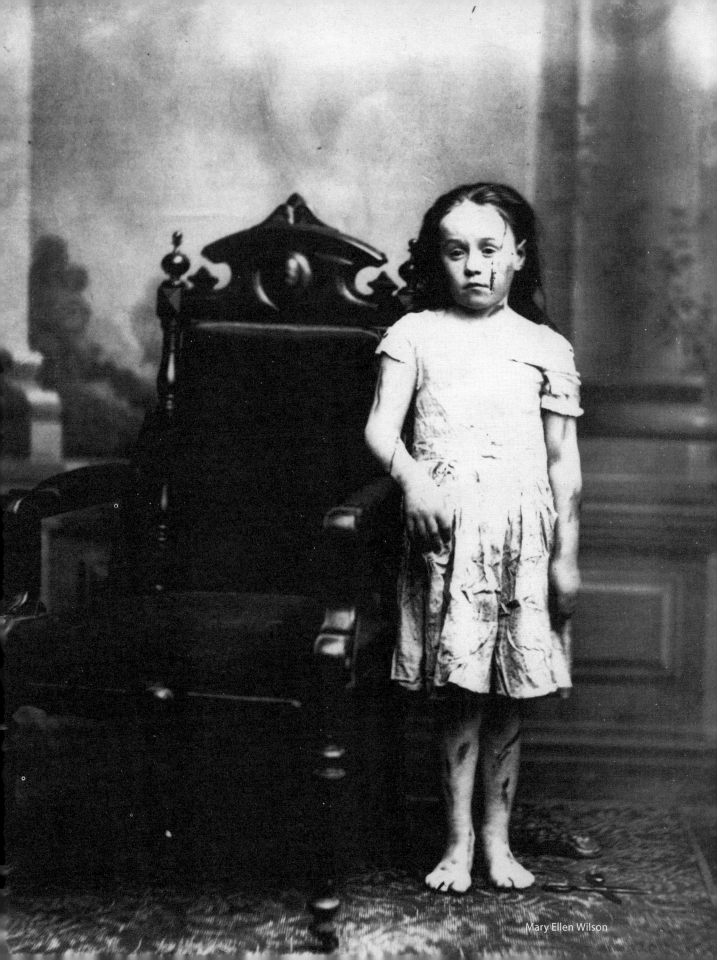

Mary Ellen Wilson

Juvenile Victims

LEARNING OBJECTIVES

Describe the history of child abuse and associated laws in the United States.

Explain the court process and its stages as they relate to victims' rights and participation.

Detail federal and state legislation and interventions that have provided additional rights, protections, and resources for victims.

Analyze statistical data regarding the age, race, and number of children affected by specific forms of victimization.

Explain efforts to collect, investigate, and disseminate information to aid missing and exploited children.

Discuss the prevalence of child victimization and mitigation efforts around the world.

Keywords

AMBER Alert system
Central registries
Electronic bullying
Group-oriented care
Individual family-oriented foster homes
Institutional reporting law
Intake
Labor trafficking

Mandated reporters
Medical neglect
Megan's Law
Missing child
Neglect or deprivation of necessities
Physical abuse
Psychological or emotional
  maltreatment

Restitution
Restorative justice
Secondary victimization
Sex trafficking
Sexual abuse
Unaccompanied alien child/minor
Victim Compensation Fund
Victimization

Introduction

Juvenile victimization rates have remained high across the United States, and increased attention has been shown both within and outside the juvenile justice system. Within the system, consideration for victims' rights has grown through providing more access to court documents, mediation programs, and the justice process overall. Outside the juvenile system, protective measures and support systems have expanded to combat a variety of crimes against children. This includes child abuse, neglect, abduction, internet crimes, and sexual offenses. Over the past decades, legislation has been passed, and other resources have been established to further assist victims and their families in both of these settings.

In this chapter, we will explore the history of how victims were treated within and outside the juvenile justice system and how and why this has changed. We will review victim trends by age and race and discuss newly established laws, as well as various resources available to victims and their families, communities, and the justice system overall. Finally, we will assess new programs and other initiatives for child victims within the United States and around the world.

Historical Treatment of Juvenile Victims in and out of the Justice System

As described in Chapter 1, many changes have occurred within the juvenile justice system for offenders as the system has evolved. These changes include juvenile offender rights, quality of detention facilities, diversion, and sentencing options. In the 19th and early 20th centuries, the original juvenile court system focused on "delinquents" and acting in what the court believed was their best interest. Juvenile court proceedings were informal, and the purpose of the system was to rehabilitate wayward and delinquent youth. However, juveniles' placement in reformatory schools and similar institutions was often criticized as far-reaching and more punitive than rehabilitative. Victims of the offenses were offered less support and were less a part of the process. Even as the system further developed, juvenile advocates and the juvenile court as a whole remained primarily focused on the offender regarding the best methods for their rehabilitation (McCord et al., 2001; National Research Council, 2013).

In the late 1980s and early 1990s, juvenile crime spiked, with almost a third of all crimes committed by juveniles. Society realized that along with those incidents came as many victims. Legislation was passed to make laws tougher on youths regarding accountability, increase the transfer of cases to adult court, and extend more punitive sentencing. Victims were also beginning to receive more support in some jurisdictions and a role in the juvenile process in terms of access to court records, giving testimony, and presenting impact statements to a judge. However, although communities and governments established programs and agencies dedicated to victim assistance and specific rights, many states restricted these rights in juvenile court proceedings because of confidentiality laws designed to protect the offender. Therefore, a number of victims in juvenile court did not have much of a participatory role during this time, beyond limited court information and sometimes **restitution**. Restitution is defined as compensation to a victim for harm or for something that was stolen or damaged, in the form of money, acknowledgment of guilt, or community service (Bourque & Cronin, 1993; Finkelhor et al., 2005).

Expansion of Victim Services and Programs

As we will read throughout this chapter, into the 21st century, the expansion of available resources and programs directed toward victims' protection and well-being has continued. Victims' rights have also increased in terms of participation in the court process, access to case documents, even when the offender is a juvenile, and assistance in court. Court advocates are generally assigned to victims. They provide access to resources and services and assist with answering questions about the court process, victim's rights, and any other concerns that may be raised. They also assist victims in getting to court if needed, preparing victim statements, and accessing counseling services, restitution, and, more recently, restorative justice programs.

Restorative Justice

Restorative justice focuses both on an acknowledgment by the offender of wrongdoing and an attempt to repair the harm to the victim and the community in the form of mediation and restitution. Restorative justice has become more prevalent since the beginning of the 21st century. Although there are varied components of and definitions for this process, it has been commonly referred to as a "contemporary justice mechanism to address crime, disputes, and bounded community conflict. The mechanism is a meeting of affected individuals, facilitated by one or more impartial people" (Daly, 2016, p. 21). Its purpose is to mitigate the effects of a crime or wrongdoing by focusing on the victim and the harm caused (Wilson et al., 2017).

Research has shown that restorative justice methods not only have had effects on recidivism rates but also have benefited victims of crime, who have indicated being more satisfied with this type of sanction as opposed to a more offender-focused punitive resolution (Posick, 2019; Strang et al., 2013; Wilson et al., 2017).

In addition to an expansion of services and support available to victims, particular attention has also been given to avoid **secondary victimization**, additional trauma experienced by the victim as a result of stress, confusion, the anxiety of the court process, violation of rights, or inadequate treatment (Rasho et al., 2019). In addition to assigning court advocates for victims, efforts to avoid revictimization have been incorporated into the court process and its specific stages.

The Court Process

To initiate the court process, an allegation of a crime against the victim is made via a complaint report or referral to law enforcement; if there is suspected child abuse or neglect, a notification can be made either to a police entity or to Child Protective Services. After an investigation that may include interviewing the victim, witnesses, or the accused, by either entity, if the complaint is founded, the offender(s) will be taken into custody by the police.

If the offense is an allegation of child abuse or neglect within the home, emergency removal of the child from a residence deemed unsuitable or dangerous could occur by the police or Child Protective Services. Although laws vary by state, the child could be placed with another family member or put into a government-run or private child care facility, including a foster home.

After an arrest, the offender will enter the first stage of either juvenile or criminal court based on the seriousness of the alleged offense, the state, and the age of the offender. Because stages differ between the juvenile justice system and the criminal system, so do the rights of both juvenile and adult victims, depending on the municipality. However, there are typically intake, initial and fact-finding hearing, adjudication, and disposition stages in the juvenile court and an arraignment, grand jury, trial, and sentencing hearing in criminal court (also see Chapter 8, "Juvenile Courts"). Generally, during **intake**, specifically within the juvenile justice system, the victim and their family can play an essential role in assisting the intake officer. The intake officer will consider the victim's input to help determine if the case should be handled formally within the juvenile system or diverted to an alternative program such as restorative justice or other type of mediation and treatment service. If the case proceeds formally, the victim continues to be part of the process in terms of testifying, making an impact statement to the judge about how the crime has affected them and voluntarily participating in various ordered sanctions, including forms of restitution (see Figure 6.1). It should also be noted that if the offender was diverted or does not adhere to the judge's probationary order, they can be brought back to the court and their case handled formally. Sentencing may then include stricter penalties, including incarceration. Victims can receive support and guidance during and after the court process and can even sue offenders for monetary compensation in civil court.

The overarching goal for the court system and professionals within it is it to work with the victim to provide support, safety, and ultimately justice (Kratcoski, 2017).

Overall Victimization and Statistics

Victimization can occur in many ways. In this section (and as indicated by Tables 6.1, 6.2, 6.3, and 6.4), we take an overall look at crimes inflicted on juveniles. Throughout the rest of the chapter, we will discuss in more detail the specific forms of child victimization and how and when these crimes can occur.

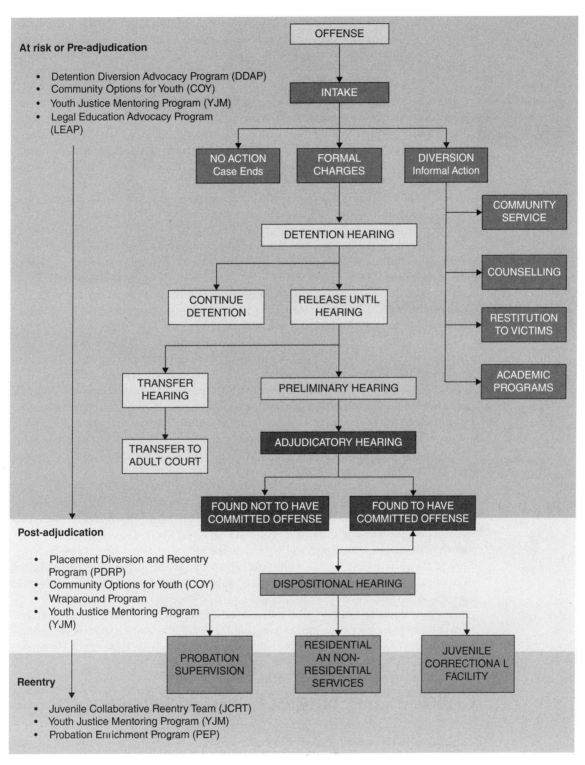

At risk or Pre-adjudication

- Detention Diversion Advocacy Program (DDAP)
- Community Options for Youth (COY)
- Youth Justice Mentoring Program (YJM)
- Legal Education Advocacy Program (LEAP)

Post-adjudication

- Placement Diversion and Recentry Program (PDRP)
- Community Options for Youth (COY)
- Wraparound Program
- Youth Justice Mentoring Program (YJM)

Reentry

- Juvenile Collaborative Reentry Team (JCRT)
- Youth Justice Mentoring Program (YJM)
- Probation Enrichment Program (PEP)

OFFENSE

INTAKE

NO ACTION
Case Ends

FORMAL
CHARGES

DIVERSION
Informal Action

COMMUNITY
SERVICE

COUNSELLING

RESTITUTION
TO VICTIMS

ACADEMIC
PROGRAMS

DETENTION HEARING

CONTINUE
DETENTION

RELEASE UNTIL
HEARING

TRANSFER
HEARING

PRELIMINARY HEARING

TRANSFER TO
ADULT COURT

ADJUDICATORY HEARING

FOUND NOT TO HAVE
COMMITTED OFFENSE

FOUND TO HAVE
COMMITTED OFFENSE

DISPOSITIONAL HEARING

PROBATION
SUPERVISION

RESIDENTIAL
AN NON-
RESIDENTIAL
SERVICES

JUVENILE
CORRECTIONA L
FACILITY

Figure 6.1 Center on Juvenile and Criminal Justice Continuum of Care

Three things to note: 1. Victims are also provided with services and counseling throughout these stages, including placement outside homes where crimes have occurred. 2. Victims can testify during the preliminary/fact-finding stage (also see Chapter 8, "Juvenile Courts" chapter). 3. Victims can provide an impact statement and be part of adjudication and disposition (e.g., restitution, mediation, and restorative justice).

Source: Center on Juvenile and Criminal Justice

According to the FBI's Uniform Crime Report, in 2018, there were 1,126 juvenile homicide victims under 18 as compared to 1,208 in 2017, representing a 6.7% decrease. Of the 1,126 homicides occurring in 2018, close to half (43%) were female victims, nearly half (47%) were African American, and over a third of children killed were under the age of 4 (see Table 6.1).

Juveniles have also been victims of other violent crimes. Data are collected through self-reporting in the National Crime Victimization Survey, as well as the FBI's Uniform Crime Reporting Program. As we learned in Chapter 2, data can vary between these crime measuring tools because of how data are collected. Therefore, trends in crimes can sometimes be more revealing. As you may recall, the Summary Reporting System and the National Incident-Based Reporting System rely on reporting to the police. The National Crime Victimization Survey is based on interviews with individuals 12 and older who may or may not have reported the crime to law enforcement (see Chapter 2 for more information regarding these crime measuring tools).

The Bureau of Justice Statistics defines violent crimes as misdemeanor and felony assault, rape and sexual assaults, and robbery. According to the National Crime Victimization Survey, youth ages 12 to 17 were 1.5 times more likely to be victims of violent incidents than expected based on their percentage of the population. However, the number of victims of serious crimes aged 12–17 decreased by approximately 49,000, or 9%, from 2017 to 2018 (Morgan & Oudekerk, 2019; also see Table 6.2).

Tables 6.3 and 6.4 represent 2018 and 2017 data collected by the National Incident-Based Reporting System to gather more detailed crime information regarding the victim and the offense. These data are snapshots of crimes reported to law enforcement in 2017 and 2018. Based on the National Incident-Based Reporting System, there were over half a million (574,056) total crimes against individuals under 21 in 2018, approximately a 3% increase from the year before. Of those under 21, youth between 11 and 15 years old had the highest growth of overall victimization, almost 5% from the year before, and for both 2017 and 2018, children between 11 and 15 were victims of the highest number of sexual offenses (U.S. Department of Justice, 2019).

Juveniles have also been victims of maltreatment, neglect, exploitation, child pornography, and physical and sexual abuse both in and outside families. These crimes can overlap with traditional crimes of assault and sexual offenses. They can be reported directly to law enforcement and Child Protective Services, who will work together to support the victim and investigate and prosecute the offender. These efforts among agencies and the variety of services and resources provided to the victim and their families, although sometimes compartmentalized, have been referred to as the juvenile victim justice system (Finkelhor et al., 2005).

As you will read in more detail in the next section, in child abuse and neglect cases, services and resources have expanded throughout the decades as a result of increased awareness, education, and legislation directed at protecting victims from these types of crimes.

Child Abuse, Neglect, and Maltreatment

Until the early 19th-century, child protection services both sporadically and informally existed within communities and the justice system to remove child victims from abusers. These processes became more formalized in 1874 with the creation of the New York Society for the Prevention of Cruelty to Children, founded by Henry Bergh and colleagues (Fegert & Stötzel, 2016). Henry Bergh was a philanthropist and diplomat who formed the American Society for the Prevention of Cruelty to Animals in 1866. He was approached

TABLE 6.1 Murder victims by age, sex, race, and ethnicity, 2018

AGE	TOTAL	SEX			RACE				ETHNICITY		
		MALE	FEMALE	UNKNOWN	WHITE	BLACK OR AFRICAN AMERICAN	OTHER[1]	UNKNOWN	HISPANIC OR LATINO	NOT HISPANIC OR LATINO	UNKNOWN
TOTAL	14,123	10,914	3,180	29	6,088	7,407	395	233	2,173	9,066	1,840
Percent distribution[2]	100.0	77.3	22.5	0.2	43.1	52.4	2.8	1.6	16.6	69.3	14.1
Under 18[3]	1,126	784	341	1	493	577	30	26	191	704	147
Under 22[3]	2,819	2,186	632	1	1,069	1,649	53	48	504	1,745	365
18 and over[3]	12,855	10,035	2,809	11	5,544	6,784	362	165	1,966	8,314	1,635
Infant (under 1)	137	75	62	0	83	43	1	10	19	73	27
1 to 4	255	153	101	1	129	113	4	9	33	168	33
5 to 8	76	43	33	0	37	34	4	1	10	47	12
9 to 12	60	34	26	0	28	26	5	1	8	33	10
13 to 16	319	238	81	0	119	186	11	3	64	207	32
17 to 19	1,107	948	159	0	364	712	21	10	199	709	124
20 to 24	2,199	1,813	385	1	764	1,369	33	33	428	1,334	295

[1] Includes American Indian or Alaska Native, Asian, and Native Hawaiian or Other Pacific Islander.

[2] Because of rounding, the percentages may not add to 100.0.

[3] Does not include unknown ages.

Source: FBI, Uniform Crime Report

TABLE 6.2 Demographic characteristics of victims of serious crime, 2014–2018

Number and percent of persons who were victims of serious crime, by demographic characteristics of victims, 2014–2018

VICTIM DEMOGRAPHIC CHARACTERISTIC	NUMBER OF VICTIMS[a]					PERCENT OF PERSONS[b]				
	2014	2015	2016	2017	2018*	2014	2015	2016	2017	2018*
Total	5,034,030	4,793,040	4,708,410	4,529,520	4,636,730	1.89%†	1.78%	1.73%	1.66%	1.68%
Sex										
Male	2,526,190	2,304,250	2,336,240	2,268,380	2,307,130	1.94%†	1.76%	1.76%	1.71%	1.72%
Female	2,507,850	2,488,790	2,372,170	2,261,150	2,329,600	1.83%†	1.80	1.70	1.61	1.65
Race/ethnicity										
White[c]	2,813,170	2,900,140	2,664,370	2,689,950	2,687,680	1.62%	1.68%	1.54%	1.57%	1.57%
Black[c]	856,140	691,130	697,110	639,140	732,020	2.61	2.08	2.07	1.95	2.21
Hispanic	1,035,610	900,690	951,050	864,110	889,800	2.50†	2.08	2.14	1.90	1.89
Asian[c]	135,800	131,970	239,890†	156,020	124,380	1.01	0.90	1.53†	0.94	0.72
Other[c,d]	193,310	169,100	155,990	180,300	202,860	3.55	3.21	2.83	2.88	3.13
Age										
12-17	642,470†	599,550	559,090	534,530	485,480	2.56%†	2.41%	2.23%	2.15%	1.95%
18-24	854,980†	666,590‡	709,140†	618,610	553,530	2.81†	2.19	2.34†	2.07	1.86
25-34	828,380	881,650	845,940	806,790	831,150	1.92	2.02	1.91	1.82	1.85
35-49	1,234,370	1,169,990	1,097,240	1,065,690	1,115,800	2.03	1.92	1.79	1.75	1.82
50-64	1,000,210	933,420	975,470	984,320	1,004,830	1.60	1.48	1.54	1.56	1.60
65 or older	473,620†	541,830‡	521,540†	519,590†	645,940	1.05	1.16	1.09	1.05‡	1.26
Marital status										
Never married	2,268,180†	2,021,850	2,042,010	1,940,140	1,920,450	2.47%†	2.17%	2.14%	2.02%	1.98%
Married	1,728,560	1,735,080	1,682,680	1,686,090	1,585,130	1.36	1.36	1.32	1.32	1.23
Widow/widower	211,140†	192,540†	199,440†	186,380†	297,020	1.44†	1.30†	1.32†	1.26†	1.96
Divorced	611,770	677,880	612,210	549,210‡	652,090	2.35	2.50	2.25	2.05‡	2.38
Separated	174,010	136,730	140,620	145,170	170,380	3.43	2.67	2.80	2.94	3.32

† Significant difference from comparison year at the 95% confidence level.

‡ Significant difference from comparison year at the 90% confidence level.

a Number of persons age 12 or older who experienced at least one serious crime during the year.

b Percentage of persons age 12 or older who experienced at least one serious crime during the year.

c Includes persons who were a victim of a serious violent crime or whose households experienced a completed burglary or completed motor-vehicle theft.

d Includes Excludes simple assault, threatened rape or sexual assault, and unwanted sexual contact (not rape) without force.

e Includes completed burglary and completed motor-vehicle theft

Source: Bureau of Justice Statistics, National Crime Victimization Survey, 2014–2018 (Morgan & Oudekerk, 2019, table 19, p. 18).

TABLE 6.3 2018 crime data.

OFFENSE CATEGORY	TOTAL VICTIMS¹	10 AND UNDER	11-15	16-20	21-25	26-30	31-35	36-40	41-45	46-50	51-55	56-60	61-65	66 AND OVER	UNKNOWN AGE
Total	**4,720,900**	84,157	139,255	350,644	533,768	575,710	517,299	463,514	375,812	371,235	332,546	299,006	226,058	385,703	66,193
Crimes Against Persons	**1,587,662**	74,943	115,280	176,935	208,118	215,653	182,052	153,088	113,428	102,622	82,535	62,967	37,010	42,327	20,704
Assault Offenses	1,454,398	49,993	85,336	153,279	194,936	204,766	173,837	146,516	109,100	99,175	80,117	61,149	35,986	40,567	19,641
Homicide Offenses	5,673	269	92	645	854	810	634	559	386	339	288	252	152	324	69
Human Trafficking Offenses	569	32	163	198	61	30	24	13	10	4	1	3	0	0	30
Kidnapping/Abduction	21,114	2,340	1,306	2,673	3,253	3,131	2,506	1,974	1,292	927	605	411	231	326	139
Sex Offenses	105,908	22,309	28,383	20,140	9,014	6,916	5,051	4,026	2,640	2,177	1,524	1,152	641	1,110	825
Crimes Against Property	**3,133,238**	9,214	23,975	173,709	325,650	360,057	335,247	310,426	262,384	268,613	250,011	236,039	189,048	343,376	45,489
Arson	11,414	239	95	355	776	1,025	1,088	1,064	969	1,061	976	925	680	1,250	911
Bribery	385	5	25	36	41	63	51	41	26	20	14	18	11	11	23
Burglary Breaking & Entering	401,855	1,719	2,324	16,717	36,610	43,593	41,918	39,298	33,352	34,979	33,635	33,139	27,193	52,285	5,093
Counterfeiting/Forgery	44,437	107	114	1,682	2,664	3,237	3,620	3,663	3,236	3,641	3,840	4,099	3,555	8,950	2,029
Destruction/Damage/Vandalism	602,224	1,296	2,015	32,900	65,785	70,836	64,761	61,680	52,691	53,724	49,569	45,944	35,941	57,763	7,319
Embezzlement	4,862	1	10	104	241	331	407	457	423	510	484	434	360	957	143
Extortion/Blackmail	5,163	17	218	928	855	523	396	360	293	311	322	280	220	410	30
Fraud Offenses	334,249	610	879	15,023	27,566	31,113	31,093	30,656	26,875	29,170	28,049	27,772	24,171	55,031	6,241
Larceny/Theft Offenses	1,344,243	4,174	15,006	81,983	146,617	160,018	148,250	133,559	111,602	112,514	103,725	96,556	77,441	137,661	15,137
Motor Vehicle Theft	249,976	206	123	9,596	26,543	32,113	29,390	27,275	23,337	23,056	20,930	18,890	14,230	21,497	2,790
Robbery	87,458	653	2,938	12,509	13,866	12,210	9,632	7,930	5,915	5,694	5,093	4,371	2,760	3,299	588
Stolen Property Offenses	46,972	187	228	1,876	4,086	4,995	4,641	4,443	3,665	3,933	3,374	3,611	2,486	4,262	5,185

AGE

¹ This table includes only data for the victim types of individual and law enforcement officer. It does not include business, financial institution, offense type to which they are connected.

Source: FBI. Uniform Crime Report

TABLE 6.4 2017 Crime Data.

OFFENSE CATEGORY	TOTAL VICTIMS[1]	AGE													
		10 AND UNDER	11-15	16-20	21-25	26-30	31-35	36-40	41-45	46-50	51-55	56-60	61-65	66 AND OVER	UNKNOWN AGE
Total	**4,524,968**	81,314	133,006	343,030	519,331	539,476	486,214	431,308	362,615	364,005	329,274	288,204	213,285	370,552	63,354
Crimes Against Persons	**1,448,085**	71,725	106,321	165,503	196,695	194,677	163,908	135,273	103,163	94,541	75,921	54,586	30,932	35,842	18,998
Assault Offenses	1,325,786	48,033	78,439	143,843	184,421	185,117	156,378	129,787	99,220	91,301	73,764	53,050	30,096	34,332	18,005
Homicide Offenses	5,542	264	89	628	840	800	622	485	374	384	312	238	164	258	84
Human Trafficking Offenses	431	11	92	159	42	31	19	8	6	3	3	5	0	0	52
Kidnapping/Abduction	19,505	2,094	1,215	2,598	3,063	2,860	2,415	1,681	1,165	875	550	368	194	298	129
Sex Offenses	91,208	20,570	22,900	17,147	8,284	5,845	4,460	3,302	2,389	1,967	1,291	924	476	948	705
Sex Offenses, Nonforcible	5,613	753	3,586	1,128	45	24	14	10	9	11	1	1	2	6	23
Crimes Against Property	**3,076,883**	9,589	26,685	177,527	322,636	344,799	322,306	296,035	259,452	269,464	253,353	233,618	182,353	334,710	44,356
Arson	**11,722**	335	105	402	835	1,024	1,031	1,183	974	1,115	987	930	664	1,266	871
Bribery	**264**	3	11	28	31	41	40	30	15	15	9	9	4	8	20
Burglary/Breaking & Entering	**418,978**	1,627	2,319	17,705	39,136	44,657	43,387	40,089	34,883	36,948	35,976	35,103	27,857	54,023	5,268
Counterfeiting/Forgery	**44,074**	82	116	1,673	2,890	3,381	3,589	3,487	3,289	3,758	3,832	4,015	3,419	8,657	1,886
Destruction/Damage/Vandalism	**617,807**	1,295	2,052	35,114	67,752	70,222	65,174	61,298	54,467	56,479	52,649	47,215	36,064	60,121	7,905
Embezzlement	**4,505**	2	13	95	226	303	364	393	403	485	464	416	341	828	172
Extortion/Blackmail	**3,521**	18	162	693	578	390	292	225	190	242	185	173	104	228	41
Fraud Offenses	**319,591**	600	774	13,985	25,513	28,869	28,814	28,807	26,986	28,798	28,480	27,534	23,745	51,165	5,521
Larceny/Theft Offenses	**1,304,989**	4,538	17,694	84,683	142,873	151,299	140,332	125,775	108,525	111,532	103,517	94,453	73,087	132,225	14,456
Motor Vehicle Theft	**225,211**	182	136	9,118	24,933	28,653	26,054	23,812	20,844	21,135	19,246	16,646	12,390	19,219	2,843
Robbery	**81,680**	712	3,011	12,127	13,749	11,408	8,913	6,971	5,326	5,031	4,695	3,826	2,511	2,925	475
Stolen Property Offenses	**44,541**	195	292	1,904	4,120	4,552	4,316	3,965	3,550	3,926	3,313	3,298	2,167	4,045	4,898

[1] This table includes only data for the victim type of individual and law enforcement officer. It does not include business, financial institution, government, religious organization, or other victim types. Victims are counted once for each offense type to which they are connected.

Source: FBI, Uniform Crime Report

by a Methodist mission worker, Etta Wheeler, who had become aware that 9-year-old Mary Ellen Wilson was being physically abused and neglected by her guardian. Because there were limited resources at the time, Ms. Wheeler had been unsuccessful in getting help. Through Henry Bergh's attorney, Elbridge Gerry, filing a petition with the court, along with the fact that Mary Ellen's guardian was not her biological parent, Mary Ellen was removed from the home and assault charges were brought against her guardian (there were no specific child abuse and neglect laws at this time; Myers, 2006; Palusci, 2017). Because of this incident and because Ms. Wheeler persuaded Mr. Bergh that just as there was a society to protect against cruelty to animals, there should be one to protect against abuses toward children, Bergh, Gerry, and philanthropist John D. Wright formed the first child protective agency (New York Society for the Prevention of Cruelty to Children, 2017). Gerry then announced to the world the agency's purpose:

> To rescue little children from the cruelty and demoralization which neglect, abandonment, and improper treatment engender; to aid by all lawful means in the enforcement of the laws intended for their protection and benefit; to secure by like means the prompt conviction and punishment of all persons violating such laws and especially such persons as cruelly ill-treat and shamefully neglect such little children of whom they claim the care, custody or control. (Cregan & Cuthbert, 2014, p. 40)

DEEPER DIVE

Mary Ellen Wilson

Mary Ellen Wilson, whose parents had died, was placed with a guardian, Mary Connolly, at age 4. Connolly physically and emotionally abused and neglected Mary Ellen from her arrival until age 9, when the abuse was reported by philanthropist Henry Bergh, his attorney, and Ms. Etta Wheeler, a Methodist mission worker. Mary Ellen testified that she had been beaten and whipped with rawhide almost every day. She also spoke about never being hugged or kissed.

Mary Ellen was removed from the home and, through Ms. Wheeler's efforts, was allowed to live with Ms. Wheeler's mother and sister. She later married and had two daughters who became schoolteachers. She lived until 92 years of age.

Mary Connolly was convicted of felony assault (child abuse laws did not exist yet), which, along with similar cases, prompted the creation of the New York Society for the Prevention of Cruelty to Children in 1874. This was the first institution dedicated to child protective services.

Mary Ellen Wilson.

After the creation of the New York Society for the Prevention of Cruelty to Children, although they had no government affiliation, 300 independent child services agencies were formed across the United States throughout the 19th century. As we read in Chapter 1, it was also during this time, in 1899, that the juvenile justice system was created in Illinois. Although the justice system had the power to remove children from their homes, its focus remained on the juvenile offender. Although independent agencies did spread, many areas in the early 1900s relied on family and friends intervening in order to stop situations of child abuse and neglect.

It was not until 1912 that the federal government created the Federal Children's Bureau. This was followed by the Social Security Act in 1935, which included provisions that the Children's Bureau work with state public welfare agencies to create or enhance services for the protection and care of children who were neglected, homeless, or on a path toward delinquency (Petersen et al., 2014).

Into the 1940s and 1950s, after experiencing financial hardships from the Great Depression, many independent child protective agencies took a reverse turn, and many began to close. It was not until the 1960s that the medical field sparked attention to this topic. An article entitled "The Battered Child Syndrome," written by Dr. C. Henry Kempe and colleagues (Kempe, et al., 1962), generated national media coverage of child abuse. Their paper described the prevalence of child abuse and neglect and how to identify and report it. This brought national awareness to these occurrences, and further efforts to combat child abuse grew. Dr. Kempe also founded the Kempe Center for the Prevention and Treatment of Child Abuse and Neglect. He advocated for a multimodal approach that involved families, communities, and available resources to care for child victims (Kempe, 2021).

Following this momentum, in 1962, the Social Security Act was amended, making child protective services more a part of social welfare to encourage governments to offer child welfare and protective services statewide. This also prompted Henry Kempe and Vincent de Francis, director of the Children's Division of the American Humane Association, to consult with other experts and officials regarding the enhancement of the Federal Children's Bureau, also known as the Children's Bureau of the U.S. Department of Health, Education, and Welfare. Shortly after, the bureau released a report revealing rising incidents of child and infant abuse within families. The Children's Bureau, along with other organizations such as the American Medical Association, the Council of State Governments, and the American Humane Society, outlined reporting laws that states could follow (Petersen et al., 2014).

The Children's Bureau's definition of child abuse was limited in scope, however; it was described as an intentional injury inflicted on a child by a parent or caregiver that only medical professionals could be mandated to report. The definition and the ways in which individuals identified child abuse were expanded by many states. These states believed that identifying child abuse and neglect did not require specific medical expertise, could be reported by other professionals, and should be wide-ranging. For example, Nebraska defined child abuse as

> knowingly, intentionally, or negligently causing or permitting a minor child or an incompetent or disabled person to be: (a) placed in a situation that may endanger [the child's] life or health; (b) tortured, cruelly confined, or cruelly punished; (c) deprived of necessary food, clothing, shelter, or care; or (d) left unattended in a motor vehicle, if such minor child is six years of age or younger. (Child Welfare Information Gateway, 2019b, p. 54, § 28-710)

As a result of these efforts, since 1967, all states have some form of child abuse and neglect definitions and reporting laws, but they vary from state to state (Myers, 2008).

Definitions generally separate child abuse into subsections that include physical, sexual, and emotional abuse and neglect (McCabe & Murphy, 2016). More recently, child trafficking has been included in child abuse. Federal funding contingencies have mandated states to put more preventative and investigative efforts into this area (see the section "Federal Interventions").

Mandated Reporting Laws

States not only have varying definitions of child abuse and neglect, but also various mandated reported laws. Since the Children's Bureau recommendations in the early 1960s, many states have amended these mandates (Petersen et al., 2014). Although all states have some type of reporting laws, they can differ widely, from only specific professionals being mandated to report suspected child abuse to all individuals being obligated to report it. **Mandated reporters** are generally individuals who are required by law to report suspected child abuse and neglect because of their occupation or affiliation with a designated profession. Specific professions and associated mandates can vary from state to state, but those selected as reporters have a responsibility to report suspected or witnessed child abuse or neglect. The abuse can be reported to a supervisor within the agency, law enforcement, or a Child Protective Services agency, depending on state laws. For example, in New York, physicians, dentists, licensed therapists, school officials, peace officers, and district attorneys are required to report directly to either law enforcement or child protective service agencies. In other states, such as Alaska and Florida, employees or volunteers who work for mandated reporting agencies are required to report suspected abuse to their supervisor, who in turn will report it to law enforcement or Child Protective Services, also known as **institutional reporting law**. Eighteen states mandate anyone who suspects child abuse, regardless of profession or affiliation, to report it.

States also have varied penalties for mandatory reporters who neglect to report abuse. They can range from fines to misdemeanor and felony charges, depending on the severity of the abuse and its consequences on the child victim. There are federal and state protections for reports made in good faith, even when an investigation determines the case to be unfounded or results in no abuse findings. Individuals who file reports known to be false can be fined civilly and, in some cases, criminal charges can be filed (Child Welfare Information Gateway, 2019b).

Reports of Abuse

With the recognition of child abuse and neglect, by the mid-1970s with mandated reporting laws enacted, over 60,000 cases were reported, and this number continued to grow. By the 1980s and 1990s, the number of reported cases was in the millions. Although declines have been seen since the beginning of the 21st century, the number of reported cases remains in the hundreds of thousands. In 2018, there were 678,000 reported cases of child abuse in the United States (Myers, 2011; U.S. Department of Health & Human Services [HHS], 2020; U.S. Department of Justice, 2020; also see the section "Child abuse and Neglect Trends and Statistics" for more child abuse statistics).

In 2018, most child abuse and neglect reports (67.3%) were filed by professionals who had contact with a potentially maltreated victim in the course of their job, such as law enforcement, teachers, and social service providers. Of those professionals, teachers had the highest reporting percentage, followed by those associated with the justice system and social services. The remaining reporters are labeled as nonprofessionals and can include friends, neighbors, and relatives of the victim (HHS, 2020; see Figure 6.2).

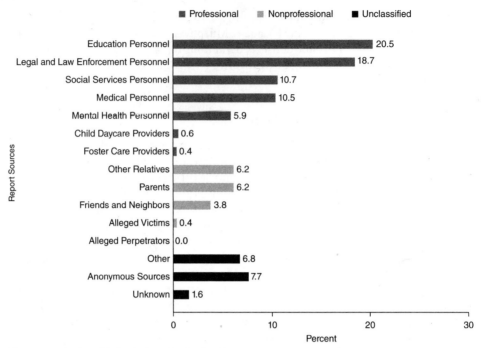

Figure 6.2 Referral Submissions by Profession.

Based on data from 49 states. Data are from the Child File. States were excluded from this analysis if more than 25.0 percent had an "other" or unknown report source. Supporting data not shown.
Source: Child Maltreatment Report, 2018. (ACF, 2020)

The Process: What Happens After a Report Is Filed?

Reports can be made to law enforcement or child protective service agencies. Information can be written or called in confidentially and is documented by that state's registry (see the following discussion of national and local registries). Reports are then reviewed for reliability and jurisdiction. The decision of which allegations to investigate, and in what manner, varies by states; however, reports of drug use, sexual and severe physical abuse, and evidence directly showing other forms of maltreatment generally are investigated by either law enforcement or an official from a child protective agency.

Investigations can be conducted independently by child protective employees or in conjunction with police agencies and the prosecutor/district attorney's office, depending on state laws and guidelines. These investigations can include home visits, medical exams, and interviews with the child, the alleged abuser, other family members, witnesses, and other persons deemed necessary. Children can be immediately removed from a home while the investigation takes place depending on the seriousness of the allegation, initial evidence presented, and determination by the investigator. Children can be placed with other family members or put into a state facility while awaiting the outcome of the investigation. If the allegation is proven to be false, the child is then returned. If there is not enough evidence, continued monitoring may be put in place or a record of the event may be generated for later reference if further allegations are received. If an allegation is founded, the case may be prosecuted in criminal or juvenile court depending on who the offender is, their age, and the offense committed (Child Welfare Information Gateway, 2019b).

In 1997, to further monitor and set additional guidelines for children to be removed and returned to their homes, Congress passed the Adoption and Safe Families Act. This act created stipulations for time limits for long-term foster care, termination of parental rights, and returning children to their homes. It also allowed states to automatically move to terminate parental rights for cases of sexual abuse (ACF, 2019).

If a guardian is incarcerated and no family member, or in some states, no competent adult, can take care of the child, the youth will remain in a state-run or private facility. In some cases, even if the parent/guardian is released, courts can terminate parental rights, whereby the child could be placed for adoption. The goal of these agencies is to provide a safe family environment for the child when possible by preventing further abuse, and they may offer offenders treatment, counseling services, parenting education, and other supportive resources (Swenson & Schaeffer, 2019). These services can also be provided in conjunction with or as part of a court sanction (see Figure 6.3).

Since 1974, the government has taken a more active role in protecting children by passing legislation that directly affects the prevention of child abuse and neglect across the United States. The first action was the Child Abuse Prevention and Treatment Act (CAPTA).

Federal Interventions

Child Abuse Prevention and Treatment Act

CAPTA was enacted in 1974 and has been amended several times, most recently in 2019 through the Victims of Child Abuse Act (GovTrack, 2020b). In 1974, CAPTA established state responsibilities for child protection and directed state funding toward training and investigating child abuse and neglect. It also provided funding for nonprofit organizations and established both the Federal Inter-Agency Work Group on Child Abuse & Neglect and a national clearinghouse of child abuse and neglect research and statistics. Although CAPTA does not provide federal mandates to report child abuse and neglect, it does require states to maintain their own mandating reporter laws to continue receiving federal funds (ACF, 2020).

The 1988 amendment to CAPTA mandated the HHS to establish a national data collection and analysis program called the National Child Abuse and Neglect Data Systems. It is federally sponsored and collects and analyzes annual data volunteered from states on child abuse and neglect. The data are collected and analyzed by the Children's Bureau, Youth and Families, and the ACF within the HHS (ACF, 2012).

CAPTA also requires states to keep confidential records of child abuse and neglect in child abuse and neglect **central registries** to receive federal funding. Although these records are generally confidential, states do allow access to specific individuals, such as physicians, court personnel, police personnel, potential child care employers, and a child victim and their parent or guardian. There is generally no public access, but state registry information regarding cases that have resulted in a fatality is made publicly available (Child Welfare Information Gateway, 2019a).

States requesting CAPTA funding as of 2017 are required to investigate reports of child trafficking, which are now included in the federal child abuse definition (see the following discussion of the Justice for Victims of Trafficking Act). States are also required to provide training for social service workers and coordinate efforts between social services, law enforcement, the juvenile justice system, and homeless and runaway shelters to identify victims of trafficking. It also provides guidelines for minimal

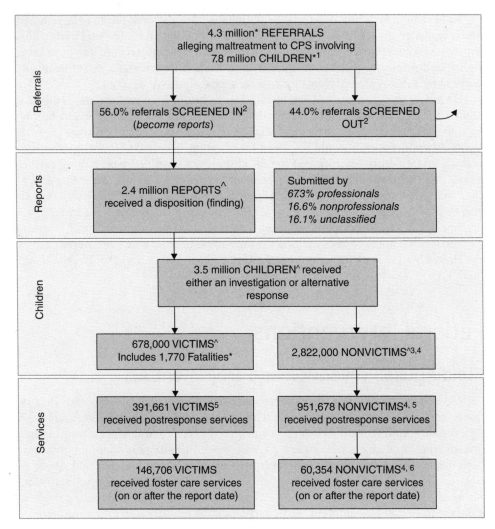

Indicates a nationally estimated number. ^indicates a rounded number.

1 *The average number of children included in a referral was (1.8).*
2 *For the states that reported both screened-in and screened-out referrals.*
3 *The estimated number of unique nonvictims was calculated by subtracting the unique count of victims from the unique count of children.*
4 *Includes children who received an alternative response.*
5 *Based on data from 50 states.*
6 *Based on data from 49 states.*

Figure 6.3 Referral to Child Protective Services Flow Chart

Source: Child Maltreatment Report, 2018. (ACF, 2020)

conduct that constitutes child abuse and neglect for states to include in their own legal definitions. CAPTA defines abuse and neglect as

> any recent act or failure to act on the part of a parent or caretaker which results in death, serious physical or emotional harm, sexual abuse or exploitation; or an act or failure to act, which presents an imminent risk of serious harm. CAPTA, PL 111–320. (ACF, 2020)

CAPTA also expands the definition of sexual abuse to include the production of child pornography, statutory rape, and prostitution of children (Brown & Gallagher, 2014; Child Welfare Information Gateway, 2019a; Stuart, 1975).

As discussed, each state has its own definition of child abuse and neglect. The federal definitions discussed next have further guided states in formulating or amending their child abuse laws and protections.

Types of Child Maltreatment and Their Associated Federal Definitions

- **Neglect or deprivation of necessities:** failure by the caregiver to provide needed, age-appropriate care, although they are financially able or have been offered the financial or other means to do so. This includes not meeting a child's educational needs.

- **Medical neglect:** caused by the caregiver's failure to provide for the appropriate health care of the child, although they are financially able or have been offered financial or other resources to do so

- **Psychological or emotional maltreatment:** acts or omissions—other than physical abuse or sexual abuse—that caused or could have caused conduct, cognitive, affective, or other behavioral or mental disorders; frequently occurs as verbal abuse or excessive demands on a child's performance

- **Physical abuse:** the disregard of a child's physical needs and physical safety, including abandonment, illegal transfers of custody, expulsion from the home, failure to seek remedial health care or delay in seeking care, or inadequate supervision, food, hygiene, clothing, or shelter Includes acts that caused or could have caused physical injury to the child, including excessive corporal punishment

- **Sexual abuse:** the involvement of the child in sexual activity to provide sexual gratification or financial benefit to the perpetrator, including contacts for sexual purposes, molestation, statutory rape, prostitution, pornography, exposure, incest, or other sexually exploitative activities

- **Sex trafficking:** a subtype of sexual abuse that refers to the recruitment, harboring, transportation, provision, or obtaining of a person for the purpose of a commercial sex act. States have the option to report to NCANDS any sex trafficking victim who is younger than age 24. Prior to data published for Fiscal Year 2018, sex trafficking was not distinct from sexual abuse. (OJJDP, 2020a)

Additional federal acts have also guided states in their child maltreatment investigations. They have provided technical support, training, access to central repositories of court data and records, additional funding for agencies and counseling, and other forms of treatment for victims.

Additional Legislation to Protect Children

As we read in Chapter 2, in the 1980s and early 1990s, crime had escalated across the United States, as well as in other parts of the world, and the focus turned to drugs, gangs, and juveniles. In response, the Violent Crime Control and Law Enforcement Act was passed in 1994 by then-President Bill Clinton. The act called for stricter sentencing by states for drug dealers, gang crimes, and prosecuting juveniles as adults at younger ages for more severe crimes. The act also advocated for victims, encouraging states to enhance their records and investigations of sex offenders and to allow victims of federal violent and sex crimes to speak at sentencing and receive restitution from their offender (U.S. Department of Justice, 1994).

Maintaining a Central Registry

As part of the Federal Violent Crime Control and Law Enforcement Act of 1994, the Jacob Wetterling Crimes Against Children and Sexually Violent Offender Registration Act, also known as the Wetterling Act, was enacted. It mandated states to maintain a registry of offenders convicted of sexual offenses and other crimes against children. It also required that law enforcement keep updated records, including current addresses of those offenders, for 10 years after their release. In 1989, 11-year-old Jacob Wetterling went missing. He was abducted by a stranger and his remains were found almost 27 years later, which prompted the creation of the Wetterling Act. The act was amended in 1996 with **Megan's Law**, named after Megan Kanka, a 7-year-old girl from New Jersey who was sexually assaulted and murdered by a child molester who moved into the area. In 1994, New Jersey passed a state-sanctioned "Megan's Law," and in 1996, it was enacted on a federal level. Megan's Law expands on the Wetterling Act by requiring law enforcement entities to release to the public sex offender information that it deems necessary for public safety. That same year, the FBI established a tracking system through the Pam Lychner Sexual Offender Tracking and Identification Act to assist local law enforcement when a sex offender crosses state lines. In 1998, the Wetterling Act was amended to allow for expanded discretion by states to ensure databases were updated with more detailed information. The amendment also required offenders to register in states where they were attending school and mandated registration by federal and military employees (GovTrack, 2020a).

In addition to state registries, the Adam Walsh Child Protection and Safety Act passed in 2006 required the HHS to develop a national center on child abuse and neglect. It also called for an accessible national registry to be established through CAPTA for a variety of record checks, such as for employment and background checks of potential adoptive and foster parents (National Academy of Sciences, 2014). See more on the Adam Walsh story and its effects on state and federal legislation and central registries under "Missing and Exploited Children."

Enhanced Support and Investigation of Child Abuse Cases

The Children's Justice Act was formed in 1986 through CAPTA. It has since been amended and provides grant funds for projects to support abuse victims and prosecution of child abuse and neglect cases. It also targets the handling of homicide cases suspected to be the result of abuse and neglect (ACF, 2019). Children's Justice Act activities also include training for law enforcement members, child protective services, health and mental health professionals, and other members of the judicial system.

Family First

The Family First Prevention Services Act was signed into law by then-President Donald Trump in 2018. It provides provisions to safely keep children with their families when interacting with the child welfare system and enhance foster care when children must be placed outside their families. Under this act, federal funds can be utilized for children's preventative services to avoid foster care and instead have them stay with family members. If children must be placed in foster care, the act also incentivizes states through funding to put children in **individual family-oriented foster homes**. This type of personalized setting, composed of six or fewer children, is in contrast to **group-oriented care**, which typically supervises larger groups of children (National Conference of State Legislatures, 2020). If group care is the only option, it should be temporary and generally not exceed 2 weeks. If a child is in a residential treatment program, the act also mandates that a licensed health care professional evaluate the child to assess if their needs could be met elsewhere, for example, by family members or in a family-oriented foster home.

Protecting Victims of Human Trafficking

The Trafficking Victims Protection Act, established in 2000, was the first federal act that provided prevention and protection to trafficking victims and the comprehensive prosecution of offenders. The act has been updated several times, most recently in 2017. It also defines and addresses two forms of trafficking, sex and labor, and associated federal laws.

- **Sex trafficking** is the recruitment, harboring, transportation, provision, obtaining, patronizing, or soliciting of a person for the purposes of a commercial sex act, in which the commercial sex act is induced by force, fraud, or coercion or in which the person induced to perform such an act has not attained 18 years of age. (22 U.S.C. § 7102)
- **Labor trafficking** is the recruitment, harboring, transportation, provision, or obtaining of a person for labor or services through force, fraud, or coercion for the purposes of subjection to involuntary servitude, peonage, debt bondage, or slavery. (22 U.S.C. § 7102)

The act enabled the State Department to monitor the trafficking and established the President's Interagency Task Force to coordinate efforts to mitigate it. It has also created the Trafficking in Persons Report to include 168 country governments around the world to track and address all forms of human trafficking (OJJDP, 2019a).

More recently, in 2015, the Justice for Victims of Trafficking Act was signed into law. The act's purpose was to enable fines and penalties for human trafficking and child pornography offenders, making them one and the same. The funds are then used to assist trafficking and child pornography victims. The act provides local law enforcement and justice agencies funds to establish trafficking task forces, enhance prosecution of these cases, and provide additional victim services. The act additionally expands the federal definitions of "child abuse and neglect" and "sexual abuse" to include a child who is identified as a victim of sex trafficking or other forms of child trafficking, such as that resulting in forced labor and exploitation (Child Welfare Information Gateway, 2019b; Congressional Research Service, 2015).

Compensating Victims

In 1984, the Victims of Crime Act was passed, creating the Crime Victims Fund. The act allows the transfer of monetary penalties and fines taken from federal criminals to a crime victims' fund to assist a wide range of victims of various offenses. This assistance can include financial compensation for victims as well as funding for agencies such as Child Advocacy Centers to provide forensic medical exams and mental health counseling, as well as other necessary and supportive services. Each year, the Department of Justice distributes this money to states and organizations that assist victims of crime. In 2016, updated guidelines of the act further expanded the definition of child abuse to include child pornography offenses and to permit funding for victim services in detention facilities and trafficking victims in shelters (Department of Justice Rule, 2016; Office for Victims of Crime, 2020).

The Victims of Crime Act also established the **Victim Compensation Fund**, which permits states to distribute funds to victims of crimes who have suffered a monetary loss directly related to the offense. Victim compensation can vary by state, but typically includes some kind of medical treatment and financial support, even if no arrest is made, if a need is established as a result of the crime (Office for Victims of Crime, 2020).

In 2000, the Child Abuse Prevention and Enforcement Act was signed into law to increase funding for the Victims of Crime Act from $10 million to up to $20 million to be split between child abuse prevention and treatment efforts and the Victim Compensation Fund. The act also provides current justice programs and additional training and equipment for personnel, along with access to criminal records such as conviction information and orders of protection (House Report 764, 2000).

State Legislation to Expand Reporting and Child Protection

States have also passed legislation to support victims of child abuse. For example, amendments to the Child Victims Act in New York and other states have recently extended the statute of limitations for reporting child abuse. This is because many times, these cases are not brought forward until the victim enters adulthood.

Prior legislation in New York only gave an individual until age 23 to report abuse, but in 2019 this was amended to extend the age to 55 to file a civil case, 28 to file charges in criminal court for felonies, and 25 for misdemeanors. It also provided a "lookback window" in 2019 for 1 year to file a civil suit at any age for a past abuse (State of New York 2019–2020).

In California, Assembly Bill 218 changed the childhood sexual assault statute of limitations laws from a maximum age of 26 to age 40 to file a lawsuit; for adults who have realized in adulthood that their psychological injury or illness was a result of childhood abuse, it raises the limitation from 3 to 5 years to file suit (State of California, 2019–2020).

Safe Haven Laws

Safe Haven laws, also referred to as Baby Moses laws (a biblical reference), Safe Place laws, and Safe Delivery laws, began in the state of Texas in 1999 to dissuade parents from abandoning an infant child and putting them in a fatal environment. These laws were enacted in states across the United States to address a rising number of infant abandonments (Child Welfare Information Gateway, 2017). A parent or someone representing the parent can anonymously and with protection from prosecution bring the baby to a designated "safe haven," which can include a police station, fire department, hospital, or social service agency, depending on state guidelines. States also vary with regard to how old the infant can be for the parent to be protected by these laws, ranging from up to 72 hours to up to 1 year after birth (National Academy of Sciences, 2014).

Despite all these federal and state efforts to protect victims and prosecute offenders, child abuse and neglect cases increased from 2014 to 2018. It should be noted that this increase could in part be a result of greater awareness of the signs of abuse and additional reporting resources (HHS, 2020; OJJDP, 2020c). In the next section, we explore the prevalence, trends, and demographics of these types of crimes.

Child Abuse and Neglect Trends and Statistics

As cited earlier, according to the National Criminal Justice Reference Service, in 2018, there were approximately 678,000 victims of child abuse and neglect in the United States, of which 1,770 died as a result, and almost half (46.6%) were under the age of 1. Before their first birthday, children are victimized at the highest rate, at 26.7 per 1,000 children of the same age across the United States (; HHS, 2020; U.S. Department of Justice, 2020). Additionally, 35% of child maltreatment victims were under age 3, and over 50% were under age 7. Of these victims, 44% were White, followed by 25% Hispanic and 13.7% African American; the majority (61%) experienced neglect in the form of maltreatment (see Tables 6.5–6.6).

The majority of offenders (77.5%) were the victims' parents (HHS, 2020; OJJDP, 2020c). Tables 6.5 and 6.6 and figures 6.4 to 6.7 further represent this and other child abuse data.

In 2018, an estimated 3.5 million children received an investigation or an alternative response, an increase of 18% since 2014.

The following sections discuss the victimization of children in other settings and contexts.

TABLE 6.5 Characteristics of Child Maltreatment Victims, 2018

Estimated number of unique victims	678,000
Victimization rate[a]	9.2
Age	
0 to 3	35%
4 to 7	23%
8 to 11	20%
12 to 15	16%
16 to 17	6%
Gender	
Male	49%
Female	51%
Race/ethnicity	
White	44%
Black	21%

(Continued)

TABLE 6.5 continued	
Hispanic	22%
American Indian/Alaskan Native	1%
Asian/Pacific Islander	1%
Multiple race	5%
Unknown/missing	5%
Maltreatment type[b]	
Neglect only	61%
Physical abuse only	11%
Sexual abuse only	7%
Psychological maltreatment only	2%
Medical neglect only	1%
Other abuse	3%
Multiple maltreatment types	16%
Unknown/missing	<0.5%
Victim relationship to perpetrator[c]	
Parent	92%
Mother only	39%
Father only	22%
Mother and Father	21%
Mother, father, and other nonparent	1%
Mother and other nonparent	7%
Father and other nonparent	1%
Relative	5%
Unmarried partner of parent	3%
Other nonparent[d]	2%
Professional[e]	1%
Other/unknown	6%

Note: Percentages are based on the unique count of child victims and should not be compared to years prior to 2010. Data are based on sample data reported by a varying number of states.

[a] Rate is per 1,000 children under 18 in the U.S. population.

[b] If a child has been a victim of two or more maltreatment types, they are counted once in the multiple maltreatment category. In 2018, "sex trafficking" was introduced as a new maltreatment type; counts were reported by 18 states. These counts are included in the "sex abuse only" category.

[c] A child may be victimized by multiple perpetrators; therefore, the percentages total more than 100.0%.

[d] Other nonparent includes friends and neighbors, legal guardians, or more than one nonparental perpetrator.

[e] Professional includes adults who care for children as part of their employment duties, such as child day care providers, foster parents (nonrelative), and group home staff, as well as other professionals.

Source: U.S. Department of Health and Human Services, Administration on Children, Youth, and Families. *Child Maltreatment 2019*. Washington, D.C.: U.S. Government Printing Office.

TABLE 6.6 Characteristics of Fatality Victims of Child Maltreatment, 2018	
Estimated number of fatality victims	1,710
Fatality rate[a]	2.3
Age	
Under 1	50%
1	13%
2	9%
3	6%
4 to 7	11%
8 to 11	6%
12 to 17	6%
Unknown/missing	<1%
Gender	
Male	58%
Female	42%
Unknown/missing	<1%
Race/ethnicity	
White	40%
Black	33%
Hispanic	14%
Asian/Pacific Islander	1%
American Indian/Alaskan Native	1%
Other/multiple race	6%
Unknown/missing	5%
Reported maltreatment types of child fatalities[b]	
Neglect	73%
Physical abuse	46%
Other	8%
Medical neglect	8%
Psycological abuse	46%
Sexual abuse	<1%
Unknown	0%

(Continued)

TABLE 6.6 continued

Child fatalities by prepetrator relationship	
Parent	80%
Mother only	27%
Father only	16%
Mother and Father	22%
Mother and other nonparent	11%
Father and other nonparent	22%
Mother, father, and other nonparent	2%
Other relative	3%
Unmarried partner of parent	2%
Professional[c]	2%
Other[d]	8%
Unknown	5%

Note. In 2018, half of all victims were under the age of 1, the majority (58%) were male, and 40% were White.

Notes: Demographic and perpetrator relationship information is based on sample data reported by a varying number of states. Because the national estimate of child fatalities is influenced by which states report, even small fluctuations in the data can affect the national estimate and the national rate.

* Rate is per 100,000 children under 18 in the U.S. population.

**** Professional includes adults who care for children as part of their employment duties, such as child daycare providers, foster parents (non-relative), and group home staff, as well as other professionals.

**** Other includes friends and neighbors, legal guardians, and other.

Source: U.S. Department of Health and Human Services, Administration on Children, Youth, and Families. *Child Maltreatment 2019.* Washington, D.C.: U.S. Government Printing Office.

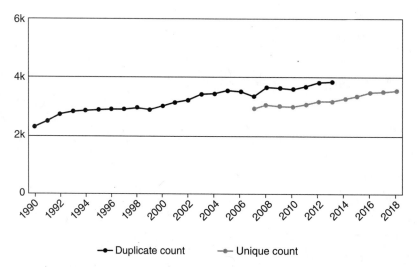

Figure 6.4 Number of Child Reports of Maltreatment (in thousands) 1990–2018

Note: Child reports are counts of children who are the subject of reports. Duplicate count: an individual child is the subject of more than one report during a year. Unique count: a child is counted once regardless of the number times he or she was the subject of a report.
Source: OJJDP (2020c)

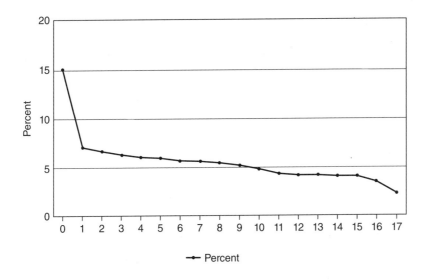

Figure 6.5 Age Distribution of Child Maltreatment Victims, 2018

Note: In 2018, infants and toddlers (ages 0 to 3) accounted for the majority of victims (35%), the highest proportion of victims were youth under one (15.0%). Older youth accounted for the smallest proportion of victims; 17-year-olds were just 2% of child maltreatment victims in 2018
Source: OJJDP (2020c).

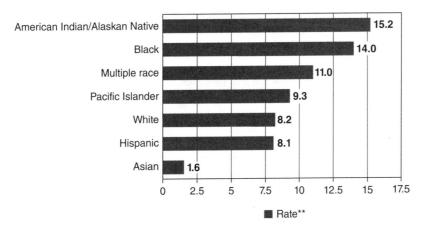

Figure 6.6 Maltreatment Victimization Rate by Race/Ethnicity*, 2018

Of the maltreatment types, neglect was the most common; 61% experienced neglect in 2018

Source: OJJDP (2020c)

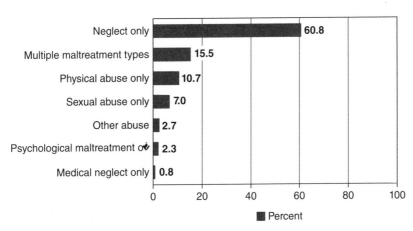

Figure 6.7 Percent of Victims by Maltreatment Type, 2018

Note: Of the maltreatment types, neglect was the most common; 61% experienced neglect in 2018. In 2018, "Sex Trafficking" was introduced as a new maltreatment type; counts were reported by 18 states. These counts are included in the "Sex abuse only" category. This graph is based on sample data reported by a varying number of states.
Source: OJJDP (2020c)

Violence and Victimization in School Settings

Victimization in school can range from bullying to fighting to other violent crimes, all of which can lead to emotional and physical injury and, in some cases, fatalities. There are a variety of indicators to measure the occurrence of victimization in schools that can help inform programs to provide support to children who have been victimized (see the end of the chapter for examples of these types of interventional programs). The following are some of the tools used to measure victimization in school.

The School Crime Supplement to the National Crime Victimization Survey was first conducted in 1989. It was created by the National Center for Education Statistics (NCES) and the Bureau of Justice Statistics. It collects information regarding school violence and victimization, gangs at school, gang violence, fighting, and bullying. The School Crime Supplement defines a bullying incident as when

> another student had made fun of them, called them names, or insulted them; spread rumors about them; threatened them with harm; pushed or shoved them; forced them to do something they did not want to do; excluded them from activities; or destroyed their property on purpose. (Musu et al., 2019, p. 240)

The survey also measures a variety of other student victimizations for the prior 6 months, including felony assaults such as those with serious injuries or with weapons, sexual assault, and robbery, as well as misdemeanor offenses such as assaults with minor injuries and without weapons, and violent threats. It also includes theft or attempted theft, excluding motor vehicle theft. Crimes must have occurred going to, at, or coming home from school to be counted. The self-reporting survey is administered every 2 years and surveys 9,500 students ages 12–18 in public and private schools across the United States.

The Youth Risk Behavior Surveillance System was developed in 1990 by the Centers for Disease Control and Prevention and began surveying individuals in 1991. This tool assesses a variety of risks and behaviors that contribute to tobacco use, violence, alcohol and drug use, and other detrimental activities that can lead to social problems, disability, and sometimes death. Since its inception, data have been collected from over 4 million high school students.

The NCES is considered the primary source of education data and draws on data sets from a variety of sources, including the School Crime Supplement and the Youth Risk Behavior Surveillance System. Results from their 2018 Indicators of School Crime and Safety report show that from 2015 to 2016, there were 38 school-associated violent deaths, which included 7 suicides. In 2017, 827,000 total victimizations occurred "at school," which includes going to and from school and on school property (NCES, 2019).

Suicides

The NCES also showed that there were 1,941 total suicides of school-aged children between 2015 and 2016. Suicide has also been found to be the second leading cause of death in school-aged children 10 years old and older in both 2017 and 2018 data (Centers for Disease Control and Prevention, 2020; National Institute of Mental Health, 2019). In fact, in 2018, there were twice as many youths who died as a result of suicide as opposed to homicide. In 2018, about half (51%) of all youth suicides were the result of some form of suffocation (e.g., hanging), 40% were committed with a firearm, and about 10% were performed by a different method (e.g., poisoning) (OJJDP, 2020c). There are many possible emotional and mental causes of suicide, and recognizing early indicators has been shown to provide beneficial and necessary interventions (Burstein et al., 2019).

Bullying

The latest NCES data, from 2017, reveal that 20% of students 12–18 were bullied at school during the school year and 15% reported what was described as **electronic bullying**, bullying that occurs by electronic means, for example, via texting or on social media platforms (Musu et al., 2019; also see the discussion of cyberbullying in Chapter 12, "Juvenile Justice and the Digital Age").

Bullying can lead to various emotional issues for children, including anxiety and depression, which can lead to risk-taking behaviors such as drug use, suicidal ideation, and self-harm (Eastman et al., 2018; Smalley et al., 2017; Yanez & Seldin, 2019).

Although debate exists with regard to the association between bullying and suicide, according to a report from the Centers for Disease Control and Prevention, the majority of children who are bullied do not become involved in suicide-related behavior. However, involvement with bullying along with other risk factors, such as emotional distress, family conflict, lack of connectedness to school, or lack of access to resources and support, increases the odds of a youth engaging in suicide-related behaviors (Centers for Disease Control and Prevention, 2020).

Active Shooter Incidents

This NCES also reports on active shooter incidents. According to their report, there were 52 active shooting incidents in school settings from 2000 to 2017. Thirty-seven of these incidents occurred in elementary and secondary schools, and 15 incidents occurred at postsecondary institutions. However, approximately 45% of active shooter incidents overall occur in work settings.

From 2000 to 2017, active shooter incidents in school settings have resulted in 67 students killed and 86 wounded in elementary and secondary schools and 70 killed and 73 wounded in postsecondary settings (Musu et al., 2019). The FBI defines an active shooting incident as "one or more individuals actively engaged in killing or attempting to kill people in a populated area" (Musu et al., 2019, p. 22). Countless victims who witnessed or were associated with or related to those who were killed or wounded are treated as victims as well.

Schools have also implemented zero-tolerance policies, have mandatory reporters, and must report to law enforcement criminal acts that have led to suspension and expulsion. In 2017, students were more likely to be victims of a serious violent crime away from school (not associated with) than they were at or on their way to school. Figures 6.8 and 6.9 present these statistics and related data.

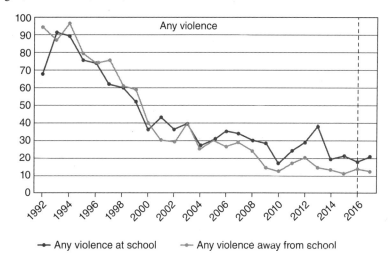

Figure 6.8 Violence per 1,000 Students, Ages 12–18, 1992–2017

Source: OJJDP (2020c)

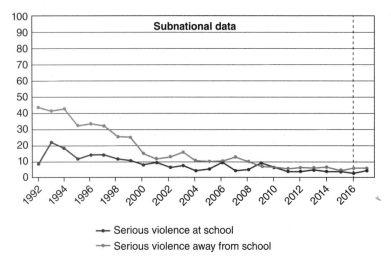

Figure 6.9 Serious Violence per 1,000 Students, Ages 12–18, 1992–2017

Note: Serious violence includes rape, sexual assault, robbery, and aggravated assault. Violent victimization includes serious violence and simple assault.

Source: OJJDP (2020c)

Unaccompanied Minors at U.S. Borders

A minor with unlawful immigration status, referred to as an "**unaccompanied alien child/minor**," is defined in Section 462(g)(2) of the Homeland Security Act of 2002 as a child: (1) who has no lawful immigration status in the United States; (2) who has not reached 18 years of age; and (3) with respect to whom there is no parent or legal guardian in the United States, or there is no parent or legal guardian in the United States available to provide care and physical custody (United States Department of Homeland Security, 2002)

In 2019, 76,020 unaccompanied minors were apprehended. This was a 52% increase from 2018. Some children come with their families, others are brought in by smugglers or nonrelatives, and some arrive alone to escape violence or poverty or to attempt to reunite with relatives. There have been criticisms and allegations of human rights violations in the process of taking minors from arriving families who enter the U.S. illegally, which by legal definition makes the children unaccompanied because the parent(s) are detained/arrested and therefore are not able to properly care for them (Council on Foreign Relations, 2020).

When children are detained at the U.S. border, there is a multiagency response and shared responsibility between the Department of Homeland Security and the HHS to provide care under the Homeland Security Act of 2002. As a result of various laws, including the Trafficking Victims Protection Reauthorization Act, which was last amended in 2018, children are not to be held for more than a month, but exceptions can be made because of emergencies and volume. While these children are detained in the United States, they are entitled to the least restrictive setting possible under HHS guidelines and often are placed in private facilities across the United States that are required to provide food, shelter, and education until they are released to family or sponsors, are deported, or, if they are turning 18, are transferred to adult facilities. In some cases, asylum is given, which allows the child to remain in the United States permanently (see Figure 6.10).

There has also been a focus on the care and treatment of these children, because many of them have fallen victim to a variety of crimes while being held in governmentally responsible private facilities. There have been reports of sexual abuse and harassment of unaccompanied or separated children who are in facilities under the auspices of the HHS's Office of Refugee Resettlement while awaiting decisions on their cases. In 2014, additional standards and reporting measures were established, which mandated facilities to base reports on federal definitions of sexual abuse and sexual harassment. Formerly, these facilities reported abuse based on a given state's required reporting laws and definitions. These federal definitions include expanded forms of sexual abuse and harassment to include simulated sexual acts; attempts, threats, or requests to engage in sexual activities; and voyeurism. In 2017, 1,069 allegations of sexual misconduct were reported. Although approximately 80% of these allegations were between the minors in the facility,

19% involved adult staff members. Mandated reporting and efforts to mitigate these occurrences continue (ACF, 2020).

Missing and Exploited Children

The terms missing and exploited, although they have distinct characteristics, have overlapped for children across the United States (Fernandes-Alcantara, 2019). Historically, however, the focus was on children who were missing because they ran away and became reliant on social welfare agencies. In 1974, the Runaway and Homeless Youth Act was passed to ensure assistance in terms of shelters and other social services was provided to both homeless and runaway children. In the following years, into the early 1980s, cases of children who were missing, abducted, sexually exploited, and sometimes murdered began to surface in increasing numbers. Many cases were publicized, and the approximately 1.8 million children reported missing annually to the police at the time prompted Congress to pass the Missing Children Act in 1982. It defined **missing children** as "a person under 18 whose whereabouts are unknown by his/her parent or guardian" (Fernandes-Alcantara, 2019, p. 20). The act mandated a federal database of missing children to be maintained and made available to state and local governments. In 1983, the Missing Children's Assistance Act was established and prompted federal efforts to investigate missing children cases and develop national resource centers and a national toll-free tip line to provide information about a child who was reported missing.

Figure 6.10 What Happens When a Child Arrives at the U.S. Border?

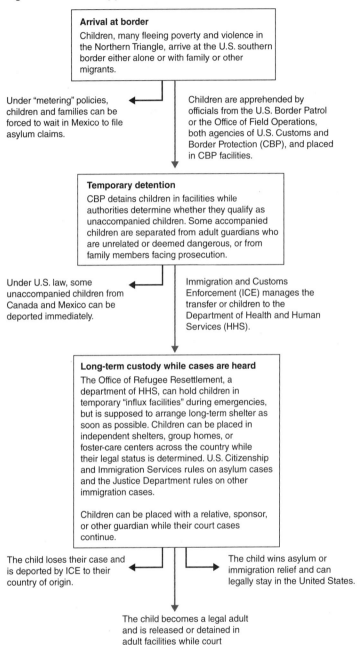

Source: Council on Foreign Relations. (2020).

The National Center for Missing & Exploited Children

The National Center for Missing & Exploited Children (NCMEC) was founded in 1984 by several child advocates, including John and Reve Walsh. The nonprofit organization serves as a resource and repository for information regarding missing and exploited children. Adam Walsh, the son of John and Reve, was abducted in 1981 at the age of

6 and later found murdered. NCMEC assists law enforcement with missing children cases reported to the FBI's national database, the National Crime Information Center, which in 2019 had 421,394 reported cases (NCMEC, 2020). It should be noted that these cases can include multiple incidents by the same child, such as running away. In 2019, NCMEC provided support for numerous families and assisted law enforcement with nearly 30,000 cases of missing children. Of those cases, 4% were family abductions, less than 1% were nonfamily abductions,1% were lost or injured, and 4% were missing young adults (18–20) because of critical circumstances surrounding their disappearance; the majority (91%) were endangered runaways. It is also estimated that 1 in 6 reported runaways are likely victims of child sex trafficking (FBI, 2020b; NCMEC, 2020).

In 2018, the Missing Children's Assistance Act was reauthorized and amended to allot $40 million per year until Fiscal Year 2023 for funding of activities and programs through the OJJDP. A portion of these funds is also to be distributed to the NCMEC to continue its efforts to assist children missing from government foster care agencies and to coordinate with the justice system with missing children investigations, including those at risk for sex trafficking. To date, NCMEC has received approximately 5 million calls, assisted in the recovery of over 300,000 missing children, and facilitated training for over 365,000 law enforcement and other professionals associated with the criminal and juvenile justice system. NCMEC also participates in an alert system for instantaneously disseminating detailed information for missing children in real time, also known as the AMBER Alert system.

The AMBER Alert System

The Amber Alert system was created in Texas in 1996 as a result of a collaboration between law enforcement and the media. That same year, a 9-year-old girl, Amber Hagerman, who lived in Arlington, Texas, was abducted while riding her bike. A man in a black truck was seen taking her, as later reported by witnesses. Four days later, she was found deceased. Community members wrote to radio stations suggesting that the already established Emergency Alert system should also be utilized when a child is abducted. In response and named after Amber, the **AMBER Alert system** was created locally in Dallas–Fort Worth. Similar alert systems then began spreading to other states throughout the country. This system was eventually adopted by the NCMEC as part of a national initiative.

AMBER stands for America's Missing: Broadcast Emergency Response and the system is run by coordinators in all 50 states. It has expanded from broadcast agencies to include wireless communication, transportation facilities, and social media to instantly disseminate information and involve the entire community's assistance (Office of Justice Programs, 2019). The Prosecutorial Remedies and Other Tools to End the Exploitation of Children Today Act (PROTECT) was signed into law on April 30, 2003, creating the National AMBER Alert System and support to local and state agencies utilizing an AMBER system. It created a national coordinator and advisory group to help states and law enforcement investigations and arrests. Additionally, the PROTECT Act provides funds for stricter laws regarding offenses against children in terms of sentencing and bail and enhanced investigatory tools, including monitoring internet transmissions.

Protecting Children Online

The PROTECT Act also authorized the Internet Crimes Against Children Task Force Program, which began in 1998 as a result of a growing number of children falling victim to a

DEEPER DIVE

Adam Walsh

In July 1981, 6-year-old Adam Walsh went with his mother to a department store. He asked to watch some older boys play video games while she shopped close by. After a fight broke out between the other boys, a 17-year-old part-time security guard had all the boys disperse and leave the store, including Adam. Adam was abducted outside and later murdered. In 1996, an individual made a bedside confession, stating he was Adam's killer.

Following this and other incidents, national databases, coordinated missing person alerts, law enforcement training, and investigative funding for missing and exploited children were developed, mostly through the efforts of Adam's parents.

Adam Walsh

variety of crimes online. These crimes include unsolicited sexual contact over the internet, online predator trading of child pornography, and requests to meet unsuspecting children in person, leading to abductions, sexual assaults, and, in some cases, homicide (OJJDP, 2020).

The task force assists local and state agencies with training, resources, community awareness, and victim services. In 2017, the program was reauthorized until 2022. Since its inception, over 700,000 individuals have been trained, along with almost a million online sexual victimization cases investigated, which have resulted in over 100,000 arrests. (OJJDP, 2020a; also see Chapter 12, "Juvenile Justice and the Digital Age," for more information regarding online victimization). Many other programs exist to support juvenile victims both in and out of the system. Some examples follow.

Additional Programs for Victims

Balanced and Restorative Justice Project

The Balanced and Restorative Justice Project advocates for restorative justice and a "balanced approach" by those within the juvenile justice field. Accordingly, equal attention should be given to the well-being of victims and communities and juvenile offenders. This includes taking responsibility for the crime and the harm it has caused, restitution to the victim(s), and building skills for the offender to successfully reintegrate into the community. The project has provided training and resources to agencies across the country and has encouraged legislation that supports restorative justice practices as a viable alternative to the traditional handling and adjudication of juvenile cases (OJJDP, 2019b).

Project Safe Childhood

Project Safe childhood began in 2006 through the Department of Justice to combat child exploitation both in person and on the internet. It addresses international risks of child pornography and sexual exploitation of children, including sex trafficking. This is accomplished by working with a multitude of federal and local agencies to conduct joint investigations leading to offenders' prosecution.

More recently, Project Safe has expanded its federal partners to include the Department of Homeland Security, the U.S. Secret Service, the U.S. Postal Inspector, and the U.S. Marshals Service; it has also expanded investigations to include those who fail to register as sex offenders. An increase in indictments for a range of crimes from the production of child pornography to sexual abuse of minors has been credited to this program (U.S. Department of Justice, 2016).

Nurse–Family Partnership

The Nurse–Family Partnership is a visitation program for first-time mothers who would otherwise lack the necessary resources and treatment for their child and themselves because of lack of financial means. Nurses visit homes, starting during pregnancy and continuing until the child is 2 years old. They provide support and education for prenatal care and assist mothers in finding physical and mental health care.

Nurses also assist in parenting skills, finding employment, and building positive futures. Results have indicated that mothers enrolled in this program, compared to those in similar situations who were not, showed significant decreases in domestic violence, child abuse and neglect cases, and child substance abuse, as well as increases in child academic achievement (Miller, 2015).

Stop School Violence Program

This program began in 2018 through the Stop School Violence Act to reduce school violence and protect students. It is administered through the Bureau of Justice Assistance and the Office of Community Oriented Policing Services. The program provides training for law enforcement to better secure schools. It makes recommendations for improved security efforts through cameras, metal detectors, and lighting and enhances communication to law enforcement during an emergency. Additionally, the program provides prevention training to school personnel and guidance on how students can protect themselves and report acts of violence. As of 2018, over 5,000 schools and 3 million students have been supported by this program (Bureau of Justice Assistance, 2019).

Worldview

*Addressing Child Victimization Around the World**

As the focus on victims' rights, treatment, support, and protection has grown in the United States, it has also grown in countries around the world.

UNICEF

In 1946, after World War II, the United Nation's General Assembly established the United Nations International Children's Emergency Fund (UNICEF) to aid children living in countries negatively impacted by the war. Years later, in 1989, UNICEF was part of drafting the U.N. Convention on the Rights of the Child. UNICEF helps to monitor and enforce the stipulations of this treaty among the now 196 member states that have signed it (UNICEF, 2019; United Nation Office on Drugs and Crime, 2019).

The U.N. Convention on the Rights of the Child was established in 1989 to unite countries around the world to legally commit to protecting children and their rights. Article 19 states,

> 1. States Parties shall take all appropriate legislative, administrative, social and educational measures to protect the child from all forms of physical or mental violence, injury or abuse, neglect or negligent treatment, maltreatment or exploitation, including sexual abuse, while in the care of parent(s), legal guardian(s) or any other person who has the care of the child.

> 2. Such protective measures should, as appropriate, include effective procedures for the establishment of social programmes to provide the necessary support for the child and for those who have the care of the child, as well as for other forms of prevention and for identification, reporting, referral, investigation, treatment, and follow-up of instances of child maltreatment described heretofore, and, as appropriate, for judicial involvement. ((United Nations, 2021).

According to the World Health Organization, in 2015, an estimated 1 billion children from the ages of 2 to 17 have experienced some kind of physical, sexual, or emotional violence or neglect (Hillis et al., 2016; World Health Organization, 2019). The prevalence and efforts to combat this type of child victimization by individual countries are given in the following sections.

AUSTRALIA

During 2018–2019, over 170,000 children received protective services in Australia. Services can range from an investigation and family support services to protection orders and out-of-home placement. This figure is up from 159,000 the year prior, a 7% increase. The most common types of abuse were emotional, neglect, physical, and sexual, respectively. Since 2015, there has been an approximately 12% increase in the number of youths receiving some form of protective service. This upward trend has been attributed to increased reporting resulting from heightened awareness of these issues and expanded access to services across the country (Australian Institute of Health and Welfare, 2020). Like the United

---

*The countries included here were selected based on available and relevant material.

States, Australia has mandatory reporting laws but also encourages all residents to report suspected child abuse to law enforcement or a local child protection agency (Australian Institute of Family Studies, 2019).

CANADA

The Youth Criminal Justice Act in 2002 set forth guidelines of how victims should be treated and be involved in various stages of the juvenile justice system. The act states that "victims should be treated with courtesy, compassion, and respect for their dignity and privacy and should suffer the minimum degree of inconvenience as a result of their involvement with the youth criminal justice system" (Government of Canada, 2015, p. 1). Every jurisdiction has a child welfare agency that investigates reports of child abuse and neglect. Canada asserts that everyone in the country has a duty to report child abuse, and those who have contact with children as part of their employment have a legal responsibility to report as well (Ministry of Children, 2019).

LATIN AMERICA AND THE CARIBBEAN

Many Latin American and Caribbean countries suffer from large amounts of violence, and their children are affected by a significant portion of that type of reported crime. Over 50% of children (58%) are estimated to have experienced sexual, physical, or emotional violence each year (Devries et al., 2019).

Latin America and the Caribbean also have the highest homicide rate among children according to Guedes (2019), reported to be three times the global average, and boys up to age 19 are seven times more likely than girls to be homicide victims. This violence, which also affects adults in these regions, has been attributed to a lack of access to education and health care, weakening economies, and gang and political uprisings (Canudas-Romo & Aburto, 2019; de Ribera et al., 2019; Rodgers & Baird, 2015).

There have been global efforts by the World Health Organization to combat these issues not only in Latin America and the Caribbean, but also around the world. These efforts include providing guidelines and supportive programs to raise awareness, increased training for practitioners, and better access to resources (World Health Organization, 2020).

GERMANY

Child sexual abuse was up over 6% in Germany from 2017 to 2018, reaching over 14,000 cases in 2018 (Bundeskriminalamt, 2019). In Germany, child abuse is defined as "physical, sexual, or emotional mistreatment of children" (U.S. Embassy Berlin, 2020, p. 1). As in other countries, police in Germany fear the number of child abuse victims is much larger because it is very difficult for children to report this abuse. This is because most of its occurrence is caused by family members or those known to the victim, as is the case in many other countries, including the United States (U.S. Embassy Berlin, 2020).

The production and distribution of child pornography have also increased in Germany. In 2018, law enforcement discovered over 7,000 cases of these types of offenses, a 14% increase from 2017. It is believed that the increase may be a result of child abuse crime rings, increases in technology, and international cooperation (Bundeskriminalamt, 2020; Witt et al., 2017, 2018).

AFRICA

According to the South African Police Service Missing Bureau, since 2000, approximately 16,000 children have been reported missing, and 25% never returned home (Emser & van der Watt, 2019). The bureau is a nonprofit public organization established in 2007, after the kidnapping and murder of 7-year-old Sheldean Human and 12-year-old Anestacia Wiese, to support families in similar situations. They also work directly with police and utilize various outlets, including social media, to disseminate missing information to the public.

Last amended in 2019, the Child Justice Act of 2008 regulates the intricacies of juvenile justice in Africa. The act not only sets mandates for ages of culpability and court processes but also provides stipulations for victims' rights. These include victims being part of the legal process to either prosecute an offender or divert them from formal processing. Diversion can include participation in a restorative justice–based program with the victim to account for and help mitigate the negative impacts of their crimes (van der Watt, 2020).

Despite passing legislation aligned with the U.N. Convention on the Rights of the Child, South Africa's statistics reveal that their homicide rate is twice the world's average. In 2018, children accounted for over 1,000 murders and over 18,000 victims of rape. Unfortunately, much like Germany and other countries, these figures may be lower than what is actually occurring because of cultural issues, a lack of centralized reporting systems, and various legislative laws. Efforts are being made to centralize reporting and develop comprehensive legislation through agencies such as Missing Children South Africa and the International Center for Missing and Exploited Children (Emser & van der Watt, 2019; South African Police Service, 2019).

Human trafficking also remains an issue in Africa. It has been reported that children are targeted especially for forced labor, sex, illegal adoptions, forced marriage, and, at times, body parts (Emser & van der Watt, 2019).

ADDITIONAL GLOBAL STATISTICS

Over a million children are reported missing around the world each year. To address this on a global level, the International Centre for Missing & Exploited Children was created in 1998. They provide global statistics and training to child protection agencies and professionals each year; over 20,000 professionals have been trained globally. They have offices in approximately 30 countries and have worked with legislators and provided training for law enforcement in over 100 nations.

Following are further statistics on missing children around the world (countries were selected based on available and relevant data). As we have learned, these numbers are sometimes underreported, and some countries do not report these statistics at all. In response, the International Centre for Missing & Exploited Children has developed a Model Missing Child Framework that provides countries with guidelines and standards for not only recording and disseminating data but also carrying out efficient and productive investigations.

GLOBAL STATISTICS ON MISSING CHILDREN

In Australia, an estimated 20,000 children are reported missing every year. Australian Federal Police, National Coordination Centre

In Canada, an estimated 45,288 children are reported missing each year. Government of Canada, Canada's Missing: 2015 Fast Fact Sheet

In Germany, an estimated 100,000 children are reported missing each year. Initiative Vermisste Kinder

In India, an estimated 96,000 children go missing each year. Bachpan Bachao Andolan, Missing Children of India

In Jamaica, an estimated 1,984 children were reported missing in 2015. Jamaica's Office of Children's Registry

In Russia, an estimated 45,000 children were reported missing in 2015. Interview with Pavel Astakhov, MIA "Russia Today," April 4, 2016

In Spain, an estimated 20,000 children are reported missing every year. Spain Joins EU Hotline for Missing Children, September 22, 2010

In the United Kingdom, an estimated 112,853 children are reported missing every year. National Crime Agency, UK Missing Persons Bureau

In the United States, an estimated 460,000 children are reported missing every year. Federal Bureau of Investigation, National Crime Information Center

Source: From International Centre for Missing & Exploited Children (2020). .

Wrap-up

Children fall victim to a variety of crimes and situations, both domestically and internationally. Over the years, the U.S. juvenile justice system has developed processes, protections, and programs that focus on victims' rights and further support. State and federal interventions have created legislation that defines specific types of victimization against children, sentencing guidelines for those prosecuted, and involvement in the court process for those affected. Central registries and repositories have been created so that information on perpetrators and on child victims who have been abused, exploited, and/or reported missing can be quickly collected and disseminated to law enforcement and the public to better assist with investigations, apprehensions, and returning those children back to their homes. Public and private agencies and associated programs have also been developed to provide advocacy and services to child victims and their families, including restorative justice measures to compensate victims and help mitigate the effects of the crimes against them. Systems in the United States and around the world continue to evolve, and collaborative efforts continue to increase in an effort to better protect and support the victims of these often-devastating crimes.

Discussion Questions

1. How have child abuse and its associated laws changed in the United States over the past decades?

2. What function does the victim play during the court process and at its specific stages?

3. What specific acts have increased protections for victims and their rights?

4. What are some common characteristics of the statistical data presented in terms of demographics of victims and specific forms of victimization?

5. How do central repositories help collect, investigate, and disseminate information regarding child victimization, including for missing and exploited children?

6. What are the victimization trends and mitigation efforts in specific countries?

ONLINE RESOURCES

International Center for Missing & Exploited Children globalmissingkids.org
National Institute of Justice: Crime Solutions crimesolutions.gov
National Center for Missing & Exploited missingkids.org
National Center for Biotechnology Information ncbi.nlm.nih.gov
Office of Juvenile Justice and Delinquency Prevention ojjdp.gov
BJA BJA.gov
US Department of Justice: Office of Justice Programs ncjrs.gov
National Children's Alliance nationalchildrensalliance.org
National Juvenile Justice Network njjn.org
National Institute of Justice NIJ.gov
Youth Government youth.gov
Crime Solutions crimesolutions.gov
National Conference of State Legislatures ncsl.org
Childhelp National Child Abuse Hotline childhelp.org
Child Welfare Information Gateway childwelfare.gov

Definitions

AMBER Alert system—America's Missing: Broadcast Emergency Response alert system. It is run by coordinators in all 50 states and can instantly disseminate information and involve the entire community's assistance.

Central registries (child abuse and neglect)—a repository of confidential records of child abuse and neglect

Electronic bullying—bullying that occurs electronically, for example, via texting or on social media platforms

Group-oriented care—homes that typically supervise and provide care to larger groups of children placed away from their families

Individual family-oriented foster homes—homes that are more personalized (six or fewer children) and offer residential foster care

Institutional reporting law—mandates employees of mandated reporter agencies to report suspected abuse to their supervisor, who in turn will report it to law enforcement or Child Protective Services

Intake—an initial stage within the juvenile system where the intake officer will consider the victim's input to help determine if the case should be handled formally or diverted to an alternative program

Labor trafficking—the recruitment, harboring, transportation, or possession of an individual for labor or services through the use of force, fraud, or intimidation

Mandated reporters—individuals who are required by law to report suspected child abuse and neglect because of their profession or affiliation with a designated profession

Medical neglect—failure by a child's guardian to provide necessary health care, although they are able to do so

Megan's Law—Megan's Law expands on the Wetterling Act by requiring law enforcement entities to release to the public sex offender information that it deems necessary for public safety

Missing child—a person under 18 whose whereabouts are unknown by their parent or guardian for any length of time

Neglect or deprivation of necessities—failure by a guardian to provide care although they are able to do so, including not meeting a child's educational needs

Physical abuse—force that caused or could have caused physical injury

Psychological or emotional maltreatment—acts that can cause behavioral or mental disorders

Restitution—compensation to a victim for harm or for something that was stolen or damaged, in the form of money, acknowledgment of guilt, or community service

Restorative justice—focuses both on an acknowledgment by the offender of wrongdoing and an attempt to repair the harm to the victim and the community in the form of mediation and restitution

Secondary victimization—additional trauma experienced by the victim because of the stress, confusion, and anxiety of the court process and poor treatment sometimes received from the system

Sex trafficking—also considered a type of sexual abuse, it is the recruitment, harboring, transportation, or possession of a person for the purpose of commercial sexual activities

Sexual abuse—involving a child in sexual activity to provide sexual gratification through molestation, statutory rape, prostitution, pornography, or other types of sexual exploitation

Unaccompanied alien child/minor—a minor with no lawful immigration status in the United States; an individual under 18, with no legal guardian lawfully in the United States who can take care of them

Victim Compensation Fund—provides monetary compensation or other services to victims of crimes who have suffered a loss directly related to the offense

Victimization—trauma experienced by a victim in the form of property crimes and crimes against persons, such as sexual, physical, and emotional abuse and neglect, exploitation, trafficking, abduction, and other forms of violence and abuse

References

Administration for Children & Families. (2012, May 17). *Children's Justice Act.* U.S. Department of Health & Human Services. https://www.acf.hhs.gov/cb/resource/childrens-justice-act

Administration for Children & Families. (2020). *Report on sexual abuse and sexual harassment involving unaccompanied alien children: 2017.* U.S. Department of Health & Human Services. https://www.hhs.gov/programs/social-services/unaccompanied-alien-children/uac-sexual-abuse-report-2017/index.html

Australian Institute of Family Studies. (2019). *Reporting child abuse and neglect: Information for service providers.* https://aifs.gov.au/cfca/publications/cfca-resource-sheet/reporting-child-abuse-and-neglect

Australian Institute of Health and Welfare. (2020). *Child protection Australia 2018–19* (Child Welfare Series 72, Cat. CWS 74). https://www.aihw.gov.au/reports/child-protection/child-protection-australia-2018-19/contents/table-of-contents

Bourque, B., & Cronin, R. (1993). *Helping victims and witnesses in the juvenile justice system: A program handbook.* U.S. Department of Justice. https://www.ncjrs.gov/pdffiles1/ojjdp/210951.pdf

Brown, L., & Gallagher, K. (2014). Mandatory reporting of abuse: A historical perspective on the evolution of states' current mandatory reporting laws with a review of the laws in the Commonwealth of Pennsylvania, 59 Vill. L. Rev. Tolle Lege 37.

Brown III, L. G., & Gallagher, K. (2014). Mandatory reporting of abuse: A historical perspective on the evolution of states' current mandatory reporting laws with a review of the laws in the Commonwealth of Pennsylvania. Vill. L. Rev. Tolle Lege, 59, 37. https://digitalcommons.law.villanova.edu/vlr/vol59/iss6/5

Bundeskriminalamt. (2019). *PCS 2018—Police crime statistics report.* https://www.bka.de/SharedDocs/Downloads/EN/Publications/PoliceCrimeStatistics/2018/pks2018_englisch.html?nn=113788

Bureau of Justice Assistance. (2019). *Student, Teachers, and Officers Preventing (STOP) School Violence program.* U.S. Department of Justice.

Burstein, B., Agostino, H., & Greenfield, B. (2019). Suicidal attempts and ideation among children and adolescents in US emergency departments, 2007–2015. *JAMA Pediatrics,173*(6), 598–600. https://doi.org/10.1001/jamapediatrics.2019.0464

Canudas-Romo, V., & Aburto, J. M. (2019). Youth lost to homicides: Disparities in survival in Latin America and the Caribbean. *BMJ Global Health, 4*(2), e001275.

Centers for Disease Control and Prevention. (2020). *Leading causes of death reports, 1981–2018.* U.S. Department of Health & Human Services. https://webappa.cdc.gov/sasweb/ncipc/leadcause.html

Child Welfare Information Gateway. (2017). *Infant Safe Haven laws.* U.S. Department of Health & Human Services.

Child Welfare Information Gateway. (2019a). *About CAPTA: A legislative history.* U.S. Department of Health & Human Services. https://www.childwelfare.gov/pubs/factsheets/about/

Child Welfare Information Gateway. (2019b). *Definitions of child abuse and neglect.* U.S. Department of Health & Human Services.

Council on Foreign Relations. (2020). *U.S. detention of child migrants.* https://www.cfr.org/backgrounder/us-detention-child-migrants

Congressional Research Service. (2015). *Justice for Victims of Trafficking Act of 2015: Changes to domestic human trafficking policies.* https://www.everycrsreport.com/files/20151217_R44315_ddd4eda7fcf8c4049f13783859b736cf-8d9a47c3.pdf

Cregan, K. & Cuthbert, D. (2014). Global childhoods: Children as objects of national and global concern.

In *Global childhoods* (pp. 35–54). SAGE. https://doi.org/10.4135/9781473909656.n4

Daly, K. (2016). What is restorative justice? Fresh answers to a vexed question. *Victims & Offenders, 11*(1), 9–29.

Department of Justice Rule. (2016, July 8). Victim of Crime Act Victim Assistance Program, *Federal Register, 81*(131), Rules and Regulations, p. 44524.

de Ribera, O. S., Trajtenberg, N., Shenderovich, Y., & Murray, J. (2019). Correlates of youth violence in low- and middle-income countries: A meta-analysis. *Aggression and Violent Behavior, 49*, 101306.

Devries, K., Merrill, K. G., Knight, L., Bott, S., Guedes, A., Butron-Riveros, B., Hege, C., Petzold, M., Peterman, A., Cappa, C., Maxwell, L., Williams, A., Kishor, S., & Abrahams, N. (2019). Violence against children in Latin America and the Caribbean: What do available data reveal about prevalence and perpetrators? *Revista panamericana de salud publica = Pan American Journal of Public Health, 43*, e66. https://doi.org/10.26633/RPSP.2019.66

Emser, M., & van der Watt, M. (2019). #Stillnotfound: Missing children in South Africa. *Alternation, Interdisciplinary Journal for the Study of the Arts and Humanities in Southern Africa, 26*(1), 89–120. https://doi.org/10.29086/2519-5476/2019/v26n1a5

Federal Bureau of Investigation. (2019). *2018 Crime in the United States.* U.S. Department of Justice. https://ucr.fbi.gov/crime-in-the-u.s/2018/crime-in-the-u.s.-2018/home

Federal Bureau of Investigation. (2020a). *National Center for Injury Prevention and Control, WISQARS—Web-Based Injury Statistics Query and Reporting System.* https://www.cdc.gov/injury/wisqars

Federal Bureau of Investigation. (2020b). *2019 NCIC missing person and unidentified person statistics.* National Crime Information Center. https://www.fbi.gov/file-repository/2019-ncic-missing-person-and-unidentified-person-statistics.pdf/view

Fegert, J. M., & Stötzel, M. (2016). Child protection: A universal concern and a permanent challenge in the field of child and adolescent mental health. Child Adolesc Psychiatry Ment Health 10, 18. https://doi.org/10.1186/s13034-016-0106-

Fernandes-Alcantara, A. L. (2019). *The Missing and Exploited Children's (MEC) program: Background and policies.* Congressional Research Service. https://fas.org/sgp/crs/misc/RL34050.pdf

Finkelhor, D., Cross, T. P., & Cantor, E. N. (2005). The justice system for juvenile victims: A comprehensive model of case flow. *Trauma, Violence, & Abuse, 6*(2), 83–102. https://doi.org/10.1177/1524838005275090

International Centre for Missing & Exploited Children (2020). *Missing children's statistics.* https://globalmissingkids.org/awareness/missing-children-statistics/

Government of Canada. (2015). *Victims.* https://www.icmec.org/missing-children-statistics/

GovTrack. (2020a). *H.R. 324—103rd Congress: Jacob Wetterling Crimes Against Children Registration Act.* https://www.govtrack.us/congress/bills/103/hr324

GovTrack. (2020b). *S. 2961—115th Congress: Victims of Child Abuse Act Reauthorization Act of 2018.* https://www.govtrack.us/congress/bills/115/s2961

Guedes, A. (2019). *Violence against children in Latin America and the Caribbean: Data and action.* Pan American Health Organization/World Health Organization Regional Office for the America. https://www.paho.org/hq/index.php?option=com_docman&view=download&slug=violence-against-children-in-latin-america-and-the-caribbean-data-and-action&Itemid=270&lang=en

House Report 764. (2000). Child Abuse Prevention and Enforcement Act. U.S. Government Publishing Office. https://www.govinfo.gov/content/pkg/CRPT-106hrpt360/html/CRPT-106hrpt360.htm

Hillis, S., Mercy, J., Amobi, A., & Kress, H. (2016). Global prevalence of past-year violence against children: A systematic review and minimum estimates. *Pediatrics, 137*(3), e20154079. https://bja.ojp.gov/program/stop-school-violence-program/overview

Kempe. (2021, January 14). Innovating for 45 years. The Kemp Center for Prevention and Treatment of Child Abuse and Neglect. http://www.kempe.org/about/history/

Kempe, C. H., Silverman, F. N., Steele, B. F., Droegemueller, W., & Silver, H. K. (1962). The battered-child syndrome. Jama, 181(1), 17-24.

Kratcoski, P. C. (2017). The criminal justice system in transition: Assisting victims of crime. In *Correctional counseling and treatment* (pp. 31–50). Springer.

McCabe, K. A., & Murphy, D. G. (2016). *Child abuse: Today's issues.* CRC Press.

McCord, J., Widom, C. S., & Crowell, N. A. (2001). *Juvenile crime, juvenile justice. Panel on Juvenile Crime: Prevention, Treatment, and Control.* National Academies Press.

Miller, T. R. (2015). Projected outcomes of nurse–family partnership home visitation during 1996–2013, USA. *Prevention Science: The Official Journal of the Society for Prevention Research, 16*(6), 765–777. https://doi.org/10.1007/s11121-015-0572-9

Ministry of Children. (2019). *Reporting child abuse and neglect.* Ministry of Children, Community and Social Services. http://www.children.gov.on.ca/htdocs/english/childrensaid/reportingabuse/index.aspx

Morgan, R., & Oudekerk, B. A. (2019). *Criminal victimization, 2018.* U.S. Department of Justice. https://www.bjs.gov/index.cfm?ty=pbdetail&iid=6686

Musu, L., Zhang, A., Wang, K., Zhang, J., & Oudekerk, B. A. (2019). *Indicators of school crime and safety: 2018* (NCES 2019-047/NCJ 252571). National Center for Education Statistics.

Myers, J. (2008). A short history of child protection in America. *Family Law Quarterly, 42*(3), 449–463.

Myers, J. E. (2006). *Child protection in America: Past, present, and future.* Oxford University Press.

Myers, J. E. (2011). *The APSAC handbook on child maltreatment.* Sage.

National Academy of Sciences. (2014). *New directions in child abuse and neglect research.* National Center for Biotechnology Information https://www.ncbi.nlm.nih.gov/books/NBK195993/

National Center for Education Statistics. (2019). *Indicators of school crime and safety: 2018.* U.S. Department of Education. https://nces.ed.gov/pubsearch/pubsinfo.asp?pubid=2019047

National Center for Missing and Exploited Children. (2020). *Missing children statistics.* https://www.missingkids.org/footer/media/keyfacts

National Conference of State Legislatures. (2020). *Family First Prevention Services Act.* https://www.ncsl.org/research/human-services/family-first-prevention-services-act-ffpsa.aspx

National Institute of Mental Health. (2019). *Suicide.* U.S. Department of Health & Human Services. https://www.nimh.nih.gov/health/statistics/suicide.shtml

National Research Council. (2013). *Reforming juvenile justice: A developmental approach.* National Academies Press.

New York Society for the Prevention of Cruelty to Children. (2017). *History.*

Office for Victims of Crime. (2020). *Crime Victims Fund.* U.S. Department of Justice. https://www.ovc.gov/about/victimsfund.html

Office of Justice Programs. (2019). *About AMBER Alert.* U.S. Department of Justice. https://amberalert.ojp.gov/about

Office of Juvenile Justice and Delinquency Prevention. (2018, October 22). *Statistical briefing book.* U.S. Department of Justice. https://www.ojjdp.gov/ojstatbb/victims/qa02401.asp?qaDate=2016

Office of Juvenile Justice and Delinquency Prevention. (2019a). *Human trafficking resources.* U.S. Department of Justice. https://ojjdp.ojp.gov/programs/human-trafficking-resources

Office of Juvenile Justice and Delinquency Prevention. (2019b). *The Balanced and Restorative Justice Project.* U.S. Department of Justice. https://ojjdp.ojp.gov/sites/g/files/xyckuh176/files/pubs/implementing/intro.html

Office of Juvenile Justice and Delinquency Prevention. (2020a). *Internet Crimes Against Children Task Force Program.* U.S. Department of Justice. https://ojjdp.ojp.gov/programs/internet-crimes-against-children-task-force-program

Office of Juvenile Justice and Delinquency Prevention. (2020b). *Model programs guide.* U.S. Department of Justice. https://www.ojjdp.gov/MPG/Topic/Details/1

Office of Juvenile Justice and Delinquency Prevention. (2020c, February 28). *OJJDP statistical briefing book.* https://www.ojjdp.gov/ojstatbb/

Office of Juvenile Justice and Delinquency (2020d). *OJJDP Statistical Briefing Book.* Online. Available: https://www.ojjdp.gov/ojstatbb/victims/qa02109.asp?qaDate=2018. Released on February 28, 2020.

Palusci, V. J. (2017). Child protection and the development of child abuse pediatrics in New York City. *Journal of Forensic and Legal Medicine, 52,* 159–167.

Petersen, A. C., Joseph, J., Feit, M., & National Research Council. (2014). Child Abuse and Neglect Policy. New Directions in Child Abuse and Neglect Research. https://www.ncbi.nlm.nih.gov/books/NBK195985/ doi: 10.17226/18331

Posick, C. (2019). Restorative Justice. In The Encyclopedia of Women and Crime (eds F.P. Bernat and K. Frailing). https://doi.org/10.1002/9781118929803.ewac0437

Rasho, A. R., Guarnaccia, C., & Villerbu, L. (2019). The traumatic impact of socio-judicial procedures and risk of second victimization on sexually abused children. *International Journal of Psychoanalysis and Education, 11*(2), 14–26.

Rodgers, D., & Baird, A. (2015). Understanding gangs in contemporary Latin America. In S. H. Decker & D. C. Pyrooz (Eds.), *Handbook of gangs and gang responses* (pp. 478–502). John Wiley & Sons.

Sandberg K. (2018) Children's Right to Protection Under the CRC. In: Falch-Eriksen A., Backe-Hansen E. (eds) Human Rights in Child Protection. 15-38. Palgrave Macmillan, Cham. https://doi.org/10.1007/978-3-319-94800-3_2

South African Police Service. (2019). *Crime situation in Republic of South Africa twelve months April to March 2018_19.* 5. South African Police Service. https://www.saps.gov.za/services/april_to_march2018_19_presentation.pdf

State of California. (2019–2020). *AB-218 Damages: Childhood sexual assault: Statute of limitations.* https://leginfo.legislature.ca.gov/faces/billTextClient.xhtml?bill_id=201920200AB218

State of New York. (2019–2020). *AB-2683 Child Victims Act.* https://www.nysenate.gov/legislation/bills/2019/a2683

Strang, H., Sherman, L. W., Mayo-Wilson, E., Woods, D., & Ariel, B. (2013). Restorative justice conferencing (RJC) using face-to-face meetings of offenders and victims: Effects on offender recidivism and victim satisfaction. A systematic review. Campbell Systematic Reviews, 9(1), 1-59.

Stuart, D. (1975). Comment, Mandatory Reporting of Child Abuse in Nebraska, 8 CREIGHTON L. REV. 791, 793 (1975). https://dspace2.creighton.edu/xmlui/bitstream/handle/10504/38855/61_8CreightonLRev791%281974-1975%29.pdf?sequence=1&isAllowed=y

Swenson, C. C., & Schaeffer, C. M. (2019). Who's in the child's corner: Bringing family, community, and Child Protective Services together for the protection of children. *International Journal on Child Maltreatment: Research, Policy and Practice, 2*(3), 143–163.

United Nations (2021). Convention on the Rights of the Child. United Nations Human Rights: Office of the High Commissioner. https://www.ohchr.org/en/professionalinterest/pages/crc.aspx

U.S. Department of Health and Human Services. (2020). *Child maltreatment 2018.* U.S. Government Printing Office. https://www.acf.hhs.gov/cb/resource/child-maltreatment-2018

U.S. Department of Hopmeland Security (2002). *Homeland Security Act 2002, Public Law 107-296* https://www.dhs.gov/xlibrary/assets/hr_5005_enr.pdf

U.S. Department of Justice. (1994). *Violent Crime Control and Law Enforcement Act of 1994 Fact Sheet.* https://www.ncjrs.gov/txtfiles/billfs.txt

U.S. Department of Justice. (2016). *Project Safe Childhood.* https://www.justice.gov/psc

U.S. Department of Justice. (2018). *About crime in the U.S.* FBI: Criminal Justice Information Services Division.

U.S. Department of Justice. (2019). National Incident Based Reporting System. FBI: Criminal Justice Information Services Division. https://ucr.fbi.gov/nibrs/2018/tables/data-tables

U.S. Department of Justice. (2020) *Child abuse.* https://www.ncjrs.gov/childabuse/

U.S. Embassy Berlin. (2020). *Child abuse.* U.S. Embassy and Consulates in Germany. https://de.usembassy.gov/child-abuse/

UNICEF. (2019). *For every child, every right.* https://www.unicef.org/reports/convention-rights-child-crossroads-2019

United Nations Office on Drugs and Crime. (2019). *30 years on, the Convention on the Rights of the Child remains relevant and needed.* https://www.unodc.org/dohadeclaration/en/news/2019/11/30-years-on--the-convention-on-the-rights-of-the-child-remains-relevant-and-needed.html

Van der Watt, M. (2015). *Human trafficking in South Africa: An elusive statistical nightmare.* The Conversation. https://www.researchgate.net/publication/283711191_Human_trafficking_in_South_Africa_An_elusive_statistical_nightmare

Van der Watt, M. (2020). Child trafficking and children in South Africa's sex trade: Evidence, undercounting and obfuscations. *Child Abuse Research in South Africa, 21*(1), 58–82.

Wilson, D. B., Olaghere, A., & Kimbrell, C. S. (2017). *Effectiveness of restorative justice principles in juvenile justice: A meta-analysis.* U.S Department of Justice. https://www.ncjrs.gov/pdffiles1/ojjdp/grants/250872.pdf

Witt, A., Brown, R. C., Plener, P. L., Brähler, E., & Fegert, J. M. (2017). Child maltreatment in Germany: Prevalence rates in the general population. *Child and Adolescent Psychiatry and Mental Health, 11*(1), 47.

Witt, A., Glaesmer, H., Jud, A., Plener, P. L., Brähler, E., Brown, R. C., & Fegert, J. M. (2018). Trends in child maltreatment in Germany: Comparison of two representative population-based studies. *Child and Adolescent Psychiatry and Mental Health, 12*(1), 24–12. https://doi.org/10.1186/s13034-018-0232-5

World Health Organization. (2020.) *Violence against children.* World Health Organization. https://www.who.int/news-room/fact-sheets/detail/violence-against-children

The Police and Juveniles

Keywords

Children in need of supervision
Community oriented policing
Discretion
Enforcement
Juvenile Justice and Delinquency Prevention Act
Legalistic
Mere suspicion

Minors in need of supervision
Order maintenance
Pendleton Act
Petition
Person in need of supervision
Police-initiated contact
Probable cause
Progressive Era

Protective custody
Reasonable suspicion
Service
Status offenses
Watchman
Wickersham Commission
Youth-initiated contact

Introduction

Police agencies have had a prominent role within the juvenile justice system throughout history. Even before the creation of the juvenile court, juvenile delinquents had ongoing interactions with law enforcement. Those interactions left police officers with few options in terms of handling juvenile cases. Since the establishment of the juvenile court and other diversionary opportunities, the police department has had additional choices and more discretion in managing delinquent cases. Police roles have also expanded in terms of not only making arrests but also being involved in after-school activities and protecting victims. In this chapter, we will look at the interactions between the police and juveniles throughout history and their changing role throughout the eras of policing. We will also explore various styles of policing and priorities of modern-day police departments in the United States and around the world because they often serve as the primary contact for juveniles within the criminal justice system.

History of American Law Enforcement and Juveniles

American policing has undergone significant changes since its formal inception in the early 1800s, including with regard to the treatment of juveniles. As we read in Chapter 1, the control and punishment of children were handled primarily by families and surrounding communities in the 17th and 18th centuries. Law enforcement was informal, having adopted systems from England that included volunteers watching over communities and protecting them from outsiders (*Police*, 2017). Formal part-time police departments began to form in the early 1800s, but the first 24-hour municipal police force was not established until 1845 in New York. This first major era in policing was considered the political era, wherein officers served at the pleasure of the politicians as opposed to the communities they worked in. There were no qualifications to be hired or promoted other than the influence of an elected official, also known as cronyism. Consequently, juveniles were not a priority for police departments in terms of rehabilitation and diversions, as they have become in the early 21st century (Police, 2017; Potter, 2013

Before the creation of the juvenile justice system, officers had few choices when it came to the handling of juveniles: handle the situation informally by letting the youth go free (sometimes after applying a form of corporal punishment), passing them off with no formal intervention, or formally processing them as adults. There were no juvenile officers and no specialized units, and children were prosecuted similar to adults, with no special attention given (*Police*, 2017). In England in the 1800s, a member of the Cabinet, Home Secretary Sir Robert Peel, established the 1829 Metropolitan Police Act in an effort to professionalize policing and establish a more professional and organized force. Nine principles of policing were established, and Peel put forward the notion that "the police are the public and the public are the police" (*Principles of Good Policing*, 2015, p. 2). In essence, Peel believed that the police were part of the community, and their mission was not only to protect but also to serve. As we saw in Chapter 1, during the 1800s, the Industrial Revolution in the United States displaced families, and more juveniles were left to fend for themselves on the streets. Policymakers recognized not only the need for a more organized police force overall, as was done in England, but also the need to have specific personnel care for these destitute and delinquent children. In the mid-1800s, law enforcement agencies began hiring female employees known as matrons. The first known police matrons were hired in New York City in 1854. Police matrons had no law enforcement powers and were initially hired to guard female prisoners. Eventually, matrons were further tasked with clerical work, traffic summonses, and the care of abused and neglected children and delinquents.

A Path to the Professional Era

Akin to the movement in England and the principles set forth by Sir Robert Peel, the United States recognized the need to further professionalize their police departments and in 1883 passed the Civil Service Reform Act, also known as the **Pendleton Act** for Senator George H. Pendleton, its primary sponsor. It put forward specific requirements and qualifications to become government employees, including law enforcement officers. At the same time, the U.S. Civil Service Commission was created to assist with selecting government employees solely based on qualifications, such as passing a competitive qualifying entrance exam, instead of political favor.

Early Police Matrons left to right: Marie Owens, Lola Baldwin, Alice Stebbins Wells

Society as a whole was also recognizing the need for a formal juvenile justice system. As we read in Chapter 1, during the advent of the **Progressive Era**, a period of widespread political reform and social activism (Buenker et al., 1976; *Police*, 2017), many reformists advocated for creating the first juvenile court in 1899. Although a more formalized system to handle juveniles was spreading across the United States, corruption and inefficiency still plagued policing, without much more attention paid to children (*Police*, 2017).

Federal Intervention and the Police

Shortly after the establishment of the juvenile court in 1899, the federal government established the first U.S. Children's Bureau in 1912 through the Federal Juvenile Delinquency Act. It was the first federal agency, under the auspices of the U.S. Department of Health & Human Services, that focused on the welfare of children, their guardian, and appropriate treatment programs. The bureau still exists in the early 21st century and has expanded its role to include improving child abuse prevention, foster care, and adoption. However, the way police handled juvenile delinquency and crime overall did not improve during the Progressive Era and continued to be a subject of criticism during that period (*Police*, 2017).

Recognizing the widespread corruption and apparent ineffectiveness of the police to deal with rising crime, President Hoover formed the **Wickersham Commission** in 1929, officially known as the National Commission on Law Observance and Enforcement. It was composed of national leaders and researchers who were tasked with addressing police misconduct, inadequate police investigations, lack of professionalism, and crime in general, among other issues.

August Vollmer, known as the father of modern policing, served as the police chief in Berkeley, California, in 1909, and as president of the International Association of Chiefs of Police from 1921 to 1922. He was asked to contribute to the Wickersham report and wrote the police section in 1931, addressing the need to professionalize, improve investigations, and root out corruption. The findings, published in 1931 and 1932, revealed police brutality and misconduct of adults and children, widespread corruption, and lack of enforcement. Vollmer went on to author papers regarding the appropriate methods of handling juvenile delinquency, including increased and specialized training for juvenile officers (Kelling, 1987). The commission also asked Dr. Miriam Van Waters, who was president of the National Conference of Social Work and in charge of the juvenile delinquency section of the Harvard Crime Survey, to serve as a consultant and direct the juvenile delinquency division of the Wickersham Commission. She helped produce papers from studies of juvenile delinquency for the commission regarding the handling of juvenile delinquents under age 17.

In 1948, the Interdepartmental Committee on Children and Youth was established to promote federal interagency communication regarding children and youth. In 1950, the White House Conference on Children and Youth took place in an effort to strengthen juvenile courts and develop police services for juveniles, as well as prevention and treatment strategies. In 1961, the President's Committee on Juvenile Delinquency and Youth Crime was established and helped enact the Juvenile Delinquency and Youth Offenses Control Act the same year. The act helped develop innovative methods to control and prevent juvenile delinquency. In 1968, the Omnibus Crime Control and Safe Streets Act was passed to assist all levels of government with reducing crime through interagency coordination and enhancing the effectiveness and fairness among law enforcement and the criminal justice system as a whole. In 1971, the act was amended, authorizing grants and tasking law enforcement to develop programs related to the reduction of juvenile

August Vollmer

August Vollmer wanted juvenile officers to be educated on the causes of juvenile delinquency and develop programs to help keep juveniles out of trouble. Specialized youth units and bureaus could be found in most city agencies by the mid-1900s, and their primary focus was crime prevention.

August Vollmer

delinquency. In 1972, the Juvenile Delinquency Prevention Act was enacted as an extension of the Juvenile Delinquency Prevention and Control Act to provide grants for the development of delinquency prevention programs outside the juvenile justice system. In 1973, the Omnibus Crime Control and Safe Streets Act was amended to require each state to develop a specific juvenile delinquency strategy as part of their plan to improve law enforcement strategies and their criminal justice system overall.

Juvenile Justice and Delinquency Prevention Act of 1974

In 1974, the **Juvenile Justice and Delinquency Prevention Act** (JJDPA) was enacted. The act has undergone amendments throughout the years, as we learned in Chapters 1 and 4. The four core components of this act can also be applied to law enforcement's interactions with juveniles. These provisions are also known as *core protections*.

DEINSTITUTIONALIZATION OF STATUS OFFENDERS

The majority of contacts with youth by police are the result of **status offenses**—offenses that are age specific and solely apply to juveniles. These actions, such as truancy and running away, would not be considered an offense if committed by adults (Office of Juvenile Justice and Delinquency Prevention [OJJDP], 2018a). Law enforcement is encouraged by this provision to divert children from formal processing and instead seek out family support and other nonformal treatment that protects the juvenile from secure/locked detention. This can also take place on intake by the prosecuting attorney as opposed to filing a petition (see Chapter 8, "Juvenile Courts"). In the early 21st century, status offenses exist in all states, and many juveniles are still confined for such offenses (OJJDP, 2018a).

2018 UPDATE: DEINCARCERATION OF STATUS OFFENSES

On December 13, 2018, Congress passed H.R. 6964, which made changes to the four components of the JJDPA. One item was the deincarceration of status offenders: "Youth who were arrested for a status offense and have been later found in violation of a valid court order regarding that status offense, may now only be held in detention, for no longer than seven days, if the court finds that such detention is necessary." Previously, this period was set by a judge without restrictions (Coalition of Juvenile Justice, 2018, p.1).

ADULT JAIL AND LOCK-UP REMOVAL (JAIL REMOVAL)

Juvenile delinquents who are arrested for nonstatus offenses or detained by law enforcement for nonstatus offense investigations are not allowed to be detained in adult jails for more than 6 hours and never in the same place adults are being held. However, as we read in Chapter 4, this does not apply to juveniles who would be considered juvenile offenders/adult transfers by the individual state. It should also be noted that a juvenile is allowed to be held in a nonsecure area in excess of 6 hours solely for return to their parents. However, an amendment is being written to limit this additional time to 24 hours and require a transfer of custody to child welfare or social service agency after that limit expires.

SIGHT AND SOUND SEPARATION

In instances when status offenders are temporarily placed in an adult jail or lock-up, "sight and sound" contact with adults is prohibited. Children cannot be detained or confined next to adult cells or share any other space with adults. State and local police departments have also established their own guidelines for coming in contact with juveniles. Guided by this provision, children are separated from adults, not only within the precinct but also while in transport to and from the police facility and at other locations.

2018 UPDATE: SIGHT AND SOUND/JAIL REMOVAL

States are now required

> to ensure sight and sound separation and jail removal for Juvenile Offenders/
> Adult Transfers awaiting trial. This protection previously applied only to youth
> being held on juvenile court charges. An exception continues to exist for cases,
> where a court finds, after a hearing and in writing, that it is in the interest of
> justice. (JJDPA, 2018, p. 1)

DISPROPORTIONATE MINORITY CONTACT

As discussed in previous chapters, historically, youth of color have experienced harsher punishments (Campbell et al., 2018). The JJDPA mandates states to address disproportionate minority contact by gathering statistics and assessing the causes. Despite efforts, youth of color make up approximately one third of the youth population, but two thirds of children of color are within the juvenile justice system (National Coalition of State Legislatures, 2020). Studies still indicate that youth of color receive harsher sentences and are more likely to be incarcerated than other young people even when controlling for variances in the seriousness of crimes committed (Rauner, 2021; Robles-Ramamurthy & Watson, 2019).

2018 UPDATE: RACIAL AND ETHNIC DISPARITIES

This update changes the **disproportionate minority contact** requirement to focus on racial and ethnic disparities. It requires that "states collect and analyze data on racial and ethnic disparities and requires them to determine which points create [racial and ethnic disparities], and establish a plan to address [racial and ethnic disparities]" (JJDPA, 2018, p. 1).

States are monitored for compliance with these four core protections of the JJDPA and receive grant funds based on their level of compliance. Over the years, the act has been amended to provide a national program for juvenile delinquency prevention as it relates to law enforcement and criminal justice. The Act established the Office of Juvenile Justice and Delinquency Prevention, a national advisory committee, a federal coordinating council, and the National Institute for Juvenile Justice and Delinquency Prevention. It has made available "formula grants to States based on population under 18; and provided discretionary funds to support youth programs developed by public and private youth-serving agencies" (OJJDP, 2018a, p. 2).

In 2017, the OJJDP provided new guidance on the core requirements of the JJDPA with the goal to "promote the well-being of young people and limit their contact with the justice system" (U.S. Department of Justice, 2018, p. 9), published in the *Federal Register* on January 17, 2017.

Although many of these requirements are specific to confinement in jails and prisons, the requirements of keeping adults and children separate and deinstitutionalizing youth often begin with law enforcement. States additionally have their own model policies, which they have adopted from various sources, including the OJJDP.

THE JUVENILE JUSTICE AND DELINQUENCY PREVENTION ACT OF 1974

The Juvenile Justice and Delinquency Prevention Act of 1974 was created by an act of Congress. The act directed the U.S. Children's Bureau

> to investigate and report . . . on all matters pertaining to the welfare of children and child life among all classes of our people and shall especially investigate the questions of infant mortality, the birth rate, orphanage, juvenile courts, desertion, dangerous occupations, accidents, and diseases of children, employment, legislation affecting children in the several States and Territories.

The JJDPA was considered landmark legislation due to it being the first federally supported Act to broadly address juvenile justice and delinquency prevention (OJJDP, 2020).

Source: Office of Juvenile Justice and Delinquency Prevention and the Office of Justice Programs.

The OJJDP

The OJJDP is the agency charged with the responsibility for juvenile justice at the U.S. Department of Justice. They provide a guidance manual that aligns with the requirements of the JJDPA. This manual also offers additional guidance to states for monitoring the deinstitutionalization of status offenders, separation, and jail removal requirements of the act. »

Interactions Between Youth and Law Enforcement

Police officers are often considered the juvenile justice system's gatekeepers because of the large percentage of juveniles entering the system through interactions with law enforcement. In fact, 82% of delinquency referrals to juvenile courts were made by law enforcement (Hockenberry & Puzzanchera, 2020). Police agencies interact with juvenile issues in a variety of ways, ranging from sponsorship of midnight basketball games (as we will see later in the chapter) to the aggressive enforcement of curfew and truancy laws and other street encounters. As of 2019, approximately 700,000 arrests of juveniles were made by the police across the United States (Office of Justice Programs, 2020).

Contact between law enforcement and youth can be either youth initiated or police initiated. These contacts can occur through day-to-day interactions in schools or the larger community, in police-sponsored programs, or as part of police incidents as witnesses, subjects, or victims of crimes (Goodrich et al., 2014). Specific data on these interactions are varied and difficult to generalize because who qualifies as a juvenile varies from state to state and because data tools have limitations. Youth are defined differently based on the government agency collecting the data. For example, the Centers for Disease Control and Prevention defines a youth as an individual between the ages of 10 and 24 (Centers for Disease Control and Prevention, 2020); the FBI publishes the Uniform Crime Report arrest data, which defines youth as those ages 10 to 17; and the Bureau of Justice Statistics provides data for juveniles, which they define as being between the ages of 16 and 24 (Bureau of Justice Statistics (2017).

The OJJDP defines a **youth-initiated contact** as one that is initiated by youth, is considered voluntary, and usually involves a child reporting a crime or requesting police assistance for a noncriminal matter (OJJDP, 2018c). In 2015, the Bureau of Justice Statistics estimated that 27 million residents age 16 and older requested police assistance at least once (Davis et al., 2018). Of the total number of police requests for assistance, 10.9% were from individuals ages 16 to 24.. Police were contacted by these youth most commonly to report a crime/disturbance/suspicious activity, followed by reporting a noncriminal emergency.

Police-initiated contact is defined as "contact that is initiated by the police, usually involuntary, and involves a police officer stopping a youth on the street or a youth who is driving or riding in a car" (OJJDP, 2018c, p. 1). Over 80% of delinquency referrals to juvenile courts were made by law enforcement (Hockenberry & Puzzanchera, 2020). The Bureau of Justice Statistics estimated that 23% of police–youth contact occurs during traffic stops (Davis et al., 2018). Drivers ages 16 to 24 were most likely to be involved in a traffic stop and most likely to be warned or ticketed by law enforcement. With regard to stops on the street, 24.1% of young people ages 16 to 24 were involved in street stops during 2015, a larger percentage than any other age group (Davis et al., 2018; see Table 7.1 and Figures 7.1–7.4).

TABLE 7.1 Demographic characteristics of U.S. residents age 16 or older for whom the most recent contact was police-initiated, by type of contact, 2015

DEMOGRAPHIC CHARACTERISTIC	TOTAL	DRIVER DURING TRAFFIC STOP	PASSENGER DURING TRAFFIC STOP	STREET STOP	ARREST	OTHER
Total	100%	67.5%	17.6%	6.7%	1.9%	6.3%
Sex	100%					
Male	100%	70.5%	13.3%	7.7%	2.4%	6.1%
Female	100%	63.6	23.2	5.3	1.3	6.7
Race/Hispanic origin	100%					
White	100%	68.7%	16.7%	6.1%	1.6%	6.8%
Black	100%	64.5	19.3	9.1	2.6	4.4
Hispanic	100%	64.7	20.9	7.4	2.1	4.9
Other	100%	66.2	17.0	5.8	3.3	7.7
Age	100%					
16–17	100%	38.3%	40.4%	15.2%	1.9%	4
18–24	100%	60.3	25.2	8.9	2.3	3
25–44	100%	70.2	16.2	5.8	2.2	5
45–64	100%	72.5	12.0	5.7	1.6	8
65 or older	100%	67.9	15.2	4.8	0.7	11.5

Note: In 2019, law enforcement agencies in the U.S. made an estimated 696,620 arrests of persons under age 18 (OJJDP, 2020). Although contacts can result in arrests, they account for a small percentage of police and youth interactions. (BJS, 2018; OJJDP, 2019, 2020). From the early 2000s, overall juvenile arrest rates have decreased for both boys and girls for each of the major racial and ethnic groups. The number of juvenile arrests has dropped 58 percent between 2010 and 2019.
Source: OJJDP 2020

Police and Status Offenders

Law enforcement also processes noncriminal status offenses and child victim cases. Although officers are provided with substantial **discretion**—the ability to decide which laws to enforce in these cases—their actions usually are based on keeping the child safe, such as in cases of runaways and truants. This also provides a way to intervene with a wayward youth before delinquent acts are committed. The number of petitioned status offense cases involving detention fell by 79% between 2005 and 2018 (OJJDP, 2020; see Figure 7.4).

Between 2005 and 2018, law enforcement agencies were the primary source of total delinquency/status offense referrals for each year. In 2018, law enforcement referred 82% of all juvenile cases. However, there were variations across offense categories. Law enforcement agencies referred 90% of drug law violation cases, 92% of property offense cases, 88% of person offense cases, and 58% of public order offense cases in 2018 (Hockenberry & Puzzanchera, 2020).

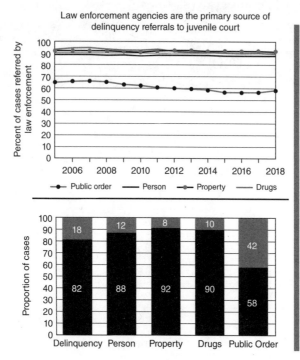

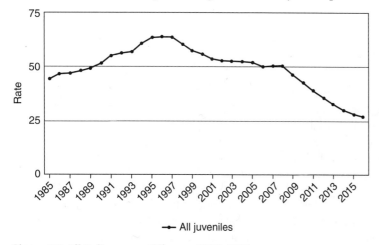

Figure 7.1 Status Offense Referrals

Source: OJJDP, 2020

The Other 18%

Status offense cases are also referred to court intake by a number of other sources, including school officials and relatives of the offender, parents, social service agencies, probation officers, and even victims. The court allows petitions for court processing/proceedings to be filed by other parties under certain circumstances. These petitions are termed slightly differently depending on the state. For example, some states use the terms **person in need of supervision** (PINS), **children in need of supervision** (CHINS), and **minors in need of supervision** (MINS). In essence, all follow a similar process and application. If a child under the age of 18 is beyond the control of their parents or other authoritative figures, is not attending school, or is a general behavioral problem, the law allows for a petition to be filed so that the matter can be handled formally through the juvenile court.

Police can also come in contact with youth for a variety of other reasons, including police involvement in schools, community-based prevention programs, victimization, and protective custody.

Figure 7.2 All Delinquency Offenses, 1985–2015

The total delinquency case rate increased gradually from 1985 through the late 1990s and then declined through 2018.

Source: OJJDP, 2020

TABLE 7.2 Estimated number of petitioned status offense cases, 2016				
MOST SERIOUS OFFENSE	**NUMBER OF CASES**	**2007-2016**	**2012-2016**	**2015-2016**
Total*	94,700	−47%	−23%	−4%
Runaway	8,000	−50%	−21%	1%
Truancy	54,100	−25%	−3%	−1%
Curfew	5,400	−69%	−56%	−23%
Ungovernable	8,600	−57%	−36%	−10%
Liquor law violations	11,400	−71%	−46%	−6%

* Includes other offenses not shown.

Note: Percent-change based on unrounded numbers.

• Status offenses are acts that are illegal only because the persons committing them are of juvenile status.

• The juvenile court caseload for petitioned status offenses declined 47% between 2007 and 2016.

• Truancy cases accounted for the majority (57%) of petitioned status offense cases disposed in 2016.

Protective Custody: Protecting Juveniles From Victimization

An officer can take a minor into police custody to protect them from possible harm, known as **protective custody**. This type of contact can be either youth initiated or police initiated.

Although youth victimization rates have been decreasing, juveniles are still more likely than adults to be victims. According to the National Incident-Based Reporting System, one in four victims of serious violent crimes is a juvenile. Youth are the victims in 64% of sexual assaults, 10% of robberies, and 15% of aggravated assaults (Hullenaar & Ruback (2020). NIBRS, 2018).

Youths may also come to the attention

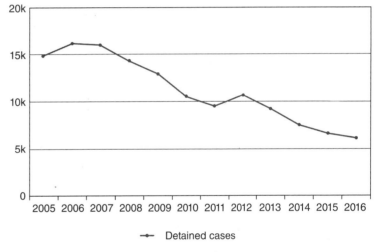

Figure 7.3 Detained Petitioned Status Offense Cases, 2005–2016

In 2018 there were 744,500 delinquency cases and 101,400 petitioned status offense cases (petitioned status offenses by category).

Source: OJJDP 2020

of law enforcement because they have witnessed domestic abuse or other violent acts. The National Survey of Children's Exposure to Violence, conducted most recently in 2014, found that about 24.5% of youths under age 18 reported witnessing violence, including 18.4% who witnessed assaults in the community and 8.4% who witnessed assaults in the family. The Coalition for Juvenile Justice and the International Association of Chiefs of Police (IACP) through the OJJDP Institute for Police Youth Engagement provide officer guidance for better responses to children exposed to violence and improved community relationships (OJJDP, 2018c). In 2017, the IACP established in 1893 and consisting of volunteer police chiefs across the country, released a toolkit for law enforcement agencies that focuses on police responses and behavior when interacting with children who were

Percentage of petitioned status
offense cases referred by law
enforcement:

Most serious

Offense	2005	2016
Total status	34%	21%
Runaway	36	46
Truancy	4	2
Curfew	96	97
Ungovernability	26	30
Liquor law	96	94

■ In 2016, law enforcement agencies
referred one-fifth (21%) of the petitioned status offense cases disposed
by juvenile courts.

■ Compared with 2005, law enforcement referred larger proportions of
runaway, curfew, and ungovernability
offense cases in 2016.

■ Schools referred 93% of the petitioned truancy cases in 2016.

■ Relatives referred 50% of the petitioned ungovernability cases in 2016.

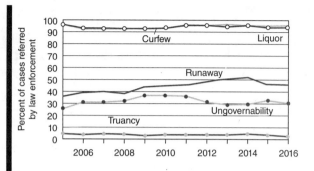

The source of referral in 2016 for petitioned status offense
cases varied with the nature of the offense

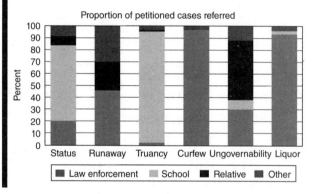

Figure 7.4 Percent of Juvenile Cases Referred by Law Enforcement and Sources of Referral

Source: OJJDP 2020

exposed to violence. It emphasizes just how vital police officers' interactions are with
youths who are victims (International Association of Chiefs of Police, 2017).

Positive interactions between the police and youth are essential in terms of not only
protecting a child victim but also influencing a delinquent child's future. Police behavior and how it affects police action have been studied not only in relation to the general
public but also with regard to how it further impacts juveniles.

Police Behavior: James Q. Wilson

James Q. Wilson is credited with contributing to the professional era and police behavior. Wilson was a political scientist and scholar who contributed to the professional
movement through his book *Police Administration* (Forst, 2013; Liederbach & Travis,
2008). Additionally, he authored *Varieties of Police Behavior: The Management of Law
and Order in Eight Communities.* (Wilson, 1970). In 1968, he observed patterns of behavior by officers. He concluded that officers generally operate within three operational
styles of policing: legalistic (law enforcement), watchman (order maintenance), and service (the combination of enforcement and order maintenance). Although his work was
conducted many years ago, Wilson's policing style typology is still used to characterize
police behavior in the early 21st century. It can be applied to their handling of juveniles,

specifically deterring and preventing youth crime. According to Wilson, the typology or combination thereof followed by the officer can explain their behavior. This includes the discretion to decide which laws to enforce when interacting with juvenile delinquents and finding an alternate means to handle a situation (Liederbach, & Travis, 2008).

Three Styles of Policing

James Q. Wilson, in *Varieties of Police Behavior*, identified the following three styles of policing.

SERVICE

The **service** style can include both enforcement and maintaining order, but focuses on a **community oriented policing** mentality—working with those within the community to solve problems. In terms of interacting with juveniles, officers using this policing style adopt the role of a surrogate parent seeking to prevent delinquency. These officers seek fewer arrests and lean more toward giving verbal warnings and returning juveniles home or to other services/social agencies.

WATCHMAN

The **watchman** style focuses on **order maintenance**, being less proactive and overlooking certain minor offenses while maintaining order. When interacting with juveniles, officers using this policing style utilize discretion and verbal warnings, but do not typically take the next step to become further involved or refer children to other agencies.

LEGALISTIC

The **legalistic** style focuses strictly on **enforcement**, exercising little discretion, and enforcing the law by writing tickets and making arrests. Community contact is formal. Officers using this policing style approach juvenile matters "by the book," with little or no discretion, enforcing the law with a focus on the crime at hand, without considering extralegal factors.

An officer may also utilize a combination of these styles depending on the situation and their particular assignment.

Incident and legal factors can guide police behavior with juveniles as well. Factors considered include the seriousness of the offense, evidence, whether the youth appears to be under the influence of alcohol or drugs, and whether the victim requests that the police make an arrest (T. T. Allen, 2005).

Legal Rights of Juveniles

As you will read in Chapter 8 ("Juvenile Courts"), the juvenile court system's goal is to rehabilitate youth, and proceedings are intended to be informal and nonadversarial. Because of this, many due process rights guaranteed to adults in criminal court were previously thought of as unnecessary in juvenile court. Many Supreme Court decisions later, however, most due process rights were eventually applied in juvenile proceedings, and many begin with a juvenile's first contact with the system, often at the hands of the police.

The basic purpose of the constitutional protection against unlawful searches and seizures is to "safeguard the privacy and security of each and every person against all arbitrary intrusions by government" (Supreme Court, 2018, p.8).. The **Fourth Amendment** to the Constitution protects against unlawful searches and seizures. It has been the focal point in many court cases involving police procedures and interactions with adults and youth. Interactions with children on the street and in schools, photographing, fingerprinting, and interrogating minors in precincts have all led to scrutiny in the courts and sometimes changes in policies. These changes have led to reinterpretations not only of the Fourth Amendment, but also of the Fifth Amendment self-incrimination clause, the Sixth Amendment right-to-counsel clause, and the Fourteenth Amendment due process clause (see Chapter 8, "Juvenile Courts").

As we have seen, the majority of interactions between law enforcement and youth are police initiated, and the majority of cases of juveniles entering the system are a result of these interactions. The upholding of due process rights by law enforcement, guaranteed by the Fourth Amendment, has been challenged in court as it pertains to individuals of all ages. One of the most famous cases that the Supreme Court heard regarding due process and the Fourth Amendment was *Terry v. Ohio*.

Street Encounters

In 1964, John Terry, along with two others, was observed by a plainclothes officer engaging in "suspicious activity," leading the officer to believe he was about to commit a crime. This was based on the time of night, the location, which was known for illicit activity, and the individuals' behavior. The officer stopped and frisked all of the individuals, explaining later for safety, and subsequently found concealed weapons on Terry and one of the other individuals. A frisk is a pat over clothing for safety, as opposed to a search, which is the process of going into the individual's clothing. The defense attorney argued that the officer did not have **probable cause**—a reasonable belief that a person has committed a crime, as stipulated in the Fourth Amendment. The case was eventually heard by the U.S. Supreme Court, which ruled that

> police may stop a person if they have a **reasonable suspicion** that the person
> has committed or is about to commit a crime, and may frisk the suspect
> for weapons, if they have reasonable suspicion that the suspect is armed
> and dangerous, without violating the Fourth Amendment prohibition on
> unreasonable searches and seizures. (*Terry v. Ohio*, 1967)

This case set a precedent for police procedures across the country when interacting with the public. What would become known as the Terry frisk and Terry stop were also applied to traffic stops. This prompted police departments to reexamine and create new internal policies regarding investigations of potential criminal activity. Other case law occurred across states, also challenging the rights of the police and citizens, for example, in New York, in the case of *People v. De Bour*.

On October 15, 1972, police officers on foot patrol noticed someone walking on the same side of the street in their direction. When the individual, later identified as Louis De Bour, was within 30 or 40 feet of the uniformed officers, he crossed the street. The two policemen approached him, and one asked what he was doing in the neighborhood. De Bour nervously told them he had just parked his car and was going to a friend's house. De Bour was asked for identification and stated he did not have any. One of the officers then noticed a bulge at his waist, under his jacket, and an officer asked him to unzip the coat, which exposed a handgun. De Bour was consequently arrested. De Bour's attorney tried to have the evidence suppressed, stating the police had no right to stop and frisk De Bour. The officers said they suspected him of being involved in narcotics and that he crossed the street to avoid apprehension. The motion to suppress was denied, and De Bour pled guilty to possession of a weapon. The case was then moved to the New York Court of Appeals, where it was determined that the officers had the right to ask pointed questions of De Bour and the right to have him unzip his jacket for their safety.

As we see with the Terry case, the U.S. Supreme Court discussed different contact/intrusion levels between police officers and the public and the necessary level of suspicion for a forcible stop and arrest (*Terry v. Ohio*, 1968). In the DeBour case, *People v. De Bour* (1976), the New York Court of Appeals presented additional levels of suspicion and the type of intrusion allowed by the officer at those corresponding levels. Courts at all levels in New York State currently follow the guidelines listed under "Four Levels of Intrusion," and other states have their own policies for law enforcement making contact with citizens of all ages. This is in addition to the stop, question, and frisk level of contact challenged in the Terry case.

Four Levels of Intrusion

The following four levels of intrusion emerged from the decision in *People v. De Bour*.

- First level: request for information (least intrusive)
  - Justification: any articulable reason to approach
  - The officer does not need to observe some kind of unusual behavior. At this level, they do not need to suspect criminality is afoot (at hand).
  - Restrictions: Cannot ask for consent to search for anything
  - Nonforcible (cannot forcibly stop an individual)
- Second level: common law inquiry
  - Justification—**mere suspicion** (founded suspicion that criminality is afoot)
  - At this level, a hunch or gut feeling that some kind of criminality is at hand is necessary.
  - Restrictions: can ask for consent, but nonforcible
- Third level—stop, question, and frisk* (forcible)
  - Justification: **reasonable suspicion** (criminality is afoot)
  - At this level, the officer needs more than a hunch or gut feeling. Must have reasonable suspicion that a crime (Felony or Penal Law Misdemeanor.) has been or is going to happen. When the case goes to court, the judge will decide if the officer was at this level.
  - Restrictions: Okay to forcibly stop. Must be in fear of physical injury in order to frisk.
- Fourth level: arrest
  - Justification—probable cause, also referred to as reasonable cause
  - At this level, the officer must have probable cause to believe a crime has been committed and that the person arrested committed it. Obviously, this is forcible. The probable cause standard falls under U.S. criminal law and the Fourth Amendment and is applicable to all states.

Please note - A lie or running away or other such action can raise the level of intrusion. A frisk may be permitted prior to Level 3 (reasonable suspicion) if the officer can articulate why they felt the individual might have had a weapon.

---

*Stop, question, and frisk is applicable to all states because of the Supreme Court ruling in *Terry v. Ohio*.

School Settings

In schools, students and their property (e.g., items located in their lockers/desks) can be searched based on reasonable suspicion, not probable cause, and therefore the warrant that would generally be required by the Fourth Amendment is not necessary. This type of ruling occurred in *New Jersey v. T.L.O.* (1985). A 14-year-old girl was caught smoking in the school's bathroom against school policy, and subsequently, her purse was searched by the school principal. Cigarettes were found in the girl's purse after the girl denied having smoked. The search revealed not only cigarettes, but also drugs and drug paraphernalia, and the student was charged accordingly as a juvenile. The case was appealed for violating her Fourth Amendment right against unreasonable searches. The case eventually made its way to the U.S. Supreme Court, which ruled the search was reasonable. The court ruled that "reasonable warrantless searches of students under their authority, notwithstanding the probable cause standard that would normally apply to searches under the Fourth Amendment, was permissible and not in violation of the 4th Amendment" (*New Jersey v. T.L.O.*, 1985, p. 1). The court put forward the notion of the balancing approach—balancing between the legitimate expectation of privacy of the individual, including the student, and the school's interest in preserving order and discipline. Because of this, "students in primary and secondary educational settings should not be afforded the same level of protection for search and seizures as adults and juveniles in non-school settings" (*New Jersey v. T.L.O.*, 1985, p. 1). Officers have also been assigned to schools as additional security, which has presented a gray area in terms of whether the officer is acting in a school official capacity or that of the police department and related restrictions.

Processing of Juvenile Delinquents

In the early 21st century, many police departments have separate divisions to process juveniles. However, the first interaction with youth is usually made by a patrol officer. States have created their own guidelines, in alignment with the core components of the JJDPA, to follow when processing juveniles, including the length of confinement and with whom they can be confined. For example, the sight and sound separated component of the JJDPA applies from the first contact with police. Juveniles and adults must be separated during transport to the police facility, confinement within the facility, transfer to juvenile court intake for further processing, and waiting for release to a parent or guardian.

Interrogation of Juveniles

In a landmark case, *In re Gault* (1967), the Supreme Court ruled that minors within the juvenile justice system are entitled to many of the same due process rights that were previously guaranteed only to those in adult criminal court (read more in Chapter 8, "Juvenile Courts"). In *Gault*, the Supreme Court made clear that juveniles were protected from self-incrimination and that they had a right to an attorney (*In re Gault*, 1967), however, it is not clear if juveniles, like adults, can waive these rights. States generally present testimony from an interrogated youth who has waived their rights if they determine the youth is able to understand their Miranda rights and the consequences of waiving them, regardless of their young age. Therefore, children as young as 10 years old (and sometimes younger) can be interrogated by police in some jurisdictions, and anything that is said can be used as evidence in a trial. As in the case of *In re Gault*, due process rights stemming from the Fifth Amendment were not always afforded to those within the juvenile court system. After 1967, however, many due process rights were guaranteed to juveniles, including the reading of their Miranda rights (see Chapter 8, "Juvenile Courts"). However, critics have expressed concerns regarding a youth's ability to understand those rights, the actual consequences of talking to police, and the ease of being manipulated into confessions (Sharf et al., 2017).

In 2010, the American Bar Association provided a resolution for municipalities, advising them to develop simpler language when reading Miranda rights to a juvenile. Although some states have passed legislation mandating edited versions, others have not changed how the rights are given (Laird, 2018). Some states, however, have developed measures to protect youths who are interrogated. For example, in New Mexico, confessions by youth under age 13 are generally inadmissible, and Wisconsin disallows any confessions by youth that were not recorded. Illinois requires an attorney to be present for children under 13. In California, starting in 2018 under Senate Bill 395, children 15 years old and younger must be provided an attorney before waiving their Miranda rights and being interrogated. The only exception is if the interrogation is in the interest of public safety.

The It was also found that almost 90% of juveniles waive their Miranda rights. In many cases, they did so not only without understanding the rights themselves but also without understanding the potential consequences of discussing the details of an incident without a parent or lawyer present (Laird, 2018).

In 2016, a petition was filed for the Supreme Court to review the case of *Joseph H. v. California. The high court was asked* to determine if a ten-year-old who was being interrogated in police custody could give a voluntary waiver of his rights against self-incrimination, without access to an unconflicted adult guardian nor an attorney (Juvenile Law Center, 2020). The Supreme Court denied this petition.

Modern Police Response

As mentioned earlier in the chapter, August Vollmer recommended that law enforcement develop programs and have specialized units dedicated to juveniles' care and processing. By the mid-1900s, following the advice or policy of Vollmer and private and government entities, most large police departments across the country had developed specialized juvenile officers and units. Smaller departments, in which entire units were not formed, generally created at least one "juvenile specialist" who was responsible for both reactive and proactive efforts regarding the community's youth. Following the trend of specialized officers and units dedicated to helping children, youth programs sponsored by police departments were being created, such as the Police Athletic League and other diversionary programs—some of which still exist in the early 21st century (see Chapter 10, "Interventions and Diversion"). Police athletic leagues were created to help build trust between the police and youth. Diversion programs attempt to divert youth from criminality by teaching responsibility and consequences and a better way to address issues that come up in their lives, no matter how challenging (Merenda, 2020). The creation and implementation of programs focused on youth has become the goal of many departments nationwide.

In May 2016, the U.S. Department of Justice's Office of Community Oriented Policing Services, in partnership with the International Association of Chiefs of Police and CNA (a nonprofit research and analysis organization), launched the Advancing 21st

Century Policing Initiative. This initiative provides evaluations and technical support to states and local law enforcement agencies regarding diverting youth from paths toward delinquency and forging relationships with communities. Modern police leaders have recommended moving toward "community-oriented policing" to bring the police back into the community (OJJDP, 2020; Sellers, 2015). Community oriented policing involves the community, both adults and youth, working together to build relationships and solve problems (Merenda et al., 2020; OJJDP, 2018c; Sellers, 2015).

Program Models Across Police Agencies

In addition to officers unofficially visiting schools to discuss gangs and drugs, formal programs were created (see the following list). One specific prevention program, Drug Abuse Resistance Education, also known as DARE, became especially popular across the country during the 1990s. Over the long term, this program has received criticism for being ineffective (Rosenbaum, 2007; Rosenbaum & Hanson, 1998). Therefore, departments stopped participating in the program or made efforts to reform it.

Police departments were also encouraged to form stronger relationships with communities to prevent crime and delinquency. In the late 1990s, under President Bill Clinton's administration, millions of dollars in funding went to school-based partnership grants. These grants supported partnerships between the police, schoolchildren, and the community to address violence in schools and relationships between law enforcement and youth.

The following are police department programs across states.

Partnership: The New Haven and Hartford, Connecticut, Police Departments created a board of "Young Adult Police Commissioners." They are chosen by their peers and ultimately appointed by the mayor. They meet regularly with the department to discuss youth issues.

Employment: Many cities run summer programs hosted by police departments in which youths work with officers in recreational, educational, and safety programs.

Problem-solving: In Seattle, Washington, a handbook entitled *RESPECT* was distributed to law enforcement and youth in the community regarding the issues of loitering and traffic stops.

After school: The Ft. Myers, Florida, Police Department created programs intended to reduce delinquency, address dropping out of school, and helping youths become better, law-abiding members of the community. The Jacksonville, Florida, Sheriff's Department initiated the "Youth Intervention Program." As part of the program, officers mentor youth ages 12–18. Other police departments have also created mentoring programs that assign officers to youth who are considered at risk.

Gang Resistance Education and Training: Also known as GREAT, this program was initiated in Phoenix, Arizona, in 1991 and adopted by the Boston Police Department and other departments across the country. It is generally taught to middle schoolers as an 8-week course by officers who focus on teamwork, leadership skills, and resolving conflict. The Federal Bureau of Alcohol, Tobacco, Firearms, and Explosives is a cosponsor.

Boston Community Centers: The Streetworkers Program has been ranked as one of the top three violence prevention programs in the United States. Officers and other members engage gang members in the streets and through home visits. The Streetworker's staff advocate for gang members in the courts (when appropriate), help the probation department with supervision, mediate disputes and gang truces, and refer gang members and their families to existing government and community programs. The New York City Police Department adopted a similar program, Operation Ceasefire. This program invites gang members to meetings with local law enforcement, representatives from the district attorney's office, and other stakeholders to offer youth services and communicate zero tolerance for firearm homicides.

Reaching Out to Chelsea Adolescents: Also known as ROCA, this youth center has the goal of building better relations with police in Chelsea and Revere, Massachusetts, through "street summits," whereby youth and police have discussions and attempt to solve issues directly.

Our Positive Posse: This is a teen empowering program established in Brockton, Massachusetts. It consists of youth organizers from housing developments in the city and sponsors workshops and events to reduce drug-related violence among youth. They work closely with the local police department, serving as a bridge between the police and local youth.

Success Through Academic and Recreational Support Program (also known as STARS): The city of Fort Myers, Florida, the school district of Lee County, the Fort Myers Police Department, and other agencies jointly provide resources and opportunities for at-risk youth from ages 8 to 14. Police officers refer juveniles who meet the criteria for the program, and there is ongoing follow-up regarding their progress.

See OJJDP (2018c, 2020) for additional information about these and other programs and their effects.

Worldview

*Policing Juveniles Around the World**

UNITED NATIONS

The United Nations established the Standard Minimum Rules for the Administration of Juvenile Justice in 1985, referred to as the Beijing Rules. In 1990, the Guidelines for the Prevention of Juvenile Delinquency, also known as the Riyadh Guidelines, were additionally adopted. These guidelines complement the Beijing Rules with the goal of a positive, proactive approach to preventing the rise of juvenile crime and the monitoring of its progress. These guidelines recommend that the rights of the child and overall discretion be considered in conjunction with individual laws. It further advocates that those who exercise discretion should be specially trained to do so "judiciously and in accordance with their functions and mandates" (United Nations General Assembly, 1990, p. 135).

*The following countries were chosen based on relevance to the chapter's content and available international data.

The importance of police professionalism in this context is emphasized by the 1989 Committee on the Rights of the Child, a treaty among nations that stipulates that "a comprehensive juvenile justice system requires both the establishment of specialized units within the police sector (among others) and specialist training for all those involved in the enforcement of juvenile justice" (p. 136). The Standard Minimum Rules stipulate that juveniles should be detained as a last resort and with specific care for the needs and vulnerabilities of young persons. It also encourages countries to increase their levels of protection to every child under the age of 18. Article 40 of the Committee on the Rights of the Child and the Beijing Rules emphasize "the need to respect the basic rights of any person deprived of freedom, to involve parents and guardians in the process, to detain juveniles separately from adults, and to promote the juveniles' overall well-being" (United Nations General Assembly, 1990, p. 135).

Nearly every nation signed these treaties; however, as we will see next, some countries have their own interpretations of how the specific guidelines of these treaties should be followed and ultimately carried out.

INDIA

India's Juvenile Justice Care and Protection of Children Act was revised in 2015, replacing the previous 2000 act, and was passed by India's parliament. However, its latest revision incurred protest regarding its provisions on child rights. Specifically, the act now allows juveniles "in conflict with Law" in the age group of 16–18, involved in heinous offenses, to be tried as adults. Previously, individuals in this age group were prosecuted as juveniles (Agarwal, 2018).

Juvenile Arrests by Police in India		
2014	**2015**	**2016**
38,455	33,433	35, 849

National Crime Records Bureau.(2016)

JUVENILE JUSTICE (CARE AND PROTECTION OF CHILDREN) ACT 2015

An Act to consolidate and amend the law relating to children alleged and found to be in conflict with law and children in need of care and protection by catering to their basic needs through proper care, protection, development, treatment, social re-integration, by adopting a child-friendly approach in the adjudication and disposal of matters in the best interest of children and for their rehabilitation through processes provided, and institutions and bodies established, hereinunder and for matters connected therewith or incidental thereto.

सत्यमेव जयते

AUSTRALIA

Each state and territory in Australia has its own youth justice legislation, policies, and police practices. Generally, however, how young people are charged and sentenced is similar across the country. As we read in Chapter 1, as in the United States, Australia has separate justice systems for young people and adults. The upper age limit for treatment under the youth system is 17, with some exceptions for those ages 18 and 19 in certain territories (Youth Justice in Australia, 2018).

Young people in Australia usually make contact with the youth justice system through interactions with the police, specifically through criminal police investigations. If a youth is arrested, police actions can be formal, in terms of charging youth and referring them to court, or informal, in terms of verbal or written warnings and referrals, such as for appropriate rehabilitative counseling. As a result, the courts may decide to dismiss a charge, transfer the youth to a specialty court, or send the juvenile to a program outside the court.

LATIN AMERICA

Rates of crime and violence in Latin America and the Caribbean region are ranked among the world's highest. Young people are the principal victims and perpetrators of violence in this region. The World Bank (2016) reports that the homicide rate in the region is 92 per 100,000 males aged 15 to 24, which is almost four times the regional average (see Figure 7.5).

Despite recommendations by the United Nations, countries around the world have set different minimum and maximum ages of criminal responsibility for children. In Latin America, a number of countries have lowered the criminal age of responsibility for police to make arrests (Mercurio et al., 2020) In 2011, Argentina proposed a reduction of the age, from 16 to 14, but it did not pass. Bolivia proposed and passed the lowering of age from 16 to 14 in 2014. In Brazil, an amendment to their constitution to lower the minimum age of criminal responsibility from 18 to 16 is being sought, and Mexico's juvenile justice system encompasses youth aged 12 to 18, with slight variations from state to state (Child Rights International Network, 2019; Mansur et al., 20194).

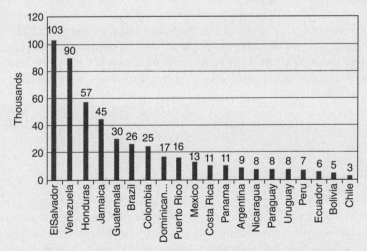

Figure 7.5 Homicide Rates in Latin American and the Caribbean, per 100,000 occupants, 2016

In 2018 there were 744,500 delinquency cases and 101, 400 petitioned status offense cases (petitioned status offenses by category).
Source: OJJDP 2020

A report commissioned by the United Nations Population Fund and the Peacebuilding Support Office found that in Colombia, the police apprehended on average 53 minors (ages 15–17) every day in 2016, several for petty theft and drug-related misdemeanors. In Mexico, a total of 16,885 adolescents were imprisoned in 2014, some 4,558 (27% of the total) for serious crimes (Muggah, 2018). According to this report, militarized police and the armed forces are also utilized to guarantee internal security.

In Bolivia, in a single night, up to 1,200 adolescents were arrested during a police raid as part of the public safety plan because they were consuming alcohol (Regional Juvenile Justice Observatory, 2014).

CANADA

The rate of youth charged by police decreased by 27% between 2012 and 2016 in Canada. As we read in Chapter 1, the Youth Criminal Justice Act, enacted in 2003, governs youth aged 12 to 17 years old involved with the Canadian justice system. The act "provides for a separate youth justice system based on the principle of diminished moral blameworthiness or culpability of youth" (M. Allen, 2018, p. 1). Youth are much more likely to be accused of a police-reported crime than people aged 25 years and older. A recent analysis for 2014 showed that rates of juveniles charged with a crime were more than twice as high as rates for individuals 25 years or older. However, until 2017, the police-reported youth crime rate has been on a downward trend, from its peak in 1991 (M. Allen, 2018). Older youth and male offenders comprise the majority of youth admissions.

In 2017, the Youth Crime Severity Index, which measures both the volume and the severity of crimes involving youth accused of committing violent and non-violent offenses (both charged and not charged), increased 3%. This was the first increase since 2007. Over half of the increase was the result of higher rates of youth accused of robbery (+13%) and homicide (+108%, from 24 to 50 homicides).

Restorative justice, focusing on youth rehabilitation through mediation with victims and the community (Wilson, 2018), is practiced across Canada, but its use varies greatly. For example, the Nova Scotia Restorative Justice Program began in 1999 and is one of the country's most extensive programs. Law enforcement can refer a youth aged 12 and older before charging them and now includes adult offenders. Additionally, a prosecutor can refer individuals after the person is charged and corrections officials can make a recommendation after the individual receives a sentence. Under the Youth Criminal Justice Act, the youth justice system, including police, additionally can refer young persons to community programs for "offending behavior" (Vaz & Baron, 2013).

Wrap-up

The role of the police as the primary contact with youth has experienced great change throughout history, from before the creation of the juvenile justice system, when police had limited options when interacting with destitute and delinquent youth, to the early 21st century, when offices have not only a variety of choices including diversionary alternatives, but also momentum to support the goal of rehabilitation. The role of the police has expanded regarding police behavior and interactions with youth, including the handling, arrest, and processing of juveniles, but not without controversy. Many law enforcement agencies in the United States and around the world have been working with private and government agencies to change their policies and implement training to improve their interactions with youth and communities overall.

Discussion Questions

1. What were the major eras leading up to modern-day policing?
2. Describe the changing role and mindset of the police when interacting with juveniles.
3. Describe the federal acts that led to changes in policing juveniles.
4. What are the main policing styles described by Wilson?
5. Describe the legal rights of juveniles and the influence of landmark cases.
6. List and explain the JJDPA core components.
7. Describe how police address the victimization of juveniles.
8. Explain discretion and how it is applied by law enforcement in terms of status offenses and referrals to diversionary programs.
9. How is the process of policing juveniles in the United States different from/similar to that of other countries around the world?

ONLINE RESOURCES

U.S. Department of Justice: Office of Justice Programs http://www.ncjrs.gov
National Partnership for Juvenile Services http://www.npjs.org
Youth Government http://www.youth.gov
Juvenile Justice Center of Philadelphia http://www.juvenilejustice.org
Bureau of Justice Statistics http://www.bjs.gov
The United States Department of Justice http://www.justice.gov
Coalition for Juvenile Justice http://www.juvjustice.org

Definitions

Children in need of supervision—a petition for children in need of supervision
Community oriented policing—the police and the community working together to solve problems
Discretion—the ability to decide which laws to enforce
Disproportionate Minority Contact—overrepresentation of minority youth in the Nation's juvenile justice system
Enforcement—enforcing the law by writing tickets and making arrests
Fourth Amendment—An amendment</related-object> to the Constitution that provides protections against unlawful searches and seizures.
Juvenile Justice Delinquency Prevention Act—provides funding and guidelines for states and the criminal justice system as a whole
Legalistic—a police style focusing on enforcement while exercising little discretion
Mere suspicion—founded suspicion that criminality is afoot
Minors in need of supervision—a petition for minors in need of supervision
Order maintenance—less proactive enforcement and overlooking of minor offenses

Pendleton Act—civil service act that created qualifications to become a government employee, including law enforcement
Petition—a legal document that includes details of an offense and can initiate the prosecution process
Person in need of supervision—a petition for persons in need of supervision
Police-initiated contact—initiated by the police, is usually involuntary and involves a police officer stopping a youth on the street or a juvenile who is driving or riding in a car
Probable cause—a reasonable belief that a person has committed a crime, as stipulated in the Fourth Amendment
Progressive Era—a period of widespread reform
Protective custody—the ability to take a minor into police custody to protect them from possible harm
Reasonable suspicion—a suspicion that a penal law misdemeanor or felony crime has been occurring or will occur
Service—a police style focusing on order maintenance
Status offenses—age-specific offenses solely applying to juveniles
Watchman—a police style focusing on both enforcement and order maintenance

Wickersham Commission—1929 National Commission on Law Observance and Enforcement to root out corruption and improve government operations, including law enforcement

Youth-initiated contact—considered voluntary and usually involves a youth reporting a crime or requesting police assistance for a noncriminal matter

References

Agarwal, D. (2018). Juvenile delinquency in India—Latest trends and entailing amendments in Juvenile Justice Act. People: International Journal of Social Sciences, 3(3), 1365-1383.

Allen, M. (2018). *Police-reported crime statistics in Canada, 2017.* Statistics Canada. https://www150.statcan.gc.ca/n1/pub/85-002-x/2018001/article/54974-eng.htm

Allen, T. T. (2005). Taking a juvenile into custody: Situational factors that influence police officers' decisions. *Journal of Sociology & Social Welfare, 32*(2), 121–129.

Buenker, J. D., Crunden, R. M., & Burnham, John C. (1976). Progressivism. Cambridge, Mass: Schenkman Pub. Co

Bureau of Justice Statistics (2017) FY 2017 BJS Visiting Fellows: Criminal Justice Statistics Programs. U.S. Department of Justice 2018 Office of Justice Programs Bureau of Justice Statistics. https://bjs.ojp.gov/sites/g/files/xyckuh236/files/media/document/fy2017bjsvfcjspsol.pdf

Campbell, N. A., Barnes, A. R., Mandalari, A., Onifade, E., Campbell, C. A., Anderson, V. R., . . . & Davidson, W. S. (2018). Disproportionate minority contact in the juvenile justice system: An investigation of ethnic disparity in program referral at disposition. Journal of ethnicity in criminal justice, 16(2), 77-98.

Centers for Disease Control and Prevention (2020). *Preventing youth violence.* National Center for Injury Prevention and Control, Division of Violence Prevention. https://www.cdc.gov/violenceprevention/pdf/yv/YV-factsheet_2020.pdf

Child Rights International Network (2019). Minimum ages of criminal responsibility in the Americas. Civil Rights International. https://archive.crin.org/en/home/ages/Americas.html

Coalition for Juvenile Justice (2018). *Summary of the Juvenile Justice Reform Act of 2018.* National Criminal Justice Association, https://www.juvjustice.org/sites/default/files/resource-files/Summary%20of%20the%20Juvenile%20Justice%20Reform%20Act%20of%202018.pdf

Davis, E., Whyde, A., & Langton, L. (2018). *Contacts between the police and the public 2015.* U.S. Department of Justice. https://www.bjs.gov/content/pub/pdf/cpp15.pdf

Forst, B. (2013). James Q. Wilson. In *Oxford bibliographies online data sets.* https://doi.org/10.1093/obo/9780195396607-0156

Goodrich, S.A., Anderson, S.A., and LaMotte, V. (2014). *Evaluation of a Program Designed to Promote Positive Police and Youth Interactions.* Journal of Juvenile Justice 3(2):55

Government of India Ministry of Women and Child Development, 2016. "The Juvenile Justice (Care and Protection of Children) Act, 2015," Working Papers id:10837, eSocialSciences.

Hockenberry, S., and Puzzanchera, C. (2020). *Juvenile Court Statistics 2018.* National Center for Juvenile Justice. https://ojjdp.ojp.gov/sites/g/files/xyckuh176/files/media/document/juvenile-court-statistics-2018.pdf

Hullenaar, K., and Ruback, B. R. (2020). Juvenile Violent Victimization, 1995–2018 U.S. Department of Justice, Office of Justice Programs. https://ojjdp.ojp.gov/juvenile-violent-victimization.pdf

In re Gault 387 U.S. 1 (1967).

International Association of Chiefs of Police (2017). *Police and Youth Engagement.* The International Association of Chiefs of Police. https://www.theiacp.org/projects/police-and-youth-engagement

Juvenile Law Center (2020) Joseph H. V California. Juvenile Law Center. https://jlc.org/cases/joseph-h-v-california-re-joseph-h

Kelling, G. L. (1987). Juveniles and police: The end of the nightstick. In *From children to citizens* (pp. 203–218). Springer.

Laird, L. (2018.). *Police routinely read juveniles their Miranda rights, but do kids really understand them?* http://www.abajournal.com/magazine/article/police_routinely_read_juveniles_their_miranda_rights_but_do_kids_really_understand

Liederbach, J., & Travis, L. F. (2008). Wilson redux. *Police Quarterly, 11*(4), 447–467. https://doi.org/10.1177/1098611108314567

Mansur, T. S., Rosa, E. M., & Trindade, Z. A. (2019). Review of Scientific Literature on the Age of Criminal Majority in Brazil. *Temas Em Psicologia, 27*(1), 113–126. https://doi.org/10.9788/tp2019.1-09

Mercurio, E., García-López, E., Morales-Quintero, L. A., Llamas, N. E., Marinaro, J. Á., & Muñoz, J. M. (2020). Adolescent brain development and progressive legal responsibility in the Latin American context. Frontiers in psychology, 11, 627.

Merenda, F. (2020). Adventure-based programming with at-risk youth: Impact upon self-confidence and school attachment. *Child & Youth Services.* https://doi.org/10.1080/0145935X.2020.1829465

Merenda, F., Ostrowski, S., & Merenda, F., II. (2020). Building blocks of resiliency. *Journal of Applied Juvenile Justice Services,* 112–130.

Muggah, R., Garzón, J. C., & Suárez, M. (2018). Mano Dura: the costs and benefits of repressive criminal justice for young people in Latin America. https://www.youth-4peace.info/system/files/2018-04/1.%20TP_Mano%20Dura_Rob%20Muggah.pdf

National Conference of State Legislatures (2020). *Racial and Ethnic Disparities in the Juvenile Justice System.* https://www.ncsl.org/research/civil-and-criminal-justice/racial-and-ethnic-disparities-in-the-juvenile-justice-system.aspx

http://www.defensapublica.org.ar/BancodeDatos/2014/2_trimestre/Segundo Informe Periódico2014.pdftPublications/CII/CII2016/pdfs/Table 5A.1.pdf

National Crime Records Bureau (2016). Crime in India: Statistics. National Crime Records Bureau Ministry of Home Affairs.NCRB (https://ncrb.gov.in/sites/default/files/Crime%20in%20India%20-%202016%20Complete%20PDF%20291117.pdf

New Jersey v. T.L.O. (1985). Oyez. Retrieved January 17, 2019, from https://www.oyez.org/cases/1983/83-712

Office of Juvenile Justice and Delinquency Prevention. (2018a). *Compliance with the core requirements of the Juvenile Justice and Delinquency Prevention Act.* U.S. Department of Justice. https://www.ojjdp.gov/compliance/index.html

Office of Juvenile Justice and Delinquency Prevention. (2018b). *Promising strategies to reduce gun violence.* U.S. Department of Justice. https://www.ojjdp.gov/pubs/gun_violence/contents.html

Office of Juvenile Justice and Delinquency Prevention. (2018c). *Enhancing law enforcement efforts and engagement with youth.* U.S. Department of Justice. https://www.ojjdp.gov/programs/law_enforcement_and_youth.html

Office of Juvenile Justice and Delinquency Prevention. (2020). *Model programs guide.* U.S. Department of Justice. https://ojjdp.ojp.gov/model-programs-guide/home

Office of Justice Programs (2020). *Statistical briefing book.* Office of Juvenile Justice and Delinquency Prevention, https://www.ojjdp.gov/ojstatbb/crime/qa05101.asp?qaDate=2019&text=yes

Law and Legal Reference Library (2017). *Police: Handling of juveniles—historical overview and organizational structure.* http://law.jrank.org/pages/1660/Police-Handling-Juveniles-Historical-overview-organizational-structure.html

People v. De Bour (1976)

Principles of good policing. (2015). Civitas. http://www.civitas.org.uk/research/crime/facts-comments/principles-of-good-policing/

Rauner, J. (2021). *Black disparities in youth incarceration.* https://www.sentencingproject.org/publications/black-disparities-youth-incarceration/The Sentencing Project.

Regional Juvenile Justice Observatory (2014). Monitoring report on juvenile justice systems in Latin America. NGO Panel on Children Deprived of Liberty. https://defenceforchildren.org/wp-content/uploads/2015/02/Monitoring-Report-Regional-Observatory_AS.pdf

Robles-Ramamurthy, B., & Watson, C. (2019). Examining racial disparities in juvenile justice. Journal of the American Academy of Psychiatry and the Law, *47*(1), 48-52.

Rosenbaum, D. P. (2007). Just say no to D.A.R.E. *Criminology & Public Policy, 6,* 815–824.

Rosenbaum, D. P., & Hanson, G. S. (1998). Assessing the effects of school-based drug education: a six-year multilevel analysis of project D.A.R.E. *Journal of Research in Crime and Delinquency, 35*(4), 381–412. https://doi.org/10.1177/0022427898035004002

Sellers, B. G. (2015). Community-based recovery and youth justice. *Criminal Justice and Behavior, 42*(1), 58–69.

Sharf, A. J., Rogers, R., & Williams, M. M. (2017). Reasoning your way out of Miranda rights: How juvenile detainees relinquish their fifth amendment protections. *Translational Issues in Psychological Science, 3*(2), 121–130.

Supreme Court (2018) *Carpenter v. United States.* United States Supreme Court 1-119. https://www.supremecourt.gov/opinions/17pdf/16-402_h315.pdf

Terry v. Ohio. (n.d.). Oyez. Retrieved January 14, 2019, from https://www.oyez.org/cases/1967/67

Terry v. Ohio, 392 U.S. 1(1968)

The World Bank (2016). *Urban violence: A challenge of epidemic proportions.* World Bank Group. https://www.worldbank.org/en/news/feature/2016/09/06/urban-violence-a-challenge-of-epidemic-proportions

United Nations General Assembly. (1990, December 14). Guidelines for the prevention of juvenile delinquency (the Riyadh guidelines). General Assembly Resolution 45/112.

U.S. Department of Justice. (2017). Juvenile Justice and Delinquency Prevention Act Formula Grant Program. *Federal Register.*

Vaz, E. & Baron, S. (2013). Juvenile delinquency. In *The Canadian encyclopedia.* https://www.thecanadianencyclopedia.ca/en/article/juvenile-delinquency

Weingartner, E., Weitz, A., Khashu, A., Hope, R., & Golden, M. (2002). A Study of the PINS System in New York City: Results and Implications. Vera Institute of Justice, March.

Wilson, D. B., Olaghere, A., & Kimbrell, C. S. (2018). Effectiveness of restorative justice principles in juvenile justice: A meta-analysis. Inter-university Consortium for Political and Social Research.

Wilson, J. Q. (1970) *Varieties of Police Behavior: The Management of Law and Order in Eight Communities.* Athenum Publishers.

Youth justice in Australia, 2016–17. (2018). Australian Institute of Health and Welfare. https://www.aihw.gov.au/getmedia/19707990-1719-4600-8fce-f0af9d61331c/aihw-juv-116.pdf.aspx?inline=true

Zedlewski, E. W. (2009). Conducting cost–benefit analyses in criminal justice evaluations: Do we dare? *European Journal on Criminal Policy and Research, 15*(4), 355–364.

Juvenile Courts

LEARNING OBJECTIVES

At the end of the chapter, students will be able to

describe the development of the juvenile court system in the 19th and 20th centuries,

explain the philosophical difference between the adult criminal justice system and the juvenile court system,

describe how due process was applied to the juvenile justice court and how and why this changed,

describe the purpose of the 1938 Juvenile Justice and Delinquency Prevention Act and its revisions passed by Congress,

describe the stages of the juvenile court,

compare and contrast the stages of the juvenile court system with the adult criminal court system, and

compare the juvenile justice court in the United States to other country's systems.

Keywords

Actus reus
Adjudication/fact-finding hearing
Beyond a reasonable doubt
Blended sentence
Child Savers
Concurrent jurisdiction
Delinquency petition
Detention hearing
Disposition hearing

Diversion
Due process
Expungement
Guardian ad litem
Initial hearing
Intake
Judicial waiver
Justice model
Legislative waivers

Mens rea
Parens patriae
Petition
Preponderance of the evidence
Prosecutorial waiver
Reverse waiver
Status offenses
Welfare model

Introduction

As we read in Chapter 1, the juvenile justice system is relatively young, with the first court established in 1899, and the system continues to evolve. Before the juvenile court's creation, prosecution for both children and adults could be identical. Although in the mid-19th century children could be sent to workhouses or some type of reformatory, even at that time and certainly prior, they could also be tried and punished as adults. Children were regarded as small adults and consequently could receive severe punishment, including being put to death. We saw a transition through the years, from families being the principal disciplinarians acting as judge and jury to the government stepping in during the 1800s under the umbrella of **parens patriae**. It was this doctrine that took ultimate authority away from the family and eventually put it in the hands of a separate specialized court. We begin this chapter with the original specialized juvenile court of 1899 and how it developed. We will then learn how it has evolved through landmark cases, policy shifts, and the overall changes in society's attitudes toward its youth.

The Development of the Juvenile Court

Throughout the 17th and 18th centuries, there were few differences in the way children and adults were handled in the criminal justice system, including within the courts. A 7-year-old child could be prosecuted and sentenced to death, just as an adult could be (Bedau, 1997). Early in history, families were also given substantial authority regarding the delivery of punishment to their children by the courts who sanctioned them. As we read in the first chapter, during the Puritan times of the 1600s, discipline could range from cutting off a child's hand to putting a child to death for disrespecting the authority of their parents and for delinquent acts against the community (American Bar Association, 2007).

The laws in the United States during the 1600s into the 1700s were influenced by English Common Law. In the 1760s, William Blackstone, an English lawyer, published Commentaries on the Laws of England (Blackstone, 1765). As part of those commentaries, he addressed two components that are generally necessary to commit a crime: that the individual has to have the will or intent to commit the crime, also known as a "guilty mind" (termed **mens rea** in Latin), and **actus reus**, meaning that the unlawful act needs to be committed. Blackstone addressed the first component by stating that individuals who could not fully understand their actions did not possess the "vicious will," the true intent to commit the crime, and were therefore incapable of committing a crime. He described this group as being composed of the mentally ill, infants, and young children who could not understand their actions. Therefore, individuals under 7 years of age could not be held accountable. However, those over 14, who were thought to be able to understand their crimes, could be tried and subjected to the same sanctions as adults. Children between 7 and 14 would be treated on a case-by-case basis depending on the court's belief that they understood what they had done and that they understood right from wrong; if this were the case, they would be punished the same as adults, with the same potential sanctions, including being put to death. In one section of the commentaries, he identified individuals whom he believed were incapable of committing a crime:

Malice Supplies the Age

The capacity of doing ill or contracting guilt, is not so much measured by years and days, as by the strength of the delinquent's understanding and judgment. For one lad of eleven years old may have as much cunning as another of fourteen, and in these cases, our maxim is that malitia supplet aetatem (malice supplies the age). Under seven years of age, indeed, an infant cannot be guilty of a felony; for then, a felonious discretion is almost an impossibility in nature: but at eight years old, he may be guilty of a felony. Also, under fourteen . . . if it appears to the court and jury that he . . . could discern between good and evil, he may be convicted and suffer death. Thus a girl of thirteen has been burnt for killing her mistress; and one boy of ten, and another of nine years old, who had killed their companions, have been sentenced to death, and he of ten years actually hanged because it appeared upon their trials, that the one hid himself and the other hid the body he had killed, which hiding manifested a consciousness of guilt and a discretion to discern between good and evil. (Blackstone,1837, p 334).

Throughout the Industrial Revolution, from the late 1700s into the 1800s, economic and social changes resulted in families becoming unstable and many juveniles becoming destitute. Supervision over juveniles began to shift toward government oversight and control. As we read in Chapter 1, social reformers created special facilities for both delinquents and neglected youth. Workhouses and reformatories were established and provided an alternative for courts, along with a new but often unfulfilled goal: to rehabilitate children. These environments were often criticized for their subpar conditions and poor results. Society, therefore, continued to call for a more appropriate method of handling its youth, and the government answered (also see Chapter 9, "Juvenile Corrections").

America's First Juvenile Court: 1899

The country's first juvenile court was created in Chicago, Illinois, in 1899, resulting from the efforts of multiple entities, including the Society of Pauperism and members of the Chicago Women's Club, also referred to as **Child Savers**, a progressive group primarily composed of women who advocated for specialized government intervention for society's youth. Through these efforts, the Illinois Juvenile Court Act of 1899 authorized a separate juvenile court. This court, strictly dedicated to society's youth between the ages of 7 and 15, could remand a child up to the age of 21 or until the child was "cured." It ruled with a distinct and primary goal of rehabilitation as opposed to punishment.

This new juvenile court would be unique from the adult criminal court. Proceedings would be civil and nonadversarial, with an intent to focus on the child, not the reason they were there. The court's rehabilitative nature and goal were based on a **welfare model**, where the focus was on the child's welfare and not the delinquent act committed. Since the court also heard noncriminal cases, such as those involving abuse and neglect, the model seemed appropriate at the time. This was the opposite of the **justice model**, which focused on accountability for the offense committed (Hudson, 1987).

The court was to act in "the best interests of the child." This was rooted in the parens patriae doctrine described previously and strictly defined as "parent of the country." It gave the individual state the ability to serve as the parent/guardian for juveniles who were neglected/abused or considered delinquent. This included, in some instances, the power to remove the child from their home.

The key provisions of the Illinois Juvenile Court Act of 1899 were as follows (Bonnie, 2013).:

1. Distinguish between criminal and noncriminal juveniles.
2. Develop informal procedures to handle juvenile cases.
3. Children and adults must be separated not only in court proceedings, but also in confinement.
4. Establish a system of probation to assist the courts.

The Illinois Juvenile Court opened on July 3, 1899, under Judge Richard Stanley Tuthill, the first juvenile court judge in the United States. Members of the Chicago Women's Club continued to work with the court to provide the backgrounds of the juveniles appearing before it. The notion of the government acting in the best interest of the child was to be the guiding principle of the court, along with the belief that children would be more receptive to rehabilitation than adults.

The first juvenile case was that of Henry Campbell, an 11-year-old boy charged with larceny. One day earlier, the boy would have been called a defendant and his case would have been heard in adult criminal court. Henry would have been held alongside adult criminals charged with a variety of serious crimes. But now, instead of being a defendant, the boy was considered a delinquent by the juvenile court. He could receive reduced sentencing options, including **diversion** from formal detention, a strategy that removes formal processing but upholds accountability, with the overarching goal of rehabilitation, not punishment. In this case, after conferring with the boy's parents, the judge agreed to have him live and be raised by his grandmother to be rehabilitated instead of being sent to formal detention.

Judge Tuthill said the following regarding his judicial philosophy: "Kindness and love for the children must be used in this work if we would hope to receive the benefits, which we should from this court, from which so much is expected" (Tanenhaus, 2004, p. 24).

ILLINOIS JUVENILE COURT ACT OF 1899

Authorized by the Illinois Juvenile Court Act of 1899, the juvenile court had jurisdiction over neglected, dependent, and delinquent children under the age of 16. The juvenile court was tasked to intervene with wayward youth but also to assist in protecting children who were abused, neglected, or abandoned. This system still exists in the early 21st century. It is important to note that during this time, children who were accused of committing violent crimes could be tried in adult criminal court, depending on the circumstances and the opinion of the judges involved in both courts. The act also provided for informality in procedures within the court. Specialized juvenile proceedings and specialized courts spread rapidly around the country, and by 1925 a juvenile court or section of a court dedicated to juvenile proceedings existed in every state except two (Schlossman, 1983). By 1945, there were juvenile courts in every state, all with the goal of rehabilitation. Although not as common, juveniles could be adjudicated at the federal level as well.

Federal Juvenile Delinquency Act of 1938: "The Act"

In 1938, the United States passed the Federal Juvenile Delinquency Act. Before 1938, legislation regarding the treatment of juveniles within the court system existed only at the state level. The Federal Juvenile Delinquency Act aligned with the state systems' goals regarding keeping juveniles separate from adults and children being sentenced to a maximum of 21 years of age. It also gave the attorney general power to decide if an individual would be prosecuted as a juvenile. The Federal Juvenile Delinquency Act was amended in 1948 and again in 1974. What would now be known as "the Act" was adopted by Congress with the purpose to "provide basic procedural rights for juveniles who came under federal jurisdiction and to bring federal procedure up to the standards set by various model acts, many state codes and court decisions" (Sessions, 1982, p. 509-510). The Act also stressed that only in severe cases would juveniles not be referred to and handled at the state and local levels (Bremner & Barnard, 1974). See the sidebar link to the U.S. Department of Justice's *Attorney's Manual*.

According to the Federal Juvenile Delinquency Act, an act of juvenile delinquency is "a violation of Federal law committed by a person before age 18, which would have been a crime if committed by an adult" (18 U.S.C. § 5031). As mentioned, juvenile proceedings in the federal system are limited, whereby prosecutors must establish that

- there is substantial federal interest,
- the state does not have jurisdiction or refuses to assume jurisdiction,
- the state with jurisdiction does not have adequate programs or services for juvenile offenders, and
- the offense charged is a violent felony, a drug trafficking or importation crime, or a firearm offense. (18 U.S.C. § 5032)

The federal government may also initiate juvenile proceedings when Native American tribal jurisdictions lack resources or jurisdiction or when there is a substantial federal

TABLE 8.1 Comparison of Adult and Juvenile Court Terms and Stages

ADULT	JUVENILE
Crime	Delinquent act
Arrest	Taken into custody
Compliant/indictment	Petition
Arraignment/pretrial conference	Initial hearing
Trial	Adjudication/fact-finding hearing
Acquitted/sentenced	Disposition
Jail	Detention
Parole	Aftercare

interest (18 U.S.C. § 1152 and 1153). Unlike individual states, the federal system does not have a separate juvenile justice court. Juveniles are adjudicated by a U.S. district court judge or magistrate in a confidential hearing with no jury. If found delinquent, a disposition hearing is held.

Although the federal government stressed the notion of basic procedural rights for juveniles, juvenile court hearings were informal, nonadversarial, and noncriminal. Offenses that would be considered a crime if an adult committed them were considered "delinquent acts" if they were instead committed by a child. Because of these differences, especially the noncriminal nature of the court proceedings, states believed that juveniles going through these proceedings did not need nor were they entitled to the **due process** rights otherwise constitutionally guaranteed (through the Bill of Rights) to adults in criminal proceedings. This included a right to an attorney, the right to cross-examine witnesses, and the right not to self-incriminate. In the years to come, this lack of due process was challenged in what became landmark cases, often rising all the way to the U.S. Supreme Court (see landmark case decisions affecting juvenile rights in Figure 8.1).

Informal Juvenile Proceedings: A Double-Edged Sword

Because the focus of juvenile proceedings was on informality and rehabilitation of the child rather than the criminality of the act, juveniles were not afforded many due process rights. Unfortunately, this sometimes resulted in youths receiving poorer treatment in the juvenile system, including much longer time in formal detention, than what an adult would receive for the same act.

Commonwealth v. Fisher, 1905

In *Commonwealth v. Fisher*, a juvenile was accused of larceny and was taken into the custody of the court and sent to a reformatory school for 7 years. The case was appealed to the superior court in Pennsylvania, stating that it was unconstitutional for Fisher to be taken into custody without formal due process and that his right to trial by jury was denied. The superior court made the following decision in 1905 regarding the constitutional rights of juveniles in juvenile court:

> The natural parent needs no process to temporarily deprive his child of its liberty by confining it in his own home, to save it and to shield it from the consequences of persistence in a career of waywardness, nor is the state, when compelled, as Parens Patriae, to take the place of the father for the same purpose, required to adopt any

process as a means of placing its hands upon the child to lead it into one of its courts. When the child gets there and the court, with the power to save it, determines its salvation, not its punishment, it is immaterial how it got there. (*Commonwealth v. Fisher*, 1905)

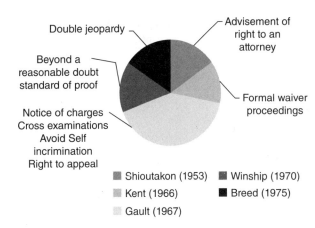

Figure 8.1 Cases Providing Additional Due Process Rights for Juveniles

In re Gault is indicated by a larger portion of the pie to exemplify a larger number of due process rights resulting from the case.

The court further explained that since juveniles are not accused or tried for crimes but instead taken into custody for delinquent acts, the constitutional rights of due process do not pertain to noncriminal cases. This ruling affirmed the court's role under parens patriae, wherein the state had the same unbridled rights over the child as their parents did, and therefore instituting due process in noncriminal cases was unnecessary. Over the next 60 years, the juvenile justice system's constitutionality generally went uncontested, with those cases that did allege unconstitutionality dismissed based on the *Fisher* ruling.

The 1950s–1960s Juvenile Court: For Better or Worse

"The worst of both worlds"—Abe Fortas, Supreme Court Justice (Kent v. United States, 1966)

Public concern grew in the 1950s and 1960s regarding the juvenile justice system's effectiveness and the disparities in treatment resulting from juvenile court judges' absolute discretion. Sometimes this opinion was not based on the crime, history, attitude, or receptiveness of the child, but instead on the "mood, temperate, or personal philosophy" of the judge (Ventrell, 1998, p. 1).

Criticism quickly ensued of the court's fairness and effectiveness, questioning features such as informal proceedings, discrimination (children who were brought before the court were primarily from low-income families, while affluent families stayed intact), and lack of due process (Ventrell, 1998). The courts had authority not only over youth who committed criminal acts, but also over those who were destitute and those who committed **status offenses**, acts considered illegal because of one's age, such as truancy and running away from home. The courts' ability to similarly detain and incarcerate all of these youth, without a formal trial or even a defense attorney, not only was reminiscent of prior proceedings associated with Houses of Refuge but also was now having the same ill-effects within the juvenile courts.

Restructuring of the Juvenile Justice System: The Cases

Shioutakon v. District of Columbia, 1956 (Ruled Upon)

On February 4, 1953, Thomas Edward Shioutakon, age 15, was taken into custody for using other people's vehicles without their permission or authority. He had committed these acts from the time he was 14. Shioutakon was not advised of his right to an attorney because the juvenile proceeding was not a criminal trial. Remember, it was the *Fisher* case that set this precedent. It was determined that since the juvenile court was civil in nature, there was no entitlement to constitutional rights that would otherwise be afforded to adults in criminal cases. The case's disposition was confinement to a training school until Shioutakon was 21, a 6-year sentence. After serving 3 years,

The Supreme Court of the United States

his case was appealed. Again, the issue of constitutional due process rights was raised, specifically that Shioutakon had not been advised of his right to a lawyer. Initially, this motion was denied. However, on appeal, the court decided that under certain circumstances, such as the potential confinement that existed in this case, a juvenile should be advised of their right to an attorney. The appeals court made it clear that they did not think that advisement of the right to an attorney impeded the spirit of the juvenile proceeding with regard to it being nonadversarial and noncriminal (*Shioutakon v. District of Columbia*, 1956).

KEY FACTS

- The juvenile was taken into custody for unauthorized use of a vehicle.
- He was sentenced to a training school for 6 years.
- An appeal was filed for being denied the constitutional right of being advised by an attorney.
- The higher court agreed, ruling that the juvenile proceeding's noncriminal spirit would not be jeopardized by the juvenile being advised of his right to an attorney.

Kent v. United States, 1966 (Ruled Upon)

In 1961, Morris Kent, who was 16 at the time of the alleged offense, was taken into custody in connection with robbery and rape. At the time, the District of Columbia's juvenile justice system defined a juvenile delinquent as an individual under 18. The case was transferred to adult court, where Kent was found guilty and sentenced to 30–90 years in prison. The case was appealed to the District of Columbia Court of Appeals because there was no due process regarding the transfer in terms of a formal investigation and attorney involvement. However, the appeals court agreed with the lower court's decision, even though the judge offered no reason for the transfer at the time.

The U.S. Supreme Court decided to review the case. This was the first juvenile case to be reviewed by the U.S. Supreme Court. In 1966, the court determined that before a juvenile case is waived to adult criminal court, there must be a formal investigation by the court, a waiver hearing, access to an attorney, and access to the juvenile's prior record, if one exists. Supreme court Justice Abe Fortas wrote, "There may be grounds for concern that the child receives the worst of both worlds: that he gets neither the protections accorded to adults nor the solicitous care and regenerative treatment postulated for children" (*Kent v. United States*, 1966). However, the Supreme Court did not rule further regarding whether other constitutional due process rights afforded to adults should now be guaranteed in juvenile court proceedings.

KEY FACTS

- The juvenile was taken into custody for a connection with a robbery and rape.
- The case was transferred to an adult court, with a sentence of 30–90 years in prison.
- An appeal was filed for transfer occurring with no due process.
- The U.S. Supreme Court agreed, ruling that before juvenile cases are transferred to adult court, there must be formal proceedings, including access to records and an attorney.

In re (in the matter of) Gault, 1967 (Ruled Upon)

On June 8, 1964, Gerald Gault, age 15, was taken into custody after his neighbor alleged Gault had made lewd prank phone calls to her residence. Gault was on probation in connection to prior petty theft, and his parents were not present when he was taken into custody. At the initial hearing, Gault's mother had still not been notified of the incident and was not present, the accuser was not present, and there were no formal statements about the facts of the case. Gerald was questioned about the telephone call, but there was no transcript of the questioning. Gault was sent back to the juvenile detention center and not released until June 12, 4 days after initially being placed in custody. At a second hearing, again the accusing neighbor was absent. There was no transcript and no attorney. The probation officer acted on behalf of Gault along with the judge. Gault's mother was present as the judge committed Gerald to Arizona's state industrial school until age 21, a 6-year sentence. Gerald was unable to appeal the sentence; Arizona only allowed appeals for adults in criminal court. The judge had legally and not criminally categorized Gerald as a delinquent child. It should be noted that if an adult committed the same offense during that time, in a criminal court, they would have been sentenced to no more than 2 months in jail or a $5 to $50 fine.

The Arizona Supreme Court held the lower court's decision, and the U.S. Supreme Court eventually reviewed the case. The constitutional question was, Were procedures used to convict and institutionalize Gault in violation of the due process clause of the 14th Amendment?

The Supreme Court, in a landmark decision, ruled that juvenile courts must protect the constitutional rights of juveniles and formal proceedings must be incorporated into the juvenile justice system, especially when there is a possibility of incarceration, to ensure equal protection of the law (U.S. Attorney's Manual, 1997). They further stated that to hold juveniles to harsher penalties than adults was a denial of constitutional safeguards. Therefore, based on their constitutional rights, youths were to be tried by many of the guarantees of the Bill of Rights made applicable to the states through the 14th Amendment. The court ruled that juveniles in juvenile court proceedings were to have the right to counsel, protection against the right against self-incrimination, a right to adequate notice of charges against them, and the right to confront and to cross-examine their accusers (*In re Gault*, 1967).

This landmark ruling, entitling juveniles to many of the same constitutional due process rights as adults, was believed to be the beginning of national reform in juvenile justice, increasing procedural formality and shifting the traditional focus from the whole child to the procedures to be followed based on the delinquent act (Bernard, & Kurlychek, 2010; Williams, 2017).

KEY FACTS

- The juvenile was taken into custody for making lewd phone calls.
- He was sentenced to an industrial school for 6 years.
- An appeal was filed for being denied due process.
- The higher court agreed, ruling that due process protections were necessary for juveniles to prevent harsher sentencing than even adults could receive. As a result, many due process rights afforded to adults through the constitution became applicable in juvenile proceedings. This included the right to counsel, no self-incrimination, a notice of charges, and the right to confront and cross-examine their accusers.

Please note that cases depicted with "v." (versus) generally denote the local, state, or federal government against a particular party. Those prefaced with "In re (the matter of)" generally refer to cases that may not have formal adverse parties or are uncontested. Although these depictions can be used in any court proceeding, remember that juvenile proceedings were not intended to be of an adversarial nature; instead, the state worked with the juvenile to find a resolution.

In re Winship, 1970 (Ruled Upon)

In 1969, Samuel Winship, age 12, was arrested for stealing $112 from a woman's pocketbook. Winship was charged and was found guilty based on the **preponderance of the evidence** (more likely than not to have committed the offense, basically a 51% certainty). Winship appealed the case, stating that the higher burden of proof, **beyond a reasonable doubt** (there is no other reasonable explanation for the crime; therefore, almost 100% certainty of knowing who committed the act is required), used in criminal cases should have been the standard used in his case. The appellate agreed with the lower court in its use of the lower burden of proof since juvenile proceedings are civil in nature. Current civil court proceedings use the preponderance of the evidence for their burden of proof.

The U.S. Supreme Court reviewed the case and found that when establishing guilt of criminal charges, the strict "reasonable doubt" standard must be applied to both adults and juveniles alike. The court noted that by establishing guilt based only on a "preponderance of the evidence," as is customary in civil cases, courts were "denying criminal defendants a fundamental constitutional safeguard against the possibility that their fate is incorrectly decided due to fact-finding errors" (*In re Winship*, 1970).

The court concluded that age differences among criminal defendants did not merit different burdens of proof when facing a "loss of liberty" as a possible sentence (*In re Winship*, n.d., p. 1).

KEY FACTS

- The juvenile was taken into custody for larceny (stealing money from a purse).
- He was found guilty based on the civil court's preponderance of the evidence burden of proof.
- An appeal was filed for the burden of proof to be raised to beyond a reasonable doubt, as it is in adult criminal court proceedings.
- The U.S. Supreme Court agreed, ruling that when establishing the guilt of criminal charges, the strict "beyond a reasonable doubt" standard must be applied to both adult and juvenile cases alike.

McKeiver v. Pennsylvania, 1971 (Ruled Upon)

Joseph McKeiver, age 16, was arrested for robbery and assault. The Philadelphia Juvenile Court denied requests for a jury trial, and the case was eventually consolidated with another juvenile case involving Edward Terry, age 15, for the same charges and denial. The cases were appealed, but the appellate court agreed with the lower court's denial.

These cases were then reviewed by the U.S. Supreme Court along with *In re Burrus* (consolidated cases of over 40 juveniles), which occurred in November and December 1968. These cases were mostly misdemeanors having to do with illegal protests against desegregation within school districts and school consolidation of multiple districts, both to obtain equal racial distribution within educational institutions. All of these cases were denied a request for a jury.

The court decided that there is no constitutional right to a jury trial for juveniles. According to the Supreme Court, the Sixth Amendment right to a jury trial clause is only meant to be applied to criminal court cases (see the '6ᵗʰ Amendment at the end of the section). Additionally, the court determined that a jury trial could jeopardize the nonadversarial proceeding of a juvenile case and its confidentiality. Reference to *Kent* and *Gault* was made to explain the court's ruling. The required aspects of due process in *Gault*, such as cross-examination and right to counsel, fulfilled the constitutional right for fact-finding and did not require a jury to accomplish: "as such, there is no requirement for a jury trial in juvenile cases" (*McKeiver v. Pennsylvania*, 1971).

This ruling is still upheld in the early 21st century; however, in some U.S. states and territories, such as New Hampshire, Kansas, and American Samoa, courts do permit jury trials in juvenile cases (Russo, 2017).

KEY FACTS

- The juvenile was taken into custody for robbery and assault.
- An appeal was filed for being denied a jury trial and was reviewed with other similar juvenile cases where a jury trial was denied.
- The U.S. Supreme Court disagreed, ruling that there is no constitutional right for a jury trial and that the right to fact-finding can be accomplished by other due process means such as cross-examination and right to counsel, which are already permitted in juvenile proceedings.

Breed v. Jones, 1975 (Ruled Upon)

Gary Jones, age 17, was taken into custody for robbery and was tried as a juvenile. The juvenile court ruled that he had committed the act and that he should be tried as an adult for the crime of robbery because of the court's belief that he was not suitable for treatment as a juvenile. The case was transferred to criminal court, where he was retried and found guilty. Jones appealed, stating that this was double jeopardy and unconstitutional. The U.S. Court of Appeals agreed with Jones, concluding that upholding the guilty verdict would reduce confidence in the judicial system. The U.S. Supreme Court also reviewed the constitutionally of the case, ruling unanimously that, in fact, this was double jeopardy and that decisions of waiving a case to criminal court should be made before adjudication (*Breed v. Jones*, 1975).

KEY FACTS

- The juvenile was taken into custody for robbery.
- The juvenile was tried in both juvenile and adult court for the same charge and was found to have committed the act by both the juvenile and the criminal court.
- An appeal was filed for violation of double jeopardy due process protection.
- The U.S. Supreme Court agreed with the U.S. Court of Appeals, ruling that decisions of waiving a case to criminal court should be made before adjudication.

Schall v. Martin, 1984 (Ruled Upon)

In 1977, 14-year-old Gregory Martin was arrested for robbery, assault, and criminal possession of a weapon. He was detained after a fact-finding hearing (see juvenile court stages later in the chapter) until trial, which is permitted under the New York Family

Court Act. Martin was held in pretrial detention, which he appealed as being equal to punishment before being found guilty. Other cases with similar consequences joined against then-Commissioner Schall of the New York City Department of Juvenile Justice.

The U.S. District Court for the Southern District of New York found, and the U.S. Court of Appeals for the Second Circuit affirmed, that the detention was a violation and unconstitutional. However, the U.S. Supreme Court, on review, ruled that the pretrial detention of juveniles does not violate the right of due process. They ruled that pretrial detention in certain cases can reduce potential harm to the community or the youths themselves (*Schall v. Martin*, 1984).

KEY FACTS

- The juvenile was taken into custody for robbery.
- The juvenile was placed in pretrial detention before being found guilty.
- An appeal was filed for being "punished" by being put in pretrial detention before being found guilty. Other similar juvenile cases were also appealed and reviewed.
- The U.S. Supreme Court ruled that the pretrial detention of juveniles does not violate the right of due process. This type of detention can serve the legitimate purpose of protecting the state and the juvenile.

14TH AMENDMENT SECTION I

No state shall make or enforce any law which shall abridge the privileges or immunities of citizens of the United States; nor shall any state deprive any person of life, liberty, or property, without due process of law; nor deny to any person within its jurisdiction the equal protection of the laws.

The Constitution of the United States

6TH AMENDMENT

> In all criminal prosecutions, the accused shall enjoy the right to a speedy and public trial, by an impartial jury of the state and district wherein the crime shall have been committed, which district shall have been previously ascertained by law, and to be informed of the nature and cause of the accusation; to be confronted with the witnesses against him; to have compulsory process for obtaining witnesses in his favor, and to have the assistance of counsel for his defense.

The Juvenile Court Process

As we have read, each state has its own juvenile justice system with its own laws and guidelines. However, all juvenile systems generally have four main stages: intake, petition, adjudication, and disposition hearing. It is also important to keep in mind that within the juvenile justice system, victims are often part of the process, especially when it comes to diversion from formal processing and restorative justice, as discussed in Chapter 10.

Although many individuals are involved with the juvenile justice court process and the main parties' roles can vary by state, there are generally four main players: the intake officer/law department representative, the prosecuting attorney, the attorney for the child, and the juvenile court judge. Some states also have courts that appoint what is sometimes termed a **guardian ad litem**, an individual in addition to the youth's attorney, who has input along with other parties such as representatives from probation, to make recommendations for sanctions. They are usually appointed for children in abuse and neglect cases (as discussed in Chapter 6) and sometimes for youth in juvenile delinquency cases who are not competent to stand trial. We will see the roles of individuals involved in the court process as we go through the stages in the following paragraphs.

The juvenile court system includes specific stages, from when the juvenile is taken into custody to adjudication and disposition (see Figure 8.2).

Entering the Juvenile Court System

In 2019, there were 722,600 delinquency cases and 90,500 petitioned status offense cases handled by U.S. courts with juvenile jurisdiction. Most juvenile court cases are referred by law enforcement. Law enforcement referrals accounted for 82% of

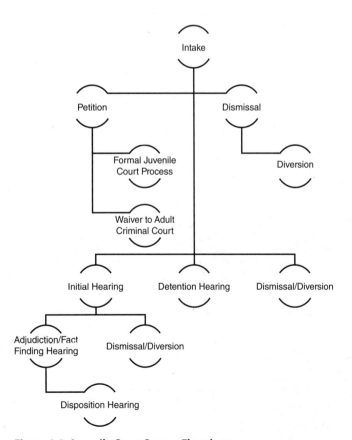

Figure 8.2 Juvenile Court System Flowchart

all delinquency cases referred to juvenile court in 2019 (Office of Juvenile Justice and Delinquency Prevention, 2021). The remaining referrals were made by others, such as parents, victims, schools, and probation officers, through **petitions**, a legal document describing what offenses the respondent is alleged to have committed.

The Stages

Intake

After the initial contact, a juvenile may continue to the first stage of the juvenile justice system, **intake**. Although states differ with regard to who performs intake, generally, it is performed by a designated intake officer within the juvenile probation department or the prosecutor's office. Unlike in the criminal justice system, a juvenile who ends up in intake will not necessarily go through the juvenile court's formal process and may not ever see a juvenile court judge. The intake officer can decide either to dismiss the case or to have the matter handled through some type of juvenile court diversion, such as probation or restitution, mediation, community service, or Teen Court (also see Chapter 10). The intake officer can also request formal intervention by the juvenile court. The victim of the offense, if one exists, can be part of this process, although to what extent depends on the state. If the law department is not involved in this process, the case is sometimes then referred to them to review the matter further. If deemed necessary, they will interview the parties involved, including who made the referral (usually the police officer). If there is a separate review by the law department, they have the same options as the intake officer.

Petition

If the decision is to formally handle the case through the court, typically two types of petitions may be filed: a petition for delinquency or a petition for a waiver to adult court. A **delinquency petition** includes the offense's details and makes a request that the cases be processed in juvenile court. A petition for waiver consists of the details of the offense and requests/justifies that the case be processed in adult court. This will be decided by a judge and ultimately carried out through a **judicial waiver**, the mechanism by which a juvenile court judge may transfer a juvenile offender to criminal court jurisdiction. In some states, the prosecutor can also file a petition, sometimes known as a **prosecutorial waiver**, to transfer the case to adult court (a judicial waiver would not be needed in this situation). In these instances, the prosecutor may file a petition to have the case adjudicated in either juvenile or criminal court based on the case's specific circumstances. This can include the type of crime, the offender's age when the crime was committed, and criminal history. The prosecutorial waiver can result in the minor being found either "delinquent" in juvenile court or guilty of a "crime" in criminal court. This kind of discretion by the prosecutor occurs through **concurrent jurisdiction**, whereby both juvenile and criminal court can have jurisdiction. At the end of 2016, 14 states, including the District of Columbia, had some kind of prosecutor discretion provision through concurrent jurisdiction.

There are also mandatory statutes called **legislative waivers** (sometimes called direct waivers), whereby states require automatic processing in criminal court based on the juvenile's age and type of crime. In some states, however, a youth can petition the criminal court to waive their case back to juvenile court, termed a **reverse waiver**. As of 2016, half of all U.S. states have reverse waiver laws in place (Thomas, 2017).

> ### RECAP OF THE ABOVE TERMS
>
> **Concurrent jurisdiction**—the ability to exercise judicial review by different courts (juvenile/criminal) at the same time
>
> **Delinquency petition**—a petition filed by the prosecuting attorney in cases where a minor (determined by the state) commits a delinquent act
>
> **Judicial waiver**—the mechanism by which a juvenile court judge may transfer a juvenile offender to criminal court jurisdiction
>
> **Legislative waiver**—requires automatic initial processing in criminal court based on a combination of the juvenile's age and type of crime
>
> **Prosecutorial waiver**—a statutory mechanism that provides a prosecutor with exclusive court discretion through concurrent jurisdiction
>
> **Reverse waiver**—statutes that allow a juvenile case that is to be prosecuted in criminal court to be transferred to juvenile court for processing, adjudication, or disposition

EXAMPLE OF JUVENILE PROCESSING

A 14-year-old is involved in a robbery. The police arrest the juvenile, and a formal proceeding is decided upon at intake and petitioned via the law department. Because of the juvenile's crime and age, there is concurrent jurisdiction between juvenile court and criminal court. The state can allow, via the prosecutor's filing of a delinquency petition, for the case to be processed through juvenile court. However, the prosecutor can also advocate, because of the case's circumstances, the child's record, and other relevant factors, that the case be prosecuted in criminal court. The prosecutor can then file a petition for a waiver to adult criminal court. A waiver hearing is held in front of the judge, who has the ultimate authority to send the case to criminal court through a *judicial waiver*. Some states will also allow what is called a *prosecutorial waiver*, which provides a prosecutor with exclusive discretion when concurrent jurisdiction exists. Under these circumstances, the prosecutor has the liberty to decide for themselves where to file the case and have it tried. While prosecutorial decisions are subject to review, the decisions are rarely reversed, therefore providing authority to the prosecutor. Finally, some states have passed a *legislative waiver*. Thirty-seven states and the District of Columbia have this type of waiver, whereby even if the juvenile meets the age range for juvenile court jurisdiction, because of the seriousness of the crime, the case will automatically be tried in adult criminal court. For example, in New York, if a 15-year-old boy commits murder, his case will go directly to criminal court. Remember, the case can be sent back to juvenile court in some states through a *reverse waiver* when deemed appropriate.

Initial Hearing

The **initial hearing** is the first appearance before the court. The court may assign a lawyer for the child at this point if the youth does not have one already and will also advise the child and their guardians of the charges and their rights. The child or the attorney for the child will enter a plea at this stage.

The child may already have had a detention hearing; if not, a **detention hearing** can take place regarding holding the child in formal custody or other placement, such as shelter care, until the adjudication hearing or allowing them to be released until the adjudication/fact-finding hearing (considered the trial in criminal court). The court may also impose other restrictions if the child is sent home, such as electronic monitoring and curfews. This determination is based on many factors, including the safety of the child and the safety of the community. It is important to note, as with every stage in the juvenile process, that the judge can dismiss the case or divert it to a nonformal rehabilitative process if deemed appropriate and in the best interests of the child (see Chapter 10, "Interventions and Diversions," and Chapter 9, "Juvenile Corrections"). If the child admits to the act, the case will proceed to disposition. Otherwise, it may proceed to the adjudication/fact-finding stage.

Adjudication/Fact-Finding Hearing

As we saw earlier in the chapter, juvenile trials require the same burden of proof, beyond a reasonable doubt, as adult criminal trials (*In re Winship*, 1970). During adjudication (the trial state in criminal court), the facts of the case are presented, along with any evidence and witness/character testimony, much like a trial in an adult criminal case. The prosecuting attorney presents evidence and must prove allegations stipulated by the delinquency petition beyond a reasonable doubt. Because of the 1967 case of Gault, a juvenile has the right to counsel, the right to hear formal charges, and the right to confront and cross-examine witnesses (*In re Gault*, 1967). The hearing is confidential and is usually only heard by a judge. As mentioned at the beginning of the chapter, there is no jury in most states (*McKeiver v. Pennsylvania*, 1971). If the court finds that the allegations have not been proven, the juvenile case is discharged. If the court finds that the allegations have been proven, a disposition hearing is scheduled. The case can still be dismissed if the judge sees fit, even if it is believed that the juvenile committed the act, if it is believed to be in the best interests of the child. The case can also still be diverted from formal processing to informal treatment or other type of rehabilitative program.

Disposition Hearing

If the youth has admitted to committing the delinquent act or has been found to have committed it by the court during adjudication, they will enter the disposition stage. The disposition stage is similar to sentencing in criminal court. However, the judge is afforded substantial discretion regarding the sanctions in a juvenile case. The judge will weigh the need for public safety and the rehabilitation needs (best interests) of the juvenile in determining sanctions. The disposition can range from probation, community service, or attending treatment/therapy to being committed to a formal juvenile detention facility. A **blended sentence** can also be enacted by a juvenile court in certain states, which blends a juvenile sentence and an adult sentence for certain serious youthful offenders. Juvenile cases can also generate a record for the youth.

Juvenile Records

After a juvenile case has gone through all of the processing stages, a record of the offense has been created. Although a juvenile record can be detrimental to a child's future, every state has its own process to expunge records. **Expungement** is defined as records being destroyed/removed from all databases and other files (Office of Juvenile Justice and

Delinquency Prevention, 2018). This term is sometimes mistakenly used interchangeably with the sealing of a record, which does not delete the account, but instead limits the public's access to it. Usually, states will allow a case to be expunged when the juvenile turns a certain age, generally 18 or 19. While some states will remove the record automatically or upon a formal request, others require a fee, potentially causing socioeconomic bias (Safiedine & Chung, 2017; Shapira, 2020).

Postdisposition Matters

In some states, even when a juvenile has been sent to a formal juvenile detention facility or is receiving another type of mandated sanction, such as community service or a mandated treatment program, juvenile courts can still retain some jurisdiction. In those states, the court can ensure that the sanctions are being followed and that the juvenile is treated appropriately through additional hearings and interventions when necessary.

Worldview

*Juvenile Courts Around the World**

Juvenile justice systems were widespread not only across America in the 20th century, but also all over the world. Canada and Great Britain started their first juvenile court in 1908, followed by Switzerland in 1910, France in 1912, Austria in 1919, Germany in 1923, and Spain in 1924. Other juvenile courts on other continents were also being developed during this time, all acknowledging that there should be different court proceedings for children and that children should be treated differently.

ITALY

Italy established its first juvenile court in 1934; like the other countries we have looked at in this text, initially, the focus was not imprisonment rather than rehabilitation. The 1988 Juvenile Justice Procedural Reform Act reorganized Italy's juvenile justice system with goals of positive embrace by communities for adjudicated juvenile delinquents, minimizing involvement with the criminal justice system, and limiting imprisonment to cases where there are no other options available. (Gatti & Verde, 1997).

The minimum age of criminal responsibility in Italy is 14. If a juvenile goes to trial, the judge only has one option, imprisonment, with some leeway to suspend sentencing. However, there are many options that can be utilized before trial, such as dismissal or pretrial probation, and higher courts have stressed their use before the case goes to trial. Typically, only minors found guilty of serious crimes face prosecution and are sent to formal detention centers in Italy (Italy National Report, 2013).

*The countries included here were chosen based on relevance to the chapter's content and available international data.

CANADA

On July 7, 1982, the Young Offenders Act was enacted, replacing the prior Juvenile Delinquents Act. Under the old act, and much like the current juvenile justice system in the United States, age limits differed from jurisdiction to jurisdiction. The court proceedings were informal, with open-ended sentences. Juveniles could also be prosecuted for status offenses (offenses based on age), and because the proceedings are informal, the youth can be brought back to court arbitrarily until they are 21 (Department of Justice, 2017). Under the new act, children are given the same rights as adults regarding due process, including a determinate sentence. The act applies to juveniles ages 12–17; those under 12 cannot be charged with crimes and those 18 and older are prosecuted in adult court. Additional protections include being kept separate from adults and making youth records confidential. If a juvenile is found guilty and only if deemed necessary, a youth can serve up to a maximum of 3 years in formal detention. Youths 14 and older can also be transferred to an adult court for certain violent crimes. In 1984, the act was amended, increasing the maximum age for youth court jurisdiction to 18. It also provides discretion to judges to permit early release and provides direction for the use of community-based sanctions. The Young Offenders Act was replaced in 2003 with the Youth Criminal Justice Act. This new act reduced the amount of discretion judges would have regarding sentencing juveniles to formal detention and permitted incarceration for only the most egregious cases. The act also provided alternatives to detention, including community supervision.

GERMANY

The first juvenile court was established on January 1, 1908, in Frankfurt and the first Juvenile Justice Act was enacted in 1923. It focused on education instead of punishment. The overall goal of Germany's current juvenile court is "normalization." Juvenile courts in Germany have jurisdiction over juvenile and young adult offenders from 14 to 21 years of age, with individuals being able to stay in juvenile detention centers until they are 24. This inclusion of young adults aged 18–21 occurred in 1953, allowing juvenile court judges to impose either juvenile or adult sentencing on a case-by-case basis. Germany's Youth Court Law was established in 1923 and has undergone amendments throughout the years: in 1953, 1990, and most recently 2008. Germany made changes similar to those made in Canada, eliminating indeterminate prison sentences for juveniles and limiting juveniles' confinement before trial. Youth courts are prohibited from transferring juveniles to adult court and instead sentence many young adults as juveniles (Ishida, 2015).

The Youth Court Law specifies three categories of youth sanctions—*educational measures* to improve socialization; *disciplinary actions* such as court-ordered community service that seeks to strengthen youth socialization through community service, social training courses, and victim–offender mediation; and *imprisonment* (often a last resort), with a maximum 10-year sentence in most cases, but up to 15 years can be given for the most egregious of acts (Chammah, 2015). Again, imprisonment is uncommon, and only 2% of youth are in formal detention (Dünkel, 2016). There is more commonly a focus on education and restorative justice measures within Germany's juvenile courts, with the overarching goal of normalization for its youth.

NEW ZEALAND

New Zealand passed the Children, Young Persons, and Their Families Act in 1989 to increase the court's focus on youths and their families' well-being. It also limited formal detention to criminal cases. The act advocates for keeping youth in their community and participating in rehabilitation programs. It encourages the notion of social justice, whereby the youth offender, their families, victims, and communities are all part of the rehabilitation process. (Spier & Wilkinson, 2016).

Juvenile·courts in New Zealand have several other disposition options for delinquents, however, and have jurisdiction over youth as young as 10 years old. Unlike Germany but similar to some states in the United States, they are allowed to transfer juveniles as young as 12 years old to adult court. They can also sanction youth to supervised community service, impose fines, and order restitution.

On July 13, 2017, the act was renamed the Children's and Young People's Well-Being Act. The newly named act reexamines the rehabilitative goals of the system. It extends youth court jurisdiction until an individual's 18th birthday, although more egregious cases can still be transferred to adult court (Ministry of Social Development, n.d.).

THE NETHERLANDS

The juvenile justice system in the Netherlands began in 1905 following the implementation of several acts, including the Penal Children's Act. This act introduced special criminal proceedings and penal provisions for children, including special sentences. In 1922, dedicated juvenile judges were introduced.

The juvenile court has jurisdiction over individuals age 12–17. Youth under 12 are not held accountable for any criminal actions. Additionally, youth who do fall under the court's jurisdiction are rarely incarcerated and are instead provided with noncustodial options for rehabilitation. No juveniles age 12–17 can be transferred to adult court; however, in rare cases, a juvenile can be sentenced through the adult penal law (equivalent to a blended sentence in the United States). Conversely, individuals age 18–21 under the adult criminal court's jurisdiction can be sentenced through the juvenile justice system, but this is also uncommon. Additionally, youth within the juvenile court can be sanctioned for noncriminal offenses such as truancy.

Due process applies to juvenile cases, including being assigned an attorney, and although all verdicts are made public, juvenile trial proceedings are private and are kept confidential from the public. Along with legislation in the 1980s that put the focus on incarceration alternatives, including various diversion programs, in 2008, noncustodial treatment was introduced and rehabilitation was further advocated for in the Netherlands' juvenile system (Gerrits, 2016).

Wrap-up

The creation of the juvenile court system was intended to provide an alternative process for wayward and destitute youth to receive assistance and rehabilitation. Before its creation, children of a certain age could be punished much in the same manner as adults in a criminal court setting, although families were traditionally left with the primary responsibility of disciplining their children. In the 1800s, as more families found themselves out of work and more children took to the street, to help these children and avoid further disruption to society, workhouses and reformatories were established (American Bar Association, 2007). Under the parens patriae doctrine, which allowed the government to act in the best interests of the child and have ultimate authority, criminal and noncriminal youth were put into these institutions to "cure" them. Following criticisms of substandard conditions, abuse, and unsuccessful results, in 1899, through the Women's Society, also known as the Child Savers, the first juvenile court was established in Illinois (Center on Juvenile and Criminal Justice, n.d.). The creation of specialized juvenile courts and proceedings not only spread across the United States but also could be seen around the world (United Nations General Assembly, 1985). The goals of this specialized court in the United States were to focus on the child, not necessarily the act; to be nonadversarial; to act in the best interests of the child; and to be available to those under 16.

The juvenile court's overarching goal was different from that of the criminal courts, which focused on punishment; juvenile proceedings were geared toward rehabilitation. However, criticism fell on this new court and the rulings that followed. Judges were thought to have too much discretion, and because the proceedings were viewed more as civil than criminal, due process laws afforded in the criminal courts did not exist in the juvenile court. As such, juveniles received harsher penalties than they would for the same crime if an adult had committed it. Youths were not given lawyers and were not allowed to cross-examine witnesses or even know the formal charges against them. Most due process rights were eventually guaranteed to children through a series of cases that made their way to the U.S. Supreme Court, which ruled in favor of their inclusion in all juvenile court proceedings.

The juvenile court continues to offer a variety of informal alternatives in addition to reforms to its own formal process in order to provide resources and maintain its original goal of rehabilitating youth.

Discussion Questions

1. What led to the formation of the first juvenile court?
2. What were the original goals/philosophies of the juvenile court?
3. What are some of the similarities and differences of the juvenile court compared to the adult criminal court?
4. What are the main stages of the juvenile court process?
5. Describe the challenges of the juvenile court in the 20th century.
6. List and describe some of the landmark cases discussed and explain how they changed the juvenile court and its process.
7. What was the purpose of the 1938 Juvenile Justice and Delinquency Prevention Act and its more current revisions?
8. How is the juvenile court in the United States different from/similar to that of other countries around the world?

ONLINE RESOURCES

U.S. Department of Justice Office of Justice Programs http://www.ncjrs.gov
National Partnership for Juvenile Services http://www.npjs.org
Youth Government http://www.youth.gov
Juvenile Justice Center of Philadelphia http://www.juvenilejustice.org
U.S. Courts http://www.uscourts.gov
U.S. Department of Justice http://www.justice.gov
Coalition for Juvenile Justice http://www.juvjustice.org

Definitions

Actus reus—the unlawful act

Adjudication/fact-finding hearing—facts of the juvenile case are presented along with other evidence, similar to a trial in an adult criminal case

Beyond a reasonable doubt—burden of proof required for both juvenile and adult criminal cases that requires that there is no other reasonable explanation for the crime, with almost 100% certainty

Blended sentence—blending of juvenile and adult sentences for specific serious youthful offenders

Child Savers—a group of reformers with the intention to save children and stabilize society

Concurrent jurisdiction—the ability to exercise judicial review by different courts at the same time

Delinquency petition—a petition that is filed by the prosecuting attorney in cases where a minor (as determined by the state) commits a delinquent act

Detention hearing—a hearing to determine formal custody of a juvenile while awaiting adjudication based on safety for the child and the community

Disposition hearing—a hearing where the juvenile court judge will give discretionary sanctions; similar to sentencing in adult criminal court

Diversion—an effort to avoid court intervention

Due process—procedural rights guaranteed by the Constitution

Expungement—court records being destroyed/removed from databases and other files

Guardian ad litem—an individual appointed by the court to act in the best interest of the child and make recommendations for sanctions

Initial hearing—a first appearance before the juvenile court, similar to an arraignment in adult criminal court

Intake—after the initial contact, a juvenile may continue to this first stage of the juvenile justice system, where a determination is made for further formal processing

Judicial waiver—the mechanism by which a juvenile court judge may transfer a juvenile offender to criminal court jurisdiction

Justice model—focuses on accountability for the offense committed

Legislative waiver—legislation that permits automatic processing in criminal court based on the juvenile's age and type of crime

Mens rea—guilty mind

Parens patriae—Latin for "parent of the country," allows the government to intervene in juvenile matters in the best interest of the child

Petition—a legal document describing what offenses the respondent is alleged to have committed

Preponderance of the evidence—a burden of proof that requires more than 50% certainty, more likely than not, of who committed the offense; required in civil cases

Prosecutorial waiver—a statutory mechanism that provides a prosecutor with exclusive discretion through concurrent jurisdiction

Reverse waiver—statutes that allow a juvenile case that is being prosecuted in criminal court to be transferred to juvenile court for processing

Status offenses—offenses that are illegal because of the offender's age, such as truancy

Welfare model—focus of the court is on the welfare of the child and not the delinquent act committed

References

American Bar Association. (2007). The history of juvenile justice. In *Dialogue on youth and justice* (pp. 5–8). https://www.americanbar.org/content/dam/aba/administrative/public_education/resources/DYJfull.pdf

Australian Bureau of Statistics. (1982–2013). *Prisoners in Australia* (various issues) (ABS Cat. 4517.0). 1982–1993 published by the Australian Institute of Criminology.

Bedau, H. A. (1997). *The Death Penalty in America: Current Controversies*. Oxford University Press.

Bernard, T. J., Kurlychek, M. C., & Kurlychek, M. C. (2010). *The cycle of juvenile justice*. Oxford University Press.

Blackstone, S. W. (1765). *Commentaries on the Laws of England: By William Blackstone*. Clarendon Press.

Blackstone, W. (1837). *Select Extracts from Blackstone's Commentaries, Carefully Adapted to the Use of Schools and Young Persons*. Maxwel Publishing.

Bonnie, R. J. (2013). *Reforming juvenile justice: a developmental approach*. National Academies Press.

Breed v. Jones, 421 U.S. 519 (1975).

Bremner, R. H., & Barnard, J. (1974). *Children and youth in America: A documentary history*. Harvard University Press.

Eekelaar & R. George (Eds.), *Routledge handbook of family law and policy* (pp. 245–256). Taylor & Francis. https://doi.org/10.4324/9780203796221.ch4_1

Center on Juvenile and Criminal Justice. (n.d.). *Juvenile justice history*. Retrieved February 5, 2020 from http://www.cjcj.org/education1/juvenile-justice-history.html

Chammah, M. (2015). *How Germany treats juveniles*. The Marshall Project. https://www.themarshallproject.org/2015/06/19/how-germany-treats-juveniles

Department of Justice. (2017). *Youth justice*. Government of Canada. http://www.justice.gc.ca/eng/csj-sjc/just/11.html

Dünkel, F. (2016-01-19). Youth justice in Germany. In *Oxford handbooks online*. Retrieved 1 Jun. 2018, from http://www.oxfordhandbooks.com/view/10.1093/oxfordhb/9780199935383.001.0001/oxfordhb-9780199935383-e-68.

Furbish, L. K. (1999, December 17). *Western European juvenile justice models*. Connecticut General Assembly. https://cga.ct.gov/PS99/rpt%5Colr%5Chtm/99-R-1157.htm.

Gatti, U., & Verde A. (1997). *Comparative Juvenile Justice: An Overview of Italy (From Juvenile Justice Systems: International Perspectives, P 177-204, 1997, John A Winterdyk, ed. - See NCJ-174323)*. U.S. Department of Justice Office of Justice Programs. https://www.ojp.gov/ncjrs/virtual-library/abstracts/comparative-juvenile-justice-overview-italy-juvenile-justice.

Gerrits, I. (2016). *The use of alternatives to detention in the Netherlands*. International Juvenile Justice Observatory. http://www.oijj.org/en/docs/general/the-use-of-alternatives-to-detention-in-the-netherlands

Ministry of Social Development (n.d.). Investing in New Zealand's Chieldren and Their Families Ministry of Justice. Retrieved on December 2, 2019 from https://www.msd.govt.nz/about-msd-and-our-work/work-programmes/investing-in-children/new-childrens-agency-established.html

Hudson, B. A. (1987). *Justice through punishment: A critique of the justice model of corrections*. St. Martin's Press.

order exception. *Arkansas Law Notes*, 29–37. http://media.law.uark.edu/arklawnotes/files/2012/01/Hughes-Overview-of-the-Juvenile-Justice-and-Delinquency-Prevention-Act-ArkansasLawNotes-2011.pdf

In re Gault, 387 U.S. 1 (1967).

In re Winship. (n.d.). Oyez. https://www.oyez.org/cases/1969/778

In re Winship, 397 U.S. 358 (1970).

Ishida, K. (2015). *Young adults in conflict with the law: Opportunities for diversion*. Juvenile Justice Initiative. http://www.modelsforchange.net/publications/799

Italy National Report. (2013). *JODA—juvenile offenders detention alternative in Europe*. European Union.

Kent v. United States, 383 U.S. 541 (1966).

Luna, B., & Wright, C. (2016). Adolescent brain development: Implications for the juvenile criminal justice system. In K. Heilbrun, D. DeMatteo, & N. E. S. Goldstein (Eds.), *APA handbook of psychology and juvenile justice* (pp. 91–116). American Psychological Association. https://doi.org/10.1037/14643-005

McKeiver v. Pennsylvania, 403 U.S. 528 (1971).

Office of Juvenile Justice and Delinquency Prevention. (2018). *Reentry starts here: A guide for youth in long-term juvenile corrections and treatment programs*. U.S. Department of Justice. https://www.ojjdp.gov/pubs/251193.pdf

Office of Juvenile Justice and Delinquency Prevention. (2021). *Statistical briefing book*. U.S. Department of Justice. https://www.ojjdp.gov/ojstatbb/court/faqs.asp

Platt, A. M. (1977). *The Child Savers—the invention of delinquency* (2nd ed.). University of Chicago Press

Russo, R. G. (2017). When is a Criminal Trial Not a Criminal Trial?-The Case Against Jury Trials in Juvenile Court. The Catholic Lawyer, *18*(2), 5.

Safiedine, S. S., & Chung, K. J. (2017). The price for justice: The economic barriers that contribute to an unfair and unjust criminal justice system. *Criminal Justice, 32*, 40 (2017-2018). https://heinonline.org/HOL/LandingPage?handle=hein.journals/cjust32&div=70&id=&page=

Schall v. Martin, 467 U.S. 253 (1984).

Schlossman, S. (1983). Juvenile justice: History and philosophy. In S. H. Kadish (Ed.). *Encyclopedia of crime and justice* (Vol. 3, pp. 961–969). Free Press.

Sessions, W. S., & Bracey, F. M. (1982). A Synopsis of the Federal Juvenile Delinquency Act. . Mary's LJ, 14, 509.

Shapira, L. R. (2020). The crippling costs of the juvenile justice system: A legal and policy argument for eliminating fines and fees for youth offenders. *Emory Law Journal, 69*(6), 1305. https://scholarlycommons.law.emory.edu/elj/vol69/iss6/4

Shioutakon v. District of Columbia, 236 F.2d 666 (1956).

Spier, P., & Wilkinson, R. (2016). *Reoffending patterns for participants of youth justice Family Group Conference's held in 2011 and 2012*. Ministry of Social Development. https://www.msd.govt.nz/about-msd-and-our-work/publications-resources/research/child-and-youth-of-fending-patterns/index.html

Tanenhaus, D. S. (2004). *Juvenile justice in the making*. Oxford University Press

Thomas, J. M. (2017). *Raising the bar: State trends in keeping youth out of adult courts (2015–2017)*. Campaign for Youth Justice.

U.N. General Assembly. *United Nations standard minimum rules for the administration of juvenile justice ("The Beijing Rules"): Resolution/adopted by the General Assembly*, November 29, 1985, A/RES/40/33. https://www.ohchr.org/documents/professionalinterest/beijingrules.pdf

U.S. Attorney's Manual. (1997). *Constitutional protections afforded to juveniles*. https://www.justice.gov/usam/criminal-resource-manual-121-constitutional-protections-afforded-juveniles

Ventrell, M. (1998). Evolution of the dependency component of the juvenile court. *Juvenile and Family Court Journal, 49*(4), 17–37. https://doi.org/10.1111/j.1755-6988.1998.tb00788.x

Williams, L.M. (2017). In re Gault. In The Encyclopedia of Juvenile Delinquency and Justice (eds C.J. Schreck, M.J. Leiber, H.V. Miller and K. Welch). https://doi.org/10.1002/9781118524275.ejdj0008

Juvenile Corrections

Introduction

Corrections for juveniles was much the same as it was for adults prior to the 19th century. Both child and adult prisoners were held temporarily behind bars for committing a crime, but instead of long-term incarceration, punishment was carried out in the form of whippings, beatings in public, and other forms of torture. As time progressed, imprisonment was still not utilized as punishment; instead, prisoners were put to work for the state or contracted out to farms and wealthy landowners. Juveniles received the same fate. It was not until organized labor felt threatened by cheap prisoner labor in the 18th century that formal institutions began to serve as punishment in and of themselves. At this time, those juvenile delinquents processed by the court, as opposed to those who were informally punished by their families, were mostly prosecuted and incarcerated with adults. It was not until the late 18th- and early 19th-century Progressive Era that the notion of separate treatment for destitute and delinquent youth existed and the first juvenile correctional institutions were created. Sometimes referred to as houses of refuge and later **industrial schools**, these institutions were designed to focus on rehabilitation by providing education and tangible skills that would help delinquent youth become productive members of society. Unfortunately, as you have read in previous chapters, these institutions more resembled adult correctional facilities, with similar hazardous conditions and abuses, rather than the positive reformatories they were intended to be. After the creation of the juvenile court in 1899, a more organized and dedicated juvenile justice system that included formal and informal detention alternatives was put in place, but it was not without its own controversies.

In this chapter, we will explore the corrections component of the juvenile system. Specifically, you will learn how it was developed throughout history and about its changing policies and objectives and its eventual direction toward a youth's best interests while attempting to keep our society safe.

History of Juvenile Correctional Systems and Their Effects on Juveniles

The notion of "**corrections**" is defined as "a network of agencies that supervise individuals in a state of incarceration, rehabilitation, parole, or probation" (Correctional Officer, 2019, p. 1). A correctional system therefore refers to a group of agencies that manage prisons and community-based programs. The correctional system is the last major component of the larger juvenile justice system, following the police and courts (Blomberg & Lucken, 2011).

However, historically corrections was generally a penal system that focused on punishment as opposed to rehabilitation and was absent of community-based programs—those that allow the offender to remain within their own community but under the court's supervision. Additionally, prisons themselves were not considered the actual punishment, as they are in the early 21st century, but instead were treated as holding areas until physical punishments such as whippings, beatings, and executions were decided on and carried out.

Ancient and Medieval Times

As you may recall from Chapter 1, in the early 1700s, before the American Revolution and the creation of the juvenile justice system, families were given the authority to inflict punishment themselves on wayward youth. It was acceptable during this time for families to deliver harsh physical punishment that could include dismembering and even killing a child for stealing or talking back to a parent. Many ancient cultures had permitted the same type of justice to be delivered by the victim or a member of the victim's family.

As territories developed, landowners and rulers preferring a more systemic and orderly method of handling criminals helped to develop criminal courts. An individual who was found guilty could be sentenced to anything from slavery, as a form of restitution for the victim's family, to physical punishment and, if warranted, death. Those arrested were usually confined until they confessed to the crime and their punishment was imposed.

During medieval times, the church occasionally used long-term incarceration to replace executions, and landowners created private prisons for those who disobeyed them. In England in 1166, King Henry II created a set of ordinances known as the Assize of Clarendon. For crimes that were considered against the "king's peace," the state began to sentence offenders to imprisonment instead of physical punishment.

Colonial America

As you read in Chapter 1, in colonial America, the focus of corrections was to deliver severe punishment to both adults and children, even for what would be considered by 21st-century standards low-level crimes (see Table 9.1). Fines were another form of punishment, but depending on the social class involved, they may not have been an option. If one was eligible, the amount of the fine was consistent with the severity of the crime and increased for repeat offenders. Children, usually from families of lower social class, were either subject to the same harsh punishment as adults, if it was determined that they could tell right from wrong, or could be **bound out**. This meant that the court ordered the child to serve as an apprentice for someone outside the institution or be sold as a servant for several years (*History of Corrections*, n.d.).

TABLE 9.1 Colonial America Crime and Punishment

CRIME	PUNISHMENT
Hog theft	Whipping, first offense Death for repeat offenders
Not attending church	Whipping or fine
Slander	Dunking stool
Theft/burglary	Branding of a "T" or "B" on the forehead
Unseemly behavior including kissing on the Lord's day	Several hours with hands and head in stock
Gossiping	A spiked piece of iron thrust into the mouth

Note. Fines were usually reserved for those with a higher social class. If a fine could not be paid, it was replaced by physical punishment.

Children who were determined to know right from wrong were subjected to the same forms of punishment.

The death penalty also existed, as it does in the 21st century, but it applied to a larger array of crimes. For example, in 1636, the Massachusetts Bay Colony listed 13 crimes that warranted execution, including practicing witchcraft and worshipping idols. In early New York, 20% of offenses, including pickpocketing, horse stealing, and robbery, warranted the death penalty (*History of Corrections*, n.d.). Although jails were used to hold prisoners as they are in the 21st century, in colonial America, the prison was not the punishment, as was the case in ancient times. Those found guilty were not sanctioned to imprisonment but instead endured harsh physical punishments. For example, the Puritans of Massachusetts believed that humans had no control over their fate, and punishment was inflicted to appease God.

An exception to these types of punishments existed in a few areas. For example, in Pennsylvania, executions were abolished under the auspices of William Penn, a Quaker and the founder of Pennsylvania, except as a punishment for homicide. Additionally, instead of physical disciplines, Penn reintroduced the idea of hard labor and imprisonment as an individual's sentence.

A Call For Reform

Pennsylvania System

In 1787 in Pennsylvania, the Philadelphia Society for Alleviating the Miseries of Public Prisons was established, composed of many Quakers. The group advocated for imprisonment as a form of punishment as opposed to the established physical sanctions, which included the death penalty. They also supported solitary confinement as a method to reform criminals by allowing them to think about their crimes, become remorseful, and ultimately repent. In 1790, Pennsylvania established the Walnut Street Jail in Philadelphia for "hardened and atrocious offenders." Continued pressure for additional prisons led to the creation of the Western Penitentiary outside Pittsburgh in 1826 and the Eastern

DEEPER DIVE

Colonial America

"Correcting" devices . . .

Stocks: a small wooden device with foot holes. A seated person's ankles were locked in while their legs were held straight out.

Pillory: This contraption had holes for a person's head and hands. It was common to have rotten fruit and rocks thrown at the criminal.

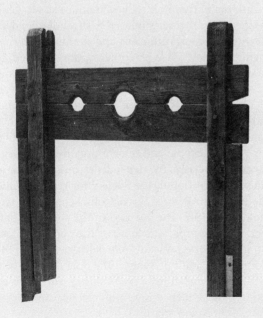

Whipping post: A place where criminals were publicly whipped in front of onlookers and neighbors.

Dunking stool: a chair to which criminals were tied and dunked into the water as punishment.

Penitentiary near Philadelphia in 1829. Individual cells measuring 12 by 8 by 10 feet were erected, maintaining the notion of the benefits of solitary confinement. Prisoners had a different opinion, however, because this type of isolation proved difficult to endure.

Auburn System

The Auburn system was used in 1819 in New York. It adopted the method of solitary confinement just described, but only at night. During the day, prisoners were put to work, and although they were held in the same space, they were not allowed to talk to or even look at each other. Supervisors could beat any prisoner with a whip or a stick for violating the rules (*History of Corrections*, n.d.).

Reformers at the time considered both the Pennsylvania and the Auburn systems both cost-effective and efficient, because they could use fewer guards by either isolating inmates in cells or grouping prisoners together to keep up the prison while at the same time instilling strict discipline. European countries generally followed the Pennsylvania system, while many American states chose the Auburn system for adults and sometimes even for children. Although these strategies could make it easier to run the prison, they did little to rehabilitate the prisoners within.

The Reform Movement

As you read previously in this chapter and as you may recall from Chapter 1, initially American colonies generally left the discipline of their children up to their parents; however, from the mid-18th to the mid-19th century, the overall population of the United States increased exponentially, from 1.5 million to 23 million, because of a variety of factors, including mass immigration. In states like New York, Massachusetts, and Pennsylvania, many immigrant families, mostly German and Irish, did not have work and were seen as unfit and incapable of handling their children, many of whom were destitute and committed minor crimes such as theft. When the 1800s began, the juvenile delinquent label was already being applied to children in the lower socioeconomic classes. Children who were apprehended and imprisoned were regularly housed with adult offenders.

In the late 18th and early 19th centuries, courts punished and confined criminal and noncriminal youth in jails and penitentiaries. Since few other options existed, it was common practice to house youth with adult criminals and the mentally ill in deplorable conditions. At the same time, American cities were confronting high poverty rates, child neglect, and unemployment. Elected officials were under pressure to help alleviate these social issues (National Research Council and Institute of Medicine, 2001).

As both children and their families suffered and became more reliant on public and private charities and other support, philanthropic and reform organizations began to form to provide additional assistance. **Pauperism**, the dependency on others for goods and services, was addressed through the creation of the Society for the Prevention of Pauperism. The society was founded by John Griscom, Isaac Collins, James W. Gerard, Hugh Maxwell, and other stakeholders in 1817. The purpose of the society was to research the causes of pauperism and provide programs to assist the poor. One issue in which the society became increasingly interested was juvenile delinquency and the potential benefits of separating children from adult prisoners. The organization believed that by instilling good judgment through education, skills building, and work ethics, there would eventually be a reduction in dependence and future pauperism (Society for the Prevention of Pauperism in the City of New York, 1818).

In 1823, the Society for the Prevention of Pauperism disbanded and reformed as the Society for the Reformation of Juvenile Delinquency to refocus their efforts on youth. They believed this area was in need of reform and in need of an institution that could provide juveniles with one of the things they needed most—refuge.

House of Refuge: The First Juvenile Correctional Institution

The newly created Society for the Reformation of Juvenile Delinquents, led by John Griscom and other wealthy businessmen and professionals, wanted to establish a reformatory for juveniles, an institution that could isolate arrested delinquents from adult criminals and provide shelter to destitute youth coming from unstable homes. They lobbied in New York State, and in 1824, a bill was passed to establish the **New York House of Refuge**, the first correctional institution solely for juveniles, on January 1, 1825.

The following goals were set by the Society for the Reformation of Juvenile Delinquents for the newly created New York House of Refuge in 1825:

> The design of the proposed institution is, to furnish, in the first place, an asylum, in which boys under a certain age, who become subject to the notice of our police, either as vagrants, or homeless, or charged with petty crimes, may be received, judiciously classed according to their degree of depravity or innocence, put to work at such employments as will tend to encourage industry and ingenuity, taught reading, writing, and arithmetic, and most carefully instructed in the nature of their moral and religious obligations while at the same time, they are subjected to a course of treatment, that will afford a prompt and energetic corrective of their vicious propensities, and hold out every possible inducement to reformation and good conduct. (Macallair, 2015, p. 21)

New York House of Refuge, Randall's Island

The New York House of Refuge, also referred to as a reformatory, initially was occupied by 9 children, 6 boys and 3 girls. Within 10 years, that number increased to almost 1,678.

Reformatories also existed outside the United States, in Britain. However, the New York reformatory differed by committing both criminal and noncriminal children to indefinite sentences. Children were required to perform supervised labor to offset operating costs, including the producing of brushes, brass nails, and shoes for boys and making uniforms, doing laundry, and other such "domestic" work for girls. Basic literacy skills were also taught, and there was an emphasis on evangelical religious instruction. The reformatory could also bind out the children, as we saw occur during colonial times through indenture agreements, where employers agreed to supervise them during their "employment." Many children were sent to work on farms and others served as domestic laborers, all in the name of rehabilitation (New York State Archives, 1989).

Between 1825 and 1855, many immigrants populated the New York House of Refuge, the majority of whom were of Irish descent (Macallair, 2015). All children in this reformatory were subjected to corporal punishment, which included severe beatings. Houses of refuge began to spread to other states in the mid-19th century. Crowding conditions became more prominent, and with overuse, these facilities began to deteriorate quickly. Practices in the houses of refuge were also questioned, because labor seemed to dominate education and skills training. The population was still a mix of juveniles who had committed crimes and those who had not committed but were considered unruly, vagrant, or destitute by the court. However, regardless of why a child was in an institution, all children were subject to the daily routine of labor and other punishments, including solitary confinement, the use of the dunking stool, and the "silent system," like the Auburn system, where complete silence among all the children was required (Center on Juvenile and Criminal Justice, n.d.; Macallair, 2015). It should also be noted that, depending on the location, African Americans and other minority groups at the time were either excluded from or segregated from White children within houses of refuge. Many scholars agree that this was a result of racial biases of the time, which followed the ideology that specific minority groups could not be rehabilitated and belonged in adult prisons (James, 2016; Kopaczewski, 2016; also see the Center on Juvenile and Criminal Justice (www.cjcj.org) for more information on further disparities during this era).

Unlike in the 21st century, no trial was required for an individual to be sent to a correctional institution like a house of refuge. Children were brought directly to the judge or magistrate, and under the doctrine of **parens patriae**, the court having the right to act as father or parent of the youth, could remove the child and sentence them to a reformatory. This could be done even if it was against the parent's wishes. A landmark case that exemplifies this is *Ex Parte (for) Crouse*.

As you read in Chapter 1, in 1838, Mary Ann Crouse, a young girl at the time, was sent to the Pennsylvania House of Refuge after her mother complained to the court that her daughter was unruly and was displaying, as determined by the court, "vicious incorrigible conduct." In 1835, a new law was passed in Pennsylvania allowing girls under the age of 18 and boys under age 21 to be committed to a house of refuge for incorrigible and vicious behavior. Although Mary Anne's father appealed the court's decision on the basis of what he described as "imprisoning" his infant child, Pennsylvania's appellate court ruled that houses of refuge were reformatories rather than prisons. Remanding a child to a house of refuge did not constitutionally require a trial or any other due process rights. The court decided that the state had the fundamental right to intervene on behalf of the best interests of the child.

It was not until 32 years after the ruling in *Ex Parte Crouse*, in 1870, that the Illinois Supreme Court decided that parents have a right to care for and educate their children, which cannot be prevented by the court without gross negligence demonstrated on the part of the caregivers. The Supreme Court ruled that a state imprisoning youth for "moral welfare and the good of society" without committing a crime was unconstitutional (see Chapter 1, *People ex rel. O'Connell v. Turner*, 55 Ill).

Reformers, including those from **Hull House**, originally founded by Jane Addams and Ellen Gates Starr in Chicago in 1889 as a settlement house providing services such as education and assistance to the poor, began to criticize the conditions of various houses of refuge across the United States and a series of court challenges emerged (see Chapter 1).

For the first half of the 19th century, houses of refuge were the primary institutions confining destitute and wayward youths. Unfortunately, as you have read in previous

DEEPER DIVE

San Francisco Industrial School

Within 3 years of the opening of the New York House of Refuge, approximately 25 more similarly-styled reformatory facilities were erected throughout the country. "Houses of Refuge were large fortress-like congregate style institutions located in urban areas for youth designated as abandoned, delinquent or incorrigible" (Center on Juvenile and Criminal Justice, n.d., p. 1). An example of a 19th-century reformatory was the San Francisco Industrial School, which was established in 1859. "Throughout its turbulent 30-year history, the Industrial School was the subject of frequent scandals stemming from physical abuse to managerial incompetence. When the facility was finally ordered closed in 1891, the city's judiciary denounced it as a failed system" (Center on Juvenile and Criminal Justice, n.d., p. 1).

INDUSTRIAL SCHOOL.

San Francisco Industrial School

chapters, houses of refuge shared many of the same issues that existed in adult jails and prisons—overcrowding, deteriorating conditions, and abuse. These reformatories have since been replaced with similarly designed youth correctional institutions that continue to follow a **congregate institutional** model, concentrating many youths in highly regimented, penitentiary-like institutions.

By the middle of the 19th century, following the creation of the houses of refuge, other types of institutions were being created, such as cottage systems and other out-of-home placements (see Chapter 1). Social reformers continued to push for changes to better serve youth and society as a whole.

More Reform . . . Illinois Juvenile Court, 1899 and Beyond

The early history of juvenile justice in the United States is characterized by "intentions falling far short of actions, and the notion of humane treatment for 'wayward' children giving way to harsh punishment, exploitation, overcrowding, and various other abuses" (U.S. Prison Culture, 2011, p. 1). By the late 1800s, reformers were again looking to improve the juvenile rehabilitation process while protecting society. These efforts eventually led to the establishment of the first juvenile court in the United States, in Chicago in 1899 (National Research Council and Institute of Medicine, 2001).

As described in earlier chapters, in 1899, the first juvenile court was established to create a judicious method of detaining youth and deciding what was in their best interest. These specialized institutions quickly spread throughout the United States. The juvenile court conducted informal hearings and then determined the most appropriate correctional treatment (Center on Juvenile and Criminal Justice, n.d.).

Through the 1930s and into the 1950s, the notion of rehabilitation seeped into correctional institutions by means of a **rehabilitation model**. This model called for qualified staff members to determine the cause of an inmate's criminal behavior and then provide treatment through group therapy and counseling. Because of limited budgets, overcrowding, and more complex cases, such as those involving violent crimes, this model was unsuccessful. Later, in the 1960s, as crime rates increased, a new approach was taken, focusing on **community corrections**. Part of community corrections was that rehabilitation needed to be completed in the community, not in jails. It favored job training, treatment, educational programs, and probation (*History of Corrections*, n.d.). This approach influenced prison models applicable to both adults and juveniles. However, by the 1950s and 1960s, the effectiveness of the juvenile justice system was in question because of informal procedures, disparities in sentencing by judges who were afforded great discretion, and institutional conditions, including juveniles being housed with adults (Center on Juvenile and Criminal Justice, n.d.).

Federal Interventions

Although states had the authority to create their own juvenile systems and disposition options, the federal government created legislation to regulate the state's handling of juveniles, especially for those being held in adult facilities and for low-level offenses.

In 1971, a National Advisory Commission was formed by the Administration of the Law Enforcement Assistance Administration. The commission was established to address various conditions within corrections affecting both adults and juveniles and was tasked to make recommendations for improvements (Morris, 1976).

In 1974, Congress passed the Juvenile Justice and Delinquency Prevention Act (JJDPA; 42 U.S.C. §§5601–5640) and at the same time created the Federal Office of Juvenile Justice and Delinquency Prevention within the Department of Justice. As you have read in previous chapters, this act called for states to make drastic reforms at all stages of the juvenile justice system, and the corrections stage was no different.

The JJDPA called for noncriminal status offenders (e.g., runaways, truants) being held in secure detention facilities be removed in order for states to receive **federal block grants**, "funds of a specified amount from the Federal government to individual states and local governments to help support various programs, such as law enforcement, social services, and community development" (Grants, 2016, p. 1). Other concerns addressed by this act were sight and sound separation of children and adults and juveniles' removal from adult jails and lockups. In 1988, the act was amended to mandate states to address disproportionate confinement of minority juveniles (also see table 9.4 for statistical data).

Despite this federal plan to keep youth out of confinement (deinstitutionalization) and other reform efforts to rehabilitate youth, states had their own agenda, and nearly half of the states created stricter legislation to handle chronic youthful offenders. This included lowering the age for juveniles to be protected by the juvenile justice system. The impact of these reforms was an increase in the juvenile detention rate by more than 50% on any given day between 1977 and 1985 (Schwartz, 1989).

However, by the early 1980s, federal intervention did result in some decreases in the number of youth being held as status offenders (National Research Council, 1982; Schneider, 1984a, as cited in National Research Council and Institute of Medicine, 2001). However, there was some question regarding states arresting more juveniles for minor offenses and incarcerating those who violated conditional court orders issued for **status offenses**. In turn, the rate of juvenile incarceration remained the same in these states, but for different offenses (Schneider, 1984b, as cited in National Research Council and Institute of Medicine, 2001).

As you read in Chapter 2, juvenile crime increased during the late 1980s and into the early 1990s. By the early 1990s, the federal government, in addition to the states, seemed to believe the solution was to get tougher on juvenile offenders. A more punitive response was believed to be the answer, and a **justice model** was implemented. This model called for putting and keeping more offenders in prison. Akin to this belief was the creation of the Violent Crime Control and Law Enforcement Act in 1994, also referred to as the Federal Crime Bill, which provided funding for those states carrying out stricter youth sentencing and prosecuting youthful offenders as adults at a younger age (Cothern, 2000; Department of Justice, 1994; *History of Corrections*, n.d.).

Many states passed harsher laws, including mandatory sentences and automatic adult court transfer for certain crimes. Stricter laws made it easier to transfer youthful offenders to the criminal justice system. By the mid-1990s, youth confinement for even minor offenses had grown exponentially (Redding, 2010).

However, by the late 1990s, as you read in Chapter 4, when juvenile crime had shown large decreases and the fear of juvenile "superpredators" and impending increases in violence had been dispelled, policies advocating for youth incarceration and laws affecting the system began to change.

Juvenile Corrections in the 21st Century

The Effects of the 1974 JJDPA on Our Current Correctional System

In the United States, the U.S. Supreme Court has described punishment as having at least four purposes: deterrence, societal retribution, rehabilitation, and incapacitation, with the latter intended to protect society by removing the offender (*History of Corrections*, n.d.). Corrections within the juvenile justice system, however, have become focused on the first three purposes of punishment, with an overarching goal of rehabilitation, not incapacitation. Recent amendments to the 1974 JJDPA have also aligned with this purpose: "On December 13, 2018, Congress passed HR 6964, amending the four core components of the JJDP Act, which affected the correctional section of the Juvenile Justice System" (Office of Juvenile Justice and Delinquency Prevention [OJJDP], 2019b).

Deincarceration of status offenses took away judges' discretion and restricted youth from being incarcerated for more than 7 hours for violation of a court order associated with a previous status offense. This was considered a loophole by some who believed it was a way to still hold status offenders in secure facilities.

Juvenile delinquents detained by law enforcement for non–status offense investigations, which falls within the *adult jail and lockup removal*, are not allowed to be detained in adult jails for more than 6 hours and never where adults are being held. States are also now required to ensure *sight and sound separation* and jail removal for juvenile offenders/adult transfers awaiting trial. As you read in Chapter 8, this protection previously applied only to youth being held on juvenile court charges. However, an exception still exists if "it is in the interest of justice" to hold certain juveniles being tried as adults in adult facilities potentially within sight and sound of adults. This judicial exception can be based on the juvenile's age, their mental and physical state, the current offense, previous delinquent behavior, and other factors deemed relevant by the judge (Knoke, 2019).

Finally, as discussed in previous chapters, historically, disparities among race and ethnicity have existed in all components of the criminal justice system, and corrections is no exception (Campbell et al., 2018). As of 2016, studies still indicate that youth of color are more likely to be incarcerated than other youth for the same offenses (Britton, 2017; OJJDP, 2018). As you have read, in 2018, the disproportionate minority contact requirement was also updated to focus on *racial and ethnic disparities (RED)*. Accordingly, it requires states to determine at which point(s) during the juvenile process, including sentencing to correctional institutions, disparities occur and improve their efforts to address this issue (OJJDP, 2019b, p. 53, 2019c; also see Table 9.2).

The Juvenile Corrections Process

As we saw in the previous chapter, there are four main stages that juvenile cases can go through: intake, petitioning, adjudication, and disposition. If a juvenile has been adjudicated delinquent (found to have committed the act), a *disposition hearing*, similar to sentencing in criminal court, is held to determine the appropriate sanction. Dispositions can include probation and placement in a group or foster home or other residential facilities. Other options can include referral to an outside agency or treatment program, the imposition of a fine, community service, restitution, or commitment to a detention center. It should be noted that at any stage during the process, even at intake, some juveniles may be held in a secure facility if the court believes it is in the best interest of the community or the child. Juvenile probation officers or detention workers (depending on the state) will review the case and decide if the juvenile should be held pending a mandatory hearing by a judge. In 2018, minors were held in detention centers in about 1 in 4 delinquency cases (26%) processed by the juvenile courts (OJJDP, 2020). In this section, we will focus on the disposition stage and the process of how dispositions are assigned and carried out by juveniles (National Research Council and Institute of Medicine, 2001).

Disposition Hearings

If the youth has admitted to committing the delinquent act or has been found to have committed it by the court during adjudication, they will enter the **disposition stage**. The disposition stage is similar to sentencing in a criminal court, and the judge is afforded substantial discretion with regard to the sanctions in a juvenile case. The judge will weigh the need for public safety and the rehabilitation needs of the juvenile, which can include treatment or custody. This can be based on input from the probation officer through a **predispositional report** that contains a recommendation for the care, treatment, or rehabilitation of the child along with the participation of the parents or guardians. Some states also have courts appoint what is sometimes termed a **guardian ad litem**, an individual in addition to the youth's attorney who has input along with other parties such as representatives from probation to make recommendations for sanctions. They are usually appointed for children in abuse and neglect cases (as discussed in Chapter 6) and sometimes for youth in juvenile delinquency cases who are not competent to stand trial. Others who can provide input are the prosecutor, the attorney for the child, the child's parents and guardians, victims, character witnesses, psychologists, counselors, and anyone else who can advocate for appropriate sanctions that fit the act committed. A judge then orders a decision by way of a disposition order (also see figure 9.1).

A **disposition order**, a written, signed document handed down by the court, can include an ordered sanction, a treatment plan, or a combination of sanctions and treatment. A **blended sentence** "that blends a juvenile sentence and an adult sentence for certain serious youthful offenders" (US Legal, n.d., p. 1) can also be enacted by a juvenile court in individual states.

Juvenile Sanctions

A **sanction** is a financial or other penalty imposed by a judge on an offender (National Juvenile Defender Center, n.d.; US Legal, n.d.2018) and for juveniles can range from probation to placement in foster homes to secure incarceration. The sanction is intended to be in the best interests of the child but also takes into account the offense, the victim, and the community at large. There can also be what are termed **graduated sanctions**, "the continuum of disposition options that juvenile court judges and court staff have at their disposal" ("Practical Approach," 2004, p. 1), discussed later in the chapter.

As we have learned throughout this text, juvenile proceedings as a whole are distinct from those of adults because they focus on rehabilitation, and we see this in the following range of sanctions/dispositions.

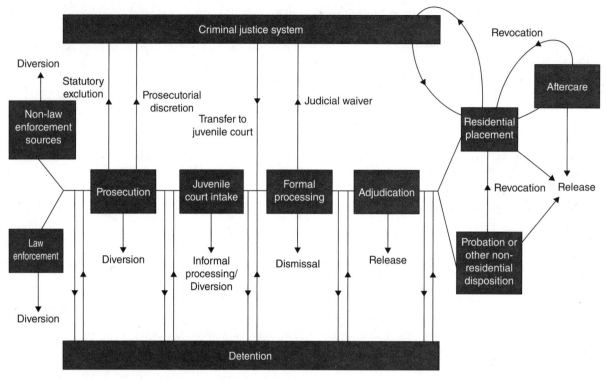

Figure 9.1 Case process through the juvenile justice system
Source: OJJDP

Probation

According to the OJJDP (2021a), "probation is the most common disposition for youth who receive a juvenile court sanction" (p. 1). Probation was ordered in 49% of the 601,700 delinquency cases that received a juvenile court sanction in 2015, compared with 11% that received placement in an out-of-home facility. In 2018, probation was ordered in 51% of nearly 505,400 delinquency cases that received a juvenile court sanction (OJJDP, 2019a).

As you read in previous chapters, John Augustus was referred to as the "Father of Probation" because his efforts are believed to have set the course for the modern-day system. In 1859, Massachusetts passed the first probation statute based on the work of Augustus (County of San Mateo Probation, 2005). This created an official probation system that quickly spread to other states. **Probation** is an alternative to confinement, whereby the youth reenters society under specific conditions for a specified period of time under the supervision of a probation officer (OJJDP, 2019a). Probation

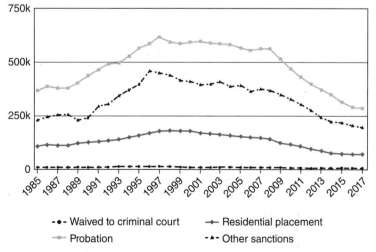

Figure 9.2 Disposition of Delinquency Cases, 1985–2017
Source: OJJDP

can be used as a diversion from the juvenile court process or as a sanction after adjudication at the disposition stage described previously.

You may remember from the previous chapters that a probation officer works with the court regarding decisions of possible diversion during the intake/adjustment stage in juvenile court, can make disposition recommendations to the court, supervises youth who were diverted from formal processing, and oversees juveniles on probation as a sanction after formal proceedings.

Probation is also considered a **community-based corrections program**—one that allows the offender to remain within their own community but under

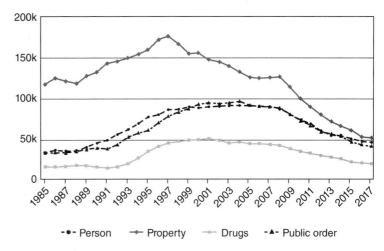

Figure 9.3 Adjudicated Delinquency Cases Placed on Probation, by Offenses, 1985–2017

Source: OJJDP

the court's supervision. It can be given not only to first-time offenders but also to those who are considered low risk and, in certain cases, to more serious offenders as an alternative to confinement in a detention center. Agreement to abide by the provisions of probation can be voluntary or involuntary. It can be voluntary if offered as a diversionary program from formal processing or mandatory if ordered by a judge after adjudicating the case. Other diversion programs will be discussed in depth in Chapter 10.

As you can see in Figure 2, formal probation sanctions doubled between 1985 and 1997, but then declined 63% through 2018. Property and drug offenses, crimes against persons, and public order cases all declined as well during this time, which resulted in declines in formal probation for these crime categories (see Figure 9.3).

The intricacies of probation can vary by jurisdiction and by the type of case. This can include both the general terms of the probation and any additional requirements dictated by specifics of the case and imposed by the judge. Juveniles are expected to abide by all of the conditions set forth, and families, along with the probation officer, can assist the child in fulfilling the probation order requirements. These conditions can include mandated school attendance, curfews, community service, counseling, and orders to not associate with specific individuals, such as in gang activity cases. Some juveniles may additionally be ordered to treatment programs or anger management, social skills building, and substance abuse classes as part of probation (Development Services Group, 2017, 2019; OJJDP, 2019a).

The court assigns a probation officer to monitor and supervise the youth's compliance with the probation order; this is also the case for minors who are sent to a juvenile facility and put on probation afterward. This can be done through spot checks and regularly scheduled meetings. Serious offenders may be required to meet with probation officers more often and be subject to stricter conditions.

Additional provisions could require paying restitution to the victim. In some states, parents may be required to pay restitution up to a specified amount for their child if the child does not have the means to do so (Department of Justice, 2017).

The term of probation may be specified or open-ended. The juvenile's progress is monitored through court hearings, and at the conclusion of probation, if all the requirements have been met, the judge will terminate the case.

Parents and guardians are encouraged to report any probation violations. This can be done at any time or during a *postdisposition hearing*, a hearing/review to determine

TABLE 9.2 Characteristics of Adjudicated Cases Ordered to Probation, 2005–2019, by Most Serious Offense, Age, Gender, and Race

	2005	2010	2011	2012	2013	2014	2015	2019
Most serious offense	100%	100%	100%	100%	100%	100%	100%	100%
Person	26%	26%	27%	26%	26%	27%	28%	33%
Property	36%	36%	35%	35%	34%	33%	34%	31%
Drugs	13%	13%	13%	13%	13%	13%	12%	11%
Public order	26%	26%	26%	26%	26%	26%	26%	25%
Sex	100%	100%	100%	100%	100%	100%	100%	100%
Male	77%	78%	78%	78%	78%	78%	77%	78%
Female	23%	22%	22%	22%	22%	22%	23%	22%
Race	100%	100%	100%	100%	100%	100%	100%	100%
White*	47%	44%	44%	44%	43%	41%	42%	41%
Black*	33%	34%	33%	33%	35%	36%	36%	35%
American Indian	2%	2%	2%	2%	2%	2%	2%	2%
Asian/NHPI*	1%	1%	1%	1%	1%	1%	1%	1%
Hispanic	17%	19%	19%	19%	19%	19%	19%	21%
Age at referral	100%	100%	100%	100%	100%	100%	100%	100%
Under 14	16%	13%	14%	14%	14%	13%	13%	14%
Age 14	17%	15%	15%	16%	15%	16%	16%	16%
Age 15	24%	23%	23%	23%	23%	23%	23%	23%
Age 16	25%	27%	27%	26%	26%	26%	26%	25%
Age 17 & older	19%	22%	22%	21%	21%	22%	22%	21%

Note. Since 2005, females annually accounted for about one-fourth of the formal probation caseload. White youth accounted for a smaller share of the formal probation caseload in 2018 than in 2005 (41% and 47%, respectively), while Black and Hispanic youth accounted for a slightly larger proportion in 2019. Youth aged 14 and under accounted for smaller proportions of the formal probation caseload in 2019 compared with 2005, while youth aged 17 and older accounted for a larger proportion. From Office of Juvenile Justice and Delinquency Prevention (2021a).

[a] Excludes persons of Hispanic ethnicity. Persons of Hispanic ethnicity can be of any race. Detail may not sum to 100% because of rounding.

if the youth, parent, or legal guardian is following the probation order. This is done to encourage collaboration between the court and the youth's family to help the juvenile fulfill their probation conditions and ultimately be released from court supervision.

If a juvenile is believed to have violated a condition of their probation, the court is notified and a *revocation hearing* is held, in which a judge will decide the validity of the violation. If it is found the youth violated their probation, the judge can warn the juvenile or, in some instances, revoke the probation and impose a harsher sentence, such as incarceration.

Other Sanctions

Alternative Nonincarceration Options

A disposition order may include other sanctions that do not include confinement and may or may not be part of a probation order. These can include the following:

Verbal warning: A judge can verbally reprimand a juvenile as a sanction, usually for low-level first offenses.

Fine/restitution: The minor may be required to pay a fine or provide compensation to the victim.

Counseling: This can be in conjunction with probation or be given as independent treatment.

Community service: Juveniles can be ordered to spend a certain number of hours in their community performing work on a needs basis or as part of compensating a victim, such as cleaning up graffiti they drew on someone's property.

Alternative Incarceration Options

Home confinement/house arrest: The judge can order the minor to spend all of their time outside school and other mandated orders, such as counseling and community service, at home. This mandate can include either **passive monitoring**, which consists of periodic phone calls to check up on the youth and verify that they are home, or **active monitoring**, which is usually prescribed for more serious offenses and can include an electronic bracelet that continually monitors the youth's location.

According to the OJJDP (2018), "the most severe sanction that a juvenile court can impose is restricting a juvenile's freedom through placement in a facility" (p. 1). In 2017, 28% of adjudicated delinquents were placed in a residential facility (OJJDP, 2019a). **Residential placement** is out-of-home placement before or more likely after an adjudication that can be secure or nonsecure and can include the following:

Juvenile Hall/Juvenile detention facility: The judge can send the minor to a juvenile detention facility for a short period of time.

Secured juvenile facilities: These facilities are designed for long-term stays, usually for more violent and chronic offenders (also see figure 9.7).

Juvenile and adult prison: In some jurisdictions, judges can send delinquent children to a juvenile facility and then order a transfer to an adult facility when the youth reaches the age of majority. As you may remember from Chapter 8, when a minor is sentenced to serve time in both a juvenile and an adult facility, it is considered a **blended sentence**.

Generally, placement occurs after a youth has been adjudicated delinquent for an offense; however, as mentioned previously, a juvenile may also be held in detention before adjudication, such as soon after arrest or during court proceedings. This depends on the case's circumstances, for example, for the offender's, victim's, and community's safety. Juveniles sanctioned to residential placement must still receive mental health and other counseling, health care, and educational services, among many other documented needs.

There were 12,219 17-year-olds in residential placement in 2017, more than any other age group (OJJDP, 2019c; more information regarding age and facility data is provided in figures 9.4-9.6 and table 9.3).

Statistical Data Reflecting Juveniles in Residential Placement by Most Serious Offense, Age, Gender, and Race

- Just under 1,000 inmates age 17 or younger were in the custody of state prisons at the end of 2018. The number of youth under age 18 in adult prisons fell 82% between 2000 and 2018.
- Since 2000, between 3% and 4% of inmates under 18 in custody were females.
- From 2000 to 2005, the count of inmates under 18 in adult facilities decreased by 43%. The count increased 24%, to 2,743 youth under age 18 held in adult facilities, by 2009 and then decreased rapidly.

As discussed, juveniles can also be detained while awaiting trial for their own safety and the safety of the community as determined by the judge. Percentages of juveniles who are in residential placement as a result of being either detained or committed is detailed in Figure 9.8)

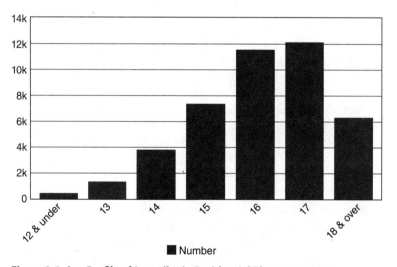

Figure 9.4 Age Profile of Juveniles in Residential Placement, 2017

- There were 545 juveniles ages 12 or younger in residential placement on the 2017 census date. These very young juveniles accounted for 1% of all youth in residential placement.
- Although comparable numbers of 16-year-olds and 17-year-olds were arrested in 2017 the number of 16-year-olds in residential placement was lower than the number involving 17-year-olds. Despite this, in 9 States 17-year-olds are excluded from the original jurisdiction of the juvenile court. In these States, all 17-year-olds are legally adults and are referred to criminal court rather than to juvenile court. Usually, fewer 17-year-olds than 16-year-olds are subject to original juvenile court jurisdiction in the United States and placed in juvenile facilities. In addition, many States have statutes that target certain older juveniles for processing directly in criminal courts (via either statutory exclusion or concurrent jurisdiction provisions). In these situations, when a youth of juvenile age is arrested, the matter goes before a criminal court rather than before a juvenile court. The census captured a small number of youth who were processed in a criminal rather than a juvenile court, but the majority of youth handled in criminal court and incarcerated at some point are held in adult jails and prisons.

Source: OJJDP

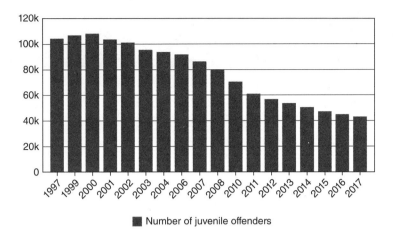

Figure 9.5 One Day Count of Juveniles in Residential Placement Facilities, 1997–2017

Nationally, 37,529 juvenile offenders were held in residential placement facilities on October 24, 2018. The residential placement rate is the number of juvenile offenders in residential placement on October 24, 2018, per 100,000 juveniles age 10 through the upper age of original juvenile court jurisdiction in each state.

Minorities include blacks, Hispanics, American Indians/Alaskan Natives, Asians/Pacific Islanders, and those identified as other race.

- In all but six states, the residential placement rate for black juvenile offenders exceeded the rate for other race/ethnicity groups.
- Nationally, the ratio of the placement rate for minorities to that for whites was 2.4 to 1.
- In 33 states, the ratio between the minority-to-white placement rate was above the national average. In 18 states, the minority-to-white placement rate was more than 4 to 1.

Source: OJJDP

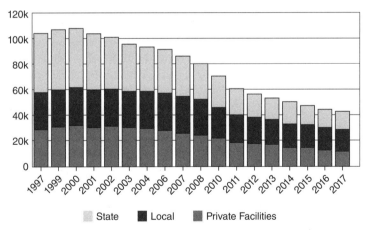

Figure 9.6 One Day Count of Juveniles in Residential Placement Facilities by Facility Operation, 1997–2017

- Information about youth in residential placement and the facilities that hold these youth are based on two OJJDP data collections: the Census of Juveniles in Residential Placement (CJRP) and the Juvenile Residential Facility Census (JRFC), respectively. Combined, these data collections provide a one-day count of the youth residential placement population.
- The vast majority of residents in juvenile residential placement facilities on October 24, 2018 were juveniles held for an offense (86%).
- The one-day count of juveniles in residential placement held for an offense fell 64% between 1997 and 2018.
- More than two-thirds (73%) of juvenile offenders were held in public facilities in 2018 - and more than half (52%) of these youth were in local facilities

Source: OJJDP

TABLE 9.3 Percent of facilities providing treatment services, by facility operation, 2018

	TOTAL	PUBLIC	STATE	LOCAL	PRIVATE
Total number of facilities	1,510	903	331	572	607
Number of facilities providing on-site treatment	932	468	250	218	464
Any treatment service	62%	52%	76%	38%	76%
On-site treatment services[a]					
Mental health	86%	90%	94%	86%	83%
Substance abuse	70%	80%	87%	72%	60%
Sex offender	36%	38%	53%	22%	34%
Violent offender	21%	30%	42%	17%	11%
Arson	10%	13%	22%	4%	8%

Note. Sixty-two percent of residential placement facilities provide on-site treatment as categorized here. A larger proportion of private facilities (76%) reported providing on-site treatment services in 2018 than public facilities (52%). From Office of Juvenile Justice and Delinquency Prevention (2019a).
[a] Percent based on number of facilities providing on-site treatment.

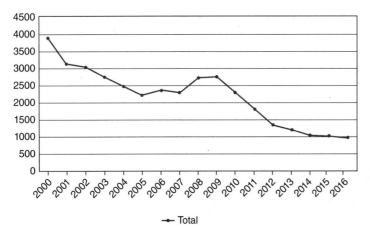

Figure 9.7 Number of Inmates Age 17 or Younger in Custody of State Prison Institutions, 2000–2016

Source: OJJDP

Graduated Sanctions

Courts can also follow the notion of **graduated sanctions**. A graduated-sanctions system can provide multiple levels of sanctions ranging from least restrictive, in the form of teen court or probation, to secure corrections (Howell, 1995; Wilson & Howell, 1993, as cited in "Practical Approach," 2004).

A GRADUATED-SANCTIONS SYSTEM

1. Immediate intervention with first-time delinquent offenders (misdemeanors and nonviolent felonies) and nonserious repeat offenders (examples include teen court, diversion, and regular probation)
2. Intermediate sanctions for first-time serious or violent offenders and also chronic and serious/violent offenders (intensive probation supervision is the main example)
3. Community confinement (secure and nonsecure residential community-based programs are examples)
4. Secure corrections for the most serious, violent, chronic offenders (e.g., training schools)
5. Aftercare (consisting of a continuum of court-based step-down program options that culminate in discharge) ("Practical Approach," 2004)

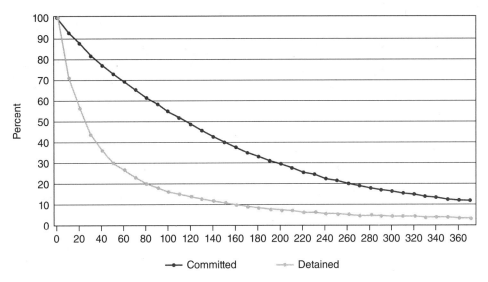

Figure 9.8 Percent of Residents Remaining in Placement by Placement Status, 2017
Source: OJJDP

These gradations and their sublevels are usually matched up to a continuum of treatment options for law enforcement, juvenile and family courts, and juvenile corrections officials ("Practical Approach," 2004, p. 1).

Multiple-problem youth,juveniles experiencing both mental health and school issues along with other problems such as drug use, gang involvement, and personal victimization are at greater risk for continued and escalating offending ("Practical Approach," 2004). These problem youth and youth in general who have suffered victimization can be revictimized after entering the system as well.

Victimization Within Juvenile Facilities

Statistics and Disparities

According to the National Survey of Youth in Custody, the rate of sexual victimization of youth in facilities declined from 9.5% in 2012 to 7.1% in 2018 (Bureau of Justice Statistics, 2018). Table 9.5 presents the most recent data available.

More than one-third (40.3%) of adjudicated youth who reported youth-on-youth sexual victimization were victimized by more than one perpetrator, as detailed in Table 9.6.

According to the OJJDP (2018), "almost one-third (32.0%) of victims of youth-on-youth sexual victimization reported being injured by the perpetrator, and about one in thirty (3.4%) youth victimized by facility staff reported being injured" (p. 1). (see Table 9.7).

Prison Rape Elimination Act of 2003

On September 4, 2003, President George W. Bush signed the Prison Rape Elimination Act of 2003 (Public Law 108-79). The act requires the Bureau of Justice Statistics to perform an analysis each year of the incidence and effects of prison rape. The Bureau of

TABLE 9.4	Demographics of Juveniles in Corrections						
MOST SERIOUS OFFENSE	**TOTAL**	**WHITE**	**TOTAL MINORITY**	**BLACK**	**HISPANIC**	**AMERICAN INDIAN**[a]	**ASIAN**[a]
Total	100%	33%	67%	41%	21%	2%	1%
Delinquency	100%	32%	68%	42%	21%	2%	1%
Person	100%	29%	71%	45%	21%	1%	1%
Criminal homicide	100%	21%	79%	47%	28%	1%	1%
Sexual assault	100%	54%	46%	26%	16%	1%	1%
Robbery	100%	11%	89%	63%	21%	1%	1%
Aggravated assault	100%	23%	77%	47%	25%	2%	1%
Simple assault	100%	37%	63%	38%	19%	2%	0%
Other person	100%	39%	61%	39%	16%	1%	1%
Property	100%	32%	68%	43%	19%	2%	1%
Burglary	100%	30%	70%	46%	18%	2%	1%
Theft	100%	36%	64%	43%	16%	1%	1%
Auto theft	100%	28%	73%	44%	24%	2%	1%
Arson	100%	47%	53%	21%	19%	6%	4%
Other property	100%	36%	64%	40%	18%	2%	1%
Drug	100%	43%	57%	29%	23%	2%	0%
Drug trafficking	100%	29%	71%	38%	32%	0%	0%
Other drug	100%	46%	54%	27%	21%	3%	0%
Public order	100%	34%	66%	38%	22%	1%	1%
Weapons	100%	17%	83%	52%	26%	1%	1%
Other public order	100%	46%	54%	29%	20%	2%	1%
Technical violation[b]	100%	33%	67%	35%	26%	2%	1%
Status	100%	54%	46%	27%	12%	2%	1%

Note. Total includes a small number of youth for whom race/ethnicity was not reported or was reported as other. Details may not add to total because of rounding. The Hispanic category includes persons of Latin American or other Spanish culture or origin regardless of race. These persons are not included in the other race/ethnicity categories. Minorities include Blacks, Hispanics, American Indians/Alaskan Natives, Asians/Pacific Islanders, and those identified as other race. From Office of Juvenile Justice and Delinquency Prevention (2018).

[a] American Indian includes Alaskan Natives; Asian includes Pacific Islanders.
[b] Technical violations include violations of probation, parole, and valid court order.

• In 2017, about 29,000 minority offenders were in residential placement in juvenile facilities across the country, 67% of the national residential placement population.
• White youths' share of juveniles held in placement was greatest for the offenses of sexual assault and status offenses and black youths' share was greatest for robbery and weapons offenses.

TABLE 9.5 National Estimates of Adjudicated Youth Reporting Sexual Victimization in Juvenile Facilities, 2012 and 2018

TYPE OF INCIDENT	2012	2018
Estimated number of adjudicated[a] youth in placement	18,140	12,750
Estimated number of victims	1,720	900
Percent of adjudicated youth reporting any sexual victimization	9.5%	7.1%
Percent of adjudicated youth reporting:		
Youth-on-youth victimization	2.5%	1.9%
Staff sexual misconduct	7.7%	5.8%
Force reported	3.5%	2.1%
No report of force	4.7%	3.9%

Note. Sexual victimization is defined as any forced or coerced sexual activity with another youth or any sexual activity with facility staff. In 2018, 1.9% of youth reported sexual victimization by another youth, down from 2.5% in 2012. In 2018, 5.8% of youth reported sexual misconduct by facility staff, and 2.1% reported sexual misconduct by facility staff that involved force or coercion, significantly below the levels reported in 2012. Data are based on the National Survey of Youth in Custody (NSYC; conducted between February and September 2012 and between March and December 2018). The NSYC is based on a multistage probability sample providing representative data on adjudicated youth residing in facilities owned or operated by a state juvenile correctional authority and all state-placed adjudicated youth held under state contract in locally or privately operated juvenile facilities. The NSYC is part of the Bureau of Justice Statistics' National Prison Rape Statistics Program, which was established to collect data on the incidence and prevalence of sexual assault in juvenile facilities under the Prison Rape Elimination Act of 2003 (PREA; P.L. 108-79). Table and notes from Office of Juvenile Justice and Delinquency Prevention (2021c).

[a] Youth were asked to report on any victimization involving another youth or facility staff in the past 12 months or since admission to the facility, if less than 12 months. Subgroups may not sum to total because youth may have reported multiple victimizations or because of item nonresponse.

Justice Statistics developed the National Prison Rape Statistics Program, which consists of four separate data collection efforts: the Survey on Sexual Violence, the National Inmate Survey, the National Survey of Youth in Custody (NSYC), and the National Former Prisoner Survey. The Survey on Sexual Violence collects information about incidents of sexual violence that have been reported to and investigated by adult and juvenile correctional authorities. The National Inmate Survey collects allegations of sexual assault self-reported by adult and juvenile inmates in correctional facilities. The NSYC retrieves self-reported sexual assault data from youth in juvenile correctional facilities. The National Former Prisoner Survey studies allegations of former inmates of sexual assault experienced during their last incarceration.

Solitary Confinement

Solitary confinement, or "seclusion," can include physical and social isolation in a cell for 22 to 24 hours per day (American Academy of Child & Adolescent Psychiatry, 2012). The American Academy of Child & Adolescent Psychiatry says solitary confinement of juveniles "can lead to depression, anxiety, and even psychosis" (American Academy of Child & Adolescent Psychiatry, 2012, p. 1). On January 26, 2016, President Barack Obama announced a ban on solitary confinement, through an executive order, for juvenile offenders

TABLE 9.6 Perpetrator Characteristics Reported by Victims of Youth-on-Youth Sexual Victimization, 2018

PERPETRATOR CHARACTERISTICS	PERCENT
More than one perpetrator	
Yes	40.3%
No	59.7%
Sex of perpetrator	
Male(s) only	67.8%
Female(s) only	26.5%
Both male(s) and female(s)	5.7%
Race of perpetrator in single-perpetrator incidents	
White only	57.1%
Black only	26.2%
Other/two or more races[a]	16.6%
Race of perpetrator in multiple-perpetrator incidents	
White only	19.9%
Black only	35.4%
Other/two or more races[a]	44.7%
Were any of the perpetrators[b]:	
Hispanic	31.6%
A gang member	45.3%
Victim's roommate	35.7%

Note. More than half (57.1%) of juvenile victims reported that at least one of their perpetrators in single-perpetrator incidents of youth-on-youth sexual victimization was White, and 26% of victims reported that one or more perpetrators were Black. More than one-third (35.7%) of reported perpetrators were the victim's roommate and 45% of perpetrators of youth-on-youth sexual victimization were gang members. Data are based on the third National Survey of Youth in Custody (NSYC) conducted between March and December 2018 (Office of Juvenile Justice and Delinquency Prevention, 2021b). The NSYC is based on a multistage probability sample providing representative data on adjudicated youth residing in facilities owned or operated by a state juvenile correctional authority and all state-placed adjudicated youth held under state contract in locally or privately operated juvenile facilities. The NSYC is part of the Bureau of Justice Statistics' National Prison Rape Statistics Program, which was established to collect data on the incidence and prevalence of sexual assault in juvenile facilities under the Prison Rape Elimination Act of 2003 (PREA; P.L. 108-79). Table and notes from Office of Juvenile Justice and Delinquency Prevention, 2021b).

[a] Includes American Indian, Alaska Native, Asian, Native Hawaiian, and other Pacific Islander.
[b] Detail sums to more than 100% because some youth reported more than one characteristic. Refers to both single- and multiple-perpetrator incidents.

TABLE 9.7 Incident Characteristics of Sexual Victimization in Juvenile Facilities, 2018

INCIDENT CHARACTERISTICS	YOUTH ON YOUTH	STAFF SEXUAL MISCONDUCT
Victim injury		
Yes	32.0%	3.4%
No	68.0%	96.6%
When victimization first happened		
During first 24 hours	12.1%	8.9%
During first week (but not first 24 hours)	17.8%	14.4%
During first month (but not first week)	20.5%	23.5%
During first 2 months (but not first month)	7.8%	11.4%
After first 2 months	35.2%	31.5%
Not reported	6.5%	10.3%
Type of pressure or force		
Gave victim drugs or alcohol	13.8%	36.5%
Threatened with physical harm	33.0%	12.8%
Physically held down/restrained	22.1%	9.7%
Threatened with a weapon	21.8%	12.8%
Pressured/hurt some other way	64.5%	37.3%
Where occurred		
In victim's room/sleeping area	24.0%	32.0%
In room/sleeping area of another youth	4.1%	NA
Shower/bathroom	13.9%	7.5%
Other area on facility grounds[a]	36.4%	21.5%
Somewhere else on or off facility grounds, unidentified, or other areas unknown	21.7%	NA
Private office	NA	20.0%
Closet or supply room	NA	14.8%
Off of facility grounds	NA	4.2%

Note. NA: does not apply. Threat of physical harm was reported by one-third of victims of youth-on-youth sexual victimization; conversely, 12.8% of victims of staff sexual misconduct reported such threats. More than one-third (36.4%) of youth-on-youth victims reported that the incident took place somewhere on the facility grounds (e.g., recreation area, library, workshop, or other common areas), and 28.1% of victims of youth-on-youth sexual victimization reported the incident took place in their room or in the room of another youth. Table and notes from the Office of Juvenile Justice and Delinquency Prevention (2021d).

[a] Includes yard or recreation area, classroom, library, workshop, kitchen, or other workplace, office, closet, supply room, bus, car, or other unknown areas.

DEEPER DIVE

The Nelson Mandela Rules in Relation to Solitary Confinement

The "Nelson Mandela Rules" are a revision of the 1955 United Nations Standard Minimum Rules on the Treatment of Prisoners. The revised rules were adopted by the UN Commission on Crime Prevention and Criminal Justice in Vienna, Austria, on May 22, 2015.

The revision focused on nine areas, including prison health care, discipline/sanctions, and restraints. One of the modifications was in the area of discipline and the use of solitary confinement. This amendment provided not only an updated definition for solitary confinement but also strict limitations for its use (Penal Reform International, 2019).

in the federal prison system. It should be noted, however, that the number of juveniles held in federal prisons is very low, fewer than 30 individuals in 2016 (Schwartzapfel, 2016). Youth can also be contracted out from federal to private institutions or transferred to local prisons, which are not governed by this order (Sawyer & Wagner, 2019). This is typically done because alternate detention centers can offer more rehabilitative programs for the youths (Schwartzapfel, 2016). Both private and state prisons, however,

◼ Statutes limiting or prohibiting juvenile solitary confinement

Figure 9.9 States Limiting or Prohibiting Juvenile Solitary Confinement.
Source: NCSL, 2020

have also been encouraged to minimize their use of solitary confinement as stipulated in the Bureau of Prisons guidelines. Solitary confinement was also addressed in the last revision of the JJDPA in 2018, which requires reporting on the use and reason for holding youth in solitary confinement in state prisons. In December 2018, the passage of the First Step Act made the prior executive order banning solitary confinement of juveniles in federal public prisons a federal law. The new law bans solitary confinement at the federal level with few exceptions. It limits solitary confinement in all federal institutions to a maximum of 3-hour periods and only in very rare cases (Congressional Research Service, 2019). In those cases where behavioral issues still exist after a short time in solitary confinement, juveniles are to be transferred to another facility, as opposed to further isolated in confinement (Congressional Research Service, 2019).

In recent years, states have also begun to prohibit or limit solitary confinement through administrative policies or state law. Currently, however, as depicted in Figure 9.9, disparity still exists among individual states' guidelines and use of this type of imprisonment.

The Death Penalty to Life in Prison

As you may remember reading in previous chapters, the U.S. Supreme Court ruled in *Roper v. Simmons* in 2005 that imposing the death penalty on offenders who were younger than age 18 at the time of the offense was cruel and unusual punishment and violated the Eighth Amendment. Imposing the death penalty on children is also prohibited by international human rights law as described in the International Covenant on Civil and Political Rights, the UN Convention on the Rights of the Child, and the American Convention on Human Rights (United Nations, 1990).

Although the death penalty was banned in 2005, states were still able to automatically sanction a youth to life in prison for certain violent offenses without parole. It was not until 2010 that the Supreme Court ruled in *Graham v. Florida* that a state imposing life in prison without parole is also in violation of the Eighth Amendment and therefore is unconstitutional. This decision was made partly because, as the court notes, life sentences for juveniles for nonhomicidal crimes had already been banned across the globe. Two years later, two cases, *Miller v. Alabama* and *Jackson v. Hobbs* (2012), prompted the Supreme Court once again to rule in the area of life without parole for those under 18. The court further mandated states to avoid automatic rulings of life without parole in homicide cases and instead decide them on a case-by-case basis. Finally, in 2016, in the case of *Montgomery v. Louisiana*, the Supreme Court requested states to apply the 2012 ruling retroactively. States were to review past cases that were automatically adjudicated as life in prison with no parole and consider lesser punishment through parole hearings. Although numerous states have outlawed life without parole under any circumstance for those under age 18, over 1,40 individuals remain in correctional facilities without review because of various factors, including lack of state resources and heavy caseloads (Rovner, 2021).

Supreme Court Rulings

ROPER V. SIMMONS, *543 US 551 (2005)*

In 1993, Christopher Simmons was sentenced to death after committing a murder at age 17 in Missouri. Along with two younger friends, Charles Benjamin and John Tessmer, Simmons devised a plan that included breaking into an individual's home.

After meeting up in the middle of the night, John decided not to go with Christopher and Charles. Simmons and Benjamin broke into the house, bound the occupant's hands, and covered her eyes. After driving the homeowner to a state park, they threw her off a bridge. The defendants were charged and convicted of murder and sentenced to death. The case was appealed to the Missouri Supreme Court, and the execution was put on hold while the U.S. Supreme Court decided another case involving defendant Daryl Renard Atkins. Atkins, who was deemed to have limited mental capacity and considered "mentally retarded," was also facing the death penalty. The court ruled that because most citizens found this punishment extreme and uncommon under these circumstances, carrying out Atkins's execution would be cruel and unusual. The court also noted that this type of punishment would conflict with "evolving standards of decency" and applicability of deterrence to "mentally retarded" offenders because of their mitigated culpability. The Missouri Supreme Court then applied this logic to *Roper v. Simmons*. They believed there was also a consensus among citizens within the United States and people in other countries condemning capital punishment for minors because of their inherent impulsivity and therefore reduced culpability. The case was overturned by the Missouri Supreme Court, and in 2005 the U.S. Supreme Court ruled 5–4 to consider capital punishment cruel and unusual for those under 18 because it was a disproportionate punishment for minors and contrary to a consensus against it. Capital punishment for any minor under 18 is now considered unconstitutional for all states.

GRAHAM V. FLORIDA, *130 S. CT. 2011 (2010)*

In July 2003, Terrance Graham, age 16, along with two accomplices, attempted to rob a restaurant in Florida. Graham was arrested and charged as an adult for armed burglary. Because armed burglary is a first-degree felony that was punishable by life in the state of Florida, he plead guilty to avoid a life sentence. In 2004, Graham was arrested again for home invasion robbery. In 2006, he was sentenced by the judge to life in prison, and since there is no parole in Florida, Graham would not have a chance for an early release.

The case was reviewed by the Supreme Court, which ruled that it was unconstitutional to sanction life in prison for a nonhomicide offense if there was no realistic chance to obtain release through parole. Graham's sentence was overturned, and life in prison with no opportunity for parole was banned for nonhomicide cases.

MILLER V. ALABAMA, *NO. 10-9646,* AND JACKSON V. HOBBS, *NO. 10-9647*

In July 2003, Evan Miller and Colby Smith killed Cole Cannon. They used a baseball bat to beat Cole and then set fire to his trailer while he was still inside. Miller was 14 years old at the time. In 2004, Miller was transferred from the Lawrence County Juvenile Court to Lawrence County Circuit Court to be tried as an adult for capital murder. In 2006, he was found guilty and was sentenced to a mandatory term of life imprisonment without the possibility of parole.

In an associated case, three boys, Kuntrell Jackson, along with Derrick Shields and Travis Booker, robbed a store in 1999. All of the offenders were 14 years old at the time. During the robbery, one youth shot the store clerk before leaving the store. Even though Kuntrell did not fire the gun, being part of a robbery that led to a murder, he was tried and convicted of capital murder. He was sentenced to a mandatory term of life imprisonment without the possibility of parole.

The U.S. Supreme court reviewed both these cases. It ruled 5–4 that the Eighth Amendment prohibition against cruel and unusual punishment prohibits the mandatory sentencing of life in prison without the possibility of parole for minors. Justice Kagan wrote,

> That mandatory life without parole for those under age of 18 at the time of their crime violates the 8th Amendment's prohibition on cruel and unusual punishments. . . . Mandatory life without parole for a juvenile precludes consideration of his chronological age and its hallmark features—among them, immaturity, impetuosity, and failure to appreciate risks and consequences.

Justice Kagan further stated, "It prevents taking into account the family and home environment that surrounds him—and from which he cannot usually extricate himself—no matter how brutal or dysfunctional" (*Montgomery v. Louisiana* 136 S. Ct. 718, 2016).

The court concluded that children are constitutionally different from adults for sentencing purposes. Although a mandatory life sentence without parole did not violate the Eighth Amendment for adults, this sentence would be unconstitutionally disproportionate for children.

DEEPER DIVE

George Stinney Jr.

In 1944, at age 14, George Junius Stinney Jr., an African American teenage boy, was found guilty of the murder of two girls, ages 7 and 11, in South Carolina. Later that year, Stinney was executed by electric chair.

For more information regarding this event, please see YouTube https://www.youtube.com/watch?v=5iL1f-jV32A

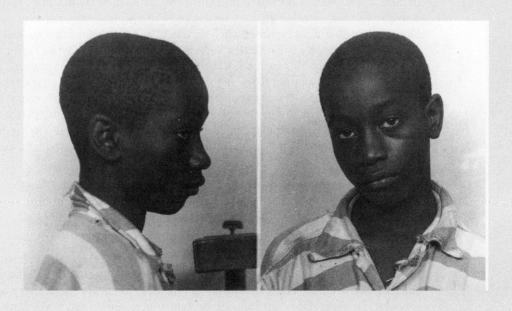

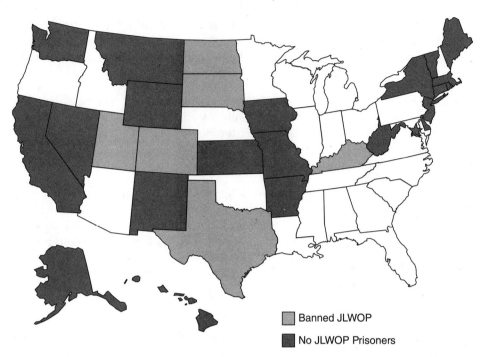

Figure 9.10 States that have banned or limited the use of juvenile life without parole sentences, 2018

It should be noted that this ruling did not make life in prison without parole for homicide offenses unconstitutional; it only made its automatic/mandatory application unconstitutional. States are only required to apply this sentence on a case-by-case basis.

MONTGOMERY V. LOUISIANA, *136 S. CT. 718 (2016)*

In 2016, the Supreme Court determined that *Miller v. Alabama* must be applied retroactively. This was decided after its review of *Henry Montgomery v. Louisiana*. Henry Montgomery committed murder when he was 17 and had been in prison in Louisiana since 1963. He was 68 years when the Supreme Court ruled 6–3 that their prior ruling be applied retroactively. This meant that those states that automatically sentenced all homicide cases involving a minor to life in prison without parole must reconsider those cases on a case-by-case basis. It was suggested that states could address the unconstitutionality of mandatory juvenile life-without-parole sentences by permitting parole hearings instead of resentencing the approximately 2,000 individuals affected. Twenty-five states still allow life without parole as a sentencing option for juveniles who have committed homicide (Rovner, 2021; also see figure 9.10)).

Aftercare and Reentry Into Society

Juvenile aftercare/reentry has been defined as "reintegrative services that prepare youths in out-of-home placements for their eventual return home by establishing the necessary collaboration with the community and its resources to ensure the delivery of needed services and supervision" (Altschuler & Armstrong, 2001; Gies, 2003; both cited in

Development Services Group, 2017, p. 1). Juvenile **aftercare** is similar to adult parole in that after release from an institution, a juvenile is often ordered to a period of aftercare. During this time, the youth is still under the court's supervision and may be recommitted if they do not follow the provisions of aftercare. Juvenile **parole** officers work in juvenile corrections to help juvenile offenders transition back into the community (National Research Council and Institute of Medicine, 2001; OJJDP, 2019a).

Recidivism

Although national recidivism rates for juveniles do not exist, a 2015 report from the Council of State Governments Justice Center compiled data from the 39 states tracking recidivism to compare state statistics. The study found that juveniles reoffend more often than adults after release in all states. The highest reported recidivism rate for juvenile offenders was 76% within 3 years and 84% within 5 years. Many of these juveniles continue to reoffend into adulthood (Council of State Governments, 2015, 2016). In another study conducted by Anna Aizer and Joseph Doyle in 2015, data on 30,000 juvenile offenders over the previous 10 years who had been involved in the Illinois juvenile justice system were analyzed. The study found that 40% of juvenile offenders were incarcerated in an adult prison for reoffending by the time they turned 25 (Aizer & Doyle, 2015).

Programs

There are many programs that provide various services and educational opportunities to assist juveniles in positive and fulfilling reintegration and prevent recidivism. These programs will be discussed more in later chapters, some of which can be found through the resources listed in the sidebar.

Expungement

If a juvenile case is not dismissed and ultimately reaches the disposition stage, a record of the offense is created. Because a juvenile record can be detrimental to a child's future, every state has its own process to expunge records. **Expungement** is defined as records being destroyed/removed from all databases and other files (Teigen, 2016). This term is sometimes incorrectly used interchangeably with the **sealing** of a record,

---

JUVENILE RE-ENTRY/AFTERCARE RESOURCES

CrimeSolutions.gov: A National Institute of Justice website that provides detailed information regarding programs that are focused on reducing recidivism and successfully reintegrating offenders into the community.

The National Institute of Justice's Serious and Violent Offender Reentry Initiative: The National Institute of Justice funded a multiyear, multisite evaluation of programs. The initiative's goal was to improve criminal justice, employment, education, health, and housing outcomes.

National Reentry Resource Center: Established by the Second Chance Act (Public Law 110-199) and administered by the Bureau of Justice Assistance in the U.S. Department of Justice, the center provides training and technical assistance to institutions working on prisoner reentry.

which does not delete the information, but instead limits access to it by the public. Usually, states will allow a case to be expunged when the juvenile turns a certain age, typically 18 or 19. However, whereas some states will remove the record automatically or upon a formal request, others require a fee (Webster, 2015). In addition, the digital age has also made the erasure of criminal records or even an arrest nearly impossible (Thompson, 2015).

Worldview

Juvenile Corrections Around the World

The United Nations Standard Minimum Rules for the Administration of Juvenile Justice (the Beijing Rules) defines the deprivation of liberty as

> any form of detention or imprisonment or the placement of a person in a public or private custodial setting, from which this person is not permitted to leave at will, by order of any judicial, administrative or other public authority. (United Nations, 1990, p. 1)

Article 37 of the UN Convention on the Rights of the Child requires that "deprivation of the liberty of a juvenile should be a disposition of last resort and for the minimum necessary period and should be limited to exceptional cases" (United Nations, 1990, p. 1). It goes on to stipulate that these rules should be applied impartially, without discrimination of any kind, and that juveniles detained in facilities

> should be guaranteed the benefit of meaningful activities and programs which would serve to promote and sustain their health and self-respect, to foster their sense of responsibility and encourage those attitudes and skills that will assist them in developing their potential as members of society. (United Nations, 1990, p. 1)

Likewise, Rule 11(b) of the Havana Rules has defined deprivation of liberty as

> any form of detention or imprisonment, or the placement of a person in a public or private custodial setting from which the child is not permitted to leave at will, by order of any judicial, administrative or other public authority. (United Nations, 1990, p. 85)

However, despite these compilations of guidelines and laws, the United Nations Children's Fund, UNICEF, has estimated that more than 1 million children are behind bars across the globe and disparity of treatment continues to exist (Human Rights Watch, 2016; also see rate of recidivism, figure 9.12).

The following countries were chosen based on relevance to the chapter's content and available international data.

GERMANY
The Vera Institute of Justice has recognized Germany's justice system as one with better outcomes for all of its prisoners, even though it is less punitive toward minors who commit

crimes (Delaney et al., 2018; VERA Institute of Justice, 2018). In Germany, a minor, defined as anyone under 18, is never prosecuted as an adult, no matter what crime they commit, even homicide. There is also a specialized prison for adolescents, but they can stay there until they reach the age of 24. These prisons house both males and females, prisoners can interact with each other, and each youth is given a paying job. Prison cells are equipped with private bathrooms and windows that open, and adolescents can leave during the day. Germany's juvenile recidivism rate is reported to be 30%.

AUSTRALIA

On an average night in June 2018, 980 young people were in youth detention in Australia; 60% were unsentenced, awaiting the outcome of their case. The majority (90%) were male, and most (84%) were aged 10–17. This reflects a rate of 3.5 per 10,000 young people aged 10–17.

Each state and territory in Australia has its own juvenile laws and policies, but many of the statutes are similar. There are separate justice systems for young people and adults. Juveniles can be charged with a criminal offense if they are aged 10 and older. The upper age limit for their youth systems is 17 (at the time of the offense).

Although Australian states and territories have set the age of criminal responsibility at 10 years old, a recommendation to raise the age to 12 has been proposed and is under review. In Victoria, individuals aged 18–20 may be sentenced to detention in a youth facility under the state's "dual-track" sentencing system, which is intended to prevent young people from entering the adult prison system at an early age. Types of youth justice supervision include supervised detention, community-based detention, unsentenced supervision, home detention, bail, supervised release, probation, and similarly suspended detention (Australian Institute of Health and Welfare, 2019; Sawyer & Wagner, 2019).

CANADA

The Youth Criminal Justice Act (YCJA) is the federal law that governs Canada's youth justice system and applies to youth aged 12 to 17. Before the YCJA, Canada had one of the highest youth incarceration rates in the Western world (Allen, 2018; Public Safety Canada, 2018).

In 2012, Canada's Parliament amended the YCJA to permit a youth sentence to include the objectives of punishment and specific deterrence. However, they stipulated that this should not result in a sentence that exceeds a proportionate response, nor should it impede rehabilitation. Additionally, all reasonable alternatives to custody should be considered first.

Although the most common sentence for youth in Canada is probation, legislation has also instituted sentences that combine imprisonment with community supervision. These sentences include a portion of the sentence to be completed in custody and the other part in the community to aid in rehabilitating and reentry into society. In 2016/2017, there were 5,937 youth who began a period of supervision in correctional services in the eight reporting jurisdictions, an 8% decrease from the previous year and a 44% decrease from 2012/2013. Among those entering the corrections system, 68% began their period of supervision in the community (also see Figure 9.11). Victims' participation in community-based approaches is also encouraged.

A general rule under the YCJA is that a young person serving a youth custody sentence is to be kept separate from adults. When a juvenile is serving the custody portion of the sentence, the YCJA requires that a youth worker assist the young person during their reentry into the community and supervise and provide support for adherence to any court mandates.

Other sentencing options include warnings, probation, attendance at special programs, or community service (Allen, 2018).

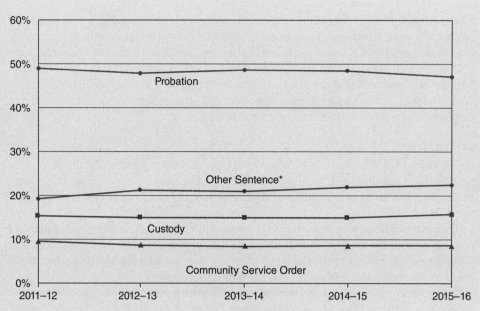

Figure 9.11 Percentage of Youth Court Sentences in Canada
Source: Public Safety Canada, 2018

LATIN AND CENTRAL AMERICA

Probation is the most common sanction in Latin American countries, as it is in the United States (Inter-American Commission on Human Rights, 2015; OJJDP, 2018). Similarly, these programs require the child to attend socioeducational programs but are supervised by social workers who have regular contact with the youth, their family, and the community. Other noncustodial measures also tend to be similar to those in the United States and include warnings by the judge and prohibiting the child from associating with specific individuals or going to certain places or events. Measures can also include requiring the child to attend counseling and restorative justice in the form of providing community services, repairing any damage done or harm caused, and other forms of restitution.

Minimum ages of responsibility vary between Latin and Central American countries. For example, Mexico's constitution states that at both the federal and the state level, "incarceration will be used only as an extreme measure and for the shortest appropriate period of time and can only be used in the case of adolescents over the age of 14 convicted of very serious, antisocial behavior" (Inter-American Commission on Human Rights, 2015, p. 4). In Nicaragua, children and adolescents between the ages of 13 and 15 cannot be sentenced to imprisonment. Some countries have age ranges of responsibility. For example, in Venezuela, the maximum custodial sentence children 12 and 13 can receive is 2 years, whereas children 14–17 can be imprisoned for up to 5 years. In Guatemala, children between 13 and 15 can be imprisoned for up to 2 years, while those between 15 and 18 can be imprisoned for up to 6 years. In Nicaragua, the maximum sentence for children age 15 to 17 is 6 years. Other areas have laws for minors of any age. For minors in Costa Rica, the maximum penalty is 15 years; it is 10 years in Chile; 8 years in Honduras, Paraguay, and Colombia; and 7 years in El Salvador. However, El Salvador antigang laws can raise the maximum sentence by 20 years for a minor, and in Peru, under their aggravated terrorism laws, children between 16 and 18 can be sentenced to no less than 25 years (Inter-American Commission on Human Rights, 2015).

In 2015, the Regional Observatory on Juvenile Justice Systems found that in the eight countries monitored in the region (Uruguay, Brazil, Argentina, Bolivia, Colombia, Costa Rica, Ecuador, and Paraguay), there are currently more than 30,000 adolescents (individuals between the ages of 12 and 18) in custody. Many of those countries had a percentage of nearly 50% or more adolescents in pretrial detention (see Table 9.8).

As you have read previously, Article 37 of the Convention on the Rights of the Child prohibits capital punishment and life imprisonment without parole for children; however, not all countries abide by this provision. For example, Saint Vincent and the Grenadines only prohibit capital punishment in the case of minors up until age 15, and therefore capital punishment could be imposed for minors 16 and older. In Argentina, juveniles can be sentenced as adults; therefore, a maximum sentence of life imprisonment without parole can be applied. Belize also permits a sentence of life in prison without the possibility of parole for crimes committed by persons under the age of 18. In Saint Lucia, Saint Vincent and the Grenadines, and Jamaica, a person who has committed a crime while still a minor can be sentenced to life imprisonment. In Barbados and Dominica, a child can be incarcerated indefinitely.

Central American countries allow a custodial measure to be replaced by a noncustodial measure. For example, in Ecuador, a judge can modify or replace the custodial sentence imposed if recommended by the institution in which the child is serving the sentence. In Brazil, noncustodial alternatives are reconsidered every 6 months while the child is incarcerated until they reach the age of 21, when they must be released. In Jamaica, 100% of the children released are automatically enrolled in postrelease programs to track their reentry into the community (Defense for Children, 2015; Inter-American Commission on Human Rights, 2015).

TABLE 9.8 Latin American Adolescents 12–18 in Custody in the Juvenile Justice System by Type of Detention

COUNTRY	TOTAL ADOLESCENTS IN CUSTODY	PRETRIAL DETENTION	SERVING A SENTENCE
Argentina	1,508	867	641
Bolivia	269	162	107
Brazil	20,023	4,315	15,708
Colombia	7,447	4,030	3,417
Costa Rica	64	32	32
Ecuador	625	294	331
Paraguay	387	356	31
Uruguay	744	No data	No data
Totals	31,067	10,056	20,267

Note. From Defense for Children (2015).

DEEPER DIVE

Executions of Juveniles Since 1990 (as of March 2018)

The use of the death penalty for youth under 18 is prohibited under international human rights law; however, some countries around the world continue to utilize it. Since 1990, Amnesty International has documented 138 executions of child offenders in nine countries: China, the Democratic Republic of Congo, Iran, Nigeria, Pakistan, Saudi Arabia, Sudan, the United States, and Yemen.

Many of these countries have changed their laws, and capital punishment for children no longer exists. However, some countries have not. For example, Iran has executed more than twice as many child offenders as the other eight countries combined and is believed by some organizations to be still enforcing this practice.

Additional resources can be found at Amnesty International https://www.amnesty.org/download/Documents/ACT5038322016ENGLISH.pdf

NORWAY

In the entire country of Norway, only nine juveniles were imprisoned as of 2020(Aebi & Tiago, 2021). Only youth who they term "juveniles of last resort," those who display serious behavior problems, have committed serious crimes, and are chronic offenders, can be imprisoned. In those cases, the juvenile can be put in prison for up to 4 weeks, with the possibility of renewal for up to 12 months (Bauer, 2019).

Norway also sets its minimum age of criminal responsibility at 15, which is higher than the minimum age of 12 that the UN Convention on the Rights of the Child recommends, and utilizes a restorative justice model that is consistent with the UN's recommendations. Akin to this philosophy, Norway does not impose life sentences. Norway has an overall recidivism rate of 20%, one of the world's lowest (Bauer, 2019).

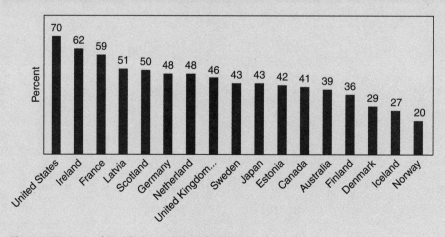

Figure 9.12 Rate of Recidivism Around the World
Source: OJJDP

**KEY INTERNATIONAL SOURCES FOR STANDARDS
AND NORMS FOR THE ADMINISTRATION OF JUSTICE
FOR CHILDREN**

- UN Convention on the Rights of the Child (CRC)
- UN Standard Minimum Rules for the Administration of Juvenile Justice (Beijing Rules)
- UN Rules for the Protection of Juveniles Deprived of Their Liberty (Havana Rules)
- UN Guidelines for the Prevention of Juvenile Delinquency (Riyadh Rules)
- Guidelines for Action on Children in the Criminal Justice System

(Penal Reform International, 2019)

Wrap-up

Although juvenile corrections have not always focused on rehabilitation and were initially administered by the youth's family, and sometimes cruelly by individual societies worldwide, as time progressed, most communities saw the need for a more fair, structured system. Through federal intervention, state policies, and a changing consensus among many societies in the United States and around the world, the juvenile correctional system has undergone significant changes. It continues to strive to provide the necessary tools to ultimately serve the best interests of the child.

Discussion Questions

1. What were the major eras leading up to modern-day corrections?
2. What were the changing roles of corrections up until the modern day?
3. What were some of the federal acts, amendments, and bodies that addressed juvenile confinement and the various guidelines implemented?
4. Describe the various court cases that affected juvenile corrections and punishment within the United States.
5. List and explain the Juvenile Justice and Delinquency Prevention Act core components as they relate to sentencing and corrections.
6. List and explain custodial and noncustodial correctional treatment options.
7. How is juvenile corrections in the United States similar/dissimilar to that in other countries around the world?

ONLINE RESOURCES

National Partnership for Juvenile Services http://www.npjs.org
U.S. Department of Justice Office of Justice Programs http://www.ncjrs.gov
Youth Government http://www.youth.gov
United States Department of Justice: Office of Justice Programs http://www.ojp.gov
Juvenile Justice Exchange Information http://www.jjie.org
Bureau of Justice Statistics http://www.BJS.gov

United States Department of Justice http://www.justice.gov
Coalition for Juvenile Justice http://www.juvjustice.org
Justice Center: The Council of State Governments http://www.csgjusticecenter.org

Definitions

Active monitoring—usually prescribed for more serious offenses and can include an electronic bracelet that continually monitors the youth's location.

Aftercare—services that prepare youths for their eventual return home from out-of-home placements

Blended sentence—blends a juvenile sentence and an adult sentence for certain serious youth offenders

Bound out—some children were sent from institutions to work on farms and others served as domestic laborers

Community-based programs—allow the offender to remain within their own community but under the court's supervision

Community corrections—rehabilitative process completed within the community, not the jails

Congregate institutional model—concentrated large numbers of youth within highly regimented, penitentiary-like institutions

Corrections—a network of agencies that supervise individuals who are incarcerated or going through rehabilitation, parole, or probation

Disposition hearing—a hearing where the judge decides on a disposition for the juvenile after input from various stakeholders

Disposition order—a written, signed document handed down by the court that states the disposition and can include an ordered sanction, a treatment plan, or a combination of sanctions and treatment

Disposition stage—stage in the juvenile justice court process whereby the juvenile has admitted to committing the delinquent act or has been found to have committed it by the court during adjudication

Expungement—criminal records that are destroyed/removed from all databases and files

Federal block grants—aid of a specified amount from the Federal government to individual states and local governments to help support various programs for law enforcement, social services, and community development

Graduated sanctions—the continuum of disposition options that court staff have at their disposal

Guardian ad litem—an individual in addition to the youth's attorney who has input along with other parties, such as representatives from probation, to make recommendations for sanctions

Hull House—a settlement house providing services such as education and assistance to the poor, many of whom were immigrants

Industrial schools—these institutions were intended to focus on rehabilitation by providing education and tangible skills to help youth become productive members of society

Justice model—A more punitive response that called for putting and keeping more offenders in prison

Multiple-problem youth—juveniles experiencing both mental health and school issues along with other problems such as drug use, gang involvement, and personal victimization

New York House of Refuge—the first correctional institution/reformatory solely for juveniles in 1825

Parens patriae—the court having the right to act as the father or parent of the youth

Parole—a period of conditional, supervised release from prison

Passive System—consists of periodic phone calls to check up on the youth and verify that they are home.

Pauperism—dependency on others for goods and services

Petition—a legal document that includes details of an offense and can initiate the prosecution process

Predispositional report—a recommendation for the care, treatment, or rehabilitation of the child along with the parents' or guardians' participation

Probation—an alternative to confinement, whereby the youth reenters society under specific conditions under the supervision of a probation officer

Rehabilitation model—treatment utilizing group therapy and counseling within the institution

Sanction—a financial or other penalty imposed by a judge on an offender

Residential Placement—out-of-home placement before or after adjudication that can be secure or non-secure.

Sealing—does not delete a record, but instead limits access to it by the public.

Status offenses—age-specific offenses solely applying to juveniles

References

Aebi, M. F., & Tiago, M. M. (2021). SPACE I – 2020 – Council of Europe Annual Penal Statistics: Prison populations. Council of Europe.

Allen, M. (2018, July 23). *Police-reported crime statistics in Canada, 2017*. Statistics Canada. https://www150.statcan.gc.ca/n1/pub/85-002-x/2018001/article/54974-eng.htm

American Academy of Child and Adolescent Psychiatry. (2012, April). *Solitary confinement of juvenile offenders.* https://www.aacap.org/aacap/Policy_Statements/2012/Solitary_Confinement_of_Juvenile_Offenders.aspx

Australian Institute of Health and Welfare. (2019). *Youth justice overview.* https://www.aihw.gov.au/reports-data/health-welfare-services/youth-justice/overview

Aizer, A., & Doyle, J. (2015). "Juvenile incarceration, human capital, and future crime: Evidence from randomly assigned judges." *The Quarterly Journal of Economics, 130*(2), 759–803.

Bauer, E. (2019, January 24). Rehabilitative promise: Why Norway uses restorative justice in juvenile law. *International Law Review.* https://www.msuilr.org/msuilr-legalforum-blogs/2019/1/24/rehabilitative-promise-why-norway-uses-restorative-justice-in-juvenile-law#_ftnref24

Blomberg, T. G., & Lucken, K. (2011). *American penology: A history of control.* Aldine Transaction.

Britton, L. (2017, September 1). *ABA enacts standards for dual-system youth.* American Bar Association. https://www.americanbar.org/groups/public_interest/child_law/resources/child_law_practiceonline/child_law_practice/vol-36/sept-oct-2017/aba-enacts-standards-for-dual-system-youth/

Bureau of Justice Statistics. (2018). *National Survey of Youth in Custody (NSYC).* Retrieved April 20, 2020, from https://bjs.ojp.gov/content/pub/pdf/svryjf18.pdf

Campbell, N. A., Barnes, A. R., Mandalari, A., Onifade, E., Campbell, C. A., Anderson, V. R., Kashy, D. A., & Davidson, W. S. (2018). Disproportionate minority contact in the juvenile justice system: An investigation of ethnic disparity in program referral at disposition. *Journal of Ethnicity in Criminal Justice, 16*(2), 77–98.

Center on Juvenile and Criminal Justice. (n.d.). *Juvenile justice history.* Retrieved March 20, 2019, from http://www.cjcj.org/education1/juvenile-justice-history.html

Council of State Governments. (2015). *Closer to home.* Retrieved from https://csgjusticecenter.org/wp-content/uploads/2020/01/texas-JJ-reform-closer-to-home.pdf

Council of State Governments. (2016). *The Second Chance Act: Juvenile reentry.* Council of State Governments, Justice Center.

Congressional Research Service. (2019, March 4). *The First Step Act of 2018: An overview.* https://fas.org/sgp/crs/misc/R45558.pdf

Correctional Officer. (2019). *U.S. correctional system.* Retrieved November 10, 2020, from https://www.correctionalofficer.org/us-correctional-system

Cothern, L. (2000, November). Juveniles and the death penalty. *Coordinating Council on Juvenile Justice and Delinquency Prevention,* 1–15. https://www.ojp.gov/pdffiles1/ojjdp/184748.pdf

County of San Mateo Probation. (2005). *The history of probation.* Retrieved on May 17, 2020 from https://probation.smcgov.org/history-probation

Defense for Children. (2015, February 24). *Monitoring report on juvenile justice systems in Latin America.* https://defenceforchildren.org/monitoring-report-on-juvenile-justice-systems-in-latin-america/

Delaney, R., Subramanian, R., Shames, A., & Turner, N. (2018, October). *Reimaging prison Web report.* VERA Institute of Justice. https://www.vera.org/reimagining-prison-web-report

Department of Justice. (1994, October 24). *Violent Crime Control and Law Enforcement Act of 1994: FactSheet.* https://www.ncjrs.gov/txtfiles/billfs.txt

Department of Justice. (2017). *Juvenile restitution.* Retrieved on February 14, 2018 from https://www.doj.state.wi.us/sites/default/files/ocvs/not-victim/Juvenile%20restitution%20outline-%20updated%20August%202017.pdf

Development Services Group. (2017). *Juvenile reentry: Literature review.* Office of Juvenile Justice and Delinquency Prevention. Retrieved on December 1, 2017 from https://files.eric.ed.gov/fulltext/ED590849.pdf

Development Services Group. (2019). *Juvenile residential programs: Literature review.* Office of Juvenile Justice and Delinquency Prevention. Retrieved May 2, 2020, from https://www.ojjdp.gov/mpg/litreviews/Residential.pdf

Graham v. Florida, 560 U.S. 48, 82 (2010).

Grants. (2016, June 15). *What is a block grant?* https://blog.grants.gov/2016/06/15/what-is-a-block-grant/

History of corrections—punishment, prevention, or rehabilitation? (n.d.). Encyclopedia.com.Retrieved on September 16, 2019 from https://www.encyclopedia.com/reference/encyclopedias-almanacs-transcripts-and-maps/history-corrections-punishment-prevention-or-rehabilitation

Howell, J. C. (Ed.). (1995). *Guide for implementing the Comprehensive Strategy for Serious, Violent, and Chronic Juvenile Offenders.* Office of Juvenile Justice and Delinquency Prevention.

Human Rights Watch. (2016, January 8). *Children behind bars.* https://www.hrw.org/news/2016/01/08/children-behind-bars

Inter-American Commission on Human Rights. (2015). *Juvenile justice and human rights in the Americas.* http://www.cidh.org/countryrep/JusticiaJuvenileng/jjiv.eng.htm

James, J. (2016, March 22). The roots of Black incarceration. *Boston Review, 24.*

Knoke, L. (2019). See no evil, hear no evil: Applying the sight and sound separation protection to all youths who are tried as adults in the criminal justice system. *Fordham Law Review, 88,* 791–821. http://fordhamlawreview.org/wp-content/uploads/2019/11/Knoke_November_N_14.pdf

Kopaczewski, J. (2016). *House of refuge.* Encyclopedia of Greater Philadelphia. https://philadelphiaencyclopedia.org/archive/house-of-refuge/

Macallair, D. (2015). *After the doors were locked: A history of youth corrections in California and the origins of twenty-first-century reform.* Rowman & Littlefield.

Morris, M. (1976). *Instead of prisons: A handbook for abolitionists*. Syracuse. Prison Research Education Action Project. https://www.prisonpolicy.org/scans/instead_of_prisons/index.shtml

National Research Council. (1982). *Neither angels nor thieves: Studies in deinstitutionalization of status offenders* (J. F. Handler & J. Zatz, Eds.). National Academies Press.

National Research Council and Institute of Medicine. (2001). *Juvenile crime, juvenile justice*. National Academies Press. https://doi.org/10.17226/9747

National Juvenile Defender Center. (n.d.) *Juvenile court terminology*. Retrieved November 20, 2019, from https://njdc.info/juvenile-court-terminology/

New York State Archives. (1989). *The greatest reform school in the world: A guide to the records of the New York House of Refuge*. New York State Archives Cultural Education Center. http://www.archives.nysed.gov/common/archives/files/res_topics_ed_reform.pdf

Office of Juvenile Justice and Delinquency Prevention. (2018.) *Statistical briefing book: Juveniles in corrections*. Retrieved December 26, 2018, from https://www.ojjdp.gov/ojstatbb/corrections/qa08205.asp?qaDate=2017&text=yes&maplink=link1

Office of Juvenile Justice and Delinquency Prevention. (2019a). *Statistical briefing book: Facility practices and services*. Retrieved September 16, 2020, from https://www.ojjdp.gov/ojstatbb/corrections/qa08520.asp?qaDate=2018&text=yes&maplink=link1

Office of Juvenile Justice and Delinquency Prevention. (2019b). *Redline Version: Juvenile Justice and Delinquency Prevention Act as Amended by the Juvenile Justice reform Act of 2018*. https://www.ojjdp.gov/about/JJDPA-REDLINED-JJRA-amendments-3-26-19.pdf

Office of Juvenile Delinquency and Prevention. (2019c). *Statistical briefing book: Juveniles in corrections: Demographics*. Retrieved May 17, 2020, from https://www.ojjdp.gov/ojstatbb/corrections/qa08204.asp?qaDate=2019

Office of Juvenile Justice and Delinquency Prevention. (2020). *Statistical briefing book: What's new*. Retrieved September 16, 2020, from https://www.ojjdp.gov/ojstatbb/

Office of Juvenile Justice and Delinquency Prevention. (2021a). *Statistical briefing book: Characteristics of adjudicated cases ordered to probation, 2005–2019*. Retrieved June 24, 2021, from https://www.ojjdp.gov/ojstatbb/probation/qa07103.asp?qaDate=2019

Office of Juvenile Justice and Delinquency Prevention. (2021b). *Statistical briefing book: Juveniles in correction, demographics*. Retrieved February 25, 2021, from https://www.ojjdp.gov/ojstatbb/corrections/qa08803.asp?qaDate=2018

Office of Juvenile Justice and Delinquency Prevention. (2021c). *Statistical briefing book: Victimization in juvenile facilities 2012 and 2018*. Retrieved February 25, 2021, from https://www.ojjdp.gov/ojstatbb/corrections/qa08801.asp?qaDate=2018

Office of Juvenile Justice and Delinquency Prevention. (2021d). *Statistical briefing book: Juveniles in corrections, circumstances surrounding sexual victimization in juvenile facilities, 2018*. Retrieved February 25, 2021, from https://www.ojjdp.gov/ojstatbb/corrections/qa08804.asp?qaDate=2018

Penal Reform International. (2019). *UN Nelson Mandela Rules (revised SMR)*. Retrieved February 25, 2020, from https://www.penalreform.org/priorities/prison-conditions/standard-minimum-rules/

A practical approach to linking graduated sanctions with a continuum of effective programs. (2004). *Juvenile Sanctions Center Training and Technical Assistance Program Bulletin*, *2*(1), 1–10. https://www.ncjfcj.org/wp-content/uploads/2012/02/linkinggraduatedsanctions_0.pdf

Public Safety Canada. (2018). *Crime prevention: Transitions from juvenile delinquency to young adult offending: A review of Canadian and international evidence*. Retrieved on July 4, 2018 from https://www.publicsafety.gc.ca/cnt/rsrcs/pblctns/2017-h05-cp/2017-h05-cp-en.pdf

Redding, R. E. (2010, June). Juvenile transfer laws: An effective deterrent to delinquency. *Juvenile Justice Bulletin*, 1–11. https://www.ojp.gov/pdffiles1/ojjdp/220595.pdf

Roper v. Simmons, 543 U.S. 551, 578 (2005).

Sawyer, W., & Wagner, P. (2019, March 19). Mass Incarceration: *The whole pie*. Prison Policy Initiative. https://www.prisonpolicy.org/reports/pie2019.html

Schneider, A. L. (1984a). Deinstitutionalization of status offenders: The impact on recidivism and secure confinement. *Criminal Justice Abstracts*, *16*, 410–432.

Schneider, A. L. (1984b). Divesting status offenses from juvenile court jurisdiction. *Crime and Delinquency*, *30*(3), 347–370.

Schwartz, I. (1989). *Justice for juveniles: Rethinking the best interests of the child*. Lexington Books, D. C. Heath.

Schwartzapfel, B. (2016, January 27). *There are practically no juveniles in federal prison—here's why: Obama takes bold action, but for a population of fewer than 30*. The Marshall Project. https://www.themarshallproject.org/2016/01/27/there-are-practically-no-juveniles-in-federal-prison-here-s-why

Society for the Prevention of Pauperism in the City of New York. (1818). *Report of a committee on the subject of pauperism*. Samuel Wood & Sons.Rovner, J (2021). *Juvenile life without parole: An overview*. Sentencing Project. https://www.sentencingproject.org/publications/juvenile-life-without-parole/

Teigen, A. (2016, July). Automatically sealing or expunging juvenile records. *National Conference of State Legislatures*, *24*(27). https://www.ncsl.org/research/civil-and-criminal-justice/automatically-sealing-or-expunging-juvenile-records.aspx

Thompson, C. (2015, September 17). *Five things you didn't know about clearing your record*. The Marshall Project. https://www.themarshallproject.org/2015/09/17/five-things-you-didn-t-know-about-clearing-your-record

United Nations. (1990). *United Nations Guidelines for the Prevention of Juvenile Delinquency (The Riyadh Guidelines)*. https://www.ohchr.org/en/ProfessionalInterest/Pages/PreventionOfJuvenileDelinquency.aspx

US Legal. (nd). Juvenile blended sentencing law and legal definition. Retrieved on May 17, 2019 from https://definitions.uslegal.com/j/juvenile-blended-sentencing/

U.S. Prison Culture. (2011, February 3). *Punishing children: Houses of refuge & juvenile justice*. http://www.usprisonculture.com/blog/2011/02/03/punishing-children-houses-of-refuge-juvenile-justice/

VERA Institute of Justice. (2018a) *Reimagining prison*. https://www.vera.org/projects/reimagining-prison

Webster, E. (2015, September 27). *California improves juvenile record sealing process*. Center on Crime and Juvenile Justice. http://www.cjcj.org/news/9817

Wilson, J. J., & Howell, J. C. (1993). *A comprehensive strategy for serious, violent and chronic juvenile offenders*. Office of Juvenile Justice and Delinquency Prevention.

Outward Bound

Interventions and Diversion

LEARNING OBJECTIVES

At the end of the chapter, students will be able to

describe the history of diversion and intervention,

evaluate associated theories of diversion and intervention,

describe the process of diversion and intervention,

discuss the points of intervention and factors weighed for services to be offered,

describe the pros and cons of diversion and intervention,

discuss various intervention and diversion programs, and

compare and contrast diversion and intervention within the United States and around the world.

Introduction

An essential component of the juvenile justice system is that children should be treated differently from adults, with the goal of rehabilitation as opposed to punishment. Akin to this process is the ability to remove justice-involved youths from the formal system and divert them into a program conducive to the needs of the juveniles, their families, and the community. These programs continue to evolve and vary in terms of access, process, benefits, and results. In addition to diversion strategies for youth who have already made contact with the juvenile system, there are intervention/preventative programs to avoid children from coming in contact with any facet of the system in the first place. This chapter will discuss the intricacies of these processes, how these programs developed, and their pros and cons. We will also explore programs in and outside the United States and their effects on juveniles, communities, and justice systems overall.

Where Did Diversion and Intervention Begin, and Why?

In the 1700s and early 1800s, juveniles who were taken into custody for delinquent acts or criminality typically faced adult processing and sentencing because the options were limited and because of the perspective that juveniles were small adults who should be treated as such. In 1825, as a result of reform efforts, houses of refuge served as the first diversion option from formal processing and incarceration with adults. They were also viewed as an intervention strategy for juveniles considered to be on a path toward delinquency. As we read in Chapter 1, however, conditions in **houses of refuge**, also referred to as "reformatories," were often similar to and sometimes worse than those of formal detention. In 1899, after the creation of the first juvenile court, the premise of diverting youth from judicial confinement continued, and the expansion of diversion options has been ongoing.

Diversion

Diversion is an "approach that redirects youths away from formal processing in the juvenile justice system, while still holding them accountable for their actions" (National Institute of Justice, 2020b, p. 1). It is important to note that diversion programs are not intended to remove responsibility. Instead, they hold a juvenile responsible through external programs to decriminalize, deinstitutionalize, and divert the youth from further justice system contact, in hopes of better rehabilitative outcomes (Loeb et al., 2015; Mackin et al., 2010).

The goal of diversion is to avoid the negative consequences of formal processing and detention, such as stigmatizing, negative peer association, overcrowding, expense, and reoffending, by providing alternatives as early as possible in the process (Development Services Group, 2017; Loeb et al., 2015). Representatives of the court, such as probation officers, attorneys, and judges, are given the ability to evaluate a delinquency case and possible alternatives to formal processing and detention based on anticipated effects on the victim and the community and, ultimately, the best interests of the child.

Intervention

Intervention attempts to prevent youth from coming into contact with the juvenile justice system. It can also redirect an individual to another path or mindset, even after encountering the justice system. Various intervention programs are utilized to assist youth faced with adversarial conditions in and out of the system. Some communities have adopted early intervention strategies to prevent youth from entering the juvenile justice system in the first place.

Other interventions are delivered in conjunction with diversion strategies, such as community-based programs. **Early intervention** "prevents the onset of delinquent behavior and supports the development of a youth's assets and resilience" (*Points of Intervention*, 2019, p. 1). Specific programs (described later in the chapter) attempt to provide skill sets, coping strategies, and other supportive resources, known as **protective factors**, for children at risk for delinquency because of environmental and social influences. Environmental and social conditions that can negatively impact an individual are known as **risk factors**. Imposing risk factors that may lead to delinquency and involvement with the justice system include poverty, exposure to violence, peer group pressure, poor coping, and problem-solving skills (Higgins & Davis, 2014; Merenda, 2020).

Theoretical Perspectives

The concept of intervention and diversion, providing short- and long-term benefits for youth, stems from three theoretical perspectives: labeling theory, differential association, and developmental theory. As you learned in Chapter 3, **labeling theory** was initially developed by Howard Becker in 1963 and applied to juveniles being processed and eventually incarcerated by the justice system. Becker argued that formal incarceration would have more negative effects, including youth feeling ostracized and negatively labeled by society, because of its potential to stigmatize them. Youth were viewed as outsiders and as belonging to a delinquent group separate from society, instead of part of a community that would be willing to accept and work with them through interventions and rehabilitation (Shulman, 2005; Skaggs, 2016).

It is theorized that youth who are labeled in this way may self-identify as such, reminiscent of a self-fulfilling prophecy, whereby the juvenile would continue fulfilling this role through chronic reoffending. It is widely accepted that diversion efforts can prevent the ill effects of stigmatizing and ostracizing youth from society and can ultimately lead to a reduction in offending (Development Services Group, 2015, 2017; Sullivan et al., 2019). See Chapter 3 for more information on labeling theory.

A second theoretical perspective justifying the benefits of diversion from formal processing and incarceration is the differential association theory. As you read in Chapter 3, "Theories of Delinquency," **differential association**, developed by Edwin Sutherland, is a social learning theory. It puts forward the notion that one adopts similar attitudes, values, and beliefs that may result in operating out of social norms through interacting with and gaining the support of others. Based on this premise, surrounding youth with individuals who have committed delinquent and criminal acts themselves could have unintended and adverse effects. This can include further adoption of antisocial and illicit behaviors. Although criticism of this theory has suggested that other factors outside negative contacts, such as environmental and psychological factors, can contribute to deviant behavior, Sutherland maintained that this type of social learning could also contribute to maladaptive behavior (Burgess & Akers, 1966; Development Services Group, 2017; Vinney, 2019).

There is also a belief that a child will naturally age out of delinquency and that their maladaptive behavior is sometimes caused by uncontrollable impulses in the early years of life. Impulsivity is believed to be a natural occurrence, because the brain is still developing through adolescence and, in many cases, becomes more controllable into adulthood (Spear, 2010). **Developmental theory** has put forward the notion that delinquency can fluctuate based on disrupted or removed social bonds with society. Therefore, instead of disconnecting bonds with society through formal detention and potentially emboldening negative behavior during childhood, a well-suited diversion program can aid in fostering ties with the community to avoid delinquency and support organically transitioning out of it (Bonnie et al., 2013; Development Services Group, 2017; Fox & Farrington, 2016; Schiraldi et al., 2015; also see developmental theory in Chapter 3).

The Process

Intervening early in a youth's life can interrupt what is sometimes referred to as the **cradle-to prison-pipeline**, whereby exposure to systematic social and environmental risk factors through one's development can cause ongoing contact with the justice system and a trajectory toward continued delinquency, criminality, and eventual incarceration (*Points of Intervention*, 2019). The intervening process starts with identifying youth who face risk factors that can lead to dropping out of school, delinquency, associating with delinquent peers, joining criminal gangs, or incarceration. Once these youth are identified, appropriate programs addressing a child's individual circumstances and needs can be located and participation offered. As mentioned previously, some intervention programs, referred to as **tertiary intervention**, are sometimes provided to youth already in contact with the justice system as part of the formal diversion process, such as community-based rehabilitation and intervention strategies (Higgins & Davis, 2014).

Although many programs can offer valuable resources and support, their accessibility is sometimes limited by availability and cost, creating a disparity of options available for those children most at risk (Feierman et al., 2016).

Points of Intervention

Formal Processing

While **formal processing**, defined as "processing juveniles through the traditional juvenile justice system without consideration of alternative sanctions or diversion" (National Institute of Justice, 2020a, p. 1), does occur, the juvenile justice system often relies on diversionary and intervention programs as a viable alternative to a more formal route. As you read in Chapter 8 and will see later in this chapter, the stages of the juvenile justice system process build in diversion options at almost every point, even after sentencing by a judge. This is especially true for first-time, nonviolent offenders.

If a juvenile's case does continue through the formal process, the law department files a **petition**, an official complaint of the charges, and the case eventually comes before a judge to be adjudicated. This can potentially result in the youth's detainment (also review the court process, Chapter 8). However, if diversion is offered, the juvenile can voluntarily agree to participate by often having to admit guilt and then agreeing to the terms of diversion. This can involve probation under court supervision, community service, diversion to a program, informal probation, or the case being dismissed completely (Mears et al., 2016).

Although slight variations may exist from state to state, diversion generally occurs in three ways: informally during an initial contact, formally during intake, or at any other stage during judicial processing, including after adjudication as a sanction.

Informal Diversion

Informal diversion, or diversion that occurs outside the juvenile justice system, often happens during initial police contact and relies on law enforcement discretion. This discretion can be based on the offense and its circumstances, as well as any risk the juvenile poses to themselves and the community at large. In this case, the child is released, no criminal record is generated, and the youth has no obligation to the court.

Formal Diversion

Diversion can also happen after an arrest and during **intake**, called **formal diversion**. This is the first stage, where the system evaluates the juvenile and the delinquent act, sometimes referred to as "adjustment." As you read in Chapter 8, there are four main stages in the juvenile justice system, the first being intake/adjustment. During this initial stage, typically administered by the probation department or the law department, the case will be evaluated in its totality. This includes considering the juvenile and their family environment, any safety threats to the community or victim(s) that a juvenile's release would impose, and other relevant factors, including what actions would best serve the youth. The case can be dismissed at this stage or the child can be diverted to anything from court supervision and counseling to community-based programs and even teen court

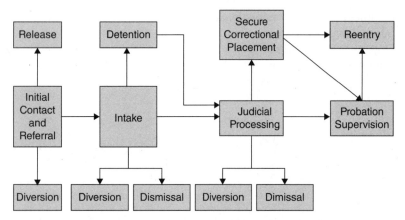

Figure 10.1 Points of intervention. Please note these are main and common stages where intervention can occur. There are other possible points of intervention based on the individual state and municipality.

Source: Center for Juvenile Justice Reform (youth.gov, 2019)

(see "Diversion Programs" later in this chapter). It should also be noted that if the provision set forth at intake/adjustment is not followed or is violated, the juvenile will be brought back into custody and be formally processed.

Finally, diversion can occur at later stages during formal processing (see Figure 10.1), including after adjudication by a judge. Diversion programs can sometimes be recommended by officers of the court and offered in the form of a sanction if it is believed that an alternate form of rehabilitation would be better suited for the youth. These types of sanctions can also be graduated.

Graduated Sanctions

Graduated sanctions are sanctions that gradually increase in severity, supervision, and confinement. As defined in Chapter 9, "Juvenile Corrections," they are "the continuum of disposition options that juvenile court judges and court staff have at their disposal" ("Practical Approach," 2004, p. 1). They can also be part of diverting a youth from formal detention, whereby the determined level of risk and need of the child can dictate the supervision and stringency of the court.

A graduated-sanctions system like that described in the previous chapter can provide multiple levels of diversionary sanctions (see the following list), ranging from least restrictive, such as teen court or probation, to secure corrections (Howell, 1995; "Practical Approach," 2004; Wilson & Howell, 1993).

Although specific sanctions and processing can differ, they generally include the following:

Immediate intervention: generally reserved for first-time offenders and those who have committed a misdemeanor or low-level, nonviolent felony. These interventions may include teen court, diversionary programs, community service, or mandated curfews.

Intermediate sanctions: usually imposed on repeat offenders or first-time violent offenders. These sanctions can include intense supervision and passive or electronic monitoring.

Passive monitoring: includes random phone calls to the youth's residence to ensure the juvenile is abiding by court mandates, including curfews and other restrictions.

Electronic monitoring: can consist of an electronic bracelet with an active global positioning system to monitor the youth's location and adherence to court orders.

Community confinement: can be given to chronic offenders as well as first-time violent offenders. It includes confinement in secure and unsecured community-based facilities such as group homes.

Secure confinement: If diversion is not appropriate, this type of sanction will likely be imposed. This type of detention is given to chronic juvenile offenders who have been found guilty of violent crimes. These facilities are often run by the city or state.

According to Howell (2003, 2009), graduated sanctions should proceed from least to most restrictive. Additionally, aftercare should mirror the least restrictive and appropriate options.

The decision to divert a youth at any stage of the juvenile justice system is also based on assessment tools explicitly designed to assess risks that may be posed by the youth's release and the ability of a specific diversion program to fulfill the needs of the juvenile.

Risk/Needs Assessment Tools

Risk and need assessment tools are instruments that help in the decision to divert a youth from formal processing and in determining an appropriate disposition after formal processing and adjudication by a judge (Development Services Group, 2015). These assessments evaluate the risk of further contact with the juvenile justice system and seek to identify factors that, if treated, can reduce **recidivism**—ongoing contact with the justice system—from occurring. According to Development Services Group (2015), these types of assessments are also helpful in developing treatment programs and determining services that will be the most effective. Risk assessment tools generally assign youth to one of three categories: low risk, for youth assessed as unlikely to reoffend; moderate risk, indicating a potential for reoffending; and high risk, which suggests a greater likelihood of reoffending exists.

Although initially risk assessments focused on "predicting and classifying risk level," these instruments have been further developed. They are currently used not only to ascertain risk levels but also to determine appropriate treatment programs that can address individual needs (see figures 10.2 and 10.3).

LOW RISK GAIN-SS & YASI Pre-Screen	**MODERATE RISK** GAIN-SS & YASI Full-Screen	**HIGH RISK** GAIN-SS & YASI Full-Screen
LOW NEED Youth and family will be educated on the juvenile justice system and case will be coded as 04 (unofficial counseling). CSB resource information will be provided if the GAIN-SS score is 3 or more. **HIGH NEED** Youth and family will be educated on the juvenile justice system and the youth will be scheduled for Core Values. Case is coded as 05 (referred to other agency for services). If Gain-SS score is 3 or more, CSB resource information will be provided.	All moderate risk youth will be referred to a Diversion Hearing or Monitored Diversion and case will be coded as 07 (diversion). • All Domestic Assaults, Status Offenses and cases in which there is increased concern for community safety will be set for Monitored Diversion • All out of jurisdiction cases will be set for a Diversion Hearing Hearing Officers will assign a service that addresses a YASI-indicated area of need. Note: Mental health and Substance abuse will be treated as priority areas.	All high risk youth will be placed on Monitored Diversion and case will be coded as 07 (diversion). • All out of jurisdiction cases will be set for a Diversion Hearing Note: Mental health and Substance abuse will be treated as priority areas.

Figure 10.2 Juvenile Intake Dispositional Matrix

Note. ALL diversion eligible youth will be assessed using the Global Appraisal of Individual Needs – Short Screener (GAIN-SS) and the Youth Assessment Screening Instrument (YASI). The GAIN-SS helps identify youth who could benefit from further psychiatric and substance use assessment. The YASI assesses a youth's risk, need and protective factors. The Pre-Screen will be utilized first and if Pre-screen results indicate moderate or high risk, the Full-Screen will be administered. The results of these assessments determine the type of intervention Juvenile Intake will utilize.

Youth who have no indicated areas contributing to risk will be considered low need. Youth who have one or more areas contributing to risk will be considered high speed.

Restitution will be encouraged to be paid within 90 days. However, no youth will be sent to court for failing to pay. Victims Services will advise victims on available civil remedies.

Source: Center for Juvenile Justice Reform

LOW RISK SERVICE OPTIONS BY YASI DOMAIN

MENTAL HEALTH SUBSTANCE ABUSE	Referral to Community Services Board • may utilize private providers out of jurisdiction cases • samhsa.gov
SCHOOL COMMUNITY/PEER FAMILY SKILLS AGGRESSION ATTITUDES	Core Values Charitable Donation Essay Firestop Letter of Apology

Figure 10.3 Youth Assessment Screening Instrument

Assessing Needs

There is also a component within assessment tools that seeks to determine what needs exist for a specific youth to assist the child and the court in providing appropriate services that will not only fulfill those needs but also promote healthy development.

Criminogenic needs factors are factors determined to be directly related to a youth's criminality that may negate further offending if changed. For example, if drug use is associated with a youth's delinquent act, treatment focuses on drug rehabilitation, with the goal of mitigating further criminality in this area. There are also **noncriminogenic needs factors**, which are indirectly associated with a youth's delinquency, such as low self-esteem and poor social skills. These, too, could be considered in determining potential diversion program options.

In assessing the need for protective factors, factors that can counteract the effects of risk factors and reduce the likelihood of delinquency are also evaluated to determine an effective treatment. The notion is that protective factors will enable the youth to cope with and be resilient toward adversities and can be instilled, for example, through community-based programs with the support of institutions such as family, schools, and other available resources (Booth & Neill, 2017; Merenda, 2020).

Finally, although they are not used to determine risk or needs, assessment tools may also consider **responsivity factors**, such as cognitive ability, willingness for change, and access to programs that can offer the most effective treatment and services.

While risk and need assessment tools share common goals, numerous versions exist not only between states but also within municipalities, and 28 states have multiple assessments that are used within their various regions (Development Services Group, 2015; Taxman, 2016). Along with varying tools are varying assessment factors (see the example in the next section). As discussed earlier, while positive results have stemmed from the removal of youth from formal processing and incarceration, there have also been unintended negative consequences of the assessment tools used to assist in those decisions and the diversion/intervention process overall (Sullivan et al., 2019).

The Pros and Cons of the Diversion and Intervention Process

Although there are many advantages of diversion for both the youth involved and the justice system overall, such as reducing caseloads, providing rehabilitation, and avoiding stigma and potential reoffending, diversion also may create net widening. **Net widening** can occur when juveniles who committed minor offenses, who might otherwise not have fallen under the court's control or incurred minor punishment, are instead controlled by the court and must abide by the strict stipulations of a given program (Mears et al., 2016). A newer but similar phenomenon has been termed **net deepening**, whereby involving youth with diversion programs through the justice system, no matter how slightly, can lead them deeper into alienation and delinquency (Schlesinger, 2018).

In addition to net widening and net deepening, although assessment tools remove some subjectivity from assessing risk, risk levels are based on protective and risk factors that may stem from the juvenile's environmental and social conditions and may sometimes lead to disparity and bias, such as assessment factors relying on neighborhood characteristics and access to resources and programs to determine risk.

Potential Bias in Assessing Risks

The assessment of risk factors in determining alternatives from formal court processing could potentially lead to bias (Development Services Group, 2015). According to Feierman et al. (2016),

> While racial disparities in the juvenile justice system arise in the context of an arrest, such disparities are also evident at multiple decision points in the delinquency system, including diversion (away from formal court processing), detention (prior to the hearing), probation, and commitment to placement. (p. 8)

The number of delinquency cases involving detention decreased by 52% between 2005 and 2018, reaching its lowest level during this time. However, disparities among racial categories continue to exist. According to the National Center for Juvenile Justice Juvenile Court statistics, cases involving White youth were less likely to be detained, whereby the juvenile is not held by the court, than cases involving all other racial groups for most years between 2005 and 2018. Further, in 2018, cases involving Black, Hispanic, American Indian, and Asian youth were less likely to be diverted than those involving White youth across all offense categories (Hockenberry & Puzzanchera, 2020).

Static and Dynamic Risk Factors

Many risk assessments consider both static and dynamic risk factors. **Static risk factors** are factors that cannot be changed. They include factors such as the individual's age at the first offense, history of violent behavior, and parental criminality within risk and need assessments. **Dynamic risk factors** are factors that can be altered, such as parenting practices, substance abuse, association with delinquent peers, and low academic achievement.

However, a focus on static risk factors such as prior offending by the youth or their families or a history of specific illicit acts and contacts with police can negatively impact a number of youths of color who disproportionately come in contact with the juvenile justice system. Since this may also only indicate which groups are more likely to come in contact with the system, rather than those who are likely to individually reoffend, some researchers believe such a focus may further perpetuate this phenomenon (Development Services Group, 2015); see Tables 10.1 and 10.2.

In addition, the number of available programs in particular areas must be considered; youth from neighborhoods with limited resources have reduced chances of being considered for potential diversionary programs and tertiary interventions available elsewhere.

TABLE 10.1 Case Processing Characteristics of Delinquency Offenses by Race, 2018

COUNTS	TOTAL	WHITE	MINORITY	BLACK	AIAN	AHPI	HISPANIC
Population (10 to upper age)	31,690,700	16,944,800	14,745,900	4,659,800	593,900	1,886,300	7,605,900
Cases referred to juvenile court	744,500	326,900	417,500	258,500	13,500	8,300	137,200
Cases diverted	192,000	102,200	89,800	48,900	3,300	2,500	35,100
Cases detained	195,400	68,500	126,900	77,400	3,600	2,100	43,900
Cases petitioned	422,100	169,000	253,000	165,200	7,800	4,500	75,600
Cases adjudicated	220,000	88,500	131,500	81,400	4,600	2,200	43,300
Adjudicated cases resulting in probation	139,000	57,300	81,700	49,400	2,900	1,700	27,700
Adjudicated cases resulting in placement	62,100	20,600	41,500	25,900	1,200	500	13,900
Cases judicially waived	3,600	1,200	2,500	1,900	<50	<50	500
RATES	**TOTAL**	**WHITE**	**MINORITY**	**BLACK**	**AIAN**	**AHPI**	**HISPANIC**
Cases referred per 1,000 population	23.5	19.3	28.3	55.5	22.8	4.4	18.0
Cases diverted per 100 cases referred	25.8	31.3	21.5	18.9	24.5	29.9	25.6
Cases detained per 100 cases referred	26.2	20.9	30.4	29.9	26.3	25.5	32.0
Cases petitioned per 100 cases referred	56.7	51.7	60.6	63.9	57.5	54.1	55.1
Cases adjudicated per 100 cases petitioned	52.1	52.4	52.0	49.3	59.1	50.0	57.3
Probation cases per 100 adjudicated cases	63.2	64.8	62.1	60.7	62.4	75.2	64.0
Placement cases per 100 adjudicated cases	28.2	23.3	31.5	31.8	27.2	20.4	32.0
Cases judicially waived per 100 cases petitioned	0.9	0.7	1.0	1.1	0.6	0.7	0.7
RATIO OF RATES[a]			**MINORITY**	**BLACK**	**AIAN**	**AHPI**	**HISPANIC**
Referral rate			1.5	2.9	1.2	0.2	0.9
Diversion rate			0.7	0.6	0.8	1.0	0.8
Detention rate			1.5	1.4	1.3	1.2	1.5
Petitioned rate			1.2	1.2	1.1	1.0	1.1
Adjudicated rate			1.0	0.9	1.1	1.0	1.1
Probation rate			1.0	0.9	1.0	1.2	1.0
Placement rate			1.4	1.4	1.2	0.9	1.4
Waiver rate			1.4	1.6	0.9	0.9	1.0

[a] The ratio of rates is created by dividing the minority rates by the white rate

AIAN: American Indian or Alaskan Native; AHPI: Asian, Hawaiian, or Pacific Islander.

Table and notes from Office of Juvenile Justice and Delinquency Prevention (2020).

Note. In 2018, cases involving Black youth were nearly three times more likely to be referred to juvenile court for a delinquency offense than cases involving White youth. The diversion rate for cases involving Black, American Indian, and Hispanic youth was less than the diversion rate for cases involving White youth. Regardless of race/ethnicity, delinquency cases involving minority youth were more likely to involve detention than cases involving White youth. Cases involving Black youth were more likely to be petitioned than cases involving White youth but were less likely to result in a delinquency adjudication. Cases involving Hispanic youth were 50% more likely to involve detention than cases involving White youth and 40% more likely to receive a placement disposition.

TABLE 10.2 Types of Legal Financial Obligations by State		
STATUTES IMPOSING DIVERSION FEES OR COSTS ON YOUTH		
STATUTE	**NO. OF STATES**	**STATES**
Mandatory	4	Idaho (if county not insured), Illinois, Michigan, Nebraska
Judicial determination	15	Arkansas, Illinois, Indiana, Iowa, Louisiana, Mississippi, Nevada, Oklahoma, Pennsylvania, South Carolina, Texas, Utah, Washington, West Virginia (municipality or county has discretion to impose mandatory fee policy), Wisconsin
STATUTES IMPOSING DIVERSION FEES OR COSTS ON PARENTS		
STATUTE	**NO. OF STATES**	**STATES**
Mandatory	6	Indiana, Nebraska, New Hampshire, New Jersey, Oklahoma, Washington
Judicial determination	8	Arizona, Arkansas, Indiana, Montana, Nevada, Oklahoma, Pennsylvania, Wisconsin

KEY FINDINGS

- Almost all states charge parents for the care and support of youth involved with the juvenile justice system, and some states charge juveniles directly.
- The inability to pay for treatment can result in youth being deprived of treatment, held in violation of probation, or held for extended periods of incarceration.
- Twenty-two states charge juveniles fees for diversion. Survey respondents in 14 states indicated that the inability to pay for diversion sometimes resulted in a formal petition being filed, and respondents in 6 states reported that it resulted in youth being put in juvenile justice placements.
- Thirty-one states charge fees for evaluation or testing (e.g., DNA, mental health evaluations).
- Youth and families are assessed fines in 29 states and court fees in 28 states.
- Youth and families in 20 states reported payment requirements associated with sealing or expungement.

From Feierman et al. (2016).
Research and monitoring in this area continue.

Disproportionate Minority Contact

As discussed in previous chapters, the Juvenile Justice and Delinquency Prevention Act, last amended in 2018, collects data and sets targets for states to receive federal funding. One of the areas addressed is to provide the tracking of and state efforts to reduce **disproportionate minority contact**. The National Research Council provided a statement prior to this amendment regarding how risk and need assessment tools may contribute to this trend.

> These instruments thus provide estimates of the likelihood of detection, apprehension, and prosecution for illegal acts, not involvement in illegal activity. Given the well-documented patterns of selective law enforcement, gender differences in processing, and disproportionate minority contact (DMC), this means that risk/needs instruments might be conflating risk with ongoing biases in the juvenile justice system and enforcing the status quo in juvenile justice processing. (National Research Council, 2013, p. 148)

Assessment tools determining risk continue to be reviewed and modified in an effort to reduce these effects, although the trend continues (Development Services Group, 2015; Office of Juvenile Justice and Delinquency Prevention, n.d.; Sullivan et al., 2019).

Socioeconomic Disparities

As you read in Chapter 9, "Juvenile Corrections," in some states, a juvenile can only have a record **expunged** (erased) for a fee, and you will now see that charging for services is not limited to that aspect of the court process.

Disparities in the diversion process can also be caused by what some refer to as **socioeconomic bias**, whereby the basis for providing diversion for juveniles with similarly qualifying criminal history, age, offense, and risk and need assessments can include consideration of the financial means to pay for the program as a deciding factor. These and other financial responsibilities in the juvenile system that we have learned about, such as costs for erasing criminal records, restitution, and probation services, can all contribute to socioeconomic disparities and adversely affect children from poverty, who have been shown to be overrepresented in the system. According to the Juvenile Law Center, such things as access to quality counsel, treatment, tertiary intervention services, and high crossover from the welfare system can be impacted, and these financial burdens from the court can also increase racial disparities in the juvenile justice system (Feierman et al., 2016).

Types of Intervention and Diversion Programs

As discussed, diversion can occur informally; for example, the police give a youth a warning, and no further contact with the justice system is made. It can also occur formally, whereby juveniles have made contact with the system and at some stage have been offered to be diverted from formal processing through an agreement to participate in an appropriate program or receive treatment outside the court. These formal programs can be further broken down into category types such as **restorative justice**—mediation between the offender, the victim, and other community stakeholders. Programs can also include direct and case-managed referrals to individual and family treatment programs intended to address addiction and skills-building, community service, or transfer to teen and other specialized courts. The following paragraph will detail some of the programs across the country that attempt to address youth needs through a variety of methods (Farrell et al., 2018). For information on the effects of these and other types of model programs, please see Office of Juvenile Justice and Delinquency Prevention (n.d.).

Diversion Programs

FRONT-END DIVERSION INITIATIVE

The Front-End Diversion Initiative focuses on youth with mental health needs who would be more negatively impacted within a juvenile facility as opposed to being diverted to specialized programs under the supervision of case managers. The National Institute of Justice estimates that 50%–75% of justice-involved youth often suffer from mental health issues such as depression, anxiety, and attention deficit hyperactivity disorder (Underwood & Washington, 2016). This program attempts to directly address those issues by involving family and therapists in determining treatment needs, such as crisis intervention and behavioral health management.

Adolescent Diversion Project The Adolescent Diversion Project is a strength-based program that began in collaboration with the justice system, Michigan State University, and the community to divert juveniles who had been arrested from formal processing. The program's goals are to reduce stigmatization and reoffending through reinforcing bonds with family and the community and providing access to any needed resources. This intervention takes place over the course of 18 weeks and is provided in phases. During the first 12 weeks, student volunteers work one on one with participants and focus on school, employment, and extracurricular activities, as well as access to available resources in their community. In the last weeks of the program, the volunteers take more of a consulting and follow-up role to allow participants to be more independent and active in using what they have learned to achieve the program's and individual's goals (National Institute of Justice, 2020a).

INDIANAPOLIS FAMILY GROUP CONFERENCING EXPERIMENT

The Indianapolis Family Group Conferencing Experiment is a restorative justice diversion program generally for first-time offenders age 14 or younger who have committed minor, nonviolent offenses. Juveniles with their family members, along with the victim(s) and community stakeholders, all get together to focus on the victim and conduct a mediation in order to understand and accept responsibility. These youth must admit guilt and are provided supportive services after assessment and mediation, such as job skills training, counseling, and other available community services.

YOUTH ADVOCATE PROGRAMS, INC.

Youth Advocate Programs, Inc. operates in multiple states across the country. After being diverted from the justice system, paid mentors work with youth who are chronic offenders at risk of formal detention and their families. The program provides individual service plans that include setting up positive peer relationships and providing a multitude of available resources to achieve both personal and court-mandated goals. Such goals and mandates can include fulfilling interests such as joining sports teams and becoming involved in other extracurricular activities to achieving counseling, educational, and employment requirements. This is accomplished by doing a series of assessments that can provide **wraparound services**, needed services that are coordinated and "wrapped around" the youth and their families, schools, and communities to align strategies and offer a single plan of care.

MAINE JUVENILE DRUG TREATMENT COURTS

The Maine Juvenile Drug Treatment Courts provide community-based diversion programs to treat juveniles with substance abuse issues. The program focuses on youth who are considered at medium or high risk for recidivism and substance abuse but are willing to participate with their families in treatment programs. The goal of the program is to deter the youth from drug abuse and reoffending through a collaborative effort between the youth and their family, the court, and other state agencies and drug treatment offices. This program typically runs for an entire year and encompasses assessment, support, instilling skills, and monitoring progress. Similar programs exist across other states (National Institute of Justice, 2020a).

DEEPER DIVE

Teen Court

The purpose of the teen court is to divert teens from the formal justice system to an alternate adjudication process that provides positive influence by their peers. It is composed of youth volunteers who serve as the prosecutor, defense attorney, and jury. Typically, adult supervisors help facilitate the process and also serve as judges. Teen court is usually reserved for first-time offenders who have committed low-level crimes. These courts are legally authorized by the juvenile court system. Juveniles going through the process and abiding by the teen court's disposition (e.g., community service, agreeing to future juvenile court service, or restitution) will not incur a criminal record for the offense, nor will they have to go back to a juvenile court if their offending ceases.

For more information, visit PBS Teen Connection https://www.pbs.org/video/teen-connection-teens-and-teen-courts/

Maryland Teen Court

Intervention Programs

Intervention programs focus on a variety of areas within a youth's life. Butts et al. (2010) created a positive youth justice model that attempts to guide the goals and aspects of these programs to align with the domains of work, education, health, relationships, creativity, and community. They further assert, as do other researchers, that programs should include practice in multiple domains with the goals of learning, doing, attaching, and belonging (Coulton et al., 2017; Korpershoek et al., 2020; Merenda et al., 2020). The following programs are examples of these types of interventions. For information on the effects of these and other types of model programs, please see Office of Juvenile Justice and Delinquency Prevention (n.d.).

OUTWARD BOUND

Outward Bound focuses on intervention and reentry and is considered adventure/wilderness-based programming. This type of programming places youth in a natural setting and presents challenges to them, such as hiking, building tents, and other collaborative activities. This is done to build skills, coping strategies, and resilience to overcome adversarial conditions, not only in conjunction with the program but also for environmental and societal risks they may face in the future. Developed skills can include problem-solving, decision-making, conflict resolution, communicating, and self-confidence.

THE CHILDREN'S VILLAGE

The Children's Village is an early intervention program that attempts to build educational and work skills and self-sufficiency for youth at risk for delinquency who were runaways or are homeless and who are leaving their current short-term residential programs. Staff gradually work with children by first assigning unpaid chores within the residence. The program then expands to paid tasks and eventually to fully paid work within the community. The program does not end when individuals leave; follow-up and support continue for years to help youth complete school and remain employed.

RITE OF PASSAGE

Rite of Passage is a program that exists across the United States with a focus on physical activity and involvement in social groups and events, such as sports and other physical activities, to promote communication and teamwork skills. They focus on the child's needs in terms of building self-confidence, prosocial bonding/behavior with social groups, and other developmental strategies. This program exists as both an intervention and a diversion for children already involved with the justice system (Butts et al., 2010).

GANG RESISTANCE EDUCATION AND TRAINING

Gang Resistance Education and Training is a nationwide school-based program focused on teaching youth ages 9–17 about avoiding joining a gang and other criminal activity, including drug use. Police officers typically do the training inside classrooms and try to establish a rapport with the students. Children are taught about taking responsibility for their actions and how those actions can affect others and impact communities. A component of the program that takes place during the summer months includes activities outside the classroom, such as field trips and other outdoor activities that promote cultural awareness, conflict resolution, and personal growth (National Institute of Justice, 2020a).

FAMILIES AND SCHOOLS TOGETHER

Families and Schools Together is a multifaceted approach that involves families, schools, and communities. It focuses on children ages 4 to 12 and their families. The program attempts to build protective factors such as academic and socialization skills and overall strengths for youth considered at risk. It is centered on a group approach of family members, school officials, peers, and community stakeholders to instill skills and build support for participants to help avoid dropping out of school and engaging in drug use, violence, or delinquency (National Institute of Justice, 2020a).

Worldview

Diversion and Intervention for Youth Around the World

THE UNITED NATIONS

The United Nations Standard Minimum Rules for the Administration of Juvenile Justice (Beijing Rules) in 1985 provided general principles on the handling, detention, and diversion of justice-involved youth. Specifically, Rule 11 (Diversion) states that consideration should be given wherever appropriate to avoid formal detention and that sources such as temporary supervision and guidance, restitution, or community programs should be offered. Programs should be on a volunteer basis, requiring consent from the youth and their family. The rule goes on to say that this approach does not need to be reserved for petty cases and that courts should consider the specifics of the case (first offense, peer pressure, etc.). The rules overall promote proactive efforts by member states to prevent juveniles from engaging in delinquency or criminality through the utilization of multiple resources such as family, community, and schools. The UN Convention on the Rights of the Child, an international human rights treaty, also advocates in Article 13 that prison be the last resort for youth and that confinement should be for the shortest appropriate amount of time possible (United Nations, 2002, 2008).

As you will see, countries around the world, most of which are member states of the UN General Assembly, attempt to fulfill these guidelines in a variety of ways. The following countries were chosen based on related and available data.

AUSTRALIA

The aim of diversionary/intervention programs in Australia is similar to the aim of such programs in the United States, with individuals diverted from formal processing and offered treatment and training to avoid the negative influences of incarceration and having a criminal record. They address the importance of mitigating risk factors such as substance misuse and conflict resolution. They have also offered restorative justice programs focusing on rehabilitation that involve a collaborative approach between the offender, victim, and community stakeholders to avoid detention. If a juvenile agrees to this approach and makes amends, they can be diverted from the justice system and participate in other forms of treatment.

However, Australia's diversion programs also face challenges. Factors similar to the United States, such as disparity of the youth coming in contact with the system and able to take advantage of diversionary options because of economic disadvantage and discrimination, have been shown to exist (Child Family Community Australia, 2020; Higgins & Davis, 2014).

LATIN AMERICA

Youth in Latin America are in the majority when it comes to victims and offenders of violent crime. In fact, the homicide rate for boys aged 15–24 is four times the region's average (American Institute for Research, 2019). Because of this disproportionate statistic and the large amount of violence in general occurring in this region, many Latin American countries continue to prosecute even minor offenses and pass down harsh sentencing for both adults and children alike.

However, initiatives have been put forward suggesting the notion of acting in the best interests of the child and restorative justice. In countries such as Brazil, Colombia, Ecuador, Nicaragua, Panama, Peru, and Haiti, risk factors such as broken families, lack of education and resources, exploitation, and inequality are being considered within justice systems to determine the best course of action for the youth (Atienzo et al., 2017).

The idea of long prison sentences, potentially leading juveniles to more involvement in criminality, has led to the development of alternative programs to divert youth from formal prosecution in areas throughout Latin America. Alternative measures such as mediation and restorative justice approaches, whereby the juvenile, victim, and community members work together to offer solutions besides a prison sentence, have been implemented in many of these countries, and efforts to provide diversion from formal processing continue (Terre des Hommes International Federation, 2019).

ASIA

The Association of Southern Asian Nations is composed of 10 countries, Brunei, Cambodia, Indonesia, Laos, Malaysia, Myanmar, the Philippines, Singapore, Thailand, and Vietnam, which work collaboratively on issues affecting education, security, sociocultural, and other government initiatives including those within their justice systems. Although the number of juveniles who have been formally charged in these member states is relatively low number compared to Europe and the United States, under 100,000, the number of children coming in contact with justice systems is increasing. Therefore, alternate strategies beyond formal processing and prosecution have been explored and implemented.

Most countries in the Association of Southern Asian Nations provide some diversion option as part of their juvenile court processing; however, the availability of these options is not consistent because of a variety of opposing factors, such as lack of programs, facilities, and workers available. The most common is police diversion, whereby an officer lets a youth go with a warning. If a child is formally charged, diversion from trial is determined by the attorney prosecuting the case. This determination can be based on various factors, including school records and criminal history (Raoul Wallenberg Institute, 2015).

Similar to Latin American countries, many of these countries' diversion programs utilize a restorative justice model. Types of treatments can include community-based and government-supervised programs that include caseworkers and may result in community work and restitution to the victim or the victim's family as alternatives to formal detention (Foussard & Melotti, 2016; United Nations Children's Fund, 2017).

EUROPE

There are various juvenile justice systems across Europe, and there has been momentum over the past decade toward expanding diversion efforts within these systems. Restorative justice practices can be seen in many European countries, such as Germany, Switzerland, Northern Ireland, and Belgium (Dünkel, 2014; Matthews et al., 2018). The European Council of Europe, a forum of European member states that collaborate on economic, social, and humanitarian issues, has recommended treating juvenile offenders through more community-based initiatives that serve the best interests of the community, the victim, and the juveniles themselves (Dünkel, 2014). Based on the reforms and the support of the United Nations Children's Fund, both Europe and Asia experienced an almost 60% decrease in youth detention between 2006 and 2012 in many of their countries and territories (United Nations Children's Fund, 2018).

Restorative justice efforts across Europe include mediation, reconciliation between the victim and the juvenile offender, and showing remorse for one's actions through acknowledgment of responsibility. In England, this consists of restitution to the victim, and in Germany it may include reconciliation through mediation.

In Italy, where juvenile systems have focused on both punitive and rehabilitative efforts, restorative justice initiatives have become more prevalent, and various forms of mediation with the victim have been offered at multiple stages during formal processing. Sweden reserves imprisonment of youth as a last resort and most often offers some type of diversion. In Poland, roughly 2% of all adjudicated cases result in incarceration. In Northern Ireland, police are encouraged to offer diversion after coming into contact with a maladaptive youth. In Hungary, the number of children formally processed has also been reduced, resulting in less formal involvement and more community-based diversion programs. Finally, Germany has implemented mediation and community service for most justice-involved youth, with a very small percentage, around 2–5%, formally prosecuted, most of whom serve short sentences, not exceeding 4 weeks (Matthews et al., 2018).

AFRICA

Like other countries, Africa has explored ways to both divert youth from formal processing within the justice system and provide interventions to proactively avoid involvement. One such intervention program that began in South Africa in 2001 is Youth Build International. This program focuses on youth who have dropped out of school and are unemployed and instills life skills and participation in community services. The program also provides employment and long-term follow-up to help keep participants as productive members of society (Miller et al., 2018).

There have also been many initiatives and legislation passed throughout the years to focus on diversion and restorative justice within courts in Africa. The National Institute for Crime Prevention and the Reintegration of Offenders, for example, launched the first diversion initiative in 1990 in South Africa. In 1997, the Inter-Ministerial Committee on Young People at Risk drafted a bill that formalized the diversion process and its availability at multiple stages throughout the formal processing of a justice-involved youth. The Child Justice Act of 2008 was also passed in South Africa, under the auspices of the UN Convention on the Rights of the Child, and created a nonpunitive justice system that is dedicated to serving justice-involved youth. This juvenile-centered court applies restorative justice principles and other diversionary procedures built into the system, based on the best interests of the child, while also considering the rights of victims and society at large (Songca, 2019; Terblanche, 2012; Wood, 2003).

Within Africa, there are also other external programs and services such as drug treatment, anger management, skills-based training, and restorative justice programs that are offered based on youth assessments and recommendations by the court. Both external and court-supervised diversion is typically offered by the prosecutor of the case, but can also be initiated through the magistrate (judge). It is important to note that, much like other jurisdictions and countries across the world, juveniles in Africa are still held accountable for their behavior. Therefore, the first step in the diversionary process is often having the youth admit guilt and taking responsibility for their actions (Sloth-Nielsen, 2016; Songca, 2019).

CANADA

Similar to the United States, Canada has implemented many programs to intervene and divert youth from the formal juvenile system. Children experiencing emotional and behavioral issues that cause them to be at risk for delinquency are met with a wraparound collaborative approach. This proactive approach addresses the child's needs. It encompasses the youth, their family, social workers, court supervisors, and community stakeholders to link strategies and treatment to instill problem-solving skills, self-control, and conflict resolution and to bridge gaps in the services offered (Public Safety Canada, 2018).

Canada also has implemented the Youth Intervention and Diversion Program, which began in 2009 with a focus on juveniles at various risk levels. Low-risk youth are often diverted from the justice system completely, while those at moderate and high risk, after undergoing a risk/need assessment/responsivity assessment, can be diverted to community-based services. Police officers can also divert youth to diversion teams that assess the case and offer services to reduce offending and potential incarceration by finding the root cause of the maladaptive behavior and providing responses that are in the best interests of the child and the community (Public Safety Canada, 2013).

Through the implementation of these intervention programs and diversion within the court process, whereby juveniles can be enrolled in a variety of programs that focus on employment, education, mediation, and other forms of treatment, Canada has described both promising and positive results from these programs (Public Safety Canada, 2018).

Wrap-up

The purpose of the juvenile justice system is twofold: to rehabilitate youth demonstrating delinquent behavior and to keep society safe. In some cases, it is believed that this goal can only be attained through formal processing and incarceration, specifically for chronic and violent offenders. However, it is also recognized that there are unintended consequences of formally adjudicating, detaining, and imprisoning a child. In this chapter we have seen alternatives to formal processing and incarceration that, despite setbacks, could benefit both the juvenile and society at large while maintaining the overarching goals of the system.

Discussion Questions

1. Explain the historical development of diversion and intervention within and outside the United States.
2. Choose and discuss the theories you believe best explain why diversion/intervention is necessary or not.
3. What are the different methods of diversion that can be offered to a juvenile?
4. What are some pros and cons of diversion and intervention?
5. Describe how diversion options can be biased to certain groups.
6. Evaluate diversion and intervention programs between the United States and other countries around the world.

ONLINE RESOURCES

National Partnership for Juvenile Services http://www.npjs.org
U.S. Department of Justice Office of Justice Programs http://www.ncjrs.gov
Youth Government http://www.youth.gov
United States Department of Justice: Office of Justice Programs http://www.ojp.gov
Juvenile Justice Exchange Information http://www.jjie.org
Bureau of Justice Statistics http://www.BJS.gov
United States Department of Justice http://www.justice.gov
Coalition for Juvenile Justice http://www.juvjustice.org
Justice Center: The Council of State Governments http://www.csgjusticecenter.org
UNICEF https://www.unicef.org
National Institute of Justice: Crime Solutions https://www.crimesolutions.gov
Office of Justice Programs: Diversion Programs https://www.ojjdp.gov/mpg-iguides/topics/diversion-programs/

Definitions

Community confinement—this type of confinement can be given to chronic offenders as well as first-time violent offenders. It includes confinement in secure and insecure community-based facilities such as group homes

Cradle-to-prison pipeline—exposure to systematic social and environmental risk factors through one's development can cause ongoing contact with the justice system and a trajectory toward continued delinquency, criminality, and eventual incarceration

Criminogenic needs factors—factors determined to be directly related to a youth's criminality, which may negate further offending if changed

Developmental theory—delinquency can fluctuate based on natural development, brain maturity, and disrupted or removed social bonds with society

Differential association—a social learning theory that puts forward the notion that one adopts similar attitudes, values, and beliefs that may result in operating out of social norms through interacting with and gaining the support of others

Disproportionate minority contact—contact with the justice system that is disproportionate to that of other race(s)

Diversion—an approach that, while holding juveniles accountable, provides alternatives to formal detention

Dynamic risk factors—factors that can be changed, such as parenting practices, substance abuse, association with delinquent peers, and low academic achievement

Early intervention—attempts to provide skill sets, coping strategies, and other supportive resources

Electronic monitoring—can include an electronic bracelet with an active global positioning system to monitor and restrict the youth's location and adherence to court orders

Expunged—the erasing of a criminal record (sometimes at a cost)

Formal diversion—diversion that occurs after an arrest at any stage during formal processing

Formal processing—processing through the traditional juvenile justice system without alternative sanctions or diversion

Graduated sanctions—sanctions that gradually increase in their severity, supervision, and confinement

Houses of refuge—also referred to as "reformatories," institutions that were intended to provide skills, educations, and character building for diverted delinquent and at-risk juveniles

Immediate interventions—generally reserved for first-time offenders and those who have committed a misdemeanor or low-level, nonviolent felony; may include teen court, a diversionary program, community service, or mandated curfews

Informal diversion—diversion that occurs outside the juvenile justice system; often takes place during initial police contact and relies on law enforcement discretion

Intake—the first stage of processing where the system evaluates the juvenile and delinquent act, sometimes referred to as "adjustment"

Intermediate sanctions—usually imposed on repeat offenders or first-time violent offenders; can include intense supervision or passive or electronic monitoring

Intervention—strategies to prevent youth from coming into contact with the juvenile justice system.

Labeling theory—characterizations that lead to adverse effects such as stigmatizing and feeling ostracized

Net deepening—involving youth, no matter how slightly, with diversion programs through the justice system, leading them deeper into alienation and delinquency

Net widening—occurs when juveniles who committed minor offenses, who might otherwise not have fallen under the control of the court and could have been released, must abide by the strict stipulations of any given "diversion" program

Noncriminogenic needs factors—factors indirectly associated with a youths' delinquency, such as low self-esteem and poor social skills, that are considered in determining potential diversion program options

Passive monitoring—includes random phone calls to the youth's residence to ensure the juvenile is abiding by court mandates

Petition—an official complaint of charges against an individual

Protective factors—skill sets, coping strategies, and other supportive resources

Recidivism—ongoing contact with the justice system

Responsivity factors—factors such as cognitive ability, willingness for change, and access to services

Restorative justice—a collaborative approach to rehabilitation that includes mediation between the offender, victim, and other community stakeholders

Risk and need assessment tools—instruments that help in the decision-making to divert a juvenile from formal processing, detention, and or confinement

Risk factors—environmental and social conditions that can negatively impact an individual

Secure confinement—detention given to chronic juvenile offenders found guilty of violent crimes; the facilities are often run by the city or state

Socioeconomic bias—approach in which the basis for providing diversion for juveniles with similarly qualifying criminal history, age, offense, and risk and need assessments can include consideration of the financial means to pay for the program as a deciding factor

Static risk factors—factors that cannot be changed, such as the individual's age at first offense, history of violent behavior, and parental criminality

Tertiary intervention—programs, services, or treatment that are sometimes offered to youth already in contact with the justice system as part of the formal diversion process, such as community-based rehabilitation and intervention strategies

Wraparound services—a proactive approach that encompasses the youth, their family, social workers, court supervisors, and community stakeholders to align strategies and offer a single plan of care

References

American Institute for Research. (2019). *Latin America and the Caribbean—Youth violence prevention*. Retrieved on May 17, 2020 from https://www.air.org/project/latin-america-and-caribbean-youth-violence-prevention

Atienzo, E. E., Baxter, S. K., & Kaltenthaler, E. (2017). Interventions to prevent youth violence in Latin America: A systematic review. *International Journal of Public Health*, 62(1), 15–29.

Bonnie, R. J., Johnson, R. L., Chemers, B. M., & Schuck, J. (2013). *Reforming juvenile justice: A developmental approach*. National Academies Press.

Booth, J. W., & Neill, J. T. (2017). Coping strategies and the development of psychological resilience. *Journal of Outdoor and Environmental Education*, 20(1), 47-54.

Burgess, R. L., & Akers, R. L. (1966). A differential association-reinforcement theory of criminal behavior. *Social Problems*, 14(2), 128–147.

Butts, J. A., Bazemore, G., & Meroe, A. S. (2010). *Positive youth justice—Framing justice interventions using the concepts of positive youth development*. Coalition for Juvenile Justice.

Child Family Community Australia. (2020). Early intervention and prevention programs. Australian Institute of Family Services: Community for Children and Young People. Retrieved on September 16, 2020 from https://aifs.gov.au/cfca/topics/early-intervention-and-prevention-programs

Coulton, S., Stockdale, K., Marchand, C., Hendrie, N., Billings, J., Boniface, S., Butler, S., Deluca, P., Drummond, C., Newbury-Birch, D., Pellatt-Higgins, T., Stevens, A., Sutherland, A., & Wilson, E. (2017). Pragmatic randomised controlled trial to evaluate the effectiveness and cost effectiveness of a multi-component intervention to reduce substance use and risk-taking behaviour in adolescents involved in the criminal justice system: A trial protocol (RISKIT-CJS). *BMC Public Health*, 17(1), Article 246. http://dx.doi.org.marist.idm.oclc.org/10.1186/s12889-017-4170-6

Development Services Group. (2015, January). *Risk and needs assessment for youths: Literature review*. Office of Juvenile Justice and Delinquency Prevention. https://www.ojjdp.gov/mpg/litreviews/RiskandNeeds.pdf

Development Services Group. (2017). *MPG I-Guides: Diversion programs*. Office of Juvenile Justice and Delinquency Prevention. Retrieved on September 16, 2018 from https://www.ojjdp.gov/mpg-iguides/topics/diversion-programs/

Dünkel, F. (2014). Juvenile justice systems in Europe: Reform developments between justice, welfare, and "new punitiveness." *Kriminologijos Studijos*, 1, 31–76.

Farrell, J. Betsinger, A., & Hammond, P. (2018) *Best practices in youth diversion: Literature review for the Baltimore Youth Diversion Committee*. Institute for Innovation and Implementation, University of Maryland School of Social Work.

Feierman, J., Goldstein, N., Haney-Caron, E., & Columbo, F. (2016). *Debtor's prison for kids? The high cost of fines and fees in the juvenile justice system*. Juvenile Law Center.

Foussard, C., & Melotti, G. (2016). *Addressing juvenile justice priorities in the Asia-Pacific region*. International Juvenile Justice Observatory. http://www.apcjj.org/sites/default/files/oijj_asia-pacific_council_2016.pdf

Fox, B. H., & Farrington, D. P. (2016). Is the development of offenders related to crime scene behaviors for burglary? Including situational influences in developmental and life-course theories of crime. *International Journal of Offender Therapy and Comparative Criminology*, 60(16), 1897–1927. https://doi.org/10.1177/0306624X15621982

Higgins, D. & Davis, K. (2014). *Law and justice: Prevention and early intervention programs for Indigenous youth* (Resource sheet no. 34). Australian Institute of Health and Welfare. https://www.aihw.gov.au/getmedia/85dd676d-62ab-47cf-8a01-a1847a05a17a/ctg-rs34.pdf.aspx?inline=true

Hockenberry, S., & Puzzanchera, C. (2020). *Juvenile court statistics, 2018*. National Center for Juvenile Justice. https://ojjdp.ojp.gov/sites/g/files/xyckuh176/files/media/document/juvenile-court-statistics-2018.pdf

Howell, J. C. (1995). Trends in juvenile crime and youth violence. In J. C. Howell et al. (Eds.), *Sourcebook on serious, violent, and chronic juvenile offenders* (pp. 1–35). Sage.

Howell, J. C. (2003). Diffusing research into practice using the comprehensive strategy for serious, violent, and chronic juvenile offenders. *Youth Violence and Juvenile Justice: An Interdisciplinary Journal*, 1(3), 219–245.

Howell, J. C. (2009). *Preventing and reducing juvenile delinquency: A comprehensive framework*. Sage Publications.

Korpershoek, H., Canrinus, E. T., Fokkens-Bruinsma, M., & de Boer, H. (2020). The relationships between school belonging and students' motivational, social-emotional, behavioural, and academic outcomes in secondary education: A meta-analytic review. *Research Papers in Education*, 35(6), 641–680.

Loeb, R. C., Waung, M., & Sheeran, M. (2015). Individual and familial variables for predicting successful completion of a juvenile justice diversion program. *Journal of Offender Rehabilitation* 54(3), 212–237.

Mackin, J. R., Lucas, L. M., Lambarth, C. H., Herrera, T. A., Wallter, M. S., Carey, S. M., & Finigan, M. W. (2010). *Baltimore County Juvenile Drug Court outcome and cost evaluation*. NPC Research.

Matthews, S., Schiraldi, V., & Chester, L. (2018). Youth justice in Europe: Experience of Germany, the Netherlands, and Croatia in providing developmentally appropriate responses to emerging adults in the criminal justice system. *Justice Evaluation Journal, 1*(1), 59–81.

Mears, D. P., Kuch, J. J., Lindsey, A. M., Siennick, S. E., Pesta, G. B., Greenwald, M. A., & Blomberg, T. G. (2016). Juvenile court and contemporary diversion. *Criminology & Public Policy, 15*(3), 953–981. https://doi.org/10.1111/1745-9133.12223

Merenda, F. (2020) Adventure-based programming with at-risk youth: Impact upon self-confidence and school attachment. *Child & Youth Services*. Advance online publication. https://doi.org/10.1080/0145935X.2020.1829465

Merenda, F., Ostrowski, S., & Merenda, F., II. (2020). Building blocks of resilience: Applications for justice involved youth. *Journal of Applied Juvenile Justice Services,* 112–130. http://npjs.org/jajjs/wp-content/uploads/2020/02/Merenda-Building-Blocks-of-Resilience-1.pdf

Miller, C., Cummings, D., Millenky, M., Wiegand, A., & Long, D. (2018). *Laying a foundation: Four-year results from the National YouthBuild Evaluation.* MDRC.

National Institute of Justice. (2020a). *Formal system processing for juveniles.* Retrieved on December 15, 2020 from https://www.crimesolutions.gov/PracticeDetails.aspx?ID=9

National Institute of Justice. (2020b). *Juvenile diversion programs.* Retrieved on December 15, 2020 from https://www.crimesolutions.gov/PracticeDetails.aspx?ID=37

National Research Council. (2013). *Reforming juvenile justice: A developmental approach.* National Academies Press.

Office of Juvenile Justice and Delinquency Prevention. (n.d.). *Model programs guide.* US Department of Justice. Retrieved April 20, 2020, from https://ojjdp.ojp.gov/model-programs-guide/all-mpg-programs

Office of Juvenile Justice and Delinquency Prevention. (2020). *Racial and Ethnic Fairness, Statistical briefing book.* Retrieved April 25, 2020, from https://www.ojjdp.gov/ojstatbb/special_topics/qa11601.asp?qaDate=2018

Points of intervention. (2019). Youth.gov. Retrieved on December 26, 2020 from https://youth.gov/youth-topics/juvenile-justice/points-intervention

A practical approach to linking graduated sanctions with a continuum of effective programs. (2004). *Juvenile Sanctions Center Training and Technical Assistance Program Bulletin, 2*(1), 1–10. https://www.ncjfcj.org/wp-content/uploads/2012/02/linkinggraduatedsanctions_0.pdf

Public Safety Canada. (2013, August 1). *Youth Intervention and Diversion Program.* Government of Canada. https://www.publicsafety.gc.ca/cnt/cntrng-crm/plcng/cnmcs-plcng/ndx/snpss-en.aspx?n=54

Public Safety Canada. (2018). *Overview of direct intervention approaches to address youth gangs and youth violence.* Government of Canada. https://www.publicsafety.gc.ca/cnt/rsrcs/pblctns/2018-ddrss-yth-gngs-vlnc/index-en.aspx

Raoul Wallenberg Institute. (2015). *A measure of last resort? The current status of juvenile justice in ASEAN member states.* https://rwi.lu.se/app/uploads/2015/04/Juvenile-Justice-Report.pdf

Schlesinger, T. (2018). Decriminalizing racialized youth through juvenile diversion. *The Future of Children, 28*(1), 59–82.

Schiraldi, V., Western, B., & Bradner, K. (2015). New Thinking in Community Corrections. *Washington, DC: National Institute of Justice.*

Shulman, D. (2005). Labeling theory. In G. Ritzer (Ed.), *Encyclopedia of social theory* (Vol. 1, pp. 427–428). SAGE Publications. https://doi.org/10.4135/9781412952552.n161

Skaggs, S. L. (2016). Labeling theory. In *Encyclopedia Britannica.* Retrieved on November 20, 2018 from https://www.britannica.com/topic/labeling-theory

Sloth-Nielsen, J. (2016). *Children's rights in Africa: A legal perspective.* Routledge.

Songca, R. (2019). A comparative analysis of models of child justice and South Africa's unique contribution. *Journal for Juridical Science, 44*(1), 63–89.

Spear, L. (2010). *The behavioral neuroscience of adolescence.* W. W. Norton.

Sullivan, C. J., Strange, C., Sullivan, C., Newsome, J., Lugo, M., Mueller, D., Petkus, A., Holmes, B., Lonergan, H., & McCafferty, J. (2019). *Multi-method study on risk assessment implementation and youth outcomes in the juvenile justice system.* University of Cincinnati, Center for Criminal Justice Research.

Taxman, F. S. (Ed.). (2016). *Handbook on risk and need assessment: Theory and practice.* Taylor & Francis.

Terblanche, S. S. (2012). The Child Justice Act: A detailed consideration of Section 68 as a point of departure with respect to the sentencing of young offenders. *Potchefstroom Electronic Law Journal/Potchefstroomse Elektroniese Regsblad, 15*(5), 435.

Terre des Hommes International Federation. (2019). *Restorative juvenile justice in Latin America.* https://www.terredeshommes.org/causes/restorative-juvenile-justice/#

Underwood, L. A., & Washington, A. (2016). Mental illness and juvenile offenders. *International Journal of Environmental Research and Public Health, 13*(2), 228. https://doi.org/10.3390/ijerph13020228

United Nations. (2002). Convention on the Rights of the Child. UN Human Rights, Office of the High Commissioner. https://www.ohchr.org/en/professionalinterest/pages/crc.aspx

United Nations. (2008). The United Nations Standard Minimum Rules for the Administration of Juvenile Justice (Beijing Rules). UN General Assembly. https://www.ohchr.org/Documents/ProfessionalInterest/beijingrules.pdf

United Nations Children's Fund. (2017). *Diversion not detention: A study on diversion and other alternative measures for children in conflict with the law in East Asia and the Pacific.* UNICEF EAPRO.

United Nations Children's Fund. (2018). *Fifteen years of juvenile justice reforms in Europe and Central Asia. Key results achieved for children and remaining challenges.* https://www.unicef.org/eca/sites/unicef.org.eca/files/2018-11/Key%20Results%20in%20Juvenile%20Justice%20in%20Europe%20and%20Central%20Asia_0.pdf

Vinney, C. (2019, June 6). *Sutherland's differential association theory explained.* https://www.thoughtco.com/differential-association-theory-4689191

Wilson, J. J., & Howell, J. C. (1993). *A comprehensive strategy for serious, violent, and chronic juvenile offenders.* Office of Juvenile Justice and Delinquency Prevention.

Wood, C. (2003). Diversion in South Africa: A review of policy and practice, 1990–2003. *Institute for Security Studies Papers, 2003*(79), 22. https://www.files.ethz.ch/isn/112130/79.pdf

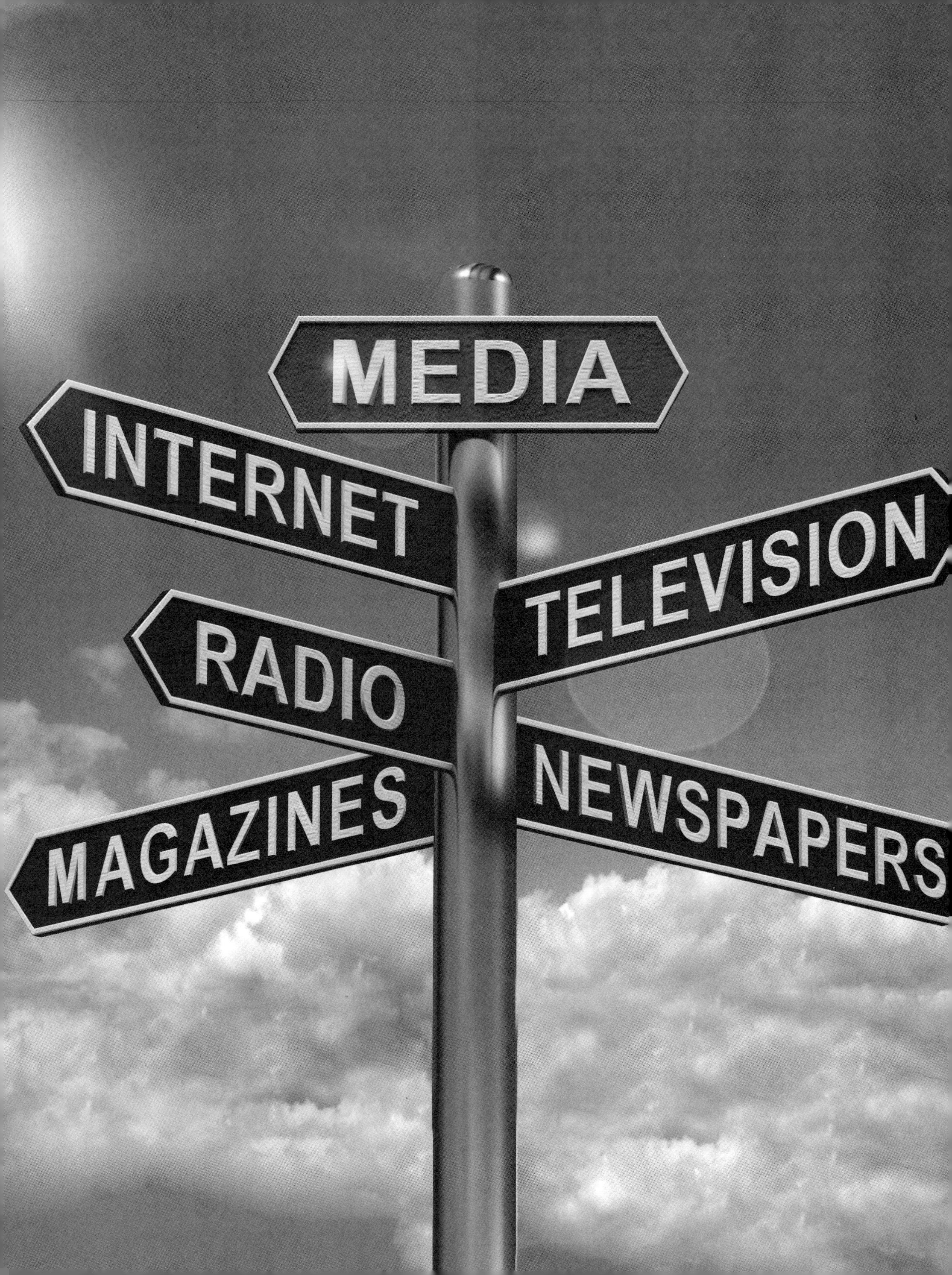
MEDIA
INTERNET
TELEVISION
RADIO
MAGAZINES
NEWSPAPERS

Media Evolution, Effects on Juveniles, and Protections Put in Place

LEARNING OBJECTIVES

At the end of the chapter, students will be able to

describe the historical development of media,

describe relevant laws and court cases affecting media and its restrictions,

describe the key components of obscenity and harmful material to children,

evaluate associated theories of the effects of media,

discuss specific modes of media and their specific effects, and

compare and contrast media regulations and child protections within the United States and around the world.

Introduction

The prevalence of media in the form of television, movies, video games, and online mediums has grown exponentially over the past few decades. With expanding media channels, the ability of individuals, specifically children, to access media content has become more widespread and that content is more easily attained. Computers, cell phones, and online game systems provide exposure to a host of content, often with almost no inherent restrictions. As media provides quick and broad access to educational resources, entertainment, and far-reaching connectivity to others, it can also provide coverage of disturbing events, misinformation, **fearmongering** (deliberately causing public alarm), exploitation and exaggeration of facts, sexual content, and violence (Rainie et al., 2019; Webb, 2017). In the worst cases, this type of content has been geared especially toward children.

In this chapter, we will look at how media has evolved and how information and images of sexuality and violence have been portrayed and regulated across such mediums as television, movies, and video games. We will study how the U.S. government and other governments around the world have tried to curtail exposure to media through attempts to control content, limit access, and provide information to parents about subject matter through rating systems. Finally, we will review the debates and studies that have measured the media's positive and negative effects in both the short and the long term in such areas as anxiety, aggression, sexuality, and violence.

What Is Media?

Media has been defined as "the means or channels of communication, that reach or influence people widely" (Bardes et al., 2016, p. 357). Historically, the means were newspapers, magazines, radio, and television, and the reach was limited to individuals who were able to come in contact with these channels directly. The subject matter communicated ranged from news to entertainment to education and other content. In the past few decades, however, that reach has expanded in many forms, not only increasing the information one is exposed to and its possible influence, but also the ease with which to access it. This includes information transmitted directly through radio and television, but also media that is accessed indirectly, through computers and any other device that can access the internet, referred to as digital media. **Digital media** is defined as any form of media that uses electronic devices for distribution (Preston, 2020). There is also two-way communication, which is referred to as **interactive media/multimedia** and is defined as

> any computer-delivered electronic system that allows the user to control, combine, and manipulate different types of media, such as text, sound, video, computer graphics, and animation. . . . Interactive media shift the user's role from observer to participant and are considered the next generation of electronic information systems. (Editors of Encyclopaedia Britannica, 2019, p. 1)

Social media is a subset of digital media and refers explicitly to "technologies, platforms, and services that enable individuals to engage in communication from one-to-one, one-to-many, and many-to-many" (Flew, 2017, p. 3). Specifically, these platforms provide digital software-based environments to exchange information. This includes such platforms as Facebook, Instagram, and Twitter (Appel et al., 2020).

Later in the chapter, we will discuss these media types in more detail along with emerging research on their effects on children.

A Little History: How Media Has Evolved and Its Growing Influence on Society

Although there is a large span of media in the early 21st century, these mediums were not always available. In fact, the first residential television set did not exist until the mid-20th century, well after trains, cars, and even planes were built.

Print Media

The first regularly printed newspaper in the United States began in Boston, Massachusetts, in 1704 (American Antiquarian Society, 2016). It initially spread information about events and activities. As time progressed, newspapers were supported by political parties and used to put forward political ideologies and **propaganda**, "an individual or group trying to influence opinion or action" (*Defining Propaganda*, n.d., p. 9). Legislators supported "freedom of the press" as described in the First Amendment to provide uncensored information so that citizens could make informed decisions, including voting for elected officials (*American Government*, 2019). The American Academy of Child and Adolescent Psychiatry described the influence of newspapers and other forms of media on youth: "Seeing and hearing about local and world events, such as natural disasters, catastrophic events, and crime reports, may cause children to experience stress, anxiety, and fears" (American Academy of Child and Adolescent Psychiatry, 2019).

In the 1800s, as printing newspapers became less expensive and more widely available, some outlets focused more on entertaining their viewership through sensationalized and sometimes scandalous stories known as **yellow journalism**. Although some people viewed this information as entertainment, others relied on it as accurate, and still others did not know what to believe because some stories conflicted with stories in other papers. Comic strips also became popular as a way to entertain both adults and children. The first appeared in 1896, and by 1910 they were seen regularly in print media.

By the late 1800s and into the 1900s, during the **Progressive Era**, a time of activism and political reform, there was a mix of what were considered serious newspapers and tabloids. Serious newspapers provided information about politics, finance, and news around the world, known as the **information model**. Tabloids often provided sensationalized and untrue stories intended for entertainment purposes, such as stories of aliens landing on earth and gossip stories. Later in the Progressive Era, legitimate newspapers began exposing fraud and corruption in private businesses as well as government, also known as **muckraking**.

As technology continued to advance, an invention to provide both news and entertainment to adults and children emerged.

Radio

Radio began in the 1920s and originally contained sponsored news programs and comedy, to be followed by music and game shows. Politicians frequently used radio as a medium to speak to the public about the state of America and new political proposals. People sat in front of the radio not only to be entertained, but also to receive current news. Information was delivered directly into the home, removing the need to seek out a newspaper to receive information. President Franklin D. Roosevelt regularly spoke over the radio, and his speeches were donned "fireside chats" as families sat together to listen to them. Radio was easily accessible to anyone by merely turning on the device.

During World War II, society sought news more regularly, and because papers took time to print, radio became the primary source of information. Radio was gaining popularity, and what was being said was thought to be shaping minds, including those of children. Because of the type of influence radio had and the fact that anyone could broadcast over a radio frequency and say just about anything at the time, the Radio Act of 1927 (preceded by the Radio Act of 1912, created to control radio wave interference by amateur broadcasters) was passed by the federal government, creating the Federal Radio Commission. The commission's purpose was to create standards and licensing and later became what is known in the early 21st century as the Federal Communications Commission (FCC) (discussed more later in the chapter). Although some critics considered the FCC a form of government censorship that violated the First Amendment, the courts ruled that radiofrequency broadcasting was not a constitutional right and that a regulated license would need to be obtained and conditionally maintained (Caterino, n.d.; Heinrich, n.d.). The FCC would eventually oversee both radio and another created medium—television.

Television

The first black and white electronic television was created in 1939 by the Radio Corporation of America and Philo Farnsworth, an independent inventor. Soon after, in the early 1950s, color television was developed, making programming even more vivid and realistic. Over time, increased availability of television content spread across the United States.

Television gained popularity into the late 1950s, providing sitcom and drama programming as well as news broadcasts, including real-time coverage of wars such as Vietnam and the Persian Gulf, in which bombs could be seen hitting targets. The

RCA Black and White Television

public began to rely on television as their primary news source. Two-thirds of all televisions belonged to families with children under 12 years of age and advertisers took advantage of this to generate millions of dollars in sales by marketing toys to children (Clark, 2020). Educational programming also developed in the 1900s and such shows as *Sesame Street* and the *Electric Company* were used to teach the millions of children tuning in each day.

In the 20th century, cable and satellite television brought movies to living rooms and bedrooms inside homes across the United States. Initially, large antennas allowed access to channels from other communities, known as community antenna television. By 1971, there were more than 80,000 subscribers in New York City alone, and by the late 1970s, such networks as Home Box Office (HBO), Cable News Network (CNN), and Nickelodeon began to appear (Stephens, 1999). As we will read later in this chapter, growing concern by the government regarding what was being shown and its effects on youth was the catalyst for much debate, restrictive legislation, and court hearings.

Motion Pictures

Photography and motion pictures were developed in the 1800s. They were initially displayed with no color (only black and white was available) and no sound. As technology advanced, so did the ability to provide color and more realistic films, as we know them today. Contemporary mainstream movies too have come a long way, offering special effects, three-dimensional experiences, and computer-generated imagery, all projected on screens as large as 70 to 100 feet, such as those found in Image Maximum (IMAX)

Magnavox Odyssey

theaters with surround sound to feel as though things are happening around the viewer. However, it was not until the 1930s that warnings of what may and may not be appropriate for children were provided to parents.

Video Games

In 1967, what was known originally as the "Brown Box," a gaming system, was released for home use, offering such games as ping pong, golf, and target shooting. It later was sold to Magnavox and renamed the Magnavox Odyssey in 1972. The popularity of arcades with adults and youth alike in the 1970s and 1980s served as an incentive to bring a form of these more intrinsic and realistic video games into homes. Although home game graphics were originally lacking compared with those found in arcades, soon home video game technology caught up and in some respects surpassed what was offered in traditional arcades, including the technology to play with other players using a computer and game console. This was most prevalent at the beginning of the 1990s as technology and connectivity further advanced.

Online Media

In 1991, the High-Performance Computing Act was passed by Congress, providing funding to create far-reaching internet browsing and connectivity for the public across the United States and eventually the world, often referred to as the **information superhighway**. In essence, this act helped create the internet as we know it today (see Chapter 12, "Juvenile Justice and the Digital Age"). With its connectivity ability, the internet provided the public with access to streaming movies and online multiplayer games, including **first-person multiplayer games**, games that offer the viewpoint of the player's character (Chikhani, 2015).

According to Johnsont (2021), in 2020, there were over 300 million internet users in the United States, and 66% (over 200 million) of the U.S. population regularly played video games. A large percentage of these users continue to be children, both in the United States and around the globe. According to the United Nations Children's Fund, children are spending more time online than ever before and a child goes online for the first time every half second (UNICEF, 2020).

In 1983, the FCC approved the DynaTAC 8000X phone, the world's first portable commercial cell phone.

Mobile Media

Smartphones are the most common mobile device. The first smartphone capable of sending and receiving an email was the Simon Personal Communicator. It was created in 1992 and was made by International Business Machines. However, the more recognized smartphone with internet access enabling access to games, news, video chats, text, and, yes, making phone calls was introduced in 2007 by Apple (Chong, 2015). Prior to the smartphone, original cell phones were portable versions of traditional landline communication and were only capable of voice communication.

In 2020, there were approximately 275 million smartphone users in the United States, and users ages 13–17 are the second-highest category of consumers, after 18- to 34-year-olds. . Content typically accessed includes social media platforms, breaking news, and gaming (Dobrilova, 2021; Johnson, 2021; Silver et al., 2019).

Into the 21st century, technology has continued to advance, and access to media has become even more readily available. Concern among communities and legislators has grown regarding the effects of media on individuals, especially children, and what can be done to regulate its content while protecting freedom of speech and freedom of the press.

Regulating Media: Attempts to Mitigate Its Effects on Children

One of the first broadcasting regulatory acts passed was the Radio Act of 1912. Because ships at the time used the same frequencies as amateur broadcasters, interference was common; such interference is believed to have led to a delay in responding to the ship *Titanic*, whose sinking killed over 1,500 people. The act required broadcast licensing. It was followed by the Radio Act of 1927 and the creation of the Federal Radio Commission, which delineated frequencies between private organizations and commercial users and networks such as the National Broadcasting Company. The commission was not given the authority to regulate radio because it was believed that the First Amendment protected radio content as a form of expression. However, the commission was authorized to regulate and prevent "obscene, indecent, or profane" content from adult and child audiences. Violations of this standard could result in fines or the removal of one's broadcast license. The Federal Radio Commission was eventually replaced by the FCC through the Communications Act of 1934. In the early 21st century the FCC still monitors radio and television, imposes fines, and revokes licenses for violations of their content guidelines.

But is censorship constitutional? What about the First Amendment?

The Cases and New Legislation

The First Amendment protects not only freedom of the press but also freedom of speech. Alleged infringements of this freedom have been challenged in the courts in terms of what kind of speech should be protected. The Supreme Court has ruled that, in fact, not all speech is protected by the First Amendment. For example, speech that incites imminent lawlessness and is intended to be taken seriously, according to the Brandenburg test, is not protected (see *Brandenburg v. Ohio*, 395 U.S. 444, 1969). Restrictions to freedom of speech within broadcasting have also been imposed on radio and television because of their easy accessibility by individuals, particularly children. State and federal courts have created laws and ruled that freedom of speech and freedom of the press are not guaranteed in cases of what would be construed by community standards as "obscene" and have tried to impose additional restrictions regarding content that could easily be heard or seen by children.

Telecommunications Act of 1996

The Telecommunications Act of 1996 is considered a revised version of the Communications Act of 1934. It attempted to address communication via television and the internet. It enabled publicly available television content to be controlled by parents through the mandatory installation of "V-chips" by manufacturers of televisions 13 inches or larger. V-chip technology allowed program access to be restricted from minors based on a rating system (see more on rating systems later in the chapter).

Children's Internet Protection Act

The Children's Internet Protection Act, passed by Congress in 2000, requires libraries and schools to restrict online access for minors to obscene and harmful material through filtering software; otherwise, they can lose funding for internet access. A U.S. district court ruled that the act violated the First Amendment because filtering software also restricts other information from being transmitted and limits adult access. However, the Supreme Court upheld the act, stating filters were necessary to block specific and ever-changing content on the internet. This ruling came with a caveat that institutions should automatically remove the filter upon request from an adult for their own access. The Children's Internet Protection Act defines "harmful to minors" as

> any picture, image, graphic image file, or other visual depiction that—(i) taken as a whole and with respect to minors, appeals to a prurient interest in nudity, sex, or excretion; (ii) depicts, describes, or represents, in a patently offensive way

with respect to what is suitable for minors, an actual or simulated sexual act or sexual contact, actual or simulated normal or perverted sexual acts, or a lewd exhibition of the genitals; and (iii) taken as a whole, lacks serious literary, artistic, political, or scientific value as to minors. (Universal Service, 2020, p. 2)

"The Big Bad Wolf"? The Current FCC

The Broadcast Decency Enforcement Act signed by George W. Bush in 2005 amended the Communications Act of 1934. It increased fines against broadcasters who violated obscenity and indecency laws from $32,500 per incident to $325,000. Additionally, if a broadcast that violated the laws was aired on multiple stations, the fine could increase to $3 million for a single incident.

As discussed previously, the FCC is considered by some to be an enforcement arm of censorship for the federal government, and court cases have alleged violations of First Amendment rights and questioned how such terms as obscenity and harmful material should be defined and interpreted. However, the courts continue to hold the position that radio and television broadcasting is not a constitutional right and, because of its open access, imposed regulations and restrictions are not in violation of the Constitution.

The FCC regulates broadcasts to ensure they adhere to these guidelines and can impose warnings and fines and even remove licenses from violators. The public can also make complaints to the FCC. The FCC further breaks down what constitutes obscene, indecent, and profane content as follows:

Obscene content is not protected by the First Amendment. For content to be ruled obscene, it must meet a three-pronged test established by the Supreme Court: It must appeal to an average person's prurient interest; depict or describe sexual conduct in a "patently offensive" way; and, taken as a whole, lack serious literary, artistic, political, or scientific value.

Indecent content portrays sexual or excretory organs or activities in a way that is patently offensive but does not meet the three-prong test for obscenity.

Profane content includes "grossly offensive" language that is considered a public nuisance (Federal Communications Commission, 2021).

Upon a complaint, the FCC conducts an investigation that considers the content, the time of day, and the context of the program. Federal law specifically prohibits "indecent" or "profane" content between the hours of 6:00 a.m. and 10:00 p.m., when the majority of children could be exposed to it. Paid subscription services do not have time restrictions for airing material that could be deemed profane or indecent based on FCC standards and definitions according to the Cable Communications Policy Act of 1984; however, obscene material is prohibited.

Rating System to Protect Children

The Telecommunications Act of 1996, in addition to the provision stated earlier, also determined that adults should be provided information about particular programs on television to assess their appropriateness for minors effectively. In addition to the mandatory installation of V-chips in televisions, the act gave television and other distributors of video programming the ability to voluntarily devise a rating system that would work with the V-chip by describing the content of a given show and its appropriateness for different age groups. News and sports programming were excluded from the rating system.

Within a year and after consultation with parents, individuals in the medical profession, religious and child advocacy groups, and other stakeholders, the National Association of Broadcasters, the National Cable Television Association, and the Motion Picture Association of America (MPAA) devised a rating system that was approved by the FCC.

An industry oversight group called the TV Parental Guidelines Oversight Monitoring Board, composed of industry experts, was voluntarily created in 1998 to assist with the consistency of the rating system. The board still exists in the early 21st century and provides an annual report. Additionally, the FCC is directed through the Consolidated Appropriations Act of 2019 to report on the accuracy of these rating systems and the ability of the TV Parental Guidelines Oversight Monitoring Board to oversee the rating system and address public concerns. The television rating system includes TV-Y (children of all ages), TV-Y7 (age 7 and above), TV-G (general audiences), TV-PG (may be inappropriate for younger children), TV-14 (may be inappropriate for children under 14), and TV-MA (inappropriate for children under 17). They also include content descriptors: D, sexual/suggestive dialogue; L, crude language; S, sexual content; V, violence; and FV, fantasy violence (*Ratings*, n.d.).

The MPAA (renamed the Motion Picture Association in 2019) had already established a quasi-rating system, what they called the Motion Picture Production Code, also known as the Hays Code, to inform audiences of the appropriateness of content. In 1966, Jack Valenti, president of the MPAA, spoke in front of the Associated Press Managing Editors at a national convention and addressed a change to the rating code to include "Suggested for Mature Audiences" for those films deemed as such. He went on to explain the need for rating films and their potential effects:

> Why should we have a code at all? The answer is simple. If we agree that motion pictures have a persuasive power beyond ordinary bounds, a potency shared by newspapers, then rational good sense demands that some form of responsible creativity be voluntarily assumed. (Motion Picture Association, 1966, p. 2)

Valenti explained that the intent was to provide parents with enough program information to decide whether their children could see and understand the content.

In 1968, the MPAA created a more informative rating system (G, general audience; M, mature audience; R, restricted (under 16 not admitted without an adult); X, persons under 16 not admitted. The MPAA created an independent board called the Code and Rating Administration, eventually renamed the Classification & Ratings Administration, to determine and administer motion picture ratings. This was to ensure consistency and comprehensive content information so that parents could make informed decisions about what their child could watch to minimize any detrimental effects. In a personal statement, Jack Valenti said regarding the new rating system that although there was "no valid evidence that movies have anything to do with anti-social behavior . . . lack of viable proof should not keep them [administration] from taking sensible steps which indicate their concern for children" (Motion Picture Association, 1966, p.2).

Ratings have changed over the years. For example, in 1984, the rating PG-13 was added to warn parents that some content may be inappropriate for children under 13. In 1990, the rating NC-17 replaced the X rating that was historically more associated with

TABLE 11.1	The Motion Picture Association of America's Rating Program, Updated in 1990
G	General audiences. All ages admitted.
PG	Parental guidance suggested. Some material may not be suitable for children.
PG-13	Parents strongly cautioned. Some material may be inappropriate for children under 13.
R	Restricted. Under 17 requires accompanying parent or adult guardian.
NC-17	No one 17 and under admitted.

Source: Motion Picture Association, 2020.

pornography. Also in 1990, more comprehensive rating descriptions were developed (*Motion Picture Association*, 2020).

In the early 21st century, in addition to film and television ratings, the video game and music industry have voluntarily created their own rating labels. The Interactive Digital Software Association (renamed the Entertainment Software Association in 2004) founded the Entertainment Software Rating Board (ESRB) in 1994 (renamed ESRB Privacy Certified in 2013), which created a five-category rating system with 17 content descriptors for game system games. In 1997, a rating system was established for online-enabled games and online gaming websites, but it was removed in 2003. In 1998, the K-A (Kid to Adult) rating was changed to E (Everyone). In 2000, an Advertising Review Council was established as part of the ESRB to monitor ESRB guidelines and impose sanctions for violations. In 2005, another rating, E10, was introduced for games that may not be appropriate for children under 10. In 2011, the ESRB developed a rating system for mobile apps at the request of CTIA, the wireless carrier association

Updated 1999 version of the ESRB Rating System for Gaming

Parental Advisory Label (PAL) of Potentially Inappropriate Music Recording Content (Recording Industry Association of America, 2020).

in the United States, and a free rating service was created in 2012 for digitally delivered games. The International Age Rating Coalition began in 2014 to continue to assign ratings to digital game content based on the ESRB guidelines (*Our History*, 2019).

The music industry voluntarily provides explicit lyrics warnings on music albums and certain digital/online music downloads through the Recording Industry Association of America. These labels can warn about sexually explicit lyrics, foul language, and drug, alcohol, or violent references in its music content. Through the Parental Advisory Label Program, music artists and record companies voluntarily decide if their content should have a warning label and what kind of warning should be provided (*Parental Advisory Label*, n.d.).

Media Effects on Juveniles

What happens when children bypass all the warnings and restrictions? As mentioned previously, with the realization that media was quickly growing and its influence was increasing, scholars and practitioners began to examine the effects of media as the government was creating methods to limit what could be seen.

Is there a link between children viewing violence and aggressive behavior? After numerous studies, there is still debate surrounding the effects of media on both adults and children. Some data show that children, as opposed to adults, are more susceptible to both short-term and long-term behavioral changes. At the same time, other studies reveal short-term effects while controlling for gender, race, and economic status, and still further research shows no media effects at all (Anderson, 2016; Ferguson et al., 2017; Huesmann et al., 2003; Smith & Ferguson, 2019; Smith et al., 2018).

Anderson and colleagues have also conducted extant research affirming adverse effects on children exposed to media violence in terms of aggression and violent behavior. Anderson defines **aggression** as "behavior that is intended to harm another person who does not wish to be harmed" and **violent behavior** as "aggressive behavior (as defined above) that has a reasonable chance of causing harm serious enough to require medical attention" (Anderson, 2016, p. 59).

However, critics argue that many studies on links between violent media and aggression in terms of predicting future serious aggression or violence are flawed, either by how aggression is measured or by how results are interpreted (R. McCarthy & Elson, 2018). For example, experiments have used putting another person's hand in cold water or giving someone different heat levels of hot sauce to measure whether viewing violent media affects short- or long-term aggressiveness in the real world (Delhove & Greitemeyer, 2019; Hollingdale & Greitemeyer, 2014). Experiments that test for aggression have also been cited as proof that viewing violent media will lead to real-world violence. However, even proponents of the violent media viewing causing aggressive behavior hypothesis acknowledge that there is no scientific evidence that exposure to media violence leads to actual violent behavior (*APA Resolution*, 2020; Ferguson et al., 2017; Smith & Ferguson, 2019).

Additionally, although numerous studies have shown how viewing violent media is associated with some form of aggressive behavior, most researchers acknowledge that media violence is only one of many factors that can cause aggression, and it is a culmination of factors or lack of a prosocial environment that can lead to an individual acting violently (Anderson et al., 2017; *APA Resolution*, 2020; Smith, et al., 2018). As stated in one review,

> It is also important to understand that no single risk factor causes a child or adolescent to behave aggressively or violently. Instead, it is the accumulation of risk factors and the relative lack of protective factors that lead to aggressive and violent acts. (Anderson et al., 2017, p. 2)

Different experiments have tested various forms of media exposure and their unique qualities in terms of causing maladaptive and aggressive behavior.

Television Effects

In the 1950s, approximately 1 in 10 family households owned a television, but in the early 21st century, 99% of households do, with an average of two or three sets in each home. It is estimated that children watch almost 3 hours of television each day, including watching movies and streaming content on other devices. This is in addition to time spent on social media and playing video games (Krantz-Kent, 2018). One of the most extensive assessments of television viewing, as it relates to its content, was performed in 1998. The study found that the average child watching television saw an average of 8,000 murders and over 100,000 acts of violence before leaving middle school (C. McCarthy, 2016). With all the additional modes of media and content now available, these statistics are likely an underestimation of the reality of the 21st century. These numbers beg the question as to what kind of short- or long-term effects exposure to media will have on children, if any.

SHORT-TERM EFFECTS

Many studies have measured the effects of television violence and aggression and show a short-term relationship (Anderson, 2016; APA Task Force on Violent Video Games, 2019). As you read in our theory chapter, Albert Bandura's social learning theory focused on learning through observation. Children imitate and model what they watch. Bandura surmised that learning could occur in a social context through observation and does not require direct reinforcement. In one of his experiments, one group of children watched a video of a clown doll, also referred to as a Bobo doll, being hit by an adult. The children then imitated the behavior when they were left alone with a similar doll even though they were provided with no further direction. Another group of children watched an adult hit the doll and then get rewarded; this group imitated the behavior the most. According to Bandura, this illustrated observational learning. This process has been related to media, wherein individuals sometimes use physical aggression to solve problems and become a hero. However, critics have pointed out that aggressive behavior differs from violent behavior, as defined previously. They have questioned whether these types of experiments indicate future real-life aggression, especially without consideration of other influencing factors (*APA Resolution*, 2020; Smith & Ferguson, 2019). In the 1980s, Bandura transitioned his social learning theory (renamed social cognitive theory) to emphasize cognitive and self-restraint processes that consider personal, social, and environmental factors and modeling behavior as equal contributors to learning (Valkenburg & Piotrowski, 2017).

LONG-TERM EFFECTS

Rowell Huesmann and colleagues (Huesmann et al., 2003) conducted a study to test for long-term effects of viewing violent television. They measured the amount of television violence viewed by second- and third-graders; 15 years later, they measured the participants' aggressive behavior as adults. Even after accounting for differences in socioeconomic status, intellectual ability, and parenting, participants who watched the most violence (upper 20%) as children were also the most aggressive as adults. This also speaks to violence on television having more significant long-term effects when viewed by a child, as opposed to a teenager or adult. The greatest impact occurs when a child identifies with the violent character or perceives the scene as being realistic and talking about life as it is.

Huesmann et al. (2003) also found that although being an aggressive child did not increase television violence viewing as an adult, more aggressive children seemed to seek out more violent television while a child. They attribute this to the justification theory, which explains how an individual attempts to justify their aggressive behavior by seeking out others acting aggressively, such as through violent media, which may in a sense normalize their behavior (Huesmann et al., 2003).

A more recent meta-analysis, a review of multiple studies by Bender et al. (2018), shows that research has moved away from asking if a relationship exists between media violence and aggression and now focuses on the question of why that relationship exists. Although some studies have controlled for demographic and other factors and still found links between media violence and aggression, researchers acknowledge that one must consider multiple additional individual factors within a social and environmental context (Bender et al., 2018).

THEORIES

Seymour Feshbach's catharsis hypothesis focused on television acting as a virtual release of violence for some and found that juvenile delinquents in a detention center who were allowed to watch programs with violence behaved less aggressively after only a few weeks. However, there were many other variables involved, such as the fact that they were given the privilege of watching a more expanded variety of programs, which critics argue could have positively modified their behavior and would not reduce effects on future behavior (Feshbach, 1984; Gentile, 2013; Sani, 2019).

Cognitive script theory focuses on specific routines/sequences of tasks children learn that form "scripts" in their minds. Examples include getting up for school in the morning and making their bed, washing up, getting dressed, and eating breakfast. This theory suggests that children who watch media in which aggression is commonly used to solve a conflict will form cognitive scripts in their minds that can be carried out when facing conflicts later in life (Hanson, 2007).

The **general aggression model** was developed to explain that the relationship between media and aggression is not automatic. It suggests that other factors, such as social and environmental factors and the characteristics of the individual themselves, should be considered, including the consequences of their actions offsetting any potential aggression or violent behavior (Allen et al., 2018; Bushman & Anderson, 2002).

Another study by Engelhardt and Bartholow (2013) reviewed research of media violence predicting aggressive behavior. They suggest it can cause a **priming** effect, wherein violent responses viewed on television can translate to violent reactions in the real world. Whereas cognitive scripts may be formed for long-term effects, priming can result in aggressive responses in the short term.

Priming is also the basis of a more recent model developed by Loersch and Payne (2011) called the situated inference model. This model explains how aggressive behavior occurs when an individual who has been primed through exposure to violent responses on television is confronted with a similar cue. The individual misattributes viewed violent reactions as their own thoughts and responds to the situation accordingly. However, the authors acknowledge that based on their review, there could be many other catalysts that link violent media to aggressive behavior.

News Effects

News stories can be accessed on various media modes in addition to television, such as radio and countless social media platforms. Unlike other forms of media, news media does not provide parental ratings. As such, the effects of being exposed to accounts of real-world events and situations have also been studied. Media news studies have found that reports of "negative" events trigger more emotion than reports of "positive" events. More than 70% of news broadcasts begin their broadcast with a violent story (Rojkova et al., 2015). Additionally, on average, a third of entire news programs are devoted to retelling violent stories in addition to detailing catastrophic and devastating events. These stories can be "tweeted" and "retweeted," disseminated through cable programming, or shown on many other social media platforms through laptops, tablets, and other mobile devices 24 hours a day (American Academy of Child & Adolescent Psychiatry, 2019, p. 1).

The American Academy of Child Adolescent Psychiatry has warned of possible negative effects of children viewing the news, particularly negative stories, and has suggested that what children view should be monitored and the content of the programming discussed. They also suggest specific effects of negative media stories, such as copycatting, aggressive or violent behavior, and fear. For example, coverage of the COVID-19 pandemic that spread across the world, killing millions of people and forcing the closure of businesses and even schools, was broadcast 7 days a week for months on every media outlet. Some accounts contradicted each other in terms of the effects of COVID-19 on adults and children, how easily the disease spread, and the consequences of contracting it. People were shown wearing masks and gloves, and images of body bags piled on streets and in the backs of trucks were flashed across every form of media. Research has found that, in addition to the adverse emotions experienced regarding the coverage of the pandemic's impact, the resulting stress "can impair cognitive development and cause long-term mental health challenges" (United Nations, 2020, p. 10). Additionally, sensationalized and erroneous news coverage resulted in increased stress and anxiety (Cao et al., 2020; Kumar & Nayar, 2021; United Nations, 2020).

However, as also happens with other studies, findings regarding whether viewing the news results in increased anxiety or mood change are mixed. Rojkova et al. (2015) studied the behavior of undergraduate students and found no significant difference in anxiety or mood after they watched a prerecorded news program. Although not statistically significant, the researchers did find that some mood changes occurred, especially after watching a negative story. According to the authors, this may have been more a result of predetermined attitudes about the news than the content viewed. For example, some participants said they find the news to be misleading and hence feel anger or resentment toward news programming.

Researchers also have considered other types of programming where violence is embedded in cartoons or displayed in a humorous fashion.

Cartoon/Funny Violence Effects

On average, children ages 2–11 watch 30 hours of cartoons a week (Habib & Soliman, 2015). In 1973, Friedrich and Stein tested the effects of preschool children watching violent cartoons such as episodes of *Batman* and *Superman*. Children watched these programs three times a week for about a month. Friedrich and Stein observed the behavior of two groups of children: those who were already considered aggressive before watching the cartoons and those who were not considered aggressive. Both groups experienced increases in observed aggression, but the group that was already aggressive showed more aggressiveness than the other children (Friedrich & Stein, 1973). Additional studies throughout the years have found similar aggressive behavior results and less prosocial behavior (Hill et al., 2016; Meng et al., 2020; Rai et al., 2017).

Repeated exposure or exposure through funny/cartoon violence has also been theorized to create a desensitizing effect. Desensitization theory describes how repeated exposure to an otherwise emotionally inducing stimulus is thwarted because of repeated viewing. In a sense, ongoing exposure to media gore and violence creates a numbing effect toward it, and some researchers believe it can cause someone to think about violence and potentially commit aggressive acts more easily in the real world (Huesmann et al., 2003).

Humor through violence can also detract from the level of violent behavior being viewed and attract child audiences. Although television shows such as *Family Guy* are intended for adult viewing because of their violent/sexual content that is shown either in cartoon form or as part of comedic scenes, children can be drawn to them. Often these types of comedic scenes are extremely graphic and use the violence for comedic purposes. Again, however, research is mixed in terms of the detrimental effects it can have on viewers. One study asserts that watching violence "camouflaged" as a cartoon can reduce the harmful effects of violent imagery on aggressive behavior. Other researchers say it desensitizes violence in general and causes higher rates of aggression and lower rates of positive socialization (Anderson et al., 2010; Kirsh, 2005; Habib & Soliman, 2015).

Movies, too, can have this effect. For example, in *Scary Movie*, the killer cuts off a cheerleader's head for making fun of him and puts it in the lost and found in the school locker room. *Scary Movie* was one of the most popular "violent" movies among teenagers after its debut and was seen by over 10 million children, 1 million of whom were age 10 when they watched it (Worth et al., 2008).

Movie Effects

Although movies have qualities and effects similar to those of television, access has changed over the years in terms of children utilizing cable television and other devices to view them. Further, unlike television, films can display more sexual content and at times more violence, especially when audiences return for a sequel and are already accustomed to the violence shown in the first film (Sparks, 2016). For example, the first *Robocop* included 32 dead bodies; the second contained nearly triple that amount. The initial *Rambo* movie killed 62 people, and by *Rambo 3*, that number reached 111 (Gerbner, 1999; Mcginnis, 2013; Orbesen, 2014). We have discussed studies exploring the effects of viewing media violence in terms of aggression, but could increased violence in movies lead to violence or acceptance of violent behavior in the real world?

One study observed 1,800 preschool children ages 3 and 4 who were exposed to violent movies and programs. Four years later, teachers were asked to complete surveys rating the aggressive behavior of the same children to assess such behavior as physical aggression and emotional distress. The authors found that the children who had been exposed to violent media displayed a lack of empathy for others, lying, and other antisocial behavior (Fitzpatrick et al., 2012).

Many years ago, a study was conducted in a juvenile delinquent residential facility. Eighty-five high school juveniles viewed either aggressive or neutral movies every day for a week. The researchers found that both physical and verbal aggression increases were linked to viewing the violent films, specifically within a short time of viewing (Leyens et al.,1975).

A more recent study tested 104 children ages 8 to 12. Half the children watched a movie containing guns, and the other half watched the same film with the gun portions edited out. The children were then allowed to play in a room where a real gun (modified not to shoot) was put into a cabinet. While some children who found the weapon turned it over to an adult, a higher percentage of children in the group who had watched the film with guns held the gun longer, fired it more times, and acted more aggressively than children in the other group. The authors concluded that children who view characters holding guns in movies are more likely to use guns themselves (Dillon & Bushman, 2017).

However, in 2018, a metanalysis of 78 individual studies involving more than 7,000 participants found that although there was consistency in terms of the presence of weapons in media leading to aggressive thoughts and hostile judgments in participants, there was also an overestimation of this leading to aggressive acts being carried out; the researchers argued that other factors in one's life should also be considered (Benjamin et al., 2018).

Pornography Website Effects

The effects of being exposed to pornography and sexually charged scenes in films are also of concern. Because there are no legislative mandates, only 3% of adult sites on the internet require age verification. Further, 74% of adult websites display free content, and the largest viewers of explicit material are between the ages of 12 and 17 (Walters, n.d.).

According to Healing (2012), children viewing sexual content can lead to confusion, premature sexual activity, and sexual attitudes, specifically when children relate what they see to real-world scenarios.

An additional concern has been raised regarding the lack of education about the significant risks of sexually transmitted diseases, pregnancy, and other adverse social problems. Although curiosity is natural, many researchers believe that interventions, such as tools for parents to identify and manage negative media influences, are needed to manage the effects of viewing sexual content. This is especially important for young persons who may have difficulty distinguishing sexual media content from its applications in the real world (Collins et al., 2017; Healing, 2012; also see Chapter 12, "Juvenile Justice and the Digital Age," regarding a more in-depth review of pornography on the internet and the dangers of sexual predators).

Copycat Crimes

There is also fear that viewing violence can create **copycat crimes**. For example, in 2012, during a showing of *Dark Knight* in a movie theater in Aurora, Colorado, a mass shooting occurred, resulting in 12 people dead and 70 injured. Although the shooter did not give a motive, the fact that he had dyed his hair red, in conjunction with false rumors reported by the media that he had referred to himself as the Joker character from the movie, caused the fear of copycat crimes in other theaters to spread, resulting in additional security measures. Viewing media accounts of mass shootings has generated threats of copycat crimes in other incidents as well. For example, after a school shooting in Parkland, Florida, in 2018, there were over 600 threats of school shootings across the country (Hayes, 2018). Crimes have also been replicated or believed to be inspired by prior incidents. A student from Virginia Tech who killed faculty and students in a shooting in 2007 had written previously about a desire to repeat the acts of a prior school shooting (Flynn & Heitzmann, 2008). Studies have shown that media coverage of mass shootings can have these types of effects, prompting psychologists to urge news stations not to provide the names of shooters in order to reduce any ensuing notability and popularity. The American Psychological Association (APA) has indicated that mass shooters often achieve fame through media coverage of their picture, name, and other personal specifics. Coverage of the incident, which usually lasts for days or even weeks, can prompt others to try to outdo the crime to achieve fame themselves (Pew et al., 2019).

One study surveyed 81 juveniles in a correctional facility regarding crimes they had committed and whether they felt their crime was inspired by or linked to a violent event or fictitious violence seen in a movie or video game that had given them ideas about how to commit a crime. The researchers found that one in four juveniles in the sample admitted to "copycatting" crimes, and one in three considered copying methods they had viewed in the media. Further, one in four juveniles credited music and one in three credited visual media as inspiring them to seek out a firearm. However, the authors noted that the majority of the sample reported little or no copycat activity and determined that the amount of media consumption was not related to copycatting. Individuals who did indicate a relationship between the media and their crime also revealed a prior perception of the media as being influential and helpful for committing criminal actions in the real world (Surette, 2016).

Video Game Effects

Copycat crimes also come into question with regard to video games. In 2012, the murders of 20 schoolchildren and 6 adults in a mass shooting at Sandy Hook Elementary School by an individual who then took his own life were reported by the news media as a possible copycat crime. It was later discovered that the shooter frequently played *Combat Arms*, a first-person shooter game used to practice headshots. However, researchers agree that if the video game was indeed a factor, it was one of many, such as psychological and emotional issues that most likely existed (Valkenburg & Piotrowski, 2017).

Before the Sandy Hook incident, in 1999, 12 students and 1 teacher were killed by 2 other students, 17 and 18 years old, at their high school. Some believed their violent acts were partly influenced by another first-person shooter game, *Doom*, which allows players to customize the game environment; in this case, according to reports, the environment had been customized as a school. But was the violence caused solely or in part by the video game, or did the juveniles have violent tendencies that drew them to the game in the first place? In response to unanswered questions of this nature, some states have attempted to ban sales of violent video games to minors, but the laws have been challenged.

BROWN V. ENTERTAINMENT MERCHANTS ASSOCIATION

In 2011, the Supreme Court reviewed an appeal to a California state law that banned companies from selling or renting video games considered violent to minors. The Supreme Court ruled that the law was a violation of the freedom of expression guaranteed by the

First Amendment, and therefore, states could not ban such sales. However, video game manufacturers use voluntary rating systems and place labels on games that are sold to warn of their content. Store owners can refuse a sale to a minor based on store policies.

VIOLENT GAME AGGRESSION STUDIES

Video games have also been studied in terms of their effects on children. Although there have been warning labels on games since 1994 under the ESRB, studies have found that **violence**, defined as inflicting harm on others, was present in 97% of teen-rated games and 64% of games labeled suitable for everyone (Busching et al., 2016). Despite the ESRB rating system and many store owners refusing to sell or rent inappropriately aged games to a minor, children can access games on multiple devices, and these devices can also provide access to the internet for multiplayer games. According to the APA, over 90% of children in the United States play video games, and this number is closer to 100% for children ages 12–17.

Atari's 'Chainsaw Massacre,' 1983

Additionally, games have become more sophisticated and realistic with the development of technologies such as 3D and virtual reality. For example, compare the game "*The Texas Chainsaw Massacre*, available for the Atari 2600 in 1983, with a similarly themed game offered 20 years later, *Grand Theft Auto Vice City*, available on PlayStation, Xbox, online, and even on one's phone. Although both games involve chasing people with a chainsaw that is used to hack their bodies, the older game is barely legible, with the people and chainsaw appearing as colorful pixelated boxes. Although it is distorted, the player gets the idea and feel of chasing other characters in the game and racking up kills. The new game, however, is much more visually realistic. Although games in the 1980s were not as visually real as games in the 21st century, some certainly portrayed scenes that were just as violent. In the mid-1980s, the game *Chiller* was released and soon became available on the Nintendo Entertainment System in the United States and Australia. In the game, the player takes on the role of a torturer who mutilates and murders nonplayer characters in an underground dungeon.

PlayStation's 'GTA Vice City,' 2003

So, if children have more access to video games than in the past and the games seem to contain just as much violence as television and movies, are the effects of video games similar as well?

The APA produces a report on violent media, including video game links to aggression, every several years. The latest report affirms the APA's contention that there is an established connection between violent media and aggression. This finding is based on an abundance of research reviewed. The APA found a "consistent relation between violent video game use and increases in aggressive behavior, aggressive conditions, aggressive affect, and decreases in prosocial behavior, empathy, and sensitivity to aggression" (APA Task Force on Violent Media, 2015, p. 11). Numerous additional studies either support or contest the APA's findings.

Chris Ferguson and colleagues (Ferguson et al., 2017) conducted a study with 99 young adults randomly split into three

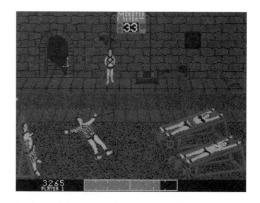

Exidy's 'Chiller,' 1986, later released by Nintendo

groups: participants either played or did not play a violent video game or were given a choice of whether to play the game. Afterward, all three groups took self-surveys and participated in an ice water test: to measure any newly formed aggression, the researchers allowed group members to choose whether to put another person's hand in ice water for a duration of time. There were no significant findings in any group to suggest that violent video game playing contributed to aggressive behavior (Ferguson et al., 2017). Another study found similar results after testing aggression levels in 59 college students, also after playing violent video games. Questionnaires measuring pre- and postaggression levels indicated no increases from playing violent games, and self-reports of preaggression were the only predictors of postaggression (Bean & Ferro, 2016). Other studies have tested participants over a period of time.

A longitudinal study published in 2018 assessed ownership of violent shooter video games in over 15,000 children and any resulting aggressive behavior throughout their lives since preschool age. Other variables in addition to aggression were also assessed, including attention deficit hyperactivity disorder, delinquency, mental health, conduct disorder, and depression. The researchers found that video game play was not predictive of delinquency or crime later in life. The authors also spoke of what they termed a catalyst model of criminal aggression, which discounts media effects, arguing that they are not long-lasting or strong enough to cause criminality; rather, personal and environmental factors are influences that are connected with aggression and antisocial behavior (Smith et al., 2018).

Researchers have also used magnetic resonance imaging to study neurological changes in the brain in relation to media effects. Pan et al. (2018) tested two groups of individuals ages 17–27. One group consisted of individuals who had played violent video games for more than 10 hours per week over the past 3 months, and the other group did not play violent video games at all. The groups were first asked to fill out a questionnaire to assess any aggression that may be linked to playing violent video games. Additionally, all participants underwent brain imaging to assess brain activity, specifically in the frontal cortex, which is related to aggression and moral judgment. Other researchers have found links between misfunction of this area of the brain and moral insensitivity. The authors found no difference in survey results measuring aggression between both groups, nor did they find any misfunction in brain activity. Based on these findings, the researchers concluded that long-term playing of violent video games does not lead to poor self-control and moral judgment or aggression. Instead, the authors assert that environmental conditions, such as childhood distress

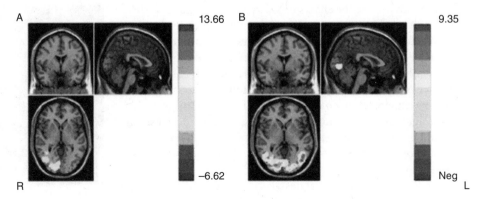

Brain Activity Imaging to Assess Possible Aggression After Extensive Video Game Playing

and family conditions, should be considered contributors to aggressive behavior, as asserted in other research studies.

However, as you read with regard to the APA report, many studies have found a link between exposure to violent video games and increased aggression and other detrimental effects. Some researchers believe that the link between violent media and aggression can stem from media changing one's perceptions of what is socially acceptable, feelings about aggression and violence, and views about the real world (Huesmann, 2007). Some critics allege that playing violent video games allows people who may be aggressive to act out their aggression in the game, but little evidence supports this theory (Busching et al., 2016). Additionally, researchers believe that viewing violent media leads not only to increased aggression in an individual, but also impulsivity, a lack of empathy, and a lack of prosocial behavior (Anderson, 2016; APA Task Force on Violent Media, 2015). In 2010, Anderson et al. conducted a meta-analysis that assessed over 130 studies of media violence with a total of over 130,000 participants. The authors concluded a causal link existed between violent video games and aggressive behavior, decreased empathy, and prosocial behavior (Anderson et al., 2010). However, critics have questioned some of the studies included in the analysis, as well as their methodologies (Ferguson & Beresin, 2017; Ferguson et al., 2017; Hilgard et al., 2017). Ferguson conducted his own meta-analysis and found no link between violent video games and aggression (2015).

A follow-up meta-analysis was conducted in 2018 to further examine Anderson et al.'s 2010 results. This meta-analysis examined 24 studies with over 17,000 participants. The studies included individuals ages 9 to 19 who played violent video games and displayed subsequent aggressive behavior. These studies were conducted in Austria, Canada, Germany, Japan, Malaysia, the Netherlands, Singapore, and the United States.

DEEPER DIVE

Shylo Kujawski

In 2006, Shylo Kujawski was charged with stealing a car in Canada, and it was revealed that he was a fan of the video game *Grand Theft Auto*, as indicated by the tattoo on his back. Investigators caught him because of the easily identifiable and incriminating tattoo (Sweet, 2006).

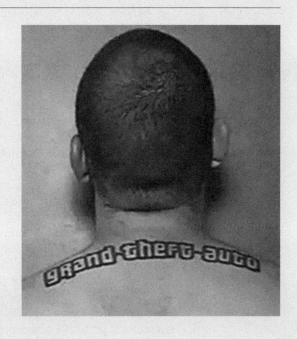

The authors found not only a link between violent video games and aggression but also a relationship with ethnicity, with White participants having the strongest effects. They determined that the conclusions resulting from Anderson et al.'s meta-analysis aligned with their results (Prescott et al., 2018).

Violent Effects

There has also been some question regarding whether violent video games beget actual violence in the real world. As you read previously with regard to mass shootings, reports blame video games for some of these incidents. In 2020, however, the APA released a resolution, based on their review of the scientific literature, indicating that no conclusive scientific evidence showed that playing violent video games leads to violent behavior.

> Whereas scientific research has demonstrated an association between violent video game use and both increases in aggressive behavior, aggressive affect, aggressive cognitions, and decreases in prosocial behavior, empathy, and moral engagement. In psychological research, aggression is usually conceptualized as behavior that is intended to harm another . . . violence can be defined as an extreme form of aggression or the intentional use of physical force or power that either results in or has a high likelihood of resulting in harm. Insufficient research has examined whether violent video game use causes lethal violence.

They also present their findings with a further caveat that reads,

> The following resolution should not be misinterpreted or misused by attributing violence, such as mass shootings, to violent video game use. Violence is a complex social problem that likely stems from many factors that warrant attention from researchers, policymakers, and the public. Attributing violence to violent video gaming is not scientifically sound and draws attention away from other factors. (*APA Resolution*, 2020, p. 1)

However, critics challenge this conclusion with their own reviews and independent research. After a review of violent media research, Bushman and Anderson (2015) found that although there is never a single cause for aggressive and violent behavior, exposure to violent media, including video games, can be a contributing factor. Researchers further assert that extreme violence occurs only when there are a multitude of risk factors present. Risk factors can include personality characteristics, life events, genetic or brain chemistry factors, and a poor family environment (Anderson, 2018; Shao & Wang, 2019).

Clearly, there are many conflicting thoughts and much research regarding the effects of violent video games, both for aggression and for real-world violence. What most researchers do agree on is that there are multiple causes for aggression, more than one factor is necessary to produce that aggression, and the causes of violent behavior are even more complex. Research continues in all of these areas.

We will now look at the effects of media around the world, as well as how media and government protections have evolved.

Worldview

Media Around the World

Media violence has been measured worldwide in such countries as Australia, Austria, Canada, China, Croatia, Germany, Japan, Malaysia, the Netherlands, Romania, and Singapore. As in the United States, results regarding links of exposure to media violence with aggression and real-world violence have been mixed (Anderson et al., 2017; Ferguson, 2015; Ferguson et al., 2017; Prescott et al., 2018; Smith & Ferguson, 2019). The secretary general of the United Nations has stated that "we must not ignore the growing risks children are facing from online violence, abuse and exploitation." He went on to say that "social media companies have a special responsibility to protect the vulnerable" (Guterres, 2020, p. 1). Scholars across the globe agree that research regarding the effects of media should continue and have implemented various strategies to protect children, as exemplified in the following paragraphs. The following countries were selected based on available information related to this topic.

THE EUROPEAN COMMISSION

The European Commission's Audiovisual Media Services Directive sets guidelines for national legislation for television and film. Its goals include protecting children while balancing freedom of expression and guaranteeing countries' independence to self-regulate media and work communities. The most recent revision was signed into law in 2018. Media providers are required to abide by individual country regulations, and rules are now extended to social media services (European Commission, 2018).

UNITED KINGDOM

Since 1913, the United Kingdom has had a rating system through its British Board of Film Classification; unlike the system in the United States, theirs is a seven-tier system. The rating system has an additional restriction between "12" and "18", classified as "15", in response to complaints of sexually violent content in "12" rated movies. Although the "15" rating allows sexual violence, its duration must be short and it must not be presented in "strong detail". They also have a "R18" rating for adult films that can only be shown in places that are specially licensed (British Board of Film Classification, 2019; see Figure 11.1).

U.K. Film Ratings

Suitable for all

Parental guidance

Cinema release suitable for 12 years and over

Video release suitable for 12 years and over

Suitable only for 15 years and over

Suitable only for adults

Adults works for licensed premises only

Figure 11.1 The British Board of Film Classification 7-tier rating system.

Unlike the United States, the UK's Video Recording Act of 2010 requires media to be submitted for classification with only a few exceptions, such as documentaries, sports, or music videos. In 2014, the act was amended to remove these exceptions if these mediums depict material that could potentially be harmful to children and would constitute a 12 rating or above.

Video games have a separate rating system designated by the Pan European Game Information. Again, unlike the United States, as of 2012, retailers are prevented by law from selling games to children that are not rated for their age (PEGI Age Ratings, 2017; see Figure 11.2).

Child access to online pornography was also a concern, and legislators tried to mandate age verification software through the Digital Economy Act in 2017. However, implementation has been delayed twice because of glitches in the system, including the ability to bypass the system and privacy issues raised by critics (Jones, 2019).

Rating	Description
3 www.pegi.info	The content of games with a PEGI 3 rating is considered suitable for all age groups. The game should not contain any sounds or pictures that are likely to frighten young children. A very mild form or violence (in a comical context or a childlike setting) is acceptable. No bad language should be heard.
7 www.pegi.info	Game content with scenes or sounds that can possibly be frightening to younger children should fall into this category. Very mild forms of violence (implied, non-detailed, or non-realistic violence) are acceptable for a game with a PEGI 7 rating.
12 www.pegi.info	Video games that show violence of a slightly more graphic nature towards fantasy characters or non-realistic violence towards human-like characters would fall in this age category. Sexual innuendo or sexual posturing can be present, while any bad language in this category must be mild. Gambling as it is normally carried out in real life in casinos or gambling halls can also be present (e.g., card games that in real life would be played for money).
16 www.pegi.info	This rating is applied once the depiction of violence (or sexual activity) reaches a stage that looks the same as would be expected in real life. The use of bad language in games with a PEGI 16 rating can be more extreme, while games of chance and the use of tobacco, alcohol, or illegal drugs can also be present.
18 www.pegi.info	The adult classification is applied when the level of violence reaches a stage where it becomes a depiction of gross violence, apparently motiveless killing, or violence towards defenseless characters. The glamorization of the use of illegal drugs and explicit sexual activity should also fall into this age category.

Figure 11.2 The Pan European Game Information rating system. In the United Kingdom, retailers are prevented by law from selling video games to children that are not rated for their age.

SOUTH AFRICA
In South Africa, 58% of children age 8 and younger watch television at least once a day, 17% use mobile devices, 14% go on the internet, and 6% play video games. The amount of time spent on these devices increases as children get older. For example, 8- to 18-year-olds spend

an estimated 7.5 hours a day on some form of media, 7 days a week (Burton et al., 2016; Film and Production Board, 2017; Phyfer et al., 2016).

The Film and Publication Board is responsible for classifying age-appropriate media for film and video games. There are more classifications than in the United States and other countries. Content is classified specifically for children ages 7–9, 10–12, 13, 16, and 18, and there are additional restrictions regardless of age (see figure 11.3). All movies and video games must be approved and classification must be assigned by the board. Additionally, those selling or renting movies must register with the board and remain in compliance (Film and Production Board, 2017).

 Material is suitable for ALL ages (only applicable to Films)

 Indicates that parents and caregivers are in the best position to decide whether or not a child in their care may view film or DVD for home entertainment purposes

 Material is not suitable for children under the age of 7. Children from the ages of 7–9 years may not be allowed to watch a film classified 7–9 unless accompanied by an adult

 Material is not suitable for children under the age of 10. Children from the ages of 10–12 years may not be allowed to watch the film unless accompanied or supervised by an adult.

 Not suitable for persons under the age of 13

 Not suitable for persons under the age of 16

 Not suitable for persons under the age of 18

 Means only a holder of a license to conduct the business of adult premises, set out in section 24 of the Act, may distribute the film to persons older than 18

 The material may not be distributed or exhibited anywhere

Figure 11.3 South Africa's Games and Films Rating System

The Films and Publication Amendment Bill of 1996 in South Africa was amended in 2015 and, after delays, was signed into law in 2019 to further stipulate authority and regulations. It also empowers the Film and Publication Board and creates mandates and criminal offenses for noncompliance with its policies. The amendment broadens regulations online in terms of holding internet service providers responsible for the content of the sites they are hosting and being susceptible to criminal and monetary sanctions for violations. Internet service providers are advised to "take all reasonable steps" to prevent the use of their services for such things as child pornography, hate speech, and advocating racism (Minister of Communications, 2015).

CANADA

In Canada, research over the years has shown, similar to research in the United States, that although a relationship between media violence and aggression may exist, it is the children who are already "at risk" for maladaptive behaviors who are most susceptible to behavioral changes (Prescott et al., 2018; Wortley et al., 2008).

On average, children in Canada under the age of 5 spend at least 2 hours watching television each day and, as in other countries, the amount of viewing increases across all media as children grow older (Canadian Pediatric Society, 2017; Tang et al., 2018). The Canadian government holds broadcasters responsible for reducing the amount of violent programming and other content they deem inappropriate on television. This mandate includes advisories throughout a program regarding violent content and limitations for violence shown on news programs. Additionally, broadcasters do not show violent programming before 9:00 p.m. Similar to other countries, Canadian broadcasters have a rating system for both television programming and cable run by the Action Group on Violence on Television.

In addition to placing responsibilities on broadcasters to protect children from exposure to violence and other inappropriate media content, the Canadian Radio–Television and Telecommunications Commission also puts forth guidelines for parents. The guidelines include information about the rating system, V-chip technology to enable parent restrictions, and methods to contact the commission about inappropriate content (History of AGVOT, n.d.).

CHINA

In China, there are stringent guidelines for collecting information from children who view media online. Through the Cyberspace Administration of China, website operators and internet service providers are mandated to obtain permission from a parent or guardian before collecting, using, transferring, or disclosing a child's personal information (Zhang & Chen, 2019, p. 1). This is to avoid websites targeting children in the future. Websites and applications are also mandated to have specific registration rules to prevent children from viewing inappropriate content. Violators of these laws can face monetary fines, have their website shut down, and have their business license revoked (Zhang & Chen, 2019).

China also has strict control over other forms of media. They utilize monitoring systems and firewalls to block specific websites, bloggers, and other news information sites they deem harmful. Although China does have freedom of speech and press for its adults and children alike, they have exceptions if it is considered a threat to state secrets or endangers the country or its citizens. However, critics say the system is too vague and allows for gross censorship. For example, the government has blocked such sites as Wikipedia, Facebook, Twitter, and YouTube and search engines such as Google, and they have implemented temporary restrictions for controversial world news (Xu & Albert, 2017).

There are numerous government bodies in China that monitor and enforce laws regarding media exposure, including the Communist Party's Central Information Department. These agencies monitor radio, television, and film to ensure appropriate content. Additionally, China employs over 2 million individual workers referred to as "public opinion analysts" to monitor the internet continually. China also has what is termed the "great firewall," which blocks access to specific websites. Violations of China's policies are met with lawsuits, fines, arrests, and even mandates to publicly confess to these violations on television (Xu & Albert, 2017).

Video game effects are also a current concern in China. In an effort to further protect children from becoming addicted, China had banned children from playing for more than 90 minutes per day on school days and disallowed play from 10:00 p.m. to 8:00 a.m. (Cuthbertson, 2019). Effective September 1, 2021, China tightened these restrictions further by completely forbidding children under 18 to play online games from Monday through Thursday. Additionally, youth can now only play for one hour, between 8 p.m. and 9 p.m., on Fridays, Saturdays, Sundays, and public holidays. These restrictions are imposed through gaming platforms (National Press and Publication Administration, 2021). These efforts are said to protect the mental and physical health of children in the country. There are also strict limitations on how much money children can spend on game add-ons and extras, with a maximum of an equivalent of about $20 per month for those under 16 and $40 for 16- to 18-years-olds (Cuthbertson, 2019; National Press and Publication Administration, 2021; Yongling, 2019).

WORLD HEALTH ORGANIZATION: GAMING ADDICTION

In addition to the previously discussed 2015 and 2020 APA reports linking violent media to aggression and other detrimental effects, the World Health Organization addressed video gaming addiction. In 2018, the World Health Organization issued a report stating that video game addiction is a mental health disorder that can cause "significant issues with functioning." Gaming disorder is defined in the 11th Revision of the *International Classification of Diseases* as

> a pattern of gaming behavior ('digital-gaming' or 'video-gaming') characterized by impaired control over gaming, increasing priority given to gaming over other activities to the extent that gaming takes precedence over other interests and daily activities, and continuation or escalation of gaming despite the occurrence of negative consequences. (World Health Organization, 2018, p. 1)

However, the World Health Organization acknowledges that based on scientific research, gaming disorder affects only a small percentage of individuals.

AUSTRALIA

In Australia, the Commonwealth Classification Act dictates how computer games and films can be sold and advertised. Individual territories can have their classification tools approved and are then permitted to enforce whatever guidelines are created. Approved tools include the International Age Rating Coalition for mobile and online games and the Netflix Classification tool for films on Netflix, for example.

Australian Classification, the agency responsible for media ratings, mandates every film, mobile app, and video game to be classified before it can be made publicly available. Television and radio are classified by industry assessors. Classifications serve as advisories to parents, as in the United States and other countries, and families make the ultimate decision as to what they feel is appropriate content for their children.

The Royal Australian & New Zealand College of Psychiatrists has recognized both the benefits and the disadvantages of children's exposure to various media content. They speak to digital skills and online services being essential attributes. For example, connecting with friends and family in a positive and healthy manner can help develop social skills and improve schoolwork. However, they also warn of possible media detriments, such as being exposed to age-inappropriate content, lack of privacy, social isolation, and mental health problems. Efforts are continually being made to protect children from these harms, and they acknowledge more research is needed in these areas.

Wrap-up

Evaluating the effects of media and how its evolution has positively or negatively contributed to society continues to garner much debate. Most researchers acknowledge the advantages these advances in technology overall and specifically media have provided, but many also caution of the potential ill effects of exposing children to some content too early. Countries around the world have adopted measures to help protect children from being exposed to content deemed inappropriate or harmful to their well-being. Responsibilities to control a child's exposure have ranged from voluntary compliance by the media industry to government mandates to the discretion of caretakers regarding what they believe is best for their child. Still, most researchers agree that media alone is not enough to create lasting behavioral changes, especially when it comes to violent acts in the real world, and that other factors in a young person's life must be considered when trying to support their healthy development.

Discussion Questions

1. Explain the historical development of media within and outside the United States.
2. What are some of the laws and acts that affected media and imposed restrictions?
3. Describe how what is considered obscene and harmful to children has changed and the reasons why.
4. Choose and discuss which theories you believe best explain media effects on children.
5. Discuss the effects of specific modes of media on children.
6. Evaluate the differences and similarities of media regulations within the United States and other countries around the world.

ONLINE RESOURCES

American Psychology Association www.apa.org
Pan European Game Information www.pegi.info
United Nations https://www.un.org/en/ www.oyez.org
Pew Research Center www.pewresearch.org
Council on Foreign Relations www.cfr.org
World Health Organization www.who.int

Definitions

Aggression—behavior that is intended to harm another person who does not wish to be harmed

Copycat crimes—crimes that are influenced by or carried out similar to another crime

Digital media—any form of media that uses electronic devices for distribution

Fearmongering—deliberately causing public alarm, exploitation and exaggeration of facts, sexual content, and violence

First-person multiplayer games—games that offer play with other people from the viewpoint of the player's character

General Aggression Model—explains that the relationship between media and aggression is not automatic and other factors should be considered.

Indecent content—portrays sexual or excretory organs or activities in a way that is patently offensive but does not meet the three-prong test for obscenity

Information model—media providing information about politics, finance, and news around the world

Information superhighway—far-reaching internet browsing and connectivity for the public across the United States and around the world

Interactive media/multimedia—two-way communication that allows the user to control, combine, and manipulate different types of media

Media—channels of communication that reach or influence people widely

Muckraking—media exposing fraud and corruption in private business as well as the government

Obscene content—appeals to an average person's prurient interest; depicts or describes sexual conduct in a blatantly offensive way; and, taken as a whole, lacks serious literary, artistic, political, or scientific value

Priming—violent responses viewed on television translating to violent responses in the real world

Profane content—includes "grossly offensive" language that is considered a public nuisance

Progressive Era—a time of activism and political reform

Propaganda—an individual or group trying to influence opinion or action

Social media—a subset of digital media that provides digital software-based environments to exchange information

Violent behavior—behavior that has a reasonable chance of causing harm serious enough to require medical attention

Yellow journalism—media entertaining its viewership through sensationalized and sometimes scandalous stories

References

Allen, J. J., Anderson, C. A., & Bushman, B. J. (2018). The general aggression model. *Current Opinion in Psychology, 19*, 75–80.

American Academy of Child Adolescent Psychiatry. (2019, January). *News and children*. Retrieved on April 20, 2020 from https://www.aacap.org/AACAP/Families_and_Youth/Facts_for_Families/FFF-Guide/Children-And-The-News-067.aspx

American Antiquarian Society. (2016, September). *The news media and the making of America: 1730–1865*. https://www.americanantiquarian.org/news-media-and-making-america-1730-1865

American government: First Amendment rights. (2019). USHistory.org. Retrieved on December 26, 2020 from https://www.ushistory.org/gov/10b.asp

Anderson, C. A. (2016). Media violence effects on children, adolescents and young adults. *Health Progress, 97*(4), 59–62. http://www.craiganderson.org/wp-content/uploads/caa/abstracts/2015-2019/16A2.pdf

Anderson, C. A. (2018, March 8). Guns, media violence and mass shootings: What psychological scientists know. *Des Moines Register*. https://www.desmoinesregister.com/story/opinion/columnists/iowa-view/2018/03/08/guns-media-violence-and-mass-shootings-what-psychological-scientists-know/407283002/

Anderson, C. A., Bushman, B. J., Bartholow, B. D., Cantor, J., Christakis, D., Coyne, S. M., & Huesmann, R. (2017). Screen violence and youth behavior. *Pediatrics, 140*(Suppl. 2), S142–S147.

Anderson, C. A., Shibuya, A., Ihori, N., Swing, E. L., Bushman, B. J., Sakamoto, A., & Saleem, M. (2010). Violent video game effects on aggression, empathy, and prosocial behavior in Eastern and Western countries: A meta-analytic review. *Psychological Bulletin, 136*(2), 151–173. https://doi.org/10.1037/a0018251

APA resolution on violent video games: February 2020 revision to the 2015 resolution. (2020). American Psychological Association. https://www.apa.org/about/policy/resolution-violent-video-games.pdf

APA Task Force on Violent Media. (2015). *Technical report on the review of the violent video game literature*. American Psychological Association. https://www.apa.org/pi/families/review-video-games.pdf

APA Task Force on Violent Video Games. (2019). *Technical report on the review of the violent video game literature*. American Psychological Association.

Appel, G., Grewal, L., Hadi, R., & Stephen, A. T. (2020). The future of social media in marketing. *Journal of the Academy of Marketing Science, 48*, 79–95. https://doi.org/10.1007/s11747-019-00695-1

Bardes, B. A., Shelley, M. C., & Schmidt, S. W. (2016). *American government and politics today: Essentials 2017–2018 edition*. Nelson Education.

Bean, A. M., & Ferro, L. (2016). Predictors of video game console aggression. *Revista Argentina De Ciencias Del Comportamiento, 8*(1).

Bender, P. K., Plante, C., & Gentile, D. A. (2018). The effects of violent media content on aggression. *Current Opinion in Psychology, 19*, 104–108.

Benjamin, A. J., Jr., Kepes, S., & Bushman, B. J. (2018). Effects of weapons on aggressive thoughts, angry feelings, hostile appraisals, and aggressive behavior: A meta-analytic review of the weapons effect literature. *Personality and Social Psychology Review, 22*(4), 347–377.

British Board of Film Classification. (2019). *BBFC classification guidelines*. Retrieved on February 25, 2020 from https://www.bbfc.co.uk/about-classification/classification-guidelines

Burton, P., Leoschut, L., & Phyfer, J. (2016). *South African Kids Online: A glimpse into children's internet use and online activities*. Centre for Justice and Crime Prevention.

Busching, R., Allen, J. J., & Anderson, C. A. (2016). Violent media content and effects. In J. Nussbaum (Ed.), *Oxford research encyclopedia of communication*. Oxford University Press. https://doi.org/10.1093/acrefore/9780190228613.013.1

Bushman, B. J., & Anderson, C. A. (2002). Violent video games and hostile expectations: A test of the general aggression model. *Personality and Social Psychology Bulletin, 28*(12), 1679–1686. https://doi.org/10.1177/014616702237649

Bushman, B. J., & Anderson, C. A. (2015). Understanding causality in the effects of media violence. *American Behavioral Scientist, 59*(14), 1807–1821.

Canadian Pediatric Society Digital Health Task Force. (2017). Screen time and young children: Promoting health and development in a digital world. *Pediatrics & Child Health, 22*(8), 461–477. https://doi.org/10.1093/pch/pxx123

Cao, W., Fang, Z., Hou, G., Han, M., Xu, X., Dong, J., & Zheng, J. (2020). The psychological impact of the COVID-19 epidemic on college students in China. *Psychiatry Research, 287*, Article 112934. https://doi.org/10.1016/j.psychres.2020.112934

Caterino, B. (n.d.). Federal Communications Commission. In *The First Amendment Encyclopedia*. Free Speech Center at Middle Tennessee State University. Retrieved from November 20, 2020 from https://www.mtsu.edu/first-amendment/article/804/federal-communications-commission

Chikhani, R. (2015, October 15). *The history of gaming: An evolving community*. Tech Crunch. https://techcrunch.com/2015/10/31/the-history-of-gaming-an-evolving-community/

Chong, C. (2015, July 6). The inventor that inspired Elon Musk and Larry Page predicted smartphones nearly 100 years ago. *Business Insider India*. https://www.businessinsider.in/The-inventor-that-inspired-Elon-Musk-and-Larry-Page-predicted-smartphones-nearly-100-years-ago/articleshow/47964129.cms

Clark, L. B. (2020). Influence on children media. Education Encyclopedia. Retrieved on May 2, 2020 from https://education.stateuniversity.com/pages/2212/Media-Influence-on-Children.html

Collins, R. L., Strasburger, V. C., Brown, J. D., Donnerstein, E., Lenhart, A., & Ward, L. M. (2017). Sexual media and childhood well-being and health. *Pediatrics, 140*(Suppl. 2), S162–S166.

Cuthbertson, A. (2019, November 7). China bans children playing video games for more than 90 minutes a day or at night. *Independent*. https://www.independent.co.uk/life-style/gadgets-and-tech/gaming/china-gaming-ban-video-game-addiction-a9188806.html

Defining propaganda. (n.d.). American Historical Association. Retrieved December 25, 2020, from https://www.historians.org/about-aha-and-membership/aha-history-and-archives/gi-roundtable-series/pamphlets/em-2-what-is-propaganda-(1944)/defining-propaganda-i

Delhove, M., & Greitemeyer, T. (2019). Can violent video game–related aggression spread to others? Effects on retaliatory and displaced aggression. *International Review of Social Psychology, 32*(1), 14. https://doi.org/10.5334/irsp.242

Dillon, K. P., & Bushman, B. J. (2017). Effects of exposure to gun violence in movies on children's interest in real guns [published correction appears in *JAMA Pediatrics, 173*(7):704]. *JAMA Pediatrics, 171*(11), 1057–1062. https://doi.org/10.1001/jamapediatrics.2017.2229

Dobrilova, T. (2021). *23+ mobile gaming statistics for 2021—insights into a $76B games market*. Tech Jury. Retrieved on August 10, 2021 from https://techjury.net/blog/mobile-gaming-statistics/#gref

Editors of Encyclopaedia Britannica. (2019). *Interactive media*. Encyclopedia Britannica. Retrieved on December 26, 2019 from https://www.britannica.com/technology/interactive-media

Engelhardt, C. R., & Bartholow, B. D. (2013). Effects of situational cues on aggressive behavior. Social and Personality Psychology Compass, 7(10), 762-774.

European Commission. (2018) *Protection of minors: Audiovisual Media Services Directive*. Retrieved on May 2, 2019 from https://ec.europa.eu/digital-single-market/en/protection-minors-avmsd

Federal Communication Commission. (2021). *Obscene, indecent, and profane broadcasts*. Retrieved on February 25, 2021 from https://www.fcc.gov/consumers/guides/obscene-indecent-and-profane-broadcasts

Ferguson, C. J. (2015). Do angry birds make for angry children? A meta-analysis of video game influences on children's and adolescents' aggression, mental health, prosocial behavior, and academic performance. *Perspectives on Psychological Science*, 10(5), 646–666. https://doi.org/10.1177/1745691615592234

Ferguson, C. J., & Beresin, E. (2017). Social science's curious war with pop culture and how it was lost: The media violence debate and the risks it holds for social science. *Preventive Medicine*, 99, 69–76.

Ferguson, C. J., Colon-Motas, K., Esser, C., Lanie, C., Purvis, S., & Williams, M. (2017). The (not so) evil within? Agency in video game choice and the impact of violent content. *Simulation & Gaming*, 48(3), 329–337. https://doi.org/10.1177/1046878116683521

Feshbach, S. (1984). The catharsis hypothesis, aggressive drive, and the reduction of aggression. *Aggressive Behavior*, 10(2), 91–101.

Film and Production Board. (2017). *Classifications*. Department of Communications: Film and Production Board. Retrieved on August 1, 2019 from http://www.dac.gov.za/sites/default/files/Draft-Revised-Classification-Guidelines.pdf

Fitzpatrick, C., Barnett, T., & Pagani, L. S. (2012). Early exposure to media violence and later child adjustment. *Journal of Developmental & Behavioral Pediatrics*, 33(4), 291–297.

Flew, T. (2017). Media convergence. In *Encyclopedia Britannica*. https://www.britannica.com/topic/media-convergence

Flynn, C., & Heitzmann, D. (2008). Tragedy at Virginia Tech: Trauma and its aftermath. *The Counseling Psychologist*, 36(3), 479–489.

Friedrich, L. K., & Stein, A. H. (1973). Aggressive and prosocial television programs and the natural behavior of preschool children. *Monographs of the Society for Research in Child Development*, 38(4), 63. https://doi.org/10.2307/1165725

Gentile, D. A. (2013). Catharsis and media violence: A conceptual analysis. *Societies*, 3(4), 491–510.

Gerbner, G. (1999). The stories we tell. *Peace Review*, 11(1), 9–15.

Guterres, A. (2020, April 16). *Protect our children*. United Nations. https://www.un.org/en/un-coronavirus-communications-team/protect-our-children

Habib, K., & Soliman, T. (2015). Cartoons' effect in changing children mental response and behavior. *Open Journal of Social Sciences*, 3(9), 248–264. https://doi.org/10.4236/jss.2015.39033

Hanson, K. (2007). Cognitive script theory. In J. J. Arnett (Ed.), *Encyclopedia of children, adolescents, and the media* (Vol. 1, pp. 186–187). SAGE Publications. https://www.doi.org/10.4135/9781412952606.n89

Hayes, C. (2018, March 7). After Florida shooting, more than 600 copycat threats have targeted schools. *USA Today*. https://www.usatoday.com/story/news/2018/03/07/within-nine-days-after-florida-shooting-there-were-more-than-100-threats-schools-across-u-s-its-not/359986002/

Healing, R. (2012, August 13). Overexposed and underprepared: The effects of early exposure to sexual content. *Psychology Today*. https://www.psychologytoday.com/us/blog/real-healing/201208/overexposed-and-under-prepared-the-effects-early-exposure-sexual-content

Heinrich, R. (n.d.). Federal Radio Commission. In *The First Amendment Encyclopedia*. Free Speech Center at Middle Tennessee State University. Retrieved on May 2, 2020 from https://www.mtsu.edu/first-amendment/article/809/federal-radio-commission

Hilgard, J., Engelhardt, C. R., & Rouder, J. N. (2017). Overstated evidence for short-term effects of violent games on affect and behavior: A reanalysis of Anderson et al. (2010). *Psychological Bulletin*, 143(7), 757–774. https://doi.org/10.1037/bul0000074

Hill, D., Ameenuddin, N., Chassiakos, Y., Fagbuyi, D., Hutchinson, J., Levine, A., McCarthy, C., Mendelson, R., Moreno, M., Swanson, W. S., & Kaliebe, K. (2016). Virtual violence. *Council on Communications and Media Pediatrics*, 138(1), Article e20161298.

History of AGVOT and ratings classifications in Canada. (n.d.). Canadian Broadcast Standards Council. Retrieved on September 16, 2020 from from https://www.cbsc.ca/tools/history/

Hollingdale, J., & Greitemeyer, T. (2014). The effect of online violent video games on levels of aggression. *PLoS ONE*, 9(11), Article e111790. https://doi.org/10.1371/journal.pone.0111790

Huesmann, L. R. (2007). The impact of electronic media violence: Scientific theory and research. *The Journal of Adolescent Health: Official Publication of the Society for Adolescent Medicine*, 41(6 Suppl. 1), S6–S13. https://doi.org/10.1016/j.jadohealth.2007.09.005

Huesmann, L. R., Moise-Titus, J., Podolski, C.-L., & Eron, L. D. (2003). Longitudinal relations between children's exposure to TV violence and their aggressive and violent behavior in young adulthood: 1977–1992. *Developmental Psychology*, 39, 201–221.

Johnson, J,(2021). Internet usage in the United States—statistics & facts. Statista. Retrieved August 15, 2021 from https://www.statista.com/topics/2237/internet-usage-in-the-united-states/

Jones, C.J.British Broadcasting Corporation. (2019, October 16). UK's controversial "porn blocker" plan dropped. BBCNews. https://www.bbc.com/news/technology-50073102

Kirsh, S. J. (2005). Cartoon violence and aggression in youth. *Aggression and behavior*, 11, 547–557.Krantz-Kent, R. (2018, September). Television, capturing America's attention at prime time and beyond. *Beyond the Numbers: Special Studies & Research*, 7(14). https://www.bls.gov/opub/btn/volume-7/television-capturing-americas-attention.htm

Kumar, A., & Nayar, K. R. (2021). COVID 19 and its mental health consequences. *Journal of Mental Health*, *30*(1), 1–2. https://doi.org/10.1080/09638237.2020.1757052

Leyens, J., Camino, L., Parke, R. D., & Berkowitz, L. (1975). Effects of movie violence on aggression in a field setting as a function of group dominance and cohesion. *Journal of Personality and Social Psychology*, *32*(2), 346–360. https://doi.org/10.1037/0022-3514.32.2.346

Loersch, C., & Payne, B. K. (2011). The situated inference model: An integrative account of the effects of primes on perception, behavior, and motivation. Perspectives on Psychological Science, 6(3), 234-252.

McCarthy, C. (2016, August 2). *Protecting children from the dangers of "virtual violence."* Harvard Health.

McCarthy, R. J., & Elson, M. (2018). A conceptual review of lab-based aggression paradigms. *Collabra: Psychology*, *4*(1), 4. https://doi.org/10.1525/collabra.104

Mcginnis, S. (2013, November 12). Top PG-13 movies have more gun violence than R rated films. *LA Times*. https://ktla.com/news/local-news/top-pg-13-movies-have-more-gun-violence-than-r-rated-films/

Meng, Q., Sheng, X., Zhao, J., Wang, Y., & Su, Z. (2020). Influence of mothers/grandmothers coviewing cartoons with children on children's viewing experience. *Frontiers in Psychology*, *11*, 1232. https://doi.org/10.3389/fpsyg.2020.01232

Minister of Communications. (2015). Films and Publications Amendment Bill. Republic of South Africa. https://www.parliament.gov.za/storage/app/media/Pages/2019/october/14-10-2019_NCOP_Permanent_Delegates_Training/docs/14_B37B-2015_Films_and_Publications.pdf

Motion Picture Association. (1966). *Valenti Remarks on the Production Code*. Retrieved on January 6, 2018 from https://www.scribd.com/document/391133158/Valenti-Remarks-on-the-Production-Code-1966

Motion Picture Association. (2020). *A half century of rating films and informing parents. Motion Picture Association, Inc.* Retrieved on January 6, 2021 from https://www.motionpictures.org/film-ratings/of violent content. Simulation Gaming 48, 329–337. doi: 10.1177/1046878116683521

National Press and Publication Administration. (2021). Notice of the National Press and Publication Administration on Further Strict Management and Practically Preventing Minors from Indulging in Online Games. http://www.nppa.gov.cn/nppa/contents/279/98792.shtml

Orbesen, J. (2014, February 20). The *RoboCop* rule: When remakes have more killing, but less gore. *The Atlantic*. https://www.theatlantic.com/entertainment/archive/2014/02/the-em-robocop-em-rule-when-remakes-have-more-killing-but-less-gore/283914/

Our history. (2019). Entertainment Software Rating Board. Retrieved on December 1, 2020 from https://www.esrb.org/history/

Pan, W., Gao, X., Shi, S., Liu, F., & Li, C. (2018). Spontaneous brain activity did not show the effect of violent video games on aggression: A resting-state fMRI study. *Frontiers in Psychology*, *8*, 2219. https://doi.org/10.3389/fpsyg.2017.02219

PEGI age ratings. (2017). Pan European Game Information. https://pegi.info/page/pegi-age-ratings

Parental advisory label. (n.d.). Recording Industry Association of America. Retrieved on May 17, 2020 from https://www.riaa.com/resources-learning/parental-advisory-label/

Pew, A., Goldbeck, L., Halsted, C., & Zuckerman, D. (2019). Does media coverage inspire copy cat mass shootings? National Center for Health Research.

Phyfer, J., Burton, P., & Leoschut, L. (2016). Global Kids Online South Africa: Barriers, opportunities and risks. A glimpse into South African children's internet use and online activities. In L. Jossel (Ed.), *Global Kids Online*. Centre for Justice and Crime Prevention.

Prescott, A. T., Sargent, J. D., & Hull, J. G. (2018). Meta-analysis of the relationship between violent video game play and physical aggression over time. *Proceedings of the National Academy of Sciences*, *115*(40), 9882–9888.

Preston, L. (2020). What is digital media? *Digital Logic*. https://www.digitallogic.co/blog/what-is-digital-media/

Rai, S., Waskel, B., Sakalle, S., Dixit, S., & Mahore, R. (2017). Effects of cartoon programs on behavioural, habitual and communicative changes in children. *International Journal of Community Medicine and Public Health*, *3*(6), 1375–1378.

Rainie, L., Keeter, S., & Perrin, A. (2019). Trust and distrust in America: Many Americans think declining trust in the government and in each other makes it harder to solve key problems. They have a wealth of ideas about what's gone wrong and how to fix it. Pew Research Center.

Ratings. (n.d.). TV Parental Guidelines. Retrieved on April 20, 2020 from http://www.tvguidelines.org/ratings.html

Rojkova, Z., Kováčová, K., & Šarmírová, J. (2015). The effect of television news media contents on anxiety and mood of individuals in the context of neuroticism. *Journal of Education, Psychology and Social Sciences*, *3*(2), 122–131.

Sani, A. (2019). Media violence and the cathartic effect on televisuals. *International Journal of Innovative Literature, Language & Art Studies* *7*(4),14-23. http://seahipaj.org/journals-ci/dec-2019/IJILLAS/full/IJILLAS-D-3-2019.pdf

Shao, R., & Wang, Y. (2019). The relation of violent video games to adolescent aggression: An examination of moderated mediation effect. *Frontiers in Psychology*, *10*, 384.

Silver, L, Smith, A., Johnson, C., Jiang, J., Anderson, M., & Rainie, L. (2019). Use of smartphones and social media is common across most emerging economies. Pew Research Center.

Smith, S., & Ferguson, C. J. (2019). The effects of violent media on children. In E. V. Beresin & C. K. Olson (Eds.), *Child and adolescent psychiatry and the media* (pp. 1–9). Elsevier. https://doi.org/10.1016/B978-0-323-54854-0.00001-1

Smith, S., Ferguson, C., & Beaver, K. (2018). A longitudinal analysis of shooter games and their relationship with conduct disorder and self-reported delinquency. *International Journal of Law and Psychiatry*, *58*, 48–53. https://doi.org/10.1016/j.ijlp.2018.02.008

Sparks, G. G. (2016). *Media effects research: A basic overview*. Cengage Learning.

Stephens, M. (1999). History of television In *Grolier Multimedia Encyclopedia* (2000 ed.). https://nyuscholars.nyu.edu/en/publications/the-history-of-television

Surette, R. (2016). Self-reported copycat crime among a population of serious and violent juvenile offenders. *Crime and Delinquency*, *48*(1), 46–69. https://doi.org/10.1177/0011128702048001002

Sweet, R. (2006, October 19). Newsquirks. *Salt Lake City Weekly*. https://www.cityweekly.net/utah/newsquirks/Content?oid=2128809

Tang, L., Darlington, G., Ma, D. W., & Haines, J. (2018). Mothers' and fathers' media parenting practices associated with young children's screen-time: A cross-sectional study. *BMC Obesity*, *5*(1), 37.

United Nations. (2020). *Policy brief: The impact of COVID-19 on children.*

UNICEF. (2020). *Protecting children online*. Retrieved on December 26, 2020 from https://www.unicef.org/protection/violence-against-children-online

Universal Service. (2020). *CIPA*. Universal Service. Retrieved on December 26, 2020 from https://www.usac.org/e-rate/applicant-process/starting-services/cipa/

Valkenburg, P., & Piotrowski, J. (2017). Media and violence. In *Plugged in: How media attract and affect youth* (pp. 96–115). Yale University Press.

Walters, L. (n.d.). The end of the age of innocence—and the beginning of responsible age verification. Walters Law Group. Retrieved on January 6, 2021 from https://www.firstamendment.com/innocence/

Webb, P. (2017). How the media contribute to disproportionate confinement of minority youth. Juvenile Justice Information Exchange.

World Health Organization. (2018, September 14). *Gaming disorder*. https://www.who.int/news-room/q-a-detail/gaming-disorder

Worth, K. A., Gibson Chambers, J., Nassau, D. H., Rakhra, B. K., & Sargent, J. D. (2008). Exposure of US adolescents to extremely violent movies. *Pediatrics*, *122*(2), 306–312.

Wortley, S., Seepersad, R., Mccalla, A., Singh, R., Madon, N., Greene, C., & Roswell, T. (2008). *Review of the roots of youth violence: Literature reviews*. Service Ontario Publications. Retrieved on May 2, 2019 from http://www.children.gov.on.ca/htdocs/english/documents/youthandthelaw/rootsofyouthviolence-vol5.pdf

Xu, B., & Albert, E. (2017). *Media censorship in China*. Council on Foreign Relations. https://www.cfr.org/backgrounder/media-censorship-china

Yongling, W. (2019). *China further prevents minors' addiction to online games*. Xinhuanet. Retrieved on May, 17, 2020 from http://www.xinhuanet.com/english/2019-11/05/c_138530228.htm

Zhang, J., & Chen, T. (2019, September 20). China's First Regulation on the Protection of Children's Personal Information. Lexology. https://www.lexology.com/library/detail.aspx?g=8a1da201-15a8-4e15-8c33-64fda8fbf621

Juvenile Justice and the Digital Age

LEARNING OBJECTIVES

At the end of the chapter, students will be able to

describe how the internet has changed over the past 3 decades;

explain the evolution of the internet digital age;

define what a cybercrime is and associated crimes affecting children;

explain the increase in predators on the internet, the use of social media, and growing trends; and

list the various forms of technology and their growing effects on children, both nationally and across the globe.

Keywords

Active predator
Aggressive predator
Approach avoidance modelArpanet
Child pornography
Cyberbullying
Cybercrimes
Cyberstalking
Flaming
Fight or flight response

General strain theory
High-Performance Computing and
 Communication Act
Internet
Intimacy stalker
Morphing
Obscene material
Passive predator
Power differential

Predatory stalker
Rejected stalker
Resentful stalker
Sexting
Suicide ideology
Traditional bullying
Transactional model
World Wide Web

Introduction

Before 1991, the internet was only available to the military and universities. If a student wanted to access a computer and communicate in cyberspace with other people, they could only do so at a few select schools and only for a legitimate educational purpose. The lack of widespread personal computers was understandable, because the first computers took up about 680 square feet and weighed 30 tons. It was not until the 1980s that personal computers became smaller and started popping up in people's homes. One of the major companies contributing to this phenomenon was the former Computing Tabulating Recording Corporation, which changed its name in 1924 to International Business Machines (now known as IBM). There were no modern-day cell phones, tablets, or advanced gaming systems. Social media was limited to chat lines that used a landline phone. Society had nothing near the extent of connectivity experienced in the early 21st century.

This chapter will discuss the advent of the widespread availability of the internet, the rapid technological advances that occurred in the years that followed, and how those advances have impacted youth in what is known as the digital age.

The Advent of the Internet

Access to what we now know as the internet, initially called the **Arpanet** in 1969, was limited to government use, private corporations, and universities. It was not until over 2 decades later, in 1991, that the **High-Performance Computing and Communication Act** was passed, expanding access and connectivity to any network, by anyone, anywhere around the world. However, the **internet** is just the vehicle to access all of the data available online. The **World Wide Web** is responsible for the data. The World Wide Web holds vast amounts of websites that offer access to educational material, entertainment, social media, and spaces for common interests. However, along with an all-access pass to cyberspace come caveats that include a vast array of **cybercrimes**—crimes committed via an electronic device. These cybercrimes include cyberbullying, cyberstalking, child pornography, and other illicit acts by internet predators. These cybercrimes significantly affect the primary users of the internet: our nation's youth.

Cyberbullying Versus Traditional Bullying

The National Crime Prevention Council defines **cyberbullying** as when "someone repeatedly harasses, mistreats, or makes fun of another person online or while using cell phones or other electronic devices" (Patchin, 2015, p. 1). Cyberbullying is comparable to traditional bullying, because **traditional bullying** is defined as intentional and repeated harmful behavior, but is usually face to face. There is also some commonality between the effects of offline and online bullying. In fact, C. W. Wang et al. (2019) found that almost half of high school cyberbullying victims were also bullied in school, causing severe detrimental effects. All forms of bullying can have similar and, in some cases, worse long-term adverse effects on young adults' mental health than even being neglected or maltreated. Both have been shown to cause substance abuse, violent behavior, lower academic achievement, hyperactive behavior conduct problems, less prosocial group behaviors, and severe depression, which in some cases have led to **suicide ideology**—thoughts of suicide, actual attempts, and suicide itself (John et al., 2018; Litwiller & Brausch, 2013; C. W. Wang et al., 2019).

So, why is there a separate category for cyberbullying? What makes it different from traditional bullying? Although the effects of cyberbullying resemble traditional bullying, there are some strong differences in its impact, and these effects are augmented by particular features of how cyberbullying is delivered. Unlike traditional bullying, where harmful behavior is commonly delivered face to face, in the case of cyberbullying, harmful behavior is delivered using tools that can provide harmful messages 24 hours a day, 7 days a week. It can be done anonymously and quickly and can be distributed to a worldwide audience, who can all join in. A single act of cyberbullying has the potential to be repeated without additional involvement of the original cyberbully because of the communal nature of online communication (Agatston et al., 2012; Chassiakos et al., 2016; Slonje et al., 2012). What is worse is that whatever is communicated, such as a post with embarrassing or harmful pictures, will be there forever, continuing to hurt the victim. A term sometimes used to describe this specific exchange of insults is **flaming**, an antagonistic and insulting interaction between internet users, generally using profanity. It can also include exchanging insults, with many groups teaming up on a single victim (Lingam & Aripin, 2017; Moore et al., 2010).

There is another unique phenomenon associated with cyberbullying: boundless power. Traditional bullying usually has a **power differential**—the imbalance of power and strength between the bully and the victim. However, this power differential does not exist online. In fact, many cyberbullies were bullied themselves in the traditional sense, and because the keyboard can replace muscle, these victims can now be the offenders in cyberspace (Lyndall et al., 2013; C. W. Wang et al., 2019). According to Bauman et al. (2013), "The dynamics of cyber-bullying may be different from traditional bullying as cyberbullying may be more of a reciprocal behavior and less about power differential" (p. 341).

Is It Illegal to Cyberbully?

Only 34 states have laws specifically against cyberbullying, and there is no specific federal law that makes cyberbullying illegal. In Ohio, for example, House Bill 116, also known as the Jessica Logan Act, named after a student who committed suicide as a result of bullying via texting, addresses cyberbullying. The bill expanded the scope of Ohio's antibullying law to prohibit harassment by electronic means. Although this state bill addressed cyberbullying and expanded antiharassment policies for Ohio, in some cases,

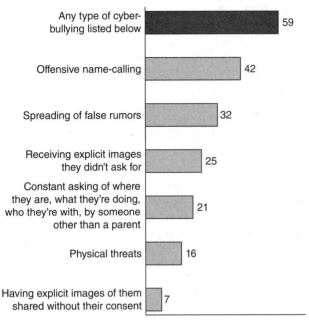

Any type of cyber-bullying listed below — 59

Offensive name-calling — 42

Spreading of false rumors — 32

Receiving explicit images they didn't ask for — 25

Constant asking of where they are, what they're doing, who they're with, by someone other than a parent — 21

Physical threats — 16

Having explicit images of them shared without their consent — 7

Figure 12.1 Percent of U.S. teens who say they have experienced some kind of cyberbullying, online or on their cellphone.

Source: Pew Research Center

cyberbullying can only be prosecuted as aggravated harassment based on a lack of state laws and as a hate crime if other motivating factors are involved, such as race or ethnicity. Educational institutions, however, are legally obligated to address cyberbullying.

Scope of Cyberbullying

Cyberbullying is a problem of growing concern for school-aged students. Almost 100% of youth in the United States are connected to the internet in one way or another, and 95% have access to smartphones with the same capabilities as computers. YouTube, Instagram, and Snapchat are the most popular online platforms, and 45% of teens have said they are online "almost constantly" (Anderson & Jiang, 2018). As technology is abused, the use of the internet and cell phones' text messages, pictures, and videos make youth more vulnerable. Regular users of the internet are significantly more likely to be impacted by cyberbullying and often can become victims. In fact, a 2018 report by the Pew Research Foundation found that 59% of U.S. teens have been bullied or harassed online, and 63% say it is a huge issue for adolescents (Anderson, 2018; also see Figure 12.1).

As stated earlier in the chapter, cyberbullying, much like traditional bullying, has caused skipping and dropping out of school, low self-esteem, and depression. Because of the ease of bullying, widespread accessibility, and permanency, messages can easily be seen by a larger audience, and they can never be erased. Cyberbullying affects many more children at greater rates and often with more detrimental effects than traditional bullying (Chassiakos et al., 2016; Schneider et al., 2012).

The National Center for Education Statistics shows that approximately 22% of students ages 12 through 18 experienced some kind of bullying and 16% of high school students experienced cyberbullying within the past twelve months (National Center for Education Statistics, 2021). This amounts to over 2 million victims, up from 6.2% in prior years. However, other studies report that the percentages of young people in the United States who have been cyberbullied range from 37% to as high as 52%. Twenty-five percent of teenagers report that they have experienced repeated bullying via their cell phones or over the internet. Unfortunately, many cases of cyberbullying, as well as traditional bullying, go unreported. Most experts believe that cyberbullying is increasing and so are its damaging effects (*Cyberbullying Statistics*, 2021; National Center for Education Statistics, 2021; Noll, 2016; K. Wang et al., 2020).

Of the students who reported being cyberbullied,

- 47% of young people have received intimidating, threatening messages online;
- 25% of teens on social media reported an incident that resulted in a face-to-face confrontation;
- 13% reported they did not want to go to school the next day;
- 12% reported being called negative names via text messages;

- 11% received other types of negative text messages; and
- 8% reported having physical altercations because of an incident on social media (*Cyberbullying Statistics*, 2021).

On December 2, 2016, 18-year-old Brandy Vela sent a text message to her family telling them that she loved them. Shortly after, as her family entered her bedroom, Brandy stood in front of her closet in tears and pressed a gun against her chest. She fired a bullet into her heart, killing herself in front of her family. Brandy had been the victim of cyberbullying in the prior months. It began almost a year earlier, when someone used her picture to create a fake profile online and solicit sex. Anonymous bullies joined in and used encrypted applications to send hateful messages; they made fake profiles of her asking for sex on dating websites. Even after Brandy's suicide, the hateful posts and cyberbullying continued.

There is no conclusive evidence that cyberbullying in and of itself causes teens to hurt themselves. Teen who commit suicide, even if it occurs directly following cyberbullying, may have other significant issues impacting their mental health and overall well-being. However, there are strong correlations between being a victim of cyberbullying and the devastating outcomes that can follow (John et al., 2018; *What Is Cyberbullying?*, 2020).

Impact on the Victim

Cases like Brandy's and others that result in severe depression and suicide ideation are becoming more and more correlated with cyberbullying. Although there is debate concerning whether individuals who commit suicide directly after cyberbullying could also be experiencing other significant issues that impact their mental health (Centers for Disease Control and Prevention, 2014; Hinduja & Patchin, 2010; John et al., 2018), people who are bullied by peers are more likely to think of suicide and attempt it (John et al., 2018; Van Geel et al., 2014).

Bullying and Teen Suicide Rates

According to the Centers for Disease Control and Prevention's (CDC) latest Youth Risk Behavior Survey in 2019, suicide is the second leading cause of death among young people (CDC, 2020). The CDC estimates that there are at least 100 suicide attempts for every suicide among young people. It is estimated that approximately 14% of high school students have considered suicide and nearly 7% have attempted it. Bullied victims are more than twice as likely to have suicidal thoughts (John et al., 2018). Additionally, there are many documented mental health effects of cyberbullying, including feelings such as sadness, hurt, anger, frustration, confusion, stress, and depression (Evans, 2018; *What Is Cyberbullying?*, 2020). This type of impact is not just reserved for the victim; it is sometimes experienced to an even greater degree by the offender.

Impact on the Offender (the Bully)

Bullies themselves sometimes display even more symptoms of depression than their targets and are also at high risk for suicidal behavior. Strong associations have been found in both middle school and high school students (John et al., 2018).

Who Are the Cyber Bullies, and Why Do They Do It?

Robert Agnew developed what is known as **general strain theory**, a criminological theory that focuses on what strains (inadequate opportunities) society puts on youth that could lead to criminal behavior to achieve socially desirable goals (Hay et al., 2010). Based on Agnew's theory, cyberbullying could result from low social control and is a form of coping with perceived inadequate opportunities. For example, a youth who sees themselves as powerless as the result of what they perceive as societal constraints may feel the only way to attain power is by spreading hateful messages.

The type of cyberbullying perpetrated tends to be different between genders; according to Patchin (2015), "girls are more likely to post mean comments online while boys are more likely to post hurtful pictures or videos" (p. 2). According to the National Center for Educational Statistics, over 30% of students admit to bullying classmates and peers (Cassidy et al., 2013). Youth who perpetrated cyberbullying indicated that they used online instant messages most frequently, followed by cell phones, social networking sites, emails, and chat rooms. Ninety-one percent said they knew their victims, and the primary motive was revenge, followed by "just not liking them," followed by doing it for fun or to demonstrate power. The majority of cyberbullying is perpetrated from the bully's personal computer, and most of the time, girls engage in more indirect types of bullying, such as spreading rumors.

The offender often believes that the aggressive and morally disengaged behavior is normal (Kowalski et al., 2014). Their victimization can be linked to maladaptive behaviors such as externalizing aggressive behavior, deviant behavior, alcohol and drug abuse, delinquency, property damage, physical assaults, and assaults with weapons (Hinduja & Patchin, 2012).

Bullies who engage in cyberbullying for revenge may have been avenging bullying or harassment they received themselves. Therefore, there is often an interchangeable role within cyberbullying that we do not generally see in traditional bullying, where the victim can become the bully and the bully can become the victim.

The Dual-Role Phenomenon

The dual role of being both the victim and the offender emerged as a new classification of bullying that categorized many youths who engage in bullying online (Bauman et al., 2013). As we saw earlier in the chapter, unlike traditional bullying, bullying in cyberspace is more about reciprocal behavior and less about power differential. With a keystroke on a computer or the push of a button on a cell phone, individuals who may be perceived as weaker in face-to-face confrontations can attain an even playing field on the World Wide Web. This ability to strike back as quickly as being struck upon has spawned a unique category, with the same individual in the dual role of both offender and victim. Oftentimes, this new group not only experiences the same effects that impact victims and bullies, but also experiences them to a greater degree and more frequently over time (CDC, 2014; Hellfeldt et.al., 2020).

The effects of cyberbullying seem to have greater intensity and frequency among the dual-role group, with those who take on both the role of the victim and the bully often doing so at nearly the same time. This group usually possesses lower self-esteem and even more suicidal thoughts than those who are solely a victim or a bully (Cassidy et al., 2013). Persons carrying out this dual role suffer from many of the same effects as those who experience the separate roles of victim and bully, such as low academic achievement, conduct problems, less prosocial peer group behavior, and other harsher social difficulties, which can impact the learning environment and the health and well-being of the family and the community (CDC, 2014; Hinduja & Patchin, 2012). This group also had the most negative scores on most measures of psychological and physical health and academic performance, very low self-esteem, and more suicidal ideology and attempts (Hellfeldt et al., 2020; Kowalski et al., 2012).

Community Strategies and Effects

Cyberbullying also has an effect on communities, including schools and families, and its impact is similar to that of traditional bullying (Cassidy et al., 2013). However, because cyberbullying has increased rapidly among youth, researchers are concerned that the problem is growing faster than the ability to respond effectively. Beale and Hal (2007, p. 1) wrote that to combat cyberbullying, "educators need to better understand the nature of it and be aware of the actions that they can undertake to prevent cyberbullying in the schools." Social support seems to be the best coping strategy (Armstrong et al., 2019), but even with this awareness, young victims seem very hesitant to tell teachers or parents. They do, however, often tell friends. Therefore, empowering students by teaching them skills, such as acceptance strategies to help a friend who became a victim, may be the best strategy.

Coping

We should also be reminded that cyberbullying can be carried out in many ways using various electronic methods, so preventive strategies must take these differences into account. Cassidy et al. (2013) suggest reducing the risks of cyberbullying and buffering its negative impacts. The fact that students who perpetrate bullying in the traditional sense, in cyberspace, or both face the same risks, including suicide ideation, should illustrate the importance of having effective programs (Bauman et al., 2013). There also seems to be a lapse in preventive intervention to create and maintain awareness and safety for young people. However, studies have revealed what victims can do to prevent cyberbullying and how to cope with it. Armstrong et al. (2019) identify effective ways to help deal with cyberbullying, like focusing on the positive aspects of one's life, such as social supports. Coping also should include reducing risks and buffering the negative impacts; therefore, it is essential to examine how children may attempt to cope with cyberbullying. The approach avoidance model and the transactional model provide other methods for youths to cope with these types of situations.

The **approach avoidance model** is based on the concept that when stressors occur, the individual will either address (approach) the stressor directly or avert (avoid) the stressor (Pickens et al., 2019). This can be most associated with the **fight-or-flight response**—a physiological reaction to a perceived harmful event. This type of phenomenon was first described by Walter Bradford Cannon, a famous physiologist whose work initially described animals' innate response to stress. Unlike a fight-or-flight innate response, the approach avoidance model depends not only on the individual's internal coping skills but also on the external support systems one has and the ability to rationalize and utilize that support. For example, if a student experiencing bullying uses the approach strategy, they would acknowledge the stressor (bullying) and confront it, believing they would have the support of the community (school, family, etc.). Conversely, if a student faced with bullying uses the avoidance strategy, they may rationalize that the bullying does not bother them and is not worth their time, and they will do their best to stay away from it. This strategy is most often used when the youth feels they have limited resources or when they perceive that the situation cannot be controlled.

Dr. Richard Lazarus created the **transactional model** in 1966 to explain how an individual copes with various environmental stressors (Fritz, 2017). It describes how someone will make a primary and secondary appraisal of a given threat in an attempt to cope with that specific stressor. The transaction (exchange) refers to the various interpretations of the stressor and the relationship between the individual and the environment where the stressor exists.

For example, if a student receives a potentially harmful text message, they will do a primary assessment to determine the meaning behind the message to determine if it is, in fact, a threat (cyberbullying). In that case, a secondary appraisal takes place, wherein the person assesses their coping resources to elicit certain coping reactions. Those coping reactions can include a "problem-focused" strategy by addressing the threat head-on, if the threat is perceived as being controllable, or an "emotionally focused" approach for those stressors deemed more difficult to change. This can include changing how the threat is perceived (how the person feels and thinks about the stressful situation), for example, convincing oneself there are other more important things to be concerned about. Although some may argue that confronting every stressor is a better strategy than avoiding it, what has shown to be most important is empowering the victim by providing multiple resources for further support, such as school, family, and community (Armstrong et al., 2019).

Unfortunately, cyberbullying is only one of the online risks youth face while surfing the Web. Other types of cybercrimes are perpetrated against youth every day, many times by strangers, with just as many detrimental effects and sometimes more.

Cyberstalking

With the greater access to and popularity of the internet in the 21st century, a much larger portion of youth are vulnerable online and can become targets of online aggressors through cyberstalking and harassment.

Cyberstalking is a pattern of threats to frighten/annoy, solicitations for sex, or gathering information that may be used to threaten or harass via electronic means. However, most federal laws require the victim to tell the offender to stop at least one time in order for the case to be effectively prosecuted. This is because many stalkers have used a legal defense in court claiming that the victim encouraged the ongoing communication and the offender never knew the victim wanted the behavior to stop. Unlike in cyberbullying, as many cyberstalkers are known to the victim as are not. As discussed earlier, there are more "offender known interactions" in cyberbullying. It should also be noted that the term cyberstalking is often used interchangeably with online harassment or online abuse. However, many experts agree that although online harassment is a nuisance intended to annoy, cyberstalking can often involve fear or threats and, in many cases, has led to offline stalking and violent crimes, including abductions (Shipley & Bowker, 2014).

It is important to understand that mere unsolicited actions by strangers online are not automatically illegal. It is when these actions are repeated, and when it has been made clear to the individual that the receiver does not want further contact, that it becomes stalking/harassment if the communication continues. For example, if someone receives an unsolicited instant message or email, most likely it does not constitute stalking/harassment. If, however, the person sending the messages is told to stop, any further correspondence could then be considered harassment/stalking and may violate state and federal law.

DEEPER DIVE

AMANDA MICHELLE TODD

On October 10, 2012, Amanda Michelle Todd, a 15-year-old Canadian girl, committed suicide. Prior to her death, she posted a video on YouTube. She used flashcards to tell her experience of being blackmailed into exposing her breasts via webcam and being harassed, stalked, and physically assaulted. The video has received more than 50 million cumulative views.

Amanda was in the seventh grade when she began using video chats to meet new people, and this is when her stalker convinced her to expose herself. He continued to blackmail her for the next 3 years. Eighteen months after her death, the man was finally caught and charged with harassment, extortion, and possession and distribution of child pornography. Amanda was not his only victim.

Stalking Laws

The federal government, all 50 states, the District of Columbia, and the U.S. territories have enacted criminal laws to address stalking. However, although it is a federal crime to transmit any communication containing a threat to injure a person, the state legal definition for stalking varies across jurisdictions:

- State laws vary regarding the element of a victim's fear and emotional distress and the requisite intent of the stalker.
- Some state laws specify that the victim must have been frightened by the stalking, while others require only that the stalking behavior would have caused a reasonable person to experience fear. (Catalana, 2012, p. 3)

In 1990, California became the first state to enact a specific stalking law. It prohibits threats against the victim and the victim's immediate family. Arizona only prohibits threats of violence against the victim, and in Maine, implied threats from a stalker can be criminal.

Scope of Cyberstalking

Cyberstalking generally begins via email, regardless of where the victim initially crossed paths with the stalker. The stalking can then be followed up by instant messaging and then chat.

- Approximately 1 in 6 females and 1 in 17 males have experienced stalking in their lifetime.
- Cyberstalking tactics include sending unwanted emails, instant messages, text messages, voice messages, or social media messages.
- Thirteen percent of males and 21% of females reported being stalked as minors and almost half of all victims experienced stalking before the age of 25.
- Anyone can become a victim of cyberstalking, however, statistics show that children are very frequent victims.
- Social media sites are very popular for cyberstalkers. (Anderson, 2018; CDC, 2019)

Who are cyberstalkers? Cyberstalkers can be dangerous and psychotic individuals. Some may not have any psychosis but instead want to seek revenge on the victim or get something from them.

Cyberstalker Types

The four most common types of predator stalkers include rejected, resentful, predatory, and intimacy stalkers.

- The **rejected stalker** is the most common. This is someone who may have been in a prior relationship with the victim or is currently with someone who is ending the relationship, which is not acceptable to this individual.
- The **resentful stalker** is usually looking for revenge. They try to harm the other person (who can be known to them or a stranger) for what they have done or are perceived to have done. This individual's actions are meant to scare the victim and cause distress.
- The **predatory stalker** is thankfully the least common. This is a sexual predator who solely desires sexual gratification and power. They intend to sexually assault their victim.
- The **intimacy stalker** seeks a relationship with the victim. They want to establish an intimate, loving relationship. They think the victim and the stalker were "meant to be together." (Miller, 2001; National Center for Victims of Crime, n.d.)

The majority of cyberstalkers are men and most of the victims are women, but there has been an increase in female cyberstalkers—they increased from 27% in 2000 to 38% in 2003 to 47% in 2012 (Hitchcock, 2015). However, it is important to note that there is also debate as to the accuracy of gender-related statistics because of underreporting or misreporting (Ahlgrim & Terrance, 2021).

Cyberstalking and Abduction Through Social Media

Teen social media users share more personal information in their profiles, which can include birthdates, school names, and photos (Canares, 2018; Madden et al., 2013):

- 91% post a photo of themselves (up from 79% in 2006)
- 71% post their school name (up from 49% in 2006)
- 71% post the city or town where they live (up from 61% in 2006)
- 53% post their email address (up from 29% in 2006)
- 20% post their cell phone number (up from 2% in 2006)

Older teen social media users (ages 14–17) more frequently share certain types of information on their profiles than younger teen social media users (ages 12–13):

- photos of themselves (94% vs. 82% of young teens)
- their school name (76% vs. 56% of young teens)
- their relationship status (66% vs. 50% of young teens)
- their cell phone number (23% vs. 11% of young teens) (Madden et al., 2013).

Since 2011, Twitter's teen use has grown significantly, from 16% to 24% (Pew Internet & American Life Project, 2013), and a greater proportion of middle school and high school students are now using Instagram compared to Facebook (Anderson & Jiang, 2018; Hinduja & Patchin, 2015).

In addition to stalkers who may threaten youth online, children can also be exposed to obscene material there. This is sometimes accomplished through trickery and sometimes through disingenuous actions leading to a false sense of trust. Pornography, including child pornography, continues to be readily available online, as predators continue to try to seduce children into participating in one of the most egregious of cybercrimes.

The Pornography Industry and Child Pornography on the World Wide Web

What industry generates $97 billion annually, with $20 billion coming directly from the internet, of which $13 billion is in the United States alone? Is it the tobacco industry? The drug industry? It is actually generated from the pornography industry. In fact, pornographic content encompasses over 12% of the internet: that is 600 million pages of pornography, all owned by fewer than 50 companies.

Here are some more statistics:

- Two in five adults visit porn sites.
- Eighty-seven percent of college students visit virtual sex sites.
- There are nearly 100 million unique visitors annually.
- What may be even more surprising is that the largest group of viewers of pornography on the internet is between the ages of 12 and 17.

Here are some even more shocking statistics:

- The average age of first internet exposure to pornography is 11 years old.
- Eighty percent of 15- to 17-year-olds have had multiple hard-core exposures.
- Ninety percent of 8- to 16-year-olds have viewed pornography online (mostly while doing homework). (*Age of First Exposure*, 2017; Internet Safety 101, 2020)

How does this happen? Children possess a natural curiosity, and that interest, combined with much easier access to adult material through laptops, smartphones, and even game systems, removes traditional obstacles society had put in place to prevent youth from exposure. Simply clicking "yes" to verify you are 18 is the only barrier between children and many adult sites, including gambling and pornography. Sometimes, children can stumble on sites accidentally or use a wrong website extension or even see inappropriate content through a nonfiltered web search. When children are surfing the Web, many predators in cyberspace try to direct them to sex sites and convince them to be active participants.

Although viewing pornography on the internet is only against the law for those under 18, child pornography is a crime for anyone to possess, produce, and distribute, and its prevalence is growing at alarming rates.

Child Pornography

The U.S. criminal code defines **child pornography** as images that depict a minor engaged in explicit sexual activity or having as its dominant characteristic the depiction of a minor's sexual organs.

Child pornography on the internet is growing at a disturbing rate. The FBI reports continued increases in the number of child pornography images on the internet since 1996 (U.S. Department of Justice, 2020a). In 2016, in a report to Congress, the U.S. Department of Justice (2016) stated, "The Internet has ushered in an explosion in the online distribution of child sexual abuse images" (p. 68). Additionally, because children have been isolated at home and there is more social use of the internet by both children and adults as a result of the COVID-19 pandemic, there is now an increased risk of online sexual exploitation in the United States and around the world (Fegert et al., 2020). The anonymity of the internet and the World Wide Web has created a virtual safe haven for child pornographers that continues to expand.

Evolution of Obscenity and Child Pornography Laws

Prior to 1973, state laws generally defined **obscene material** as speech or expression that was "**utterly without redeeming social value.**" In 1973, however, *Miller v. California* changed that definition. In 1971, Marvin Miller, the owner of a mail-order business, sent out a brochure that graphically depicted sexual activity between men and women. Five of the brochures were mailed to a restaurant, and the owner and his mother called the police upon seeing them. Miller was arrested and convicted. The case was appealed to the Supreme Court, which not only upheld the conviction but also, based on the case, broadened the definition that states could use for obscene material. These additional qualifiers are referred to as the Miller test.

It is important to note that although obscene material in and of itself is not illegal, it can be depending on who it is solicited to and in what manner. In the years following *Miller*, child pornography also became a focus. Many states, including New York, set

> ### *NEW YORK V. FERBER* (1982)
>
> Paul Ferber, the owner of an adult bookstore in Manhattan, sold an undercover police officer two movies depicting young boys masturbating. He was charged with promoting obscene sexual performances and indecent sexual performances. At trial, he was found not guilty of obscene sexual performance, but guilty of indecent sexual performance. The New York Court of Appeals overturned the conviction. They found that the obscenity law was unconstitutional under the First Amendment. However, the Supreme Court upheld the constitutionality of New York's obscenity law, ruling that it did not violate the First Amendment, and reversed and remanded the case.

forth legislation that did not require material to be obscene to be unlawful. It was made unlawful to solely depict minors in sexual acts and sexually provocative conduct. New York also had an obscenity law that made it illegal for an individual to promote any performance, including sexual conduct, by a child younger than 16 years of age.

This law was challenged in the 1982 case *New York v. Ferber*. The U.S. Supreme Court ruled unanimously that the First Amendment right to free speech does not preclude states from banning the sale of material depicting children engaged in sexual activity, even if the material is not considered obscene.

The Child Pornography Prevention Act of 1996

The **Child Pornography Prevention Act of 1996** (CPPA) was a U.S. federal law restricting child pornography on the internet, including virtual child pornography. Before 1996, Congress defined child pornography according to *New York v. Ferber*. The CPPA prohibited "any visual depiction, including any photograph, film, video, picture, or computer or computer-generated image or picture that is, or appears to be, of a minor engaging in sexually explicit conduct" (U.S. Department of Justice, 2020b, p. 1).

Simulated and Computer-Generated Child Pornography

Forms of simulated child pornography include modified photographs of real children and fictitious images generated by a computer designed to look like children (Wells et al., 2007). The Free Speech Coalition, an adult-entertainment association, and others brought a suit against the state claiming that the wording "appears to be" and "conveys the impression" in the CPPA was too broad and could prevent other First Amendment–protected material from being produced. The Supreme Court agreed and struck down CPPA in 2002 for being overly broad. The court ruled that the wording was unconstitutional because it would prevent a substantial amount of lawful speech. The court found the CPPA unconstitutional because the CPPA prohibits speech that records no crime and creates no victims by its production.

A year after the Supreme Court found the CPPA to be unconstitutional, Congress passed another act that readdressed the issue of simulated/computer-generated child pornography. Congress passed the Prosecutorial Remedies and Other Tools to End the Exploitation of Children (**PROTECT**) **Act of 2003**. The PROTECT Act made substantial changes to laws regarding virtual child pornography. It made illegal any computer-generated image that is *indistinguishable* from a portrayal of an actual minor in sexual situations or engaging in sexual acts. The act went so far as to include cartoons, sculptures, and any other illustrations.

The question is, How indistinguishable does the image have to be, and will this act also be deemed unconstitutional by the courts?

Online Sexual Predators

According to Lenhart et al. (2011), "There has been considerable concern among parents, teachers, policymakers, and advocates about the nature and intensity of online social encounters among teens" (p. 12). Although most teens have positive online experiences, some users relentlessly attempt to exploit and seduce children in cyberspace.

According to Netsmartz Internet Safety Statistics , 95% of teens (ages 13–17) have smart phones with internet access. Teens in that same age group also send and receive around 1,900 text messages a month (NetSmartz, 2021). In 2021 alone, the National Center for Missing and Exploited Children's CyberTipline has received 21.7 million reports of suspected child sexual exploitation. Moreover, 1 in 25 children ages 10 to 17 received an online sexual solicitation via email or text message in which the solicitor tried to make offline contact. Many more sexual predators try to solicit lude and sexual pictures for themselves and may use them for trading with others (Crimes Against Children Research Center, n.d.; National Center for Missing and Exploited Children, 2021; NetSmartz, 2021).

Types of Sexual Predators on the Internet

- Passive
- Active
- Aggressive

The **passive predator** primarily collects and trades child pornographic images. Thousands of child pornographic images have been found on predators' computers and in their sent files. Oftentimes, these individuals must go through an initiation phase to join groups and discussion boards that trade child pornography. The initiation usually requires submitting an original child pornography image. Individuals often accomplish this by putting a child's face, often found in public profiles, on the body of an older pornographic image of a different child. This method is known as **morphing**—the transforming of one image into another. Although this type of predator does not directly solicit children into online sexual chat or face-to-face meetings, there are many cases of these individuals' activities eventually escalating to that level.

The **active predator** attempts to sexually exploit children by trading pictures and engaging them in sexual online chat. While in a chat room and through instant messaging, a predator can mislead children and persuade them to engage in uncharacteristic behavior. The Child Abuse Prevention Act of 1990, last amended in 2010, and the Child Protection and Sexual Predator Punishment Act of 1998 are both specific to the victimization of children.

The Child Abuse Prevention Act of 1990 was designed to protect the rights of victims of crime. It established a federal victims' bill of rights for children and improved the response of the criminal justice system and associated organizations to instances of child abuse. It was reauthorized in 2013 to continue funding programs through 2018 to help child abuse victims.

The Child Protection and Sexual Predator Punishment Act of 1998 bans the transfer of obscene material to minors, prohibits engaging them in sexual activity, and increases the penalties for both. It also provides federal funding to states. It was reauthorized in 2003.

Approximately 116,000 child pornography requests are made daily on the internet. The **aggressive predator** seduces children by phone, which often leads to face-to-face meetings and, in many cases, abductions. As many as 1 in 33 children under age 18 receive aggressive solicitations, and only 25% tell a parent. In 2019, there were over 400,000 entries for missing children under the age of 21 into the FBI's National Crime Information Center (National Crime Information Center, 2020). One such case was that of Kacie Rene Reynolds, a 13-year-old girl living in Arkansas who, like many other teens her age online, believed that she could meet the boy of her dreams.

DEEPER DIVE

Kacie Rene Reynolds was a good student, a member of the school band, and like most typical 13-year-olds, she enjoyed going online. Kacie often visited Christian chat rooms and one day met 18-year-old David Fagan. David posted a profile picture that revealed a brown hair, blue-eyed boy in his high school football uniform. What Kacie did not know was that David Fagan did not really exist; instead, she was talking to 47-year-old David Fuller. Kacie shared personal information through her profile and conversations, and on a cold December evening, Fuller showed up at Kacie's home and abducted her. The next day the police found Fuller with a gunshot wound to his head and Kacie inside a rented van. Her arms and legs had been chained; she had been raped and fatally shot.

Profile of a Sexual Predator

Unfortunately, there is no specific profile of a sexual predator. They come from all walks of life. Some are married, some are single, and some are professionals, and they can be any age. Investigations and prosecutions are therefore difficult, but many primary agencies investigate these crimes.

Primary Investigative Agencies

- FBI
- Customs Service
- Postal Inspection Service
- Department of Justice (child exploitation and obscenity section)
- State and National Center for Missing and Exploited Children

In relation to child pornography, U.S. federal criminal code prohibits these three activities with the following sanctions:

- production/child exploitation (18 U.S.C. §2251): prison term from 15 to 30 years
- distribution (18 U.S.C. § 2252a): prison term from 5 to 20 years
- possessing child pornography (18 U.S.C. § 2252a): prison term from 0 to 20 years

Sanctions can increase based on the age of the victim, prior offense history, number of images, and other extenuating circumstances (U.S. Department of Justice, 2020b).

Children Who Are Deemed Sexual Offenders

Although nonconsensual sexual crimes against minors constitute the majority of these types of crimes, consensual sexual incidents between children are also against the law. These incidents come in many forms, such as statutory rape and other statutory criminal sexual acts. A newer phenomenon whose incidence has been increasing each year is the act of sexting, which is perpetrated electronically and is punished with similar fervor (Madigan et al., 2018).

Sexting

Sexting is a term used for the act of teens exchanging sexually explicit images with each other through their cell phones (Döring, 2014). Although sexting is legal among adults, in cases where the photo or the intended receiver is a minor, it is considered a crime. Even if one teen sends consensual photos to another teen, for example, between a boyfriend and girlfriend, felony charges for child pornography can result. Charges can range from possession to distribution of child pornography. Even if specific sexting laws do not exist in a given state, sexting by or to a minor can fall within the reach of other child pornography laws.

In 2016, a teenage couple in North Carolina was charged with felony crimes for sexting and possessing nude photos of each other. The male in the incident was charged with five felonies—two for taking naked pictures of himself (possession of child pornography), two for sending the pictures (distributing child pornography), and one for having a photo of his girlfriend (possession of child pornography). He faced up to 10 years in prison. His girlfriend was charged with two felonies for taking and sending a nude selfie (possessing and distributing child pornography), and she faced 4 years in prison. Both teens accepted a plea deal that consisted of pleading guilty to a misdemeanor and agreeing to stay out of legal trouble for a year. In exchange, the two would receive lesser sentences and avoid being registered as sex offenders for the rest of their lives. They were to be charged as adults, although they were considered minors with regard to part of the statute they broke; this was a result of conflicting governing state laws. Although the law in North Carolina at the time considered children under 18 minors, youths 16 and over were prosecuted as adults (see Chapter 13, "Juvenile Justice: Trends and Reforms," for new state laws that raised the age for adult prosecution).

In 2014, Pennsylvania's Supreme Court ruled that mandatory lifetime sex-offender registration for juveniles was unconstitutional. However, not all states have adopted this perspective. In either case, children can still be charged with a multitude of sexually oriented crimes and become victims as well, with both situations affecting them now and for many years to come.

We have seen various forms of criminality and accountability in the digital age across the United States, from cyberbullying to sexual predators to new sexting laws affecting our youth. Unfortunately, these issues also extend to other parts of the world. In fact, many countries across the globe struggle with the same problems. We will now look at how the digital age has affected youth across the globe.

Worldview

The Digital Age and Its Effects on Children Around the World

According to the International Centre for Missing & Exploited Children (ICMEC, 2016), "The rapid growth of the Internet and other information and communication tools over the past 20 years has created unparalleled opportunities for children and adults alike to learn and explore the world around them" (p. 5). As we saw in the United States, the advent of the internet and the World Wide Web created opportunities that otherwise would not have been available for both adults and children. Opportunities within education, entertainment, and communication with people from all walks of life were created and affected the rest of the world in similar ways. But as in the United States, these tools have also proven susceptible to misuse around the world by individuals with bad intentions.

CYBERBULLYING ACROSS THE GLOBE

Cyberbullying is a significant problem not only in the United States but also around the world and has negatively impacted children and adolescents. It is estimated that half of the world's adolescents have been victims of cyberbullying, and one in three children have been victims of online cyberthreats (Woda, 2014).

Although studies geared toward revealing these behaviors are limited worldwide, the World Health Organization indicated that one-third of students report being involved in a fight. Males are two to three times more likely than females to fight. In 27 countries, the majority of 13-year-olds participated in bullying at least some of the time. Also, many of the individuals who were bullies when they were younger experienced legal and criminal problems as adults. Sixty percent of youth who were considered bullies in Grades 6–9 had at least one criminal conviction by age 24 (Olweus, 1993).

As we saw earlier in the chapter, there is a strong correlation between bullying and suicide-related behaviors. According to Hertz et al. (2013), "Those bullied by peers were more likely to think of suicide and even attempt it" (S1). This is true not only within the United States but also around the world. An estimated 804,000 suicide deaths occurred worldwide in 2012, representing an annual global age-standardized suicide rate of 11.4 per 100,000 (Statistics & Citations, 2021). In some countries, suicide rates are highest among the young, and globally, suicide is the second leading cause of death in 15- to 29-year-olds. Because cyberbullying has become such a prevalent and devastating issue, lawmakers around the world have designed cyberbullying laws to shield victims and bring offenders to justice.

Some countries have implemented strong laws pertaining to cyberstalking, harassment, and cyberbullying, but laws differ around the world. The following countries have some of the strongest cyberbullying laws:

- **Canada:** Under the Education Act, individuals who engage in cyberbullying face suspension from school. Repeat bullies may also face expulsion and possible jail time.
- **United Kingdom:** Under the Malicious Communications Act, cyberbullying could result in 6 months or more in prison and a hefty fine.

Countries with medium to low-level cyberbullying laws include the following:

- **The Philippines:** Under the Republic Act 10627, it is up to schools to implement cyberbullying policies. If school administrators do not comply with the Republic Act, they face sanctions.
- **Australia:** Under the Federal Nature of Law, cyberbullying laws vary from territory to territory. Each territory's laws take three forms: actions by state, a lawsuit by the victim, and "Articulate of Industry Codes," which are enforceable rules for the particular industry. Nonetheless, statistics show that 1 in 5 children in Australia aged 8 to 15 have experienced cyberbullying.
- **United States:** California, Connecticut, Colorado, and Illinois have implemented cyberbullying laws that punish the cyberbully with suspension or expulsion. In New Jersey, the punishment for cyberbullying ranges from detention to expulsion. In Vermont, the punishment is expulsion. (Woda, 2014)

Although there are few cross-cultural studies involving cyberbullying, studies have examined the prevalence rates of cyberbullying in specific countries across the world. These countries have published their own statistics (Hinduja, 2011):

European Union

- 6% of teens ages 9–16 using the internet reported being sent "nasty" or hurtful messages online, while 3% said they sent such messages to others.

Belgium

- 34.3% of Belgian teenagers have reported being bullied via the internet or mobile phone.

Poland

- 52% of Polish internet users aged 12–17 have been exposed to abuse on the Web or via mobile phones.

Germany

- 14.1% of students reported experiencing the kinds of incidents (harassment, denigration, outing and trickery, and exclusion) that constitute cyberbullying.

Japan

- 10% of high school students said they had been harassed through emails, websites, or blogs.

Spain

- Between 25% and 29% of all teenagers have been bullied via their mobile phone or the internet over the past year.

South Korea

- A survey of 272 students at four South Korean universities found that three-fourths of students knew a victim of cyberbullying and more than half knew a cyberbully.

Cyberbullying is not just a national problem, but also a global one, because its impact on victims has no boundaries. As we saw earlier in the chapter, teen victims suffer from these additional stressors, in some cases causing deep depression and even suicidal ideology with the hope of ending the emotional and psychological pain.

GLOBAL SEXUAL EXPLOITATION OF CHILDREN

According to ICMEC, in April 2016, the Internet Watch Foundation in the United Kingdom reported "a staggering increase (417%) in the number of reports of illegal child sexual abuse images and videos [child pornography], that is removed from the internet in 2015. 69% of the children in the images were ten years old or younger" (p. 1). Online sexual exploitation of children continues to be a complicated issue around the globe. As technology continues to change and evolve, so do the methods perpetrators use to exploit children, often creating a game of catch-up for law enforcement. The Canadian Centre for Child Protection also showed an increase in the number of reports received by Cybertip.ca in the past few years. In 2015, the tip line processed 37,352 reports, and of those, 78.30% (34,133) of children in the images and videos were estimated to be younger than 12 years of age, and 63.40% (21,640) of those younger than 12 were under 8 years old.

As we look at the world as a whole, between 2012 and 2014, INHOPE hotlines (nonprofit child abuse centers) around the world received more than 1.5 million reports of illegal content in 2014, and 57% of the reports were confirmed to be child sexual abuse material. Although the exact number of victims worldwide is difficult to determine, the impact on child victims is all too apparent. We have seen effects from country to country, including psychological, physical, and emotional consequences that can negatively impact our youth for the rest of their lives. We have seen countries passing legislation to combat these issues, but many experts believe this is only a first step and that enforcement of the newly created laws and appropriate sanctions must follow.

There have also been significant legislative changes over the past 10 years as more countries have developed laws to protect children from sexual abuse and exploitation, focusing on child pornography. Child pornography has evolved into an industry that often originates in one country and is completed in several others. The international nature of this illicit activity makes it essential for the coordination of cross-border law enforcement. To be successful, countries around the world have collaborated to combat these abusive crimes. According to the ICMEC (2016), "Child pornography is a multi-jurisdictional problem that demands a global response. Successfully combating child pornography and child exploitation on a global scale requires uniform legislation" (p. 1). Because child predators tend to gravitate toward countries with the weakest laws, it is essential to have no weak links in the enforcement chain.

CHILD PORNOGRAPHY LAWS ACROSS THE GLOBE

Despite the increase in global child protection laws, many countries still do not consider child pornography a crime. The global problem of child pornography has exploded with the advent of the internet, increasing child abuse material through access and anonymity (ICMEC, 2016). Although more countries now have laws to protect children and the number of prosecutions of individuals who target youth has increased, many countries still do not have sufficient regulations. In fact, the latest report by ICMEC in 2016, which reviewed child pornography legislation in 196 countries, found that only 82 countries have adequate laws to protect children from this crime. Further, 35 countries have no laws that specifically criminalize child pornography, and 114 countries still do not have sufficient legislation pertaining to child pornography and the sexual exploitation of children.

The following 35 countries currently have no laws on child pornography: Afghanistan, Antigua, Benin, Burkina Faso, Chad, Dominica, Equatorial Guinea, Eritrea, Ethiopia, Gabon, Guinea Bissau, Guyana, Iran, Iraq, Kiribati, Kuwait, Lebanon, Libya, Maldives, Marshall Islands, Micronesia, Mozambique, Nauru, Nepal, North Korea, Pakistan, Palau, St. Lucia, Samoa, Solomon Islands, Somalia, Syria, Tuvalu, Yemen, and Zimbabwe.

Wrap-up

The digital age of the internet and the World Wide Web has brought with it access to great educational opportunities, people with like interests, social media, and other forms of entertainment. We have seen in this chapter, however, that it has also become a vehicle for bullies, stalkers, sexual content, and sexual predators. Society around the world has taken steps to combat these types of cybercrimes through education, support mechanisms, and specific cyberlaws. If communities continue to be involved and supportive, governments continue to pass laws, and law enforcement continues to work together, the World Wide Web can be a safe place for exploration, as it was intended to be, in the digital age.

Discussion Questions

1. Describe how the internet and the World Wide Web developed over the past 3 decades.
2. Explain the advantages and disadvantages of the World Wide Web.
3. List the various cybercrimes discussed in the chapter and how those crimes affect children.
4. Compare and contrast traditional bullying and cyberbullying.
5. Explain the increase in stalkers and sexual predators on the internet, the use of social media, and growing trends across the globe.

ONLINE RESOURCES

International Centre for Missing & Exploited Children http://www.icmec.org
Cyberbullying Research Center http://cyberbullying.us
National Center for Missing & Exploited Children http://www.missingkids.com
Clemson University http://www.olweus.sites.clemson.edu
Megan Meier Foundation http://www.meganmeierfoundation.org
U.S. Department of Justice Office of Justice Programs http://www.ojp.usdoj.gov
America for Effective Law Enforcement http://www.aele.org

Definitions

Active predator—someone who attempts to sexually exploit children by trading pictures and engaging them in sexual online chat

Aggressive predator—someone who seduces children by phone and sometimes face-to-face meetings

Approach avoidance model—based on the concept/premise that when stressors occur, the individual will either address (approach) the stressor directly or avert (avoid) the stressor

Arpanet—online communication limited to only government use, private corporations, and universities.

Child pornography—images that depict a minor engaged in explicit sexual activity or having as its dominant characteristic the depiction of a minor's sexual organs

Cyberbullying—repeated harassment over the internet or while utilizing other electronic devices

Cybercrimes—crimes that are committed via an electronic device

Cyberstalking—a pattern of threats to frighten/annoy, solicitations for sex, or gathering information that may be used to threaten or harass via electronic means

Flaming—an antagonistic and insulting interaction between internet users, generally using profanity; it can also include exchanging insults with many groups teaming up on a single victim

Fight-or-flight response—a physiological reaction to a perceived harmful event.

General strain theory—developed by Robert Agnew, a criminological theory that focuses on what strains (inadequate opportunities) society puts on youth that could lead to criminal behavior to achieve socially desirable goals

High-Performance Computing and Communication Act—passed in 1991, expanding access and connectivity to any network, by anyone, anywhere around the world

Internet—interconnected networks to access data online

Intimacy stalker—someone who seeks to establish an intimate, loving relationship with their victim. The victim and the stalker were "meant to be together." These types of individuals think that the victim owes them love and affection because of all the time and effort it took for the perpetrator to stalk them.

Morphing—the transforming of one image into another

Obscene material—speech or expression that is "utterly without redeeming social value"

Passive predator—someone who primarily collects and trades child pornographic images

Power differential—the imbalance of power and strength between the bully and the victim

Predatory stalker—someone who intends to physically or sexually attack their victim. They are motivated purely by the desire for sexual gratification and power over their victim.

Rejected stalker—someone obsessed with a former romantic partner or friend who has ended the relationship or indicates that they intend to end the relationship

Resentful stalker—someone who seeks revenge against someone who is known to them or even a stranger that has offended them. Their behavior is meant to frighten and distress the victim.

Sexting—the act of sending a sexually explicit photo or text message via a mobile phone

Suicide ideology—thoughts of suicide, actual attempts, and suicide

Traditional bullying—intentional and repeated harmful behavior, typically face to face

Transactional model—explains how an individual copes with various environmental stressors. It describes how someone will make a primary and secondary appraisal of a given threat in an attempt to cope with that specific stressor

World Wide Web—online data system

References

Agatston, P., Kowalski, R., & Limber, S. (2012).Youth views on cyberbullying. In J. W. Patchin & S. Hinduja (Eds.), *Cyberbullying prevention and response: Expert perspectives* (pp. 57–71). Routledge.

Age of first exposure to pornography shapes men's attitudes toward women. (2017, August 3). American Psychological Association. https://www.apa.org/news/press/releases/2017/08/pornography-exposure

Ahlgrim, B., & Terrance, C. (2021). Perceptions of cyberstalking: Impact of perpetrator gender and cyberstalker/victim relationship. *Journal of Interpersonal Violence, 36*(7–8), NP4074–4093. https://doi.org/10.1177/0886260518784590

Anderson, M. (2018, September 27). A majority of teens have experienced some form of cyberbullying. Pew Research Center. https://www.pewresearch.org/internet/2018/09/27/a-majority-of-teens-have-experienced-some-form-of-cyberbullying/

Anderson, M., & Jiang, J. (2018, May 31). Teens, social media and technology 2018. Pew Research Center. https://www.pewresearch.org/internet/2018/05/31/teens-social-media-technology-2018/

Armstrong, S. B., Dubow, E. F., & Domoff, S. E. (2019). Adolescent coping: In-person and cyber-victimization. *Cyberpsychology: Journal of Psychosocial Research on Cyberspace, 13*(4), Article 2. https://cyberpsychology.eu/article/view/12559/10906

Bauman, S., Toomey, R. B., & Walker, J. L. (2013). Associations among bullying, cyberbullying, and suicide in high school students. *Journal of Adolescence, 36*(2), 341–350.

Beale, A., & Hall, K. (2007). Cyberbullying: What school administrators (and parents) can do. *The Clearing House, 81*(1), 8–12. http://www.jstor.org/stable/30189945

Canares, M. (2018). Online Privacy: Will they Care?, Teenagers Use of Social Media and their Understanding of Privacy Issues in Developing Countries, World Wide Web Foundation. Retrieved December 26, 2020 from http://webfoundation.org/ docs/ 2018/ 08/WebFoundationSocialMediaPrivacyReport_Screen.pdf

Cassidy, W., Faucher, C., & Jackson, M. (2013). Cyberbullying among youth: A comprehensive review of current international research and its implications and application to policy and practice. *School Psychology International, 34*(6), 575–612. https://doi.org/10.1177/0143034313479697

Catalano, S. (2012). *Stalking victims in the United States—Revised.* Age, 18(19), 1-9.

Centers for Disease Control and Prevention. (2014). *The relationship between bullying and suicide: What we know and what it means for schools.* National Center for Injury and Control, Division of Violence Prevention. https://www.cdc.gov/violenceprevention/pdf/bullying-suicide-translation-final-a.pdf

Centers for Disease Control and Prevention. (2019). *Preventing stalking.* National Center for Injury Prevention and Control, Division of Violence Prevention. https://www.cdc.gov/violenceprevention/intimatepartnerviolence/stalking/fastfact.html

Centers for Disease Control and Prevention. (2020). Youth Risk Behavior Surveillance—United States, 2019.

Morbidity and Mortality Weekly Report, 69(1, Suppl.), 1–83. https://www.cdc.gov/healthyyouth/data/yrbs/pdf/2019/su6901-H.pdf

Chassiakos, Y. L. R., Radesky, J., Christakis, D., Moreno, M. A., & Cross, C. (2016). Children and adolescents and digital media. *Pediatrics, 138*(5), Article e20162593.

Crimes Against Children Research Center (n.d.). *Internet Safety Education for Teens: Getting It Right*. Retrieved on May 17, 2021, from http://unh.edu/ccrc/internet-crimes/Internet%20Factsheet_portrait%20version_2-6-08_khf.pdf

Cyberbullying statistics. (2021). Enough Is Enough. Retrieved on March 20, 2021 from https://enough.org/stats_cyberbullying

Döring, N. (2014). Consensual sexting among adolescents: Risk prevention through abstinence education or safer sexting? *Cyberpsychology: Journal of Psychosocial Research on Cyberspace, 8*(1).

Evans, Y. N. (2018). *Cyberbullying takes physical, psychological toll: What you can do*. American Association of Pediatrics. https://www.aappublications.org/news/2018/01/24/MasteringMedia012418

Fegert, J. M., Vitiello, B., Plener, P. L., & Clemens, V. (2020). Challenges and burden of the Coronavirus 2019 (COVID-19) pandemic for child and adolescent mental health: A narrative review to highlight clinical and research needs in the acute phase and the long return to normality. *Child and Adolescent Psychiatry and Mental Health, 14*, Article 20.

Fritz, L. (2017). How much digitalization can a human tolerate? In *Conference Proceedings Trends in Business Communication 2016* (pp. 107–113). Wiesbaden: Springer Gabler.

Hay, C., Meldrum, R., & Mann, K. (2010). Traditional bullying, cyber bullying, and deviance: A general strain theory approach. *Journal of Contemporary Criminal Justice, 26*(2), 130–147. https://doi.org/10.1177/1043986209359557

Hellfeldt, K., López-Romero, L., & Andershed, H. (2020). Cyberbullying and psychological well-being in young adolescence: The potential protective mediation effects of social support from family, friends, and teachers. *International Journal of Environmental Research and Public Health, 17*(1), 45.

Hertz, M. F., Donato, H., & Wright, J. (2013). The relationship between youth involvement in bullying and suicide. *Journal of Adolescent Health, 53*(1), S1–S3.

Hinduja, S. (2011). *Cyberbullying rates across the world, and the role of culture*. Cyberbullying Research Center. https://cyberbullying.org/cyberbullying-rates-across-the-world-and-the-role-of-culture

Hinduja, S., & Patchin, J. W. (2010). Bullying, cyberbullying, and suicide. *Archives of Suicide Research, 14*(3), 206–221.

Hinduja, S., & Patchin, J. W. (2012). Cyberbullying: Neither an epidemic nor a rarity. *European Journal of Developmental Psychology, 9*(5), 539–543.

Hinduja, S., & Patchin, J. W. (2015). *Bullying beyond the schoolyard: Preventing and responding to cyberbullying* (2nd ed.). Sage (Corwin Press).

Hitchcock, J. (2015). *Online harassment and cyber stalking statistics*. Working to Halt Online Abuse https://www.haltabuse.org/resources/stats/index.shtml

International Centre for Missing & Exploited Children. (2016). *Child pornography: Model legislation and global review* (8th ed.). Koons Family Institute for International Law & Policy. https://www.icmec.org/wp-content/uploads/2016/02/Child-Pornography-Model-Law-8th-Ed-Final-linked.pdf

International Centre for Missing & Exploited Children. (2017). *Framing implementation: A supplement to child pornography: Model legislation & global review*. Koons Family Institute on International Law & Policy. https://dev.icmec.org/wp-content/uploads/2017/02/Framing-Implementation_2017.pdf

Internet Safety 101. (2020). *Social media, mobile phones, and sexting*. Enough Is Enough. Retrieved on January 6, 2021from https://internetsafety101.org/Socialmediastats

John, A., Glendenning, A. C., Marchant, A., Montgomery, P., Stewart, A., Wood, S., Lloyd, K., & Hawton, K. (2018). Self-harm, suicidal behaviours, and cyberbullying in children and young people: Systematic review. *Journal of Medical Internet Research, 20*(4), e129. https://doi.org/10.2196/jmir.9044

Kowalski, R. M., Giumetti, G. W., Schroeder, A. N., & Lattanner, M. R. (2014). Bullying in the digital age: A critical review and meta-analysis of cyberbullying research among youth. *Psychology Bulletin, 140*(4), 1073–1137.

Kowalski, R. M., Limber, S. P., & Agatston, P. W. (2012). *Cyberbullying: Bullying in the digital age* (2nd ed). Wiley–Blackwell.

Lenhart, A., Madder, M., Smith, A., Purcell, K., Zickuhr, K., & Raine, L. (2011, November 9). *Teens, kindness, and cruelty on social networking sites*. Pew Research Center.

Lingam, R. A., & Aripin, N. (2017). Comments on fire! Classifying flaming comments on YouTube videos in Malaysia. *Malaysian Journal of Communication, 33*(4), 104–118.

Litwiller, B. J., & Brausch A. M. (2013). Cyberbullying and physical bullying in adolescent suicide: The role of violent behavior and substance use. *Journal of Youth and Adolescence, 42*(5), 675–684.

Lyndall, S., Craig, W., & Rosu, A. (2013). Power differentials in bullying. *Journal of Interpersonal Violence, 29*(5), 846–865.

Madden, M., Lenhart, A., Cortesi, S., Gasser, U., Duggan, M., Smith, A., & Beaton, M. (2013). Teens, social media, and privacy. *Pew Research Center, 21*(1055), 2-86.

Madigan, S., Ly, A., Rash, C. L., Van Ouytsel, J., & Temple, J. R. (2018). Prevalence of multiple forms of sexting behavior among youth: A systematic review and meta-analysis. *JAMA Pediatrics, 172*(4), 327–335. https://doi.org/10.1001/jamapediatrics.2017.5314

Miller, N. (2001). Stalking laws and implementation practices: A national review for policymakers and practitioners. Institute for Law and Justice Domestic Violence

Moore, R., Guntupelli, N. T., & Lee, T. (2010). Parental regulation and online activities: Examining factors that influence a youth's potential to become a victim of online harassment. *International Journal of Cyber Criminology*, 4(1 & 2), 685–698.

National Center for Education Statistics (2021). Bullying at School and Electronic Bullying. Retrieved on June 1, 2021, from https://nces.ed.gov /programs /coe/ indicator/a10

National Center for Missing and Exploited Children (2021). *By the Numbers*. Retrieved on February, 14, 2021 from https://www.missingkids.org/ gethelpnow/ cyber-tipline# bythenumbers

National Center for Victims of Crime (n.d.). *Stalking Resource Center*. Retrieved on May 17, 2020 from https:// victimsofcrime.org/stalking-resource-center/

National Crime Information Center. (2020). *2019 National Crime Information Center (NCIC) missing person and unidentified person statistics pursuant to the requirements of the Crime Control Act of 1990*, Pub. L. No. 101–647, 104 Stat. 4789. https://www.fbi.gov/file-repository/2019-ncic-missing-person-and-unidentified-person-statistics.pdf

NetSmartz (2020). *Smartphones*. Retrieved on September 16, 2020 from https:// www. missingkids.org/netsmartz/ topics/smartphones

Noll, H. (2016). *Cyberbullying: Impacting today's youth*. Semantic Scholar. https://www.semanticscholar.org/ paper/Cyberbullying%3A-Impacting-Today%E2%80% 99s-Youth-Noll/5394b744b55ee33d560c1021647617b733 ac001f

Olweus, D. (1993). *Bullying at school: What we know and what we can do*. Blackwell.

Patchin, J. (2015). *Cyberbullying victimization*. Cyberbullying Research Center. https://cyberbullying.org/2015-data

Pickens, B. C., Mckinney, R., & Bell, S. C. (2019). A hierarchical model of coping in the college student population. *Journal of Interdisciplinary Studies in Education*, 7(2), 1–19.

Schneider, S. K., O'Donnell, L., Stueve, A., & Coulter, R. W. (2012). Cyberbullying, school bullying, and psychological distress: A regional census of high school students. *American Journal of Public Health*, 102(1), 171–177.

Shipley, T. G., & Bowker, A. (2014). *Investigating internet crimes: An introduction to solving crimes in cyberspace*. Newnes.

Slonje, R., Smith, K. S., & Frisen, A. (2012). *The nature of cyberbullying and strategies for prevention. Computers in Human Behavior*, 29(1), 26–32. https://doi.org/10.1016/j. chb.2012.05.024

Statistics & citations. (2021, June). Megan Meier Foundation. https://static1.squarespace.com/static/5b33ed96372b96 4a1d83073a/t/60d619fd4d52ae0ca2c07a3e/1624644094476/ Updated+Statistics+2021.pdf

U.S. Department of Justice. (2016) *The national strategy for child exploitation prevention and interdiction: USDOJ report to Congress*. https://www.justice.gov/psc/file/ 842411/download

U.S. Department of Justice. (2020a). *Child pornography*. https://www.justice.gov/criminal-ceos/child-pornography

U.S. Department of Justice. (2020b). *Citizen's guide to U.S. federal law on child pornography*. https://www.justice. gov/criminal-ceos/citizens-guide-us-federal-law-child-pornography

Van Geel, M., Vedder, P., & Tanilon, J. (2014). *Relationship between peer victimization, cyberbullying, and suicide in children and adolescents: A meta-analysis. JAMA Pediatrics*, 168(5), 435–442. https://doi.org/10.1001/ jamapediatrics.2013.4143

Wang, C. W., Musumari, P. M., & Techasrivichien, T. (2019). Overlap of traditional bullying and cyberbullying and correlates of bullying among Taiwanese adolescents: A cross-sectional study. *BMC Public Health*, 19, Article 1756. https://doi.org/10.1186/ s12889-019-8116-z

Wang, K., Chen, Y., Zhang, J., & Oudekerk, B. A. (2020). *Indicators of school crime and safety: 2019* (NCES 2020-063/NCJ 254485). National Center for Education Statistics.

Wells, M., Finkelhor, D., Wolak, J., & Mitchell, K. J. (2007). Defining child pornography: Law enforcement dilemmas in investigations of internet child pornography possession, 1. *Police Practice and Research*, 8(3), 269–283.

What is cyberbullying? (2020). Stopbullying.gov. Retrieved on February 25, 2021 from https://www.stopbullying. gov/cyberbullying/what-is-it

Woda, S. (2014, October 16). *Cyberbullying laws around the globe: Where is legislation strongest?* UKnowKids. https://resources.uknowkids.com/blog/cyberbullying-laws-around-the-globe-where-is-legislation-strongest

Juvenile Justice: Trends and Reforms

CHAPTER OUTLINE

LEARNING OBJECTIVES

At the end of the chapter, students will be able to

describe arrest trends within the juvenile justice system and disproportionate contacts based on gender, race, and ethnicity;

describe relevant laws and court cases affecting jurisdiction and processing of juveniles;

describe initiatives of law enforcement to engage youth and communities;

evaluate sentencing trends of juveniles within and outside the system;

discuss specific factors associated with reentry and measuring success; and

compare and contrast juvenile justice reforms and initiatives within the United States and around the world.

Keywords

Alternative care communities
Child abuse and neglect
Community-based corrections
Cottage system
Cycle of justice
Deficit-based model
Diminished culpability
Emerging adults

Evidence-based initiatives
Gender-responsive programs
Implicit bias
Incorrigible
Legalistic style
Parole
Probation
Procedural justice

Prosocial bonds
Protective factors
Restorative justice
Risk factors
Service style
Strength-based perspective
Strength-based wraparound services

Introduction

As you have read throughout this text, there have been many changes to the juvenile justice system from its creation in 1899 through its evolution over the past century. We have also seen statistics and studied theories of offending to understand what factors contribute to delinquency and criminality. This understanding has also helped create interventions that not only provide support to juveniles within the justice system but also attempt to prevent children from getting involved with the system in the first place.

In this chapter, we will look at trends and reforms of the juvenile system within the United States and across the globe. Specifically, we will explore efforts by law enforcement, the courts, and corrections, as well as developing state and federal interventions and diversion programs to support vulnerable youth. We will also look at efforts to further protect child victims and enhancements to the system overall. This includes expanded jurisdiction over older juveniles and aftercare and support of children both within and outside the system.

Disproportionality Within the System

Contact With the System: Juvenile Arrest Trends

As we read in Chapters 2 and 4, although predictions in the late 1980s described "juvenile predators" lurking on our streets and warned of an increase in juvenile crime, juvenile crime actually began to plummet in the early 1990s and has continued to decrease since then. The latest data showed a decrease of 60% in the number of arrests of juveniles by law enforcement in 2018 compared to 2009. However, the number of arrests was still over 700,000, and arrests were disproportionate in terms of gender, race, and ethnicity (Puzzanchera, 2020).

Female Youth Involved in the Justice System

Arrest rates for females are less than half of arrest rates for males under the age of 18. The rates for both genders have steadily decreased from 1996 and are at their lowest since 1980 (Puzzanchera, 2020). Of those arrested, approximately 37,000 are being held by the system on any given day. Fifteen percent of juveniles held are female. There are not many differences in terms of offense and gender and being held by the system; however, the data show that females were held three times as often as males for status offenses (Office of Juvenile Delinquency and Prevention [OJJDP], 2021b).

Although arrests of female juveniles under 18 have continued to decrease, the federal government supports states that are developing initiatives that specifically address female youth involved with the system. The OJJDP developed a program entitled "Reducing Risk for Girls in the Juvenile Justice System" in 2020. This program provides funds to states looking forward and developing plans to offer alternatives to girls who become involved with the justice system by diverting them to service providers that can meet their individual needs. It also provides funds for states developing intervention plans specific to girls as well as training for officers, probation, judges, and other justice professionals to ensure they have the knowledge and skills to implement and refer girls to these programs (OJJDP, 2021a).

Gender-Responsive Programs

Gender-responsive programs consider and respond to the specific needs of a particular gender. States rely on these programs to divert and rehabilitate girls involved in the system. For example, Girls Circle, which was developed in the mid-1990s, continues to be adopted by agencies to address risks and provide support for female delinquents. The program calls for weekly support groups and gender-responsive discussions that recognize cultural differences and trauma-informed care. Staff are provided with gender-responsive, skills-building, and resilience training. States that have implemented the program, such as Illinois, have shown more reductions in delinquent behavior than states in which girls receive more traditional forms of treatment (Treskon & Bright, 2017; see Figure 13.1 regarding arrest rates by gender of youth ages 10–17).

SNAP Girls, which stands for Stop Now and Plan, is another program that continues to be adopted. It specifically addresses crime prevention among teenage girls who exhibit aggression. It is a collaborative intervention approach that involves educators, the child's family, and supportive services to encourage relationship building, positive choices, and positive school engagement for healthy development (*BRAVE*, n.d.). See the Deeper Dive box for a list of common components of gender-responsive programs.

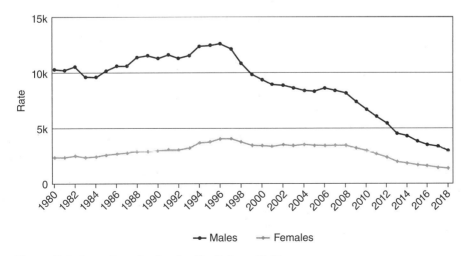

Figure 13.1 Arrest Rates by Gender, Youth Ages 10-17

Source: OJJDP

DEEPER DIVE

COMMON COMPONENTS OF GENDER-RESPONSIVE PROGRAMMING

PRINCIPLES

Focus on relationships. Relationships are used as the basis for personal change. Because of the relational nature of female development, attention is paid to relationships between staff members and clients and between clients and essential people in their lives.

Safety. Physical and emotional safety is essential, given the high rates of trauma and maltreatment in the populations served. Clients must be able to express themselves without fear of harm or reprisal.

Attention to health, mental health, and substance use. Healthy living is a focus, and attention is paid to physical, behavioral, and reproductive health issues relevant to women.

Cultural appropriateness and competence. Services are consistent with clients' cultural values. Racism and discrimination in the broader society are recognized, and services are designed to promote equality. Given that women of color are overrepresented in criminal and juvenile justice systems, cultural competence, or the ability to interact with people of different cultures, and an intersectional approach, in which each person is understood as having a complex social identity, are particularly relevant.

Response to sexism. Female development is central to service provision, focusing on the broader social forces that perpetuate sexism and gender-based discrimination.

Strengths-based approach. Rather than concentrating on deficits, staff members actively identify and build on clients' strengths to promote their empowerment.

Holistic approach. Services focus on the well-being of the whole person rather than treating a particular symptom or problem, recognizing the complexities of girls' development.

Family involvement. Resolution of family conflict, which is common in girls' histories, and the development of positive family connections are critical components of services. Family members are included in decisions and treatment.

SERVICES

Treatment for abuse and trauma. Individual and group activities focus on acknowledging and responding to interpersonal trauma and maltreatment, which are more commonly experienced by females than by males.

Life skills. Clients develop skills needed to make the transition to adulthood. This may reduce reliance on unhealthy relationships and promote women's independence.

Educational and vocational opportunities. Clients learn about and have access to educational and job-related opportunities that prepare them to pursue any field of interest, not just female-dominated professions.

Community opportunities. Connections to the broader community are encouraged through introductions and opportunities to join organizations or volunteer. (Treskon & Bright, 2017, pp. 3–4)

Society also pays attention to the demographics of who is being arrested in terms of race and ethnicity.

Racial and Ethnic Disparities

We have seen racial disparities in the system, from arrests to processing to dispositions. Although there have been efforts at the federal and state levels to reduce these differences, current studies show they still exist (Robles-Ramamurthy & Watson, 2019). According to the National Conference of State Legislatures, youth of color, although they account for just one-third of the teen population, account for approximately two-thirds of incarcerated juveniles (National Conference of State Legislatures, 2020).

Debate exists as to whether this is a result of bias in the system or systemic risks associated with factors such as lack of social and environmental resources and supports within communities, but efforts continue to address and reduce these disparities. As you have learned, the Juvenile Justice Reform Act has four core requirements, one of which has provided guidelines for states to not only track but also make efforts to reduce these disparities.

In 2018, the act was amended to better address its "disproportionate minority contact" core component and was renamed Racial and Ethnic Disparities (RED). The amendment provides research-based direction to states to manage this condition. It requires that states identify how they measure success and utilize an outcome-based evaluation of that success. States that do not follow these mandates and fail to reduce disparities in their justice systems will lose 20% of their federal funding.

In addition to measuring general effects, the act also calls for measuring disparity at five points of contact with a juvenile. These points of contact are arrest, diversion, pretrial detention, disposition, and transfer to adult court. Guidance for plans of action is also provided. Some strategies to reduce disparity have included expanding eligibility for diversion before arrest, automatic diversion for specific offenses, and working with educational institutions to reduce law enforcement's handling of school issues (Bala & Mooney, 2019; OJJDP, 2019).

Since the amendment, states have continued to adopt various programs and initiatives. Some of these initiatives include cultural competency training for school officers, standard reporting of ethnic and racial data, and "race-neutral" risk assessments (National Conference of State Legislatures, 2020; OJJDP, 2019).

Vermont has proposed "legislation inclusion" that calls for collaboration with racial equity advisory panels and other stakeholders and has been advocated for regarding laws that would affect people of color. Additionally, Vermont has advocated for the use of risk assessments that can illustrate societal inequalities and help courts make informed and objective decisions and reduce **implicit bias**, stereotypes, or attitudes that subconsciously affect one's thought process and actions.

After an analysis of its counties with the most racial and ethnic disparities, Georgia found that the most critical stage for disparity is referrals. They assert that the decision-makers, such as police officers or school resource officers, are critical players. Additionally, they found that counties with schools that carried out harsh punishments had disproportionate referrals of African American students. In response, Georgia provides implicit bias training for decision-makers they believe can be positively influenced in terms of their discretionary behavior, empathy, and positive relationships with the community. Law enforcement has also begun to take steps to mend and further form positive relationships with juveniles and communities as a whole.

Law Enforcement and Juvenile Directions

As you have read, most youths who become involved with the juvenile justice system do so through interactions with law enforcement. Therefore, positive relationships between the police and the community are believed to be paramount when it comes to preventing crime and working together to solve community problems. These relationships should be based on trust and on interaction between the police and community being carried out in a procedurally just manner (Merenda et al., 2021). **Procedural justice** includes carrying out police functions in a fair, unbiased, and transparent manner with community members while actively listening to their concerns (Community Oriented Policing Services, n.d.). Controversial police incidents and those in which officers are fired or arrested and found guilty of excessive force, assault, sexual misconduct, and even manslaughter and murder have created hostile relationships with and negative perceptions by the community that can extend to children of all ages. According to a variety of stakeholders, it is therefore imperative that law enforcement create channels of communication and initiatives that allow them to effectively reach out to young people as well as adults to foster productive interactions, transparency, and ultimately trusting relationships (Community Oriented Policing Services, n.d.; Deal, 2020).

In response to these tenuous relationships, police departments across the country are creating new initiatives and have committed to new strategies in the future. These strategies include listening to the concerns and the needs of the community and responding in a procedurally just way. They also include understanding the unique characteristics of communities and the public and their youths' specific needs.

General and specific training for law enforcement, including training to be more sensitive to the needs of those they come in contact with, is a central part of this response and their interactions, specifically with youth. For example, the Changing Minds campaign funded by the OJJDP is an educational program that is utilized by law enforcement and other professionals and caregivers. It considers environmental risks that may affect youth and additionally offers tools to teaching institutions. It attempts to raise awareness and increase the skills of professionals coming in contact with children who were victims of various childhood traumas (OJJDP, 2020d).

Another program, entitled Enhancing Law Enforcement Response to Children Exposed to Violence and Childhood Trauma, is sponsored by the International Association of Chiefs of Police and the OJJDP and has been developed to train agencies and develop law enforcement's ability to identify and effectively respond to young persons exposed to trauma and violence. It attempts to teach officers to be more sensitive to these incidents so that they can be further empathetic and supportive of these youth (Deal, 2020; International Association of Chiefs of Police, 2017).

Child Abuse Prevention

As you learned in previous chapters, the Federal Child Abuse Prevention and Treatment Act (CAPTA) defines **child abuse and neglect** as

> any recent act or failure to act on the part of a parent or caretaker which results in death, serious physical or emotional harm, sexual abuse or exploitation; or an act or failure to act which presents an imminent risk of serious harm. (42 USCA § 5106g, p. 1)

CAPTA provides minimum qualifiers, and states have not only expanded on the definition, but also created initiatives to reduce neglect and physical, emotional, and sexual abuse.

The Office of Justice Programs was established in 1984 and coordinates initiatives between the federal government and state and local municipalities. Specifically, their Office of Juvenile Justice and Delinquency Prevention (OJJDP) is responsible for reducing youth crime and violence, including abuse against children. The OJJDP has provided grants to states over past decades for initiatives focused on juveniles within and outside the system, and in 2019, they funded over $19 million toward these initiatives.

One such initiative is the National Children's Alliance, which provides support for individuals who were sexually abused as children. A multiyear campaign entitled SHINE supports communities serving victims of child abuse by providing advocates and working with child advocacy centers. Another initiative is the National Mentoring Resource Center sponsored by the OJJDP. This free resource offers training, mentoring tools, and materials at no charge to agencies and private organizations that want to provide support services to assist youth and their families (OJJDP, n.d., 2020a). The Bureau of Justice Assistance, the National Institute of Justice, and the Office for Victims of Crime also fall under the U.S. Office of Justice Programs and have directed continued efforts to sponsor and improve juvenile justice initiatives.

Youth-Focused Policing Strategies for Diversion and Interventions

In addition to the preventative and intervention programs you read about in Chapter 10, other components of the juvenile justice system also incorporate these types of initiatives. As such, youth-focused policing is a proactive strategy to enable police to intervene with juveniles before criminality and victimization occur by mitigating involvement with the system.

The President's Task Force on 21st-Century Policing

In 2016, the President's Task Force on 21st-Century Policing created six pillars of youth-focused policing (see Table 13.1). These pillars include "(1) building trust, (2) policy and oversight, (3) technology and social media, (4) community policing and crime reduction, (5) training and education, and (6) officer safety and wellness" (Rosiak, 2016, p. 1). Recent protests over excessive force and officer arrests have focused on these pillars to reestablish trust and communication with the community and its youth, now and in the future (Perez et al., 2021; Rosiak, 2016).

This drive toward future policing with regard to interacting with youth has resulted in the creation of programs that focus on officers more as mediators and practicing more of a **service style** of policing—intervening by providing informal services such as taking the youth home. This is in opposition to the **legalistic style**, which tends to be more by the book and is centered on enforcement and arrests (Zhao et al., 2006).

For example, in 2015, the New York City Police Department initiated neighborhood policing, which created "neighborhood policing officers" who focused on forging relationships and collaborations with communities as a whole. Now the department uses youth coordination officers to focus on prevention and collaboration efforts specifically geared toward youths. Aligned with the youth-focused policing strategy, this proactive approach prevents children from becoming involved with the system in the first place.

TABLE 13.1	The Six Pillars of Youth-Focused Policing				
I	II	III	IV	V	VI
Trust and legitimacy	Policy and oversight	Technology and social media	Community policing and crime reduction	Training and education	Officer safety and wellness
When it comes to engaging young people, law enforcement agencies must find various ways to encourage officers to build trust and legitimacy with youth. Officers must exhibit a "guardian" rather than a "warrior" mentality.	Law enforcement leadership can work with local schools to develop policies that help lessen youth involvement in the justice system. Most recently, school resource officers are to avoid enforcing school discipline rules.	Police agencies are using tools such as setting up their own Facebook pages and tweeting information that provides details that may be left out by mainstream media. This can target youths who more often use this technology.	Engaging youth in the process of community safety, including their voice in testimony about problems facing the community, and joint problem-solving	Law enforcement must be trained in a wide variety of areas involving youth. This includes how to engage young people positively, de-escalation techniques, understanding youth brain development, the impact of trauma and other mental health issues, and cultural differences among youth populations.	Enhancing relationships with youth and the rest of the community will, in and of itself, improve officer safety along with discussing how and why threats were perceived for mutual understanding.

Source: Rosiak (2016).

Officers are assigned to sections of a precinct and work with school safety officers in educational settings and community stakeholders to keep track of youth trends and develop strategies to prevent delinquency and criminal acts. Additionally, departments around the country are implementing various programs and activities to engage youth and their communities.

Police-Initiated Diversion for Youth to Prevent Future Delinquent Behavior Program

There is also an immerging trend to divert more youth at the law enforcement level before even reaching the stages of the formal justice system. Through the National Institute of Justice, the Police-Initiated Diversion for Youth to Prevent Future Delinquent Behavior Program focuses on low-risk youth before court interventions as an alternative to formally processing a delinquent. Officers are empowered to divert youth toward services outside the justice system that can address the root of problems, such as services that treat psychosocial needs and other contributing factors to risk behavior.

Gang Prevention Efforts

As we read earlier in the text, juvenile gangs, and gangs in general, pose a risk to children who become affiliated with individuals who carry out illegal acts. We have read about efforts to combat gangs that both prevent children from joining and help those who have joined get out. Although some efforts by the police, schools, or other agencies have been siloed, a trend to work collaboratively with outside agencies to tackle this issue is occurring.

Specifically, when addressing gangs within schools, law enforcement has begun to work collaboratively with administrators to address surrounding issues. Even school resource officer approaches seem to be changing in terms of the police serving a supportive role and school officials taking the initial response. Similar responses seem to be expanding to a variety of behavioral issues within schools. Through the OJJDP, the National Gang Center developed the Gangs in School's Guide so that officers and administrators can learn to identify and suppress criminal and gang activity in schools through police and school officials working together (OJJDP, 2020b).

Initiatives continue to develop within law enforcement to improve their operational skills in a variety of ways as new processes within the court system are developed.

Reforming the Court System

Initiatives both within and outside the court system continue to evolve. These initiatives were sometimes dependent on what we termed earlier in the text the **cycle of justice**, in which perceptions of juvenile crime instead of actual crime conditions influenced juvenile justice policy and an inefficient cycle of failed responses. Now more **evidence-based initiatives**, which have been effected by scientific evidence and prior success, have been occurring. Campaigns such as Raise the Age have carried momentum across the country to raise the maximum age for children who can be formally processed under the auspices of the juvenile system.

As you may recall from our juvenile offender chapter, Harvard University found that the part of the brain (the prefrontal cortex region) that controls impulsivity does not fully mature until age 24. As a result, older juveniles have been referred to as **emerging adults**—individuals ages 18–24 who are transitioning from a dependent child to an independent adult. This has led some policymakers to consider these young adults as juveniles developmentally and keep them within the juvenile justice system to receive rehabilitation through education, treatment, and skills-building (Schiraldi et al., 2015). Aligning juvenile justice policy with this notion is gaining more popularity, as illustrated by many states proposing and passing legislation to raise the age at which young people are processed outside the adult criminal justice system (Chester & Schiraldi, 2016).

For example, in 2007, Connecticut passed legislation raising the age at which juveniles fall under the juvenile court's jurisdiction from 15 to 17. Connecticut is now proposing raising the age again, to 20. The state reports that not only have new arrests of juveniles decreased 40% since the age was increased, but also rearrests for children on probation decreased by almost 8% (Juvenile Justice & Youth Development, 2020).

In Vermont, a study compared 16- and 17-year-olds who were charged with similar offenses, some of whom were processed in juvenile court and others who were prosecuted in adult court. The study found that youths prosecuted in juvenile court had lower recidivism rates (Crime Research Group, 2015). Senate Bill S.234, passed in Vermont in 2018, raised the age for a young adult to be processed in their juvenile system to the highest in the country over the course of 4 years. As of July 2020, Vermont is the only state to have 18-years-olds fall under the jurisdiction of their family division (juvenile court); in 2022, the age limit will increase to 19 and in 2024 to 20.

In California, Senate Bill 889 has proposed raising the maximum age for juvenile justice jurisdiction from 17 to 19 based on the previously illustrated research, which considers these juveniles "immerging adults." The bill's legislators intend for these

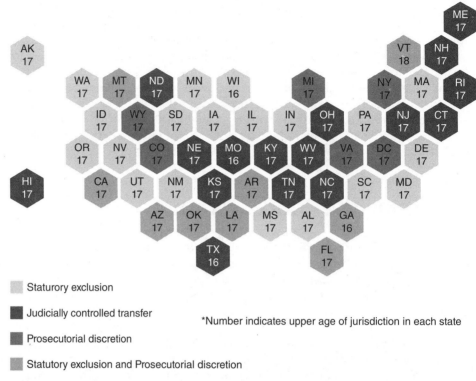

Figure 13.2 Juvenile Age of Jurisdiction and Transfer to Adult Court Laws by State.

Youth offenders are persons aged 10 to 17 years. Rate per 100,000 persons aged 10-17 years (see explanatory notes).
Source: NCSL.

young adults to receive services tailored to their specific needs to put them on a path toward rehabilitation.

Researchers have found that processing young adults through the juvenile justice system results in reductions in future arrests, court cases, and incarceration costs (Chester & Schiraldi, 2016). It is important to remember, however, that automatic transfers to criminal court for some violent felony offenses continue to exist, even in states that have raised the age for juvenile justice jurisdiction (OJJDP, 2020c). Raising the minimum age for prosecution is also being considered because 30 states have no minimum age for prosecution in the juvenile court (OJJDP, 2020c). Figure 13.2 illustrates juvenile transfer jurisdiction across the Unites States.

Sentencing

The sentencing of juveniles has also garnered substantial debate throughout the years. As you have read, even after 2005, when the Supreme Court ruled in *Roper v. United States* (Roper, 543 U.S.) that imposing the death penalty for anyone under 18 is unconstitutional, states still had mandated sentencing of youth to life with no opportunity for parole for certain offenses. These mandates changed in 2010 to solely include youth who committed murder, as decided in *Graham v. Florida* (*Graham v. Florida*

560 U.S.). Finally, the Supreme Court banned all mandates and directed judges to only impose life without parole on a case-by-case basis, considering factors such as age and home environment and only when it was determined that the juvenile was permanently **incorrigible**—not able to be rehabilitated (American Psychological Association, n.d.; *Jackson v. Hobbs*, 2011; *Miller v. Alabama*, 2012). The court decided that children have **diminished culpability** and cannot be held fully criminally liable but can be rehabilitated. Supreme Justice Elena Kagan asserted that judges and juries must evaluate "mitigating qualities" of youth such as immaturity, impulsivity, and failure to consider risk and consequence, along with their potential for rehabilitation. This should be evaluated even when they have committed the most violent of crimes, namely murder (Davidson, 2012).

The American Psychological Association agreed and highlighted three areas that substantiate a juvenile's diminished culpability. Those are:

> 1) immaturity (that juveniles have an underdeveloped sense of responsibility, which can result in ill-considered actions and decisions), 2) vulnerability (that juveniles are more susceptible to negative influences and peer pressure), and 3) changeability (that the character of juveniles is not as well-formed as that of an adult, thereby giving juveniles greater potential for rehabilitation). (American Psychological Association, 2012, p. 1)

The American Psychological Association also references research on juveniles' delayed brain development in the areas of impulsivity and control cited in these cases.

In an uncommon decision in *Montgomery v. Louisiana* in 2016 (*Montgomery v. Louisiana* 577 U.S.), the Supreme Court called for states to reexamine prior mandated sentences of juveniles serving life without parole. This was to determine if they should be released based on the court's rulings in *Miller v. Alabama* and *Jackson v. Hobbs* in 2012. As such, juveniles serving life sentences have been released, and states continue to review cases and remove previously convicted juveniles. Although some states have foregone any attempt for further review of some juvenile life sentences, current trends reveal that other states have completely banned a sentence of life without the possibility of parole for anyone under 18, under any circumstance (Campaign for the Fair Sentencing of Youth, n.d.; Rovner, 2020). Figure 13.3 shows the states that have banned life sentences without parole for children.

Restorative Justice

As you may recall from the juvenile victims chapter, **restorative justice** is an effort to divert a juvenile from formal processing and is sometimes imposed as an alternative sanction. It is a process to both maintain offender accountability and provide validation and amends to the victim and the community (Speed, 2020). When restorative justice occurs at the beginning of the juvenile justice process, it is intended to divert a juvenile from formal processing. However, it can also be utilized as a part of sentencing that moves toward the system's goal of rehabilitation.

Restorative justice as a diversion from the court process is becoming more prevalent and has yielded positive results, because it has been shown to reduce future offending. In recent years, increasing and broadening the use of restorative justice at different points in the system has been shown to decrease crime and lower incarceration, and how and where it is applied can impact racial and ethnic disproportionalities (O'Neil, 2016; Speed, 2020).

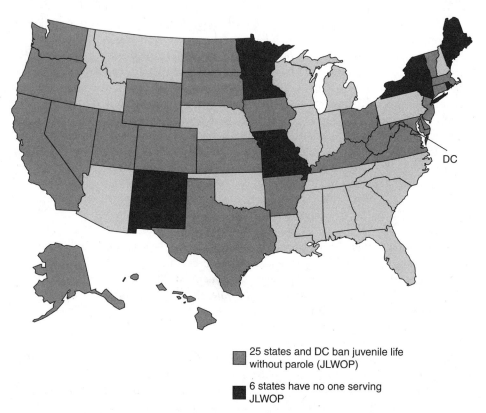

DC

25 states and DC ban juvenile life without parole (JLWOP)

6 states have no one serving JLWOP

Figure 13.3 31 States and the District of Columbia Have Banned Juvenile Life without Parole Sentences or Have No One Serving

Source: Campaign for the Fair Sentencing of Youth

Characteristics of the restorative justice process also continue to widen. Although the focus has remained on the victim and the community along with accountability for the offender, programs are also considering long-term effects beyond liability to the victim and community. To break the cycle of recidivism, restorative justice initiatives are looking not only to incorporate culpability but also to enhance protective factors and reduce future risk for the offender. This can be accomplished through building competencies, increasing access to community resources, and skills-building through affiliated programs such as the balanced and restorative justice model. Such programs focus on offender accountability to the victim and the community with the additional goals of long-term community safety and competency development (Dillard et al., 2019).

Training regarding the intricacies of restorative justice is also being made available. The Bureau of Justice Assistance created the National Center on Restorative Justice in 2019, which provides new restorative justice approaches to criminal justice professionals, students in higher education, social service providers, and other stakeholders within the community at the local, state, and federal levels (Bureau of Justice Statistics, 2020).

Implementing restorative justice methods in schools is also gaining popularity. For example, the Oakland School District continues to implement restorative justice programs in their schools as an alternative to suspensions. The district, in conjunction with **Restorative Justice for Oakland Youth**, a nonprofit in Oakland, California, has moved the program along. This organization provides training to communities and schools and pays particular attention to race and ethnic groups that disproportionally end up in the system (Restorative Justice for Oakland Youth, n.d.). Similar initiatives and collaborations with these types of organizations are spreading across the country (*In These Times* Editors, 2019).

Juvenile Detention Center Overhauls: Within and Outside the System

Solitary Confinement

As you have read, juvenile detention centers have received substantial criticism throughout the years, from the harsh conditions in the original reform schools to more recent events of violence and abuse that occur in institutions across the United States. There is also criticism regarding permitted procedures to shackle youth, appearances in the courtroom creating stigma and humiliation, and the ability to utilize solitary confinement in detention facilities (Teigan, 2020).

According to the American Academy of Child & Adolescent Psychiatry's Juvenile Justice Reform Committee, solitary confinement can increase stress, anxiety, and psychosis (Juvenile Justice Reform Committee, 2012). As you have read, the United Nations opposes solitary confinement for juveniles and young people (United Nations, 2020) and the American Academy of Child & Adolescent Psychiatry stipulates that if a youth is held for more than 24 hours in solitary confinement, they should be evaluated by a mental health professional (Juvenile Justice Reform Committee, 2012). The National Commission on Correctional Health Care has called for the least amount of time possible in solitary confinement. They have asserted that prolonged confinement is inhumane and degrading and that it should only be used for safety and not as a form of punishment (National Commission on Correctional Health Care, 2016; Teigan, 2020).

As a result, recent legislation has advocated that solitary confinement only be used for safety purposes and not as a punitive measure. However, some states limit or ban solitary confinement altogether because of the psychological and emotional stress and other detrimental effects that have resulted (see Figure 13.4) (Clark, 2017; Juvenile Justice Reform Committee, 2012; Teigan, 2020).

Some states are limiting or banning solitary confinement all together because of psychological and emotional stress and other detrimental effects that have resulted.

Community Corrections

As we have learned, there are economic, social, and psychological reasons why some experts have recommended that juvenile detention centers need to make both logistical and structural changes. There has been a call for more community-based corrections. **Community-based corrections** are programs that supervise offenders outside detention centers and prisons. This can be in the form of **probation**, which can replace time in a correctional institution, or **parole**, allowing offenders to be released from incarceration early to finish part of their sentence within the community under court supervision (National Institute of Justice, 2016).

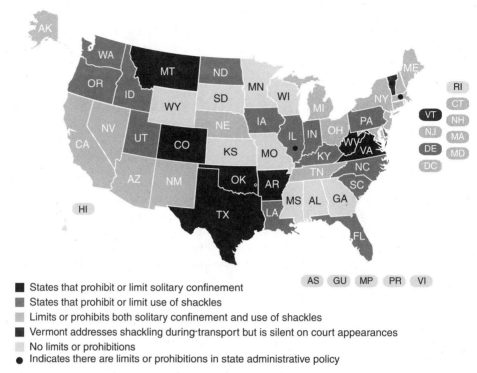

States that prohibit or limit solitary confinement
States that prohibit or limit use of shackles
Limits or prohibits both solitary confinement and use of shackles
Vermont addresses shackling during·transport but is silent on court appearances
No limits or prohibitions
● Indicates there are limits or prohibitions in state administrative policy

Figure 13.4 Some States Limit or Ban Solitary Confinement and/or The Use of Shackles.
Source: NCSL

As you read in Chapter 2, although the United States has led the world in the number of juveniles removed from their residences and put in some form of detention, these numbers have seen a downward trend since the beginning of the 20th century, down 60% from 2000 (Sawyer, 2019). Although some juvenile detention centers have shut down because of a lack of funding as a result of fewer juveniles being processed through the system, as you learned in Chapter 10, "Interventions and Diversions," there seem to be added benefits of keeping children out of incarceration. They can include reduced recidivism and avoidance of detrimental and abusive environments. As a result, along with reforms within facilities, many areas now utilize alternatives to detention for reasons other than economics.

In 2016, Harvard's Kennedy School published a report entitled *The Future of Youth Justice: A Community-Based Alternative to the Youth Prison Model* (McCarthy et al., 2016). The report describes a "four-pronged strategy" for abolishing youth prisons and imposing juvenile sanctions that focus on rehabilitation and healthy development. The four prongs are entitled reduce, reform, replace, and reinvest. The report further details these areas as follows:

(1) reduce the number of youth committed to out-of-home placement,
(2) reform programs, practices, and culture to focus on achieving positive outcomes for youth, (3) replace youth prisons with small, home-like facilities for the small number of youth for whom secure placement is necessary, and
(4) reinvest savings to expand options for youth in their communities.
(McCarthy et al., 2016, p. 2)

These philosophies seem to be gaining momentum across the United States. For example, in response to video footage and other evidence revealing juvenile detention guards arranging fights between incarcerated youth, termed "fight clubs," Florida's juvenile system was overhauled. This included efforts to hire more qualified staff to make facilities safer and spend over $9 million on intervention programs to provide rehabilitation and support to juveniles outside the correctional system (Funcheon, 2017; Miller, 2017, 2018).

In California, nine juvenile facilities have closed since 2017 in the city of Los Angeles alone. Youth have been diverted from detention and put into supervised, community-based alternatives that focus on education, community restitution, and treatment and counseling. This is based on comprehensive risk assessments to reduce potential detriments of correctional facilities, meet the youth's needs, and ensure community safety. The Los Angeles probation department reported significant decreases in juvenile crime and incarceration as a result of this initiative (Webb, 2019).

Comprehensive risk assessments can also help determine the specific needs of youth with mental illness through a collaboration between their families and trained professionals. Approximately 65% of all youth in detention have some kind of diagnosable mental health condition (Knaappila et al., 2019). Some states have even developed juvenile crisis intervention teams that can assist with diverting youth from formal processing to outside treatment and resources as part of a community-based alternative (Knaappila et al., 2019; Underwood & Washington, 2016).

Reentry

Aligned with the juvenile justice system's rehabilitation goal, reentry efforts take a holistic approach. This strategy involves community members, social services, family participation, and other resources. There have been several programs to address these objectives.

Thousands of youth reenter communities every day, and reoffending rates can range from 40% to 75%, with an average of 55% from reporting states (Department of Juvenile Justice, 2020a; OJJDP, 2017). Although some form of comprehensive reentry has been growing over the years, many justice systems are now planning for reentry earlier, well before a youth's release. Programs range from supervised aftercare to those that provide access to the previously mentioned resources that involve communities, families, and other stakeholders. Programs have also changed focus.

Focus on Strengths Versus Weaknesses

A **strength-based perspective** considers a youth's strengths and family and community input for positive adjustment and development. This is different from the traditional **deficit-based model**, which focused on the youth's problems and weaknesses to promote rehabilitation and eventual reentry into the community. Focusing on problems puts more emphasis on the child as opposed to looking at their attributes and the ability of their families and the communities to support their strengths, thereby leading them to healthy development (Juvenile Justice Information Exchange, 2020; Ttofi et al., 2016).

Focusing on a youth's strengths, protective factors, and community support has yielded more positive results than when the focus is on their weaknesses and susceptibility to internal and external risk factors (Merenda, 2020). **Risk factors** are the aspects of one's life that cause one to be more susceptible to maladaptive and criminal behavior. Examples include adverse social and environmental conditions and a lack of bonds with societal institutions. **Protective factors** are factors that can help promote healthy development and reduce the effects of risk factors. Examples include prosocial involvement with their community and positive perspectives of the world around them (Juvenile Justice Information Exchange, 2020; Ortega-Campos et al., 2016; Ttofi et al., 2016).

Other types of reentry programs continue to evolve. For example, youth (and adults) who are on parole or probation can be enrolled in Effective Practices for Community Supervision Training. In this program, developed at the University of Cincinnati, probation/parole officers are trained to work with youth collaboratively for skills development to mitigate risk and role-playing to practice healthy life choices. This and similar programs continue to be adopted by states across the country (Department of Juvenile Justice, 2020b).

Missouri has also developed new reentry programs and restructured its juvenile facilities to promote better transitions back into society. We have seen that countries like Norway and Germany have looser restrictions in detention facilities to begin to integrate inmates back into society. This includes allowing young adults to work outside with minimum supervision and to leave for the day to look for jobs and housing for when they are eventually released (Bauer, 2019; Chammah, 2015; Johnson, 2020). Missouri has followed suit by shifting from a traditional punitive correctional model to a more therapeutic one that focuses on the causes of a juvenile's delinquency to provide proper treatment to prepare them for return to their communities. They continue to restructure their system by providing smaller therapeutic facilities that offer family-like group sessions and least restrictive environments, most without cells and locks, similar to the notion of the **cottage system** that you read about in Chapter 1, which housed a lesser number of juveniles in smaller family-like facilities in the 1800s. Facilities also have better trained staff and smaller group programs close to the juvenile's home, allowing for additional family support (Division of Youth Services, 2018). Aftercare is also emphasized upon a juvenile's reentry, and "trackers" are assigned for up to 6 months to check in with the youth and assist with informal counseling, mentoring, and job searches (Juvenile Justice Information Exchange, 2020).

Other states have also begun to restructure their juvenile facilities. Virginia had closed all but one of its juvenile detention centers as of 2017, typically opting for diversion instead. The remaining center, Bon Air Juvenile Correction Center, houses just under 300 juveniles. Although fewer children are being sent to juvenile facilities in Virginia and across the United States, recidivism rates have remained high. In Virginia, for instance, reconviction rates are close to 40% for juveniles on parole placements, and approximately 55% of youths who were held in a detention center were rearrested within 12 months of release (Department of Juvenile Justice, 2020b; Pollock, 2018; Virginia Department of Juvenile Justice, n.d.). Virginia now also takes youth out of prison and allows them to stay in apartments owned by the state to encourage young people to find employment and independent living to better integrate them into society. Further reform continues, including moving the facility to a more accessible location so that visits from family are more supported, building cells with sheetrock and carpeting instead of bricks and hard floors to emulate a less harsh space, and providing therapy and skills-building to aid in healthy development (Department of Juvenile Justice, 2020b; Pollock, 2018).

Ohio has also revamped its reentry and aftercare process for juveniles. After adopting a new youth assessment tool, they have begun conducting assessments very early on to create reentry plans that include a collaboration between juveniles and

TABLE 13.2 Comparison of Traditional and Strength-Based Service Models

	TRADITIONAL SERVICE MODEL	STRENGTH-BASED SERVICE MODEL
Focus	Deficits, problems	Strengths, assets
Assessment	Risk, needs, diagnosis	Strengths discovery
Intervention	Treatment by professionals	Collaborative planning and implementation
Client role	Passive	Active, empowering
Context	Isolate client, office-based or institutional	Inclusion, mainstreaming, community-based
Goal	Symptom amelioration	Optimal developmental functioning

Source: Western Criminology Review 7(2), 48–61 (2006)

the community. They also work with multiple agencies to further ensure that specific guidance and support will be provided and positive results obtained (Department of Youth Services, 2020).

Ohio, as well as other states, is also participating in the Second Chance Act Two-Phase Re-entry Program. This grant program is sponsored by the OJJDP and provides states with funding to create and implement reentry plans to reduce recidivism rates and produce positive youth outcomes. Phases can include risk and need assessments, evidence-based interventions, community case management, support for job placement, substance abuse and mental health counseling, medical care, and ongoing mentoring. Additional grants focused on collaboration efforts for successful juvenile reentry programs have been offered and adopted across the country (Bureau of Justice Statistics, 2020; National Reentry Resource Center, 2021).

Finally, many municipalities embrace **strength-based wraparound services**, which create support teams composed of family and community members, other stakeholders, and agency personnel "wrapped" around youth to develop research-based individual reentry plans for healthy development (National Center for Innovation and Excellence, n.d.).

Measuring Success

More accurately measuring the success of reentry and rehabilitation has become the goal of many states. Although reduced recidivism is a traditional measure of success, the U.S. Office of Justice Programs has provided further standards through the efforts of the Performance-Based Standards learning institute, the Council of Juvenile Correctional Administration, and the VERA Institute of Justice to better streamline reentry programs and more accurately assess progress and needs for improvements. Suggested standards include the ability of programs to instill fairness, accountability, family engagement, and collaborations. Programs should also strive for continuous quality improvement (Deal, 2020; Godfrey, 2019).

The use of both short-term and long-term outcome assessments has been suggested. Short-term assessments should include measuring engagement in education and employment and developing well-being and **prosocial bonds**—attachment to societal institutions and engagement with the community (Intravia et al., 2017). Long-term outcomes should be assessed through community safety, program efficiency, and reoffending rates (Godfrey, 2019).

Innovations and directions for juvenile justice systems and alternative programs to incarceration are also being developed around the world.

Worldview

The Outlook of Justice Around the World

THE UNITED NATIONS

The United Nations advocates for children's rights to countries worldwide through its Committee on the Rights of the Child and the World Program of Action for Youth. The Committee on the Rights of the Child monitors countries' implementation of the standards dictated from the Convention on the Rights of the Child (United Nations, n.d.). The World Program of Action for Youth was adopted in 1995 by the United Nations and provides guidelines across the globe to improve young people's lives, assisting with promoting the United Nation's youth agenda.

In their program of action, the United Nations puts forward ongoing guidelines for juvenile delinquency preventative measures, prevention of violence, and rehabilitation services. The excerpts that continue to guide member countries and other countries around the world are provided next. In this section, we will look at specific trends and reforms of these countries' juvenile justice systems.

JUVENILE DELINQUENCY, PROPOSALS FOR ACTION

1. PRIORITY TO PREVENTIVE MEASURES

Governments should give priority to issues and problems of juvenile delinquency and youth criminality, with particular attention to preventive policies and programmes. Rural areas should be provided with adequate socioeconomic opportunities and administrative services, which could discourage young people from migrating to urban areas. Youth from poor urban settings should have access to specific educational, employment, and leisure programmes, particularly during long school holidays. Young people who drop out of school or come from broken families should benefit from specific social programmes that help them build self-esteem and confidence conducive to responsible adulthood.

2. PREVENTION OF VIOLENCE

Governments and other relevant organizations, particularly youth organizations, should consider organizing information campaigns and educational and training programmes to sensitize youth to the personally and socially detrimental effects of violence in the family, community, and society, to teach them how to communicate without violence and to promote training so that they can protect themselves and others against violence. Governments should also develop programmes to promote tolerance and better understanding among youth, with a view to eradicating contemporary forms of racism, racial discrimination, xenophobia and related intolerance and thereby prevent violence.

To prevent violence and crime, the development of social organization, particularly through youth organizations and community involvement, should be fostered by a supportive social policy and within a legal framework. Government assistance should focus on facilitating the ability of community and youth organizations to express and evaluate their needs concerning the prevention of violence and crime, to formulate and implement actions for themselves, and to cooperate with each other.

3. REHABILITATION SERVICES AND PROGRAMS
Destitution, poor living conditions, inadequate education, malnutrition, illiteracy, unemployment, and lack of leisure-time activities are factors that marginalize young people, which makes some of them vulnerable to exploitation as well as to involvement in criminal and other deviant behaviour. If preventive measures address the very causes of criminality, rehabilitation programmes and services should be made available to those who already have a criminal history. In general, youth delinquency begins with petty offences such as robbery or violent behaviour, which can be easily traced by and corrected through institutions and community and family environments. Indeed law enforcement should be a part of rehabilitation measures. Finally, the human rights of young people who are imprisoned should be protected, and principles of penal majority according to penal laws should be given great attention. (United Nations, 2007, pp. 23–25)

INDIA
As you have read in previous chapters, India passed the latest amendment to its Juvenile Justice Care and Protection of Children Act in 2015 to give more attention to juveniles' mental health and substance abuse issues. According to recent research, involvement with the justice system and mental health issues are interrelated in India and continued focus on these types of risk factors can help deter future offending (Snehil & Sagar, 2020).

Mental health professionals are utilized in India to assist both within and outside the system. A holistic approach that encompasses families and communities supporting youth has been found to be essential for healthy development (Hossain & Purohit, 2019). Further research has found that mental health referrals through the justice system have reduced recidivism (Zeola et al., 2017).

India also has a high rate of missing and trafficked children, with the number increasing from 63,407 in 2016 to 67,134 in 2018, an almost 6% increase. Similar to the United States and other countries, India has adopted a national missing and vulnerable child tracking system. The system was created in 2007 and has now been integrated to provides resources including "trackchild" for child protection agencies, police, child welfare agencies, shelters, and the community to receive statistical information and tools to investigate these types of crimes. The system is bolstered to combat the growing number of missing children through mobile access and additional resources, including a real-time map to communicate areas with high reports of missing individuals and efforts by police in those areas (National Crime Records Bureau, 2019).

EUROPE

The European Council for Juvenile Justice has made efforts to strengthen their juvenile justice systems through implementing restorative justice programs. Through international conferences and collaboration with European countries, supporting and protecting victims of crime are addressed.

A 2012 directive of the European Parliament and Council defined restorative justice as "any process whereby the victim and the offender are enabled if they freely consent to participate actively in the resolution of matters arising from the criminal offence through the help of an impartial third party" (European Parliament Directive, E. U., 2012, article 2). This can include victim–offender mediation and family group conferencing.

Aligning with the Victim's Directive of 2012, which advanced victim's rights, countries that have already implemented restorative justice and those at the beginning stages have shared ideas, tools for implementation, and successes through international conferences (see Figure 13.5). The latest session occurred in 2018 in Belgium and the implementation of restorative justice efforts continue (European Council for Juvenile Justice, 2018).

Many countries in Europe, including Italy, Germany, Portugal, Finland, and Spain, have partnered on a project to address mental health disorders in children involved with the justice system and to support interagency efforts to meet their needs. This project, entitled Fostering Alternative Care for Troubled Minors (FACT for Minors), considers the psychological and psychiatric concerns as well as the personality of children for referrals to appropriate alternative care communities as opposed to incarceration for delinquent acts. **Alternative care communities** place justice-involved youth with service providers in family counseling, mental health or substance abuse treatment, or other types of programs to address psychosocial needs and to prevent or mediate detention. There is a focus on holistic, multidisciplinary, and multiagency approaches to prevention and treatment (International Juvenile Justice Observatory, n.d.; Sawyer, 2019).

SOUTH AFRICA

South Africa has experienced violence in schools and continues to make efforts to reduce the risk of violence and occurrences involving weapons. Interventions have grown to avoid aggressive behavior among youth as well as their contact with the justice system. One such intervention involves discussion groups with teens in high school about knowing yourself, peer pressure, decision-making, and violence. Although program results did not show a reduction in other types of risky behavior such as smoking and drinking alcohol, it did show significantly fewer children bringing a weapon to school after these group sessions (Khuzwayo et al., 2020).

Youth empowerment has been a focus in South Africa for many years and continues to be stressed in a variety of programs that are being developed. Young African Leaders Initiative is sponsored by the United States to support young people and provide entrepreneurial opportunities and leadership skills. It also enables young people in countries across Africa to obtain a fellowship to study at an American university (Blakeney, 2019).

CANADA

Canada's Youth Criminal Justice Act recognizes both accountability and treatment in terms of a youth's immaturity and the circumstances of the crime for juveniles who become involved with the justice system. The act also calls for interventions that can be meaningful and reinforce respect for social values (Department of Justice, 2017).

The Intensive Rehabilitative Custody and Supervision program provides specialized treatment for incarcerated youth, including programs for violent youth suffering from psychological or mental disorders.

Implementing Restorative Justice with Child Victims

Mutual learning and sharing of existing and ongoing best practices between:

Mentee countries:
Latvia - State Probation Service (SPS)
Bulgaria - Social Activities and Practice Institute (SAPI)
France - IFJR and DPJJ of the Ministry of Justice

Mentor countries:
Katholieke Universiteit Leuven - **Belgium**
National Institute for Health and Welfare (THL) - **Finland**
Youth Justice Agency - Northern **Ireland**

This project is based on **mutual learning** and **sharing** of existing and on-going **best practices** between these six european countries.

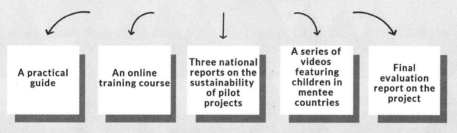

| A practical guide | An online training course | Three national reports on the sustainability of pilot projects | A series of videos featuring children in mentee countries | Final evaluation report on the project |

 This mutual learning aims to address the victims' needs through a thorough training of professionals from the three mentee countries regarding the use and implementation of a validated RJ practice in Europe throughout the implementation of national coalitions.

Final Conference:

This conference represents an opportunity to present the practical guide and the online course, as well as to produce RJ advocacy material as a mean of implementation of the 2012 victims' directive. It involves a large panel of professionals and representatives of European institutions and organisations to ensure a wide public awareness about the benefits of RJ processes for child victims.

Figure 13.5 The European Council for Juvenile Justice (ECJJ) has hosted international conferences on restorative justice programs.
Source: International Juvenile Justice Observatory

Continued focus is on preventative measures through outreach programs that place staff members in areas where youth often stay to be better able to share what positive resources are available to them. The Youth Collective Impact Program funds and assists community organizations in collaborating and offering engagement, workshops, and coaching; the Youth Research & Evaluation Exchange supports collaboration among youth organizations across various regions.

Canada also has an Enhanced Youth Action Plan. In 2012, the first action plan was developed to provide youth development programs. Now, through enhancing the program, it expands services, addresses juvenile violence, and bolsters community resources in areas that have the most need. It also considers research that has identified risk factors for delinquency and criminality and aligns support and opportunities for healthy development and community support. It is estimated that this plan helps 65,000 at-risk youth each year (Ontario Ministry of Children, 2020).

AUSTRALIA

As you have read, Australia has had reductions in juvenile crime over the past several years (Australian Bureau of Statistics , 2021). To reduce reoffending, Australia's corrections department has focused on assigning caseworkers to juveniles after release from confinement. Through this initiative, caseworkers are further tasked with assisting with reintegration into communities by helping with access to education, employment, housing, and health services (New South Wales, 2020).

Many parts of Australia focus on mitigating reoffending and diverting youth from the system in the first place. Australia implemented Youth on Track in 2016. Through the program, teachers and police officers are encouraged to refer juvenile offenders to specialized services, including counseling for behavioral issues and family support and other services to address the root causes of maladaptive behavior. Efforts for early intervention continue.

Monitoring correctional facilities that juveniles are held in continues to be a priority. In 2016, the Australian Department of Justice appointed an overseer of public and private correctional facilities. Tasks include supervising daily operations and handling complaints. Other duties include monitoring juvenile cells, prisoner transports, visitor programs, and other supportive services (New South Walses, 2020).

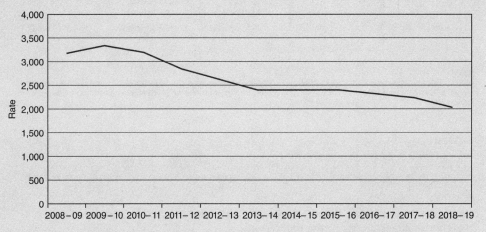

Figure 13.6 Australian Youth Offender Rate per 100,000 Persons, Aged 10 to 17 Years.
Source: Australia Bureau of Statistics

Wrap-up

Efforts to improve the juvenile justice system are continuing. Although reforms are occurring at every stage of the system, specific efforts are also being made toward avoiding juvenile involvement with the justice system in the first place. Focus is also on rehabilitating and reintegrating juveniles who do end up in detention centers back into their homes and communities.

There is also ongoing recognition of juveniles' specific health, mental, physical, and social needs within the system and how some facilities have fallen short. You have seen how diversion has become a priority in many areas, and juvenile facilities are closing as a result of reduced delinquency and efforts to utilize community-based programs. When facilities are being used, steps focus on effective youth services and better training and hiring of officers and staff. It is hoped that, through these efforts, a positive environment can be created that promotes therapeutic counseling and care, which have been shown to lead to rehabilitation, reduced reoffending, positive bonding, and better integration into society.

Wraparound strength-based approaches continue to be adopted by agencies across the United States and the world. Interagency plans that incorporate community and family collaboration and those that provide better access to resources have become paramount in rehabilitation and reentry into society. Focusing on strengths versus weaknesses has helped develop protective factors for positive youth development. Finally, proper assessments of these efforts can further lead to healthy growth in the present and well into the future.

Discussion Questions

1. Explain the disproportionate contacts with the juvenile justice systems and their effects.

2. What are some of the laws and court cases that helped shape both the jurisdiction and the processing of juveniles?

3. Describe what law enforcement initiatives you believe will have the most positive effects on juveniles and why.

4. Choose and discuss sentencing trends and what you believe their goals should be.

5. Discuss aspects of reentry initiatives and how they can be improved.

6. Evaluate the differences and similarities of juvenile justice system reforms between the United States and other countries around the world.

ONLINE RESOURCES

American Academy of Child & Adolescent Psychiatry AACAP.org
American Psychology Association APA.org
Bureau of Justice Association BJA.gov
Juvenile Justice Information Exchange JJIE.org
Office of Juvenile Justice and Delinquency Prevention OJJDP.gov
Office of Justice Programs NCJRS.gov
National Conference of State Legislatures NCSL.org
National Institute of Justice NIJ.gov
The United States Department of Justice USDOJ.gov

Definitions

Alternative care communities—communities that place justice-involved youth with service providers in family counseling, mental health or substance abuse treatment, or other types of programs to addresses psychosocial needs to prevent or mitigate detention

Child abuse and neglect—an act or failure to act by a caretaker that results in death, serious physical or emotional harm, sexual abuse or exploitation, or imminent risk of serious harm

Community-based corrections—programs that supervise offenders outside detention centers and prisons

Cottage system—housing for a lesser number of juveniles in smaller family-like facilities

Cycle of justice—perceptions of juvenile crime as opposed to actual crime conditions influenced juvenile justice policy and an inefficient cycle of failed responses

Deficit-based model—an approach that focuses on the youth's problems and weaknesses to promote rehabilitation and eventual reentry into the community

Diminished culpability—not being fully criminally liable and able to be rehabilitated

Emerging adults—individuals ages 18–24 who are transitioning from a dependent child to an independent adult

Evidence-based initiatives—initiatives that have been influenced by scientific evidence and prior success

Gender-responsive programs—programs that consider and respond to the specific needs of a particular gender

Implicit bias—stereotypes or attitudes that affect one's thought process and actions subconsciously

Incorrigible—not able to be rehabilitated

Legalistic style—by the book and centered on enforcement and making arrests

Parole—early release from incarceration

Probation—a period of supervision that can replace time in a correctional institution

Procedural justice—carrying out police functions in a fair, unbiased, and transparent manner with community members while actively listening to their concerns

Prosocial bonds—attachment to societal institutions and engagement with the community

Protective factors—factors that can help promote healthy development and reduce the effects of risk factors

Restorative justice—an effort to divert a juvenile from formal processing while maintaining offender accountability and providing validation and amends to the victim and the community

Risk factors—aspects of one's life that cause them to be more susceptible to maladaptive and criminal behavior

Service style—intervening by providing informal services such as taking the youth home

Strength-based perspective—a viewpoint that considers a youth's strengths and family and community input for positive adjustment and development

Strength-based wraparound services—services that create support teams made up of family and community members, other stakeholders, and agency personnel "wrapped" around youth to develop research-based individual reentry plans for healthy development

References

American Psychological Association. (n.d.). *Miller v. Alabama* and *Jackson v. Hobbs*. Retrieved April 20, 2019, from https://www.apa.org/about/offices/ogc/amicus/miller-hobbs

Australian Bureau of Statistics. (2021). Recorded crime—offenders, 2018–19. Retrieved on April 20, 2021 from https://www.abs.gov.au/ausstats/abs@.nsf/Lookup/by%20Subject/4519.0~2018-19~Main%20Features~Youth%20Offenders~4#:~:text=4519.0%20%2D%20Recorded%20Crime%20%2D%20Offenders%2C%202018%2D19&text=There%20were%2049%2C180%20youth%20offenders,lowest%20in%20the%20time%20series

Bala, N., & Mooney, E. (2019). Promoting equity with youth diversion. RStreet. https://www.rstreet.org/wp-content/uploads/2019/07/178.pdf

Bauer, E (2019). Rehabilitative Promise: Why Norway Uses Restorative Justice in Juvenile Law. *International Law Review*. Retrieved on November 20, 2020, from https://www.msuilr.org/msuilr-legalforum-blogs/2019/1/24/rehabilitative-promise-why-norway-uses-restorative-justice-in-juvenile-law

BRAVE/Centre for Building Resilience Through Anti-Violence Education. (n.d.). Volunteer Halifax. Retrieved on November 20, 2020 from https://volunteerhalifax.ca/nonprofit-organization/bravecentre-for-building-resilience-through-anti-violence-education/

Bureau of Justice Statistics. (2020). FY 2020 Second Chance Act community-based reentry program. U.S. Department of Justice. https://bja.ojp.gov/funding/opportunities/bja-2020-17110

Blakeney, S. (2019). Youth empowerment programs in Africa. Borgen Project. https://borgenproject.org/youth-empowerment-programs-in-africa/

Campaign for the Fair Sentencing of Youth. (n.d.). Life Without Parole. Retrieved December 26, 2020, from https://cfsy.org/?s=life+without+parole

Chammah, M. (2015). Prison Without Punishment. The Marshall Project. Retrieved on November 20, 2020, from https://www.themarshallproject.org/2015/09/25/prison-without-punishment

Chester, L., & Schiraldi, V. (2016). Public safety and emerging adults in Connecticut: Providing effective and developmentally appropriate responses for youth under age 21. Malcolm Wiener Center for Social Policy, Harvard Kennedy School.

Clark, A. B. (2017). Juvenile solitary confinement as a form of child abuse. *Journal of the American Academy of Psychiatry and the Law*, 45(3), 350–357.

Community Oriented Policing Services. (n.d.). Procedural justice. Retrieved November 24, 2020, from https://cops.usdoj.gov/prodceduraljustice#:~:text=Procedural%20justice%20refers%20to%20the,resolve%20disputes%20and%20allocate%20resources.&text=Procedural%20justice%20speaks%20to%20four,transparency%20in%20actions

Crime Research Group. (2015). Juvenile recidivism study: 2008–2011. Vermont Agency of Human Services.

Davidson, H. (2012, August 1). Juvenile defense attorneys must address mitigating factors in homicide cases. American Bar Association. https://www.americanbar.org/groups/public_interest/child_law/resources/child_law_practiceonline/child_law_practice/vol_31/august_2012/juvenile_defenseattorneysmustaddressmitigatingfactorsinhomicidec0/

Deal, T. (2020). Juvenile Justice Model Data Project: Final technical report. National Criminal Justice Reference Service. https://www.ncjrs.gov/pdffiles1/ojjdp/grants/254492.pdf

Department of Justice. (2017). Youth justice. Government of Canada. Retrieved on February 25, 2019 from https://www.justice.gc.ca/eng/csj-sjc/just/11.html

Department of Juvenile Justice. (2020a). Recidivism. In Data resource guide FY 2020 (pp. 73–86). Virginia Department of Juvenile Justice. http://www.djj.virginia.gov/pdf/about-djj/DRG/Recidivism.pdf

Department of Juvenile Justice. (2020b). Transformation plan 2020 update. Virginia Department of Juvenile Justice. http://www.djj.virginia.gov/pdf/admin/2020%20DJJ%20Transformation%20FINAL.pdf

Department of Youth Services. (2020). Ohio Ex-Offender Reentry Coalition & Juvenile Branch. https://dys.ohio.gov/wps/portal/gov/dys/youth-and-families/resources-for-youth/ohio-ex-offender-reentry-coalition-and-juvenile-branch#:~:text=The%20mission%20of%20the%20Ohio,based%20organizations%20and%20other%20stakeholders

Dillard, R., Newman, T., & Kim, M. (2019). Promoting youth competence through balanced and restorative justice: A community-based PYD approach. Journal of Youth Development, 14(4), 14–35. https://doi.org/10.5195/jyd.2019.804

Division of Youth Services. (2018). The Missouri approach. Missouri Department of Social Services. http://missouriapproach.org/

European Parliament Directive, E. U. (2012). Directive 2012/27/EU of the European Parliament and of the Council of 25 October 2012 on Energy Efficiency, Amending Directives 2009/125/EC and 2010/30/EU and Repealing Directives 2004/8/EC and 2006/32. Official Journal, L, 315, 1-56.

European Council for Juvenile Justice. (2018). Implementing restorative justice with child victims.

International Juvenile Justice Observatory. https://www.euforumrj.org/sites/default/files/2020-11/RJ%20Child%20Victims%20implementing_practical_guide_eng-2-129.pdf

Funcheon, D. (2017). Behind the Miami Herald's "inescapably powerful" juvenile justice investigation. Columbia Journalism Review. https://www.cjr.org/united_states_project/fight-club-miami-honey-bun.php

Godfrey, K. (2019). Initiative to develop juvenile re-entry measurement standards: Final technical report. National Criminal Justice Reference Service. https://www.ncjrs.gov/pdffiles1/nij/grants/254456.pdf

Hossain, M. M., & Purohit, N. (2019). Improving child and adolescent mental health in India: Status, services, policies, and way forward. Indian Journal of Psychiatry, 61(4), 415.

International Association of Chiefs of Police. (2017). Enhancing police responses to children exposed to violence: A toolkit for law enforcement. Office Juvenile Justice and Delinquency Prevention, Office of Justice Programs, U.S. Department of Justice.

International Juvenile Justice Observatory. (n.d.). FACT for Minors—Fostering Alternative Care for Troubled Minors. Retrieved May 17, 2020, from https://www.oijj.org/en/our-work/research/highlighted-research-projects/fact

In These Times Editors. (2019). Restorative justice: A much-needed alternative to mass incarceration. Institute for Public Affairs. https://inthesetimes.com/article/restorative-justice-criminal-justice-reform-mass-incarceration

Intravia, J., Pelletier, E., Wolff, K. T., & Baglivio, M. T. (2017). Community disadvantage, prosocial bonds, and juvenile reoffending: A multilevel mediation analysis. Youth Violence and Juvenile Justice, 15(3), 240–263. https://doi.org/10.1177/1541204016639350

Jackson v. Hobbs, 562 U.S. 1 (2011).

Johnson, A. M. (2020). What I Learned Touring Prisons in Finland and Norway. The California Wellness Foundation. Retrieved on April 20, 2021 from https://www.calwellness.org/stories/lessons-prisons-finland-norway/

Juvenile Justice Information Exchange. (2020). Reform trends: Re-entry. https://jjie.org/hub/reentry/reform-trends/#_edn14

Juvenile Justice & Youth Development. (2020). Fact and figures on Connecticut's juvenile justice system. State of Connecticut, Office of Policy and Management. https://portal.ct.gov/OPM/CJ-JJYD/Facts-About-Juvenile-Justice/CT-Facts--Figures-Graph-3

Juvenile Justice Reform Committee. (2012). Solitary confinement of juvenile offenders. American Academy of Child & Adolescent Psychiatry. https://www.aacap.org/aacap/Policy_Statements/2012/Solitary_Confinement_of_Juvenile_Offenders.aspx

Khuzwayo, N., Taylor, M., & Connolly, C. (2020). Changing youth behaviour in South Africa. *Health SA = SA Gesondheid*, 25, 1031. https://doi.org/10.4102/hsag.v25i0.1031

Knaappila, N., Marttunen, M., Fröjd, S., Lindberg, N., & Kaltiala-Heino, R. (2019). Changes in delinquency according to socioeconomic status among Finnish adolescents from 2000 to 2015. *Scandinavian Journal of Child and Adolescent Psychiatry and Psychology*, 7, 52.

McCarthy, P., Schiraldi, V. N., & Shark, M. (2016). The future of youth justice: A community based alternative to the youth prison model. U.S. Department of Justice, National Institute of Justicehttps://doi.org/10.7916/d8-m33x-jk51

Merenda, F. (2020). Adventure-based programming with at-risk youth: Impact upon self-confidence and school attachment. *Child & Youth Services*, 1–28.

Merenda, F., Trent, J., Rinke, C. R., & Buchanan, M. (2021). Understanding citizen satisfaction with the police: Results from a community survey. *Police Practice and Research*, 22(1), 692–710.

Miller v. Alabama, 567 U.S. (2012).

Miller, C. M. (2017). FIGHTCLUB: A Miami Herald investigation into Florida's juvenile justice system. WLRN, Miami Herald News. https://www.wlrn.org/news/2017-10-09/fightclub-a-miami-herald-investigation-into-floridas-juvenile-justice-system

Miller, C. (2018). After reports of violence, low pay, wretched conditions, Scott signs juvenile justice reforms. WLRN, Miami Herald News. https://news.wgcu.org/2018-03-27/after-reports-of-violence-low-pay-wretched-conditions-scott-signs-juvenile-justice-reforms

National Center for Innovation and Excellence. (n.d.). Wraparound. Retrieved December 24, 2020, from https://ncfie.org/our-expertise/wraparound/

National Commission on Correctional Health Care. (2016). *Solitary confinement (isolation)*. https://ncchc.org/solitary-confinement

National Conference of State Legislatures. (2020). Racial and ethnic disparities in the juvenile justice system. https://www.ncsl.org/research/civil-and-criminal-justice/racial-and-ethnic-disparities-in-the-juvenile-justice-system.aspx

National Crime Records Bureau. (2019). Report on missing women and children in India. National Crime Records Bureau Ministry of Home Affairs, Government of India. https://ncrb.gov.in/sites/default/files/missingpage-merged.pdf

National Institute of Justice. (2016). Community corrections. U.S. Department of Justice, Office of Justice Programs. https://nij.ojp.gov/topics/corrections/community-corrections

The National Reentry Resource Center (2021). Juvenile Reentry Measurement Standards. Retrieved from https://nationalreentryresourcecenter.org/resources/juvenile-reentry-measurement-standards

New South Wales (2020). Department of Communities and Justice 2019-20 Annual Report - Volume 1 - Performance and Activities. State of New South Wales. Retrieved on March 20, 2020 from https://www.opengov.nsw.gov.au/publications/ 19041;jsessionid =7C619DD1F6818E0EA8D92320E67D8761

Office of Juvenile Justice and Delinquency Prevention. (n.d.). Mentoring. U.S. Department of Justice, Office of Justice Programs. Retrieved March 8, 2020, from https://ojjdp.ojp.gov/programs/mentoring

Office of Juvenile Justice and Delinquency Prevention. (2017). Juvenile reentry. https://www.ojjdp.gov/mpg/lit-reviews/Aftercare.pdf

Office of Juvenile Justice and Delinquency Prevention. (2019). Racial and ethnic disparities. U.S. Department of Justice, Office of Justice Programs. http://ojjdp.ojp.gov/programs/racial-and-ethnic-disparities

Office of Juvenile Justice and Delinquency Prevention. (2020a). Responding to child abuse. U.S. Department of Justice, Office of Justice Programs. https://ojjdp.ojp.gov/programs/child-abuse

Office of Juvenile Justice and Delinquency Prevention. (2020b). Responding to gangs in schools: Creating a collaborative process between schools & law enforcement. U.S. Department of Justice, Office of Justice Programs. https://ojjdp.ojp.gov/media/video/9406

Office of Juvenile Justice and Delinquency Prevention. (2020c). Statistical briefing book: Juveniles tried as adults. U.S. Department of Justice, Office of Justice Programs. https://www.ojjdp.gov/ojstatbb/structure_process/qa04105.asp

Office of Juvenile Justice and Delinquency Prevention. (2020d). Children exposed to violence. U.S. Department of Justice, Office of Justice Programs. https://ojjdp.ojp.gov/programs/children-exposed-violence

Office of Juvenile Justice and Delinquency Prevention. (2021a). OJJDP FY 2021 reducing risk for girls in the juvenile justice system. U.S. Department of Justice, Office of Justice Programs. https://ojjdp.ojp.gov/funding/fy2021/O-OJJDP-2021-47008

Office of Juvenile Delinquency and Prevention. (2021b). Statistical briefing book: Juveniles in corrections, demographics. U.S. Department of Justice, Office of Justice Programs. https://www.ojjdp.gov/ojstatbb/corrections/qa08202.asp?qaDate=2019

O'Neil, C. M. (2016). Advanced policy analysis. https://pdfs.semanticscholar.org/ae42/d9def4dfc4b00354a02af-c531ad893946a08.pdf

Ontario Ministry of Children, Community, and Social Services. (2020). Enhanced youth action plan. http://www.children.gov.on.ca/htdocs/English/professionals/oyap/index.aspx

Ortega-Campos, E., Garcia-Garcia, J., Gil-Fenoy, M. J., & Zaldivar-Basurto, F. (2016). Identifying risk and protective factors in recidivist juvenile offenders: A decision tree approach. *PLOS One*, 11(9), e0160423.

Perez, N. M., Nguyen, T., & Vogel, B. (2021). Community–police dialogues: Evaluating the effects on adult, youth, and police participants. *Policing: A Journal of Policy and Practice*, 15(2), 1232–1244.

Pollock, N. (2018). The last kids locked up in Virginia. *The Atlantic*. https://www.theatlantic.com/projects/juvenile-justice/#correction-ref-1

Puzzanchera, C. (2020). Juvenile justice statistics: Juvenile arrests, 2018. U.S. Department of Justice, Office of Justice Programs. https://ojjdp.ojp.gov/sites/g/files/xyckuh176/files/media/document/254499.pdf

Restorative Justice for Oakland Youth. (2019). *Restorative justice*. Retrieved May 2, 2020, from http://rjoyoakland.org/

Robles-Ramamurthy, B., & Watson, C. (2019). Examining racial disparities in juvenile justice. *The Journal of the American Academy of Psychiatry and the Law*, 47(1), 48–52.

Rosiak, J. (2016). The pillars of 21st century youth-focused policing. https://cops.usdoj.gov/html/dispatch/04-2016/plliars_of_21st_century.asp

Rovner, J. (2020). Juvenile life without parole: An overview. The Sentencing Project. https://www.sentencingproject.org/publications/juvenile-life-without-parole/#:~:text=Having%20banned%20the%20use%20of,juveniles%20not%20convicted%20of%20homicide

Sawyer, W. (2019). Youth confinement: The whole pie. Prison Policy Initiative. https://www.prisonpolicy.org/reports/youth2019.html#:~:text=The%20number%20of%20youth%20confined,fallen%20just%2010%25%20since%202007.&text=The%20number%20of%20youth%20in%20adult%20prisons%20and%20jails%20has,by%20over%2060%25%20since%202000

Schiraldi, V., Western, B., & Bradner, K. (2015). Community-based responses to justice-involved young adults. National Institute of Justice.

Snehil, G., & Sagar, R. (2020). Juvenile justice system, juvenile mental health, and the role of MHPs: Challenges and opportunities. *Indian Journal of Psychological Medicine,* 42(3), 304–310.

Speed, J. (2020). Restorative justice: Emergence, institutionalization, and critiques. *Peace, Justice, and Strong Institutions*, 1–13.

Teigan, A. (2020). States that limit or prohibit juvenile shackling and solitary confinement. National Conference of State Legislatures. https://www.ncsl.org/research/civil-and-criminal-justice/states-that-limit-or-prohibit-juvenile-shackling-and-solitary-confinement635572628.aspx

Treskon, L., & Bright, C. L. (2017). Bringing gender-responsive principles into practice. MDRC. https://www.mdrc.org/sites/default/files/PACE_brief_March2017_web.pdf

Ttofi, M. M., Farrington, D. P., Piquero, A. R., & DeLisi, M. (2016). Protective factors against offending and violence: Results from prospective longitudinal studies. *Journal of Criminal Justice,* 45, 1–3. https://doi.org/10.1016/j.jcrimjus.2016.02.001

Underwood, L. A., & Washington, A. (2016). Mental illness and juvenile offenders. *International Journal of Environmental Research and Public Health*, 13(2), 228. https://doi.org/10.3390/ijerph13020228

United Nations. (n.d.). Committee on the Rights of the Child. United Nations Human Rights, Office of the High Commissioner. https://ohchr.org/en/hrbodies/crc/pages/crcindex.aspx

United Nations. (2007). World Programme of Action for Youth: A/RES/50/81 and A/RES/62/116. UN Department of Economic and Social Affairs Youth. Retrieved on May 2, 2020 from https://www.un.org/development/desa/youth/juvenile-justice-wpay.html

United Nations. (2020). United States: Prolonged solitary confinement amounts to psychological torture, says UN expert. United Nations Human Rights, Office of the High Commissioner. https://www.ohchr.org/EN/NewsEvents/Pages/DisplayNews.aspx?NewsID=25633#:~:text=OHCHR%20%7C%20United%20States%3A%20prolonged%20solitary,psychological%20torture%2C%20says%20UN%20expert&text=GENEVA%20(28%20February%202020)%20%E2%80%93,facilities%20in%20the%20United%20States

Virginia Department of Juvenile Justice. (n.d.). Bon Air Juvenile Correctional Center. Retrieved on January 11, 2021 from http://www.djj.virginia.gov/pages/residential/bon-air.htm

Webb, K. (2019). LA probation completes facility consolidation plan by closing nine juvenile facilities in two years. County of Los Angeles Probation. https://probation.lacounty.gov/l-a-probation-completes-facility-consolidation-plan-by-closing-nine-juvenile-facilities-in-two-years/

Zeola, M. P. Guina, J., & Nahhas, R. W. (2017). Mental health referrals reduce recidivism in first-time juvenile offenders, but how do we determine who is referred? *Psychiatric Quarterly*, 88(1), 167–183.

Zhao, J., He, N., & Lovrich, N. (2006). The effect of local political culture on policing behaviors in the 1990s: A retest of Wilson's theory in more contemporary times. *Journal of Criminal Justice*, 34(6), 569–578.

Credits

Chapter 1

[photo CO.1] © Glasshouse Images/Shutterstock. [photo 1.1] © Fritz Grögel/Wikipedia. [photo 1.2] © John Strype/Wikipedia. [photo 1.3] © Wikipedia.

Chapter 2

[photo CO.2] © Tang Yan Song/Shutterstock.

Chapter 3

[photo CO.3] © Historia/Shutterstock. [photo 3.2] © UCL Digital Media, All Rights Reserved. [photo 3.3] © Jeff Hartzog/The Collector of Experiences. [photo 3.4] © https://www.simplypsychology.org/bobo-doll.html.

Chapter 4

[photo CO.4] © ibreakstock/Shutterstock.

Chapter 5

[photo CO.5] © Shawn Ishihara/Wikipedia. [photo 5.1] © General Research Division, The New York Public Library. "Five Points, 1827" New York Public Library Digital Collections. [photo 5.2] © ANGELOUX/Wikipedia. [photo 5.3] © Walking the Tracks/Wikipedia.

Chapter 6

[photo CO.6] © The NYSPCC Archives, The New York Society for the Prevention of Cruelty to Children (NYSPCC). [photo 6.1] © The NYSPCC Archives, The New York Society for the Prevention of Cruelty to Children (NYSPCC). [photo 6.2] © Walsh, 1981.

Chapter 7

[photo CO.7] © maystra/Vectorstock. [photo 7.1] © a) https://en.wikipedia.org/wiki/Marie_Owens#/media/File:Marie_Owens_Photograph_Portrait_Chicago_Daily_Tribune.png b) https://www.opb.org/artsandlife/series/historical-photo/oregon-historical-photo-lola-g-baldwin-portland-policewoman/ c) https://en.wikipedia.org/wiki/File:Alice_stebbins_wells.jpg. [photo 7.2] © Underwood & Underwood/Wikipedia. [photo 7.4] © Ministry of Home Affairs/Wikipedia.

Chapter 8

[photo CO.8] © Fabian Junge/Shutterstock. [photo 8.1] © Niko28/Shutterstock. [photo 8.2] © Photo by Mr. Kjetil Ree/Wikipedia. [photo 8.3] © giftlegacy/iStockphoto.

Chapter 9

[photo CO.9] © luoman/iStockphoto. [photo 9.1, upper left] © Pearson Scott Foresman/Wikipedia. [photo 9.2, lower left] © IMG4FreeRgood1/Pixabay. [photo 9.3, upper right] © Library of Congress Prints and Photographs Division Washington, D.C. 20540 US. [photo 9.4, lower right] © Wikipedia. [photo 9.5] © Wikipedia. [photo 9.5] © California Department of Corrections and Rehabilitation. [photo 9.7] © State of South Carolina/Wikipedia.

Chapter 10

[photo CO.10] © Crisp0022/Shutterstock. [photo 10.1] © states.attorney@montgomerycountymd.gov - April 8, 23.

Chapter 11

[photo CO.11] © stuartmiles/GoGraph. [photo 11.1] © Gottscho-Schleisner Collection, Library of Congress, Prints and Photographs Division. [photo 11.2] © Evan-Amos/Wikipedia. [photo 11.4] © replicated from esrb.org. [photo 11.6] © Defunctgames.com. [photo 11.7] © Mobygames.com. [photo 11.8] © Arcade-history.com. [photo 11.9] © Gao, Xuemei & Pan, Wei & Li, Chao & Weng, Lei & Yao, Mengyun & Chen, Antao. (2017). Long-Time Exposure to Violent Video Games Does Not Show Desensitization on Empathy for Pain: An fMRI Study. Frontiers in Psychology. 8. 10.3389/fpsyg.2017.00650. [photo 11.10] gamespot.com.

Chapter 12

[photo CO.12] © Peshkova/Shutterstock. [photo 12.1] © By permission of Carol Todd.

Chapter 13

[photo CO.13] © SDI Productions/iStockphoto. [photo 13.1] © karenfoleyphotography/Shutterstock.

Index

Note: Page references followed by an "*t*" indicate table; "*f*" indicate figure.